Atlas
of
Scottish
History
to 1707

Edited by

Peter G B McNeill
and
Hector L MacQueen

Cartographer: Anona Lyons

Edinburgh: The Scottish Medievalists and Department of Geography, University of Edinburgh, 1996

Published jointly by The Scottish Medievalists and Department of Geography, University of Edinburgh, Drummond Street, Edinburgh EH8 9XP

First published 1996

ISBN 0 9503904 1 0

Printed and bound in Great Britain at Antony Rowe Ltd., Chippenham, Wiltshire.

Contents

The MAPS

Introductory   Edited by Ian A Morrison

Events to about 850   Edited by Lisbeth M Thoms

Events from about 850 to 1460   Edited by Norman F Shead

Events from 1460 to 1707   Edited by Norman T Macdougall

Administration   Edited by Hector L MacQueen

Economic development   Edited by Michael Lynch and David Ditchburn

The church   Edited by D E R Watt

Social and cultural　　Edited by Geoffrey Stell

Regional and local　　Edited by G W S Barrow

Introduction

This atlas appears under the joint names of the Scottish Medievalists and the Department of Geography of the University of Edinburgh.

The atlas replaces an earlier atlas, entitled *An Historical Atlas of Scotland c. 400 to c. 1600.* It was published in 1975. The present atlas has been about fifteen years in the making. An account of the making of *Atlas II* would amount to a substantial monograph: I propose to limit myself here to indicating what I have attempted to achieve in this atlas. I hope that the final maps have, within the limits of black and white, done justice to the draft maps which the various experts had submitted.

The earlier atlas was in two parts: one part contained the texts and the other the maps; and each part had a separate editor. In the present atlas, the texts and maps have been kept together, and, because of their greater bulk, the topics in the atlas have been divided into nine sections, according to subject, with the load being spread between each of the sectional editors, but with an overall general editor who was the liaison between the sectional editors and the cartographer.

The first section is an introductory one which, among other things, sets the physical and geographical basis of the maps which follow in the succeeding sections. The next three sections are chronological, covering the period from the beginning to 1707. The remaining five sections deal with important aspects of Scottish history. The classification is not wholly satisfactory and there is an element of cross-reference. The names of the editors appear in the list of over 80 contributors (there were 30 or so contributors in the earlier atlas).

As before, the elaboration of the maps is governed by the absence of colour and the need to keep the cost of production down to be within the purse of students.

The present atlas has about four or five times more maps than were in the first atlas. Also, the structure of the two atlases is different. The fairly substantial texts of the first atlas together with the linking passages amounted to a short history of Scotland for the period covered by the maps; whereas the present atlas has concentrated on the maps: it was the agreed policy that the associated texts would be briefer and have a different function. The texts are intended to indicate the principle on which the map or diagram is constructed and the lessons which can be drawn from it. As a result, most maps together with their texts make a self-contained unit of one or more pages. Where possible, the atlas attempts to have one map for one idea: this is the case in the distribution maps, such as the map showing the distribution of Pictish names. On the other hand, some maps are inventory maps, such as the map of Lowland schools, where listing of the schools by name is as important as their distribution.

I have tried for a degree of consistency in lay-out of each page or fascicle of pages. In most cases I have used the same map of Scotland so as to make it easier to compare like with like; and in most of the maps of Scotland, I have inserted in a light stipple the 800' (about 244 m) contour layer: most items of mappable interest appear below that height. Throughout, where weights and measures are mentioned, I have shown imperial and metric equivalents. Most of the readers of the atlas will no longer understand the former imperial coinage: accordingly I have made a table of imperial and metrical equivalents.

I have standardised the use of different type faces and type sizes to represent different features on the maps: these are shown in the general key.

The spelling of British place-names generally follows that shown in the 1:50,000 ordnance survey maps; and for foreign names, I have followed the spelling in *The Times Atlas of the World*

As general editor, I wish to acknowledge the forbearance of the atlas trustees, the contributors and the sectional editors during the delays which were never anticipated by me - or anyone else. Special mention must be made of the indispensable work of Professor D E R Watt. Professor Watt has been our business manager and convenor of the atlas trustees. As with the first atlas, so with this one, he was the driving force in the planning of the undertaking; he husbanded the resources created by the sales of the first atlas and acquired further large resources in cash and in kind from a variety of benefactors; and he has dealt with every aspect of the commercial production of the atlas. As a result, in the words of the preface to the first atlas, he has been able 'to keep the selling price to as low a figure as possible so that virtually no-one who has an interest in Scottish history may be debarred from obtaining a copy'.

I also wish to acknowledge the help and assistance which I have received in a variety of ways from Mr Douglas Watt, the staffs of the National Library of Scotland (including the Map Building), Historic Scotland and the Scottish Record Office. Thanks are especially due to the academic and technical staff of the Department of Geography of the University of Edinburgh who undertook the cartographic work, including Mr Ray Harris, Dr David Munro, Dr David A Gray and Anona Lyons. Over the years, there have been different hands involved on the cartographic side; but by far the largest part has been the work of the cartographer, Anona Lyons. Mrs Lyons has produced all proof maps and texts which are the basis of the atlas.

Individual mention must be made of the great assistance and encouragement which I received from Sheriff D B Smith over a decade and a half: he probably does not realise the value of his help.

Lastly I would like to dedicate this edition to my wife whose help, support and patience over the years made my 'second job' possible.

Shortly after I had drafted this introduction, I decided that, for several reasons, I had to give up editing the atlas. Thereafter, the editorial work has been continued by other hands.

Peter G B McNeill

Although I had been long involved with this atlas as one of its sectional editors, my more general activities in relation to it began in the summer of 1995 when Peter McNeill felt compelled to give up sole responsibility. It must be said immediately that the atlas now presented remains in all essential points the concept described above by Dr McNeill, and that my role has been entirely one of bringing it to fruition, happily with his continuing involvement and support in the work. Without him, there would be no atlas. In the role of carrying the project to completion I was also greatly assisted by Professor Michael Lynch and Geoffrey Stell, who gave freely of advice, time and support at a critical moment when the future of the atlas hung in the balance. Professor Donald Watt continued as a tower of strength throughout, mixing cajolery, encouragement and participation in the task in hand in equal and generous measures. Professor Charles Withers of the Department of Geography at the University of Edinburgh showed extra-ordinary patience with a troublesome lawyer let loose in his department as well as much good

will and enthusiasm for the whole atlas project. Much invaluable work of photocopying, posting and liaison was efficiently handled by Nicola Graham and Isabel Reid, and I am also grateful for the facilities afforded me by the Faculty of Law and the Department of Scottish History in the University of Edinburgh. The sectional editors and individual contributors all showed good grace and efficiency in complying with my importunate and persistent requests, and I apologise for any difficulties which attention to my demands may have caused them. I also express my personal appreciation of the cartographic labours of Anona Lyons, who responded with patience, determination and good humour to the very heavy demands of a project which turned out to be far bigger and more onerous than any of those involved had ever anticipated or realised. Lastly, I thank my wife Frances, who once again has found herself drawn into the projects of her spouse and has willingly helped with proofs and other essential checking.

Hector L MacQueen

We both wish to acknowledge here the support of The Carnegie Trust for the Universities of Scotland, and of the Russell Trust, without which publication of the atlas would not have been possible.

PGBM, HLM

Key to initials of contributors

Initials	Contributor
MA	† Marinell Ash
PA	Patrick Ashmore
JWMB	J W M Bannerman
IB	Ishbel Barnes
GWSB	**G W S Barrow**
SB	Stephen Boardman
AB	Alan Borthwick
DJB	David J Breeze
JB	James Brown
DHC	D H Caldwell
JSC	† J S Cameron
EC	Ewan Campbell
RGC	R G Cant
TMC	T M Chalmers
PC	Peter Corser
IBC	† I B Cowan
BEC	B E Crawford
EPD	E P Dennison
HD	Helen Dingwall
DDi	**David Ditchburn**
PD	Philip Dixon
DDo	David Dobson
RAD	R A Dodgshon
JGD	J G Dunbar
AAMD	A A M Duncan
JD	John Durkan
AE	Alexis Easson
WKE	W K Emond
EE	Elizabeth Ewan
RF	Richard Fawcett
EF	Elaine Finnie
IF	Ian Fisher
JDG	J D Galbraith
AGi	Alexander Gibson
JMG	John M Gilbert
AGr	Alexander Grant
WSH	W S Hanson
CH	Caroline Hardie
IBH	I B Henderson
LJFK	L J F Keppie
JK	James Kirk
JFL	J F Lydon
ML	**Michael Lynch**
NATM	**N A T Macdougall**
CAM	C A McGladdery
LJM	L J MacGregor
AIM	A I Macinnes
PGBM	**Peter G B McNeill**
AM	Alan Macquarrie
HLM	**Hector L MacQueen**
GSM	G S Maxwell
MM	Maureen Meikle
MHM	Marcus H Merriman
RM	Rosiland Mitchison
IAM	**Ian A Morrison**
JM	Jean Munro
RWM	R W Munro

Key to lettering

Civil divisions

ENGLAND	Kingdoms, modern states
GALLOWAY	Provinces
DARIEN	Imperial provinces, continents
TAYSIDE	Regions 1975
SHETLAND	Islands areas 1975
Fife	Lesser provinces, earldoms, counties, sheriffdoms, bailieries of Ayrshire, stewartries of Perthshire, modern districts (1975), economic regions, quarters of burghs

Ecclesiastical divisions

GLASGOW	Province
Glasgow	Diocese, synod, presbytery
Glasgow	Archdeaconry
Glasgow	Cathedral city, abbey
Glasgow	Deanery

Geographical features

North Sea	Firths, bays, rivers, islands, seas, lochs, capes, points, glens
DRUIMALBAN	Mountains
LEITHEN	Forests
HADRIAN'S WALL	Roman walls
Aberdeen	Towns, castles, forts, camps, parish churches and similar places

Other features

CALEDONII	Tribes
CRAWFORD	Families
Margaret Erskine	Persons
BC	Before Christ, chronological dating
bc	Before Christ, carbon dating

Introductory

Scotland: geography in history

Location is not a geographical constant: people tend to behave in terms of their subjective perceptions rather then objective geography. This atlas runs from before the Roman period up to 1707: viewed either from Rome or from London (in 1707 or indeed today in terms of the heartland of the European community) Scotland may look "peripheral", but not everyone has seen it as so.

The first map shows Scotland's situation on the north-west frontier of the Roman Empire. The second map shows Scotland and other places which are within a 600 mile radius of London.

On "the North West Frontier"...

——— Extent of Roman Empire, early first century

Scotland's place in the world: the view from Rome

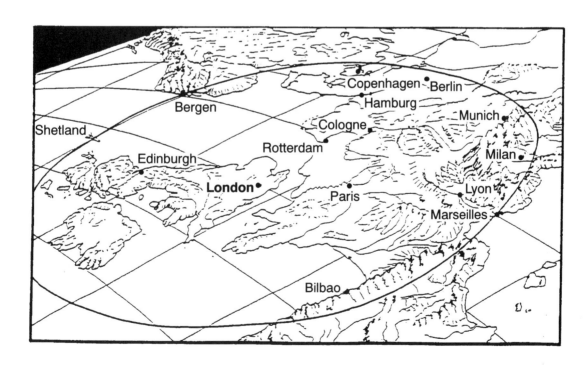

Scotland's place in the world: the view from London

IAM

1

The location and shape of Scotland

Although perceptual mapping is a modern concept, our fore-bears must have had their own mental image of Scotland. These images will inevitably have differed from ours: not only from period to period, but according to their particular cultural, political and economic affiliations. As we embark as twentieth century people on using an atlas set out in conventional modern cartography, it seems desirable to remind ourselves that we can not afford to disregard the likelihood of differences in outlook embodied in the mental maps by which our predecessors lived. One way of doing this is to consider maps with alternative perspectives. This map offers a view of Scotland in which the North Atlantic islands are envisaged as stepping stones on Viking Seaways.

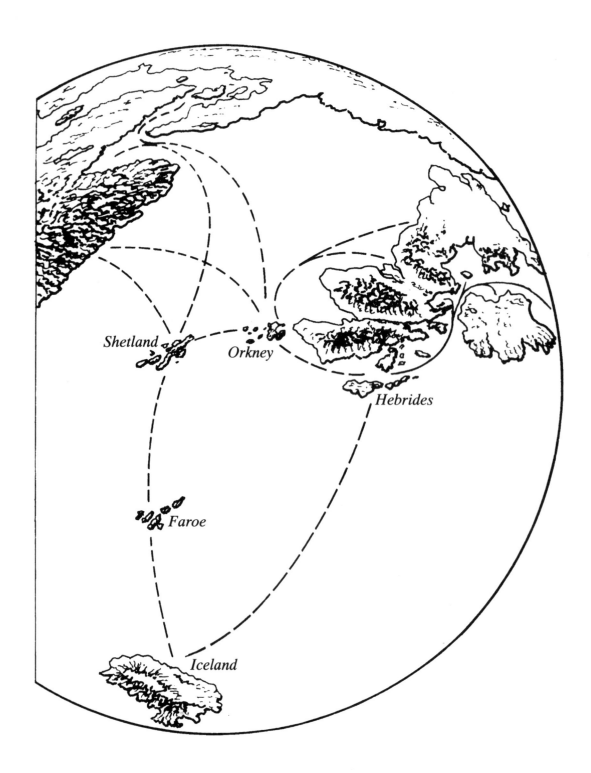

Stepping stones on the Viking seaways

IAM

The location and shape of Scotland

These maps are designed to remind us that the relative importance of different regions within Scotland is likely to have been perceived in contrasting ways by groups with differing cultural and political affiliations.

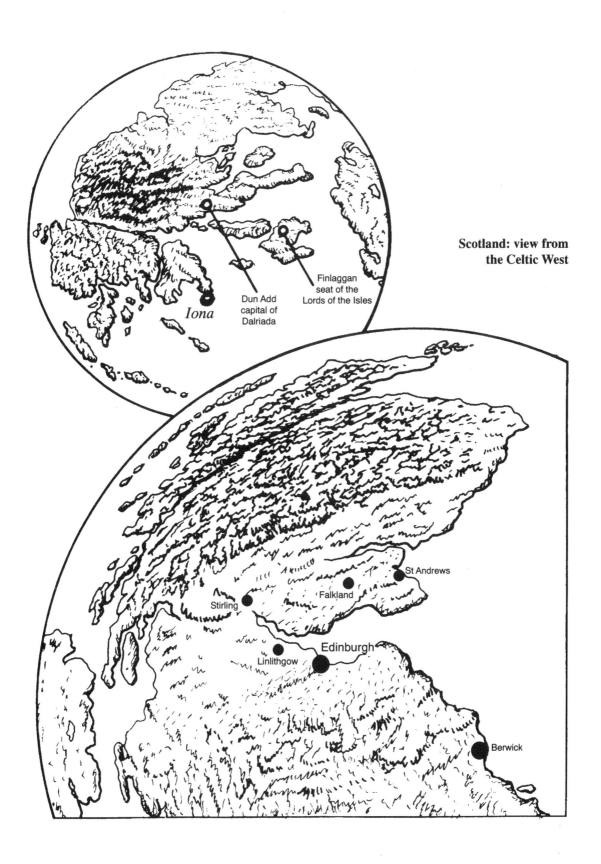

Scotland: view from the Celtic West

Dun Add capital of Dalriada

Finlaggan seat of the Lords of the Isles

Iona

St Andrews

Falkland

Stirling

Edinburgh

Linlithgow

Berwick

Scotland: view from the feudalising South-east

IAM

Routeways

Our motorcar minds tend to condition our perception of Scotland; but throughout the period covered by this atlas, much of the country was not an easy land for wheels. Seaways, river and loch routes were of major significance. This was so not only to groups whom we stereotype as seafarers, such as the Vikings or those of the lordship of the Isles.

Thus, for example, in interpreting much of the settlement pattern and history of Galloway, it can be profitable to regard the region not as " the bottom left hand corner of mainland Scotland", but rather as a peninsula integral to a maritime province. This is shown in the first map where the view is towards the West.

Equally, the Firth of Forth is perhaps better regarded as a conduit leading to the North Sea and indeed Baltic for the medieval traders of the Fife and Lothian ports, rather than as a local barrier within central Scotland.

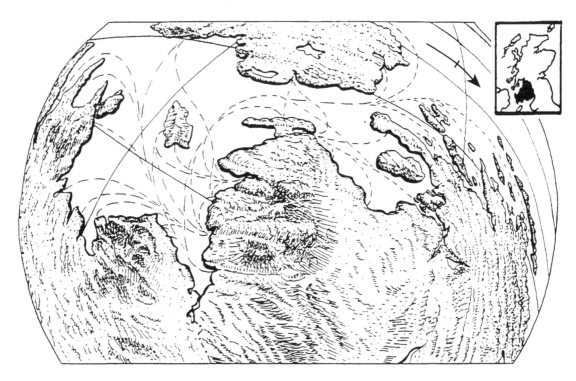

Galloway in context

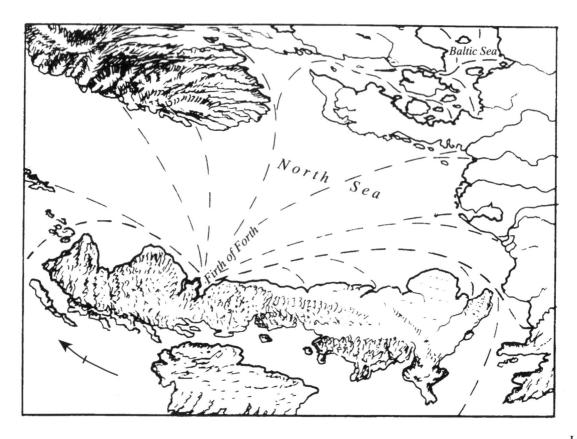

Firth of Forth and the North Sea

IAM

4

Routeways

Within the landmass of Scotland itself, the bedrock configuration together with the recency and severity of glaciation are key factors in the landscape patterns within which Scotland's history has been acted out.

Because of glacial disruption of drainage, outwith the major Firths of Forth, Clyde and Tay, Scotland has few navigable rivers. The long freshwater and sea-lochs are, however, a positive legacy from glaciation, offering fast routes to boatmen through rugged mountain country, though characteristically in directions controlled by south-west to north-east orientation of the "Caledonian trend" of bedrock structures.

This trend, and the way the structures were trenched out by the ice, has certainly influenced the pattern of overland routeways, lending special value in trade and war to valleys breaching the trend. Though the heyday of Scotland's drove roads was largely after the formal limit of this atlas, they offer a good indication of routes feasible in topographic terms throughout history. Those actually favoured in different periods of course reflected human factors ranging from politics and lawlessness to market forces, as much as physiography.

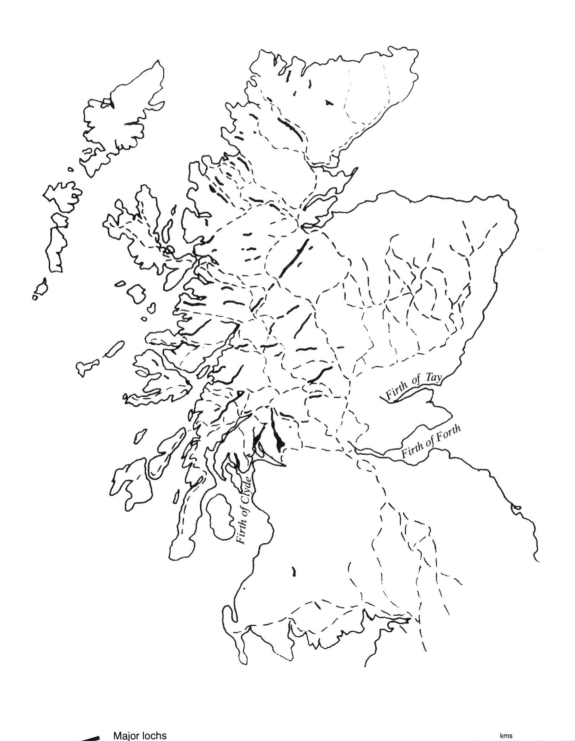

Major lochs
Drove roads

kms
0   25   50   75   100
0   10   20   30   40   50   60
miles

IAM

Routeways: major lochs and drove roads

Glaciation

Although there is truth in the stereotype of a rugged Highland "North" and a more fecund "South", both the rocks and glacial effects show west/east distinctions with important human implications. This is further reinforced by their interactions with climatic patterns, as appears in later maps: in particular, the essentially easterly distribution of Old Red Sandstone, (first map), important from Merse to Orkney for giving friable, well-drained soils, which warm up earlier in the spring than heavy clay tills.

With the weather coming in off the Atlantic in glacial times, as at the present day, the mountains of the west tended to engender the heaviest precipitation, giving severe glacial scouring on that side of the country, as shown in the next map. Combined with the intransigence of the metamorphically hardened bedrocks characteristic of the north-west, this has often given landscapes with poor soil cover and very limited agricultural potential. This is illustrated in the last map.

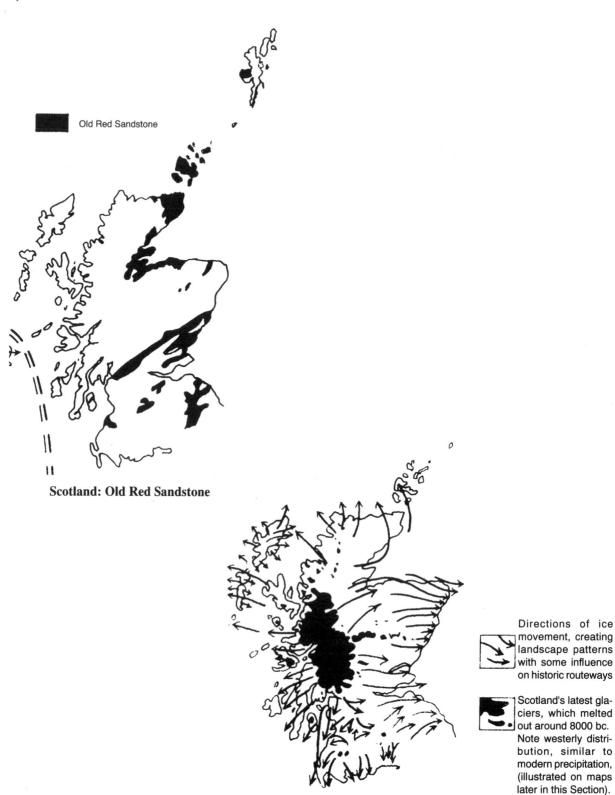

■ Old Red Sandstone

Scotland: Old Red Sandstone

Directions of ice movement, creating landscape patterns with some influence on historic routeways

Scotland's latest glaciers, which melted out around 8000 bc. Note westerly distribution, similar to modern precipitation, (illustrated on maps later in this Section).

Scotland: glaciation   IAM

6

Glaciation

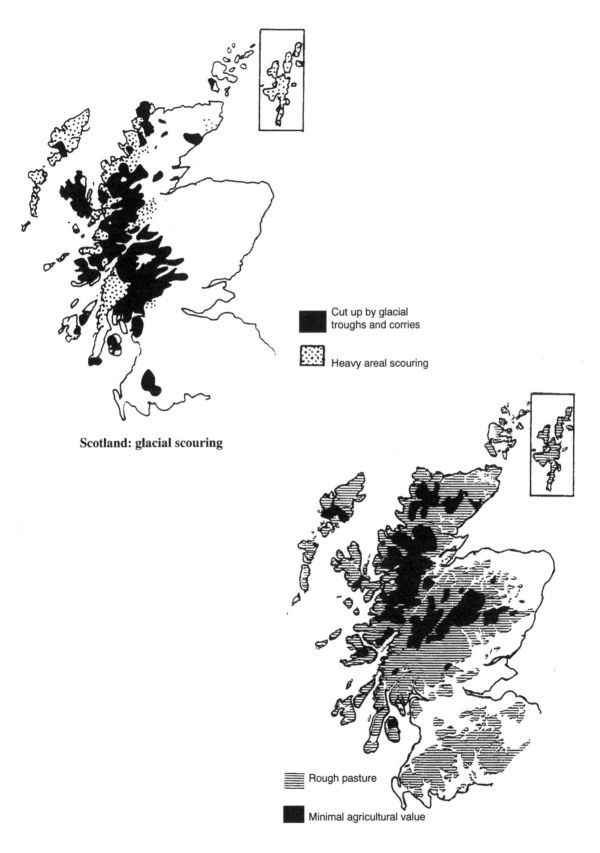

Cut up by glacial troughs and corries

Heavy areal scouring

Scotland: glacial scouring

Rough pasture

Minimal agricultural value

Scotland: agricultural potential

IAM

Land- and sea-level changes

The last major valley glaciers in Scotland melted around 10,000 bc (by uncalibrated radiocarbon dating). For several millennia, a race ensued. Sea level rose sporadically, as ice masses elsewhere melted and restored their water to the world's oceans. The earth's crust in Scotland was also rising, but not equally in all places: recovery tended to be greater where the ice loading had caused the most depression. Towards the periphery of Scotland, the overall result tended to be submergence, but everywhere the sequence was complex and raised beaches are widespread. Often their sands have improved land use potential, by lightening glacial tills (for example, in the Fringe o' Gowd round the East Neuk of Fife).

The carse clays (which are shown in the last map) are another kind of legacy of agricultural importance: rich estuarine muds largely emerging above sea-level from around 4000 bc (radiocarbon dating). For example, the carselands flanking the meanders east of Stirling were highly regarded: "The links o' Forth are worth an Earldom in the North." This potential was not always realised, however. Thus west of Stirling the deep peat that had colonised the carse surface was not cleared until the eighteenth century and even now Lochar Moss still covers much of the carse by Dumfries.

The first map shows the distortion over the last six thousand years or so: this is shown by the uplift contours derived from the main post glacial shore lines. The two remaining maps show the Dumfries area as an example of the extent to which parts of Scotland's coastline have changed during the period of known human occupation.

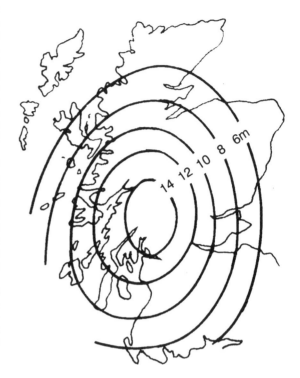

Scotland: uplift contours

Dumfries area

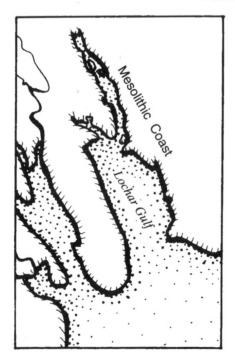

Before deposit of carse clay

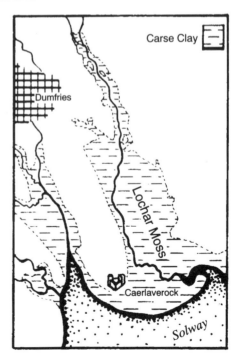

After deposit of carse clay

IAM

8

Land- and sea-level changes

Carse clays and other major expanses of post-glacial raised beaches

IAM

The shaping of settlements

Many criteria affecting the configuration of settlements are of course purely cultural and economic (and may indeed even reflect the influence of individuals). In Scotland, however, topographic patterning is also often evident. Sometimes motifs repeat themselves with remarkable consistency. For example, the geomorphological evolution of the coast line is reflected in the linear layout of the older parts of the East Neuk burghs. Part of a maritime culture involving both fishing and trading, they are perched just above present sea-level on an ancient wave-cut rock platform, constrained from spreading landwards by the fossil cliffline at their backs.

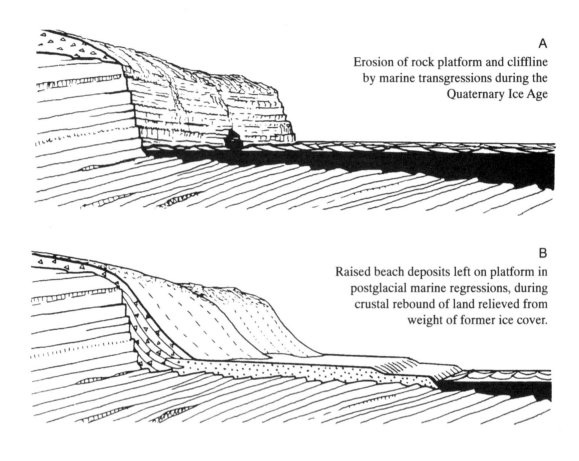

A

Erosion of rock platform and cliffline by marine transgressions during the Quaternary Ice Age

B

Raised beach deposits left on platform in postglacial marine regressions, during crustal rebound of land relieved from weight of former ice cover.

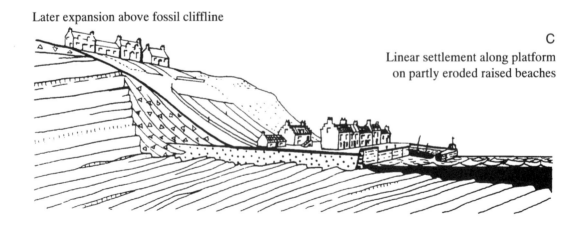

Later expansion above fossil cliffline

C

Linear settlement along platform on partly eroded raised beaches

Evolution of the coastline: East Neuk burghs

IAM

10

The shaping of settlements

Larger settlements too can reflect remarkable consistency in the ways that the potential of topographic features was appraised and exploited. Thus, the sites on which medieval Stirling and Edinburgh were developed both consist of crag and tail landforms, created where the glacial flow encountered resistant volcanic features.

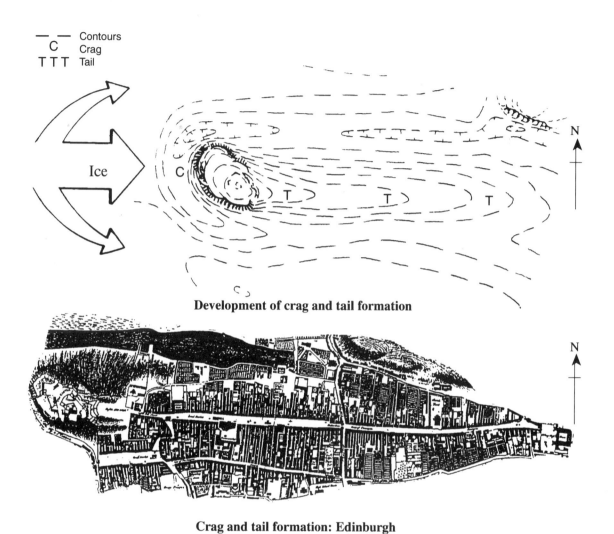

Development of crag and tail formation

Crag and tail formation: Edinburgh

Crag and tail formation: Stirling

IAM

11

The siting of settlements

As with the shaping of settlements, so too does their siting, of course, reflect very human criteria. What has seemed desirable to different groups has varied with social aims, political and economic circumstances, and technological developments. Patterns of siting have thus certainly tended to change through time. Nevertheless, some themes appear to recur, and two that seem particularly notable in Scotland are subsistence and strife.

Scotland's long history of strife has been at every level, from local lawlessness through regional factionalism to major invasions.

Crannog lake dwellings were one extreme but remarkably persistent response to this, featuring in Scotland's loch-strewn landscape from prehistory through to the seventeenth century. Not all were refuges; some were bases for aggression. Their detailed siting often exhibits a compromise between security from natural and human hazards, and convenient access to subsistence. The same seems true of the placing of many of Scotland's tower houses.

The tower houses of the more ambitious magnates also suggest sites chosen to combine local tactical advantages with a wider view of strategic potential for regional control. An example of this is the stronghold of the Black Douglases at Threave. This commands a nodal point of route ways, from the security of an island in the River Dee.

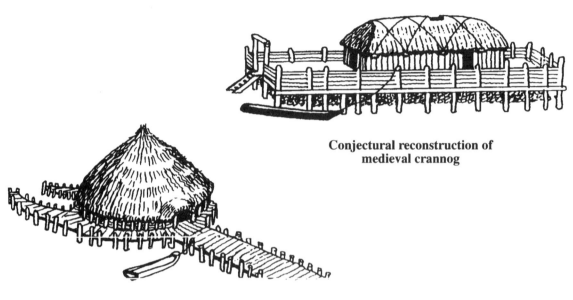

Conjectural reconstruction of medieval crannog

Conjectural reconstruction of prehistoric crannog

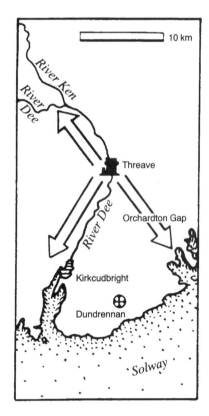

Threave Castle: strategic location

Threave Castle: tactical location on islet on the River Dee

IAM

The siting of settlements

Similar factors also seem involved in the siting of major centres of power, evolving to dominate routes in strategic nodal zones, but, within these, seeking sites offering local security. Stirling on its crag and tail is one example of this.

Perched on its strongpoint at the head of tidal navigation, Stirling had access to the North Sea, but also controlled internal routes. Until the major peat clearance in the late eighteenth century the importance of its siting as a strategic bridgepoint at the head of the Forth estuary was enhanced by the difficulty of crossing the deep bog which had overlain the carse clay to the west since perhistoric times.

In pre-industrial Scotland, most people were in need of fairly direct access to the basic components of subsistence: reliable water supply; food from land or sea or both; fuel, often peat. This pattern is still apparent in areas not subjected to later industrialisation and urbanisation. For example, in parts of the Northern and Western Isles, continuity of Viking steading names right through to present day crofts illustrates the persistence of these basic criteria in siting, for at least a millennium.

Stirling: strategic position

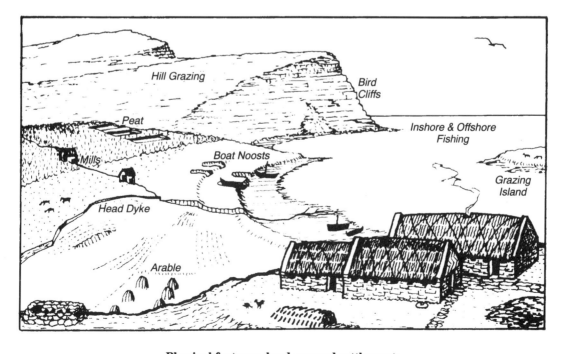

Physical features, land use and settlements

IAM

Subsistence potential of the land

Through much of the period covered by this atlas, when so many of the people got their subsistence immediately from the land, the population of Scotland has been of the order of only one-tenth of that of mainland Britain. Many factors are of course involved. However, this is in such striking contrast to the more closely comparable surface areas that it nevertheless highlights the limited land use potential characteristic of much of Scotland.

This is not merely a matter of the legacies of bedrock geology and glacial processes, though these are cardinal in pro-ducing the basic pattern with its west to east as well as south to north components.

Altitude is another major element, with its implications for temperature and precipitation. However, considerable areas of "harsh" lands lie not only at the level of the Grampian tops, but right down at sea level in the west. The phenomenon of "oceanicity" has affected Scotland's climate in ways important, throughout history, to those seeking to make their living from the land.

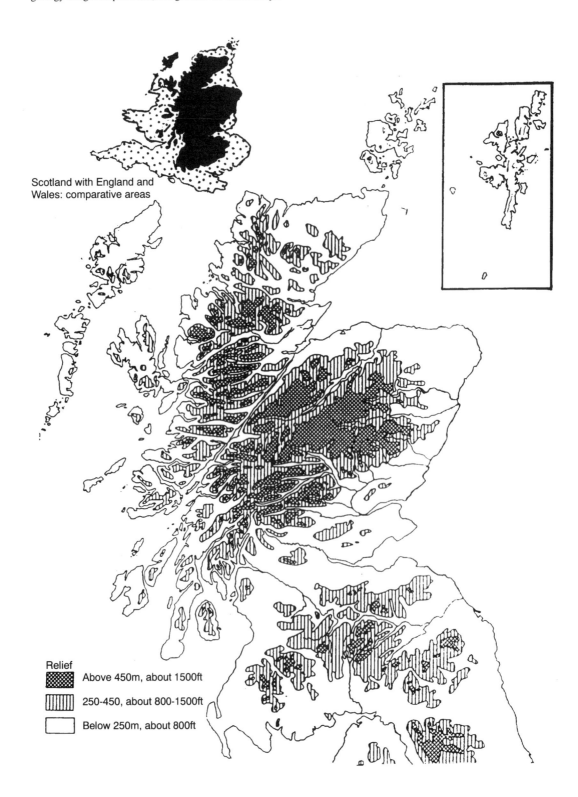

Scotland with England and Wales: comparative areas

Relief

▨	Above 450m, about 1500ft
▥	250-450, about 800-1500ft
☐	Below 250m, about 800ft

Scotland: relief

IAM

14

Subsistence potential of the land

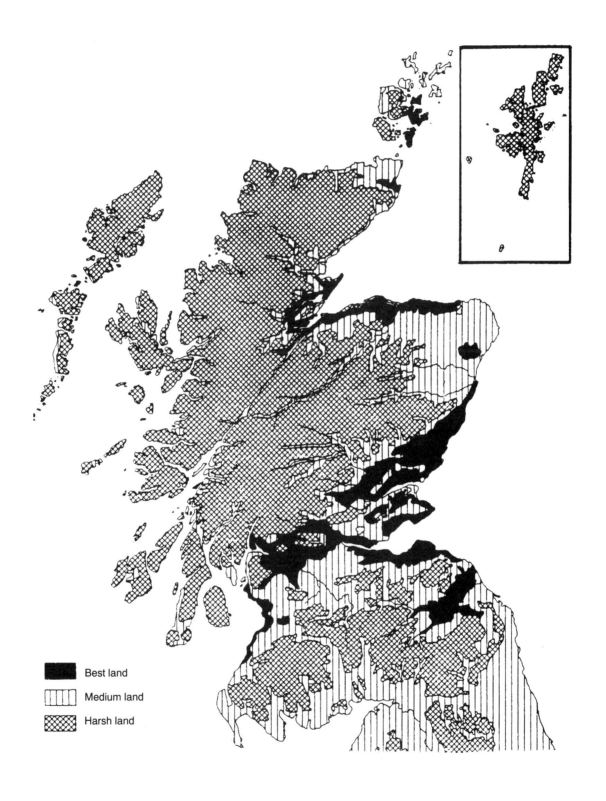

Best land

Medium land

Harsh land

Scotland: land quality

IAM

Climatic processes

With the predominant westerly winds bringing weather in off the Atlantic, the effect of the ocean on Scotland's climate is a profound but paradoxical one. Thus, despite a latitude reaching that of Greenland, warmth from the waters of the North Atlantic Drift keeps winters relatively mild. Yet in summer the heat-sink effect of the deep ocean holds down growing season temperatures, making crop ripening more marginal than in countries with more continental regimes, though these tend to have much more severe winters. Thus even southern Finland is better for ripening crops than much of Scotland.

Also within Scotland, cereals ripen to much higher altitudes in the east, which is not only farther from the Atlantic heat-sink, but in the rainshadow of the mountains, with clearer skies. The shallow North Sea downwind is of much less climatic significance. Sandier soils in the east also dry out faster

and warm up quicker in the spring.

The flatter "oceanic" annual temperature curve in the west seriously reduces the amount of heat (measured in "accumulated day degrees") available above the threshold temperature needed for crops to grow. Thus, in contrast to the high-peaked curves of continental inlands, even a small change in conditions can be critical - whether due to climatic variations through time, or to altitude locally.

Thus, vertical distances in, say, the Alps are of much less practical importance than in Scotland, and in particular, in Atlantic Scotland. There, even a small vertical change can severely constrain agriculture, while to ascend Ben Nevis from the relatively bland lowland at Fort William is to approach the climate of Greenland.

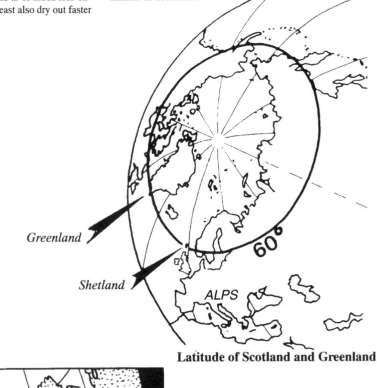

Latitude of Scotland and Greenland

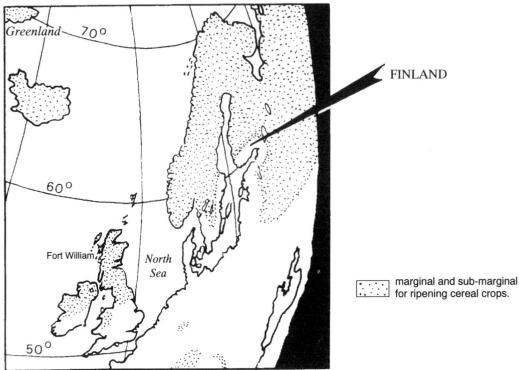

marginal and sub-marginal
for ripening cereal crops.

Ripening of cereal crops in northern Europe

IAM

16

Climatic processes

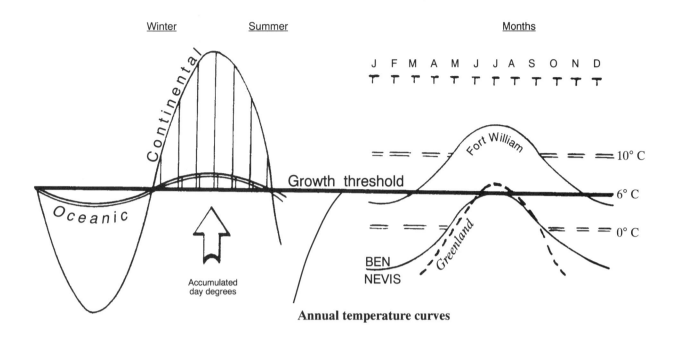

Annual temperature curves

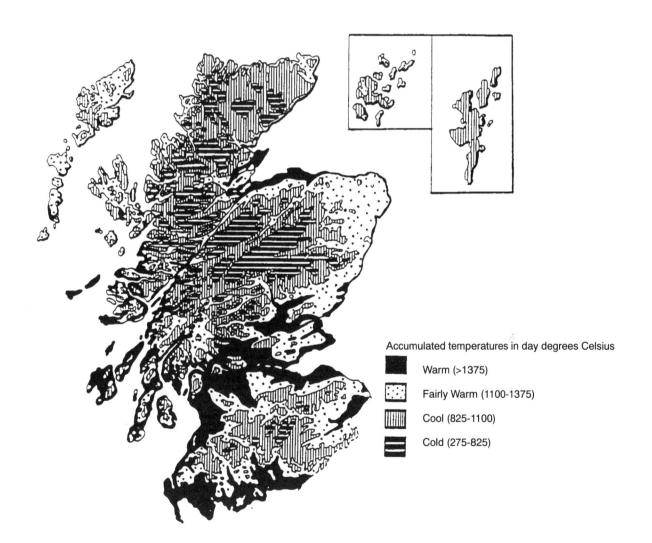

Accumulated temperatures in day degrees Celsius

■ Warm (>1375)

Fairly Warm (1100-1375)

Cool (825-1100)

Cold (275-825)

Accumulated temperatures in day degrees Celsius

IAM

17

Regional climates

As Scottish farmers are well aware, climate can vary significantly on a very local scale, with difference of exposure to wind and rain, and the aspect of slopes to the sun's rays. Neverthe-less, the general length of the growing season is one indicator which offers a broad overview of regional differences in the potential of Scotland for agriculture.

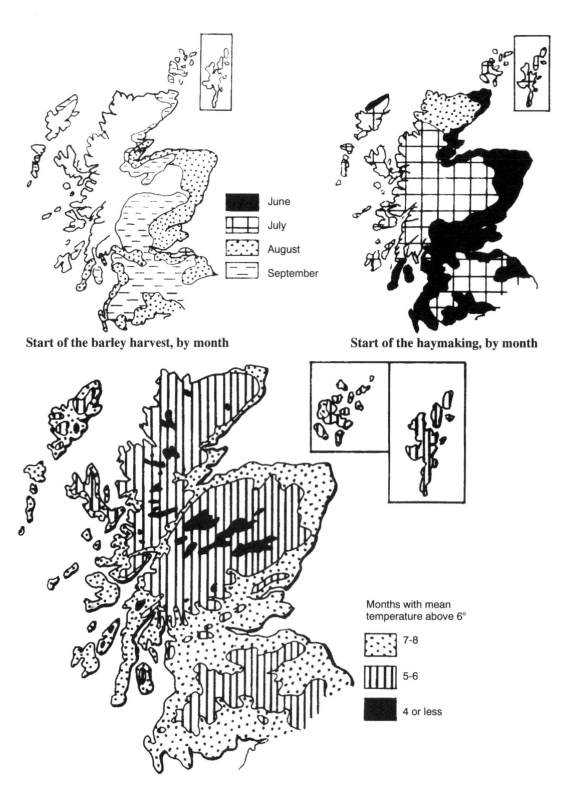

Start of the barley harvest, by month

Start of the haymaking, by month

June

July

August

September

Months with mean
temperature above 6°

7-8

5-6

4 or less

Length of growing season

IAM

18

Regional climates

To complement this, of more use than the basic rainfall map is an index which takes account of both warmth and precipitation to bring out where the moisture balance is most and least favourable for agriculture. Again, this calculation emphasises that we should keep in mind that climate conspires with soil geology and topography to favour the east for agriculture, to considerably higher altitudes than in the oceanic west, and as far north as Dornoch and indeed Orkney.

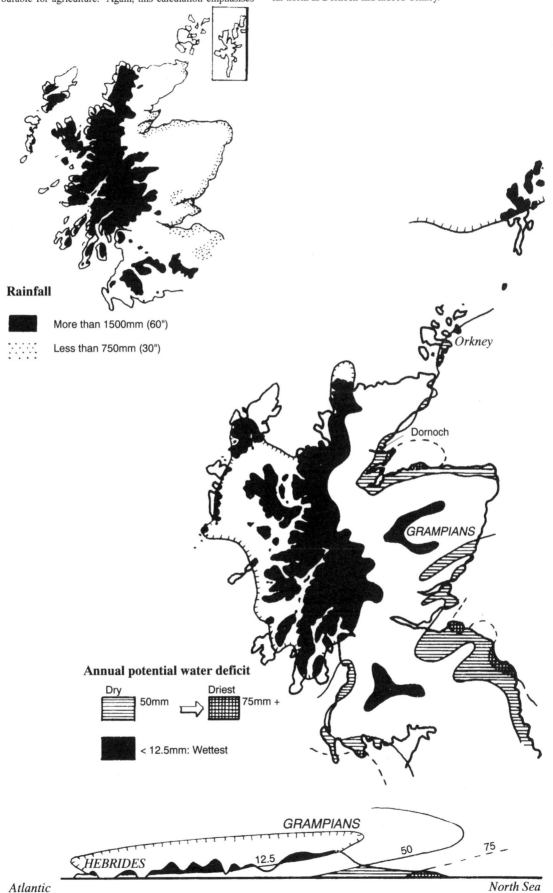

Rainfall

■ More than 1500mm (60")

⠿ Less than 750mm (30")

Orkney

Dornoch

GRAMPIANS

Annual potential water deficit

Dry ▤ 50mm ⟹ Driest ▦ 75mm +

■ < 12.5mm: Wettest

GRAMPIANS

HEBRIDES 12.5 50 75

Atlantic *North Sea*

IAM

Climatic changes

Much of the information presented in the rest of the atlas comprises data derived from archive sources unlikely to be changed in radical ways by future finds of fresh material. In contrast, since historical documentary evidence for climate change tends to be indirect and problematic, palaeoclimatologists actively pursue new data, from a whole range of laboratory and field sciences. Because of concern over global warming, governments are now financing extensive research into former climatic changes, in the hope that the past may cast its shadow into the future. Our picture of climatic change is thus under constant reassessment, so no definitive model can be offered here. Nonetheless, as historians we would be injudicious to neglect the basic fact that the physical environment which was the context for the activities of our forebears was characterised by almost constant change. The aim of what follows is therefore to give a general indication of the nature of the variations involved, with the proviso that revisions may certainly be expected.

Before exploring the sequences of change, it is important to emphasise that the interaction between Scotland's global position and physiography produces a basic climate, with characteristic regional subdivisions, and that the patterns illustrated in the previous pages have been largely characteristic of Scotland during the whole period covered by the atlas. These patterns have been modified but never obliterated by the postglacial climatic variations. Thus, while the margins between zones have been shifting almost continuously, the major positive and negative core areas of high and low "climatic productivity potential" have remained dominant features of our Scottish landscapes, throughout medieval and recent times. A basic fact of life in Scotland of which we must not lose sight is that a large portion of the country has always remained a harsh environment for subsistence agriculturalists.

Nevertheless, what people actually choose to do is by no means necessarily synonymous with what is theoretically possible in terms of their physical environment. For example, people may farm farther up the hill even in climatically adverse periods because they rate the risks of using more marginal land as being less dangerous than the hazard of living down in the lowlands in time of strife. Alternatively, people may descend from the hills even in times of better climate if more land becomes available below, because of forest or peat clearance, say. Furthermore, pressure on land resources may change through demographic trends much less dramatic than, say, the Black Death. Changes in spatial patterns may also arise from alterations in the balance between subsistence agriculture and more commercially oriented types of land use. These in turn may reflect either relatively local economic changes, or large scale changes of the pattern of international markets, and of political access to them.

In considering relationships between people and their environments, it seems that we must keep in mind changes in climates of opinion as much as changes in meteorological ones.

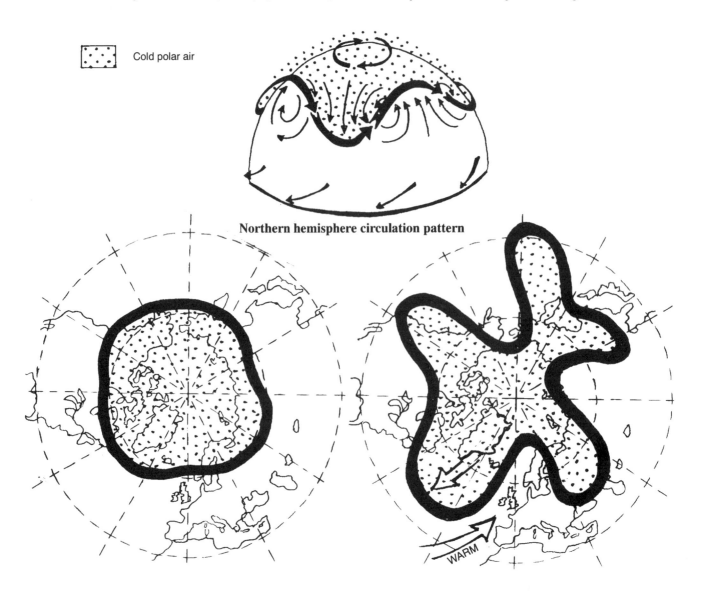

Cold polar air

Northern hemisphere circulation pattern

Common zonal pattern

Phase of meridional thrusts

WARM

IAM

20

Climatic changes

Prelude

The era in which we live seems to be merely one of the many interglacials which have temporarily intervened in the Quaternary Ice Age which has occupied most of the last 2.6 million years. Indeed, the ten thousand years of the present 'post-glacial' period probably passed its best over five thousand years ago, in its climatic optimum. Scotland came close to the re-establishment of glaciers during much of the medieval and post-medieval period. In many parts of the world, glaciers did in fact reassert themselves and this has become known as "the Little Ice Age".

Early medieval warm phase

The last really warm phase before the onset of the Little Ice Age ran from about AD 970 towards 1200, with much of the world perhaps at times approaching the warmth of the Climatic Optimum of approximately 5000 to 3000 BC. This amelioration would certainly have affected Scotland, since in Norway corn was grown to almost 70° north from AD 880 until the eleventh century. There were vineyards in England, and in many parts of Britain tillage was extended uphill to greater heights than for some time previously or since: Kelso Abbey for example had a grange at 300 metres (about 1000 feet), with over 100 hectares of tillage.

Complex end of the warm phase

The way that the warm phase ended demonstrates that it is an oversimplification to expect changes to involve mere north-south shifts in temperature zones. Thus, though the warm phase passed its peak in Greenland in the twelfth century, it probably persisted in Europe until 1300 or 1310, though with an increase in severe storms affecting the North Sea, with sea-storm flooding on the low-lying coasts. The warmth may even have reached its maximum at this late stormy stage, for there is some evidence that in the 1280s tillage reached notably high levels. This would be meteorologically consistent, suggesting a strong outward thrust of the Arctic regimes in the longitudes of Greenland and Iceland, distorting the pattern of the circumpolar vortex with a sharp salient there being balanced by a recurrent warm sector over western Europe. This type of change is illustrated N.B.

The Little Ice Age begins

Soon after 1300 the cooling trend abruptly began to affect Europe. In Scotland the growing season was shortened, perhaps typically by three weeks or more; the accumulated warmth for growing and ripening crops decreased; and the frequency of harvest failures increased. The Little Ice Age was underway worldwide, and, though there were some significant intermissions, it can be said to have continued right up to Victorian times.

The greater part of the fifteenth century was a time of frequent cold winters and wretched summers. Within the last thousand years, only the 1690s seem to have produced so many severe winter spells within the span of one decade as the 1430s.

An early sixteenth century intermission

Evidence widespread round the world suggests some amelioration at the beginning of the sixteenth century. Scotland seems to have benefited from the rather frequent anticyclones affecting the latitudes 45° to 50° north, with westerly winds bringing the moderating influence off the waters of the North Atlantic Drift into northern Europe. The effect was warmth approaching that of the post-Little Ice Age phase of the first half of the twentieth century. This ended suddenly. The winter of 1564-6 exceeded in length and harshness any winter since the 1430s.

Little Ice Age

Sea Ice

Northern limits of Gulf Stream influence

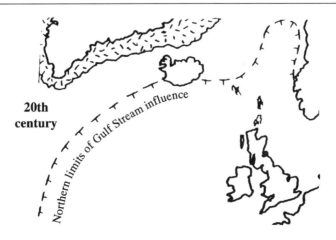

20th century

Northern limits of Gulf Stream influence

IAM

Climatic changes

The climax of the Little Ice Age

Although there were some variations, overall the next 150 years in all parts of the world saw a substantially colder regime than now, with phases representing the coldest regimes since the last Ice Age ended ten thousand years ago. Broadly, from the 1550s until 1700 the severity in Scotland tended to involve a high frequency of anticyclones centred north of 60° north, the latitude of Shetland, with winds from the north-east, and south-east ones from Europe to the south of that latitude. The north-east winds brought polar, air and in the winter- the south-east ones entrained air from the rapidly cooling continental interior.

The heat-bank of the North Atlantic Ocean soon began to cool down. By the 1580s, in several summers navigators found the seas between Iceland and Greenland impassable because of sea ice. The Arctic water spread right across the North Atlantic, with several consequences for Scotland's climate in the late sixteenth and seventeenth centuries. Thus the enhanced thermal gradient between latitudes 50 and 65 north created cyclonic wind storms which could exceed most of those of the present century, with sandblows transforming landscapes at Culbin and Udal. This strengthened gradient implicit in the low sea temperatures, with temperatures depressed significantly farther in parts of Scotland than in central England.

Intermissions

Although in general the conditions for agriculturalists from the 1550s on through into the eighteenth century were less propitious than the first half of the sixteenth century, they were not always of unmitigated harshness. Around 1670 however the climate deteriorated seriously again.

The most severe phase of the Little Ice Age

The final decades of the seventeenth century are now widely agreed to have been the harshest phase of the Little Ice Age, for most areas of the world. In Scotland as in many other areas, it was not only winter which became harder. Cool summers caused harvest failures, and clusters of these brought disaster to subsistence farmers by forcing them to eat their reserves of seed corn, thus leaving them with nothing to plant for later years. Between 1693 and 1700, the harvests failed in seven years out of eight in many upland areas.

Remission

The opening of the eighteenth century, leading up to the Union of the parliaments when coverage of this atlas ends, brought a welcome remission. Soon after 1700 around the world there was a widespread and rapid shift to warmer conditions. Even in this warming period however there were severe winters and poor harvests, and the Age of Improvement was not to prove an easy one for Scottish farmers as the harsh conditions returned in the later part of the eighteenth century.

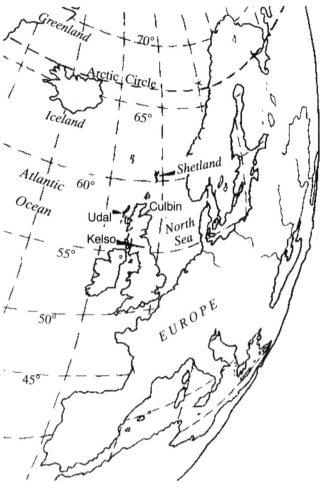

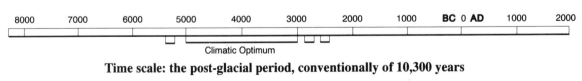

Time scale: the post-glacial period, conventionally of 10,300 years

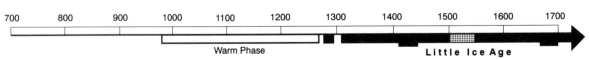

Time scale: AD 700 to 1700

IAM

22

Interaction of natural and anthropogenic processes

In the habitat offered by Scotland, throughout historic time natural elements have been varying of their own accord, and have also been affected in complex ways, directly and indirectly, by the actions (deliberate and inadvertent) of people and their animals.

And although in popular usage the word "environment" has tended to become shorthand for the physical and biological aspects of our planet, as historians we cannot but be conscious that the effective "environment" of any group also embraces their human interactions in peace and war with other cultures beyond their own land.

These physical and human interactions often involve complex networks of interlinked paths, with patterns which have continuously changed their configurations through time.

Thus, in contemplating the maps which lie ahead in this atlas, we can seldom afford to regard them as individual entities with a simple message. We need to consider how far each may reflect physical and human patterns both within Scotland and elsewhere in the world - and we need to remind ourselves both that these patterns were subject to changes within themselves, and also that they could interact in dynamic ways. These ideas have been represented by some authors in a diagrammatic way. One possibility is offered here:-

Network diagram to suggest the multi-directional interplay of local and distant factors

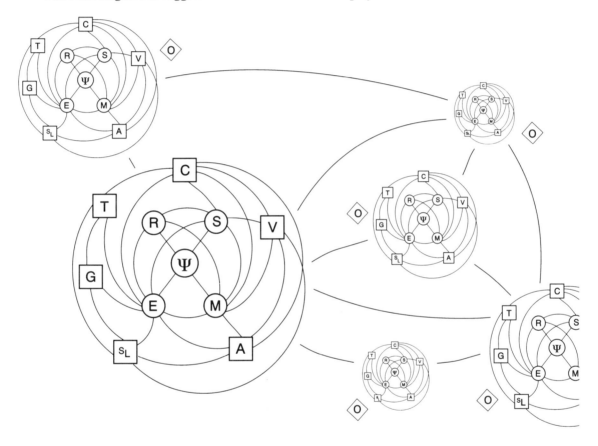

Ψ	Psychological attitude to innovation	G	Geology: bedrock and surface deposits
S	Social aspirations and constraints	T	Terrain: landscape and configuration
R	Religious outlook	C	Climate and microclimates
E	Economic resources and organisation	sL	Soil
M	Material culture and technology	V	Vegetation and crops
		A	Animals: domestic and wild

O   Other sociocultural units: also changing through time, and involved in interactions with each other as well as with Scotland

Drawn from Le Play's *Lieu, Travail, Famille* and developed by Daryll Forde as 'Habitat, Economy, Society', Patrick Geddes's concept of multi-way interaction between 'Place, Work, Folk' remains a simple but useful tool to help us keep in mind the realities of life in Scotland. His son, Arthur Geddes, used the matrix form to emphasise the multidirectional nature of the interplay.

PLACE ⇌ WORK ⇌ FOLK

FOLK ⇌ PLACE ⇌ WORK

WORK ⇌ FOLK ⇌ PLACE

IAM

Provinces and districts

This is an inventory map of some provinces, districts and other areas which have acquired a degree of unity by reason of history or geography. Some are islands; others are well defined peninsulas, such as Ardnamurchan. Some are geographical features such as promontories (like the Mull of Kintyre) or river valleys, like Strathnaver. Other areas acquired a degree of cohesion by virtue of ownership or lordship exercised by laymen or clergymen or the crown. Another group correspond - to some extent, at least - to the later counties: one of these is Tweeddale, the later county of Peebles. The area to which a particular name referred could fluctuate greatly over the centuries: thus, Moray in the early period stretched across Scotland, but latterly, it was a county of middle size. Elsewhere in the atlas, many of these reappear as lordships, baronies, thanages, regalities, stewartries, sheriffdoms, bishoprics and parishes.

Scotland from abroad

The map which bears the name "Matthew Paris" belongs to thirteenth century England and is in the form of four maps of England and Scotland. The maps are very limited and only record 36 places in Scotland. Many of the places indicated are consistent with this being a traveller's map: several religious houses are shown, as are crossing places such as Queensferry, Earlsferry and a bridge at Stirling.

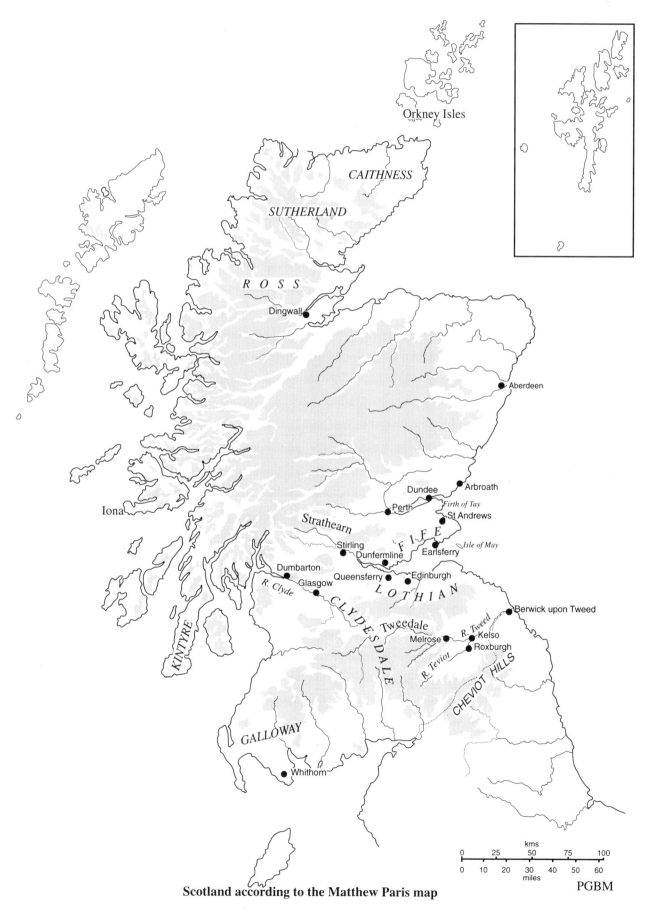

Scotland according to the Matthew Paris map

PGBM

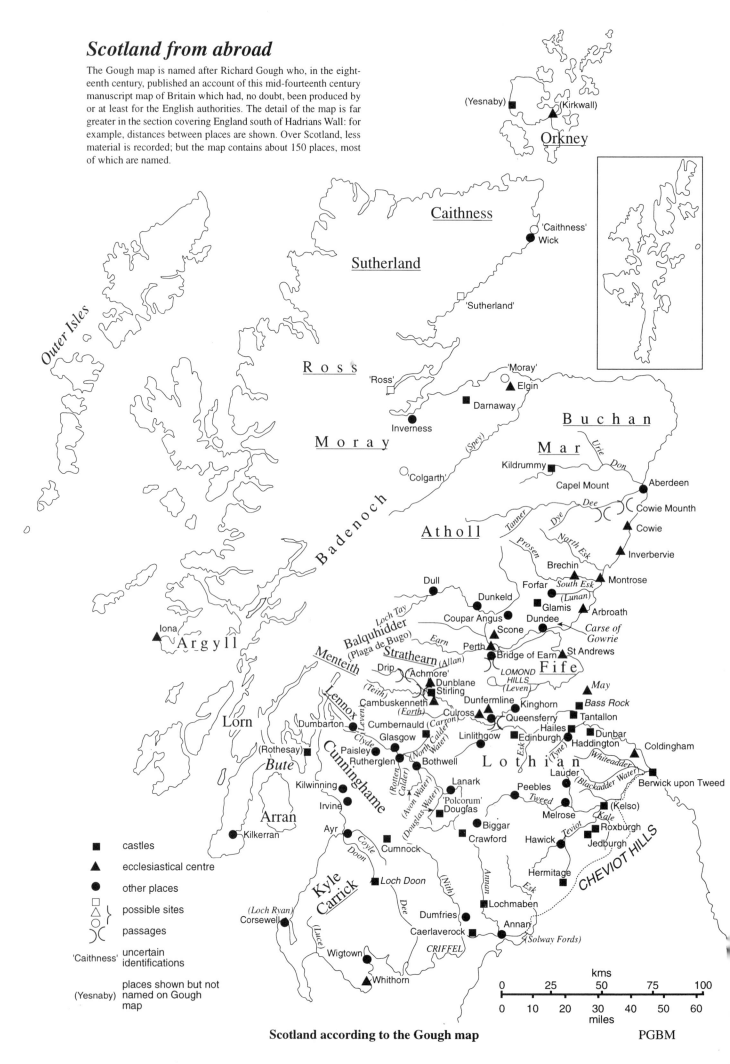

Scotland from abroad

The Gough map is named after Richard Gough who, in the eighteenth century, published an account of this mid-fourteenth century manuscript map of Britain which had, no doubt, been produced by or at least for the English authorities. The detail of the map is far greater in the section covering England south of Hadrians Wall: for example, distances between places are shown. Over Scotland, less material is recorded; but the map contains about 150 places, most of which are named.

Orkney

(Yesnaby)
(Kirkwall)

Caithness

'Caithness'
Wick

Sutherland

'Sutherland'

Outer Isles

R o s s

'Ross'

'Moray'
Elgin
Darnaway

B u c h a n

M a r

M o r a y

Inverness

'Colgarth'

Kildrummy

Capel Mount

Aberdeen

Cowie Mounth

(Spey)

B a d e n o c h

(Urie)

(Don)

A t h o l l

(Dee)

(Dye)

(Tanner)

Cowie

Inverbervie

(North Esk)

(Prosen)

Brechin

Montrose

Dull

Dunkeld

Forfar

(South Esk)

Glamis

(Lunan)

Arbroath

Iona

A r g y l l

Loch Tay

Balquhidder
(Plaga de Bugo)

S t r a t h e a r n

Coupar Angus

Scone

Dundee

Carse of
Gowrie

(Earn)

Perth

M e n t e i t h

Drip

'Achmore'

(Allan)

Bridge of Earn

St Andrews

LOMOND
HILLS
(Leven)

F i f e

Lennox

(Teith)

Dunblane
Stirling

May

Cambuskenneth

Dunfermline

Kinghorn

Bass Rock

L o r n

Dumbarton

(Forth)

Culross

Queensferry

Tantallon

Cumbernauld

(Carron)

Hailes

Dunbar

(Rothesay)

Glasgow

(North Calder
Water)

Linlithgow

Edinburgh

Haddington

Coldingham

B u t e

Paisley

Rutherglen

Bothwell

L o t h i a n

(Tyne)

(Whiteadder)

C u n n i n g h a m e

(Clyde)

(Leven)

(Rotten
Calder)

Lanark

Lauder

(Blackadder Water)

Berwick upon Tweed

Kilwinning

(Avon Water)

(Douglas Water)

'Polcorum'
Douglas

Peebles

(Tweed)

(Kelso)

A r r a n

Irvine

Biggar

Melrose

(Kale)

Roxburgh

Kilkerran

Ayr

(Coyle)

(Doon)

Crawford

Hawick

(Teviot)

Jedburgh

■ castles

▲ ecclesiastical centre

● other places

□ possible sites

△ }

)(passages

'Caithness' uncertain
identifications

(Yesnaby) places shown but not
named on Gough
map

Cumnock

K y l e
C a r r i c k

Loch Doon

(Nith)

(Dee)

(Esk)

Hermitage

C H E V I O T   H I L L S

(Loch Ryan)

Corsewell

(Luce)

Wigtown

Whithorn

Lochmaben

Dumfries

Caerlaverock

Annan

(Annan)

(Solway Fords)

CRIFFEL

kms
0   25   50   75   100

0   10   20   30   40   50   60
miles

Scotland according to the Gough map

PGBM

26

Administrative regions

In the course of the Middle Ages, the unity of the sheriffdoms had been breached by the appearance of enclaves of part of one sheriffdom within another. Similar disjunctions were common in baronial, burghal and ecclesiastical lands and jurisdictions. The sheriffdoms came to be referred to as shires, then as counties. There had been earlier attempts to rationalise county boundaries, but until 1748 apart for the arrangements made for Cromarty and Kinross these had had little effect. In 1748, with respect to jurisdiction only, lands which were disunited from a shire were to be restored or annexed to the shire or shires respectively within which the lands locally lay; and where the lands lay between two shires, they were annexed to the shire of the head burgh of which they were nearest adjacent.

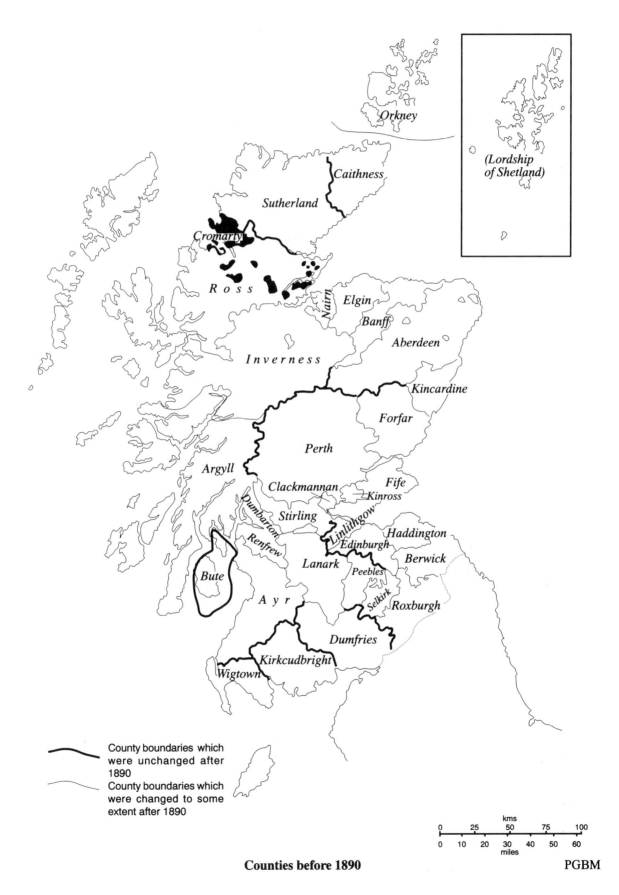

County boundaries which were unchanged after 1890

County boundaries which were changed to some extent after 1890

kms

miles

Counties before 1890

PGBM

Administrative regions

Under the Local Government (Scotland) Act 1889 and associated subordinate legislation there came a radical rationalisation which is shown in the two maps which show the position before and after 1890. Briefly, the effect of the legislation and the orders made under it, was that there was no change in the cases of Caithness, Sutherland, Bute, Wigtown, Kirkcudbright and Dumfries; the "county of Orkney and the lordship of Shetland" were made into two separate counties; but Ross and the greatly fragmented county of Cromarty were made into one single county. Apart from Dumbarton which was left with a detached portion, all the enclaves were absorbed into the surrounding county. Most of the boundaries in the mountainous areas were at the watershed. An example of the effect of the changes at a local level can be seen in the case of Coupar Angus: before 1890 the parish and burgh had been partly in Perthshire and partly in Angus; thereafter they were wholly in Perthshire.

kms
0   25   50   75   100

0 10 20 30 40 50 60
miles

Counties after 1890

PGBM

Administrative regions

In 1975 the former local government units - chiefly the counties and the burghs - which had been modified considerably in the nineteenth and twentieth centuries were replaced by a two-tier system of local government consisting of nine regions and three island areas at the top and 53 districts under them. The largest region - Strathclyde - stretched from Skye to Carrick and had a population of about 2½ million; whereas Orkney had only about 20,000.

The districts in many cases - for example, West Lothian - corresponded in area to the former counties; but the larger and more populous counties were divided into several districts: thus, the county of Ayr was divided into the districts of Kyle and Carrick, Cumnock and Doon Valley, Kilmarnock and Loudon and Cunninghame (which also included Arran and the Cumbraes). The system of 1975 was itself replaced in April 1996 with a system of 32 single tier districts.

Until the nineteenth century there had been one sheriffdom for each county. Finally they were organized in nine groups of counties with one sheriff principal each - except Lanark, which was a single county sheriffdom. After 1975 there were five sheriffdoms based on the regions and the sheriffdom of Glasgow and Strathkelvin.

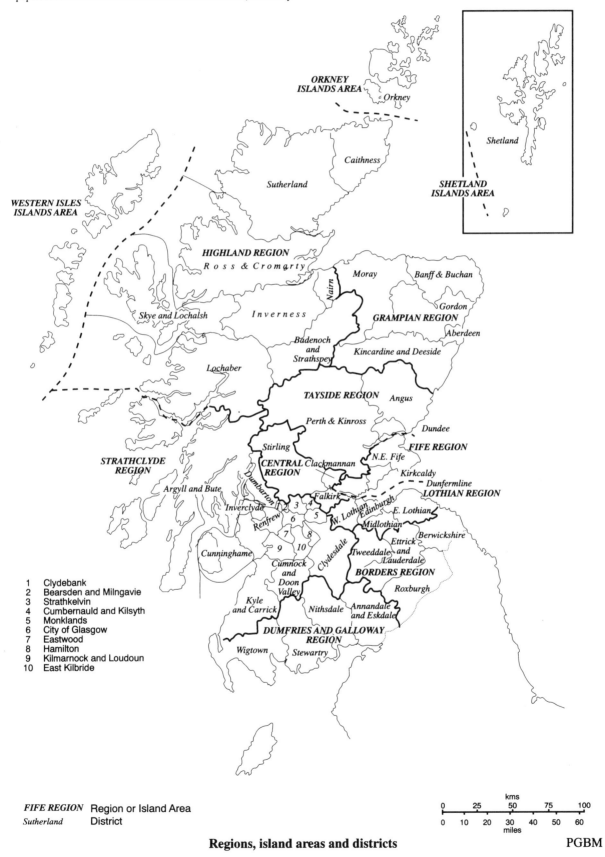

1 Clydebank
2 Bearsden and Milngavie
3 Strathkelvin
4 Cumbernauld and Kilsyth
5 Monklands
6 City of Glasgow
7 Eastwood
8 Hamilton
9 Kilmarnock and Loudoun
10 East Kilbride

FIFE REGION Region or Island Area
Sutherland District

Regions, island areas and districts

PGBM

Territorial extent of Scotland

By 1098 the territorial extent of Scotland was limited to the mainland: the Western Isles and the Northern Isles had become part of the Scandinavian dominions; but the earldom of Caithness came under the Scottish crown.

The attempts of the Scottish crown to extend their dominion over northern England did not endure - especially after the accession of the energetic Henry II. In 1237 the Scottish claims to the northern English counties were abandoned. The Scottish kings did retain lands and honours in England.

By about 1250 or even earlier Arran and Bute had come under the control of the king of Scots. In 1266, after the battle of Largs (1263), the king of Norway ceded the Western Isles - including Man - to Scotland. Man was retained by Scotland between 1266 and about 1290, restored to Scotland in 1293 until 1296, and between 1315 and 1333; therafter it remained in English hands.

Berwick was taken and sacked by Edward I in 1296; it was held by Scotland intermittently until 1482 and was thereafter lost to Scotland; but in 1551, it was made independent of both England and Scotland. For a few years (1315-1318), the Scots under Edward Bruce campaigned in Ireland, but no permanent conquest was achieved.

In 1468-69 the rights of the king of Norway in Orkney and Shetland were given to the Scottish crown as a pledge for the unpaid dowry of the wife of James III; and in 1472, the earldom of Orkney and the lordship of Shet-

land were annexed to the Scottish crown.

The borders contained areas which had been disputed between Scotland and England. In the south-west, there was an area, probably between the river Sark and river Esk, which came to be referred to as the "debateable land". The dispute was resolved in 1551 by assigning the parish of Canonbie to Scotland and the parish of Kirkandrews to England. Other lesser areas of dispute on the Borders - from the river Tweed at Redden Burn, at Gamel's Path Walls and near Liddesdale - persisted but they became of little significance after the Union of the Crowns in 1603.

The changes in sovereignty resulted in changes in ecclesiastical organisation.

Overseas, the Scots began a plantation of Nova Scotia. The lordship of Canada was not followed up by occupation; and the settlement at Darien did not last long. After 1707, imperial expansion took place under the Union flag.

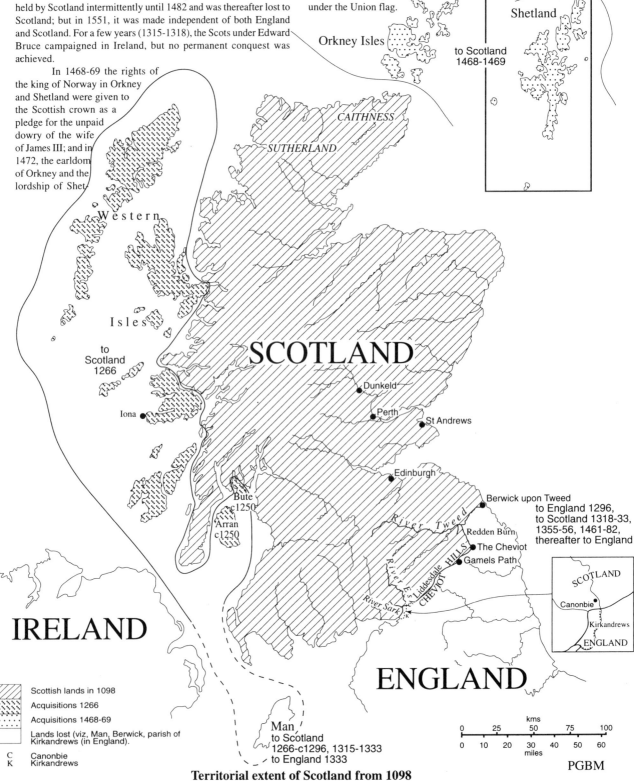

Territorial extent of Scotland from 1098

Scottish lands in 1098
Acquisitions 1266
Acquisitions 1468-69
Lands lost (viz, Man, Berwick, parish of Kirkandrews (in England).
C Canonbie
K Kirkandrews

PGBM

30

Appendix: coinage

The present metric system of money, consisting of a pound of one hundred pence, was introduced into the United Kingdom on 15 February 1971: it replaced the former system which was partially duo-decimal. The unit - the pound - was retained in the new system, but the other units - the shilling of which there were twenty to the pound, and the penny of which there were 12 to the shilling (or 240 to the pound) - were superseded.

In Scotland and in England the pound had been units of account and actual denominations. In addition, in both countries there were units of account which had never been coins or had long since ceased to be coins: respective examples of these are the mark which was $2/3$ of a pound (that is 13 shillings and fourpence) and the guinea which became one pound, one shilling, / lings. The units of the old currency were known b' *Libra, solidi* and *denarii* which were universal written thus "iij li. ix s. vj d." or later "£3 9s. 6 were witten as 7/4$^{1/}$2d, the stroke representing 7 shillings and 4 pence ha'penny; and someti especially if it was a round number of shillings, suc.. .

Although the denominations were the same in Scotland a... England, the value of the Scottish currency had depreciated greatly against that of England. By the time of the union a pound Scots was worth 1s. 8d. sterling (ie 20 old pence or 8 new pence). After the union English sterling applied in Scotland as well as in England.

Decimal coinage		Imperial coinage			
£	p	£	s	d	Name
			21		guinea
1	=100	1	20	=240	pound (paper note or gold sovreign)
	66.66		13/4	=160	merk (=$2/3$ of £1)
	50		10	=120	ten shillings
	33.3		6/8	=80	half merk (= $1/3$ of £1)
	25		5	=60	crown
	22.5		2/6	=30	half (a) crown
	10		2	=24	florin, or two shilling piece
	5		1	=12	shilling

Table (Imperial)

4 farthings	= 2 half pence
	= 1 penny
12 pennies	= 1 shilling
20 shillings	= 1 pound
	= 240 pence

Decimal	Imperial	Name
5	12	shilling
2.5	6	sixpence
	4	groat
	3	threepence
	1	penny
$1/2$		halfpenny
$1/4$		farthing

Imperial and decimal coinage   PGBM

Events to about 850

Introduction

From its initial conceptualising and planning stages this atlas was intended to supersede its predecessor, not simply supplement it. In this section therefore the topics covered extend the content of the previous atlas in terms of both chronology and subject matter, with the inclusion of an extensive Roman contribution and also settlement, burial and artefact distributions at various periods. The integration of maps with texts in this atlas is essential to the explanation and interpretation of much of the content of the section and users are urged to make reference to both. I am indebted to all contributors for their forbearance and generous assistance over what has been the very lengthy period of development and production of the atlas. It is only fair to point out that contributions were first prepared in 1985 and so largely reflect the state of knowledge and understanding of the subjects at that time. With the delivery of proofs during the course of this year (1996) it has been possible to exten-

sively revise the contents of some of the maps and texts where deemed essential due to major changes and developments in the last ten years. There will always be advancement of knowledge in all subjects but perhaps the changes are particularly rapid in the case of archaeological material. Indeed one contributor, Gordon Maxwell, observes that 'in certain areas of archaeological research the recent contributions of aerial survey have been on such a scale that with the existing resource base it has been difficult if not impossible to assimilate the new data. Where it has appeared likely that such enhancement will appreciably alter our understanding of a specific period or category of structures, an attempt has been made to indicate the character and extent of the actual impact.' In other cases however, where the increase in data has not significantly altered the distribution pattern and conclusions to be drawn, then no updating has been undertaken.

LMT

The Roman Empire and Roman Britain

The Roman empire, which by the mid-second century AD covered an area of about four million square kilometres (1.5 million square miles), was divided into provinces: the more peaceful were governed by proconsuls appointed by the Roman senate and the less developed provinces, where the bulk of the army had permanent bases, by legates directly responsible to the emperor.

Britain was a late addition to this empire. The island was invaded in AD 43 on the orders of the emperor Claudius. South-eastern Britain was quickly conquered, but the new province (named Britannia) was almost lost to Rome in 60-61 during a serious rebellion led by queen Boudica. However, from 71 onwards there was a new impetus under the Flavian emperors to complete the conquest. This was not achieved and the subsequent military opera-

tions in Scotland may be seen as series of episodes in a search for the best frontier line between that part of the island which was to be Roman and the tribes beyond.

Most of the garrison of Roman Britain was deployed in the north and Wales. From the later first century onwards the three legions forming the backbone of the army in Britain lay at Caerleon, Chester and York, bases carefully chosen to control all the areas likely to be troublesome. Behind the frontier, towns sprang up, and in the countryside villas were built in the Roman manner. By 200 the province had reached a high level of prosperity, which remained relatively intact throughout the third century. After about 300 the province was increasingly buffeted by external attacks, from the Picts in the north, and raiders from Ireland and northern Germany. In 409 the Roman government formally abandoned Britain.

The Roman Empire in the mid-second century

DJB, WSH, LJFK, GSM

N	Netherlands	ALB	Albania
S	Switzerland	BEL	Belgium
CR	Czech Republic	LUX	Luxembourg
SR	Slovak Republic	EST	Estonia
P	Palestine	LAT	Latvia
I	Israel	LITH	Lithuania

Modern Europe

The Roman Empire and Roman Britain

Inchtuthil

ANTONINE WALL

HADRIAN'S WALL

York

Chester

Wroxeter

WALES

Caerleon

London

kms
0   50   100   150

miles
0   50   100

Roman miles
0   50   100

Roman Britain: first and second centuries

DJB, WSH, LJFK, GSM

Northern Britain according to Ptolemy

This version of the British Isles according to Ptolemy has been adapted from the Ordnance Survey map of Roman Britain, making use of the coordinates given in Ptolemy's Geography, Book II.

Claudius Ptolemaeus, who worked in Alexandria before AD 150, and depended largely upon data collected by Marinus of Tyre as a result of the Agricolan campaigns between 77 and 83, provides a picture of north Britain which is instantly recognisable, but which has been turned through a right angle to the east, possibly in order to keep Scotland below 63° N, beyond which the Greeks believed life was impossible and therefore land nonexistent. Two classes of information are presented: coastal details, including headlands, river mouths and estuaries; and inland data, comprising poleis (literally, 'cities') and tribal areas: the tribes are located by reference to the cities.

Although explicit archaeological evidence is still lacking, it would nevertheless appear likely that Ptolemy's location of tribes to the south of the Forth-Clyde line approximates to reality, with the proviso that the boundaries between tribal areas cannot be precisely delineated.

To the north, however, the position is far from clear. Tacitus, who furnished the only account of the campaigns of Agricola, makes it reasonably certain that the Forth represented the southern boundary of a region known as Caledonia, which probably extended at least as far as the Moray Firth. The name of one tribe, the Caledonii, appears to have been extended to cover the whole of this part of Britain. The gradual amalgamation of the twelve tribes north of the Forth recorded by Ptolemy into the kingdom of the Picts can be traced through Roman documentary sources.

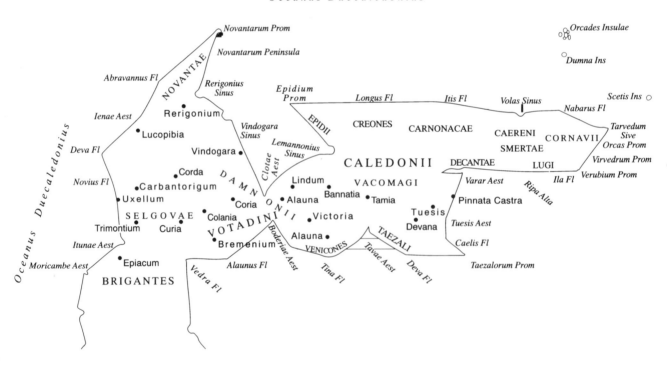

BRIGANTES	Tribes
Trimontium	Places
Orcades Insulae	Physical features

Northern Britain according to Ptolemy   DJB, WSH, LJFK, GSM

Roman Scotland in the first century (Flavian period)

The following eight maps indicate the present state of knowledge about both temporary and permanent military sites during the three periods of Roman conquest and occupation of Scotland - Flavian, Antonine and Severan. On each map, the picture is almost certainly incomplete, for new discoveries continue to be made as a result of aerial reconnaissance.

A description of the conquest of Scotland is given by Tacitus in his account of the governorship of his father-in-law Iulius Agricola (77-83). By 79 Agricola had reached the Tay and in the same season he built forts in the area overrun. Consolidation continued in 80, when he placed a series of garrisons across the Forth-Clyde isthmus. In the following year he operated in western Scotland. In 82 and 83 he campaigned in Caledonia, defeating the northern tribes at Mons Graupius. He retired to Rome the following winter and no account survives of the subsequent gradual withdrawal to the Tyne-Solway line, which appears to have been completed by about 105. Major difficulties lie in relating Tacitus's narrative to the archaeological evidence and in dating the process of abandonment.

Roman temporary camps are notoriously difficult to date, but it is reasonably certain that those with gates guarded by devices using claviculae (curving extensions of ditch and rampart) belong to Flavian times. Clavicular gates of the Stracathro type are found in camps varying in size from 1.5 to 24.5 hectares (3.7 to 60 acres) in area and though obviously serving different purposes (for example, marching and labour) probably belong to the same series of campaigns.

Other camps may be assigned to this period because of their proportions - Flavian sites tend to be square on plan - or because of their observed relationship to structures of known date. Several examples of about 18 hectares (44 acres) in size follow the main routes in Scotland from the south: they may indicate the progress of the two portions of the Agricolan army. The much larger camps of Dunning and Abernethy, each about 45 hectares (110 acres) may represent the amalgamation of those forces. A series of five camps of similar size to the north have also been claimed as Agricolan, although previously accepted as Severan. Together with the larger site at Logie Durno (58 hectares, 144 acres), these may represent the bivouacs of Agricola's army as it advanced towards Mons Graupius. In general, the marching camps indicate the lines of penetration followed by Roman armies and the extensive area over which they campaigned.

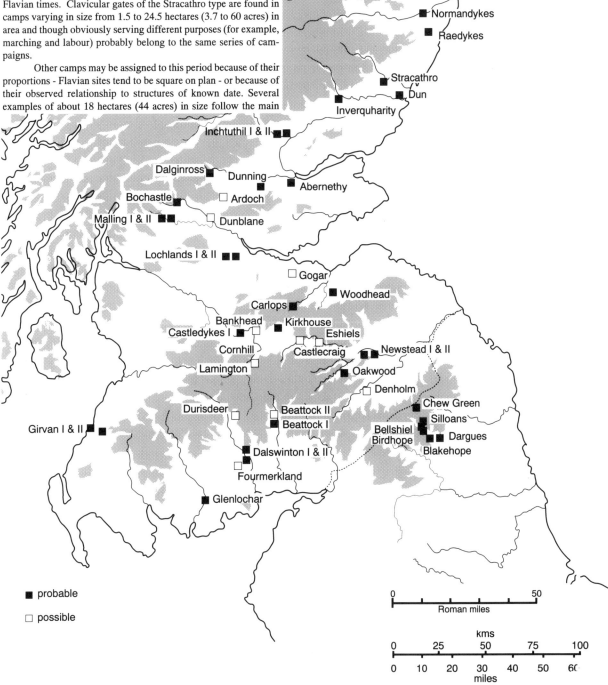

Temporary camps, late first century

DJB, WSH, LJFK, GSM

Roman Scotland in the first century (Flavian period)

Certain broad strategic patterns are clear: the distribution of forts along lines of communication in the Lowlands; the use of fortlets and smaller forts to make best use of the available manpower; the location of forts at the mouths of the glens along the south-eastern fringe of the Highlands. The concentration of sites in south-eastern Perthshire may imply different phases of occupation.

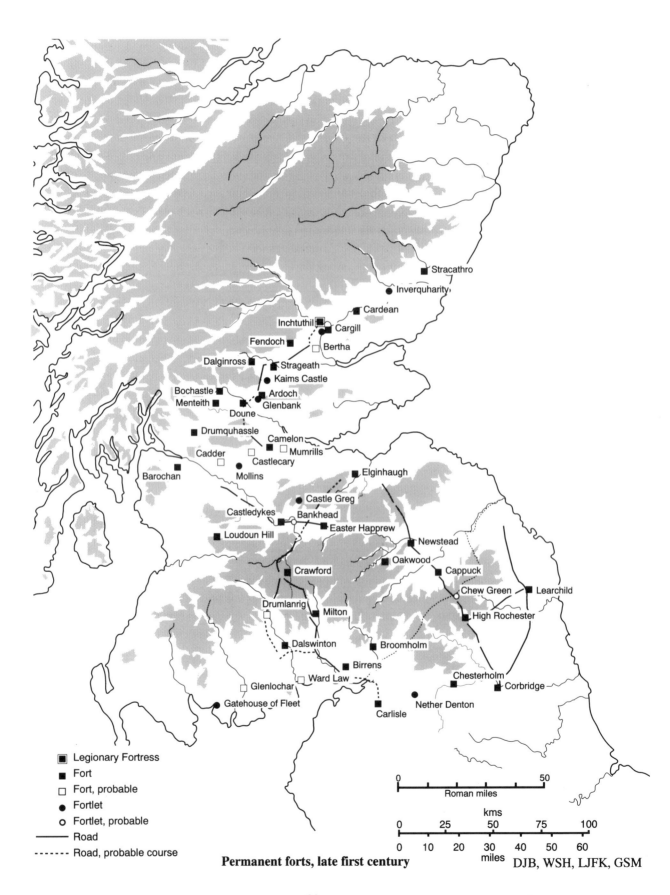

Legend:

- ■ (boxed) Legionary Fortress
- ■ Fort
- □ Fort, probable
- ● Fortlet
- ○ Fortlet, probable
- — Road
- ------- Road, probable course

Permanent forts, late first century

Roman miles: 0 — 50

kms: 0, 25, 50, 75, 100

miles: 0, 10, 20, 30, 40, 50, 60

DJB, WSH, LJFK, GSM

Map labels: Stracathro, Inverquharity, Cardean, Inchtuthil, Cargill, Fendoch, Bertha, Dalginross, Strageath, Kaims Castle, Bochastle, Ardoch, Menteith, Glenbank, Doune, Drumquhassle, Camelon, Mumrills, Cadder, Castlecary, Barochan, Mollins, Elginhaugh, Castle Greg, Castledykes, Bankhead, Easter Happrew, Loudoun Hill, Newstead, Oakwood, Cappuck, Crawford, Chew Green, Learchild, Drumlanrig, Milton, High Rochester, Dalswinton, Broomholm, Birrens, Chesterholm, Ward Law, Glenlochar, Corbridge, Gatehouse of Fleet, Nether Denton, Carlisle

Roman Scotland in the first century (Flavian period)

All these sites have afforded evidence of two structural phases in the late first century, or provided artefactual evidence of occupation after about AD 90. Comparison with previous map gives some indication of the process of Roman withdrawal from Scotland.

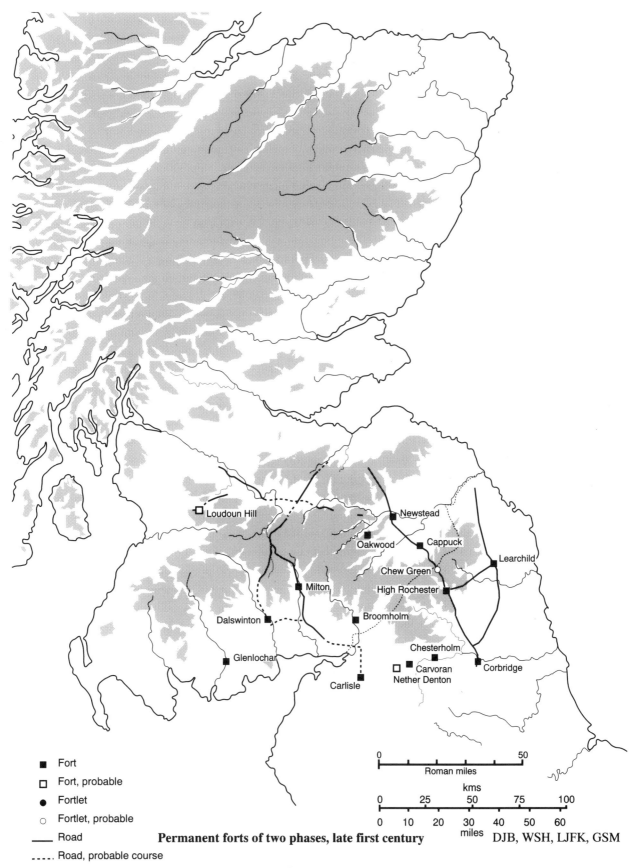

Fort
Fort, probable
Fortlet
Fortlet, probable
Road
Road, probable course

Permanent forts of two phases, late first century

Roman miles
kms
miles

DJB, WSH, LJFK, GSM

Roman Scotland in the mid-second century (Antonine period)

There are fewer examples of Roman temporary camps that can be confidently dated to the mid second century. Indeed the sites with the best credentials are the relatively small works thought to have held the legionary workforce engaged in building the Antonine Wall (not marked on the map).

Among the larger sites, those which are of tertiate plan (ie whose long sides are half as big again as their short), are more likely than not to be of second century or later date; in several cases where these are situated beside a Roman road, the longer side has been aligned parallel with the road. Two very loosely grouped classes of marching camps have thus been tentatively identified - one averaging 20 hectares in area, the other only 10 hectares; all are to be found in southern Scotland, apparently indicating passage by battle groups one or two legions strong through the major river valleys. Recent excavation has suggested that some first-century camps may have been re-used in the Antonine period.

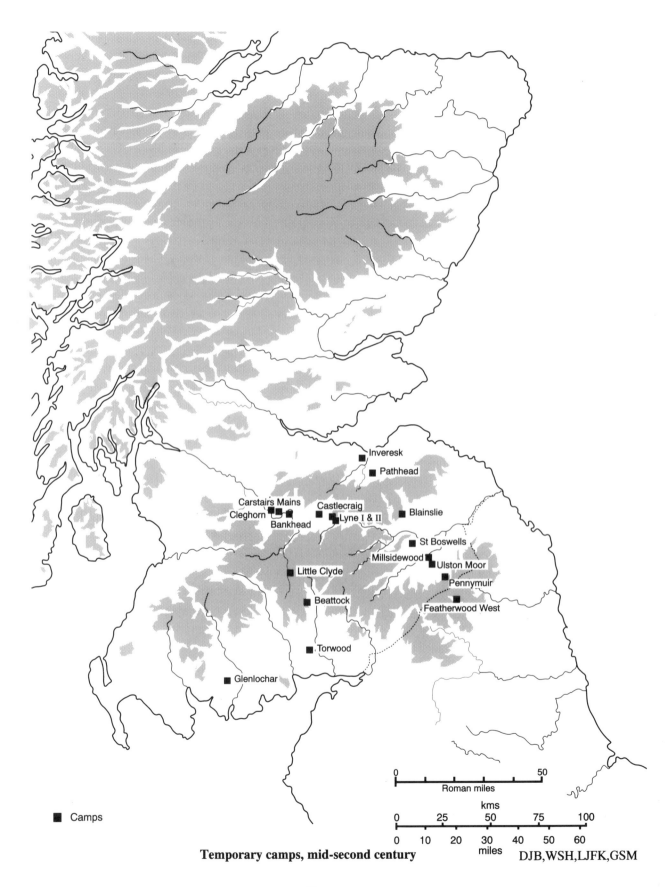

■ Camps

Roman miles

kms

Temporary camps, mid-second century

miles

DJB,WSH,LJFK,GSM

Roman Scotland in the mid-second century (Antonine period)

The disposition of forts in Lowland Scotland is, in general, similar to that of the late first century, but there is a greater use of fortlets, particularly in the south-west, suggesting not only the best use of available manpower but a concern for more localized control.

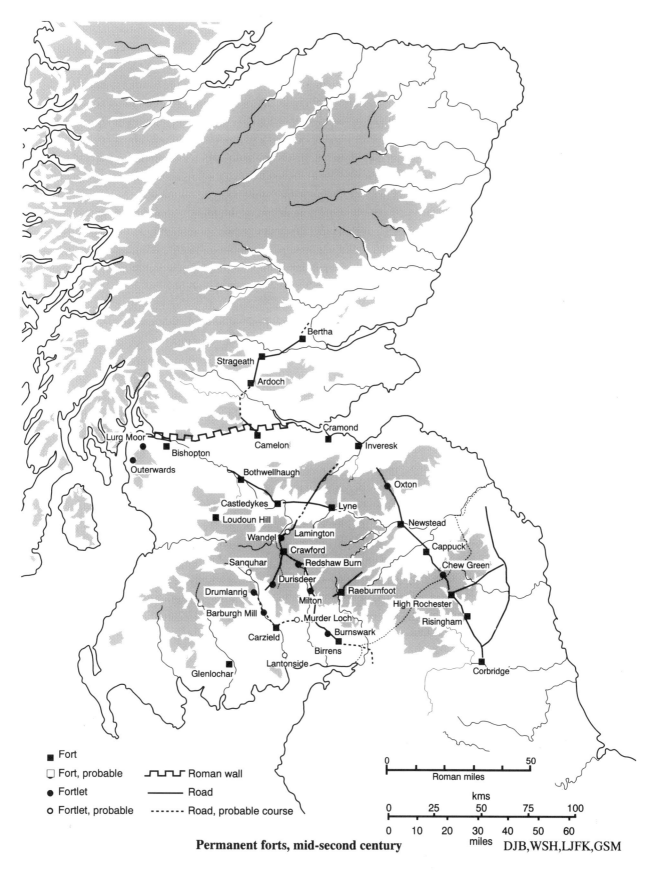

Bertha

Strageath

Ardoch

Lurg Moor

Bishopton

Outerwards

Cramond

Camelon

Inveresk

Bothwellhaugh

Oxton

Castledykes

Lyne

Loudoun Hill

Newstead

Wandel

Lamington

Crawford

Cappuck

Sanquhar

Redshaw Burn

Chew Green

Durisdeer

Drumlanrig

Milton

Raeburnfoot

Barburgh Mill

Murder Loch

High Rochester

Carzield

Burnswark

Risingham

Birrens

Lantonside

Corbridge

Glenlochar

■ Fort
□ Fort, probable   ⊓⌐⊔⌐⊔ Roman wall
● Fortlet   ──── Road
○ Fortlet, probable   ------- Road, probable course

0   50
Roman miles

kms
0   25   50   75   100

0 10 20 30 40 50 60
miles

Permanent forts, mid-second century   DJB,WSH,LJFK,GSM

41

Roman Scotland in the mid-second century (Antonine period)

All these sites have afforded evidence of two structural phases within the Antonine period. Comparison with the previous map indicates a reduction in the overall garrison and particularly in the tight control of the south-west Lowlands.

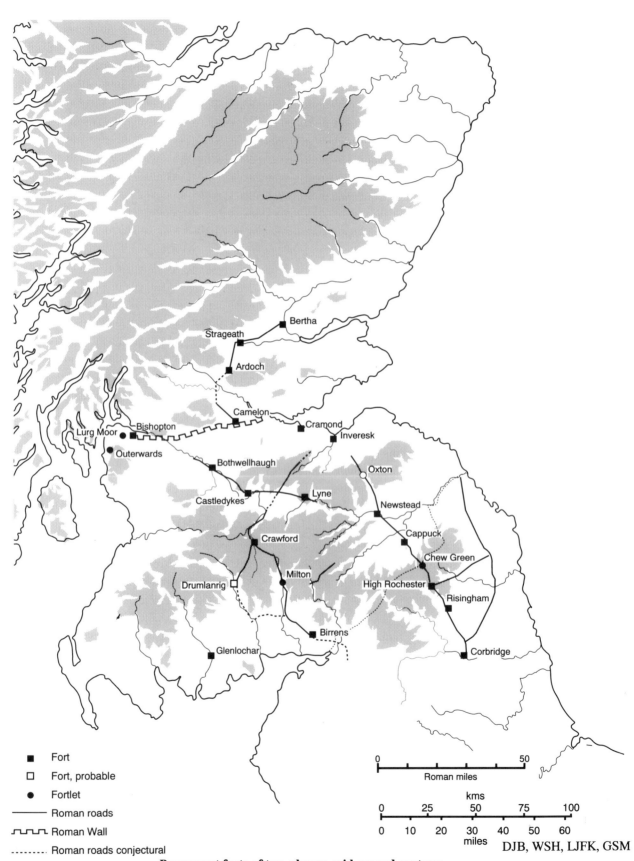

Fort ■

Fort, probable □

Fortlet ●

——— Roman roads

⊓⊔⊓⊔ Roman Wall

········· Roman roads conjectural

Bertha

Strageath

Ardoch

Camelon

Bishopton

Lurg Moor

Outerwards

Cramond

Inveresk

Bothwellhaugh

Oxton

Lyne

Castledykes

Newstead

Crawford

Cappuck

Chew Green

Drumlanrig

Milton

High Rochester

Risingham

Birrens

Glenlochar

Corbridge

0   50
Roman miles

kms
0   25   50   75   100

0   10   20   30   40   50   60
miles

DJB, WSH, LJFK, GSM

Permanent forts of two phases, mid-second century

Roman Scotland in the late second to fourth centuries

Between 208 and 211 the Emperor Septimius Severus and his son Caracalla conducted two campaigns in Scotland against the Caledonians and the Maeatae. The contemporary historian Cassius Dio records that Severus nearly reached the end of the island. After his father's death at York in February 211 Caracalla gave up the Roman conquests, abandoning forts.

For these campaigns it is argued three great series of marching camps were constructed, c. 65 hectares (160 acres), 55 hectares (140 acres), 25 hectares (62 acres) in area respectively, which indicate the line of march followed by Severan armies. They are concentrated in the east, with one unexplained outlier in Dumfriesshire.

Excavation has demonstrated that the 55 hectare camp at Ardoch is later than the 25 hectare camp. Thus it is suggested that the series of 25 hectare camps dates to the first campaign and the 55 hectare series to the second.

During the campaigns a depot seems to have been established at Cramond on the Forth, while a legionary base was constructed at Carpow on the Tay. Both appear to have been abandoned shortly after 211.

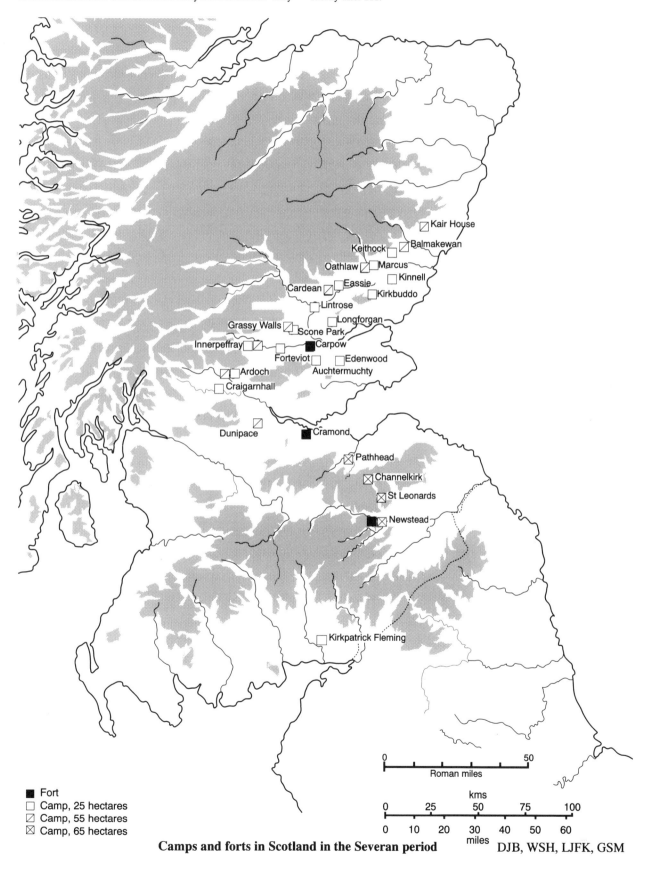

- ■ Fort
- □ Camp, 25 hectares
- ◫ Camp, 55 hectares
- ⊠ Camp, 65 hectares

Camps and forts in Scotland in the Severan period

DJB, WSH, LJFK, GSM

43

Roman Scotland in the late second to fourth centuries

After the abandonment of the Antonine Wall, its outposts and most of its hinterland forts, a number of bases continued to be maintained north of Hadrian's Wall. Birrens, Newstead and presumably Cappuck seem to have been abandoned in the 180s. Newstead was possibly re-occupied briefly in some form during the Severan campaigns; and about the same time there may have been a presence near Cappuck. The remaining four forts north of Hadrian's Wall survived into the early fourth century. Until the 'barbarian conspiracy' of 367, the Romans maintained a network of scouts beyond Hadrian's Wall, but the locations of their bases are not known.

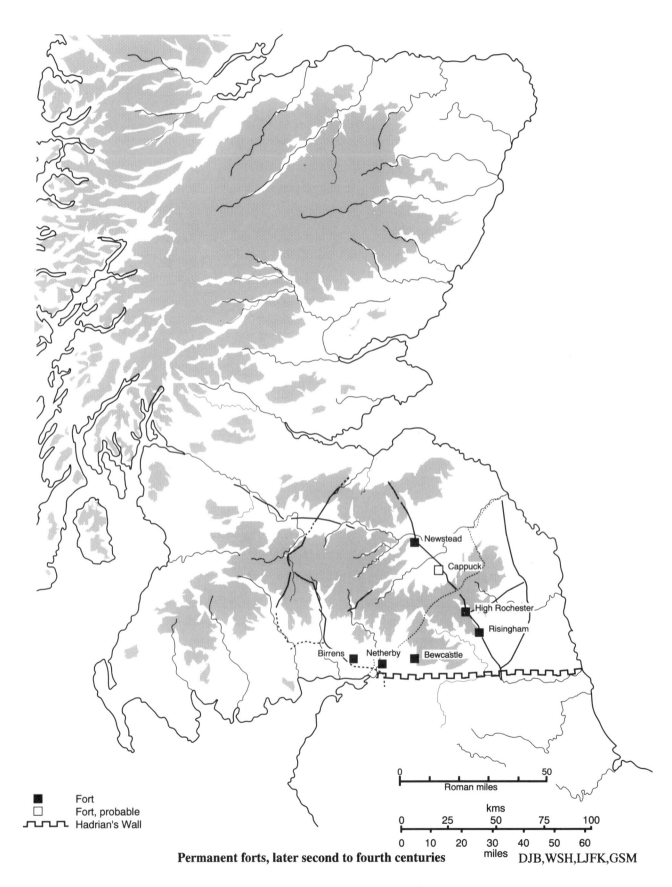

Fort
Fort, probable
Hadrian's Wall

Permanent forts, later second to fourth centuries

DJB,WSH,LJFK,GSM

Roman Scotland in the late second to fourth centuries

Roman manufactured goods are found not only on and near Roman military installations in Scotland but on settlement sites of the contemporary native population, not merely within the boundaries of empire, but also well beyond its frontiers.

This material includes coins, samian ware (imported from southern and central France), amphorae (from Spain), and jewellery in silver, bronze or gold. Other goods in wood, leather and perishable materials, as well, perhaps, as foodstuffs, can also be assumed. It may

have arrived in the hands of the native population in a variety of ways: barter, trade, diplomatic gifts, loot from abandoned Roman sites, or locally recruited Roman soldiers returning home. Much of it is of high quality - an indication, perhaps, of the owner's status in native society.

The artefacts range in date from the first to the fourth centuries: evidently Roman material was still reaching native sites in Scotland long after Roman forces had abandoned their forts there.

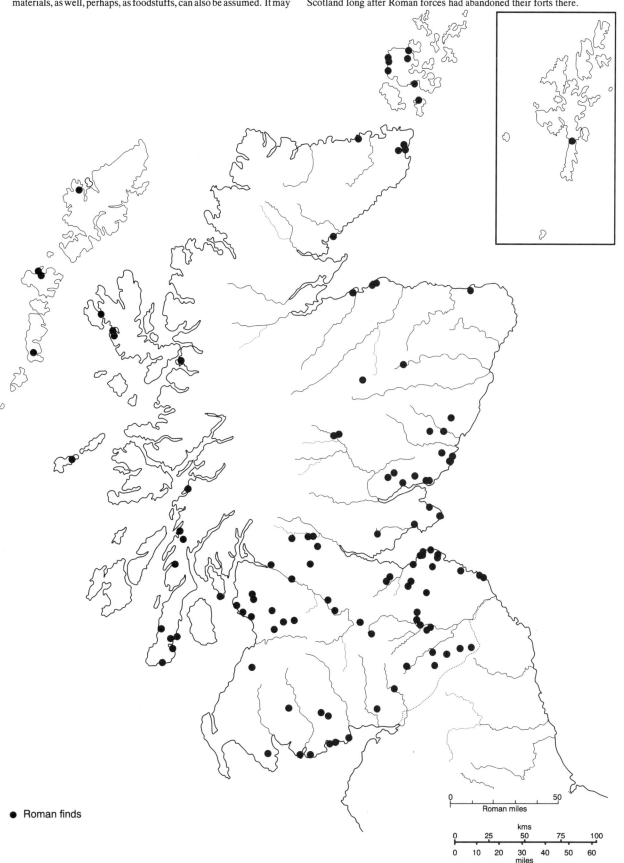

● Roman finds

Roman finds from native sites from first to fourth centuries   DJB, CH, WSH, LJFK, GSM

Roman frontiers

The halt to the expansion of the Roman empire in the first century led to the development of frontier controls. The first map reveals the limitations of our knowledge concerning Agricola's troop disposition across the Forth Clyde isthmus. The next 2 maps illustrate the development of Roman frontiers in this north-western province of the empire over a period of 60 years. The normal spacing of forts within the military zone might be about a day's march (fourteen or so miles). The role of the units in these forts was to control and protect the new provincials. The first step towards the development of a frontier was the addition of intermediate sites along the outer strand of the network, reducing the spacing to about seven miles, to which was added an extra element - the timber watchtower - to increase the army's control of movement across the frontier. Under Hadrian a new feature appeared, the linear barrier to further hinder low intensity threats, ie Hadrian's Wall; it was, however, not until later in his reign that major military forces were deployed along the barrier itself, operating in most instances from forts placed astride the Wall and in the event of attack combining to form a mobile field army. The design of the Antonine Wall reveals a closer integration between the army units and the Wall. Forts were placed on the Wall from the beginning but during building operations their number increased from an original six to at least 17 resulting in a closer spacing between forts than on any other Roman frontier.

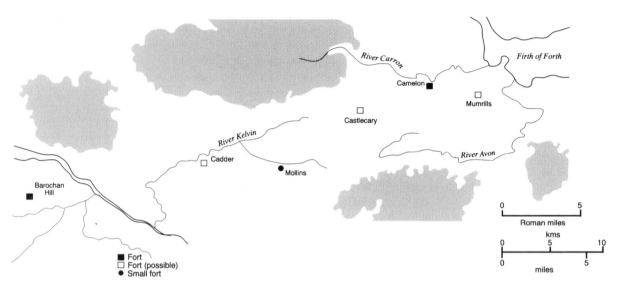

Roman frontiers, Forth-Clyde Isthmus: Agricola's troop dispositions   DJB, WSH, LJFK, GSM

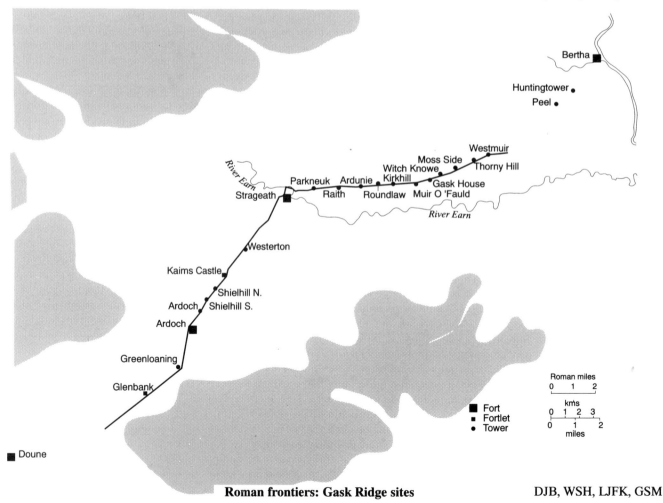

Roman frontiers: Gask Ridge sites   DJB, WSH, LJFK, GSM

Roman frontiers

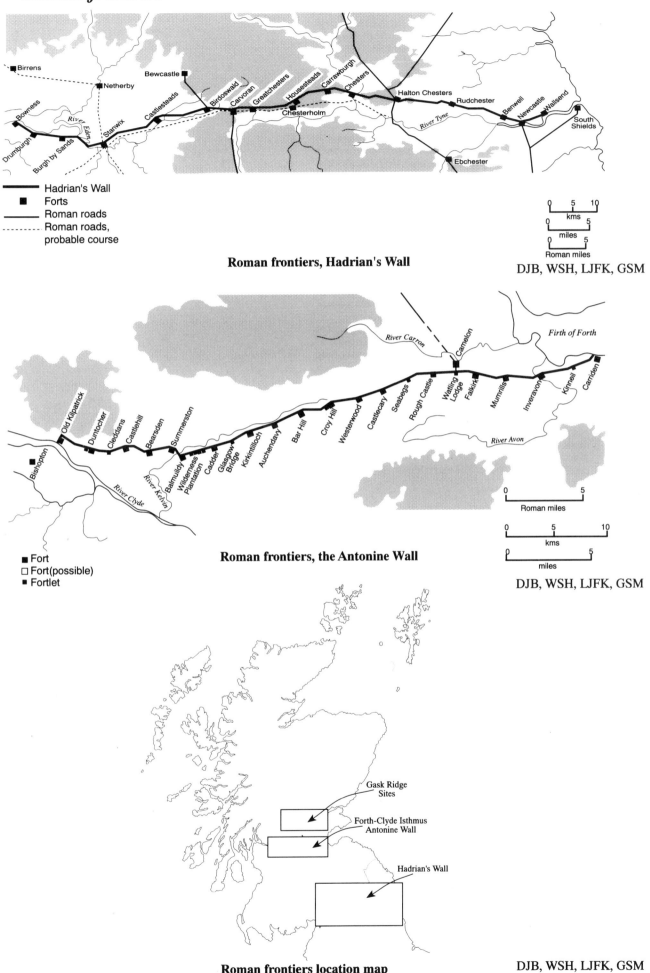

Roman frontiers, Hadrian's Wall

Hadrian's Wall
Forts
Roman roads
Roman roads, probable course

DJB, WSH, LJFK, GSM

Roman frontiers, the Antonine Wall

Fort
Fort(possible)
Fortlet

DJB, WSH, LJFK, GSM

Roman frontiers location map

DJB, WSH, LJFK, GSM

Pictish and earlier archaeological sites

Aerial survey has intensified the contrast between Iron Age patterns north and south of the Forth, and it has clarified the situation in Fife and Tayside. In the past decade the unenclosed villages of round timber houses that are typical of rural settlement in E. Scotland from the sixth century BC to the Roman period have been identified in great numbers, appearing from the air as clusters of circular or annular cropmarkings; a handful of excavations has revealed that these distinctive traces are formed by a characteristic ring-shaped or lunate hollow, 6-15m (20-50 feet) across the interior of the house. Ring-ditch houses are also found in appreciable numbers in Grampian and Highland Regions, where they appear to form a natural extension of a distribution pattern whose northern limits are not yet known, but whose southern limit coincides with that of square-barrow cemeteries (which are shown in a later map).

Of even greater interest, perhaps, has been the discovery that unenclosed settlements of the later Iron Age in those parts were frequently associated with souterrains and that these could also be identified from the air. The potential impact of this on Iron Age archaeology may be gauged from a comparison of the total number of souterrains identified in southern Pictland by a century of antiquarian endeavour, (fifty-five), with the 100-odd sites recorded by the aerial surveyor in only the past decade. Even more impressive is the quality of information thus acquired, for it is now possible to see that many settlements incorporate several souterrains, some of them of considerable size and structural complexity.

At present the implications of this sudden enhancement of information have not been fully appreciated. The distribution of souterrains now appears to be much denser than was formerly thought, the newly recorded sites occupying favoured positions in terms of drainage and soil type. The distribution is beginning to approximate to that observed for square barrows and ring-ditch houses.

(Note: Since the above was written, the picture has been complicated by the discovery that some of the settlements mentioned here include groups of sunken-floored houses of rectilinear plan; initial indications are that these may be of Early Historic date, possibly providing a bridge between prehistoric and Pictish settlement in this area.)

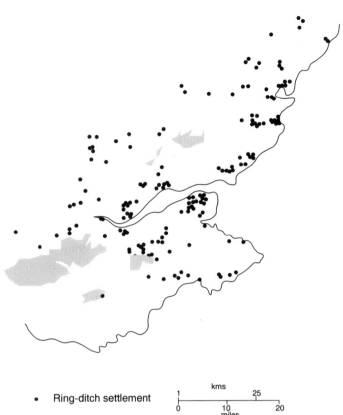

• Ring-ditch settlement

kms
1   25
0   10   20
miles

Ring-ditch houses in southern Pictland

GSM, PA

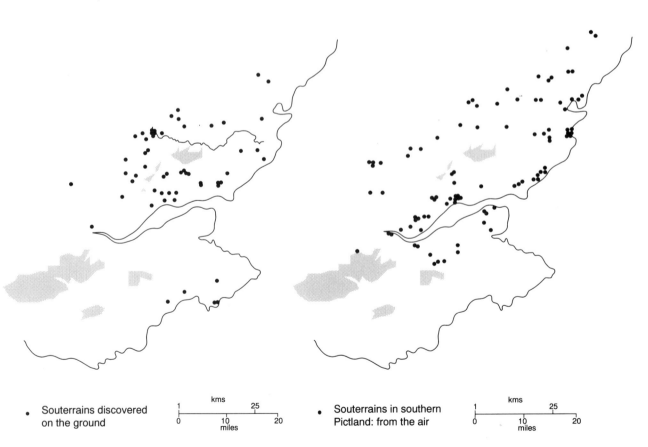

• Souterrains discovered on the ground

kms
1   25
0   10   20
miles

• Souterrains in southern Pictland: from the air

kms
1   25
0   10   20
miles

**Souterrains in southern Pictland:
on the ground**   GSM, PA

**Souterrains in southern Pictland:
from the air**   GSM, PA

Pictish and earlier archaeological sites

One of the most exciting and surprising discoveries of archaeological air survey in the past twenty years has been the identification of cemeteries including square barrows. Over much the same period scrutiny of old reports, ground surveys and excavations has revealed cemeteries of low, flat topped mounds dating between the third and eleventh centuries AD.

Air photography has revealed at least thirty cropmark square barrow cemeteries. In many of the cemeteries there are also round barrows. The vast majority lie between the Forth and the N. Esk, but there are a few in Dumfries and Galloway, Aberdeenshire, Moray and Highland. Although none of the cemeteries so far discovered is very large, the cropmarks of their shallow enclosing ditches are very tenuous, and repeated annual survey occasionally reveals new barrows and new details.

The nearest and best structural parallels for most of these cropmark burial monuments are in east Yorkshire, where some cemeteries date to the early Iron Age and others to the Roman period. However, some of the cemeteries in Scotland include square barrows with ditches interrupted at the corners which seem highly comparable to some of the broadly Pictish mounds described below. More enigmatic are the few much larger enclosures with interrupted corners which have been discovered in recent air photography of eastern Scotland.

The broadly Pictish barrows and cairns occur from Shetland to Fife. They range in diameter from under 3m (10 ft.) to (ex-ceptionally) over 12m (40ft). They have flat tops, and include two or more of the following attributes: a built or vertical slab kerb, lightly flexed inhumation in a grave sealed by a layer of redeposited subsoil or sand, and corner features, such as stones or small pillars or a square-plan ditch with causeways at the corners. These cemeteries often include round, oblong and trapezoidal mounds, some of which may be joined together, long cist burials without covering mounds, and quite often a Pictish symbol stone or a fragment of one. Radiocarbon dates suggest the burials took place between the third and eleventh centuries AD. Some of the cemeteries include one or more taller round mounds, which may be compared to burial mounds such as that overlying the counterscarp bank around Inchtuthil Roman fort. There is an overlap in the distributions of square barrows and long cist cemeteries in Fife, but their distributions are largely mutually exclusive.

The proportionately large number of associations of the upstanding cemeteries with Pictish symbol stones suggests a cultural relationship. The square barrows with interrupted ditch corners probably have similar affinities. Although their distribution stretches farther north than that of *pit-* placenames, recent discoveries of cropmark sites have reinforced the similarities between the distributions. The core of the distribution of the simple square barrows is in the southern Pictish heartlands. Although there is undoubtedly a relationship between the simple square barrows and those with interrupted ditch corners, the nature of that relationship will remain unclear until more sites have been excavated.

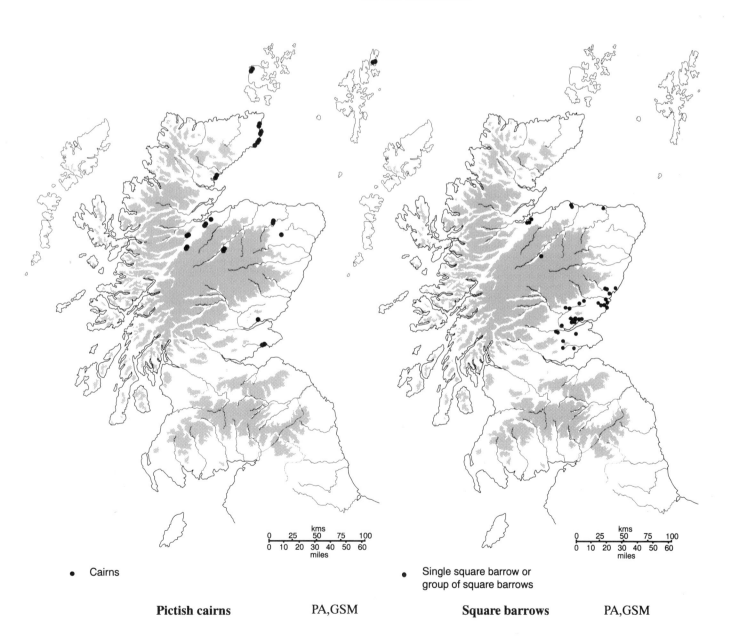

• Cairns

Pictish cairns   PA,GSM

• Single square barrow or group of square barrows

Square barrows   PA,GSM

Pictish and British place-names

Of all linguistic evidence, place-names provide the most mappable. Their known locations can be precisely pinpointed through map coordinates, and potential distribution patterns are easily discernible. Such patterns can be most directly interpreted in spatial terms but also have historical implications. Though most place names do not offer evidence for absolute dating, many of them can be placed in relative chronological sequences allowing the establishment of linguistic strata concerning both the relationship of different languages to each other and the postulation of strata within the same linguistic stratum. Naturally, the chronological dimension of spatial patterns has to be treated very carefully, bearing in mind that they usually say more about the end of the productivity of a certain name element or type than about its beginning. Place-names become the more valuable as raw material the further back we go in history, and an important approach to their study and interpretation can be termed "linguistic (or onomastic) archaeology".

The earliest Celtic settlers in Scotland did not speak Gaelic but languages more akin to Gaulish, Cornish, Breton and particularly Welsh. The two main Scottish branches were Pictish and Cumbric (British) although evidently there were also Picts whose language was not Celtic. That relationship of these languages among each other, to the other p-Celtic languages and to Gaelic was complex is demonstrated by the four maps showing the distribution of place-name generics that can be ascribed to them.

The maps display the kind of toponymic evidence that would argue for Cumbric and Pictish as separate, though related, languages. The generic *cair* 'fort, manor house, stockaded farm', as in Cramond (Midlothian), Caerlanrig (Roxburghshire), and Carfrae (Berwickshire and East Lothian), occurs almost exclusively south of the Forth Clyde line, apparently limiting Cumbric to that region in Scotland, while linking it with a small cluster of names in northwest England, i.e. the former kingdom of Rheged (Carlisle), and also with Wales (Cardiff, Caernarvon,

Cardigan). In contrast, names containing the element *pett* 'portion, share', like Pitlochry (Perthshire), Pittenweem (Fife), Pitcaple (Aberdeenshire), and more than 300 others, are found, with a few exceptions, to the north and east of the *cair*-area, and their distribution is usually interpreted as delineating the settlement area of the Celtic-speaking Picts. This assumption is probably correct, despite the fact that many *Pit*-names have Gaelic specifics, like Pitcarmick (Perthshire), Pitcox (East Lothian). Pitmedden (several). Some of these names may be part-translations; most of them are likely to have been coined during a Pictish - Gaelic bilingual period in the ninth and tenth centuries, or perhaps even later.

Maps 3c and 3d provide evidence that modifies this impression of separate linguistic entities. Names containing such elements as *lanerc* 'clear space' (Lanrick, Perthshire, Lanark, Lanarkshire), *pert* 'wood, copse' (Perth, Perthshire; Pappert Law, Selkirkshire), *pevr* 'radiant, beautiful' (Innerpeffray, Perthshire; Peffer Burn, East Lothian), *pren* 'tree' (Primrose, Fife; Primside, Roxburghshire) are found in both 'Pictish' and 'Cumbric' territory, and *aber* 'river-mouth' (Aberdeen, Aberdeenshire; Aberlady, East Lothian) in addition has especially strong links with Wales (Abergavenny, Aberythwyth, etc.). The generic *tref* 'dwelling, village' is also common in Wales (Tredegar, Tregaron) and Cornwall (Trefecca, Tregoyd), respectively, but its distribution (map d) in Scotland adds a different wrinkle to the complexity of the linguistic situation. While its distribution approximates that of *cair* when it is the first element in a compound name (Tranent, East Lothian; Tralorg, Ayrshire; Terregles, Kirkcudbrightshire), it is like *lanerc*, *pert* and *pren*, evident in both 'Cumbric' and 'Pictish' territory when it is preceded by the specific, but whereas south of the Antonine Wall this specific is always Cumbric (Niddrie, Midlothian; Ochiltree, Wigtownshire; Trostrie, Kirkcudbrightshire), in the majority of names north of the wall (Clentry, Fife; Fintry, several; Fortry, Banffshire) it is Gaelic, not unlike the hybrid Pictish-Gaelic composition of many *Pit*-names.

Pictish and British place-names

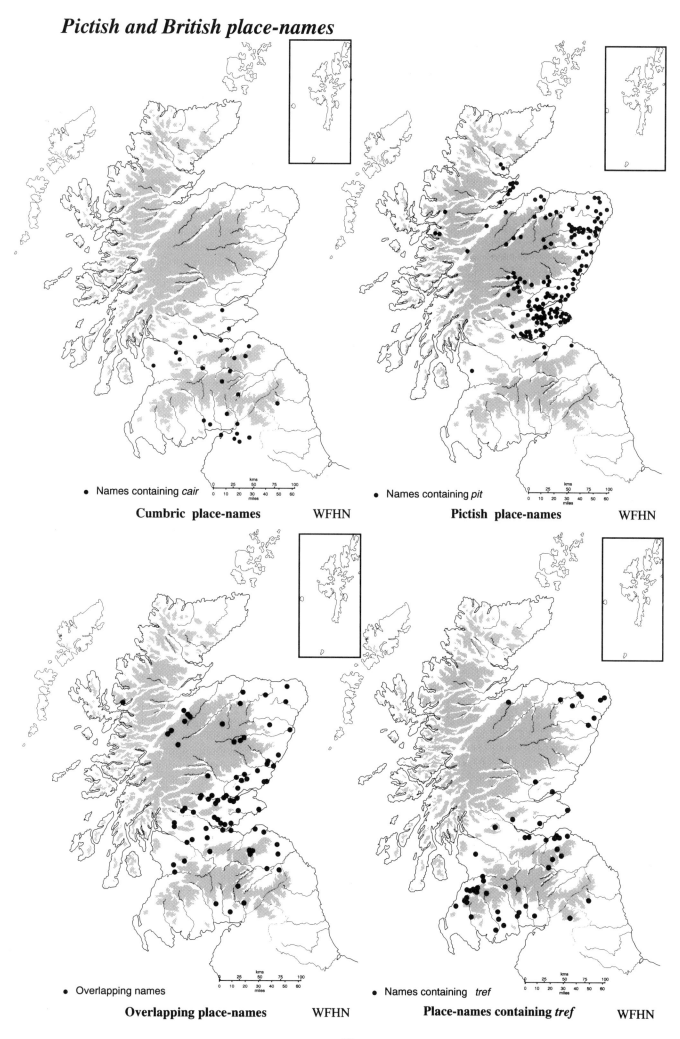

• Names containing *cair*

Cumbric place-names   WFHN

• Names containing *pit*

Pictish place-names   WFHN

• Overlapping names

Overlapping place-names   WFHN

• Names containing *tref*

Place-names containing *tref*   WFHN

Pictish territorial divisions

The most authentic version of the list of Pictish kings begins with the names of the seven sons of Cruithne (the Irish for Pict). Three of the sons appear as names of districts in entries relating to events of the seventh and eighth centuries in contemporary Irish annals: so it is reasonable to assume that all seven are eponyms referring to names of regions in the Pictish part of north Britain. In the manuscript containing the king list, there is also a tract known as *De Situ Albanie* - a collection of topographical surveys of Scotland written in the twelfth century. One survey refers to the ancient division of the land into seven regions by seven brothers, and adds that each region was divided into two parts ruled by a king and a sub-king. Another survey defines the geographical boundaries of the seven regions not all of which are consistent with the pairs of districts attributed to the ancient sevenfold division. The administrative pairs may be reflected in Adomnán of Iona's description, written about 700, of Columba's contemporary, the Pictish king Bridei as a *rex* who controlled Orkney through a local *regulus*. Adomnán had Bridei ruling over a *regio* or *provincia*, whereas Bede, writing about 730, has his contemporary, the Pictish king Nechtan, ruling over a *natio*

with *provinciae*. It is uncertain whether this change of terminology implies a centralisation of power. Bede and late classical writers thought of the Picts as having once been divided into confederacies on either side of the Mounth. The single lineage represented by the king list, and the homogeneity of Pictish sculpture suggest that most of the time from the sixth to the ninth century the Picts enjoyed cultural unity and attempted to maintain political unity. References in Adomnán's *Life of* *Columba* make it clear that by the end of the seventh century the boundary between the Picts and the Scots of Dalriada was the mountain range of Druim Alban.

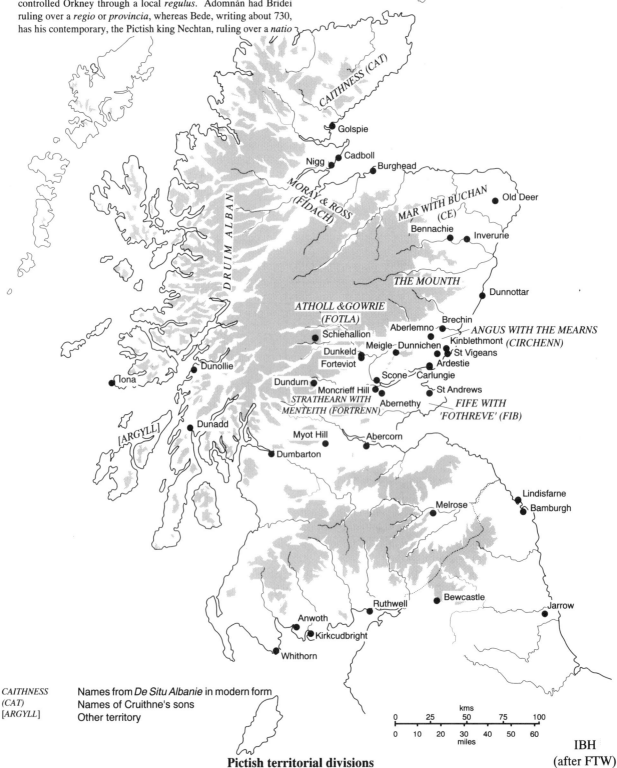

CAITHNESS
(CAT)   Names from *De Situ Albanie* in modern form
[ARGYLL]   Names of Cruithne's sons
              Other territory

kms
0   25   50   75   100
0 10 20 30 40 50 60
miles

IBH
(after FTW)

Pictish territorial divisions

52

Pictish monuments

The map shows the find spots of boulder stones incised with the unique Pictish symbol designs. It will be seen that symbol stones are found north of the Forth-Clyde line in the districts which Bede, writing in the eighth century, knew to be populated by Picts. Symbol stones are not found in the regions where the Scots settled in the early sixth century. The designs for some of the animal symbols are related to the designs used for three of the Evangelist Symbols in illuminated Gospel Books written in the second half of the seventh century.

Whether the Pictish animal symbols come before or after the manuscript creatures is a matter of controversy; but it can be said with confidence that symbol stones were being put up in the seventh century. The meaning of the Pictish symbols and the function of the stones is not known. Some of the symbol designs are engraved on silver neck chains and some are incised on the walls of caves. Recently a number of stones incised with a range of symbols have been shown to be directly associated with burials.

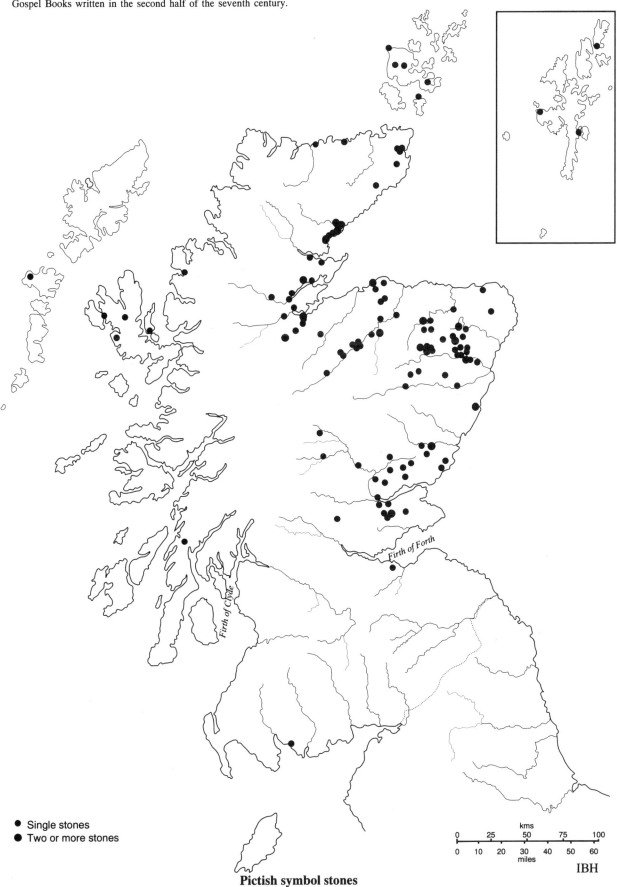

● Single stones
● Two or more stones

kms
0   25   50   75   100
0 10 20 30 40 50 60
miles

IBH

Pictish symbol stones

Pictish monuments

The map shows the find spots of dressed slabs carved in relief bearing on one side a full-length decorated cross and on the other Pictish symbols. Animal ornament surrounds the cross. The symbols accompany figurative scenes many of which depict hunting on horseback. The best known scene is the unique three-tier battle scene on the back of the cross slab in Aberlemno churchyard in Angus. Because of technical and decorative connections it is agreed that the Picts learned to cut and carve stone in relief from Northumbrian masons and sculptors some time in the eighth century. Towards the end of the century the Picts were carving ambitious monuments in high relief. The finest of these closely resemble the free-standing crosses of the Iona school of sculptors, and both sets of monuments have links with the art of the Book of Kells. This phase of Pictish sculpture provides evidence for widespread patronage by Christian Picts and for artistic contacts with Iona, Ireland, and England, north and south of the Humber. The map shows the distribution of some of the sculpture in north Britain, demonstrating these links.

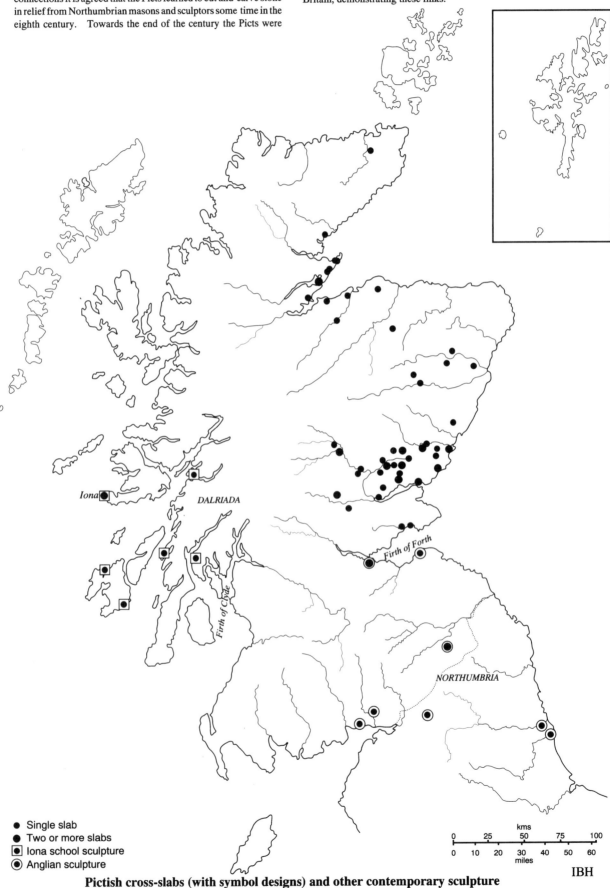

- ● Single slab
- ● Two or more slabs
- ▣ Iona school sculpture
- ◉ Anglian sculpture

kms
0   25   50   75   100

0   10   20   30   40   50   60
miles

IBH

Pictish cross-slabs (with symbol designs) and other contemporary sculpture

Pictish monuments

Some of this sculpture belongs with mainstream Pictish art, for example, the carved sarcophagus in the Cathedral Museum at St. Andrews, and the massive recumbent grave covers in the Pictish sculpture museum at Meigle, Perthshire. Other sculpture reflects the presence of the Scots of Dalriada in eastern Pictland after the takeover by Kenneth mac Alpin in the mid-ninth century, for example, the freestanding cross at Dupplin. On the other hand a large fragment of a cross-slab recently discovered at Applecross has ornament closely paralleled at St. Vigeans which suggests that sculptors trained in the east were working for patrons in the Dalriadic west. The sculpture without symbols shows late-North-umbrian traits such as the spreading of vine-scroll over the cross-head. This hybrid sculpture is less accomplished than the sculpture of earlier periods, but its value as evidence for strains of influence in the religious life of Scotland in the ninth and tenth centuries is considerable.

Two slightly later schools of sculpture are characterised by a collection of sculpture in the parish church of Govan Strathclyde, and the hogback (and kindred) monuments.

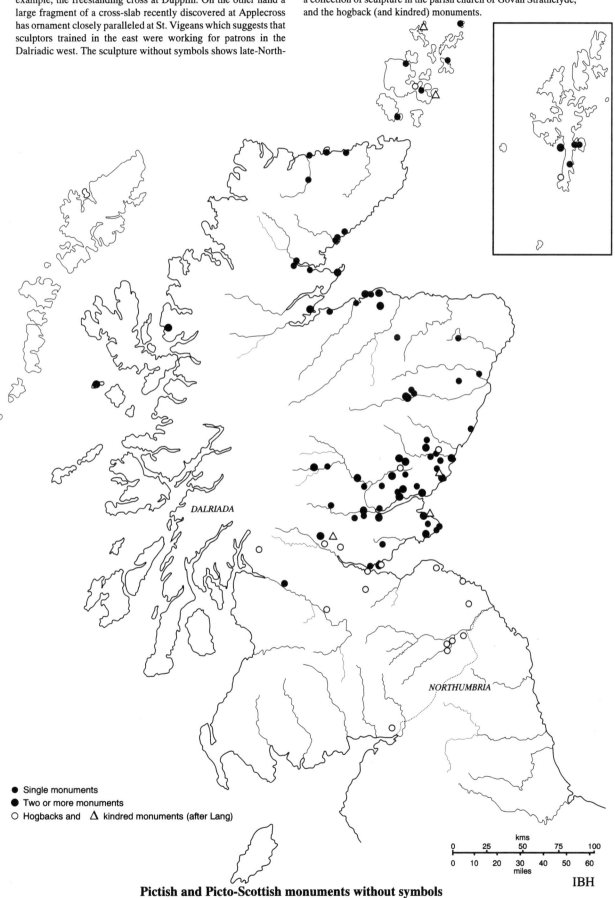

● Single monuments
● Two or more monuments
○ Hogbacks and △ kindred monuments (after Lang)

DALRIADA

NORTHUMBRIA

kms
0   25   50   75   100

0 10 20 30 40 50 60
miles

IBH

Pictish and Picto-Scottish monuments without symbols

55

Pictish monuments

Scotland's first Christian stone monuments were probably in the form of boulder stones incised with crosses used to mark graves and sanctified places. Simple monuments of this type are of uncertain date but some of the cross-types can be compared with those found on similar more datable monuments in Ireland and Wales and on this basis the Scottish stones with incised crosses can be treated as a class of potentially early medieval monumental sculpture. The incised, encircled, equal-armed crosses of eastern Pictland have been directly associated with the encircled chi-rho monograms depicted on monuments associated with the British Ninianic church at Kirkmadrine and Whithorn. Less controversially, the incised crosses of northern Britain have been interpreted as an index of the beginnings and progress of Christianity brought by the Columban church centre on

Iona. In form and technique the incised cross-bearing stones relate to the Pictish symbol stones (in the first of these Pictish maps) but the cross symbol links them to the Pictish cross-slabs (in the second map). The map is based on a preliminary list compiled in 1985 from published sources. It shows, in addition, cross-marked stones recorded by the Royal Commission in the *Argyll* inventories, and a considerable number of stones recorded by N M Robertson of Perth, as a result of field work, mainly in Highland Perthshire.

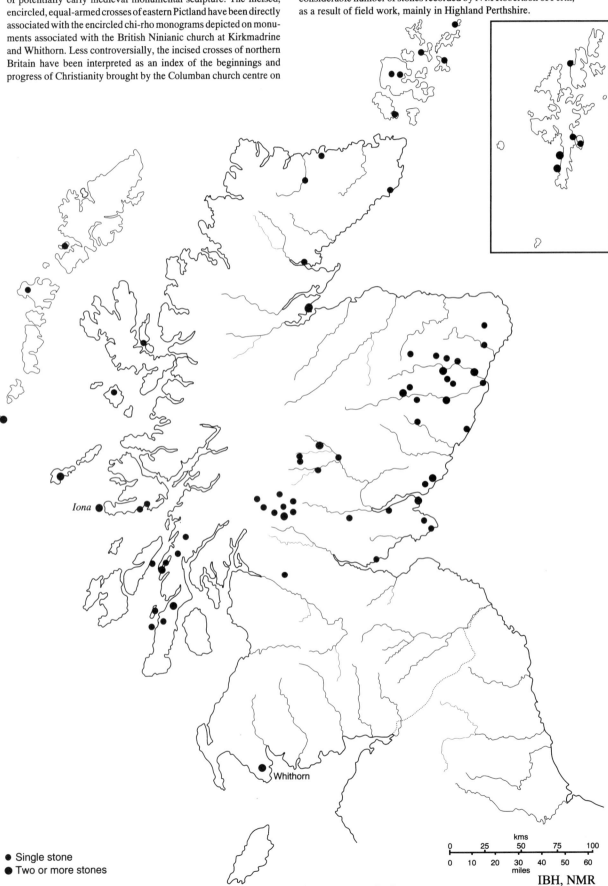

Iona

Whithorn

● Single stone
● Two or more stones

kms
0   25   50   75   100
0   10   20   30   40   50   60
miles

IBH, NMR

Pictish, and related Dalriadic, cross-marked stones

Imported pottery 400 to 1000

The distribution of E ware vessels shows concentrations at a few centres of importation, with probable redistribution from these centres to surrounding sites. The variety of forms of E ware, and of other continental imports (including glassware) found on these major sites confirms the special status of such sites. It seems likely that these major secular sites controlled the exchange of goods, and that surpluses were available for exchange. None of the undoubtedly early sixth century Mediterranean wares, which are found in the south-west of Britain, are present in Scotland. This perhaps indicates that importation did not begin until the later sixth century in Scotland. The small amounts of E ware on the major Pictish sites perhaps reflect political contacts with Dalriada.

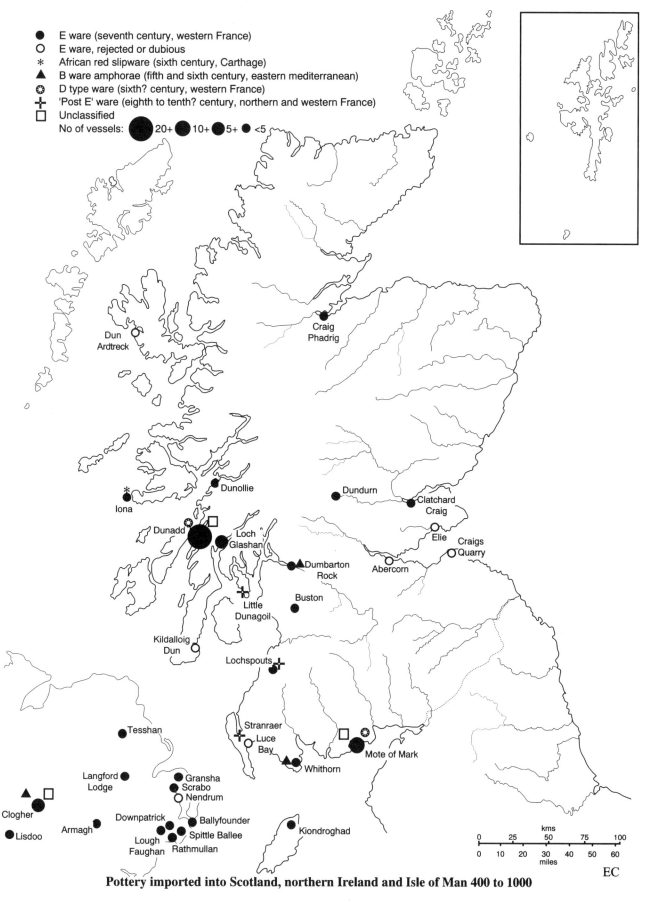

● E ware (seventh century, western France)
○ E ware, rejected or dubious
∗ African red slipware (sixth century, Carthage)
▲ B ware amphorae (fifth and sixth century, eastern mediterranean)
◉ D type ware (sixth? century, western France)
✝ 'Post E' ware (eighth to tenth? century, northern and western France)
□ Unclassified

No of vessels: ● 20+ ● 10+ ● 5+ ● <5

Pottery imported into Scotland, northern Ireland and Isle of Man 400 to 1000

EC

57

Gaelic place-names

The selective interpretation of maps showing the distribution of Gaelic place-names affords us an opportunity to discern historical strata within a stratum. Not only do the maps depicting the geographical scatter of names containing Gaelic *baile* "settlement" and *achadh* "field" reflect the largest extent to which Gaelic was once spoken in Scotland in the Middle Ages but the maps indicating the distribution of *sliabh* "hill" and *cill* "hermit's cell, church" throw light on earlier phases of Gaelic-speaking settlement before Gaelic had become the language of most of Scotland, with the notable exception of the Northern Isles, the northeastern half of Caithness and the Scottish south-east. It is worth remembering, though, that not every name represented within the boundaries of a certain distribution pattern was necessarily given before the settlement behind that pattern reached its fullest expansion the opposite is probably true in all cases, i.e. the element in question remained productive well after the limits of its distribution had been established.

This is particularly applicable to the interpretation of the location of names containing early elements like *sliabh*, and it would therefore be misleading to expect all *sliabh* names (Slewdonan, Slewfad, Slewcairn, Slogarie [Galloway], Sliabh Mor, na Moine, Fada, Meadhonach, Gaoil, nan Dearc, a'Chuir [Highlands and Islands] to have been coined before, let us say, the seventh century. Their limited extent of toponymic productivity nevertheless points to them as being closely associated with the known area of the original Dalriadic settlement of Gaelic-speaking "Scots" from Ireland in the fifth and sixth centuries AD and an equally early "Scots" colony in Galloway, especially in the Rinns. The distribution of place-names containing *cill* (Kilbride, Kilpatrick [Ayrshire], Kildonan, Killantringan, Kilmichael [Galloway], Kilblain [Dumfriesshire], East Kilbride [Lanarkshire], Kilbucho [Peeblesshire], Kilmacolm [Renfrewshire], Killeonan, Kilchenzie, Kilbarr, Kilchieran, Kilmaluag, Kilchintorn, Kilbrandon, Kilchalman, Kilmachalmaig, Kilpheder [Highlands and Islands]) indicates that this generic appears to have remained productive in Gaelic-speaking settlement areas beyond those typical of *sliabh*. While many of these names characteristically commemorate saints known to have lived in the sixth and seventh centuries, their productivity seems to have come to an end not until the ninth and tenth centuries when Gaelic speakers moved into the Pictish territory of the Scottish north-east in large numbers and also confronted the Scandinavians in Caithness.

Baile and *achadh* are important toponymic witnesses not only because of the chronological implications of their distribution patterns and the frequency of their occurrence but also because they directly refer to human settlement. Their patterns of distribution, though not completely congruous, largely confirm each other and point to the same conclusions. Examples from south of the Forth - Clyde line are Balbeg, Baldoon, Balmaghie, Ballaggan, Balbackie, Ballencrieff, Balerno, Balmuir, Balgreen, Auchenbrain, Auchleach, Auchenfad, Auchencairn, Auchentibber, Auchendinny, Auchinhard, Auchneagh; north of that line we find Ballindean, Baldragon, Balhagarty, Baldornoch, Balbeg, Balblair, Balgownie, Balintore, Baleloch, Balemartine, Achnaba, Auchenreoch, Auchmithie, Auchmacoy, Auchenreath, Auchintoul, Achluachrach, Achintraid, Achrimsdale.

Gaelic place-names

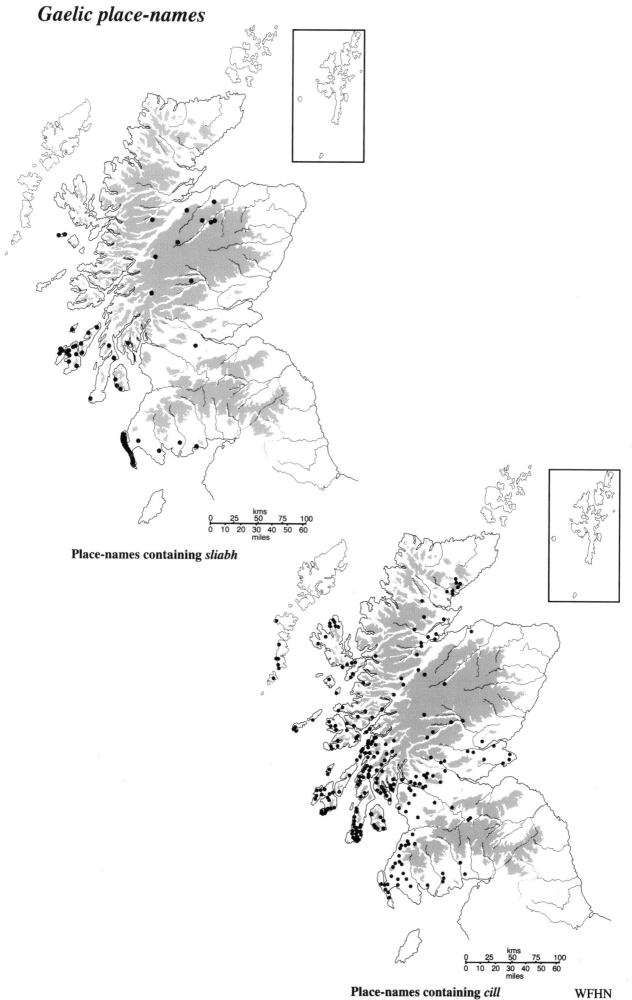

Place-names containing *sliabh*

kms
0   25   50   75   100
0 10 20 30 40 50 60
miles

Place-names containing *cill*

WFHN

Gaelic place-names

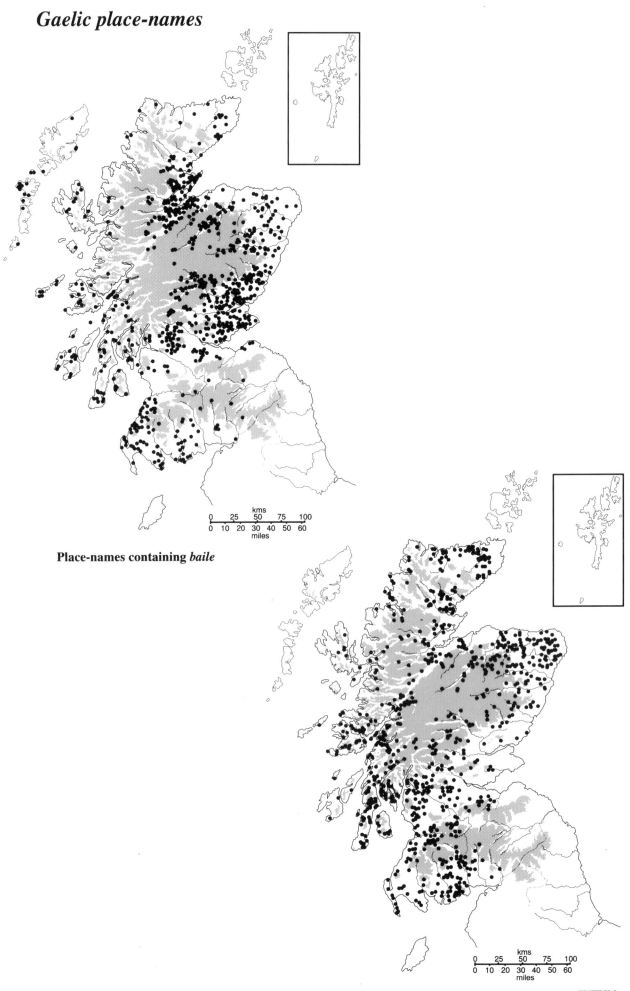

Place-names containing *baile*

Place-names containing *achadh*

WFHN

Anglian place-names

The earliest English (Anglian) place-names in Scotland cannot be dated before the second quarter of the seventh century AD. Among these are names ending in Old English (OE) -*ingham*, like Coldingham (Berwickshire), Whittinghame and Tynninghame (East Lothian) and Penninghame (Wigtownshire). Equally early, but remaining productive longer, are names containing OE *ham* "village, homestead", as, for example, Ednam, Midlem, Oxnam, Smailholm, Yetholm (Roxburghshire), Birgham, Edrom, Kimmerghame, Leitholm (Berwickshire), Morham, Oldham(stocks) (East Lothian), and Smallholm (Dumfriesshire). Unlike ham which ceased to be creative in the formation of place-names before the Middle Ages, OE *tun* "enclosure, enclosed place" continued to be productive for many centuries. While it is therefore itself not a reliable guide to the chronology of English place-names in Scot-

land, it occurs in early names, perhaps till the end of the seventh century or a little later, when combined with -*ing*-, as in Edrington, Edington, Mersington, Renton, Thirlington, Upsettlington (Berwickshire) and some others. Generics like OE *worth* "enclosure", as in Polwarth (Berwickshire), Cessford and Judburgh (Roxburghshire), *bothl*, *botl* "dwelling", as in Bolton, Eldbotle (East Lothian), Newbatte (Midlothian), Morebattle (Roxburghshire) and Buittle (Kirkcudbrightshire), and *wic*, (minor) settlement", as in Berwick (now Northumberland), North Berwick (East Lothian), Borthwick (several), Darnick, Fenwick, Hawick (Roxburghshire), Dawick (Peeblesshire), Fishwick (Berwickshire), and Hedderwick (East Lothian, Berwickshire) also occur in this early Anglian stratum. Remarkable and not fully explained is the occurrence of names like Prestwick, Previck and Fenwick in Ayrshire.

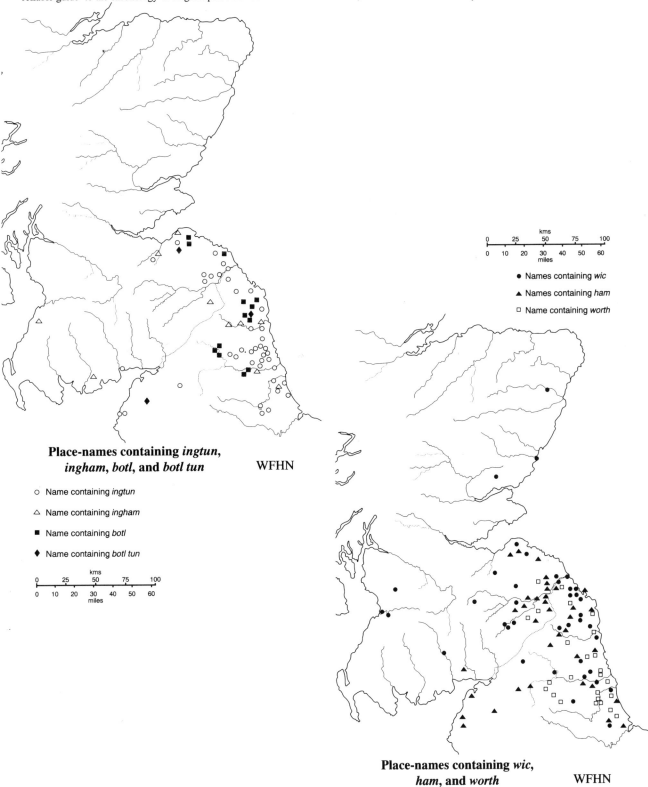

Place-names containing *ingtun*, *ingham*, *botl*, and *botl tun*   WFHN

○ Name containing *ingtun*

△ Name containing *ingham*

■ Name containing *botl*

◆ Name containing *botl tun*

kms
0   25   50   75   100
0   10   20   30   40   50   60
miles

kms
0   25   50   75   100
0   10   20   30   40   50   60
miles

● Names containing *wic*

▲ Names containing *ham*

□ Name containing *worth*

Place-names containing *wic*, *ham*, and *worth*   WFHN

The Scots of Dalriada

Dalriada, the embryonic kingdom of the Scots, was founded about 500 AD when its royal family in the person of Fergus Mor, son of Erc, forsook Dunseverick, capital of Dalriada in Ireland, and took up permanent residence across the North Channel in Scotland. The northern limits of the Scottish Dalriada are depicted as they probably were in the second half of the sixth century. To the east the ridge of mountains known in Gaelic as Druim Alban separated Scot from Pict at this time. The extent of the territories occupied by the three chief peoples of Dalriada, the Cenel nGabrain, Cenel nOengusa and Cenel Loairn, is delimited according to mid seventh century evidence, although the boundary between the Cenel Loairn and the Cenel nGabrain on the mainland was drawn to take account of the fact that early in the following century Dunadd and Tarbert were their respective strongholds in the area. Dunollie was another important and contemporary Cenel Loairn stronghold, while Dunaverty belonged to the Cenel nGabrain. Finally, by the year 700 the temporary decline of the previously dominant Cenel nGabrain had allowed that section of it which inhabited Cowal and doubtless also the neighbouring island of Bute to emerge as the Cenel Comgaill and take its place alongside the other three peoples of Dalriada.

A continuing theme in the history of the Scots of Dalriada from the period of migration onwards was their policy of territorial expansion, perhaps best exemplified by the career of Aedan, son of Gabran. Ordained king of Dalriada by Columba on Iona in 574, in 575 he was in Ireland attending the now famous Convention of Druim Cett. There are records of battles fought by him in the Isle of Man, in Orkney, in the Pictish province of Circinn and against the Maeatae of Central Scotland. His only real setback appears to have been the defeat inflicted on him in 603 by the Angles at the unidentified Degsastan somewhere in Northumbria. His grandson, Domhnall Brecc, equally ambitious, is also on record in Ireland and he was killed fighting the Britons at Strathcarron about 642. The first that is heard of Aed Find, king of Dalriada, is a battle fought by him in 768 in Fortriu, a Pictish province neighbouring Dalriada. Four of the next six kings of Dalriada are named kings of Fortriu implying that the process of establishing Scottish rule in Pictland was well underway. It was brought to its conclusion when Kenneth, mac Alpin, as king of Scots engineered the political union of Scots and Picts. However, it may be said that the church had long since prepared the way. Shortly after the advent of Columba in 563, perhaps even before he founded his monastery on Iona, he went on a mission to Pictland, winning the friendship of, and probably converting to Christianity Brude, son of Maelchu, overking of all the Picts.. The Gaelic cultural penetration accompanying the resultant spread of Christianity throughout Pictland seems to have been so deep and all pervasive as to lead to the virtual disappearance of the Picts from history in an otherwise remarkably short period of time after the union was effected.

The administrative centre of the church moved from Iona to Dunkeld in 849, following the shift in political power, and Scone became the caput or legal centre of the greatly enlarged kingdom of the Scots,whose southern boundary was now the Forth-Clyde line.

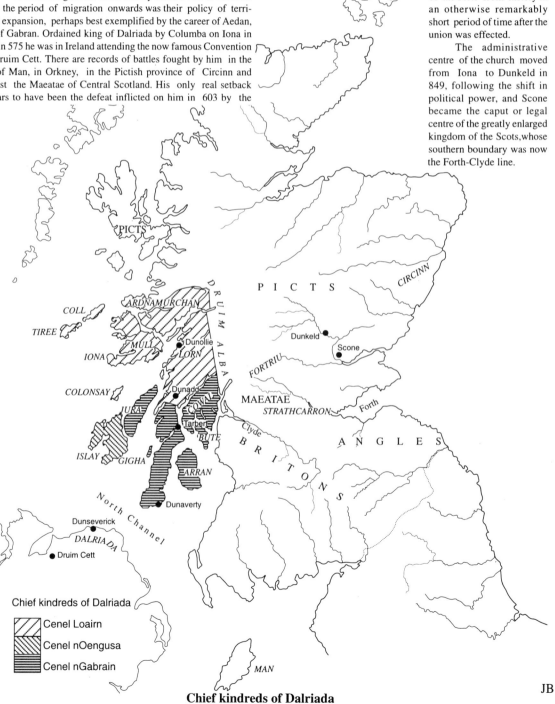

Chief kindreds of Dalriada

JB

Place-names according to Bede

The names of northern Britain which appear on this map come from Bede's *History*. Bede was born probably in 673 and he died in 735; the *History* was completed in 731. He was a monk for most of his life at Jarrow situated in the English kingdom of Northumbria. Most of the names mentioned by Bede are in the English kingdoms - particularly, Northumbria which had authority over what later became south-east Scotland up to the Forth; hence the inclusion of the ecclesiastical foundations of Abercorn, Coldingham Melrose and Whithorn. Similarly, there is an un-named reference to 'Nechtanesmere' where Egfrith, the king of Northumbria, was killed and Northumbrian power in Pictland was removed. That and other unnamed but recognisable references are shown in parenthesis. Some less certain places are also shown.

Place-names from Bede *Ecclesiastical History* in Scotland, northern England and northern Ireland

PGBM

Scandinavian place-names and settlements

Though the maps of place-names of Scandinavian origin indicate the distribution and density of settlement, they are inevitably incomplete. Many farms with Scandinavian names have long since disappeared or have been renamed. Nor do distribution maps reveal the chronology of settlement, relationships with pre-existing populations or different types of settlement established contemporaneously. Most of the Scandinavian names in Scotland were coined in the ninth to thirteenth centuries, the majority in the first half of that period and three different regions of Scandinavian settlement can be identified: the Northern Isles and north-east Scotland where the majority of names are Norse; the Western Isles and western seaboard of mainland Scotland where Norse names compete with Gaelic names; and the south-east of Scotland where Norse, Gaelic and Anglian names are all represented.

There are two categories of place-name to consider. The first is topographical names such as ON *dalr* (dale), *nes* (ness), *vagr* (voe) and *vik* (bay). Many central, primary farms bear names either in simplex form (Wick, Dale, Voe) or in compounds (Sandness, Lerwick, Snizort). There are in addition a vast number of topographical names associated with marginal farms which could have been coined at any time when the Norse language was current. The second group of names contain habitative generics such as *bolstaðr*, *staðir* and *setr*, *saetr*. The first two generics are generally rendered simply as "farm" though they probably had implications beyond that for their names. *Bolstaðr* names, for example, tend to be attached to large, fertile farms found in clusters of two, three or more and were probably given to farms resulting from division of an earlier, larger unit, indicated by the frequency with which they are compounded with locational specifics such as *norðr* (north) and *suðr* (south) in the Northern Isles. *Bolstaðr* takes various forms in Northern and Western Scotland - Urabister, (Shetland); Kirbist, (Orkney); Scrabster, (Caithness); Habost, (Lewis), Carbost, (Skye); Cornabus, (Islay); Eriboll, Skibo, (Sutherland); Ullapool, (W Ross); Crossapoll, (Tiree).

Staðir farms are also large but unlike the *bolstaðr* farms they tend to be independent units rather than divisions. Examples are: Oddsta, (Shetland); Costa, Tenston, (Orkney); Tolsta, (Lewis); Scarasta, (Harris); Connista, (Skye); Hosta, (N Uist); Olistadh, (Islay).

The third element, *setr/saetr*, was applied to more marginal farms established on pasture land, some of which may have originated as shielings. Examples include: Setter, Russetter, (Shetland); Inkster, (Orkney); Wester, Brackside, (Caithness); Grimshader, (Lewis); Drineshader, (Harris); Uigshader, (Skye); Earshader, (North Uist); Ellister, (Islay); Linside, (Sutherland).

In south-west Scotland the Scandinavian elements *bekkr* (stream); *byr* (farmstead, village); and *þveit* (clearing, meadow, paddock); and *fell* or *fjall* (hill, mountain) indicate that Scandinavian settlement in this area should be considered along with that of north-west England where these elements are common. Examples include: Allerbeck, Denbie, Cowthat, Crowthwaite and Borgue Fell.

The Old Norse *kirkja* (church) appears in a number of names, for example, Kirkbryde and Kirkgunzeon. These so-called inversion compounds imitate Gaelic words order rather than Scandinavian. Some, like Kirkcudbright and Kirkoswald, demonstrate an Anglian ambience (St Cuthbert, St Oswald).

Scandinavian place-names and settlements

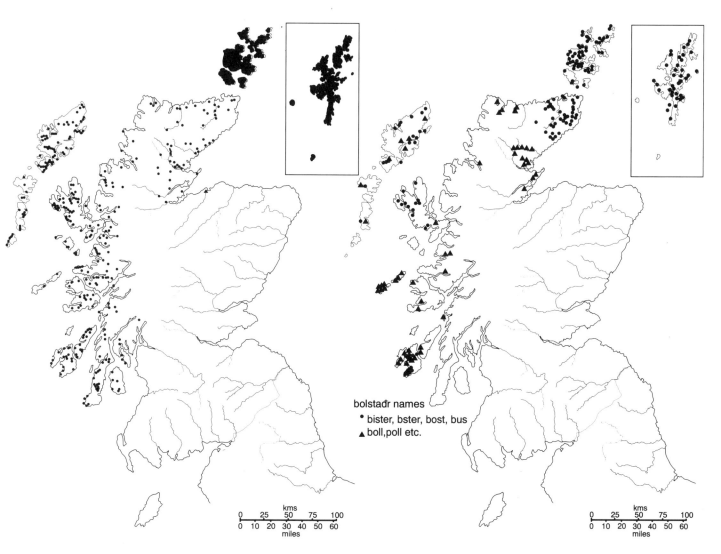

bolstaðr names
• bister, bster, bost, bus
▲ boll, poll etc.

kms
0   25   50   75   100
0 10 20 30 40 50 60
miles

kms
0   25   50   75   100
0 10 20 30 40 50 60
miles

Place-names containing *dalr*

Place-names containing *bolstaðr*

WFHN, LJM, ASm

Scandinavian place-names and settlements

Place-names containing *staðr*

Place-names containing *setr*

WFHN, LJM, ASm

Scandinavian place-names and settlements

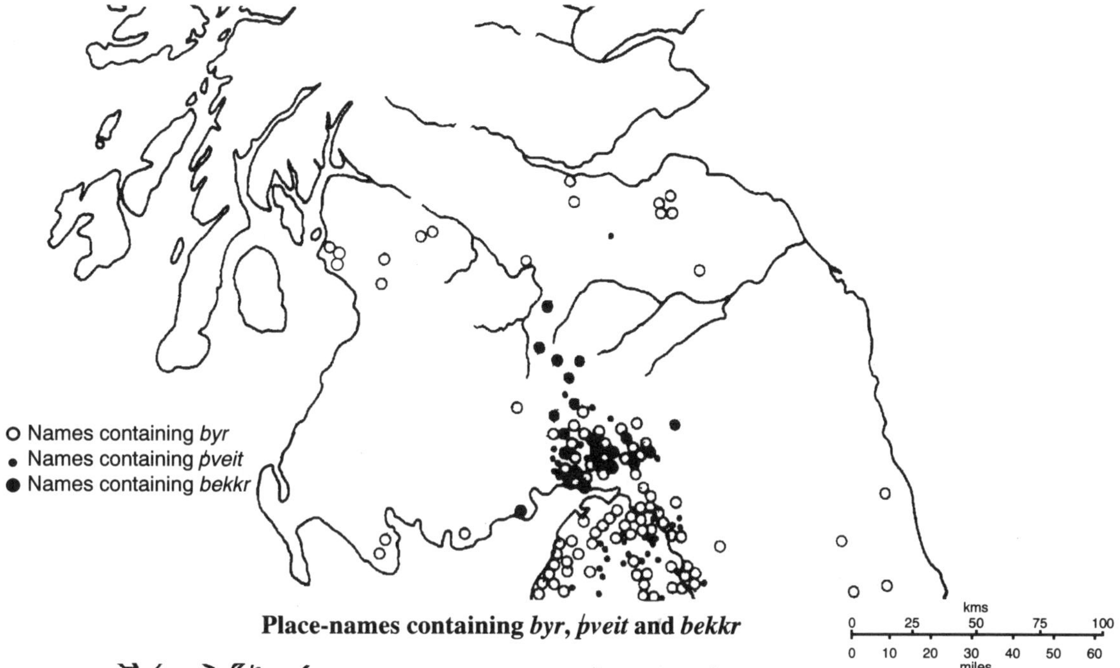

Place-names containing *byr*, *þveit* and *bekkr*

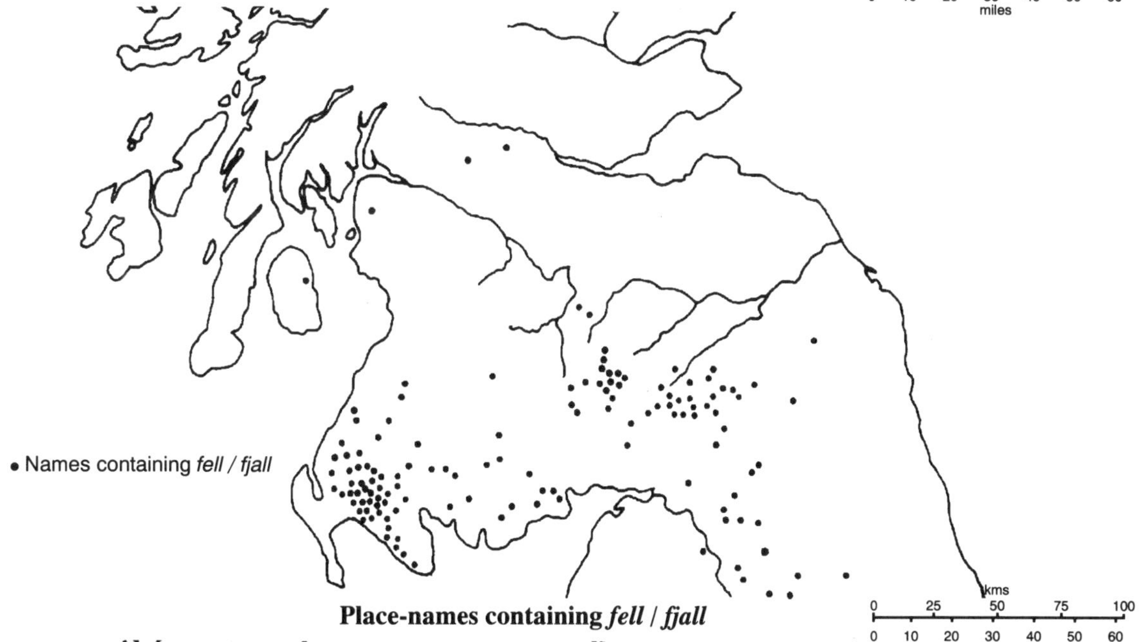

Legend:
- ○ Names containing *byr*
- · Names containing *þveit*
- ● Names containing *bekkr*

Scale: kms 0 25 50 75 100 / miles 0 10 20 30 40 50 60

Place-names containing *fell* / *fjall*

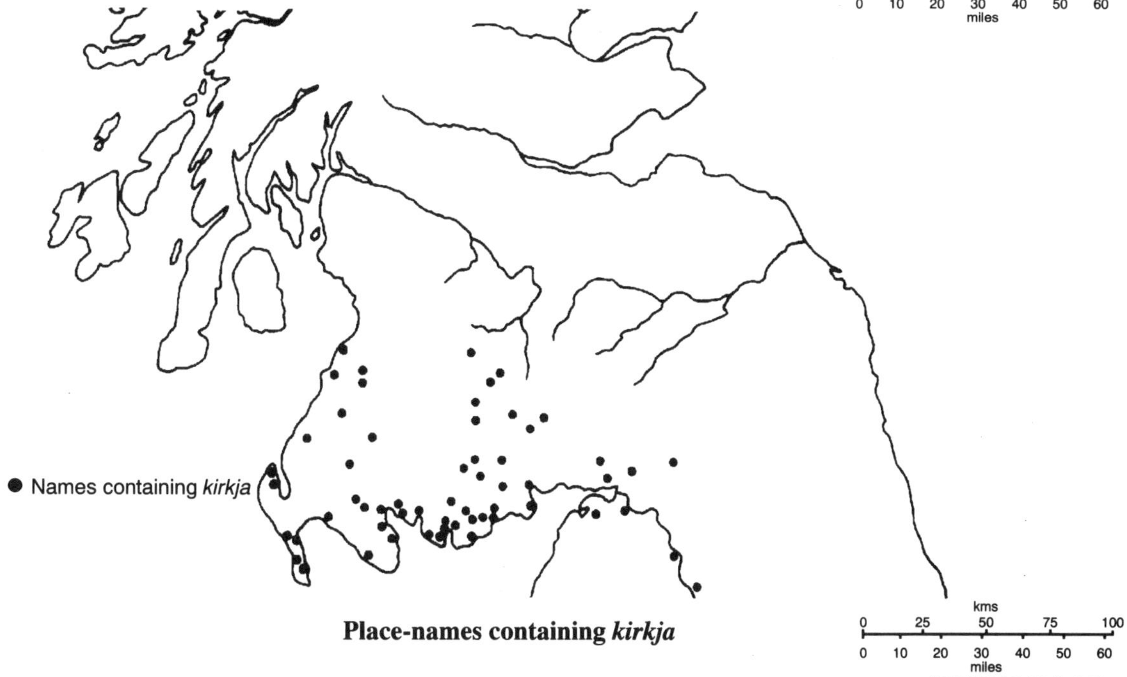

- · Names containing *fell* / *fjall*

Scale: kms 0 25 50 75 100 / miles 0 10 20 30 40 50 60

Place-names containing *kirkja*

- ● Names containing *kirkja*

Scale: kms 0 25 50 75 100 / miles 0 10 20 30 40 50 60

WFHN,LJM,ASm

Scandinavian place-names and settlements

Though there are few written sources for the Northern and Western Isles of Scotland prior to about 1200, other types of evidence can contribute to the reconstruction of settlement patterns. Settlement may be distinguished as primary, secondary or marginal according to geographical factors. Primary farms in Shetland tend to be coastal with a sheltered harbour reflected in place-names descriptive of the major coastal feature - perhaps a bay, voe (inlet), ness or sound, extensive fertile land for arable and pastoral farming, a high land assessment, calculated in Orkney and Shetland in pennylands and ouncelands for tax purposes (a system probably adopted and adapted for the Western Isles by the earls of Orkney) and merklands for rent; a nearby proprietorial chapel site and very often a broch or fort site, indicating continuity of settlement districts from at least the Iron Age. These settlement districts are represented in Shetland by scattalds, each with the necessary features of a mixed pastoral and maritime economy.

The territorial divisions of Norse Scotland (scattalds in Shetland) provide a useful key for understanding the interdependency of all those features which make up settlement patterns - location, nomenclature, secondary expansion, land use, social organisation and administration.

There are about two hundred scattalds in Shetland, twenty-four on the northern island of Unst. Most centre on coastal features favourable for settlement, on bays, firths, nesses and in dales, with arable and meadow land around and a hinterland of pasture making up the essential components of the districts. Within each scattald there can generally be identified a focus of settlement, usually at a prime coastal site, such as Wick, Burrafirth or Sandwick on Unst, around which have developed townships with secondary settlement at some distance along the coast or inland on the hill-grazing land. Primary farms often have simplex topographical names such as Wick (ON *vik*, bay); Skaw (ON *skagi*, low ness, cape); Sound (ON *sund*, sound); or compound topographical names like Sandwick (ON *sandr-vik*, sand-bay); Burrafirth (ON *borg-fjordr*, fort-firth); and Norwick (ON *nordr-vik*, north-bay).

Settlement expansion from the primary sites could take various forms. The best secondary sites had good arable land and extensive grazing though without all the favourable factors of primary sites - perhaps inland with no immediate access to a beach, like Ungirsta, or coastal but lacking a sheltered natural harbour, like Clivocast. Farms established at some distance from the primary farm are often represented by the *stadr* element (Shetland, *-sta*) and occasionally they become the focus of scattalds in their own right, like Baliasta, Ungirsta and Hoversta. Other farms could be established on existing cultivated lands, represented by the generic *bolstadr* (Shetland, - *bister*), such as Wadbister (ON *vatn*, loch), associated with the primary farm of Snarravoe, and Crossbister (ON *kross*, cross), associated with Underhoull. Like *stadr*-farms, *bolstadr*-farms could also become scattald farms in their own right. Both types of farms are represented amongst the most highly assessed on Unst.

More marginal farms could be established on or beyond the hill-dyke, the former represented by the element *gardr/gerdi* (Shetland *garth*, *gert*, *gord*), including Hundigarth (ON *hund*, dog) and Grisgarth (ON *gris*, pig); the latter represented by *setr/saetr*-farms (Shetland *setter*, *ster*), including Murrister (ON *myrr*, moor) and Collaster (ON *kollr*, hill-top, Kollr, man's name). Houses esablished in the close vicinity of the primary farm, creating townships, most often took the generics *hus* (house), *skali* (hall) (Shetland, *skaill*), *stofa* (timber house) (Shetland, *stove*), and topt (*ruin*) (Shetland, *toft*, *taft*).

Another indication of status is land assessment. There were two forms of land valuation in Norse Shetland - tax (*scat*), assessed in urislands and pennylands; and rent, assessed in merks. In Underhoull scattald, Unst there were four tax-paying farms - Underhoull (51 merks); Vinstrick (16 merks); Baila (9 merks) and Crossbister (18 merks), 94 merks in total. The whole scattald was 1 1/6 urislands or 21 penny lands, 4 1/2 merks per pennyland

Within many of the scattalds is a broch or fort which provided the focus of Iron Age settlement. For the Iron Age population had similar requirements to the Norse settlers. On Unst there are ten fort-sites.

The final indicator of primary sites is a church-site. As churches were proprietorial, they were often established at the primary farm, belonging to the most powerful family in the scattald. On Unst fifteen of the twenty-four scattalds have church-sites.

Scandinavian place-names and settlements

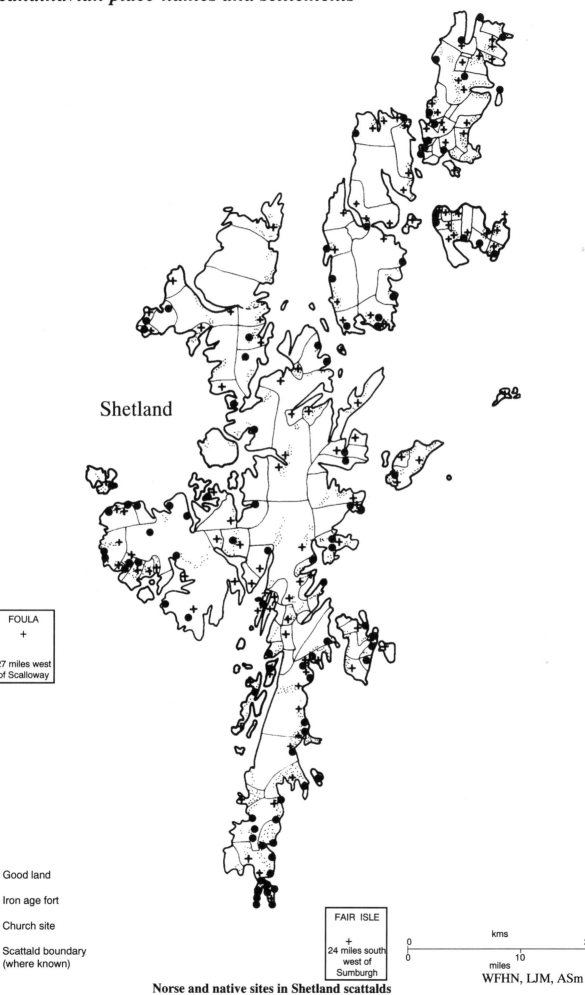

Shetland

FOULA
+

27 miles west
of Scalloway

Good land

●   Iron age fort

+   Church site

——   Scattald boundary
(where known)

FAIR ISLE

+
24 miles south
west of
Sumburgh

kms

0   25

0   10

miles

WFHN, LJM, ASm

Norse and native sites in Shetland scattalds

Scandinavian place-names and settlements

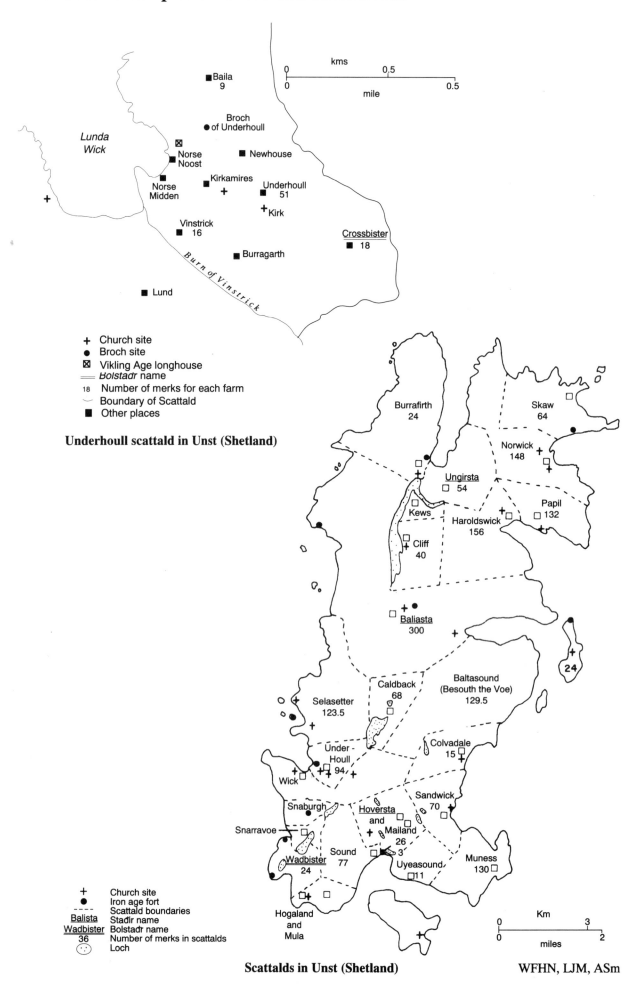

kms
0   0.5
0   0.5
mile

■ Baila
9

● Broch
of Underhoull

⊠
Norse
Noost

■ Newhouse

■ Norse
Midden

■ Kirkamires

+

■ Underhoull
51

+ Kirk

*Lunda
Wick*

+

■ Vinstrick
16

■ Burragarth

Crossbister
18

Burn of Vinstrick

■ Lund

+ Church site
● Broch site
⊠ Vikling Age longhouse
= *Bolstaðr* name
18 Number of merks for each farm
⁓ Boundary of Scattald
■ Other places

Underhoull scattald in Unst (Shetland)

Burrafirth
24

Skaw
64

Norwick
148

Ungirsta
54

Papil
132

Kews

Haroldswick
156

Cliff
40

Baliasta
300

24

Caldback
68

Baltasound
(Besouth the Voe)
129.5

Selasetter
123.5

Colvadale
15

Under-
Houll
94

Wick

Sandwick
70

Snaburgh

Hoversta
and
Mailand
26

Snarravoe

Sound
77

Wadbister
24

Uyeasound
11

Muness
130

Hogaland
and
Mula

+ Church site
● Iron age fort
--- Scattald boundaries
Balista Staðir name
Wadbister Bolstaðr name
36 Number of merks in scattalds
⊙ Loch

Km
0   3
0   2
miles

Scattalds in Unst (Shetland)   WFHN, LJM, ASm

70

Viking graves

The graves of the pagan Norsemen and women are a most important body of archaeological evidence from the early medieval period of Scottish history. They are evidence for the settlement of peoples of Norse culture with direct links with Western Norway and evidence for their adoption of some elements of local Celtic culture, and possibly for their intermingling with the local Celtic population. They are also rare evidence of early medieval society in a world where Christianised populations had long foregone the custom of burying goods with the dead, and the archaeological record is otherwise very meagre. Not only do the graves include ornaments and weapons, but also the tools of craftsmen and of farmers, as well as a variety of domestic implements. Several of them have traces of boats which had formed part of the grave furniture, as well as the skeletal material of domestic animals.

There are difficulties in dating these graves precisely, but they support in general the dates for the Viking invasions known from historical sources, which span the ninth century (with a late eighth century beginning) and spread into the tenth century, at any rate in the Northern Isles. They fit into the place-name evidence which maps the area of Norse settlement so precisely, and confirm the maritime nature of this settlement, in the Western Isles and Man, Orkney, Caithness and the Dornoch area of Sutherland. Strangely, very few graves have ever been found in Shetland. The eventual decline of the practice can be linked to conversion to Christianity which took place formally in Orkney in the late tenth and early eleventh centuries. But influence from native practice probably also played a part in changing custom and perhaps accounts for the rather small number of graves found in total - something like nearly one hundred individual graves, whereas over three hundred have been found in Iceland, which was moreover not settled until the late ninth century.

← St Kilda

▲ Male grave
■ Female grave
○ Find where sex not indicated, or uncertain if find comes from a grave
✳ Pagan cemetery
✗ Grave or find of Norse artefact in a Church yard
? Exact location uncertain
● Family boat burial in Sanday, Orkney

Viking graves

BEC

71

The Norse in Scotland

The silver hoards of the Vikings are a class of archaeological material which opens up a completely different aspect of our knowledge of the Norse in Scotland. They tell us about the trading/raiding side of these sea-borne colonisers and give an indication of the breadth of their trading activities. Viking hoards are recognisable from the variety of silver objects included:- arm-rings, brooches, necklets, ingots, and 'hack-silver' (cut-up pieces of objects which were used as bullion according to weight), as well as a variety of coins from the countries of Western Europe and the East, which came within the Viking trading network. The sheer size of some of these hoards (8kg found at the Bay of Skaill in Orkney), gives us a glimpse of the impressive wealth engendered by the Norse communities in Scotland and particularly in Ireland, where the coastal trading cities probably played a large part in stimulating the growth of the Viking economy. This wealth was carried around all the Norse communities of Scotland, including the Isle of Man, where the number of hoards

(c.20) dating from the late 10th and 11th centuries shows what an important centre of Viking activity the island had then become. How did these personal fortunes come to be buried in the ground? In times of uncertainty it was the only way of protecting one's valuables and if the owner did not survive to retrieve his hidden treasure then we can assume that times were uncertain indeed. Evidence for hoards is based on J.G-Campbell, *The Viking-Age Gold and Silver Hoards of Scotland (1995).*

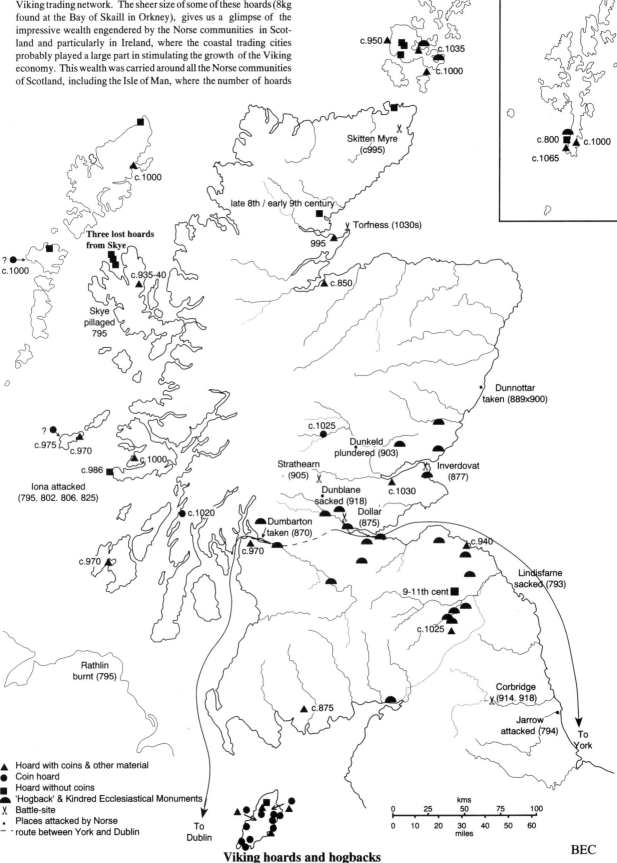

Viking hoards and hogbacks

BEC

72

Events from about 850 to 1460

Scotland from about 842 to 1286

The kingdom of Scotia or Alba, although probably not called such in Latin or Gaelic respectively until 900, came into being as a result of the takeover of Pictland by the Scots of Dalriada under their king, Kenneth MacAlpin (d.858). The traditional date for this event is 842 but the process had begun much earlier. It had certainly been completed by the year 849 when the relics of Colum Cille were taken from Iona to Dunkeld thereby marking the new administrative centre of the Church. At about the same time, Scone became the *caput* or legal centre, doubtless because it had already functioned as such for the important Pictish province of Fortriu, perhaps also for the whole of Pictland. This explains why tradition brings the inauguration stone of the kings of Scots, commonly known as the Stone of Destiny, from Iona to Scone rather than Dunkeld. The abbot of the royal (*regalis*) monastery at Scone, probably a community of Culdees, seems to have taken over the mantle of the Abbot of Iona in respect of taking part in the inaugural ceremonies associated with accession to the kingship of the Scots. The southern boundary of the enlarged kingdom of the Scots was now the Forth - Clyde line, though perhaps not precisely located on the Clyde until the final destruction of the British stronghold of Dumbarton by the Norse of Dublin in 870. It is likely to be at this point that Lennox, the northernmost province of the kingdom of Strathclyde, became part of Scotia. Control of the north depended upon the military presence there of the Norse and, for a time at least, their power extended as far south as Dingwall. Indeed, for the first fifty years or so of its existence, Scotia suffered a number of destructive raids by Scandinavians who plundered Dunkeld before 858 and probably also in 878 and again 903. But in the following year they were defeated in Strathearn by Constantine, king of Scots, who had the *bachall* or crozier of Colum Cille carried before his army. Constantine reigned from 900 to 943 and if nothing else was known

about him the length of his reign, remarkable for this period, would be sufficient testimony to his success as a ruler. In 918 the Scots again defeated the Scandinavians, this time well outside the confines of Scotia on the banks of the River Tyne in Northern England. Constantine's retirement in 943 to become Abbot of the Culdee monastery of Kilrimont at St. Andrews 'on the brow of the wave' is an indication of his confidence that the seaborne threat to Scotia from the Scandinavians had receded. More significantly, perhaps, it was apparently in his reign that the administrative centre of the church was removed from Dunkeld to St. Andrews where it remained until the Reformation.

Much of what little is known of the history of Scotia has to do with succession to the kingship under the terms of the system now generally labelled tanistry. After Constantine's reign it seems no longer to have operated peacefully, hence a long period of feud and faction between rival claimants productive of strife at such identifiable locations as Fetteresso in 954, Duncrub in 965, Fettercairn in 995 and Rathinveramon in 997. Another theme, that goes back to Dalriada, indeed to the initial period of migration from Ireland, was the constant urge of the Scots to expand into new territories. Kenneth MacAlpin himself invaded Lothian on no less than six occasions, the stronghold of Edinburgh was captured by the Scots in the reign of their King Indulf (954-62), and victory at the battle of Carham about 1018 by Malcolm II finally secured the district of Lothian. About the same time, Malcolm's grandson, Duncan became king of Strathclyde which had been in a client relationship to the kings of Scots ever since the late ninth century, exemplified as much as anything by the influx of Gaelic speakers into the area in the interval, so that when Duncan succeeded to the kingship of the Scots on the death of his grandfather in 1034, Scotia had become Scotland more or less as we know it today.

Scotland from about 842 to 1286

SHETLAND (inset map, top right)

Dingwall

PICTLAND

• Fetteresso
• Fettercairn

Iona

DALRIADA

FORTRIU
• Dunkeld
• Rathinveramon
Scone
St. Andrews
(Kilrimont)
STRATHEARN
• Duncrub

LENNOX
Firth of Forth
• Dumbarton
STRATHCLYDE
• Edinburgh
Firth of Clyde

LOTHIAN
• Carham

River Tyne

IRELAND

ENGLAND

Scotia from about 842 to 1034

kms
0   25   50   75   100
0 10 20 30 40 50 60
miles

JWMB

Scotland from about 842 to 1286

The period (1040 to 1107) saw the kingdom of Scotland take on its recognisable medieval shape both geographically and constitutionally. The rivalry between the Moray line of the royal house (represented by Macbeth (1040-57) and his step-son Lulach (1057-58)) and the direct descendants of Kenneth MacAlpin (represented by Malcolm II's grandson Duncan I, (1034-40) and his sons Malcolm III Canmore (1058-93) and Donald Ban (1093, 1094-97)) was marked by old-fashioned slayings of Duncan I at Pitgaveny, of Macbeth at Lumphanan and of Lulach at Essie. The anti-foreign reaction which followed Malcolm III's death in 1093 entailed the killing of Duncan II at Mondynes in the interests of Donald Ban who in turn was fatally wounded at Rescobie. The way was clear for Edgar (1097-1107) to exploit the territorial advantages built up under the two Malcolms and rule effectively from the northern Highlands to the Tweed. But in the 1090s the king of Scots lost English Cumbria to William Rufus and the Western Isles to Magnus Barelegs king of Norway.

Orkney
(to Norway)

Western Isles
(Sudreyiar)

(to Norway)

M O R A Y

● Pitgaveny
● Elgin

● Essie

● Lumphanan

S C O T I A

● Mondynes

Lismore

A T H O L L

● Rescobie

● Dunkeld
● Dunsinnan (✕ 1054)
● Perth

● Kilrymont (St Andrews)

● Lochleven
● Stirling
● Dunfermline

● Edinburgh

Bute

● Glasgow   L O T H I A N   ● Coldingham

(to Norway
1098-)

● Berwick upon Tweed

● Melrose   ● Bamburgh

C
U
M
B
R
I
A

● Alnwick

G A L L O W A Y

Earldom of Northumbria
(Northern Division)

● Newcastle upon Tyne
(1080)

● Carlisle
(castle 1092)

● Durham

(To King of
Scots 1018-1092,
1136-1157)

(Harterness &
Sadberge)

Earldom of Northumbria
(Southern Division)

Man
(to Norway)

Haliwerfolc or St. Cuthbert's Land
Boundary of Cumbria
Boundary of earldom of
Northumbria (northern division)
Boundary between 'English' and
'Scottish' Cumbria established by
William Rufus, 1092
Boundary between Scottish and
Norwegian suzerainty

kms
0   25   50   75   100
0 10 20 30 40 50 60
miles

GWSB

Scotland about 1040 to 1107

Scotland from about 842 to 1286

Although the Hebrides and Northern Isles remained Norwegian, the kingdom ruled by David I, especially from 1141 to 1153, represented the widest extent of Scottish royal government hitherto experienced. In the south, Cumberland, North Westmorland and Northumberland were brought under David's control after 1141, while the king took care to exercise royal authority in Argyll, Kintyre and Caithness, as well as establishing castle/burgh strongpoints in Moray, a province secured by the battle of Stracathro (1130). The centre of gravity however, in politics and government remained in the southern Lowlands, from Fife to the northernmost sheriffdoms of England.

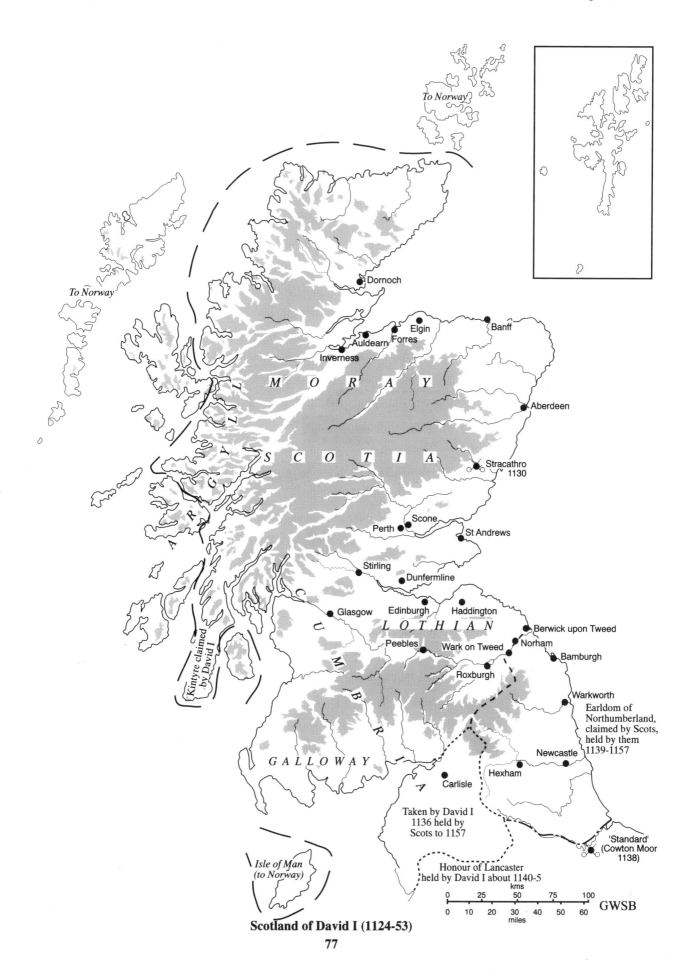

Scotland of David I (1124-53)

77

Scotland from about 842 to 1286

The political power struggle between the Comyn and Durward parties during the tense minority of King Alexander III cannot be fully understood without the awareness of their rival landed interests and ambitions, especially between about 1230 and about 1260.

The Comyn ascendancy of the 1230s was threatened in 1242 by the loss of the earldoms of Atholl and Angus from family control and more especially in 1244 by the promotion of Alan Durward as Justiciar of Scotia, chief adviser of Alexander II. This office, the main political office of state, would play a crucial role when Alexander II died in 1249 and the minority of the young Alexander III began. Durward sought to use the office to realise the long-held family ambition for the earldom of Mar.

The Comyns had had their first tussle with the Durwards over the earldom of Atholl. Alan Durward had himself briefly held the title of earl of Atholl around 1233 x 1235, his right probably based on wardenship of the heir rather than marriage to the heiress - but the earldom remained in the Comyn family circle until 1242 when it fell to David de Hastings. A longer and more passionate dispute existed over the earldom of Mar. Malcolm of Lundie, an Angus lord and the king's doorward (hence the name 'Durward') had been given land on marriage to the daughter of Gilbert, earl of

Mar, about 1203 x 1211. Thomas Durward pressed a claim to the earldom when it fell vacant about 1210 - 1220 but had to be satisfied with the important lordship of Coull between Don and Dee. When the earldom of Mar also came under Comyn influence around 1242 x 1244 - through the marriage of William, earl of Mar to the daughter of William Comyn, earl of Buchan - Durward resentment was understandable. It is hardly surprising that, after exclusion from political power from 1251 to 1255 during another period of Comyn ascendancy, Alan Durward took full advantage of his renewed Justiciarship of Scotia to pursue personal profit. He challenged the legitimacy of the earl of Mar's father and grandfather in order to obtain the earldom himself. Earl William's delaying tactics and a counter-coup by the Comyns in 1257 thwarted the Durwards again.

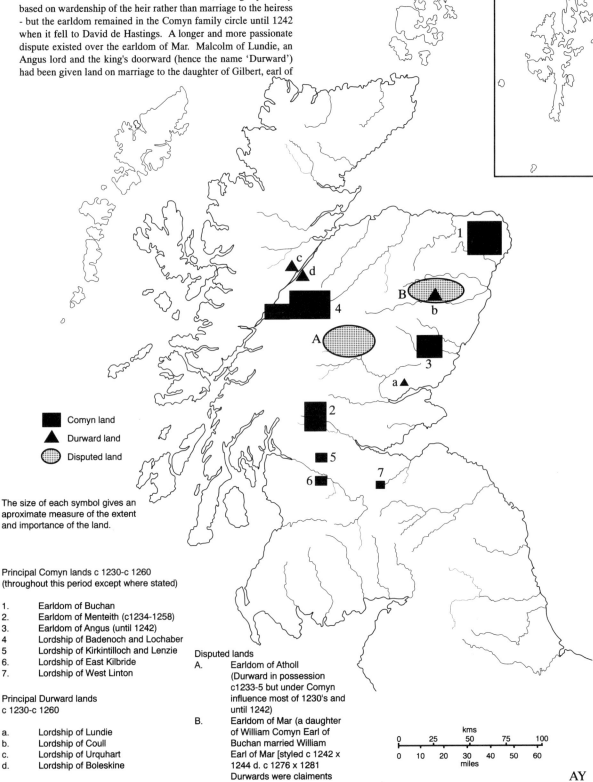

Comyn land

Durward land

Disputed land

The size of each symbol gives an aproximate measure of the extent and importance of the land.

Principal Comyn lands c 1230-c 1260
(throughout this period except where stated)

1. Earldom of Buchan
2. Earldom of Menteith (c1234-1258)
3. Earldom of Angus (until 1242)
4. Lordship of Badenoch and Lochaber
5. Lordship of Kirkintilloch and Lenzie
6. Lordship of East Kilbride
7. Lordship of West Linton

Principal Durward lands
c 1230-c 1260

a. Lordship of Lundie
b. Lordship of Coull
c. Lordship of Urquhart
d. Lordship of Boleskine

Disputed lands

A. Earldom of Atholl (Durward in possession c1233-5 but under Comyn influence most of 1230's and until 1242)

B. Earldom of Mar (a daughter of William Comyn Earl of Buchan married William Earl of Mar [styled c 1242 x 1244 d. c 1276 x 1281 Durwards were claiments c 1210-1220 and 1255-1257.

kms

0   25   50   75   100

0 10 20 30 40 50 60
miles

AY

The Comyns versus the Durwards in 1250s

78

The Anglo-Scottish Border

The Anglo-Scottish frontier clearly delineated on the eve of the first war of independence was the product of a lengthy and complex process beginning around the middle of the tenth century when the kings of Scots pushed their eastern boundary through Lothian to the Tweed. By the early eleventh century they had taken over Cumbria or Strathclyde, giving them a foothold on the north-west boundary of Yorkshire. In 1092 this Scottish southward drive was reversed by William Rufus's annexation of 'English' Cumbria and building of Carlisle castle, but in 1136 the Scots re-asserted their suzerainty over Cumbria and attempted to annex Northumberland - successfully from 1139 to 1157, but thereafter thwarted by strong English resistance. At the same time, the kings of Scots acquired the extensive lordship - later 'liberty' of Tynedale, i.e. the dales of North and South Tyne. By the treaty of York (1237) Alexander II effectively recognised English possession of Northumberland, Cumberland and Westmorland but in return was confirmed in Tynedale and was given the newly-created 'honour of Penrith'. A striking feature of the Border thus evolved and established was that the Scottish side was marked by relatively thickly-populated districts and important towns while much of the English side consisted of sparsely settled wastes and moorlands.

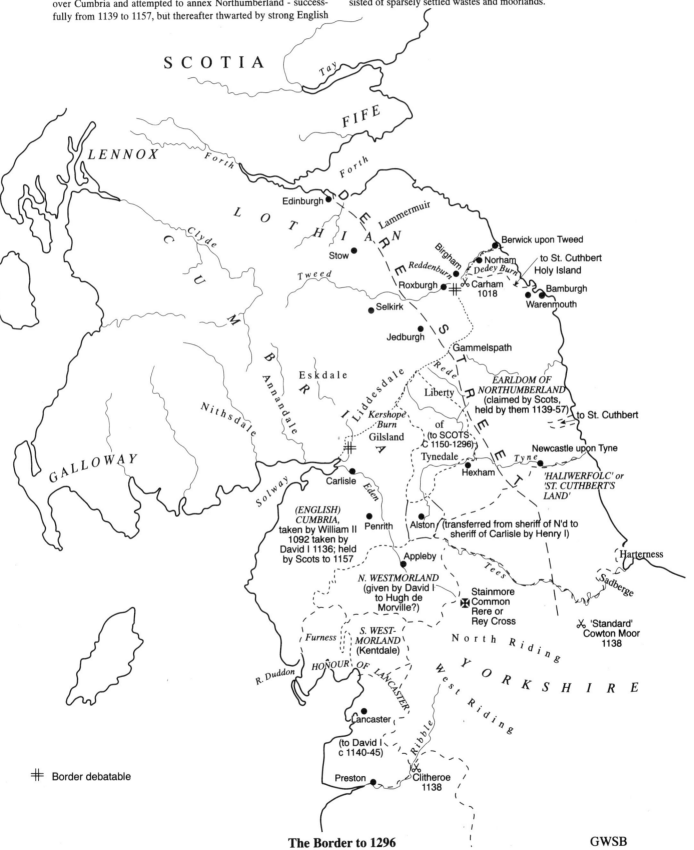

The Border to 1296

GWSB

79

The Anglo-Scottish Border

On the English side there were generally two marches. An exception was the middle march, created for the earl of Northumberland (1381-4) and again in existence from 1470 (combined with the east march until 1536). Its revival was perhaps intended to match its Scottish counterpart, referred to from the mid fifteenth century, and additional to the Scottish east and west marches (mentioned in 1355 and 1364 respectively).

The wardens, usually provided by the families of Percy and Neville on the English side and March and Douglas on the Scottish side, were to meet on March Days, often at Liliot Cross during the English occupation to Teviotdale.

Warfare was largely a matter of raids and sieges, for example, the siege of Roxburgh by the Scots during which James II was killed in 1460. The debateable land on the west march resulted from the uncertain allegiance of the Storeys and later the Grahams.

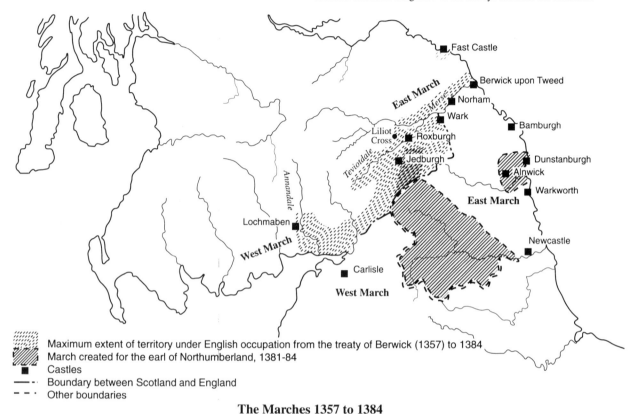

Maximum extent of territory under English occupation from the treaty of Berwick (1357) to 1384
March created for the earl of Northumberland, 1381-84
Castles
Boundary between Scotland and England
Other boundaries

The Marches 1357 to 1384

Debateable land
Territory under English control
Castles
Boundaries of the Scottish marches
Boundary of the English middle march

The Marches in the fifteenth century

AT

Anglo-Scottish relations: David I to Alexander III

The accession of David I (1124-53) marked a major turning point in the inter-relationship of the Scottish and English kingdoms. David held the honour of Huntingdon in the English eastern midlands from 1113, and he had no wish to give it up when he became king. Moreover, he encouraged immigration from other parts of England, especially the Welsh marches, of young men prepared to serve him militarily as feudal vassals; and from 1141 to 1153 the king pressed his claims effectively to rule over the earldom of Northumberland and southern or 'English' Cumbria. On the ecclesiastical side, David successfully deprived Durham diocese of Teviotdale and Tweeddale,

transferring them to Glasgow, but on the other hand Glasgow lost English Cumbria in 1133 when Henry I (1100-35) created the new diocese of Carlisle and assigned it to the province of York. The warfare of Stephen's reign (1135-54) played surprisingly little part in Anglo-Scottish relations.

Although the Scottish army led by David I and his son sustained a heavy defeat near Northallerton in 1138 (the battle of the Standard), the Scots were able to control most of the northern English counties during David's last decade; and David himself died at Carlisle.

Anglo-Scottish relations: David I (1124-53)

Anglo-Scottish relations: David I to Alexander III

William I's policies were to regain the earldom of Northumberland (of which he had been deprived by Henry II in 1157) and other northern English counties once ruled by David I, and to maintain Scottish independence.

Diplomatic attempts having failed, William allied with Louis VII and supported the rebellion of the "Young King" Henry against Henry II. William led three expeditions into England (1173-74), with little success, but Earl David helped to win control of the midland counties of England.

After capture at Alnwick (1174), William was taken to Normandy. The treaty of Falaise, confirmed at York (1175), made Scotland effectively a subject kingdom: Huntingdon was forfeit, and English garrisons stationed at Berwick, Roxburgh and Edinburgh castles.

English influence was seen in help given to William to restore his authority in Galloway and Carrick following revolts, and in intervention over a disputed election to the see of St Andrews. However, in 1185 the honour of Huntingdon was restored, and, on William's arranged marriage to Ermengarde of Beaumont, Edinburgh castle was returned.

Richard I, anxious to go crusading, accepted money to cancel the treaty of Falaise and restore Berwick and Roxburgh castles. William met John on three occasions between 1200 and 1207. A crisis over the Scottish destruction of the recently built Tweedmouth castle could not be resolved by a conference at Bolton (1209), and at Norham John obtained a ransom, the surrender of William's daughters, Margaret and Isobel, with a view to their future marriage, and the sons of nobles as hostages. The price of English help to suppress a revolt in Ross (1212) seems to have been a confirmation of this treaty and a concession that John should control the marriage of Prince Alexander, who was knighted by John. The kings last met, in a better atmosphere, in 1212.

Anglo-Scottish relations: William I (1165-1214)

WWS

82

Anglo-Scottish relations: David I to Alexander III

The baronial rebellion against King John enabled Alexander II to repudiate the treaties of 1209 and 1212 and claim the Border counties. The map illustrates the strength of the Scots' strategic position when they invaded (Oct. 1215) and assists in following the vicissitudes of the campaign. The 'Northerners' regarded Alexander as a natural ally in their struggle, and Northumberland, Cumberland and Westmorland were formally adjudged to him by the Twenty-five barons of Magna Carta. The Yorkshire rebels paid Alexander homage on 11 January 1216. But during John's northern drive (Jan.-Feb. 1216), sixteen rebel castles fell, and he conducted a devastating counter-invasion of Scotland. The Scots recovered Carlisle in August; Alexander had his candidate elected to the vacant bishopric; Alan, lord of Galloway, seized north Westmorland. The rebellions of the count of Aumale and the earl of Surrey, whose castles included Skipton, Sandal and Conisbrough, opened the way south, and Alex-

ander marched to Dover, easily the deepest penetration of England by a hostile Scottish force. About mid-September, he offered homage at Dover to Prince Louis of France, who as claimant to the English throne acknowledged Alexander's right to the three Border counties (but not to Yorkshire).

On John's death (Oct. 1216) moderates rallied behind the young Henry III. The rebel army, including a Scottish contingent, was routed at Lincoln (20 May 1217), and the ground cut from beneath the Scots, whose war aims had always depended chiefly on the strength of the baronial movement. On 1 December Alexander relinquished Carlisle; at Northampton by 19 December he returned to the allegiance of the English crown, as lord of the Huntingdon honour and Tynedale. Despite Alexander's greater initial advantages, as in 1173-4 an enterprise confidently begun ended in abject failure, and that helped to introduce new realism into the conduct of Anglo-Scottish relations.

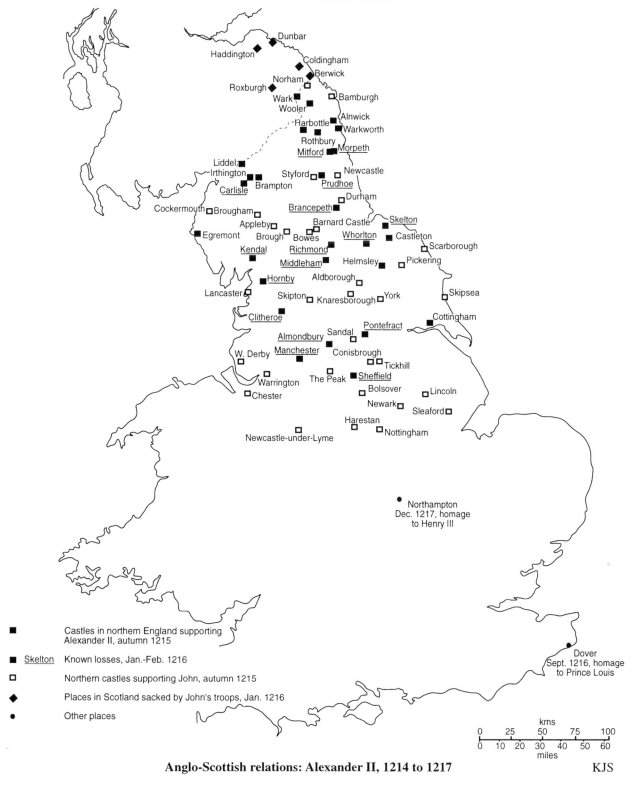

Anglo-Scottish relations: Alexander II, 1214 to 1217   KJS

83

Anglo-Scottish relations: David I to Alexander III

From December 1217 to March 1296 Scotland and England were continuously at peace. This long period of stability, unparalleled in the Middle Ages, owed much to the readiness of Alexander II and Henry III to settle or play down differences. Alexander's marriage to Henry's sister Joan at York (19 June 1221) reinforced the peace concluded at Northampton in 1217. Most significant was the treaty of York (25 Sept. 1237), a major landmark in the making of the Scots kingdom. Alexander renounced in perpetuity all claims to Northumberland, Cumberland and Westmorland for lands worth £200, and at last the Scots recognised the futility of continuing to pursue the traditional goal of southern expansion.

In 1244 the kingdoms verged on war. Alexander had married secondly Marie de Coucy, a match deemed provocative by Henry III who feared a Franco-Scottish alliance. Another cause of dispute was the fortification of Border castles, probably Hermitage and Caerlaverock as illustrated. But by the treaty of Newcastle upon Tyne (14 Aug. 1244) Alexander promised to refrain from any hostile act against Henry and that his son, the future Alexander III, would marry Henry's daughter Margaret.

The map cannot cover every important aspect of Anglo-Scottish relations in this period. Many of the barons of Scotland who swore to uphold the treaties of York and Newcastle were cross-Border landlords with a vested interest in harmony. The pope, England's overlord and protector, also encouraged peace. Unresolved by negotiation was the key question of the constitutional relationship between Scotland and the English crown. But Scottish independence was not jeopardised, and in 1217, 1237 and 1244 Henry III implicitly accepted Scotland's status as a separate kingdom.

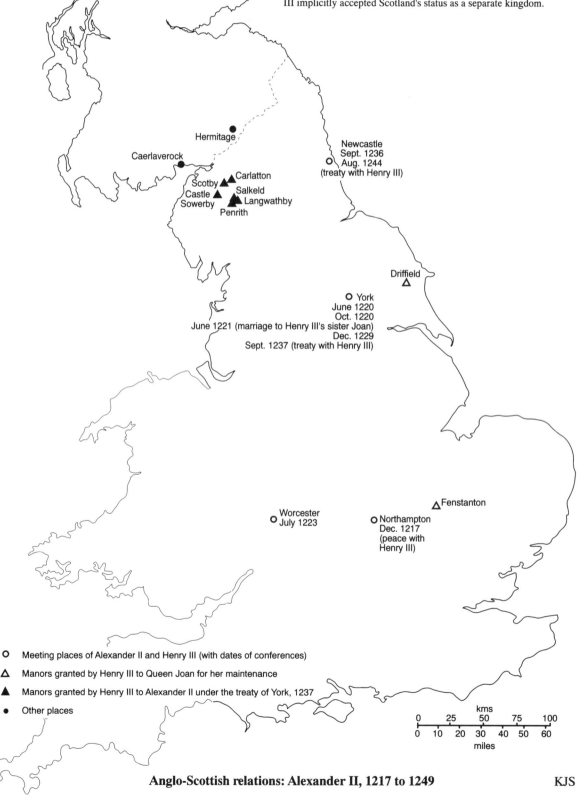

○   Meeting places of Alexander II and Henry III (with dates of conferences)

△   Manors granted by Henry III to Queen Joan for her maintenance

▲   Manors granted by Henry III to Alexander II under the treaty of York, 1237

●   Other places

Anglo-Scottish relations: Alexander II, 1217 to 1249

KJS

Anglo-Scottish relations: David I to Alexander III

It is natural to place Alexander III's reign (1249-86) in the context of the subsequent war of independence. Despite signs of tension such as increased frequency of embassies (1275-78) and discussion of border disputes in 1278, the relationship between England and Scotland was close in Alexander III's reign, and, between about 1260 and 1286, probably friendlier than at any period because of Alexander's marriage to Henry III's daughter Margaret (1251). Much political activity in the minority years 1249- about 1260 sprang from Henry's concern for the young couple and for the stability of Scotland. Both political groups, Comyns and Durwards, recognised the need for Henry's support.

After the minority, there was a very good personal relationship between the two royal families. Another stabilising force was a politically active group of magnates with land in both kingdoms. For example, John de Balliol and Robert de Ros were guardians of the young Scots king and queen (1251-55), Alan Durward served Henry III in Gascony (1254), had Henry's support for his "takeover" in Scotland in 1255, and took refuge in England after 1257. On five occasions (1257-1261) Roger de Quincy took part in embassies to Scotland. The Bruce, Comyn and Balliol families were represented on Henry's side at the battle of Lewes (1264). John de Vescy accompanied Edward I (1272-1307) on crusade and then was a leader of Alexander III's expedition to the Isle of Man (1275).

These forces of stability helped to keep in abeyance possible tensions over English claims to suzerainty and border disputes. Tensions increased after Queen Margaret's death (1275), but it was a set of tragic circumstances - the deaths of Alexander III's children, David (1281), Margaret (1283), and Alexander (1284), and of Alexander himself (1286) - which finally broke a "tie of indissoluble affection".

Edinburgh

Haddington (1)

1268 Princes Edward and Edmund on holiday at court.

1265 x 1266 Prince Edward visits (1) Margaret (11) Alexander

Kelso

(11) Roxburgh

1255 Visit of Henry III

Wark

Alexander III knighted by Henry III. Marriage of Alexander to Henry III's daughter Margaret

York

Embassies of Roger de Quincy, earl of Winchester and Constable of Scotland in 1257, 1258, 1259, 1260 and 1261

1278 meeting of Edward I and Alexander III

Tewkesbury

Woodstock

1260 visit of Scottish king and queen

1274 Scottish king and queen attend Edward I's coronation

1256 visit of Scottish king and queen

Windsor

London

Canterbury

Alexander III on pilgrimage and renders homage to Henry III

1261 birth of Princess Margaret

Lewes (1265)

kms
0 25 50 75 100
0 10 20 30 40 50 60
miles

Anglo-Scottish relations: Alexander III (1249-86)

AY

Edward I in Scotland

This series of maps shows the routes that Edward I (1272-1307) took on his expeditions to Scotland. The maps do not show every apparent foray which the king took, for example, when he wintered in Dunfermline from November 1303 until March 1304. However, the itinerary of 1296 is described in a contemporary account.

The first journey in Scotland came in the summer of 1291 after Edward's overlordship of Scotland had been acknowledged: he returned south in August for the assembly at Berwick at which the petitions in the great cause were to be presented.

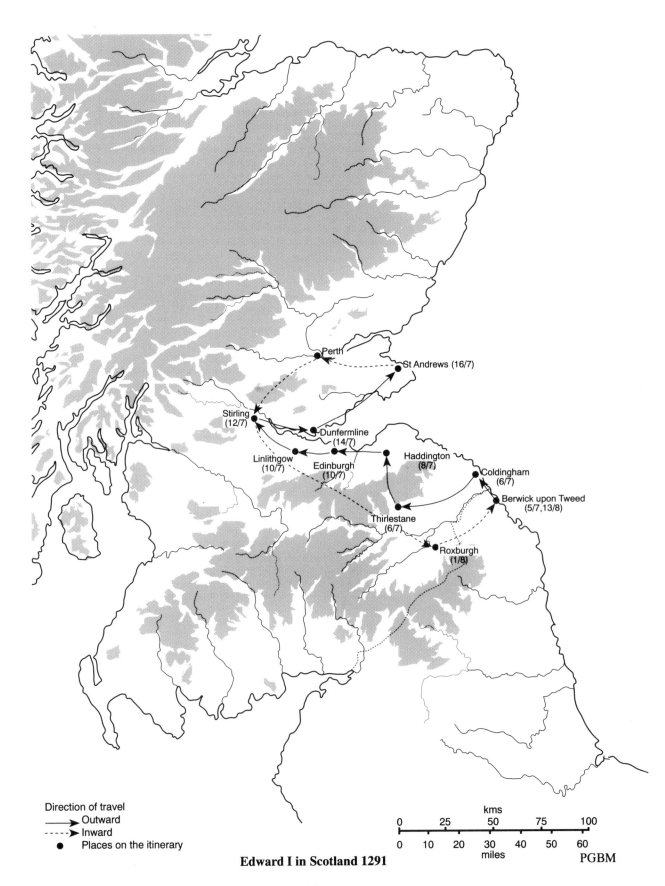

Direction of travel
→ Outward
--→ Inward
● Places on the itinerary

kms
0   25   50   75   100

0   10   20   30   40   50   60
miles

Edward I in Scotland 1291

PGBM

Edward I in Scotland

The itinerary of 1296 was a campaign of conquest which followed upon the Scottish declarations of independence and the ratification of the treaty between Scots and the French. The campaign lasted twenty-one weeks, beginning in March. After Berwick fell, it was sacked and the inhabitants were slaughtered. Edward travelled as far north as Elgin; on the way north he received King John's renunciation of the French treaty at Strathcathro (7 July) and his abdication of the throne at Brechin (10 July). Edward was back in Berwick by mid-September.

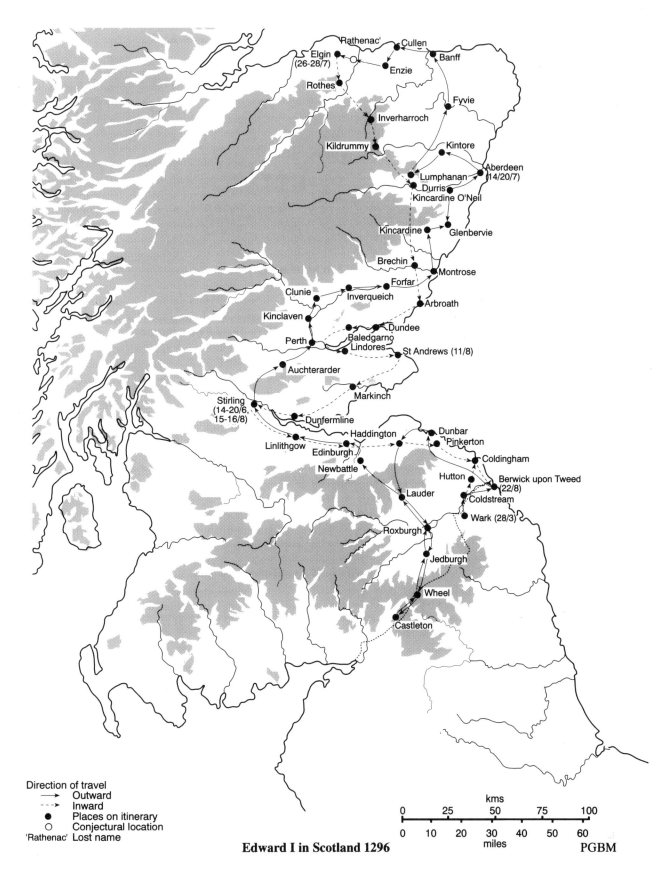

Direction of travel
→ Outward
--→ Inward
● Places on itinerary
○ Conjectural location
'Rathenac' Lost name

Edward I in Scotland 1296

PGBM

Edward I in Scotland

The military expedition of 1298 was designed to reverse the effect of Wallace's victory over the English at Stirling on 11 September 1297. After some difficulty, Edward's forces travelled as far as Falkirk where they defeated the Scots under Wallace. Edward's campaign took him to Ayr, from where he went to Dumfriesshire and back to Carlisle: but Edward had returned to Scotland because Jedburgh had held out.

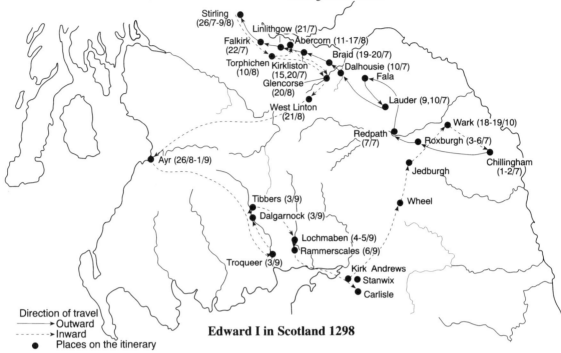

Edward I in Scotland 1298

Direction of travel
→ Outward
→ Inward (dashed)
● Places on the itinerary

The campaign of 1300 was designed to subjugate the south west: and it ended in a truce to last to May 1301.

Edward I in Scotland 1300

● Places on the itinerary
○ Conjectural locations
'Rotheland' Lost names
→ Direction of travel

After the truce ended, there was no prospect of peace; while King Edward took a larger force to Berwick from where he went across Scotland to the upper Clyde and down the Clyde valley to Glasgow. The king wintered in Linlithgow and left Scotland in February.

Edward I in Scotland 1301 to 1302

Direction of travel
→ Outward
→ Inward (dashed)
● Places on the itinerary

PGBM

88

Edward I in Scotland

On 24 February 1303, the Scots defeated an English contingent at Roslin; and on 20 May in the peace between England and France, Scotland was not comprehended. Edward's summer campaign was a full-scale invasion in which the English forces went as far north as Kinloss. After a long siege (May to 20 July) Stirling castle was taken by Edward. Thereafter, he wintered in Dunfermline and returned to England in August 1304. After this subjugation, Edward tried to stabilise the situation by a constitutional settlement. The resurgence of Scottish independence under Robert I - who had been made king on 25 March 1306 - had been kept in check by Edward's lieutenants, but Edward himself, although seriously ill, planned to undertake a futher campaign in July 1306, but he was incapacitated until March 1307. He heard of Robert's victory at Loudon Hill (10 May 1307) and decided to lead another Scottish expediton in person. He only got as far as Burgh by Sands (not far from Carlisle) were he died on 7 July at the age of 68.

The composite map of all of Edward I's Scottish campaigns shows that apart from occasional forays such as the ones to Ayr in 1298 and to Boat of Garten in 1303 the main area which he covered was the eastern part of Scotland; and most of his routes were within reasonable distance from the sea, so that he could call upon the support of the fleet. Edward's lieutenants went further afield.

The maps give mainly a picture of places at which writs were issued: some of the places must have been of little significance. The Gough map (which is shown in the first section of this atlas), on the other hand, shows major places - cities, castles and passages - which would have been of use to travellers or invaders.

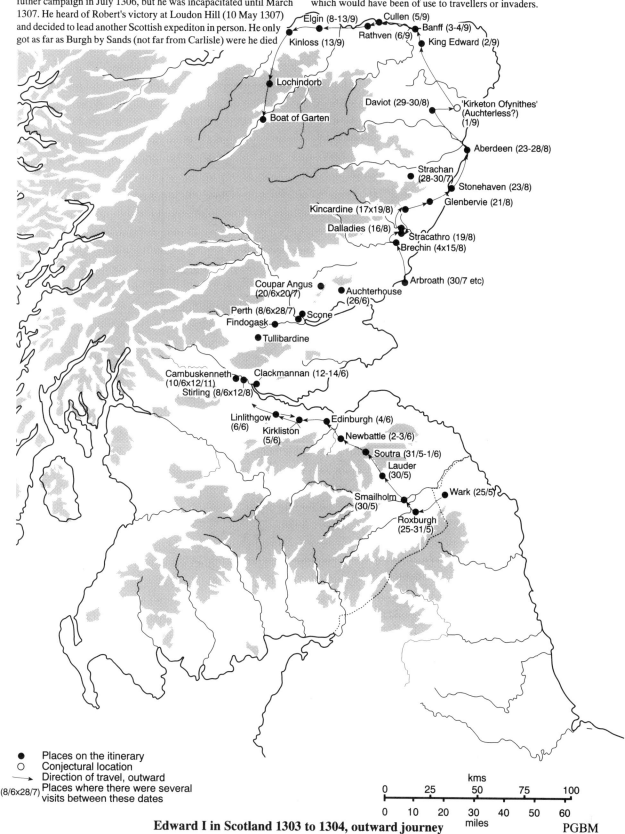

Key:
- ● Places on the itinerary
- ○ Conjectural location
- → Direction of travel, outward
- (8/6x28/7) Places where there were several visits between these dates

kms
0 25 50 75 100

0 10 20 30 40 50 60
miles

Edward I in Scotland 1303 to 1304, outward journey

PGBM

Edward I in Scotland

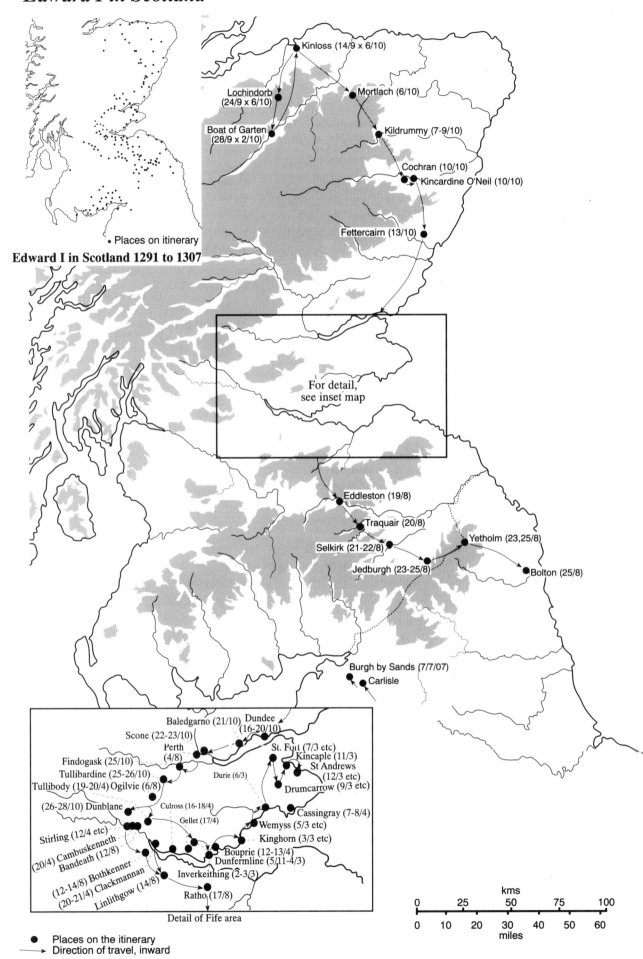

Places on itinerary

Edward I in Scotland 1291 to 1307

Kinloss (14/9 x 6/10)

Lochindorb (24/9 x 6/10)

Mortlach (6/10)

Boat of Garten (28/9 x 2/10)

Kildrummy (7-9/10)

Cochran (10/10)

Kincardine O'Neil (10/10)

Fettercairn (13/10)

For detail, see inset map

Eddleston (19/8)

Traquair (20/8)

Selkirk (21-22/8)

Yetholm (23,25/8)

Jedburgh (23-25/8)

Bolton (25/8)

Burgh by Sands (7/7/07)

Carlisle

Baledgarno (21/10)   Dundee (16-20/10)

Scone (22-23/10)

Perth (4/8)

St. Fort (7/3 etc)

Kincaple (11/3)

Findogask (25/10)

St Andrews (12/3 etc)

Tullibardine (25-26/10)

Durie (6/3)

Tullibody (19-20/4) Ogilvie (6/8)

Drumcarrow (9/3 etc)

(26-28/10) Dunblane

Culross (16-18/4)

Cassingray (7-8/4)

Stirling (12/4 etc)

Gellet (17/4)

Wemyss (5/3 etc)

(20/4) Cambuskenneth

Kinghorn (3/3 etc)

Bandeath (12/8)

Bouprie (12-13/4)

(12-14/8) Bothkenner

Dunfermline (5/11-4/3)

(20-21/4) Clackmannan

Inverkeithing (2-3/3)

Linlithgow (14/8)

Ratho (17/8)

Detail of Fife area

● Places on the itinerary
→ Direction of travel, inward

Edward I in Scotland 1303 to 1304, inward journey, and 1307

PGBM

kms
0 25 50 75 100
0 10 20 30 40 50 60
miles

The succession, diplomacy and war

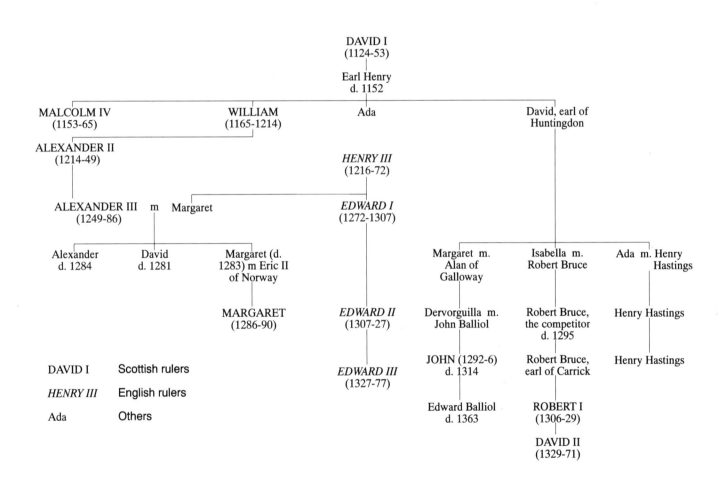

The Great Cause and after: genealogical table

PGBM

The succession, diplomacy and war

At Scone, early in 1284, following the deaths of his three children, Alexander III, with the consent of the magnates, settled the succession on his granddaughter, Margaret, the Maid of Norway. In 1285 he married Yolande of Dreux, but in March 1286, having left Edinburgh and crossed from South Queensferry to Inverkeithing to visit his wife at Kinghorn, he was killed by a fall from his horse.

After Alexander's burial at Dunfermline, a parliament at Scone chose six Guardians to govern the kingdom, and sent an embassy (instructions unknown) to Edward I. It travelled via Newcastle and London; its destination was perhaps St. Jean d'Angely, but it found Edward at Saintes and reported back to the Guardians at Clackmannan.

In 1289, the Guardians began negotiations with Norway and England for the marriage of Margaret to Edward's son. In the Treaty of Salisbury (November 1289), ratified by the Scots at Birgham in March 1290, the three countries agreed that Margaret should be sent to Scotland. The proposed marriage was arranged in the Treaty of Birgham in July 1290 and confirmed by Edward at Northampton in August. Edward sent a ship from Yarmouth to bring Margaret to Scotland (May 1290) and by June had taken control of the Isle of Man, which belonged to the Scottish Crown. However, the queen left Bergen in a Norwegian ship, only to die in the Orkneys, then Norwegian territory (late September 1290). English envoys were at Wick on 4 October, apparently to conduct further negotiations with the Norwegians. Meanwhile, the Scots magnates were gathering at Perth, perhaps for Margaret's inauguration at Scone. On 7 October Bishop Fraser of St. Andrews wrote to Edward from Leuchars telling him of rumours of the Maid's death and asking him to intervene. Although Edward announced during a parliament at Clipstone which began on 27 October 1290 that he intended to go to Scotland, the death of Queen Eleanor caused an interruption till March 1291.

The Great Cause: European setting

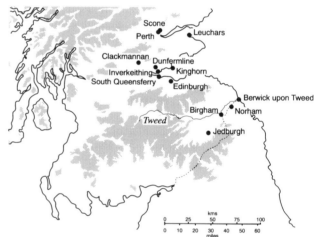

The topography of the Great Cause: Scotland and England

In early May, Edward arrived at Norham to begin the "Great Cause" to decide who should be king of Scots. The meetings took place in Norham parish church and castle, on Holywell Haugh, a field opposite the castle on the Scottish side of the Tweed, and in the castle and former Dominican friary in Berwick. On 17th November 1292 John Balliol was awarded the kingdom and on 30th inaugurated at Scone.

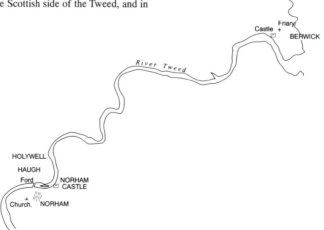

The topography of the Great Cause: Norham and Berwick upon Tweed

The succession, diplomacy and war

In the spring of 1296, Edward I sacked Berwick, defeated a Scottish army at Dunbar, and marched, virtually unopposed, as far as Elgin. On his way north, terms of surrender were dictated to the Scots at Brechin castle, and at Kincardine, Stracathro and Montrose, the royal authority of John Balliol was progressively dismantled in a series of humiliating submissions.

The general rising of 1297 was inspired by a number of prominent men, but is forever associated with only one figure, William Wallace. Unlike the other Scottish leaders, Wallace did not capitulate at Irvine in July, but went on to win the spectacular victory of Stirling Bridge. However, this was a piece of tactical opportunism, unlikely to be repeated. The Scottish massed-infantry schiltrom had many weaknesses when confronted by disciplined heavy cavalry supported by archers, as was demonstrated the next year at Falkirk, where the Scots sustained a serious defeat at the hands of a starving and near-mutinous army. For a variety of diplomatic and domestic reasons, Edward was unable to follow up this success, and the Scots recovered some ground; in particular, they regained the major Castle of Stirling.

Edward's expedition of 1300 achieved little apart from the relief of Lochmaben, the capture of Caerlaverock and the dispersal of a Scottish army at the Cree. A two-pronged attack in 1301 was more successful. The castles of Selkirk, Peebles and Bothwell were taken. However, the main English effort in the south-west was contained and did not reach Inverkip as planned, though it captured Turnberry. After wintering at Linlithgow, Edward made another in his series of intermittent truces with the Scots. It was clearly intended that the next invasion of 1303 should come to stay - Edward now had nothing to fear from the prospect of an active alliance of the Scots, the French and the Papacy. Though a probing force was defeated at Roslin, the main expedition penetrated to Kinloss before returning to winter at Dunfermline; the difficulties of supplying a large army in a hostile country, which had bedevilled earlier expeditions, had been circumvented by the use of shipping for this purpose. Edward was able to mount operations from his winter base against the Scottish stronghold of Ettrick Forest and one such raiding party defeated Wallace at Happrew. In the spring, the army moved to besiege Stirling. The general surrender of the Scottish leaders at Strathord, in February 1304, preceded the fall of the castle. Wallace, now a fugitive, engaged in at least one further skirmish near Bridge of Earn, but his capture on 3 August 1305 brought resistance to an end.

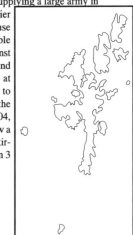

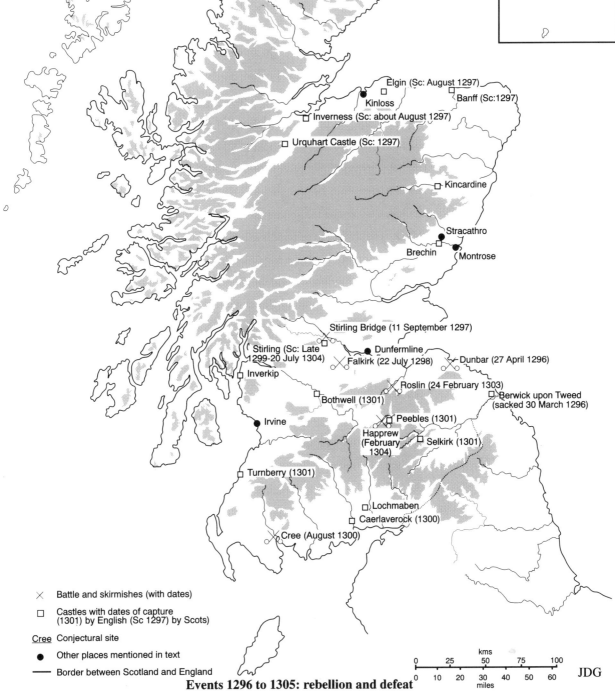

× Battle and skirmishes (with dates)

□ Castles with dates of capture (1301) by English (Sc 1297) by Scots)

<u>Cree</u> Conjectural site

● Other places mentioned in text

—— Border between Scotland and England

kms
0 25 50 75 100

0 10 20 30 40 50 60
miles

JDG

Events 1296 to 1305: rebellion and defeat

93

The succession, diplomacy and war

The seven cities shown on the map indicate the destinations of some 35 major political embassies which left Scotland between the accession of John Balliol and the death of Robert I. The cities are representative only: Paris of the French court; Avignon and Rome of the Papal curia; London and Newcastle of the English court; Bergen of the Norwegian court. The embassies do not include ecclesiastical (i.e. for the ordination of bishops) or trade missions (i.e. to the Baltic cities), unless these are known also to have been important in political terms.

Missions to France and the papacy make up the vast majority of these embassies: Dublin features only once (1315), Norway only twice (1299 and 1302) and most of the English missions took place after Bannockburn, aimed specifically at negotiating either truces or a 'final peace'.

The limited number of destinations is indicative of the relative isolation of Scotland during the war with England. Scottish envoys were consistently welcome only in the French court. (The Pope, as the leader of Christendom, had a duty to receive envoys, but it would not be true to say that the Scots were always welcome!) Scotland's active allies were few. The fact, however, that trade continued with the Italian and Baltic city states, the Empire and the Spanish kingdoms, indicates that England's allies, although many and powerful, were not necessarily anti-Scottish. Despite English protestations, trade and other peaceful links continued largely as usual. Most of Scotland's political diplomacy, however, was patently anti-English, and it is thus no surprise to find that Scottish envoys visited only powers which also had quarrels with the English

Scottish embassies abroad 1292 to 1329

NHR

Robert I (1306-29)

Robert Bruce murdered John Comyn in Greyfriars' church, Dumfries, on 12 February 1306. By the time of his coronation at Scone on 25-27 march, he had replenished his castles of Dunaverty and Loch Doon, and he and his supporters had taken, besieged, or attempted to win over the garrisons of all the castles in the South-West which are marked on map. Support for this rebellion was not confined to that area; the castle of Cupar in Fife, and the new castle of Tolibothwell in Aberdeenshire were also captured.

The English forces of occupation also seem to have reacted quickly after the Comyn murder. They took steps to reinforce the important castles of Roxburgh and Jedburgh as early as 13 February. By mid-June, Edward I's lieutenant in Scotland, Aymer de Valence, had established himself at Perth, having retaken Cupar and having received the first overtures of surrender from some of Bruce's supporters at Scotlandwell on 9 June. Bruce seems to have spent some of the period after his coronation at various places in Perthshire, presumably attempting to muster his power.

The confrontation of the two armies at Methven on 19 June proved disastrous for Bruce. Fleeing westwards, he was pursued by at least a detachment of English cavalry, and on or about 13 July suffered another major defeat at Dalry, at the hands of John Macdougall of Argyll. After his engagement, the queen and the other ladies of

Bruce's party were sent north to Kildrummy.

However, Valence also turned northwards on 13 July, reaching Aberdeen on 3 August. He quickly moved on Kildrummy. The ladies had left the castle before it fell in early September, but they were captured soon afterwards at St Duthac's sanctuary near Tain. The castles which were held for Bruce in the south-west were quickly subdued by the English local commanders, who had quelled any remaining resistance by 9 November. Bruce himself had already disappeared into the west.

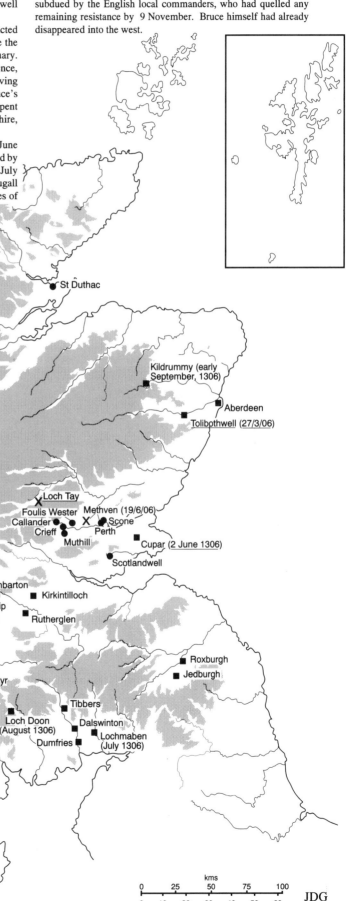

Robert I's movements 1306 to 1307

JDG

95

Robert I (1306-29)

When Robert Bruce returned to his earldom of Carrick in February 1307, he and his supporters began a highly successful guerrilla campaign. It seems that they had only two real advantages: the fact that the English local commanders, goaded by an irate Edward I, were obliged to 'come and get them' so that the superior English forces could be met on ground of the insurgents' choosing, and the ground itself, the advantage of which they had learned to exploit to the full.

Even before the death of Edward I on 7 July at Burgh-on-Sands, the forces of occupation in the south-west were in difficulties. By September, Bruce was able to turn to his enemies in the north, the Comyns of Buchan, the earl of Ross and the Macdougalls of Argyll, while leaving Sir James Douglas and others to contain and eventually dominate, the south-west. The castles of Inverlochy, Urquhart, Inverness and Nairn fell in rapid succession, though the first attempt on Elgin, in November or December was repulsed; Bruce moved instead to Banff, before turning inland. The inconclusive encounter at the Slioch between 25 and 31 December was presumably followed soon afterwards by the rout of the Comyns near Inverurie and the subjection of Buchan, for by the spring of 1308 Bruce evidently felt that this area was secure and moved westward again, this time to take

Balvenie, Duffus and Tarradale, and on 7 April, to renew the siege of Elgin.

Aberdeen, 'besieged by land and sea' in July 1308, may have held out until August. If so, Bruce himself must by then have returned to Argyll, where his campaign against the Macdougalls and their associates culminated in the victory at the Pass of Brander and the capture of Dunstaffnage. By the end of 1308, Banff was the only stronghold north of the Mounth which was still in English hands.

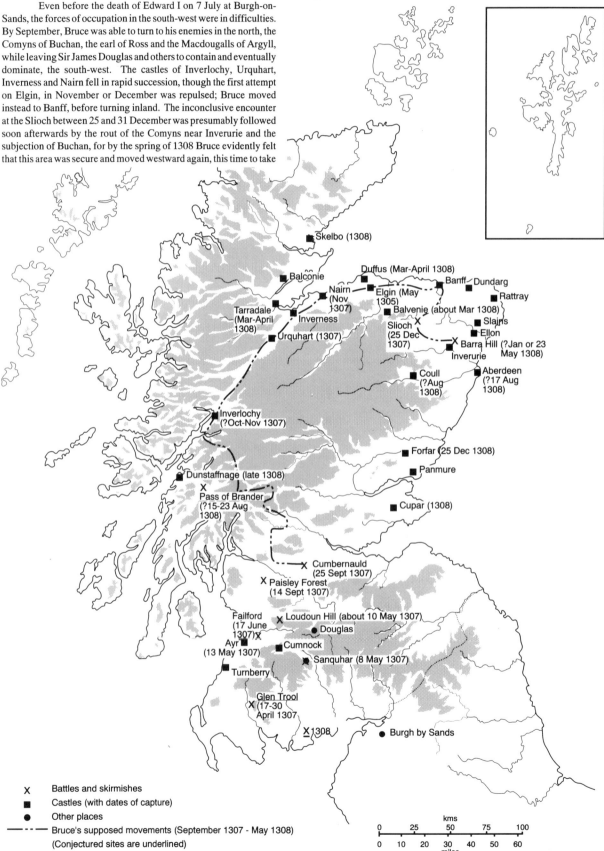

Robert I's movements February 1307 to December 1308: guerrilla warfare

JDG

X   Battles and skirmishes
■   Castles (with dates of capture)
●   Other places
—·—·— Bruce's supposed movements (September 1307 - May 1308)
(Conjectured sites are underlined)

Robert I (1306-29)

At the start of 1309, Bruce and his supporters still faced formidable opposition, particularly in the south-east and the central belt, where their enemies held the major castles of Edinburgh, Stirling, Jedburgh, the 'Marche Mont' of Roxburgh and Berwick, linked by a network of lesser fortifications. The one notable weakness in the English position was the difficulty of supplying and re-inforcing these garrisons; in this respect even the completely isolated Banff, which could (in theory at least) be supplied by sea, may have been in a rather better situation than the seemingly unassailable Stirling.

Bruce and his lieutenants now applied themselves to the gradual reduction of these obstacles, with results which were, by the standards of contemporary warfare, astonishing. Lacking sophisticated siege equipment, they employed more unorthodox methods, usually infiltration by night, the technique which disposed of Perth, Roxburgh and Edinburgh, as it already had of Forfar.

Apart from an abortive expedition in 1310-11, Edward II did little to stop the progressive destruction of the·English foothold in Scotland, until the major expedition of 1314 to relieve Stirling. At Bannockburn a conventional feudal army, relying on heavily-armed cavalry as a shock weapon, confronted a Scottish force which was inferior in all respects except the morale of its troops and the tactical skill of its leaders, particularly demonstrated on this occasion by their intelligent use of ground. Thereafter, the gradual recovery of

Scotland resumed without interruption, if we except the landing made in Fife by shipmen of the Humber which was thrown back in near-ludicrous circumstances at Auchtertool, and occasional skirmishes against local raiding parties, as at Skaithmuir and Lintalee. The initiative had passed firmly into the hands of the Scots. Long before Berwick fell, they were conducting carefully planned raids into the North of England, systematically levying blackmail, and had threatened the English hold on Man and Ireland.

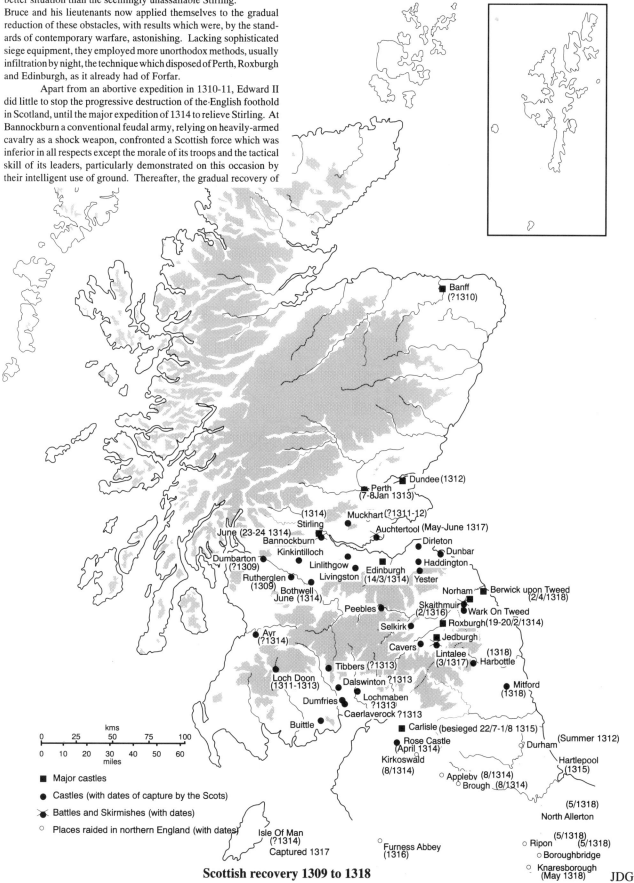

Scottish recovery 1309 to 1318

JDG

97

Robert I (1306-29)

The battle of Bannockburn (1314) occupied the greater part of two days, from the late afternoon of Sunday 23 June until the evening of Monday 24 June. There is no serious dispute about the location of the Sunday phase. The Scottish army was drawn up in four brigades at the perimeter of the 'New Park' which lay between the Bannock Burn and St. Ninians kirk. Robert I's brigade faced the oncoming English host at the 'entry', that is,where the high road entered the Park, while the brigades of the earl of Moray (close to St Ninians), Walter the Steward (in practice led by Sir James Douglas) and the king's brother Edward were stationed by the edge of the Park between the Borestone and Stirling. There were relatively small-scale but nonetheless vitally important initial clashes on the Sunday, first of all at the 'entry', then close to St Ninians, in both of which the English were repulsed with considerable loss. It is not in doubt that the English army then proceeded, largely during the short hours of darkness, to move north on to the 'carse', the low-lying boggy ground east of the Scottish position. Disagreement persists as to whether the main battle beginning early on the Monday morning, took place out on the carse or (as is suggested here) on the 'dryfield' above the 50 - largely about the 100 foot - contour. It is certain that the conflict was chiefly between English cavalry, too tightly deployed, and Scottish foot, whose three leading brigades (the king's being kept in reserve) had room to manoeuvre and give support to one another. Once the horse were repulsed, the dismounted knights were pushed back against the mass of the English foot, as yet unengaged, and many were drowned in the Bannock Burn and the Forth. Edward II, however, having vainly tried to gain entry to Stirling castle, managed to escape to Dunbar and thence to England.

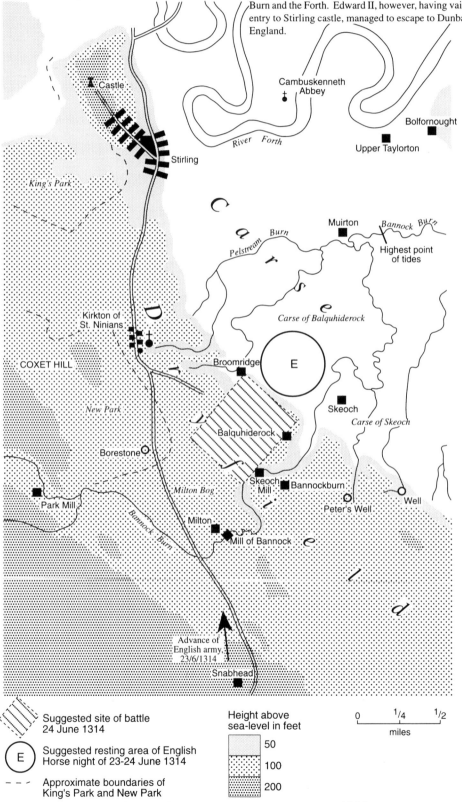

Suggested site of battle 24 June 1314

(E) Suggested resting area of English Horse night of 23-24 June 1314

- - - Approximate boundaries of King's Park and New Park

Height above sea-level in feet

50
100
200

0   1/4   1/2
miles

The battle of Bannockburn 23-24 June 1314

GWSB

Robert I (1306-29)

Edward II conducted only four major campaigns in Scotland. In 1307, he attempted a brief campaign with the army gathered by his father Edward I before his death in July of that year. In 1310, he crossed the border with a large force, but only reached Linlithgow before retreating to winter at Berwick. Gaveston was sent north to Perth and Dundee, to try to bring Scotland north of the Forth under English sway. Further operations were carried out in the east march area through the winter and in the first half of 1311. In 1314 his largest campaign ended in disaster at Bannockburn, and his last attempt, in 1322, almost ended in the same way when, forced to retreat because of starvation, the English forcer was followed south by the Scots and routed at Byland in Yorkshire. On other occasions (e.g. autumn 1319) Edward II did enter Scotland, but only with these four campaigns did he penetrate further than the border area, or pose any real threat to Scottish security.

The campaigns were limited in scope and effectiveness. Generally, restricted to areas in which the English still held strongholds, with easy communications southwards, none of the campaigns broke new ground. Their very limited number and lack of success is indicative of the inadequacy of the support for the English forces resident in Scotland for much of Edward II's reign. The inability of Edward II to exert pressure on the Scots from south of the border was undoubtedly a major factor in the success of Robert I in re-asserting Scottish independent.

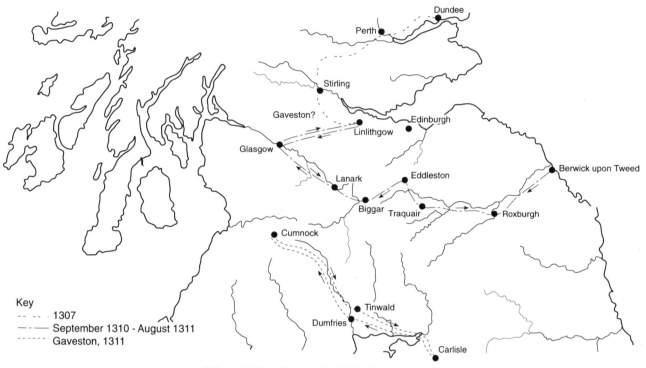

Key
- -- -- 1307
- —·— September 1310 - August 1311
- ····· Gaveston, 1311

Edward II in Scotland 1307, 1310 and 1311

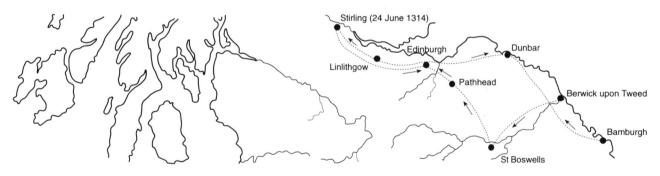

Edward II in Scotland 1314

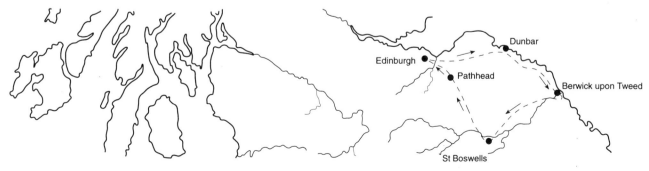

Edward II in Scotland 1322

NHR

99

Robert I (1306-29)

In 1315 Edward Bruce landed at Larne. With him was a substantial force and many important Scottish magnates. After overcoming local opposition, Bruce gained the mastery of much of the earldom of Ulster and began an invasion of English lands further south. Dundalk was sacked, as were Louth and Ardee. Bruce made a tactical retreat northwards, drawing the earl of Ulster after him and completely routing him at the battle of Connor. The campaign is shown in the first map. In a few short months Bruce and his army had exposed the weakness of the Dublin government and the inability of the local magnates to contain him successfully. But he had also seen that in a famine-stricken land he must be careful not to stretch his lines of communication too far until he was sure of widespread Gaelic support and was reinforced from Scotland. When extra men arrived from Scotland, he tried again.

This time Bruce moved through Meath, defeating Roger Mortimer, lord of Wigmore, and ravaging his lordship. He blazed a trail of destruction as far west as Granard in Longford, before turning to plunder Leinster. After looting as far south as Castledermot, he finally faced a royal army at the mote of Ardscull, not far from Athy. This was a formidable army, commanded by the justiciar, Edmund Butler, but was scattered by Bruce. There appears to have been serious quarrelling among the Anglo-Irish and soon afterwards the great magnates of Leinster and Munster solemnly issued a public declaration to defend the English king's rights and, so far as lay in their power, to destroy his enemies the Scots (1316). By then Bruce was moving northwards again, driven by famine to seek his base in Ulster. But once again he left a path of destruction behind him in Kildare and Westneath.

Edward Bruce was inaugurated High King of Ireland and began to consolidate his grip on Ulster, dispensing justice and possibly even holding a parliament. By now many Gaelic lords had taken his side or, more commonly, had used the disturbed condition which he had created to assert their independence. Even some of the Anglo-Irish of Ulster had accepted what seemed to them inevitable. The Dublin government was in a perilous state, almost bankrupt and suspicious of the attitude of many of the magnates. The terrible famine and the ravages of the Scots (supplemented by the destruction caused by the Anglo-Irish armies) had left many parts of Ireland in a desperate condition. When Carrickfergus Castle fell in 1316, after a year's siege, it seemed to signify the inevitable triumph for the Scots. The second map covers this part of the campaign.

By this time the Scots had control of the sea and King Robert joined his brother. The king brought much needed reinforcements. His presence escalated the war on to a new plane and presented the Dublin government with the gravest of perils. In 1317, most of the Scots left Ulster and, to the consternation of everybody, suddenly appeared in Meath. Their arrival at Castleknock on the outskirts of the city caused panic in Dublin. The citizens threw the earl of Ulster into prison, blaming him for not opposing the Scots. Hurriedly the city defences were repaired and part of the suburbs was fired to deprive the Scots of cover in approaching the walls. But the Bruces moved on, probably realising (especially after the experience at Carrickfergus) that a siege would be a long and expensive business. It is clear too that their main purpose was to join up with the O'Briens of Thomond. Once again no opportunity of wasting the lordship was lost; even churches and religious houses were plundered. By a slow progress through Kildare, Carlow, Kilkenny and Tipperary, the Scots were able to devastate the lands and manors of many of the greatest Anglo-Irish lords. When they reached the Shannon at Castleconnel, Donough O'Brien, who had invited them, had been ousted by his rival Murtough O'Brien and all hope of a great Gaelic uprising in Munster had been dashed. These events are shown in the third map.

Gaelic Connacht had been important since the defeat of the O'Conners at the battle of Athenry in 1316, and bitter experience had shown that there was no hope of worthwhile support from Gaelic Leinster. To make matters worse for the Scots, Roger Mortimer had just been appointed lieutenant of Ireland, and England was at last providing resources to help defeat Bruce. Famine too was taking its toll. It was time to retreat to Ulster, and it was a tired and hungry army which arrived there. A turning point had been reached; and the king went home to Scotland.

The conquest of Ireland by the Scots was now out of the question: and when Edward Bruce foolishly moved out of Ulster again in 1318, he was defeated and killed at Fochart, just north of Dundalk. The fourth map covers this last period.

Robert I (1306-29)

26 May to 10 September 1315

13 November 1315 to 20 (?) September 1316

18 February to late
April 1317

14 October 1318

Route taken
Speculative
Places on route

kms
0   25   50   75
0 10 20 30 40   50
miles

The Bruces in Ireland

JFL

101

Robert I (1306-29)

From 1311 onwards, the majority of Bruce's military efforts took place on English soil. There are, of course, exceptions: the Irish campaigns, which are treated separately; the campaign against Man in 1314 and again (under the Earl of Moray) in 1317; the defence of Scotland, most notably in 1314; and of course, the continued piecemeal reduction of English-held castles in southern Scotland.

Nonetheless, the fact remains that the bulk of the later campaigns by or on behalf of Robert I were offensive, on English soil. The king led an army across the border for the first time in 1311, and more than twenty subsequent invasions took place before a final peace was made in 1328. The area of greatest devastation was the north, but as the maps show, the incursions covered a good deal of England as far south as York. Almost annually, large amounts of tribute were raised in return for promises of local truce, and rumours spread that Bruce intended to annexe the northern counties. This may have been the case, but it seems more likely that his primary aim was to pressurise the English king to negotiate recognition of Bruce's royal status, and an end to the war. The timing of the raids, often immediately before or after negotiations for truce or peace, adds weight to this interpretation.

The eastern routes into England were most frequently used, but the western march was also subject to regular incursion. The most far-reaching raids tended to enter England by the eastern march, and return westwards. The maps are an attempt to represent 'typical' routes, the campaigns being too frequent and the evidence too patchy to allow for individual raids to be accurately shown. Not all of the excursions, of course, went so far south and some were merely quick raiding parties. Nonetheless, the serious effects of Bruce's latter campaigns on the political stability of England should not be underestimated.

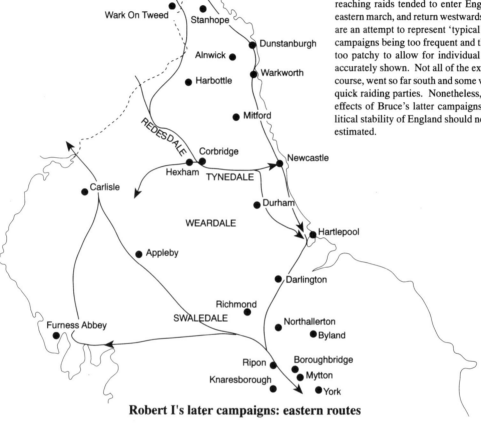

Robert I's later campaigns: eastern routes

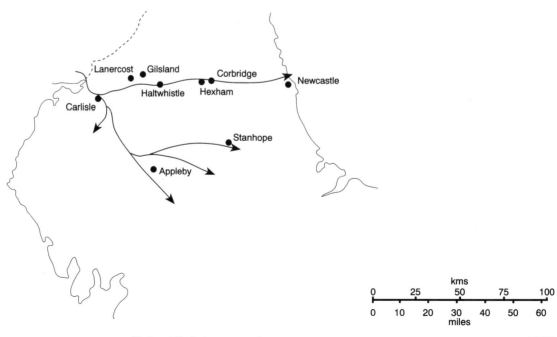

Robert I's later campaigns: western routes

NHR

Robert I (1306-29)

The map tries to show something of the political significance of the gains made by Robert I's chief supporters during the Wars of Independence. Since, however, it is very difficult to determine the exact boundaries of the lands involved, they are simply indicated by conventional symbols, the size of which roughly corresponds to the extent and importance of the lands. The greatest changes came in the Borders, where there was almost an obligation to hand over lands recovered from the English to the men who had recovered them. The map shows the lands acquired by the two Douglas brothers, James and Archibald, and by Thomas Randolph, whose families had held only a modest inheritance on the eve of the wars. Most of the lands shown were gains. The map also shows the lands of the Steward family; but their lands in Renfrewshire, Ayrshire, Bute and Kintyre had been held for generations and their gains were very small.

In 1329, there was a kind of equilibrium among these four families; but the descent of the lands, sometimes contrived, sometimes accidental, changed the situation profoundly. In 1371, the Stewards became kings, merging their lands in practice with those of the crown. In 1354, the lands of the two Douglas branches merged; and these were joined in 1388 by the lordship of Galloway, creating a predominant Douglas power in the Borders. Meantime, the Randolph inheritance had passed to the earls of March, producing as the map might suggest, a rivalry between Douglas and March which was resolved by the exile of George, earl of March in 1400, leaving the Douglas power in the Borders unchallenged until it was destroyed by the crown in the 1450s. Thus the power struggles of the next 150 years flowed in great measure from the landed settlement established by Robert I.

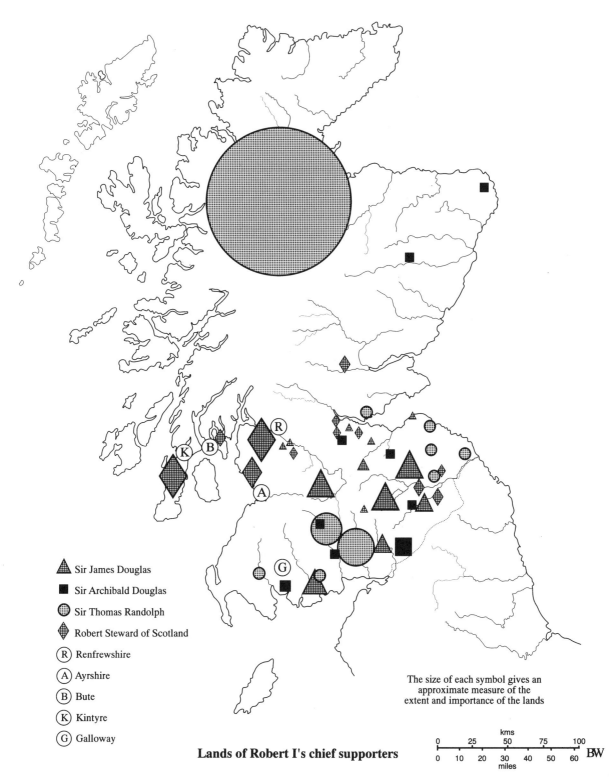

▲ Sir James Douglas

■ Sir Archibald Douglas

◉ Sir Thomas Randolph

◆ Robert Steward of Scotland

Ⓡ Renfrewshire

Ⓐ Ayrshire

Ⓑ Bute

Ⓚ Kintyre

Ⓖ Galloway

The size of each symbol gives an approximate measure of the extent and importance of the lands

Lands of Robert I's chief supporters

kms
0   25   50   75   100

0   10   20   30   40   50   60
miles

BW

Anglo-Scottish relations 1329 to 1422

The death of Robert I left his kingdom weakened by the accession of his infant son David II (b. 1324) and the successive deaths of James Douglas (1330) and Thomas Randolph, earl of Moray (1332). In this new situation, the Treaty of Edinburgh/Northampton (1328) was rapidly disregarded and first Edward Balliol, the son of King John; the 'disinherited' (barons who had lost their Scottish lands for failing to adhere to Robert I); and eventually Edward III himself tried to conquer the country. The four maps represent the course of events. This map illustrates the campaigns of 1332 and 1333, in which Edward Balliol first secured the crown after his victory at Dupplin Moor, but was ejected after a skirmish at Annan; in the following year, Edward III himself defeated the Scots at Halidon Hill, captured Berwick and re-established Balliol as a puppet ruler.

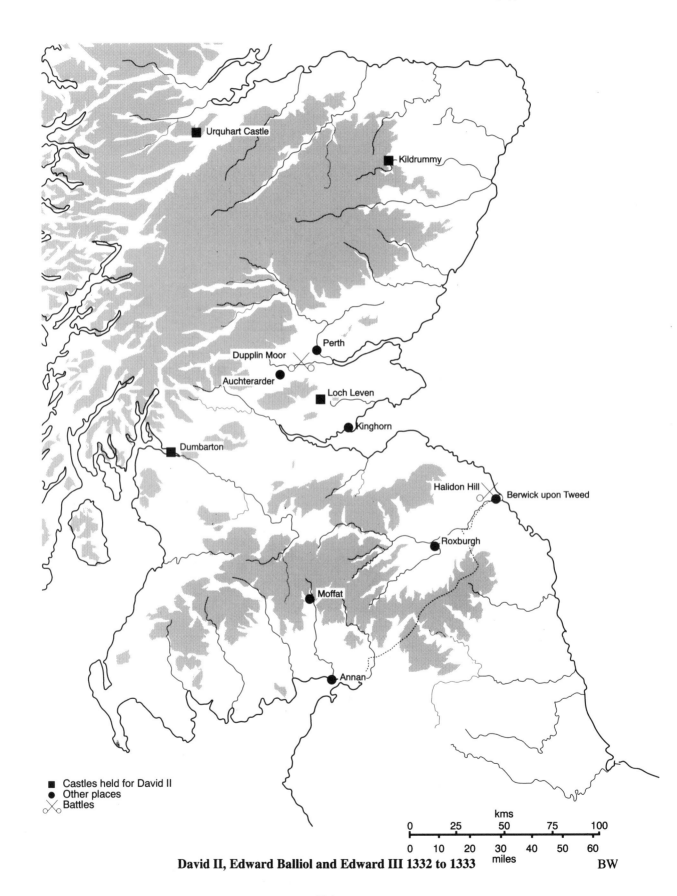

■ Castles held for David II
● Other places
✕ Battles

kms
0   25   50   75   100

0   10   20   30   40   50   60
miles

David II, Edward Balliol and Edward III 1332 to 1333   BW

104

Anglo-Scottish relations 1329 to 1422

The situation which ensued is represented in this map. Balliol, as the price of Edward's support, ceded much of the south of Scotland, and English sheriffs were established, creating an administration centred on Berwick. Balliol claimed to rule the rest of the country, but in reality was heavily supported by English garrisons at many castles, and was uneasily accepted in most of the lowlands. It seems that formal administration in the name of David II ceased; the king himself had to take refuge in France, but a number of castles were still held for him, of which the most important are shown.

- ■ Castles held for David II
- ▲ Castles held for Balliol or Edward III
- ● Other places
- ✕ Battles
- ○ English sherriffdoms
- /// Land nominally ceded by Balliol to Edward

kms

| 0 | 25 | 50 | 75 | 100 |

| 0 | 10 | 20 | 30 | 40 | 50 | 60 |
miles

BW

David II, Edward Balliol and Edward III about 1336

Anglo-Scottish relations 1329 to 1422

In 1335, David II's supporters won an important victory over David of Strathbogie, earl of Atholl, who was killed at the battle of Culblean while attempting to besiege Kildrummy. Several English expeditions failed to consolidate Balliol's position, and the outbreak of the Hundred Years' War distracted Edward; so that by 1340, David's position had improved; the English sheriffdoms no longer functioned; English garrisons were reduced to Stirling and Edinburgh and several sites in the Borders; and a number of burghs in the north-east rendered account at a session of the Scottish Exchequer held in April 1340. The Scottish administration was beginning to recover.

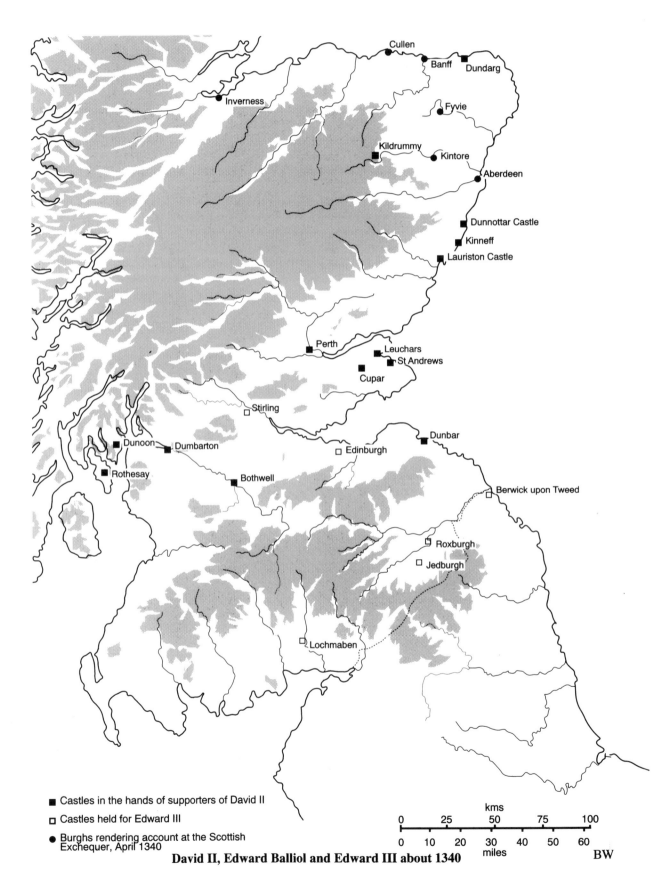

■ Castles in the hands of supporters of David II

□ Castles held for Edward III

● Burghs rendering account at the Scottish Exchequer, April 1340

kms
0   25   50   75   100

0   10   20   30   40   50   60
miles

David II, Edward Balliol and Edward III about 1340

BW

Anglo-Scottish relations 1329 to 1422

In 1341, David returned from France; and by 1343 normality was almost restored. The only English garrisons still holding out were at Lochmaben, Jedburgh and Berwick; in the rest of the country, David's administration was recognised and seems to have functioned efficiently. Balliol maintained his claim till 1356, when he formally resigned it into the hands of Edward III; but his pretensions were hardly taken seriously. David's capture in 1346 at the Battle of Neville's Cross re-awakened Edward's hopes of some sort of supremacy, but the notion of Edward Balliol as a possible king of Scots seems soon to have been abandoned.

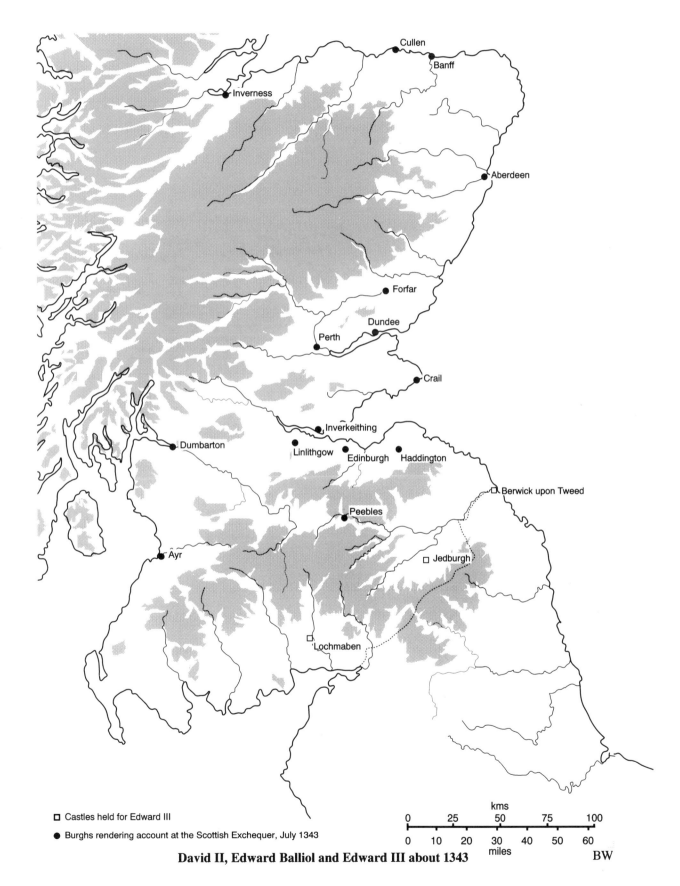

□ Castles held for Edward III

● Burghs rendering account at the Scottish Exchequer, July 1343

David II, Edward Balliol and Edward III about 1343

BW

Anglo-Scottish relations 1329 to 1422

When a truce ended in 1384, the English forces were dislodged easily from Annandale and Teviotdale, and the French became directly involved in accordance with the agreement of 1381 Robert II (1371-90) and Charles VI. After the expedition of John of Gaunt and Richard II, the French withdrew from Scotland. There were invasions of Cumberland and Northumberland (1388): the invasion of Northumberland was defeated at Otterburn, and Scotland subsequently adhered to the Anglo-French truce.

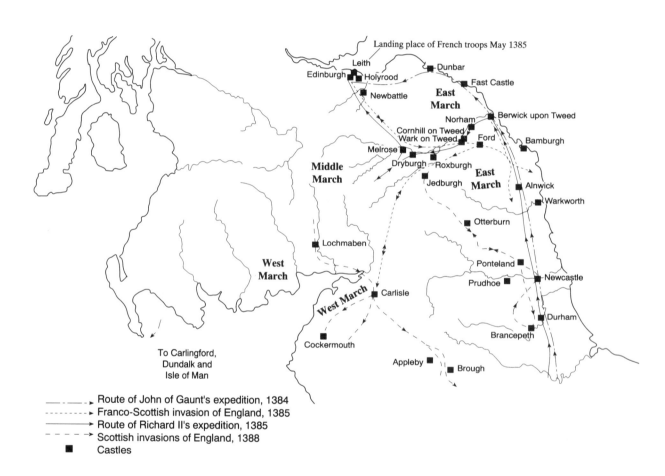

Landing place of French troops May 1385

Leith
Edinburgh
Holyrood
Newbattle
Dunbar
Fast Castle

East March

Norham
Cornhill on Tweed
Wark on Tweed
Ford
Berwick upon Tweed
Bamburgh

Melrose
Dryburgh
Roxburgh

Middle March
Jedburgh

East March
Alnwick
Warkworth

Otterburn

Lochmaben

West March

Ponteland
Prudhoe
Newcastle

West March
Carlisle

Cockermouth

Appleby
Brough

Durham
Brancepeth

To Carlingford,
Dundalk and
Isle of Man

—·—·—► Route of John of Gaunt's expedition, 1384
--------► Franco-Scottish invasion of England, 1385
————► Route of Richard II's expedition, 1385
— — — ► Scottish invasions of England, 1388
■　Castles

кмs
0　　25　　50　　75　　100
0　10　20　30　40　50　60
miles

Anglo-Scottish relations 1379 to 1388

AT

Anglo-Scottish relations 1329 to 1422

The earl of March's defection to England in 1400 led to his raid into Lothian. Henry IV's expedition and a Scottish raid defeated at Reseswyre were followed by inconclusive negotiations at Kirk Yetholm in 1401. In 1402 March won a victory at Nesbit Muir. A retaliatory raid was defeated at Humbleton Hill, but the fall of the Percies and the capture of Prince James ended this phase of Anglo-Scottish warfare, the main Scottish concerns were directed to aid to France and recovery of their prisoners.

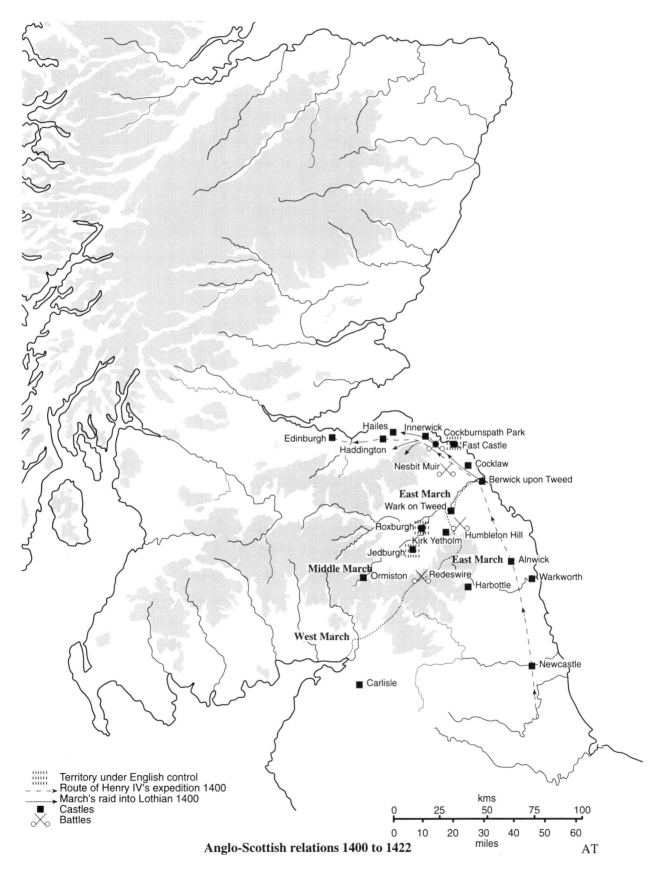

Territory under English control
Route of Henry IV's expedition 1400
March's raid into Lothian 1400
Castles
Battles

kms
0   25   50   75   100

0   10   20   30   40   50   60
miles

Anglo-Scottish relations 1400 to 1422

AT

James II (1437-60)

The deaths of James I in 1437 and Archibald, fifth earl of Douglas, lieutenant general, in 1439 left a power vacuum which allowed two baronial families, the Crichtons and the Livingstons, to rise into prominence.

Sir Alexander Livingston was given the keeping of the young James II after the removal of his mother in 1439. At various times in the 1440s, the family held the offices of justiciar, chamberlain, comptroller, warden of the mint at Stirling and custumar of Linlithgow as well as the castles shown on the map.

In 1449, shortly after the king took over the reins of government following his marriage, three of the Livingstons were imprisoned in Blackness castle: in 1450, the family was forfeited by a parliament at Edinburgh and Robert Livingston, custumar of Linlithgow was executed.

The Dundas family, who were related to the Livingstons by marriage, shared in their fall and Dundas castle was held against the king for several weeks. The chief beneficiaries of the fall of the Livingstons were the earls of Douglas and Crawford and the new queen, Mary of Guelders.

James Livingston, who had been keeper of the person of the young king during his minority, escaped to his son-in-law, John, lord of the Isles who in 1451 seized Ruthven castle. Inverness castle and possibly Urquhart castle were given to Livingston. His keepership was recognised by James II. In addition, by 1454, Livingston had been restored to royal favour.

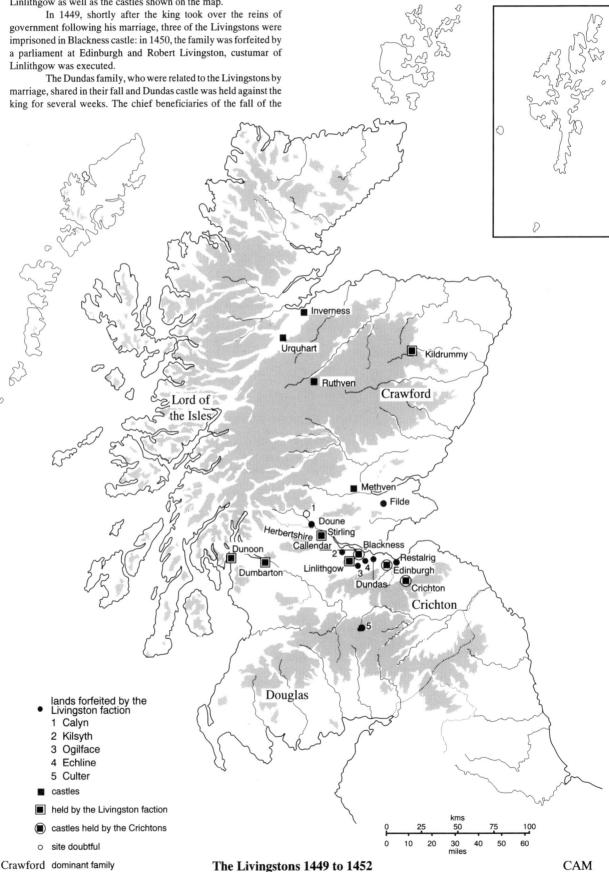

lands forfeited by the
● Livingston faction
1 Calyn
2 Kilsyth
3 Ogilface
4 Echline
5 Culter

■ castles

▣ held by the Livingston faction

◉ castles held by the Crichtons

○ site doubtful

Crawford dominant family

The Livingstons 1449 to 1452

CAM

110

James II (1437-60)

In the space of a few years, James II removed from the political scene many men who had been responsible for the government of the realm during his minority. First to go were the Livingstons, in 1449-50; James himself struck the first blow in the murder of the eighth earl of Douglas in 1452 and in 1455 after Arkinholm the Black Douglases effectively disappeared, although the ninth earl lived mainly in England until 1491. One of the most significant features of this period is that an army lacking the king's presence won the final conflict. Three years before, the earl of Huntly, claiming to bear the king's banner and be his lieutenant, had seen off the earl of Crawford at Brechin. It is probable the king feared a repetition of the events of 1437; his people were anxious to prevent any lasting threat to the stability of the realm.

The maps (based on those provided for the first atlas) show the territorial possessions of the Black Douglases and their allies; and indicate the areas where the king found support in the 1450s. The reign of James I had seen great changes in the higher nobility which meant the earls of Douglas had no peers in terms of possession of property. This allowed previous historians to see the earls as archetypal over-mighty magnates, yet the earls held public offices, and no-one is known to have petitioned for their removal. Certainly, there was tension between the Crown and the Douglases, e.g. over the right the eighth earl had to the lands of his mother; and his bond with the earl of Crawford and the Lord of the Isles was also contentious: his refusal to break it seems to have precipitated his murder, but none of this was likely to produce a Scottish War of the Roses. Indeed, although it cannot be quantified, more people were probably killed in the various outbreaks of plague during the reign than in any of the armed encounters.

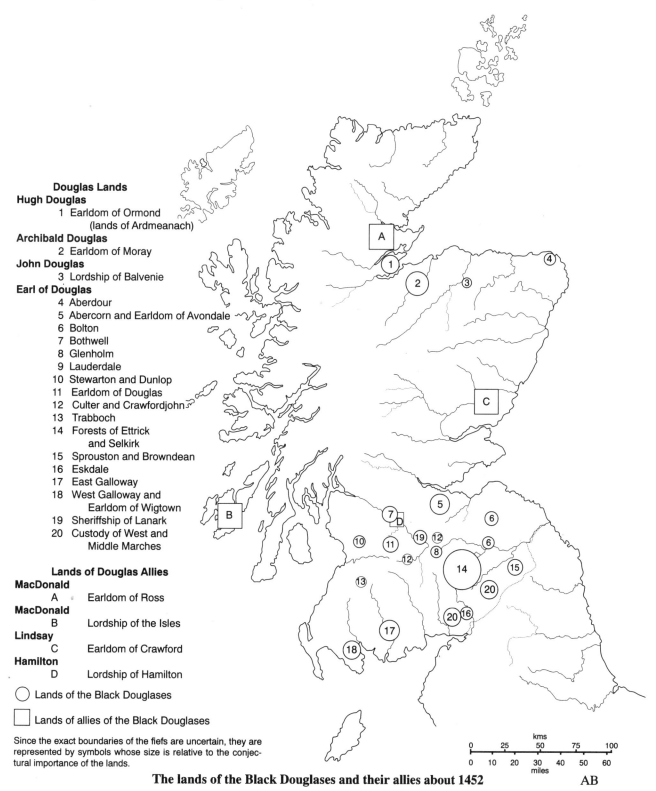

Douglas Lands
Hugh Douglas
   1 Earldom of Ormond
        (lands of Ardmeanach)
Archibald Douglas
   2 Earldom of Moray
John Douglas
   3 Lordship of Balvenie
Earl of Douglas
   4 Aberdour
   5 Abercorn and Earldom of Avondale
   6 Bolton
   7 Bothwell
   8 Glenholm
   9 Lauderdale
  10 Stewarton and Dunlop
  11 Earldom of Douglas
  12 Culter and Crawfordjohn
  13 Trabboch
  14 Forests of Ettrick
      and Selkirk
  15 Sprouston and Browndean
  16 Eskdale
  17 East Galloway
  18 West Galloway and
      Earldom of Wigtown
  19 Sheriffship of Lanark
  20 Custody of West and
      Middle Marches

Lands of Douglas Allies
MacDonald
  A   Earldom of Ross
MacDonald
  B   Lordship of the Isles
Lindsay
  C   Earldom of Crawford
Hamilton
  D   Lordship of Hamilton

◯ Lands of the Black Douglases

▢ Lands of allies of the Black Douglases

Since the exact boundaries of the fiefs are uncertain, they are represented by symbols whose size is relative to the conjectural importance of the lands.

kms
0   25   50   75   100
0 10 20 30 40 50 60
miles

The lands of the Black Douglases and their allies about 1452

AB

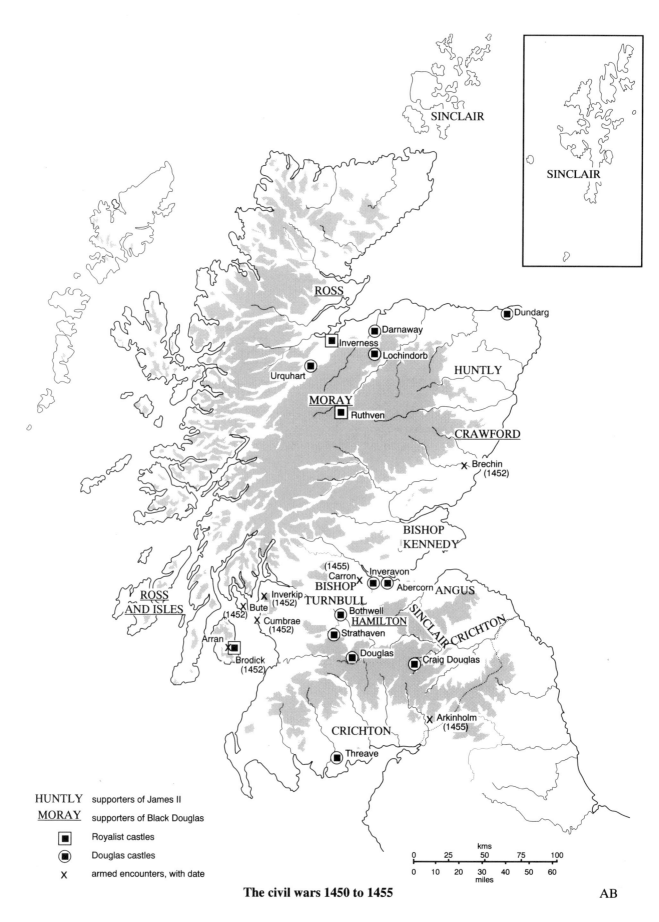

James II (1437-60)

SINCLAIR

SINCLAIR

ROSS

Dundarg

Darnaway
Inverness
Lochindorb
Urquhart

HUNTLY

MORAY
Ruthven

CRAWFORD

Brechin
(1452)

BISHOP
KENNEDY

(1455)
Carron
Inveravon
BISHOP
Abercorn
ANGUS
TURNBULL

ROSS
AND ISLES

Inverkip
(1452)
Bute
(1452)
Cumbrae
(1452)

Bothwell
HAMILTON
Strathaven

SINCLAIR
CRICHTON

Arran

Brodick
(1452)

Douglas

Craig Douglas

Arkinholm
(1455)

CRICHTON

Threave

HUNTLY	supporters of James II
MORAY	supporters of Black Douglas
■	Royalist castles
◉	Douglas castles
X	armed encounters, with date

kms
0   25   50   75   100
0 10 20 30 40 50 60
miles

The civil wars 1450 to 1455

AB

James II (1437-60)

In the parliament of August 1455, it was enacted that certain lordships and castles be annexed perpetually to the Crown. No gifts of these lands could be made without the consent of parliament; if they were made, the monarch could at any time resume them into his own hands without compensation. Many of the lands so annexed had been held by the Douglases, whose recent forfeiture had brought much land into Crown hands. It would thus be possible to see this as parliament instructing the king to retain these lands perhaps to avoid the need for taxation in the future to pay for the Crown's expenses. But this did not stop the Crown obtaining contributions, e.g. for the expenses of ambassadors, presuming the Aberdeen burgh records give a fair indication of what may have been a general occurrence. The whole customs as in the hands of James I on the day he died were also annexed: it has been estimated that this act gave the Crown an annual endowment of £6,050. The Act was to form part of the monarch's coronation oath, and indeed we find it referred to in subsequent reigns when revocations were announced.

The act of annexation 1455

AB

113

Scotland and Europe

The marriages included in these maps are those of the Scottish monarchs, their siblings and their children. The dates used are the regnal dates: thus King John's marriage to Isabella de Warenne (x1281) is included in the second map. Royal bastards are included, though they seem more important politically in the period 1107 to 1286 (map one) rather than later. Second and subsequent marriages are also included.

The first map shows how limited was the scope of royal marriages from 1107 to 1286, England being the main source; even the appearance of France is somewhat misleading, since the two brides - Ermengarde de Beaumont and Yolande de Dreux - were daughters of vassals of the English king. Apart from Norway, which comes in only at the end of the period (marriage of Alexander III's daughter Margaret to Eric II of Norway), choice is confined to the seaboard of northern Europe. The second map shows even greater limitations: Scotland seems largely to have been turned in on itself. Some of this may be explained partly by the fact that John, Robert I and Robert II were not born heirs to the crown, partly by the marriages of Robert II's numerous children, and partly by those who married two, three or four times.

The wider spread of connections shown in the third map is largely the result of the ambitious diplomacy of James II. For Scottish monarchs after 1460 France and Denmark became more important as sources of consorts.

DENMARK	Kingdom
BRITTANY	Province
(Dreux)	Other places
(2)	Number of marriages into royal family where more than one
(11)	Number of marriages into baronial family where more than one
*	Two of these daughters were vassals of the king of England

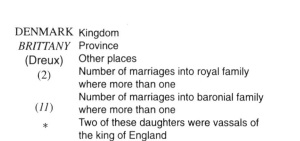

Royal marriages 1107 to 1286

Royal marriages 1292 to 1406

Royal marriages 1406 to 1603

NFS

114

Scotland and Europe

As the English conquest of northern France proceeded from mid-1417 onwards, the Dauphin Charles sought the help of foreign troops to resist the invader. Sir John Stewart of Darnley was among the first Scots mercenaries to enter his service in October 1418. Large contingents of an army sent officially by the governor and the estates of Scotland followed from the end of 1419, using La Rochelle as the port of entry, led by John, earl of Buchan and Archibald, earl of Wigtown. Wigtown was replaced by his father the fourth earl of Douglas in 1424. The Scottish component of the Dauphin's forces in the early 1420s may have at times comprised as many as 6000 men.

The places on the map are those where Scottish troops are known to have been stationed or to have taken part in operations against the English and their Burgundian supporters between 1418 and the capture of Joan of Arc in 1430. (A few individual Scots also accompanied the Dauphin on his journey to Toulouse and Carcassonne in the south of the country in the early months of 1420.) The major engagements in which they took part (underlined on the map) were at Fresnay on 3 March 1420, Baugé on 22 March 1421, Cravant on 31 July 1423, Verneuil on 17 August 1424, Rouvrey ('the battle of the herrings') on 12 February 1429 and Patay on 18 June 1429. Some were present at the coronation of the Dauphin as King Charles VII at Rheims on 16 July 1429.

Scottish leaders were awarded with grants of castles and lands from the French royal domain, since the Dauphin had notoriously little cash at his disposal. Such grants are marked in italic type on the map. It is hard to know how effective they were, for there were often other claimants with conflicting rights. The earl of Douglas certainly held the duchy of Touraine for four months in 1424 before he was killed at Verneuil; but his heirs had no success in retaining these French lands. Wigtown was granted the county of Longueville in 1421, and Stewart of Darnley the county of Evreux in 1427. Both areas were under English control, and neither man ever took possession. The county of Saintonge was promised to King James I in 1428 as part of an agreement over further military help from Scotland: but the grant was not effective, for with the advent of Joan of Arc in 1429, the tide of war moved quickly in favour of King Charles and soon a large Scottish contingent in his army was no longer needed or welcome. Only a small Scots Guard was retained thereafter.

The Scots in France in the 1420s

DERW

Events from 1460 to 1707

Major feuds in late medieval Scotland

The map illustrates some of the major baronial feuds in later fifteenth century Scotland. The last two decades of the fifteenth century saw a number of intense local and regional feuds which contributed to, and were exacerbated or initiated by, the national crises of James III's reign, particularly the contest between the king and his son and heir, Prince James, for political control of the Kingdom during 1488. In many ways, the battle of Sauchieburn was the culmination not only of the conflict between the king and his son but also of a number of regional power struggles. Much of the political violence of 1488 - 9 resulted from these pre-existing local tensions with the forces adhering to both the prince and the King reflecting these local divisions.

The map shows major pitched battles, including the four battles (Blackness, Sauchieburn, Dunkeld, Gartloaning) which took place between 'royal' and 'rebel' forces in the fifteen months from May 1488 to October 1489. In addition the map identifies the location of full scale confrontations between individual baronial families, such as the clash in Edinburgh between Lord Lyle and James, earl of Buchan during 1487. The political settlement of 1488, after James IV's accession to power, saw the wholesale removal of James III adherents from local office and gave rise to a series of feuds between members of the new regime and the men they had displaced at the local level. The most remarkable example of this type of dispute was the sustained campaign mounted by the Cunningham kindred against Hugh, Lord Montgomery's exercise of the office of bailie of Cunningham after 1488, which accounts for the series of confrontations between the two families in Irvine. Where details of any large scale confrontation are unclear or unrecorded the feud is simply numbered and the protagonists named.

List of feuds

1. Earl of Huntly - Rose of Kilravock/MacKenzies of Kintail
2. Clan Chattan/Hugh Lord Fraser of Lovat
3. Clan Chattan/Dunbars of Westfield
4. Clan Chattan/Seton of Touchfraser
5. Earl of Huntly/Lord of the Isles
6. Earl of Buchan/Gordon of Longer
7. Earl of Erroll/Lord Gordon
8. Earl of Caithness/Keith of Inverugie
9. Lord Gordon/Forbes of Skene
10. Earl of Crawford/Lindsay of Edzell
11. Master of Crawford/Alexander Lindsay of Auchtermonzie
12. Lord Glamis/Master of Crawford
13. Earl of Buchan/Earl of Erroll
14. Lord Oliphant/Lord Ruthven
15. Lord Drummond/Lord Gray
16. Lord Drummond/Buchanan of that ilk
17. Lord Oliphant/Lord Drummond
18. Lord Fleming/Lord Kennedy
19. Earl of Lennox, Lord Lyle/Lord Sempill
20. Burgh of Renfrew/burgh of Paisley
21. Lord Fleming/Lord Hamilton
22. Lord Fleming/Laird of Kincaid
23. Earl of Lennox/Lord Hamilton
24. Lord Borthwick/Lord Crichton
25. Kers of Cessford/Murrays of Touchadam
26. Lord Crichton of Sanquhar/Douglas of Drumlanrig
27. Lord Carlisle/Murray of Cockpool
28. Lord Maxwell/Douglas of Drumlanrig

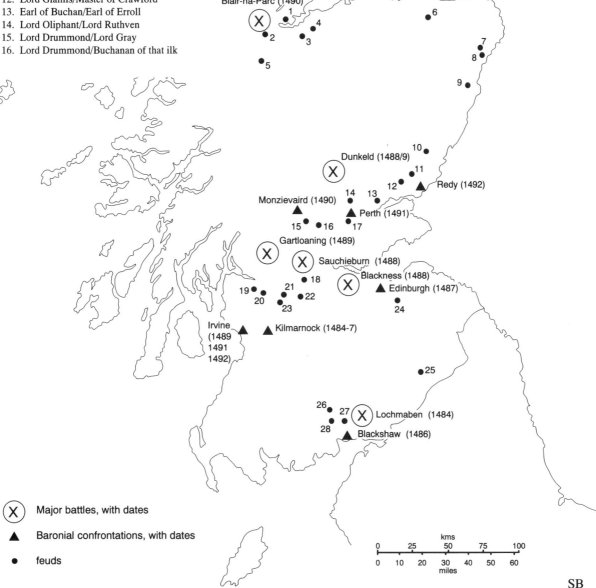

Feuds, battles and baronial confrontations 1480 to 1500

SB

117

Anglo-Scottish relations 1460 to 1465

The early 1460s saw the York-Lancaster struggle in England at its height, and English governmental weakness gave the Scots their best chance to recover their remaining border strongholds - Roxburgh and Berwick - still in English hands. James II was killed at the siege of Roxburgh (3 August 1460), but the siege was ultimately successful, and the government of James's eight-year old son fell into the capable hands of his widow, Mary of Gueldres. Initially she favoured an alliance with the deposed Lancastrian king Henry VI, and his queen, Margaret of Anjou, who ceded Berwick to the Scots in April 1461. The Lancastrian king and queen remained in Scotland a full year, dividing their time between Linlithgow and the Dominican convent in Edinburgh. Margaret of Anjou sailed from Kirkcudbright to Brittany in April to plead her cause with Louis XI of France and on her return in the autumn succeeded in capturing the northern castles of Alnwick, Bamburgh, and Dunstanburgh for the Lancastrians. But in her absence, Mary of Gueldres had already entered into negotiations with Yorkist Warwick 'the Kingmaker' at Dumfries. This pragmatic policy of playing off York and Lancaster ensured the retention of Scotland's border conquests; frustrated the treaty of 'Westminster-Ardtornish' of February 1462, whereby the Black Douglas 'fifth column' attempted to recover power in Scotland with the help of the earl of Ross and Edward IV, and prevented too heavy a Scottish reliance on the Franco-Lancastrian axis, rapidly abandoned by the cynical Louis XI in 1463. Mary of Gueldres died on 1 December 1463; but her successor at the head of government, her arch-rival Bishop James Kennedy of St. Andrews, a Lancastrian by conviction, who had forced her into conducting an abortive siege of Norham castle in the summer of 1463, was constrained by circumstances to follow her policies. Following the battles of Hedgeley Moor and Hexham (April, May 1464), the Yorkist triumph in England was complete. In June 1464 the Scots negotiated the fifteen-year truce of York with Edward IV; and this was spectacularly extended-by a further 40 years- at Newcastle in December 1465.

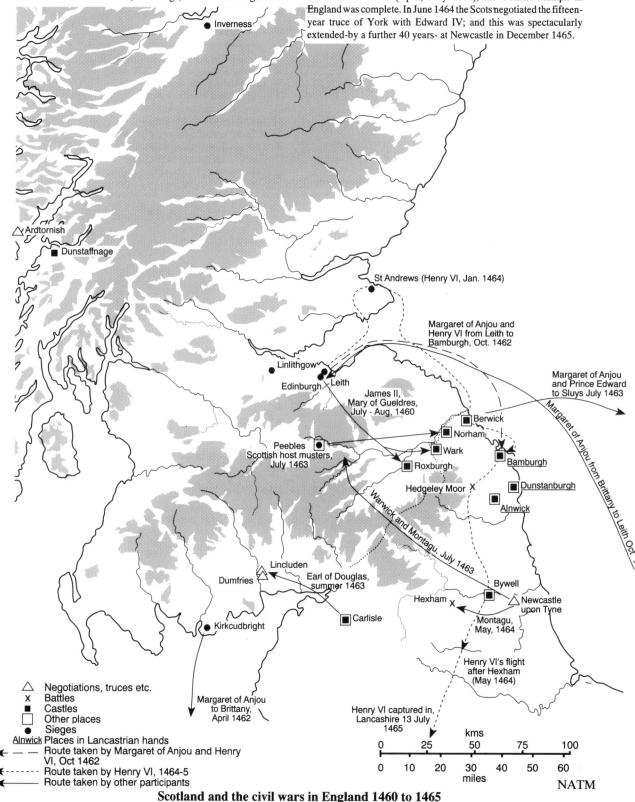

Scotland and the civil wars in England 1460 to 1465

The crises of 1482 and 1488

An English army, numbering about 20,000 men, entered Scotland late in July 1482, having first obtained the surrender of Berwick town. Its commanders were Richard, duke of Gloucester, and James III's brother, Alexander, duke of Albany, styling himself 'Alexander R'. Scottish resistance, apart from the host led by James III himself, was confined to small garrisons throughout the Marches, together with 500 mercenaries paid by James III to defend Berwick. These garrisons consisted in all of no more than 1,100 men. On 22 July James III was seized at Lauder by members of the nobility led by his half-uncles, and incarcerated in Edinburgh castle until 29 September. The route of the English army, after a brief detour to inflict £1,800 (Scots) worth of damage on Blackadder, lay by the coast to Edinburgh and Leith, supported by a fleet commanded by

Sir Robert Radcliff. Tortuous negotiations followed, with the English withdrawing from Scotland by late August, taking Berwick castle on the way (25 August), and leaving Albany to negotiate for the position of lieutenant-general. Failing to be confirmed in this office in an abortive parliament (2-11 December 1482), he retired to Dunbar and attempted to seize the king by advancing on Edinburgh (2 January 1483). Albany attacked and seized Waughton castle (defended by the loyalist David Hepburn) and his supporters killed James III's familiar, Sir Anselm Adornes, near North Berwick. But Albany failed to seize his brother, King James gradually recovered power and the death of Albany's main prop, Edward IV (9 April 1483) made his position in Scotland hopeless. He admitted an English garrison to Dunbar castle, fled to England, and was forfeited in July 1483.

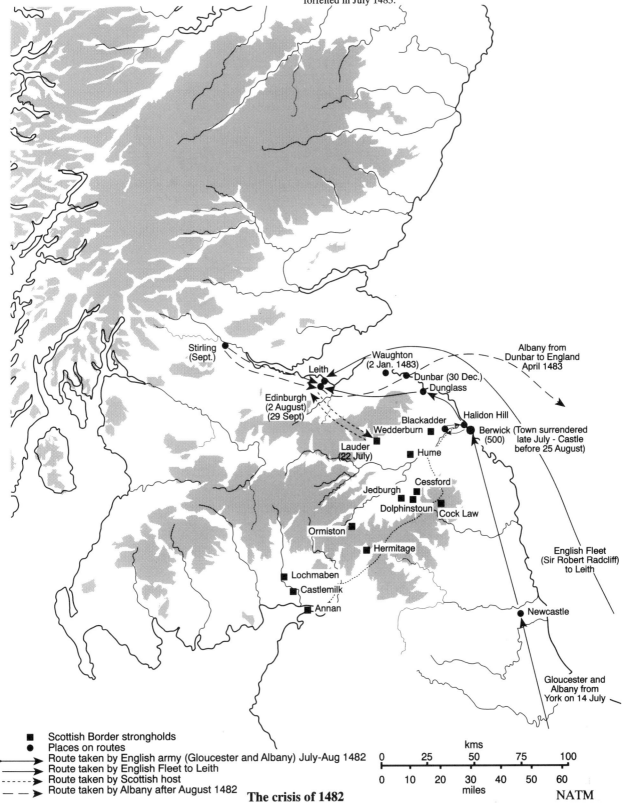

The crisis of 1482

NATM

The crises of 1482 and 1488

The background to 1488 lay in James III's determination to coerce the Humes over the revenues of the priory of Coldingham (October 1487-January 1488) and the aggressive stance he adopted in the parliament of January 1488. The major difference between the crises of 1482 and 1488 was the presence throughout the latter of the 15-year-old James, duke of Rothesay, heir to the throne, on the rebel side (from 2 February). His consistent defiance of his father over the four months of the crisis forced James III on to the defensive throughout. The map shows the principal areas of conflict and confrontation in the period March-June. Around 24 March James III left Edinburgh - with the southeast and Dunbar in rebel hands it had become too dangerous to stay - and crossed to Fife from Leith, subsequently moving north to Aberdeen (April). Here he negotiated at long distance with the rebels, but ultimately broke his written promise to send commissioners to talks (articles sometimes wrongly described as the 'Pacification of Blackness'), and came south with reduced support. There was a skirmish at Blackness (mid-May), followed by a giving of hostages by the king, a brief return to Edinburgh, and the final campaign in and around Stirling in early June. James III had short-lived success in a skirmish at Stirling Bridge, but was defeated and killed at Sauchieburn near Bannockburn (11 June), in spite of his efforts to emulate Robert Bruce by bringing the hero-king's sword to the field. James III's only really committed supporter, Alexander, master of Huntly, who had received rewards, including royal treasure, from the king (and the burgh farms of Inverness for 19 years) fought an inconclusive battle on the king's behalf at Dunkeld. But it was too late; as early as 12 June Rothesay was issuing charters as James IV.

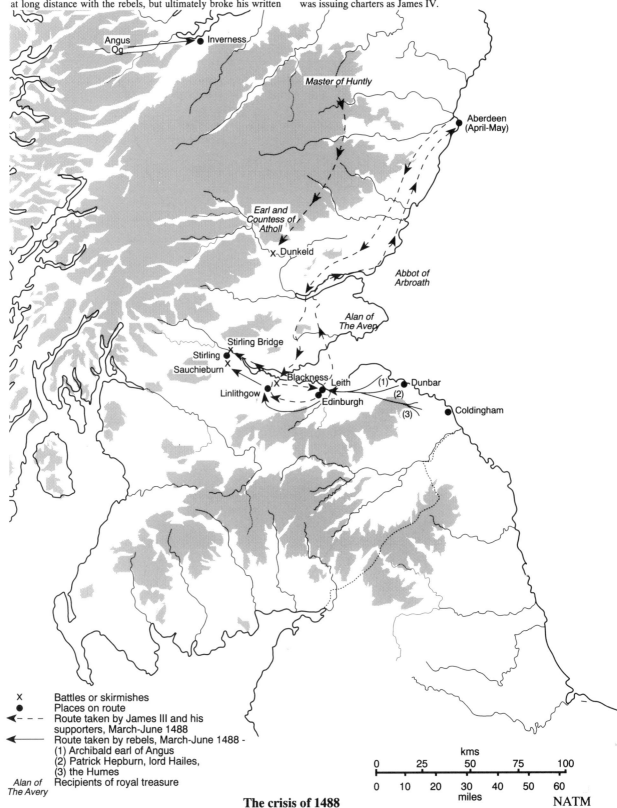

The crisis of 1488

NATM

120

Anglo-Scottish relations: James IV and Governor Albany

In the 14th century Scottish armies penetrated deep into England, burning and looting as widely as possible but avoiding strongholds and moving rapidly to avoid English forces. With the development of effective siege guns a different strategy could be adopted, and was by James IV and after him by Governor Albany. Facing the Scots across their southern border was no fortification which, when effectively attacked, could be expected to hold out longer than a few days. With sufficient manpower to blockade the chosen strongpoint and prevent relief from the neighbouring castles the Scots would hope to capture and demolish their objective and withdraw before a relief army arrived on the scene. If this all took place in late summer or autumn the lateness of the year might deter the English from doing too much damage in Scotland in revenge. While Berwick was not actually attacked at this time the successful reduction of English strongholds in the East Marches would have the effect of isolating it and it can hardly be doubted that its ultimate recovery was a major foreign policy objective of James IV and Albany.

This strategy only achieved any significant success in 1496 when Heaton Castle and several other lesser towerhouses in the East Marches were destroyed and the host had time to withdraw before the arrival of the English army of relief. Owing to the time it took to get the artillery to the Border and the excellent quality of Tudor intelligence-gathering the Scots only had four days to ply their guns against Heaton.

In the campaign of 1497 Norham was subjected to a bombardment of similar length but could not be captured. In 1513 the English were surprisingly slow to react to one of the strongest

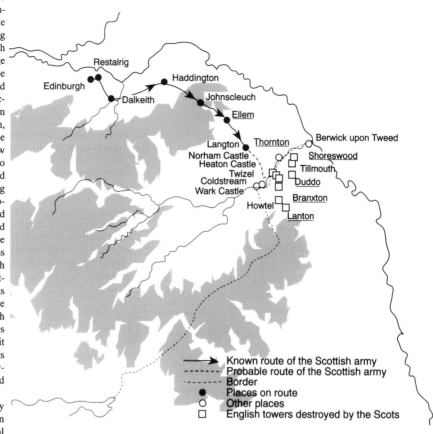

Campaign of James IV 1496

Scottish invasion forces ever, giving James ample time to reduce Norham and leading him on to the battle which the strategy was surely designed to avoid. Albany could only pursue this strategy in 1523 thanks to substantial French aid in the form of mercenary troops and money payments to the nobles but had only two days to bombard Wark, without success. His failure and the lasting impression of Flodden discredited this strategy for good.

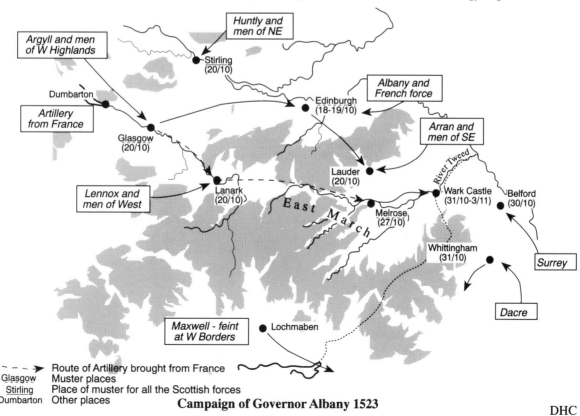

Campaign of Governor Albany 1523

DHC

James V (1513-42)

James V set out from Kirkcaldy on 1 September 1536 to sail to France to marry Mary of Bourbon, daughter of the duke of Vendome. The marriage contract was confirmed on 29 March 1536 and was not welcomed by Henry VIII. A discreet attempt to reach France by sailing around the north of Scotland had been abandoned at Whithorn in August after a storm scattered the Scots fleet. For this second trip seven ships carrying five hundred men for protection sailed down the English east coast, off which the last Scots king to travel overseas had been kidnapped. They arrived at Dieppe on 10 September where James disembarked and travelled in disguise to St Quentin to inspect his bride-to-be. He did not like the look of her and headed south to meet with Francis I. In the Loire valley James negotiated marriage with Francis' daughter Madeleine and the contract was drawn up in Blois on 26 November. After both kings had visited Fontainebleau, James retired to Cluny abbey. On 1 January 1537 he was married to Madeleine at Notre Dame in Paris. The return to Scotland was delayed by her ill-health. At Rouen, headquarters for the Scots, James issued his act of revocation (3 March.) He returned with a French escort to a peaceful Scotland on 19 May after stopping to buy fresh meat at Tynemouth. Madeleine died on 7 July at Holyrood.

James spent £82,000 on his marriages, a huge part of this in Paris New Year gifts for his French hosts, and jewels for himself cost £10,000. There were no presents for the Scots lords with him. The lavish French court and architecture of his father-in-law inspired James to increase his own expenditure in this direction

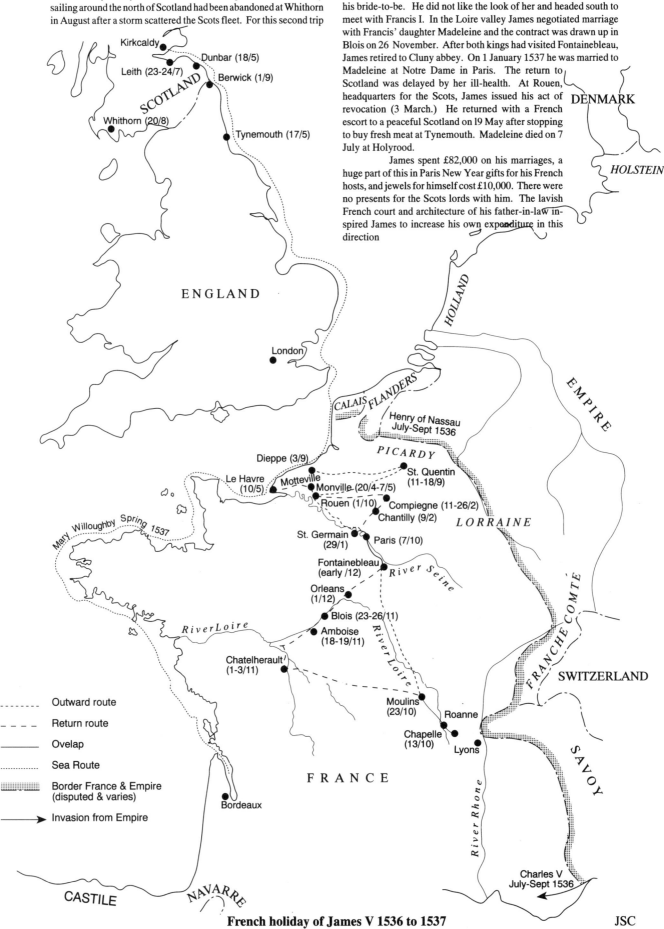

French holiday of James V 1536 to 1537

JSC

122

James V (1513-42)

Marriage in Europe was a prime concern of diplomacy for Stewart kings. The traditional ally was France but James V, like his father, concluded a perpetual peace with England before reverting to the auld alliance. The Scots first approached Francis I in 1516 (1, 2) and in the following year concluded the defensive treaty of Rouen by which a royal French princess (3, 4, 6) was promised for the young James on the understanding that the Emperor Charles V had the first refusal. Henry VIII then sought in 1523 to woo Scotland away from France with the offer of his daughter Mary (5). The Danish kings tried three times without success to attract Scottish support in their family squabbles over the Danish throne (7, 8, 10, 11). Charles

V, at odds with both France and England in 1528, saw Scotland as a possible ally (12, 13). James' uncle, the duke of Albany, tried to win Scotland over to France with the promise of Catherine of Medici (9), but by the time the Scots ambassador arrived in Rome she was betrothed to Francis I's son. In the 1530s Francis I had higher priorities for his daughters when James sought to implement Rouen (14, 15, 16). He only consented in 1536 to James marrying Madeleine (4) (d 1537) after resisting an invasion by Charles V. James himself had forgone the pleasure of marrying his mistress (17). His second bride (15), whom he married by proxy in France on 11 June 1538, expressed her own preference to become the fourth wife of Henry VIII. The French dowries were worth £166,666 Scots.

The marriages of James V

JSC

James V (1513-42)

James V was born on 10 April 1512 at Linlithgow and succeeded to the throne on 9 September 1513. The early years of the minority were spent at Stirling, until he was moved to Edinburgh for safer keeping in the Duke of Albany's absence from the summer of 1517. Thereafter he travelled rarely until his escape from the Douglases in 1528. (This is reflected in the registered great seal charters: 504 out of 596 were granted at Edinburgh in the period September 1513 - June 1528).

Apart from the journeys undertaken to use royal resources in kind and for hygienic reasons, principally between Edinburgh, Linlithgow, Stirling and Falkland, there were four main reasons for travel. These were to oversee justice, for religious reasons, for pleasure and to show himself and his brides to the people. These reasons were not mutually exclusive.

The pursuit of justice led to the trip of July 1526 with the earl of Angus, but it seems to have been ineffective because of the opposition which led to armed conflict near Melrose (at Darnick Moor) where Sir Walter Scott of Buccleuch attempted to wrest the king from Douglas control. Other trips to the Borders were made in June 1527; May-June 1529; July 1530; May 1532; June and Oct-Dec. 1534; April-May 1535; June 1536 and January 1539.

Pacification of the west and of the Isles and showing the royal flag on the fringes of the kingdom were the principal reasons for the trips to Argyll in 1533, the north in 1537 and the most famous journey of James V, round the north of Scotland via Orkney to the Western Isles in 1540.

Religious pilgrimages were made to St. Ninian's (Whithorn) in July 1531 and September 1533 and to St. Duthac's (Tain) in March 1534.

James's favourite hunting grounds were at Meggetland in the Borders (visited in August 1531 and June 1534) and at Glenartney and Benmore in Perthshire (visited in September 1531 and July 1534). He also hunted in Atholl in 1532.

Queen Madeleine's tragically early death in July 1537 was followed by a trip to Tantallon in August and thence on the northern tour through Ruthven, Inverness, Aberdeen, Dunnottar and Brechin, in September-October 1537. Marie de Guise landed at Fifeness near Crail in May 1538 and married James at St Andrews. A tour of Fife followed.

War accounted for James's final journey and he was at Lochmaben when he heard the news of the rout at Solway Moss. He returned to Marie at Linlithgow and travelled on to Falkland where he died on 14 December 1542 aged 30.

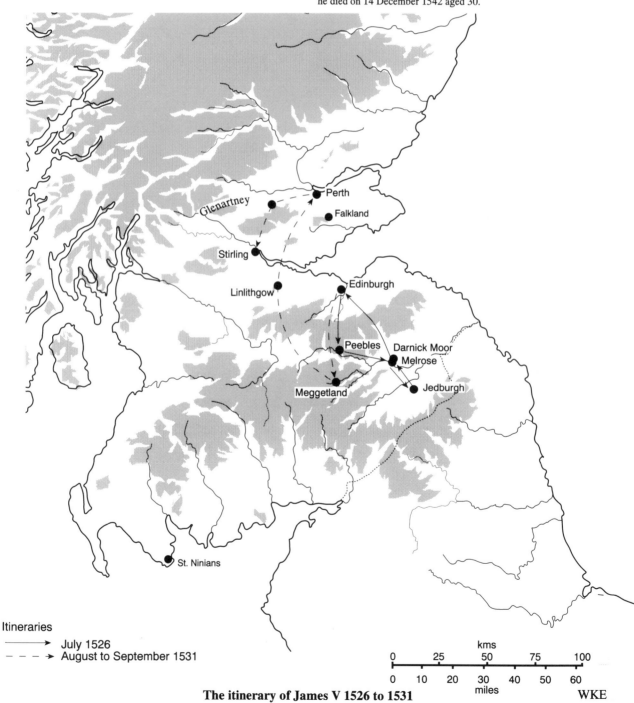

Itineraries

———→ July 1526

– – – → August to September 1531

kms

0   25   50   75   100

0   10   20   30   40   50   60
miles

The itinerary of James V 1526 to 1531   WKE

James V (1513-42)

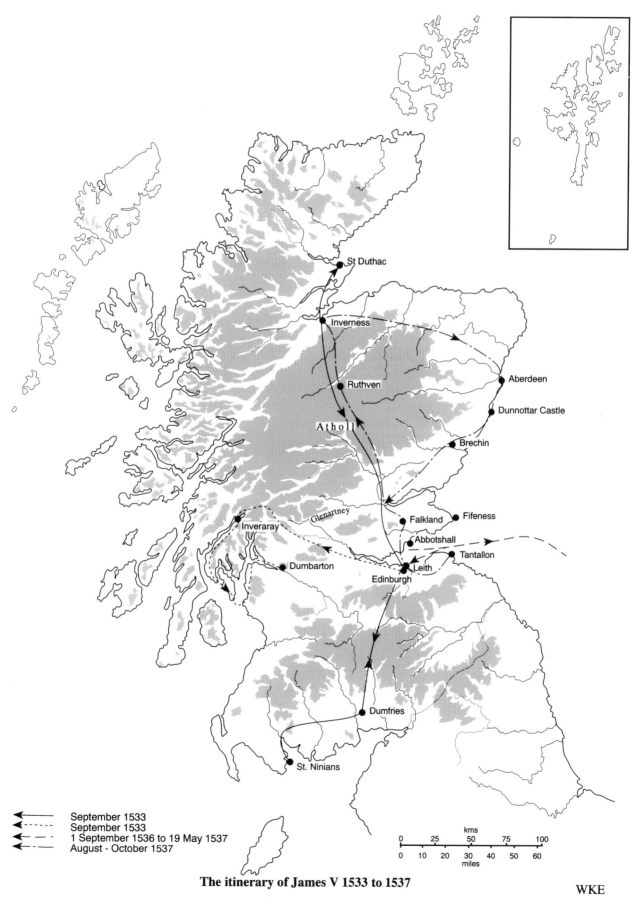

St Duthac

Inverness

Ruthven

Aberdeen

Dunnottar Castle

Brechin

Atholl

Glenartney

Inveraray

Falkland

Fifeness

Abbotshall

Dumbarton

Tantallon

Leith

Edinburgh

Dumfries

St. Ninians

	September 1533
	September 1533
	1 September 1536 to 19 May 1537
	August - October 1537

kms

0	25	50	75	100

0	10	20	30	40	50	60

miles

The itinerary of James V 1533 to 1537

WKE

James V (1513-42)

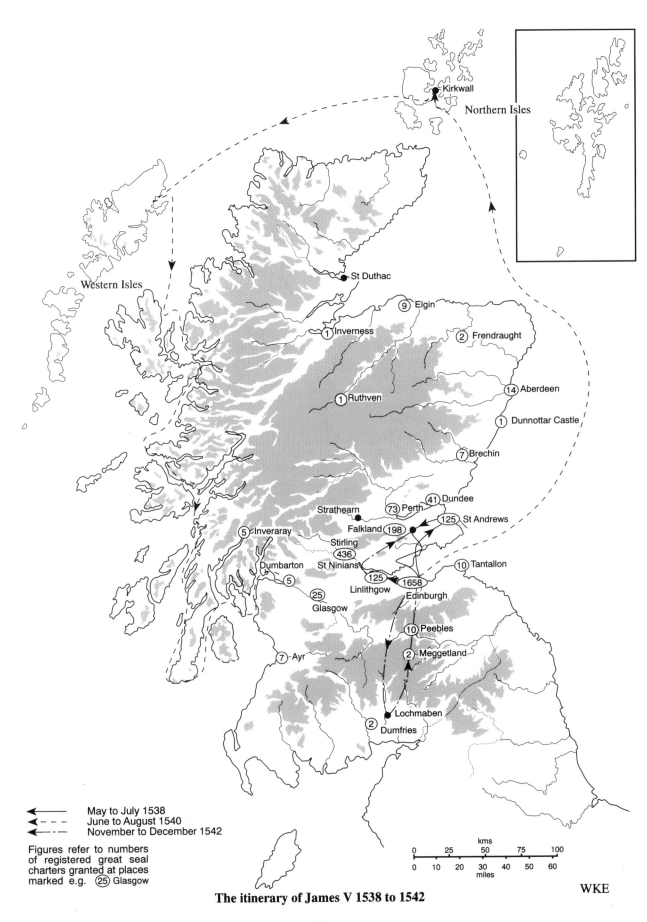

Kirkwall

Northern Isles

Western Isles

St Duthac

⑨ Elgin

① Inverness

② Frendraught

⑭ Aberdeen

① Dunnottar Castle

① Ruthven

⑦ Brechin

Strathearn

⑤ Inveraray

Dundee

㊹ Perth

⑦③ Perth

Falkland

⑫⑤ St Andrews

⑲⑧

Stirling

Dumbarton

④③⑥

St Ninians

⑤

⑩ Tantallon

⑫⑤

⑯⑤⑧

Linlithgow

Edinburgh

㉕

Glasgow

⑩ Peebles

② Meggetland

⑦ Ayr

Lochmaben

② Dumfries

⟵——— May to July 1538
⟵- - - June to August 1540
⟵-·-·- November to December 1542

Figures refer to numbers
of registered great seal
charters granted at places
marked e.g. ㉕ Glasgow

kms
0   25   50   75   100
0 10 20 30 40 50 60
miles

The itinerary of James V 1538 to 1542

WKE

Anglo-Scottish relations: the 'Rough Wooing' 1544 to 1550

The 'Rough Wooing' of 1544 to 1550 was the attempt by Henry VIII and the Protector Somerset to force the Scottish government of the earl of Arran to agree to the betrothal of Mary, queen of Scots and Henry's son, Edward and thereby to unite the two monarchies dynastically. The normal pattern of warfare during the period 1544 to 1546 was by raids into Scotland by English raiding parties based along the Marches, which caused considerable destruction from Dumfries to Hume and Coldingham. Even although the English briefly held some parts of Scotland, such as Lochmaben, Caerlaverock, Threave and Langholm, the warfare remained confined to the Borders. The invasion of a large force in May 1544 destroyed Edinburgh, and the invasion of September 1545 ravaged the Merse and Teviotdale; but the English retired on the death of Henry VIII in January 1547 without achieving the marriage.

Somerset realised that failure in that policy was due to the temporary nature of the pressure which had been put upon the Scots: he invaded Scotland in September 1547 with a large army primarily to capture strongpoints, and not just to defeat the Scots, which he did in the great set-piece battle of Pinkie (10 September). The English fleet, which shadowed the English army as it moved towards Pinkie, then captured Inchcolm and Broughty Craig; and English forces were placed in them. At the same time another English army invaded the south-west and by the end of the year Dumfries, Cockpool, Castlemilk and Lochwood were garrisoned by English troops. (These events are shown in the first map.) However, by December 1547, French assistance for the Scots was beginning to arrive. Somerset resolved to strengthen greatly the English position in Scotland.

English invasions in the east and the west resulted in the capture of Haddington, Saltoun, Ormiston and Yester. Later, modern forts were built at Balgillo, Lauder and Haddington. The mutually-protecting forts formed what the English regarded as a pale. New forts were built at Dunglass (September 1548) and Fast castle (1549). But with the French reinforcements to the Scots, there was little the English could do to maintain their position: the English pale was pushed back; and the French entrenched themselves with garrisons and fortifications, as is shown in the third map. At the time of the treaty of Boulogne (24 March 1550), only Lauder, Roxburgh, Dunglass and Eyemouth remained in English hands. The Rough Wooing had failed.

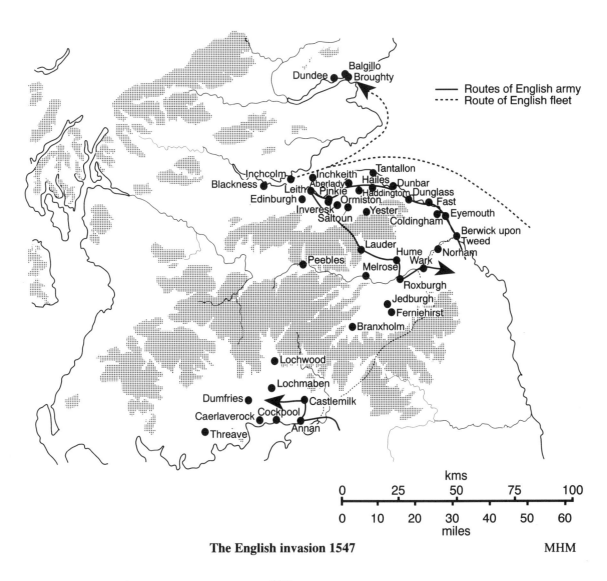

The English invasion 1547   MHM

127

Anglo- Scottish relations: the 'Rough Wooing' 1544 to 1550

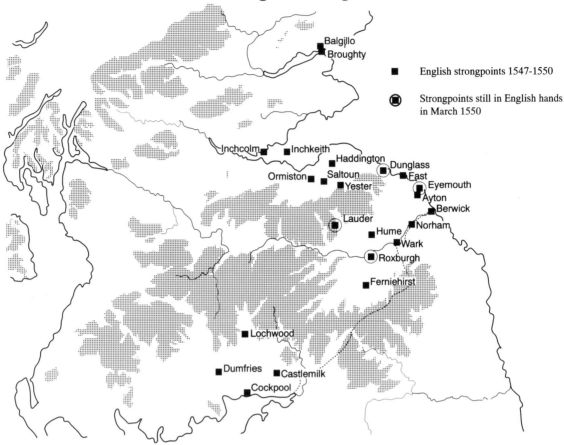

English strongpoints 1547 to 1550

■ English strongpoints 1547-1550

◉ Strongpoints still in English hands in March 1550

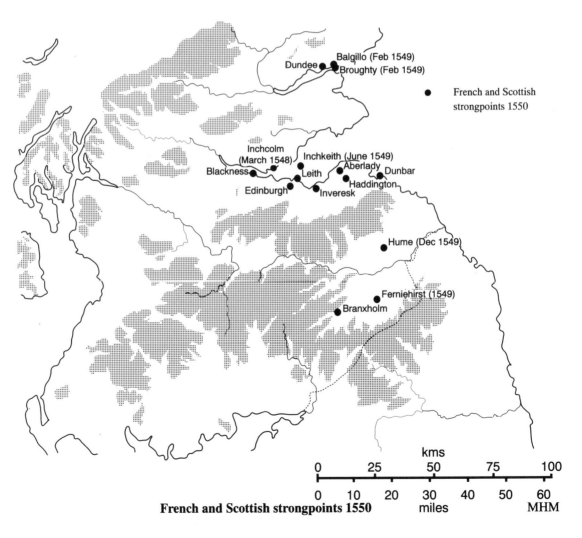

French and Scottish strongpoints 1550

● French and Scottish strongpoints 1550

kms

MHM

The Reformation parliament 1560

In the midst of the Protestant Revolution, agreement was reached in the Treaty of Edinburgh (July 1560) between England and France for a withdrawal of foreign troops from Scottish soil. With the ensuing peace, preparations went ahead for summoning parliament in Edinburgh, which was duly authorised by Queen Mary and Francis II of France to meet on 10 July and to adjourn for reassembly on 1 August. When parliament met in earnest, a week was spent debating legalities, the committee of the articles was elected, petitions accepted and, with characteristic promptitude, the assembled estates sanctioned a reformed Confession of Faith (17 August), abrogated papal authority in Scotland, prohibited idolatry and rescinded all previous legislation considered inconsistent with the protestant Confession of Faith, abolished the celebration of mass and prescribed punishment for offenders who failed to abstain from the rite (24 August). Whereas in England the Henrician 'Reformation parliament' had sat in seven sessions over seven years, its Scottish counterpart dispatched its essential business in seven days. Its work was short and swift. Concentrating on fundamentals, it assigned to others the task of working out the details. The unprecedented attendance, from far and near, of so wide a spectrum of the political community in the parliament of 1560 is indicative of the determination of the victorious revolutionaries to make a showing in the capital by rallying their adherents from many corners of the kingdom. The impressive appearance of 14 earls, led by 'the duke' who was heir presumptive to the throne, some 19 lords, half a dozen sons of peers, commissioners from 22 burghs, and a hundred or so lairds (whose right to attend by custom and use was a subject of dispute) was designed to overawe any opposition. Members of the country's most powerful and influential families evidently considered it imperative to give their presence: most were firmly protestant, some were militantly so; and the few conservatives who put in an appearance for the best part kept silent. Among the six members of the episcopate who gave their attendance, three turned protestant reformers; and the remainder showed, at least, some disposition towards wavering, if not conforming. Nor was the strong turnout of two dozen or so commendators from the monastic houses inimical to religious change, for most had shown themselves friends of the reforming party. A remarkable feature of the Reformation parliament's composition was the broad base of support which could be claimed from the political community. Its membership was drawn geographically from so far north as Inverness and its environs, along the north-eastern coastal plain, southward through Aberdeenshire, Angus and the Mearns, Perthshire (highland and lowland), to Fife, the Lothians and Merse, Stirlingshire, Lanarkshire, and Dunbartonshire.

JK

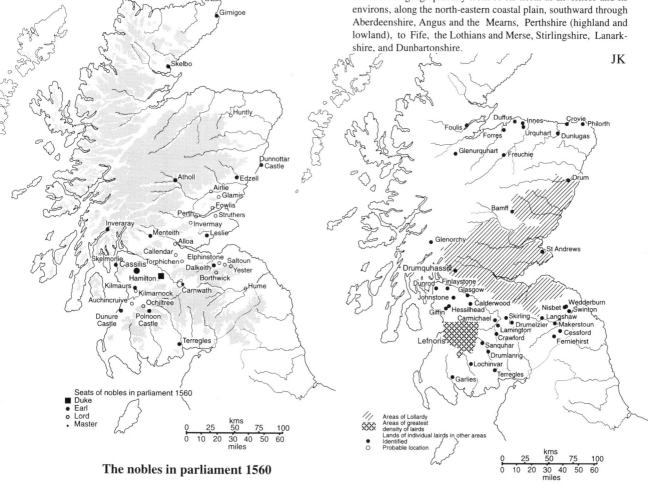

The nobles in parliament 1560

The lairds in parliament 1560

	Title	Seat						
Duke								
1	Chatelherault	Hamilton	14	Menteith	Inchtaile	27	Stewart of Innermeath	Invermay
Earls			Lords			28	Gray	Fowlis
2	Arran	Hamilton	15	Gordon	Huntly	29	Ogilvie	Airlie
3	Argyll	Inveraray	16	Erskine	Alloa	30	Glamis	Glamis
4	Atholl	Blair Atholl	17	Ruthven	Perth	31	Borthwick	Borthwick
5	Marishal	Dunnottar	18	Home	Hume	32	Cathcart	Auchincruive
6	Crawford	Edzell	19	Lindsay of the Byres	Byres	33	St. John	Torphichen
7	Morton	Dalkeith	20	Hay of Yester	Yester	Masters		
8	Glencairn	Kilmaurs	21	Somerville	Carnwath	34	Terregles	Terregles
9	Rothes	Rothes	22	Livingstone	Callendar	35	Marischal	Dunnottar
10	Eglinton	Polnoon	23	Boyd	Kilmarnock	36	Lindsay	Edzell
11	Sutherland	Skelbo	24	Stewart of Ochiltree	Ochiltree	37	Sinclair	Girnigoe
12	Cassilis	Cassilis	25	Saltoun	Saltoun	38	Glencairn	Kilmaurs
13	Caithness	Girnigoe	26	Elphinstone	Elphinstone	39	Somerville	Carnwath

IBC

The Reformation parliament 1560

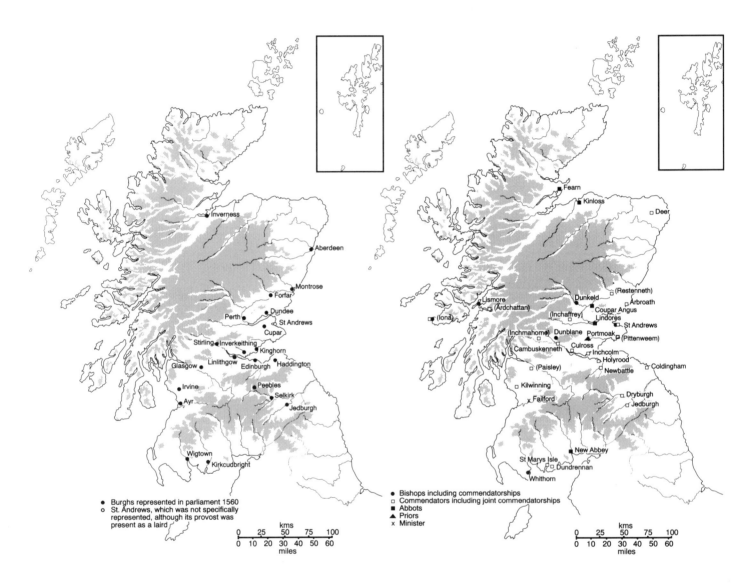

The burghs in parliament 1560

The churchmen in parliament 1560

Burghs map legend:
- ● Burghs represented in parliament 1560
- ○ St. Andrews, which was not specifically represented, although its provost was present as a laird

kms
0 25 50 75 100
0 10 20 30 40 50 60
miles

Churchmen map legend:
- ● Bishops including commendatorships
- □ Commendators including joint commendatorships
- ■ Abbots
- ▲ Priors
- x Minister

kms
0 25 50 75 100
0 10 20 30 40 50 60
miles

Burghs labels: Inverness, Aberdeen, Montrose, Forfar, Dundee, Perth, St Andrews, Cupar, Stirling, Inverkeithing, Kinghorn, Glasgow, Linlithgow, Edinburgh, Haddington, Irvine, Peebles, Selkirk, Ayr, Jedburgh, Wigtown, Kirkcudbright

Churchmen labels: Fearn, Kinloss, Deer, Lismore, (Ardchattan), (Restenneth), Dunkeld, Arbroath, Coupar Angus, (Inchaffrey), Lindores, (Iona), St Andrews, (Inchmahome), Dunblane, Portmoak, (Pittenweem), Cambuskenneth, Culross, Inchcolm, Holyrood, (Paisley), Newbattle, Coldingham, Kilwinning, Dryburgh, Failford, Jedburgh, New Abbey, St Marys Isle, Dundrennan, Whithorn

IBC

130

Mary, queen of Scots (1542-67)

First Progress of Mary Queen of Scots
11 September - 29 September 1561:
Holyrood,Edinburgh to Linlithgow Palace to Stirling Castle to Kincardine Castle making a detour to Leslie Castle in Fife en route to Perth to Dundee to St. Andrews to Cupar to Falkland Palace to Edinburgh.

First Northern Progress of Mary Queen of Scots 10 August - 21 November 1562
Edinburgh to Calder House to Linlithgow Palace to Callendar House to Stirling Castle to Kincardine Castle to Perth to Coupar Angus to Glamis to Edzell Castle to Pittarrow to Dunnottar Castle to Aberdeen to Balquhain House and Chapel of Garioch to Rothlemay Castle to Castle of Grange to Balvenie Castle to Boharm to Elgin to Kinloss Abbey to Darnaway Castle to Nairn to Inverness to Kilravock Castle to Darnaway Castle to Spynie Palace to Cullen to Boyne Castle to Banff to Gight Castle to Esslemont to Aberdeen to Dunnottar Castle to Montrose to Craig Castle to Bonnytown to Kincardine Castle to Arbroath to Dundee to Kilspindie Castle to Perth to Tullibardine to Drummond Castle to Stirling Castle to Linlithgow Palace to Edinburgh.

Western Progress of Mary Queen of Scots 30 June - 7 September 1563
Edinburgh to Glasgow to Hamilton to Glasgow to Paisley to Dumbarton Castle to Rossdhu Castle to Dumbarton Castle to Carrick Castle to Toward to Inveraray

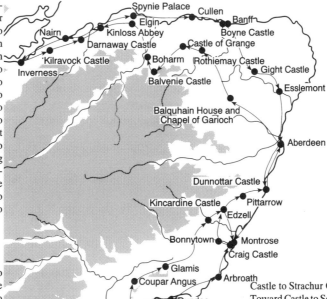

Castle to Strachur Castle to Dunoon Castle to Toward Castle to Southannan to Eglinton Castle to St. John the Baptist Monastery, Ayr to Dunure Castle to Ardmillan Castle to Ardstinchar Castle to Glenluce Abbey to Whithorn Priory to Clary House to Kenmure Castle to St. Mary's Isle Priory, Kirkcudbright to Dumfries to Drumlanrig Castle to Boghouses, Crawfordjohn to Cowthally Castle to Skirling Castle to Peebles to Borthwick Castle to Dalhousie Castle to Roslin Castle to Craigmillar Castle to Edinburgh.

Northern Progress of Mary Queen of Scots 22 July - 15 September 1564
Edinburgh to Linlithgow Palace to Stirling Castle to Kincardine Castle to Perth to Blair Atholl to Glen Tilt to Blair Atholl to Inverness to Beauly Priory to Redcastle to Dingwall to Gartly Castle to Aberdeen to Dunnottar Castle to Dundee to St. Andrews to Edinburgh.

Fife Trip early 1565 - Mary Queen of Scots 19 January - 24 February 1565
Edinburgh to Falkland Palace to Collairnie Castle to Ballinbreich Castle to Balmerino Abbey to St. Andrews to Anstruther to Newark Castle to St. Andrews to Lundie Castle to Durie Castle to Wemyss Castle to Queensferry to Edinburgh.

Trip of Mary Queen of Scots 11 May - 4 July 1565
Edinburgh to Stirling to Innerpeffray to Perth to Ruthven Castle to Dunkeld to Perth to Callendar House to Edinburgh.

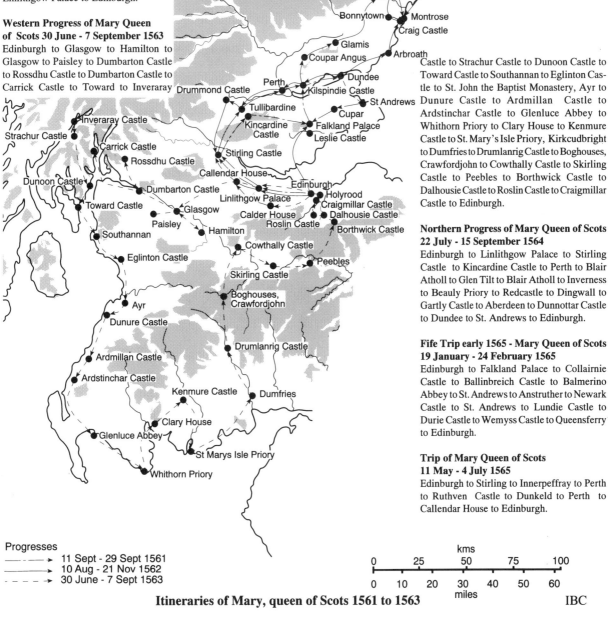

Progresses

```
— · — · —▸   11 Sept - 29 Sept 1561
————————▸   10 Aug - 21 Nov 1562
– – – – – –▸   30 June - 7 Sept 1563
```

kms
```
0      25      50      75      100
```
```
0   10   20   30   40   50   60
         miles
```

Itineraries of Mary, queen of Scots 1561 to 1563

IBC

131

Mary, queen of Scots (1542-67)

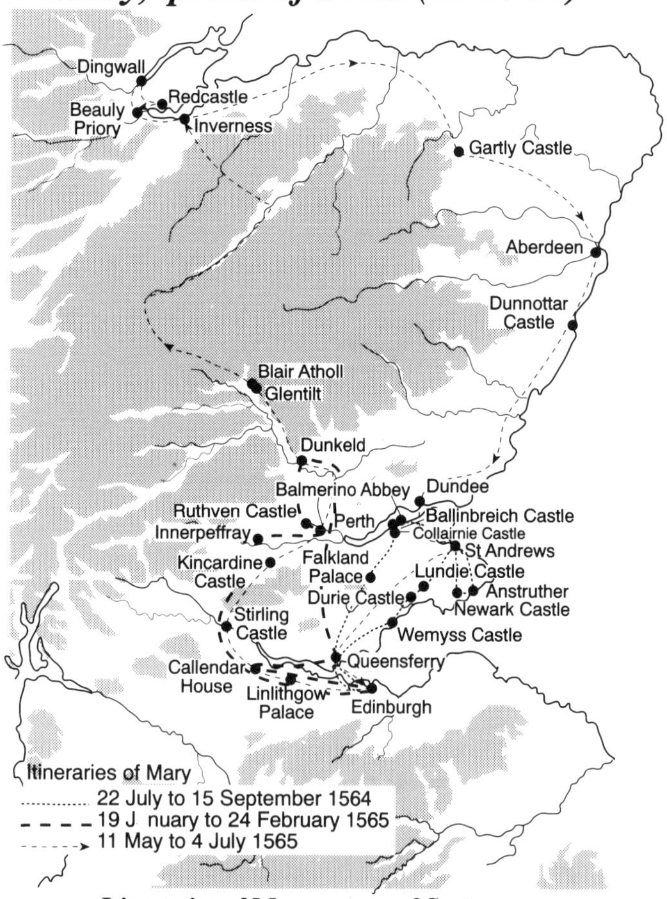

Itineraries of Mary, queen of Scots 1564 to 1565

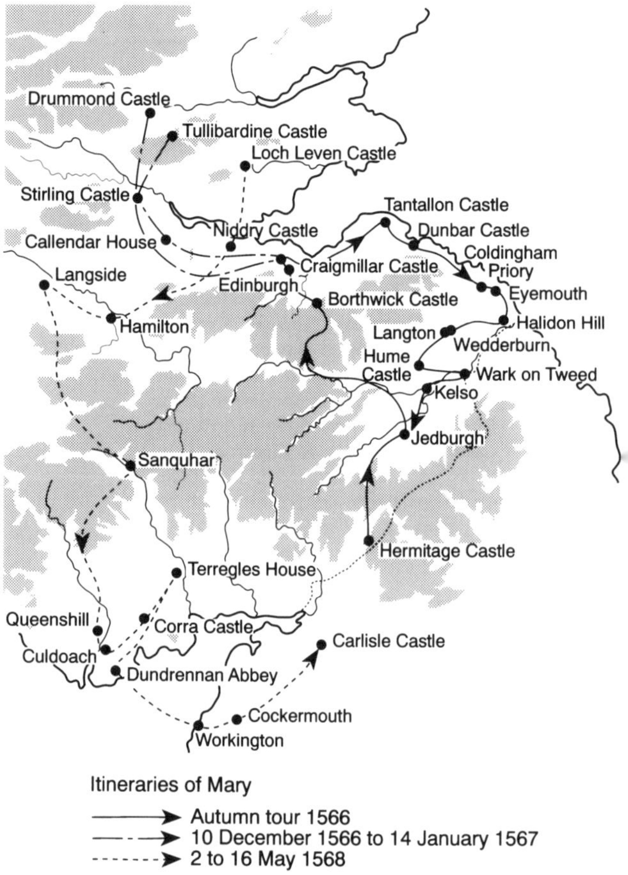

Dingwall
Redcastle
Beauly Priory
Inverness
Gartly Castle
Aberdeen
Dunnottar Castle
Blair Atholl Glentilt
Dunkeld
Balmerino Abbey
Dundee
Ruthven Castle
Ballinbreich Castle
Innerpeffray
Perth
Collairnie Castle
St Andrews
Kincardine Castle
Falkland Palace
Lundie Castle
Anstruther
Durie Castle
Newark Castle
Stirling Castle
Wemyss Castle
Callendar House
Queensferry
Linlithgow Palace
Edinburgh

Itineraries of Mary
.... 22 July to 15 September 1564
– – – – 19 January to 24 February 1565
- - -> 11 May to 4 July 1565

Itineraries of Mary, queen of Scots 1566 to 1568

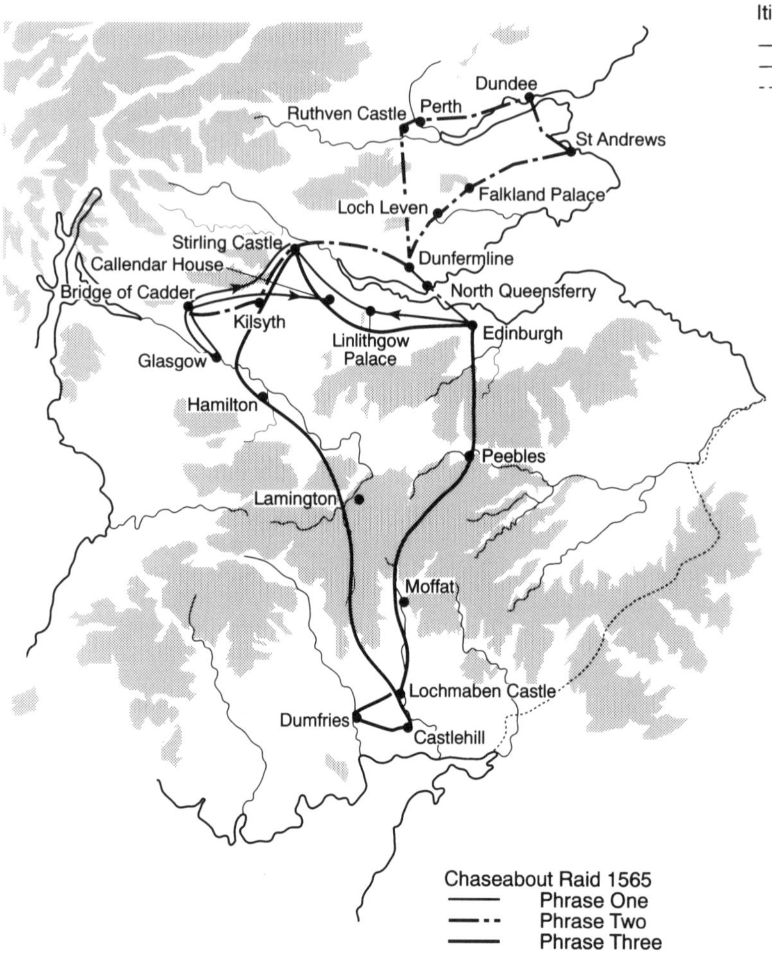

Drummond Castle
Tullibardine Castle
Loch Leven Castle
Stirling Castle
Niddry Castle
Tantallon Castle
Dunbar Castle
Callendar House
Coldingham Priory
Langside
Craigmillar Castle
Edinburgh
Eyemouth
Borthwick Castle
Halidon Hill
Hamilton
Langton
Wedderburn
Hume Castle
Wark on Tweed
Kelso
Jedburgh
Sanquhar
Hermitage Castle
Terregles House
Queenshill
Corra Castle
Carlisle Castle
Culdoach
Dundrennan Abbey
Cockermouth
Workington

Itineraries of Mary
——> Autumn tour 1566
—·—·> 10 December 1566 to 14 January 1567
- - -> 2 to 16 May 1568

Itineraries of Mary, queen of Scots: the Chaseabout Raid 1565

Dundee
Ruthven Castle
Perth
St Andrews
Loch Leven
Falkland Palace
Stirling Castle
Dunfermline
Callendar House
Bridge of Cadder
North Queensferry
Kilsyth
Linlithgow Palace
Edinburgh
Glasgow
Hamilton
Peebles
Lamington
Moffat
Lochmaben Castle
Dumfries
Castlehill

Chaseabout Raid 1565
——— Phrase One
—·—· Phrase Two
——— Phrase Three

IBC

132

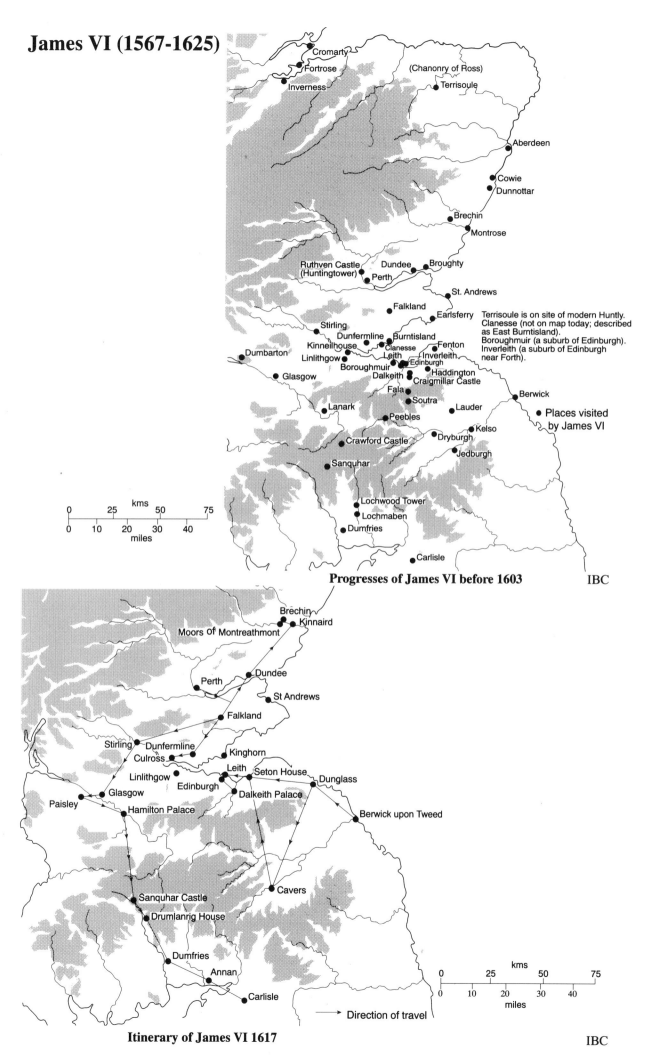

James VI (1567-1625)

Cromarty
Fortrose
Inverness
(Chanonry of Ross)
Terrisoule
Aberdeen
Cowie
Dunnottar
Brechin
Montrose
Ruthven Castle (Huntingtower)
Dundee
Broughty
Perth
St. Andrews
Falkland
Earlsferry
Stirling
Dunfermline
Burntisland
Kinneilhouse
Clanesse
Fenton
Dumbarton
Linlithgow
Leith
Inverleith
Boroughmuir
Edinburgh
Glasgow
Dalkeith
Haddington
Craigmillar Castle
Fala
Soutra
Lanark
Berwick
Peebles
Lauder
Crawford Castle
Dryburgh
Kelso
Sanquhar
Jedburgh
Lochwood Tower
Lochmaben
Dumfries
Carlisle

Terrisoule is on site of modern Huntly.
Clanesse (not on map today; described as East Burntisland).
Boroughmuir (a suburb of Edinburgh).
Inverleith (a suburb of Edinburgh near Forth).

● Places visited by James VI

kms
0   25   50   75
0 10 20 30 40
miles

Progresses of James VI before 1603   IBC

Brechin
Kinnaird
Moors of Montreathmont
Perth
Dundee
St Andrews
Falkland
Stirling
Dunfermline
Culross
Kinghorn
Linlithgow
Leith
Seton House
Edinburgh
Dunglass
Glasgow
Dalkeith Palace
Paisley
Berwick upon Tweed
Hamilton Palace
Cavers
Sanquhar Castle
Drumlanrig House
Dumfries
Annan
Carlisle

kms
0   25   50   75
0 10 20 30 40
miles

→ Direction of travel

Itinerary of James VI 1617   IBC

133

The civil war 1567 to 1573

After Mary's defeat at Carberry Hill (15 June 1567) at the hands of the confederate lords, the queen demitted her crown to her infant son James. The government was carried on by the Regent Moray. After her escape from Lochleven and her defeat at Langside (13 May 1568), Mary fled to England with little prospect of being allowed to return to Scotland, although there were in Scotland the 'queen's men' who looked for her restoration: they were opposed by the 'king's men'. After the assassination of Moray (January 1570) the opposing factions slid into civil war. By 1573 the cause of the king's men had prevailed, partly because of the support for them from Elizabeth of England who saw her position in doubt if the Marians were to succeed. The chief Marian lords acknowledged James VI as king in the pacification of Perth (23 February 1573). The maps show the location of the supporters of the queen's men and the king's men.

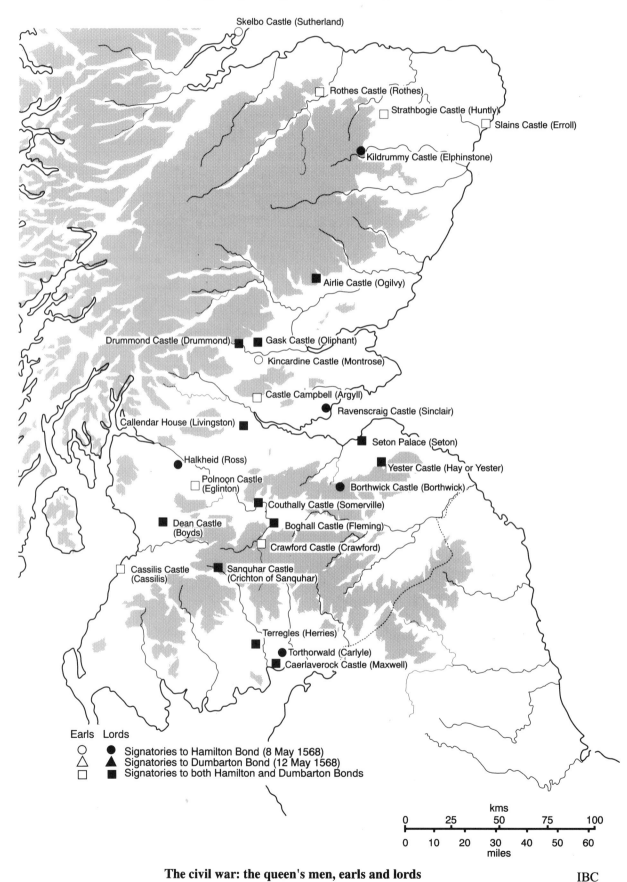

The civil war: the queen's men, earls and lords

IBC

134

The civil war 1567 to 1573

Fearn

Elgin

Fortrose Kinloss Pluscarden

Aberdeen

Brechin

Lismore Dunkeld Arbroath

Ardchattan

Inchaffray St. Andrews

Iona Lindores

Inchcolm

Paisley

Kilwinning

Kelso

Jedburgh

Crossraguel

Holywood

New Abbey

Soulseat Glenluce

Whithorn Dundrennan

	Bishops	Commendators
Signatories to Hamilton Bond (8 May 1568)	●	●
Signatories to Dumbarton Bond (12 May 1568)	▲	▲
Signatories to both Hamilton and Dumbarton Bonds	◣	◣

kms
0 25 50 75 100

0 10 20 30 40 50 60
miles

The civil war: the queen's men, bishops and commendators

IBC

The civil war 1567 to 1573

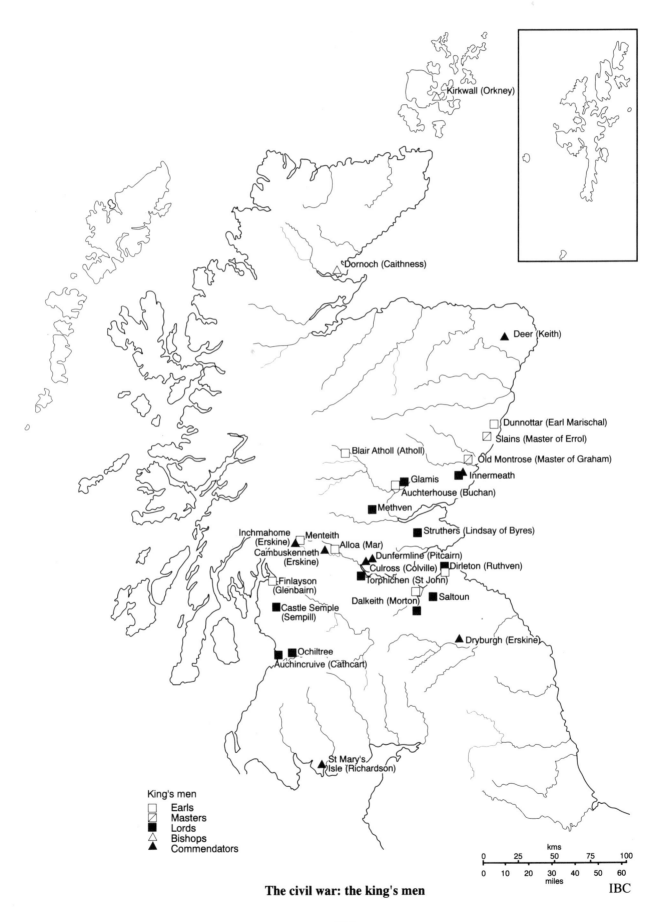

King's men

☐ Earls
▨ Masters
■ Lords
△ Bishops
▲ Commendators

Kirkwall (Orkney)

Dornoch (Caithness)

Deer (Keith)

Dunnottar (Earl Marischal)

Slains (Master of Errol)

Blair Atholl (Atholl)

Old Montrose (Master of Graham)

Glamis

Innermeath

Auchterhouse (Buchan)

Methven

Struthers (Lindsay of Byres)

Inchmahome (Erskine)

Menteith

Alloa (Mar)

Cambuskenneth (Erskine)

Dunfermline (Pitcairn)

Culross (Colville)

Dirleton (Ruthven)

Torphichen (St John)

Finlayson (Glenbairn)

Dalkeith (Morton)

Saltoun

Castle Semple (Sempill)

Dryburgh (Erskine)

Ochiltree

Auchincruive (Cathcart)

St Mary's Isle (Richardson)

kms

0   25   50   75   100

0   10   20   30   40   50   60
miles

The civil war: the king's men

IBC

136

The house of Hamilton 1554 to 1573

The strength of the house of Hamilton in the middle decades of the sixteenth century depended upon a widespread yet consolidated network of influence derived from both temporal and ecclesiastical wealth, property and positions.

In the secular sphere Hamiltons were to be found as sheriffs of Lanark, Renfrew, Linlithgow, Bute (and Arran); captains of strategic royal castles; representatives on the town councils of main burghs, in addition to controlling over 200 estates stretching from Arran to the Merse, Sanquhar to Corse in Aberdeenshire. The greatest concentrations were in Lanarkshire, Ayrshire and West Lothian around the main family fortresses, the nuclei being the baronies of Cadzow, Mauchline and Kinneil granted by Robert Bruce in 1314 to Walter, son of Gilbert, the earliest recorded ancestor, in recognition of his support during the Wars of Independence. The chief means of land accumulation was the crown grant, especially following the forfeitures of recalcitrant noble families such as the Douglases and the Boyds, but outright purchase, excambion (exchange), and marriage with sole or joint heiresses also served to increase and unify existing holdings. By a simultaneous policy of careful distribution and intermarriage, the Hamiltons ensured that their numerous offspring, whether legitimate or illegiti-mate, did not become alienated but instead were variously established as the heads of cadet branches, taken into crown service or appointed as baillies and chamberlains, thus maintaining an extensive loyalty to kin and name. Many younger or illegitimate sons were allocated pensions and positions in the ecclesiastical hierarchy, although continuity was harder to preserve as control terminated with the death of the holder. The governorship of James Hamilton, second earl of Arran and duke of Chatelherault, provided the opportunity to entrench kinsmen particularly in lucrative episcopal and monastic benefices, thus with the exception of the bishopric of Argyll and Lismore, gaining influence over an area conterminous with their secular properties. Where possible, members of the family also benefited from the feuing of church lands, mainly in the Clyde valley and north Ayrshire, and from the revenues of parish churches appropriated to the religious houses and collegiate churches or free from external influence such as Crawfordjohn, Libberton, Quothquan, Kirkmichael and Rannoch. In a period of political and religious unrest, family security ultimately mattered more than national aspirations or individual faith. Internal unity ensured that neither forfeiture nor direct attack could weaken the influential position held by the house of Hamilton in mid-sixteenth century Scotland.

B u t e	Sheriffdoms with Hamilton sheriffs
Dunbar	Castles with Hamilton captains
Edinburgh	Main burghs with Hamilton representatives on the council
•	Other Hamilton lands

ST ANDREWS	Archbishopric held by Hamiltons
Argyll	Bishopric held by Hamiltons
Kilwinning	Religious house held by Hamiltons
•	Other benefices held by Hamiltons

The house of Hamilton: secular landholding 1554 to 1573

The house of Hamilton: ecclesiastical benefices 1554 to 1573

EF

The civil wars 1639 to 1651

This map depicts Charles' strategy for subduing the Scots in the first bishops' war of 1639 - and its failure. Grandiose plans for coordinating invasions by sea and land, from both England and Ireland, with royalist risings in northern Scotland were almost uniformly unsuccessful. The covenanters took the initiative in March by seizing (without bloodshed) nearly all the castles held for the king and by sending forces to occupy Aberdeen and Arran. The royalists of the north-east twice managed to gain temporary possession of Aberdeen

(on the second occasion by a landing from ships sent from England), but this was all the success that the royalists could boast. The invasions from Ireland failed to materialise, the shores of the Firth of Forth were too strongly held by the covenanters for a landing to be risked, and the king's army on the border was too weak to invade. When in June the covenanters threateningly advanced their main army to Duns, the king agreed to open negotiations for peace, and the pacification of Berwick was signed on 18 June.

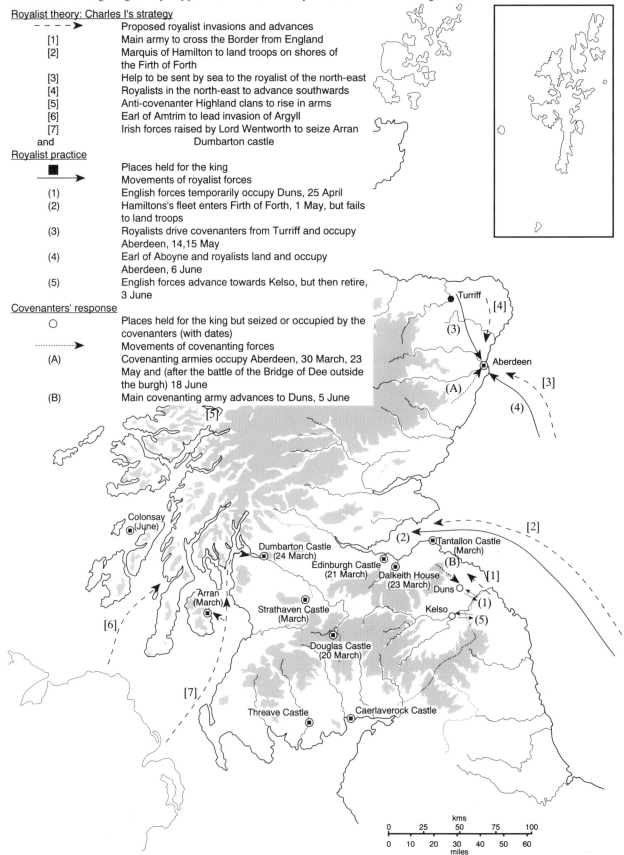

Royalist theory: Charles I's strategy

- - - - ➤	Proposed royalist invasions and advances
[1]	Main army to cross the Border from England
[2]	Marquis of Hamilton to land troops on shores of the Firth of Forth
[3]	Help to be sent by sea to the royalist of the north-east
[4]	Royalists in the north-east to advance southwards
[5]	Anti-covenanter Highland clans to rise in arms
[6]	Earl of Amtrim to lead invasion of Argyll
[7]	Irish forces raised by Lord Wentworth to seize Arran
and	Dumbarton castle

Royalist practice

■	Places held for the king
➝	Movements of royalist forces
(1)	English forces temporarily occupy Duns, 25 April
(2)	Hamiltons's fleet enters Firth of Forth, 1 May, but fails to land troops
(3)	Royalists drive covenanters from Turriff and occupy Aberdeen, 14,15 May
(4)	Earl of Aboyne and royalists land and occupy Aberdeen, 6 June
(5)	English forces advance towards Kelso, but then retire, 3 June

Covenanters' response

○	Places held for the king but seized or occupied by the covenanters (with dates)
┄┄┄➤	Movements of covenanting forces
(A)	Covenanting armies occupy Aberdeen, 30 March, 23 May and (after the battle of the Bridge of Dee outside the burgh) 18 June
(B)	Main covenanting army advances to Duns, 5 June

The first bishops' war 1639

DS

The civil wars 1639 to 1651

When war broke out again in 1640, Charles's plans were similar to those of the previous year, but the idea of a landing on the shores of the Firth of Forth was abandoned; and it was realised that there was no longer much hope of active help from the royalists in the north-east. The covenanters again seized the initiative, sending forces to occupy Aberdeen and to march through the central and southern Highlands to deter potential royalists from action. Only four castles were held for the king, but all of them required formal sieges before being forced to surrender -and three of them did not surrender until after it was clear that the king's cause was lost. As in 1639, the help expected from Ireland did not appear (except for a small scale raid in Islay long after the war was over, undertaken more for clan than royalist motives), and the king failed to assemble an army capable of invading Scotland. The covenanters therefore resolved to force a military decision by invading England. Their invasion met with complete success, and the covenanters entered Newcastle after defeating the king's forces at the battle of Newburn. Charles was forced to open negotiations and accepted the humiliating treaty of Ripon on 17 October, whereby he not only agreed that the Scots army would remain in England, but that he would pay it. The army eventually withdrew from England in August 1641, after a peace settlement had been negotiated in the treaty of London.

Royalist theory: Charles I's strategy
- - - ➤ Proposed royalist invasions and advances
[1] Main army to cross to the Border from England led by Lord Conway
[2] New army raised in Ireland by the earl of Strafford (formerly Lord Wentworth) to land somewhere in south-west Scotland
[3] Part of Strafford's Irish army to land in England to join in the main army's invasion of Scotland
[4] Possible raids on Argyll by the earl of Antrim's men and anti-covenanter refugees from the Highlands
[5] Anti-covenanter Highland clans to rise in arms

Royalist practice
■ Places held for the king
——➤ Movements of royalist forces
(1) Raid by Alasdair MacColla on Islay, November 1640

Covenanters' response
○ Places held for the king but seized or occupied by the covenanters (with dates)
········➤ Movements of covenanting forces
(A) Covenanting armies occupy Aberdeen, 5 May
(B) Marquis of Argyll's Campbell forces march through areas shown thus - Atholl - to subdue or overawe royalist sympathisers
(C) Covenanting forces based in Aberdeen oveawe north-east royalists, making expedition to Banff, August to September
(D) Main covenanting army invades England, defeating the King's forces at Newburn (28 August) and occupying Newcastle, 30 August

The second bishops' war 1640

DS

139

The civil wars 1639 to 1651

[1]   Raid on the Isles by Alasdair MacColla, November 1640.
[2]   Raid on the Isles by Alasdair MacColla, November 1642 to early 1645.
[3]   Marquis of Huntly seizes Aberdeen (March 1644) but soon forced to abandon it.
[4]   Marquis of Montrose seizes Dumfries, but forced to retreat into England.
[5]   Alasdair MacColla sails with Irish confederate expeditionary force from Wexford to Ardnamurchan, June to July 1644. After seeking support from anti-covenanter clans joins Montrose at Blair Atholl, July to August 1644.
[6]   Montrose campaigns, August 1644 to August 1645 (shown in the next two maps).
[7]   Montrose advances south after his final victory at Kilsyth. Attempts to establish a royalist regime, but defeated at Philiphaugh by forces sent home by the Scottish army in England, August to September 1645.
[8]   Montrose goes into exile, having failed to recruit a new army after Philiphaugh, 3 September 1646.
[9]   Alasdair MacColla driven back to Ireland, June 1647, and killed in battle later in the year.
[10] Pluscardine's rising: royalists from Atholl and the north led by Sir Thomas Pluscardine and others were dispersed at Balvenie, March to May 1649.
[11] Montrose's men occupy Orkney, September 1649, and (Montrose himself having joined them) land on the mainland in April 1650: they are routed at Carbisdale, and Montrose was subsequently executed.

ORKNEY

[11]

Carbisdale
27 April 1650

[10]

Balvenie
8 May 1649

[3]

KINTAIL

Glenelg

Kingussie

Aberdeen

[5]

Mingary Castle

ARDNAMURCHAN

[6]   Blair Atholl

[8]

Kinlochaline Castle

Montrose

Duart Castle

Kilsyth
15 Aug 1645

Glasgow

[7]

Bothwell

[1], [2]

Melrose

Philiphaugh
13 Sept 1645

Kelso

[9]

Selkirk   Jedburgh

[4]

Dumfries

[5]

kms
0   25   50   75   100
0 10 20 30 40 50 60
miles

Royalist risings and invasions 1640 to 1650

DS

140

The civil wars 1639 to 1651

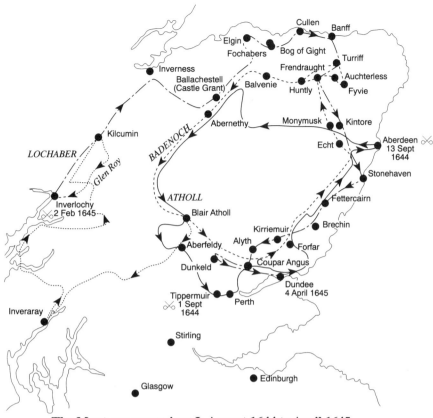

The Montrose campaigns I: August 1644 to April 1645

──────▶ First circuit of the eastern Highlands (Blair Atholl to Blair Atholl) August to October 1644
--------▶ Second circuit of the eastern Highlands (Blair Atholl to Blair Atholl) October to November 1644
··········▶ Ravaging of Argyll (Blair Atholl to Inverlochy) December 1644 to February 1645
─ · ─ ·▶ Inverlochy to Dundee, February to April 1645

DS

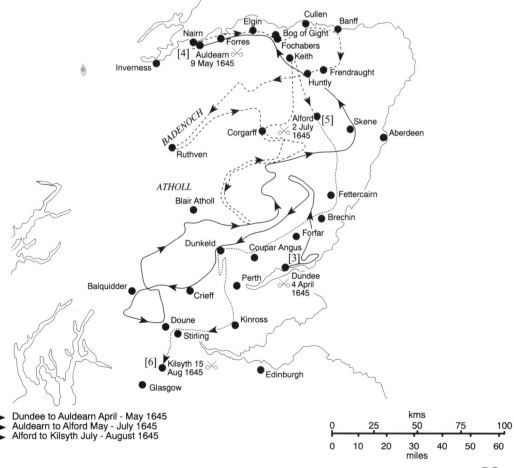

──────▶ Dundee to Auldearn April - May 1645
--------▶ Auldearn to Alford May - July 1645
··········▶ Alford to Kilsyth July - August 1645

The Montrose campaigns II: April - August 1645

DS

The civil wars 1639 to 1651

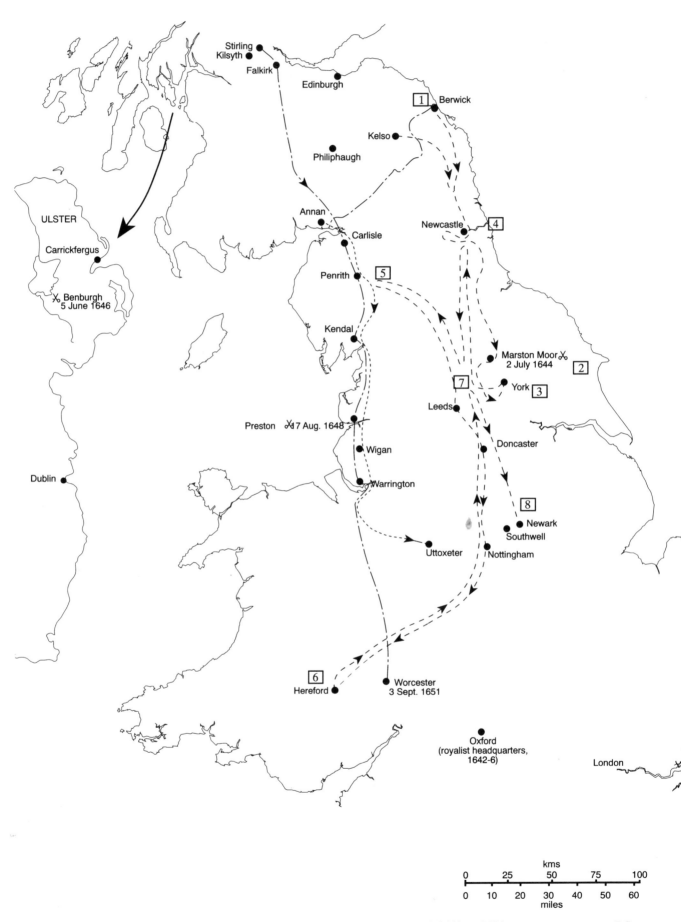

The Scottish armies in England and Ireland 1642 to 1651

DS

The Scottish army in Ireland, 1642-8. The army occupied north-east Ulster, with its headquarters at Carrickfergus. It was successful in preventing the Irish Catholic confederates from over-running all Ulster and destroying the Ulster plantation (a Scottish and English colony), but was defeated in the only major pitched battle it fought at Benburgh. The remnants of the army was dispersed in 1648 by forces of the English parliament after part of the army had left to join the Engagers' invasion of England.

The Scottish army in England, 1644-7. The army played an important role in swinging the balance in the English civil war in favour of parliament, but failed to play the dominant role in defeating the king that the covenanters had hoped for.

[1]   The army crossed the border to England, 19 January 1644.

[2]   The army joined with the armies of the English parliament in defeating the royalist army of Prince Rupert at Marston Moor, 2 July 1644.

[3]   The army took part in the siege of York which surrendered 16 July 1644.

[4]   The army stormed Newcastle, 19 October 1644, and then quartered for the winter.

[5]   In 1645 the army was reluctant to venture south, as Montrose was defeating covenanting armies in Scotland, and there were fears that the king would try to break into Scotland to join him. In May and June it moved west to block a move north by the king. When the army did march south it left forces to help in the siege of Carlisle which surrendered on 28 June 1645.

[6]   After pausing at Nottingham, 22 June to 2 July, the army laid siege to Hereford on 30 July 1645

[7]   Fears of a new attempt of Charles I to reach Scotland led to part of the army marching back north, and in September, the rest of the army followed on news of Montrose's victory at Kilsyth and the king's advance to Worcester.

[8]   In November 1645 the army moved south again (Montrose having been defeated at Philiphaugh) and laid siege to Newark. The siege lasted until May 1645 when the defeated king put himself in the hands of the Scots army and Newark surrendered. In February 1647 it moved back into Scotland, leaving the king to fall into the hands of the English parliament.

The army of the Engagement (a treaty with the imprisoned king) crossed the Border on 8 July 1648, hoping to be joined by English royalist forces and then rescue the king. But English royalist risings had already been defeated; and Cromwell routed the Engagers' army (led by the duke of Hamilton) at Preston. Remnants of the army, cut off from Scotland, retreated south before surrendering at Uttoxeter on 25 August. Cromwell later led forces into Scotland to support the Kirk Party regime which overthew the Engagers after Preston.

Charles II's despairing invasion of England, undertaken after the English invaders had outflanked his army at Stirling. The Scots army left Stirling on 31 July 1651; while it marched through England to the west of the Pennines, Cromwell hastened his army south on the east catching the Scottish army and destroying it at Worcester on 3 September.

The Scottish armies in England and Ireland 1642 to 1651   DS

The civil wars 1639 to 1651

- → The route of English armies
- ⇢ The route of Scottish armies
- ▨ Counties forming the Western Association
- [1] Cromwell leads the English army into Scotland, 22 July 1650.
- [2] English attempts to capture Edinburgh are thwarted, and Cromwell retires to Dunbar, July to August 1650.
- [3] Scottish army defeated at Dunbar, after which all south-east Scotland is occupied by the English. Charles and the Kirk Party regime of the covenanters establish themselves in Perth and Stirling.
- [4] Western Association organises its own virtually autonomous army to resist the English. This godly army of the west disowns the cause of the king, claiming to fight for God alone. The Kirk Party resolves to use force if necessary to crush the Western Association, but before it acts the English advance and defeat the Western army at Hamilton. The Association collapses and the south-west is occupied by the English.
- [5] The Start. Royalists in Fife and in the north plan to rise in arms and seize Perth, freeing Charles II from Kirk Party control. The plot fails, and by a treaty at Strathbogie on 4 November 1650 the royalists lay down arms. But the Kirk Party is now on the verge of collapse, and the royalists soon infiltrate and take over the regime.
- [6] English forces cross the Firth of Forth, rout the Scots at Inverkeithing, and then march north occupying Perth on 2 August 1651, before moving on Stirling and (via Dundee) the north-east. By the end of 1651 all the Lowlands (with the exception of a few castles) are in English hands.
- [7] Charles and the Scottish army, outflanked and cut off from hoped for recruits and supplies from the north by the English advance, leave Stirling on 31 July 1651. They undertake a desperate invasion of England, hoping that English royalists will join them, but are defeated at Worcester.

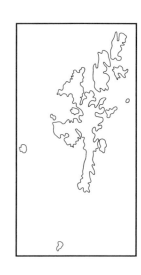

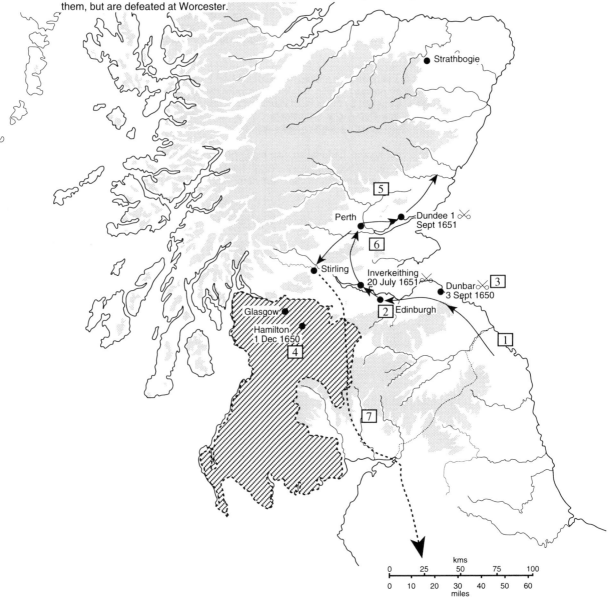

The Cromwellian conquest of Scotland 1650 to 1651

DS

The Pentland Rising of 1666

The Pentland Rising was a popular revolt triggered by the military occupation of the southwest. What began as a local dispute between a contingent of foot guards collecting recusancy fines near Dalry on 13 November 1666 and a handful of vigilantes who objected to the soldiers' methods escalated quickly into a nation-wide rebellion involving over 3,000 Scots. Yet apart from the initial attack on Corporal Deane's troop, the call to assemble at Irongray church two days later, and the subsequent march on Dumfries of 16 November, the uprising was characterised by its spontaneity. In terms of their immediate objectives, for instance, the leaders of the uprising - who were mainly conventicle preachers and small heritors - possessed only a vague plan of having their grievances redressed by marching on the capital, Edinburgh. Ironically, this element of uncertainty lent as much strength as weakness to the revolt. Although the lack of decisive leadership contributed to the rout of the rebels by government troops in the Pentland hills, nonetheless it made the rebels' actions more unpredictable, thereby allowing them to elude the authorities for almost a fortnight.

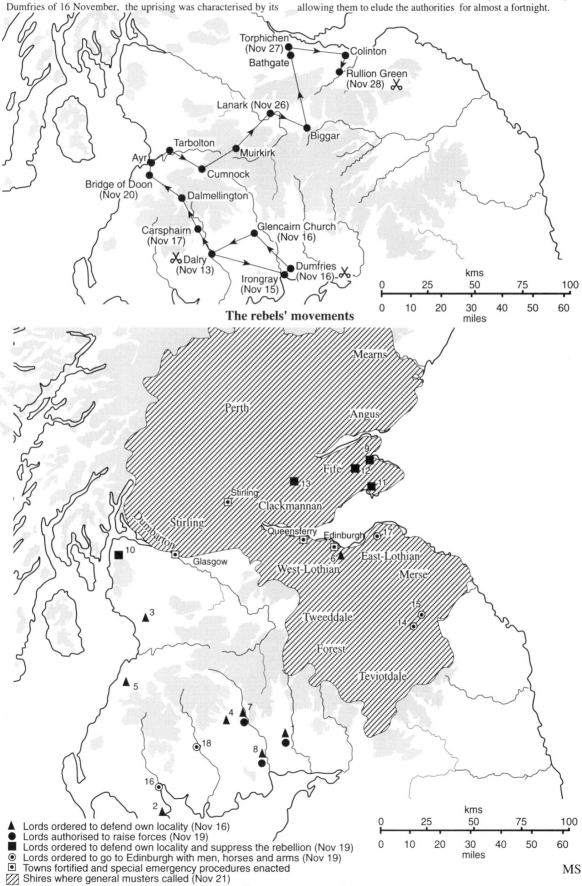

The rebels' movements

The Government reaction

145

The Pentland Rising of 1666

Government response to the rising was initially traditional. In addition to mobilising troops under General Dalziel, the privy council ordered local heritors in the disaffected areas of the southwest as well as the earl of Lothian to defend their own localities and suppress the insurrection. But this conventional solution had to be abandoned when it became evident that the degree of anti-government sentiment in the country had been underestimated. Moreover, it soon became apparent too that heritors in the west who were largely sympathetic to the rebels' case could not be relied on to suppress the uprising. Therefore, a general muster of fencible men was called on 19 November in the eastern shires from the Mearns in the north to the south-eastern Borders where covenanting sentiment was thought to be weaker. As a result, the Pentland Rising saw the lowlands split regionally between the west and east with anti- and pro- government forces emerging from these parts of Scotland respectively.

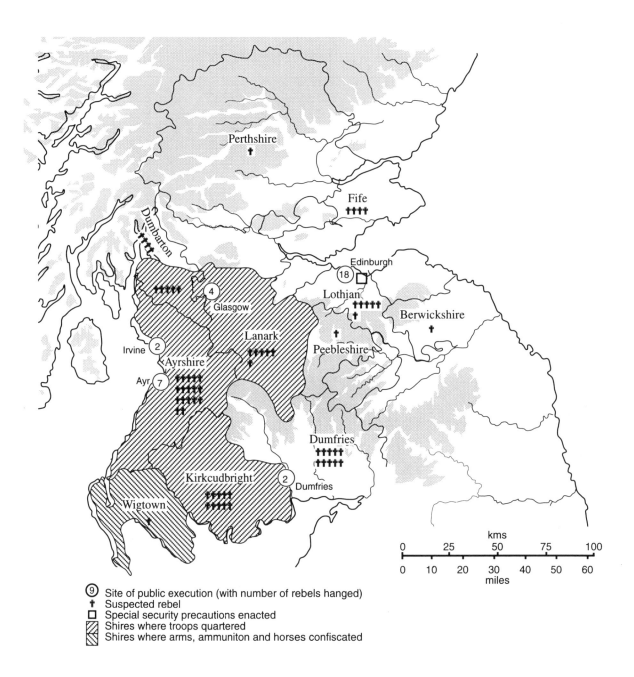

Site of public execution (with number of rebels hanged)
Suspected rebel
Special security precautions enacted
Shires where troops quartered
Shires where arms, ammuniton and horses confiscated

Aftermath and repercussions

MS

Bothwell Brig Rebellion 1679

Tensions between the state and militant nonconformists came to a head in May of 1679 when the murder of Archbishop Sharp on Magus Muir precipitated a series of acts of defiance by conventiclers in different parts of the country which together constituted an uprising. In essence, then, circumstances rather than any orchestrated conspiracy forced the dissidents to take a more aggressive public posture. For example, if the dozen men who met at Gilston and then travelled to Baldinnie on 2 May had not decided at the last minute to kill the Archbishop of St. Andrews - rather than the local sheriff, Sheriff Carmichael - there would have been neither the necessity nor the determination to foment rebellion. However, with the murder of a chief minister of the crown, the assassins had provoked a serious crisis for the government that could only be settled by armed confrontation. Yet for three weeks thereafter little activity took place to confirm the authorities' suspicions that the long-awaited rebellion was imminent. The main conspirators

including Hackston of Rathillet had gone into hiding only to surface again on 25 May at a large, ambulatory conventicle in Avondale led by Robert Hamilton. Here, with the support of over 3,000 devoted followers, Hamilton advocated the need for a popular rising: a decision further legitimised by the creation of a manifesto which was written in Glasgow, approved in Strathaven and, finally, published in Rutherglen on 29 May to coincide with the king's birthday celebrations. The Caroline government's response to this declaration of war was essentially two-fold. Firstly, not only were general musters called in nearly all Scottish shires with the exception of those in the southwest but English troops were dispatched by sea to Berwick. Secondly, in addition to fortifying the eastern burghs of Berwick, Stirling, Blackness, East Wemyss and Linlithgow, a ring of garrisons was strategically placed around the capital, Edinburgh. These precautions reflected the widely-held belief that apart from some limited support evident among the radical conventiclers of Fife, the rebellion could be contained

The Bothwell Brig Rebellion: the progress of the rebellion   MS

within the bounds of the western shires of Ayr, Dumbarton, Renfrew and Lanark. Of the five major battles or skirmishes which took place between 1 June and 22 June, the early battles fought at Loudoun Hill and Glasgow ended in victory for the rebels. However, both the skirmish at Gala Water and West Calder involving smaller numbers of combatants turned into a rout of the dissidents. Thus when the king's army gathered at Kirk of Shotts on 21 June prepared to march on the main rebel camp at Bothwell Bridge neither side could entertain the expectation that an easy victory was assured.

Bothwell Bridge proved to be the rebels' last stand. Military inferiority compounded by a lack of martial discipline and

effective leadership among the dissident forces account for much of the ease with which the king's army won the battle. And, apart from a final armed encounter at Aird's Moss on 22 July 1680 where some of the leading insurgents including Richard Cameron, Hackston of Rathillet and Donald Cargill were captured or killed, no other large-scale manifestations of popular discontent took place. Instead the dissidents were forced into a more protracted, guerilla warfare where acts of civil disobedience took other forms such as the publication of anti-government declarations. In the immediate aftermath of the rising, the government showed itself to be more concerned with moderation than retribution. Although 36 southern lairds were forfeited for their failure to join the king's host and two circuit courts - roughly one for eastern Scotland and another for the west - were set up to administer pardons and loyalty oaths to rank and file participants, no large scale executions or show trials were organised. However, given that 800 rebels (20%) were killed in battle, this approach may have been part of a conscious effort by the government to avoid the creation of any more covenanting martyrs.

The Bothwell Brig Rebellion: the aftermath   MS

Clan support for the house of Stuart

The clans - the Gaelic-speaking, patriarchal amalgams of kinship, local association and feudal deference-were the bedrock of both the Royalist campaigns of 1644-47 and the fist Jacobite rising of 1689-90. The persistence of hosting and the ready mobilisation of the clans by passing round the fiery cross meant a lower threshold in the Highlands than the Lowlands for the resort to arms. The militarism of the clans can be overplayed, however. The resolution of territorial disputes by the wholesale recourse of clans to arms was becoming less of an occasional practice, more of a rarity in the course of the seventeenth century. Technological change meant that it was becoming no longer fashionable to take arms off trees. The chiefs and leading gentry of the clans were increasingly reluctant to meet the expense of providing guns. The professional backbone to the Royalist and Jacobite campaigns was formed by Irish troops. Three regiments served under James Graham, marquis of Montrose during the civil war, and John Graham, viscount Dundee from 1689. The "Highland charge" deployed successfully on both campaigns was probably introduced to Scotland by Montrose's major-general, Alasdair MacColla, who can be said to have imported from Ulster in the summer of 1644 a tactic for irregular infantry which was designed to suit highland terrain, the technology clans could afford and the effectiveness of the sword and targe in close-quarters after the discharge of firearms.

In terms of strategy, clan support for the house of Stuart was most effective in the pursuit of guerilla warfare. After joining forces in August 1644, Montrose and MacColla commenced a twelve-month campaign of continuous movement running up a series of six bloody victories that culminated in the defeat of Covenanting forces at Kilsyth. Each victory attracted increased support from the clans. However, the military success of guerilla warfare was not converted into political achievement, notably the capture of leading towns, the key to control in the Lowlands. Within a month of parting from MacColla and the western clans, Montrose's fortunes went into rapid decline. From his defeat at Philiphaugh in September 1645, until his departure into exile twelve months later, Montrose was a spent force in Scotland. Although he was eventually forced to retire to Ireland by July 1647, MacColla fared relatively better on the western seaboard where his continued pursuit of guerilla warfare was distinctly less naive and more constructive. Other than the MacDonalds of Sleat who preferred to remain rather than accept his leadership, MacColla's affiliations to the lineal descendants of the Lords of the Isles created a ready reservoir of support. Unrivalled charisma based on his personal valour in battle and the fact that he was not required to lay siege to large towns enabled MacColla to occupy Kintyre and Islay and thus maintain, for eighteen months, a Royalist bridgehead with Ireland. Nor did the successful pursuit of guerilla warfare prove politically remunerative during the first Jacobite rising. Dundee's stunning victory at Killiecrankie in July 1689, was neutralised by his death in the course of battle. The burgeoning clan support occasioned by his personal charisma and his inspired generalship was soon dissipated by insipid and inept leadership from his officers with the Irish forces who assumed command but failed to make a military breakthrough either into central Lowlands or areas of Jacobite affinity in the north-east. Admittedly, the Stuart cause was not helped by the fluctuating nature of clan support during the Jacobite rising as during the civil war. While undoubtedly influenced by their desire to return home with booty, this fluctuating support was attributable more to the clans' reluctance to disrupt the agrarian cycle of sowing and harvesting and, above all, to their aversion to prolonged absence from their patrimonies which sustained campaigning left exposed to the ravages of cateran bands or reprisals by political opponents. For although around 5,000 clansmen were mobilised during the civil war and again for the Jacobite rising, the 47 foremost clans were never united in their support for the Stewarts albeit over 60% of the clans actively supported or shifted their support in favour of the royal house on both occasions.

Clan support for the house of Stuart as hereditary rulers of Scotland was based primarily on the projection of traditional values of clanship onto the national political stage. As the chiefs were the protectors of the clan patrimonies, so were the Stuarts trustees for Scotland. At the same time, clan support for Charles I during the civil war was essentially reactionary. The 21 clans who declared unequivocally for the Royalist cause were fighting less in favour of that absentee monarch than against the Covenanting Movement which was making unprecedented demands for ideological, financial and military commitment. More especially the clans were reacting against powerful nobles whose public espousal of the Covenanting cause masked the private pursuit of territorial ambitions. Thus, the Mackays took up the Royalist mantle to defend their patrimony of Strathnaver against the acquisitive overtures of John Gordon, earl of Sutherland. The most acquisitive influence, however, was undoubtedly that of the Clan Campbell, the main beneficiaries of the expropriation of MacDonalds from Kintyre, Islay, Jura and Ardnamurchan since the outset of the seventeenth century. Having been evicted by Campbells from Colonsay in 1639, the determination of MacColla to perpetuate the feud under the Royalist mantle was endorsed by the Irish regiments under his command which were recruited almost exclusively from among his kinsmen on the Ulster estates of Randal MacDonnell, earl of Antrim, whose own territorial ambitions on the western seaboard had encouraged Campbell forces enlisted in the Covenanting army despatched to Ireland in 1642 to wreak havoc on the isle of Rathlin and the glens of Antrim. The deliberate but wanton ravaging of Argyll and northern Perthshire during the winters of 1644 and 1645 persuaded six clans hitherto contained within the territorial spheres of Campbell influence to cut loose in support of the Royalist cause albeit the two most prominent, the Lamonts and MacDougalls, were subsequently massacred for their temerity to switch sides and plunder Campbell estates. The polarizing impact of the Campbells was not confined to the western seaboard since their chief, Archibald, marquis of Argyle, in the four years prior to the outbreak of the civil war, had utilised military commissions not only to harry suspect Royalists in Atholl, braes of Angus, Braemar and Deeside, but also to push his territorial claims over Badenoch and Lochaber. Because their chief was in the tutelage of the marquis, Camerons of Lochiel who held their lands of the house of Argyle, maintained a prudent neutrality throughout the civil war. Conversely, aversion to the hitherto pervasive influence of the Royalist magnate, George Gordon, marquis of Huntly, in the central Highlands, persuaded the Frasers and originally the Grants to declare for the Covenanters and for the Mackintoshes, but not all of the Clan Chattan to remain neutral. The willingness of the Royalist commanders to despoil territories of clans reluctant to join their cause convinced the Grants of the expediency of switching sides. The MacLeods of Dunvegan and the Sinclairs limited their support for the Covenanting Movement to the protection of their clan patrimonies. Torn between the defence of their clan patrimonies and the political ambitioning of their vacillating chief, George, second earl of Seaforth, the MacKenzies, together with their allies, the MacRaes and MacLeods of Assynt, demonstrated an unparalleled lack of touch in switching adversely whenever Royalist or Covenanting forces enjoyed ascendancy.

While the Campbells and the other clans who campaigned offensively for the Covenanting Movement were in broad sympathy with presbyterianism, the militant catholicism of the Irish forces, while espoused by MacColla and the leading branches of the ClanDonald, was certainly not shared by the majority of the Royalist clans. However, religion was a principal factor influencing clans to come out for the first Jacobite rising. The sporadic inroads of Catholic missions served to solidify the opposition of former Royalist clans to the disposition of James VII. More significant in attracting support from hitherto neutral clans and in persuading Covenanting clans to adopt a neutral standpoint was the spread of episcopalianism during the Restoration era, which not only provided a religious complement to the hierarchical nature of clanship, but inculated a spirit of obedience and submission to royal authority throughout Gaeldom. Accordingly, the replacement of James VII by William of Orange was interpreted as a breach of patriarchal duty by Gaelic poets for whom the sundering of genealogical continuity imperilled the lawful exercise of government which, in turn, subverted the maintenance of a just political order. Far from being tyrannical or oppressive, James VII had won a favourable press from the clans. When duke of York, he had instituted the commission for pacifying the Highlands in 1682 which, for the next three years, had sought the co-operation of chiefs and leading gentry in maintaining law and order. This commission represented a brief, but welcome, respite from the grasping and intimidatory policies of successive regimes in the Restoration era which had sought to tarnish the Highlands as an area of endemic lawlessness in order to maintain a standing army and facilitate the collection of onerous taxes. Moreover, James had proved notably responsive in redressing the

Clan support for the house of Stuart

acquisitiveness of the house of Argyle. Although the marquis had been executed in 1661, when his son Archibald was restored as ninth earl two years later he embarked upon a credit squeeze that revived his father's policy of forcing heavily indebted chiefs and leading gentry to accept the feudal superiority of their house. By exploiting the legal technicalities of public and private indebtedness, Argyle even had chiefs and leading gentry of the Macleans of Duart expropriated from Tiree, Mull and Morven by 1679. Six years later, when the ninth earl rebelled against the accession of James VII who had engineered his forfeiture in 1681, over 4000 clansmen under the command of John Murray, marquis of Atholl, drawn from clans throughout Gaeldom, but predominantly from the victims of Argyle's acquisitiveness, systematically ravaged mid-Argyll, Cowal and Kintyre. This "Atholl Raid" gave a foretaste of the simple antipathy to the restoration of the house of Argyle at the Revolution. Clans within Campbell spheres of influence who had switched their allegiance in the course of the civil war declared openly for James

VII in 1689. Only the MacAllisters declared for the Whigs, as earlier for the Covenanters, before switching sides.

The 27 clans that declared unequivocally for the Jacobite cause demonstrated not just an increased willingness to support the royal house at the outset of campaigning, but also masked a pronounced movement of 10 clans in favour of James VII with a loss of 4 former supporters of Charles I. The only Royalist clan actually to declare for the Whigs were the Mackays, principally because one of their leading gentry, major-general Hugh Macrae of Scourbie, commanded William of Orange's forces in Scotland. Although the MacDonnells of Antrim opted to concentrate their political energies on Irish affairs, a small contingent from the Isle of Rathlin served with the Kintyre clans fighting for James VII. Of the 25 clans who maintained the same political standpoint towards

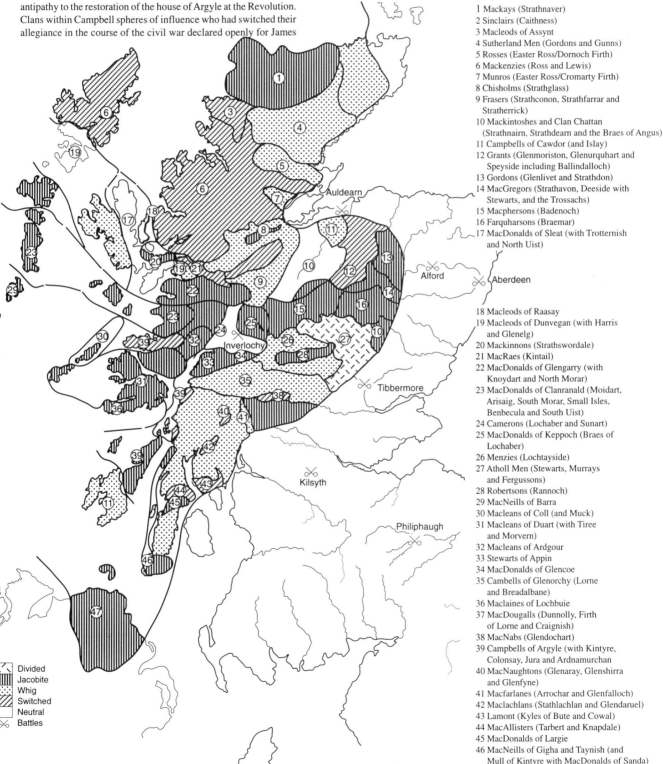

1 Mackays (Strathnaver)
2 Sinclairs (Caithness)
3 Macleods of Assynt
4 Sutherland Men (Gordons and Gunns)
5 Rosses (Easter Ross/Dornoch Firth)
6 Mackenzies (Ross and Lewis)
7 Munros (Easter Ross/Cromarty Firth)
8 Chisholms (Strathglass)
9 Frasers (Strathconon, Strathfarrar and Stratherrick)
10 Mackintoshes and Clan Chattan (Strathnairn, Strathdearn and the Braes of Angus)
11 Campbells of Cawdor (and Islay)
12 Grants (Glenmoriston, Glenurquhart and Speyside including Ballindalloch)
13 Gordons (Glenlivet and Strathdon)
14 MacGregors (Strathavon, Deeside with Stewarts, and the Trossachs)
15 Macphersons (Badenoch)
16 Farquharsons (Braemar)
17 MacDonalds of Sleat (with Trotternish and North Uist)
18 Macleods of Raasay
19 Macleods of Dunvegan (with Harris and Glenelg)
20 Mackinnons (Strathswordale)
21 MacRaes (Kintail)
22 MacDonalds of Glengarry (with Knoydart and North Morar)
23 MacDonalds of Clanranald (Moidart, Arisaig, South Morar, Small Isles, Benbecula and South Uist)
24 Camerons (Lochaber and Sunart)
25 MacDonalds of Keppoch (Braes of Lochaber)
26 Menzies (Lochtayside)
27 Atholl Men (Stewarts, Murrays and Fergussons)
28 Robertsons (Rannoch)
29 MacNeills of Barra
30 Macleans of Coll (and Muck)
31 Macleans of Duart (with Tiree and Morvern)
32 Macleans of Ardgour
33 Stewarts of Appin
34 MacDonalds of Glencoe
35 Cambells of Glenorchy (Lorne and Breadalbane)
36 Maclaines of Lochbuie
37 MacDougalls (Dunnolly, Firth of Lorne and Craignish)
38 MacNabs (Glendochart)
39 Campbells of Argyle (with Kintyre, Colonsay, Jura and Ardnamurchan
40 MacNaughtons (Glenaray, Glenshirra and Glenfyne)
41 Macfarlanes (Arrochar and Glenfalloch)
42 Maclachlans (Stathlachlan and Glendaruel)
43 Lamont (Kyles of Bute and Cowal)
44 MacAllisters (Tarbert and Knapdale)
45 MacDonalds of Largie
46 MacNeills of Gigha and Taynish (and Mull of Kintyre with MacDonalds of Sanda)
47 MacDonnells of Antrim (including the Rathlin Isles).

Clan support for the Stuarts: the Scottish civil war 1644 to 1647   AIM

Clan support for the house of Stuart

the house of Stuart, 17 loyal to Charles I remained loyal to James VII, albeit the MacDonalds of Keppoch remained apart from the main contingent of Jacobite forces, being more committed to plunder than military campaigning. The Mackintoshes, against whom they fought the last clan battle at Mulroy on the braes of Lochaber in August 1688, were the only clan to remain neutral during the Jacobite rising as during the civil war. No more than 3 clans committed to the Covenanting cause sided with William of Orange, albeit 12 actually fought exclusively for the former and 8 for the latter. The most notable loss arose from the breaking of ranks within the Clan Campbell. Not only did clansmen in territories appropriated by the Campbells in the course of the seventeenth century fail to adhere to the Whig cause, but the principal cadet, John Campbell of Glenorchy, recently ennobled as the earl of Breadalbane, affirmed his political independence of the house of Argyle by remaining neutral. That family solidarity was less pronounced during the first

Jacobite rising than during the civil war was borne out by the split allegiance of Grants and the Atholl Men. Whereas the majority of Grants in Strathspey followed their chief in declaring for William of Orange, the Grants of Ballindalloch consistently adhered to the Jacobite cause while the Grants in Glenmoriston and Glenurquhart, after an intimidatory measure of persuasion from neighbours, switched in favour of James VII. Although the marquis distanced himself from commitment to either cause, a small contingent of Atholl Men supported the Whigs at the instigation of his eldest son, Lord Murray; but the majority switched to Jacobitism in the aftermath of Killiecrankie under the leadership of his second son, Lord James. While the extension of civil war between as well as among the clans was the most innovatory feature of the first Jacobite rising, the MacKenzies and their associates were again afflicted by inept leadership. Although Jacobite in sympathy they were neutral by default because Kenneth, fourth earl of Seaforth, dallied with James VII on his hapless Irish venture. When Seaforth belatedly returned to rally his clansmen in the spring of 1690, the discredit of the Irish officers commanding the Jacobite clans was all but complete. It is important to stress, in conclusion, that the clans were contained rather than defeated in the course of the first Jacobite rising. That the Whig government should instigate the massacre of MacDonalds of Glencoe in February 1692, because of the technical default of their aged chief in making timely acceptance of its offer of indemnity, served to consolidate support among the clans for the exiled house of Stuart.

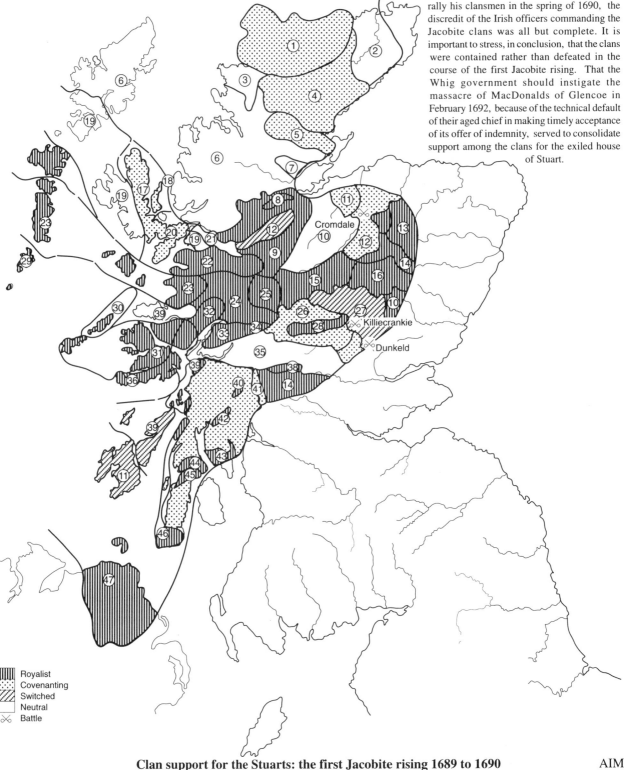

Royalist
Covenanting
Switched
Neutral
Battle

Clan support for the Stuarts: the first Jacobite rising 1689 to 1690

AIM

150

The 1707 Union: support and opposition

The treaty of union of 1707 was the product of diplomatic brinkmanship, military intimidation and political manipulation on the part of an English ministry intent on an incorporating parliamentary union and of economic defeatism, financial chicanery and political ineptitude on the part of Scottish politicians intent on personal advantage from the loss of national independence.

By 1702, Anglo-Scottish relations were crystallizing into constitutional crisis which made the continuance of the regal union no longer a viable political option. The thirteen-year rule of William of Orange had witnessed the blatant sacrificing of Scottish trade on the altar of English foreign policy. The death of the last surviving child of Anna, the new queen, and the recognition of the Jacobite pretender as James VIII and III by Louis XIV of France, meant there was a real danger that the current continental imbroglio, the war of the Spanish succession, would spill over into the war of the British succession. In the event, Anglo-Scottish hostilities were restricted to a legislative war. The English parliament having passed the act of settlement in 1701, unilaterally vesting the succession on the house of Hanover, the Scottish estates retaliated with a tripartite package in 1703. The act of security and the wine act upheld respectively the independent right of the Scottish estates to fix the succession and authorise trade with France; the act meant peace and asserted the estates' right to assume an independent foreign policy on the death of Queen Anne. The Scottish bluff was called in 1705 when the English parliament passed the alien act which threatened to treat Scots as foreigners unless the Hanoverian succession was accepted unequivocally by the estates. At the same time, the Scottish estates were invited to resume the discussions for a closer union which had been an early casualty of the legislative war.

Economic and social factors played an important part in persuading Scottish politicians, in particular the aristocratic factions which dominated parliamentary politics, to treat for union. There was undoubtedly an aura of economic defeatism in the country at large occasioned by the swallowing up of Scottish venture capital in the Darien fiasco and compounded by five years of intensive dearth and famine that ended in 1700. More immediately, the alien act had posed a direct challenge to the rent-rolls of the aristocracy which depended heavily on open access to English markets for such commodities as coal, linen and, above all, livestock. That 1 in 7 Scottish nobles had English wives at the resumption of negotiations, testifies not only the their steady assimilation into the British ruling class, but also to their growing dependence on the English marriage market to build up disposable income.

Notwithstanding these factors, the accomplishment of union within two years must be attributed primarily to political considerations. The English ministry guiding the queen had a clearly defined objective - an incorporating parliamentary union to shut permanently the Scottish back-door to military invasion by a foreign power. The English treasury was prepared to advance $20,000 sterling (£240,000 Scots) to influence voting in the Scottish estates. For their part, the Scottish estates, though initially not inclined to accept a parliamentary union, were unable to sustain a common front in support of alternative options which ranged from complete separation to federalism. Moreover, politicians across the political spectrum were becoming conditioned to seek the support and clientage of the English ministry in their competitive drive for office. The Court party, which had favoured shoring up the regal union until its leader, the duke of Queensberry, was threatened with loss of backing by the English ministry, espoused parliamentary union in a salvage operation to retain office. Opposed to the Court was the Country, not so much a party as a confederation. At the one extreme was a rump of constitutional reformers, the only principled opponents of parliamentary union, who were intent on freeing Scotland from the shackles of aristocratic privilege as of the English ministry. At the other extreme were the Jacobites, the one political grouping prepared to condone the military option, but weakened by the defection of episcopalians who placed the prospect of toleration before the restoration of the house of Stuart. The dominant grouping within the Country was the old party frustrated placemen and the disappointed investors in Darien, led by a quixotic vacillator, the duke of Hamilton, whose indecisiveness occasioned this defection of aristocratic associates, the formation of the new party - known as the "flying Squadron' or the "Squadrone Volante" for their desperate pursuit of office - and, most crucially, the choice of commissioners to treat for an incorporating union being left to the queen not the estates. As a result, the twenty-four articles of the treaty of union presented for the approval of the Scottish estates on 3 October 1706, were not so much the fruits of diplomatic negotiations as the dictates of the English ministry. To underline the seriousness of their intent, the English ministry had moved troops to Berwick and northern Ireland to be held within striking distance of Edinburgh and the west of Scotland, the main areas of anticipated opposition to the union.

From the crucial vote on the first article of union on 4 November, which revealed a majority of 33 in favour of a united kingdom of Great Britain, the Country confederation mounted a continuous barrage of protests and amendments to negate, alter and delay the passage of the remaining articles. Addresses against the union were also forthcoming from around half the shires (18) and about a third (21) of the royal burghs. Nonetheless, despite the general assembly of the Kirk expressing its reservations and the convention of royal burghs its outright opposition, the treaty was ratified on 16 January 1707, when the majority in favour was augmented to 41. In only two shires did the parliamentary commissioners respond positively to the addresses and vote solidly against the ratification. The burgh commissioners were no more responsive: eight continued to vote in favour of the union though one did abstain on the ratification. While these addresses were undoubtedly instigated and concerted by the parliamentary opposition, the Court party was unable to mobilize any addresses in favour of the union. Instead, its influence was applied, particularly in the Highlands and south-west, to suppress the endeavours of gentry and burgesses to petition against the union. Although the addresses led no significant shift in the voting pattern against ratification, their presentation enabled the Country confederation to claim that the treaty of union lacked public support, a claim given further plausibility by popular protests against the union and recalcitrant magistrates in the burghs of Glasgow, Dumfries and Edinburgh and more convincingly, by sixty-two exceptional and unsolicited addresses from presbyteries (3), towns (9) and parishes (50), the latter usually in clusters. These addresses against the union came predominantly from west-central and south-western Scotland, where local communities drew consciously on covenanting traditions of supplicating in support of religious and civil liberties. The extreme Cameronians in the south-west went so far as to submit their own eclectic band against the union. The leavening of petitions from around the firth of Forth, from communities involved in the burgeoning coal and salt industry, were also inspired, perhaps, by the union's threatened eradication of differential trading tariffs.

The voting pattern for the first article and the final ratification is noteworthy not just for the demonstrable lack of response from the estates to public opinion as expressed through addresses and popular protests, but for the increase in abstentions and absentees, from 25 members at the vote on the first article to 46 on the ratification. In effect, the union was ratified by default rather than by an absolute majority. No more than 6 members actually switched sides at a net loss of 2 votes to the Country confederation yet, only 15 members abstained or were absent on both occasions. Thus, the increase in abstentions and absences masks considerable volatility in voting among the estates. The net loss to the Court party from such volatility was 8 votes as against 12 votes for the Country confederation. Equally, the Court vote was appreciably more resolute. 102 members voted for both the first article and the ratification; whereas only 59 members voted against both.

The relative solidity of the Court party and the greater volatility in voting exhibited by adherents of the Country confederation cannot be dissociated from the politics of influence, or, less politely, bribery. The court, with the backing of the English ministry, was undoubtedly able to use the spoils of office to shore up its own voting and retain the commitment of aristocratic defectors, including the new party. The principal fund of influence was the advance of £20,000 sterling from the English treasury ostensibly to pay arrears of pensions and allowances from the civil list. Only 26 members of the estates eligible to vote actually received part payments of arrears. In only 1 instance did a recipient actually switch sides, though 2 opponents of the first article did abstain at the ratification of the treaty. More pertinently, 9 recipients had no apparent claim to arrears and another 6 were not required to

The 1707 Union: support and opposition

acknowledge receipt for sums paid, fuelling suspicions that they were again reimbursed from the capital equivalent (of £308,085-10/-) conceded to compensate Scottish interests materially disadvantaged through alignment to higher English fiscal dues, exchange rates and national debt. This expectation that over 58% of the capital equivalent would be utilized to make reparations for venture capital lost at Darien was a further powerful inducement for members of the estates not to oppose the union. The bulk of the sum advanced for arrears of salary (£12,325 sterling) was placed at the personal disposal of Queensberry, as the queen's commissioner to the estates, and was certainly distributed covertly, not only to shore up the Court, but also to pay informers and, perhaps, agents provocateur in order to expose and discredit any recourse to the military option by the parliamentary opposition or their adherents in the country. That the estates' proceedings on the union were conducted against a continuous background of popular disturbances in the capital and well-founded rumours of risings involving Cameronians in the south-west and clans in the Highlands served also to justify the intimidatory presence of standing forces as a parliamentary guard to expedite the passage and ratification of the treaty.

But the accomplishment of parliamentary union cannot wholly be attributed to the politics of influence and military intimidation nor even to the Court's concession of an act within the treaty confirming the Presbyterian establishment, a political masterstroke which removed the Kirk as the galvaniser of addresses against the union from presbyteries and local communities. A large measure of responsibility for the eventual ratification of the treaty

of union rests with the inept political leadership of the Country confederation also, in particular with the duke of Hamilton, who personally sabotaged three manoeuvres to stem the parliamentary tide running in favour of the Court. Following the estates' approval of the first article, moves were set afoot to mobilize the political extremes in the country, the Cameronians and the clans, to effect a coup d'etat. The order to rendezvous outside the town of Hamilton was countermanded peremptorily by the duke who had taken fright at the prospect of dissolving the estates by force of arms. Instead of the anticipated 7-8000 fighting men, less than 50 kept the rendezvous. Hamilton secreted himself in his mansion until the potential insurgents dispersed leaderless. As the Court was now on guard against the possibility of an armed rising, the opposition, again inspired primarily by the Jacobites, decided upon a mass lobby of parliament-house by the gentry who had submitted addresses from the shires against the union. Although over 500

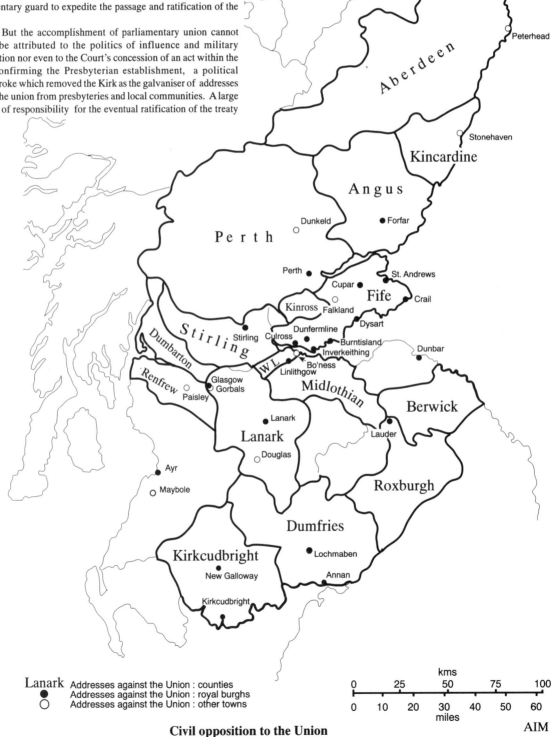

Lanark	Addresses against the Union : counties
●	Addresses against the Union : royal burghs
○	Addresses against the Union : other towns

Civil opposition to the Union

AIM

152

The 1707 Union: support and opposition

gentry were mobilized to demand that the estates suspend proceedings until the queen be acquainted with the true extent of public antipathy towards the union, the lobby was forestalled by Hamilton's insistence that any address to the Crown must acknowledge the Hanoverian succession. The same condition was later repeated by Hamilton to renege on his commitment to present a protest against the estates proceeding to ratify the treaty. This protest was intended as a prelude to the wholesale secession of the Country confederation from the estates, a tactic used successfully to scupper proposals for union in 1702, in order to force a general election in which the Court would be obliged to campaign for specific mandate to ratify the treaty. Thus, the shortfall of 17 votes in the number opposing ratification as against those opposing the first article was essentially a reflection of Jacobite disillusionment with the duke of Hamilton.

Two months after the treaty of union had been ratified with comparative ease in English parliament, the parliamentary incorporation of Scotland into the united kingdom came into force on 1 May 1707. The accomplishment of union resulted in a drastic reduction in the number of voting members in the last session of the Scottish estates eligible to sit in both houses at Westminster. In the Lords, the representation of Scottish peers was reduced from 7 to 16. In the Commons, the gentry as shire commissioners were reduced from 82 to 30 and the burgesses from 66 to 15. Ultimately, therefore, the treaty of union was a self-inflicted act of political laceration on the part of the Scottish estates.

● Addresses against the Union : individual parishes
○ Addresses against the Union : clusters of parishes (with names of parishes alongside)

Ecclesiastical / parochial opposition to the Union

Total Voting Membership - 225

First Article (4 November, 1706)

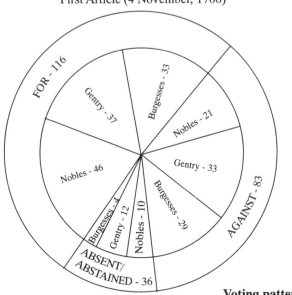

Ratification (16 January, 1707)

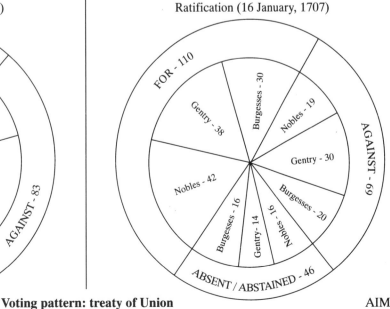

Voting pattern: treaty of Union

AIM

153

Scotland and the New World

In 1621 James VI granted to Sir William Alexander the lands in Canada between the English lands of Newfoundland and New England and up to the St Lawrence. Later the crown granted baronies of 16,000 acres from land that Alexander surrendered from his grant. Quite separately, in 1628. Charles created in his favour a strip of land 100 leagues across North America, but not extending to lands effectively possessed by the king or other Christian princes in league with the king. The charter apparently proceeds on the representation of the area by Ortelius whose map does not show the Great Lakes. and has the St Lawrence rising in the modern states of Indiana or Illinois. The two lordships did not endure and succumbed to the rivalries of the European powers.

Approximate boundary of Lordship and Lieutenancy of Nova Scotia, 1621

Approximate boundary of Lordship of Canada, 1628

Erroneous course of upper St Lawrence (Ortelius)

NEW FRANCE   Lands possessed by kings and princes of Europe

Lordship of Nova Scotia: the lordship of Canada   PGBM

Scotland and the New World

In general, people associate Scottish settlement in early seventeenth century America with Nova Scotia and overlook the virtually permanent Scottish presence in the contemporary West Indies, which had a far greater impact on the society and economy of Scotland.

The earliest mention of a Scottish merchant ship leaving for the West Indies is 1611. In 1626 a Scotsman, James Hay, earl of Carlisle, was first to be appointed by Charles I as Proprietor of Barbados. Subsequently a number of Scots were sent there as administrators. William Powrie, planter from Peebles was one such. There is evidence of direct trade links between Scotland and Barbados, Martinique and other Caribbean islands during the 1630s and 1640s, which led to settlement by merchants and planters. The English Civil War led to a marked increase in the numbers of Scots in these islands because of the transportation of hundreds of Scottish prisoners-of war by Cromwell after the battles of Dunbar and Worcester 1650-1651. After the Restoration, the Scottish Privy Council followed the English precedent by banishing criminals, social undesirables and religious dissidents to the English Plantations in the West Indies. Its records outline numerous requests by merchant-skippers for felons to be shipped to the English colonies. Scottish indentured servants were also sailing via the English ports of London, Bristol and Liverpool. During the 1660s the Dutch islands of Curacao, Saba and St Eustacia also were home to numbers of Scots. By the 1680s serious consideration was being given to the establishment of an independent Scots colony in the West Indies, but this plan did not come to fruition.

The Scottish connection began with small scale success in Barbados but ended in large scale failure in Darien. These links, however, were the foundation of the substantial trade and settlement in the following century.

Places with Scottish presence
- (1)   1625 to 1650
- (2)   1651 to 1675
- (3)   1676 to 1707

The Scots in the Caribbean 1626 to 1707

DDo

Scotland and the New World

Darien was the name given to the entire isthmus now known as Panama. It was the Spanish province in central America between Veragua and New Granada; but the name came to be applied later to the smaller area between the Gulf of S Miguel on the east and the Gulf of Uraba on the west. This is where the Scottish settlement was. After 1821, Panama became a province of the independent republic of Colombia; and in 1903, Panama, with the backing of the United States of America, declared itself to be a separate republic. Now, the republic is divided into nine provinces of which two are Panama and Darien; and part of the original Darien is still within the republic of Colombia.

There are other places called Darien: Santa Maria Antiqua del Darien, known as "Darien", is situated on the western shore of the Gulf of Ubara: it was the first Spanish settlement on the American mainland (1509). There are other Dariens on the river Tuva, and in the modern Canal Zone. (These places are seldom marked on modern maps.)

The project of a passage across central America at the point chosen by the Scots was no more fanciful than the passage from Colon to (Old) Panama which the Spaniards used for three centuries. The Spaniards had tried the Darien passage before and the English were considering a colony there. Across the Serrania del Darien, was the river Tuira, which was navigable for 100 miles of its length of 190 miles.

In 1698, the Scottish colonists landed near Punta Escoces and founded a colony called New Caledonia: its capital was New Edinburgh and its fort, New St Andrews. In February 1700 the Scots with Indian allies defeated a Spanish force at Tubuganti, but were themselves besieged by the Spaniards and had to surrender to them in March. That was the end of the Darien project.

The expedition left some Scottish effect on the place-names of central America: Punta Escoces, Caledonia Bay and the Caledonian Mountains.

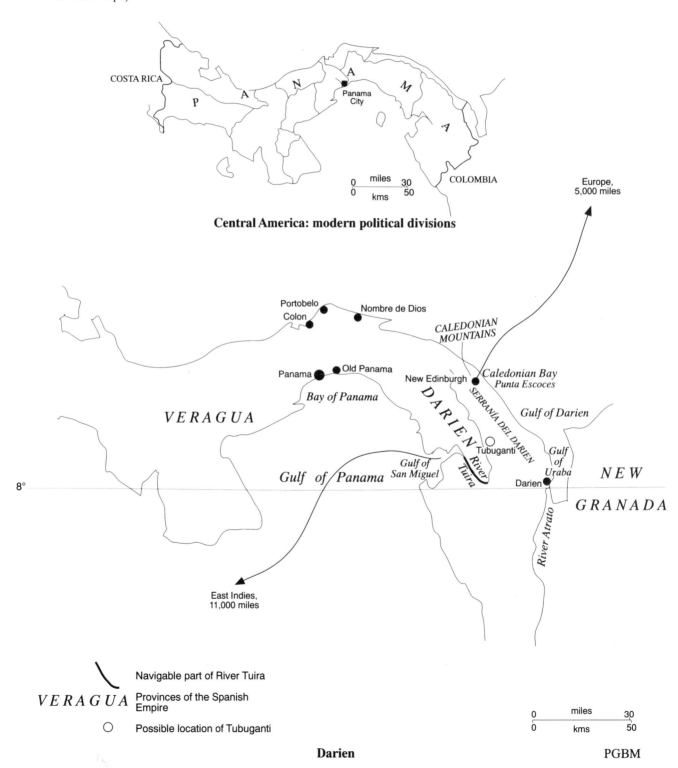

Central America: modern political divisions

VERAGUA   Navigable part of River Tuira

VERAGUA   Provinces of the Spanish Empire

○   Possible location of Tubuganti

Darien

Administration

Place-dates of royal charters to 1296

The practice of adding a date of place (i.e. 'given, *datum*, at Edinburgh') to written acts or charters authenticated by the king's seal seems to have begun in Scotland early in the twelfth century, possibly as early as the reign of Alexander I (1107-24). By the later years of David I (1124-53) it was unusual to omit the place-date. A date of time, in the form of the day of the month only, was added from 1195, the year being added about 1222. There are occasional examples of time-dates (normally indicating the year only) in royal acts from David I's reign onwards, almost certainly supplied by ecclesiastical beneficiaries who were more conscious of chronology than their lay contemporaries. Clearly, the provision of a place-date gives the historian extremely valuable information about the areas and places where king and court were normally located, although a word of caution is necessary in respect of these maps. Firstly, the mappable place-dates are obviously only those recorded in acts whose texts (whether in original or in copy) happen to survive. Secondly, and particularly in the earlier period, the king would tend to be asked for brieves and charters mainly in those parts of his realm where this kind of documentation was familiar and in regular use.

GWSB

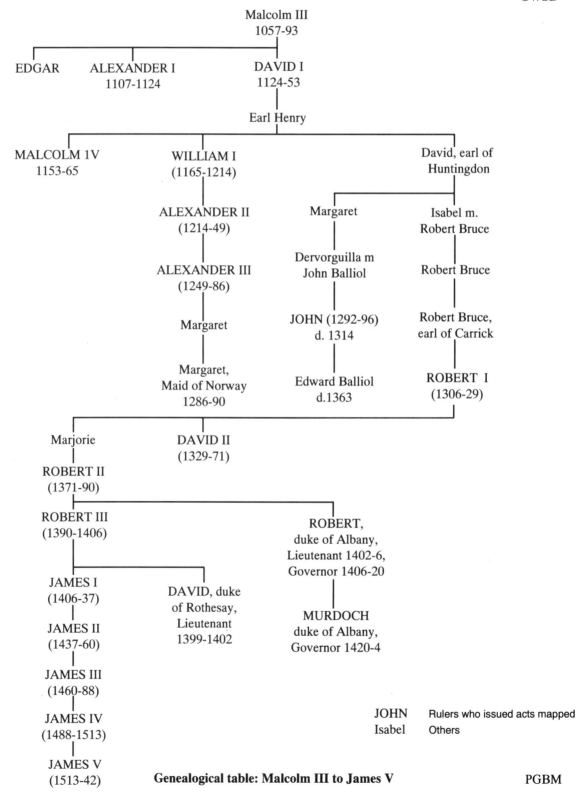

Genealogical table: Malcolm III to James V

PGBM

Place-dates of royal charters to 1296

The accident of survival means that the place dates shown form only a small proportion of the places recorded by the royal scribes of the period, as well as reflecting the unbalanced pattern of survival of royal acts as a whole. For example, the loss of record relating to almost all the religious houses of south-western Scotland (except Paisley) is undoubtedly reflected in the noticeable absence of place-dates in this area. Further, if acts were issued only where sought, then the virtual absence of place-dates throughout the Highlands is not safe evidence that the kings never set foot there, although the maps allow a reasonable inference that the court spent more time in the eastern and southern lowlands, especially between Forfar and the Tweed, than in other regions. A few localities in northern England are included to demonstrate the Scottish interest in Northumberland and English Cumbria during the twelfth century. Place-dates -not shown here- also illustrate the lordship of the midland English honour of Huntingdon enjoyed by the Scots kings for much of the period.

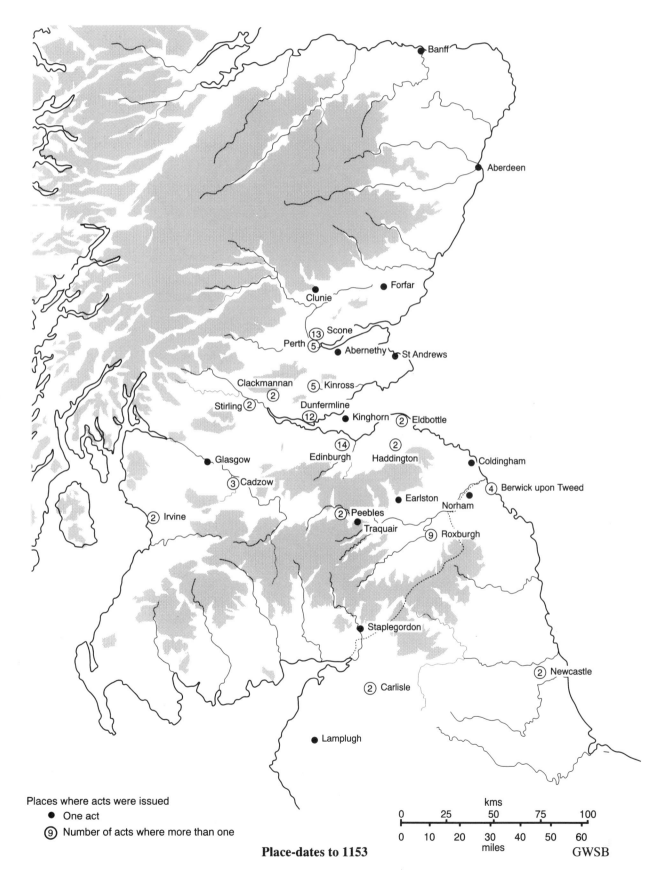

Places where acts were issued
- ● One act
- ⑨ Number of acts where more than one

kms

Place-dates to 1153

GWSB

159

Place-dates of royal charters to 1296

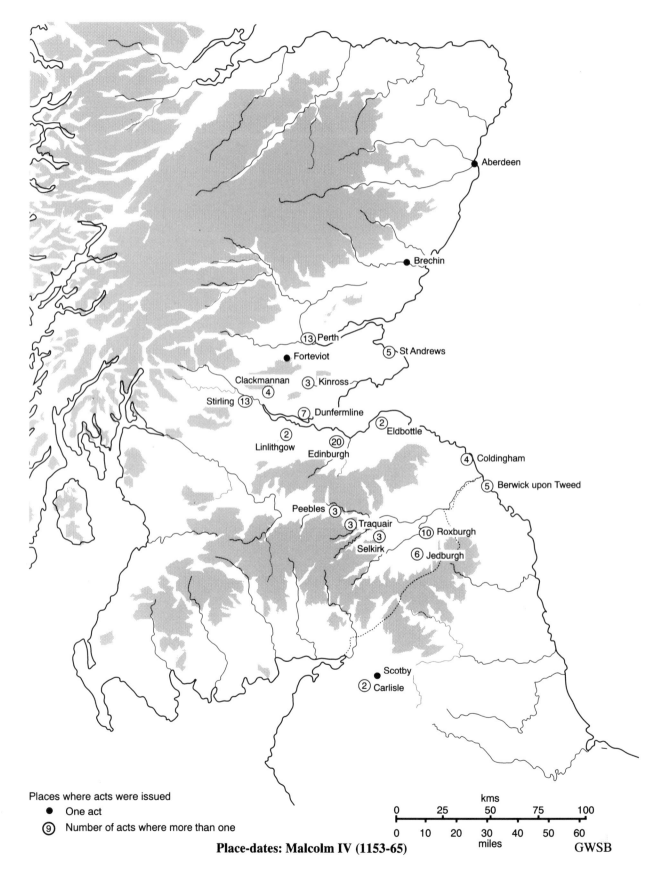

Aberdeen

Brechin

(13) Perth

(5) St Andrews

Forteviot

Clackmannan
(4)

(3) Kinross

Stirling (13)

(7) Dunfermline

(2) Eldbottle

(2)

Linlithgow

(20)

Edinburgh

(4) Coldingham

(5) Berwick upon Tweed

Peebles (3)

(3) Traquair

(10) Roxburgh

(3)

Selkirk

(6) Jedburgh

Scotby

(2) Carlisle

Places where acts were issued

●   One act

(9)   Number of acts where more than one

kms

0   25   50   75   100

0   10   20   30   40   50   60

miles

Place-dates: Malcolm IV (1153-65)

GWSB

160

Place-dates of royal charters to 1296

Places where acts were issued
- ● One act
- ⑨ Number of acts where more than one

kms

miles

Place-dates: William I (1165-1214)

GWSB

Place-dates of royal charters to 1296

Alexander II directed his attention towards asserting royal authority in the outer reaches of the kingdom more fully than had any of his twelfth-century predecessors. But little of the king's vigorous policy can in fact be recovered simply by mapping the place-dates of his extant written acts. Quite apart from the general limitations of such evidence, there are two specific considerations to bear in mind. First, Alexander's military campaigns in Galloway, Argyll, Moray and Caithness were effective but brief, and it is unlikely that many royal acts could have been issued on these occasions. Second, it seems clear that the king endeavoured to consolidate military gains not through regular personal itineration but primarily by delegating royal authority and power to trusted subordinates like the de Moravias in Strathnaver and Sutherland, Farquhar Mactaggart in Ross and North Argyll, the Comyns in Badenoch, Lochaber and Galloway, and the Stewarts in Cowal and Bute. Arguably the most significant place-date is the island of Kerrera, at the entrance to Oban Bay, where a charter was issued on 8 July 1249 while Alexander lay dying during a great naval expedition to the west. At the time of his sudden death, not only had he secured control of the western seaboard from Kintyre to Ardnamurchan, but he may also have been on the verge of annexing the Western Isles, then under Norwegian hegemony. Yet in general the place-dates reveal a pattern of royal sojourns, concentrated in the eastern lowlands between the English border and the Mounth, that is not dissimilar to William the Lion's, save that Edinburgh (occupied by Angevin castellans from 1175 to 1186) had evidently resumed its position as the principal seat of government. Alexander's negotiations with Henry III account for two of the English place-dates shown, and these serve as a useful reminder that peaceful relations with England were fundamental to the successful assertion of royal authority in the north and west. Off the map are York and Accrington.

Places where acts were issued

- ● One act
- ⑨ Number of acts where more than one

Place-dates: Alexander II (1214-49)

KJS

162

Place-dates of royal charters to 1296

It may be significant that, with one exception (Kincardine 1251), no acts survive from the minority years (1249-59) place-dated in the north or south west of the country. In 1260, however, when the king was assuming personal control of government, his single act dated at Inverness appears. Possibly this act, and another close in date from Durris, are the remaining evidence, of a royal progress to assert the young king's authority. Thereafter, northern place-dates are not unusual: the king, although not far-travelled, does appear to have visited the north-east with some regularity. In general the surviving place-date evidence is consistent in its distribution with earlier reigns. The reign was above all a period of consolidation. Relatively few of Alexander's acts are new grants: a high proportion are confirmations. The scarcity of his acts may therefore be an indication of the stable and consolidatory nature of the reign.

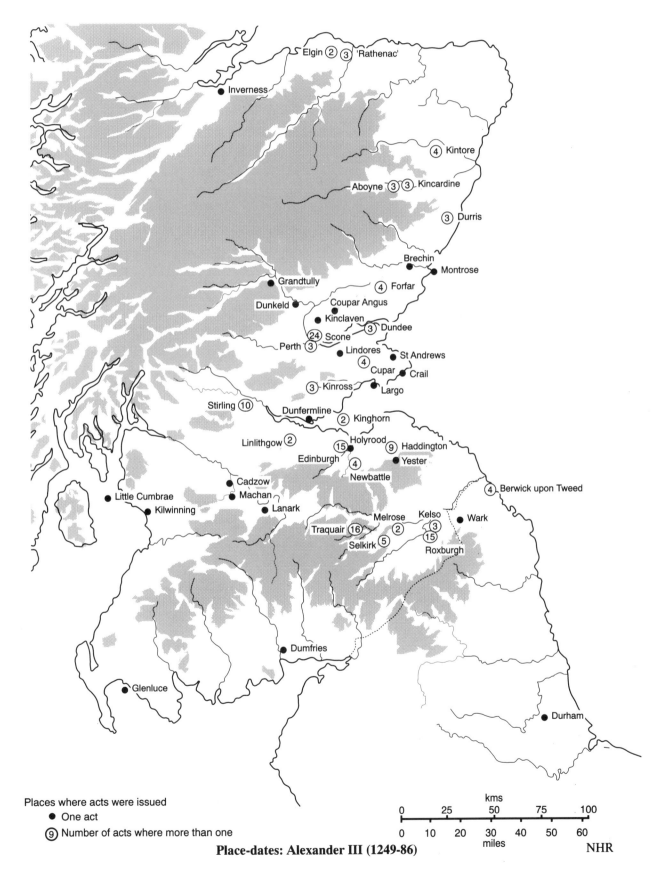

Places where acts were issued
- ● One act
- ⑨ Number of acts where more than one

Place-dates: Alexander III (1249-86)

NHR

163

Place-dates of royal charters to 1296

The committee of guardianship which ruled Scotland from 1286 until 1292 had no easy task. To keep the wheels of government turning, whilst refraining from jeopardising the rights of the Crown which they represented cannot have been simple. Their unique and spectacular seal of government is perhaps symbolic of their constitutional difficulty: they had the authority of the nation - a conceptual entity - which was impressive in terms of national identity, but was hardly a strong legal basis for the authority of their dictate. Their acts were thus limited to the strictly necessary. No grants of land survive, and the vast majority of their acts are brieves regarding overdue payments, settlement of disputed and other legal matters, or concern the negotiations aimed at settling Scotland's constitutional problems.

As for the distribution of the acts, half of those which bear place-dates were made in Edinburgh. A few acts specify that only some of the guardians were present, which may indicate that normally the whole group, or at least a majority, met to conduct the business of government in committee on a fairly regular basis, normally in Edinburgh. The group of acts place-dated on the border with England were all made during either the period of negotiation leading to the treaty of Birgham (1290) or the 'Great Cause' (1291-92).

Places where acts were issued

- ● One act
- ⑨ Number of acts where more than one

kms
| 0 | 25 | 50 | 75 | 100 |

| 0 | 10 | 20 | 30 | 40 | 50 | 60 |
miles

Place-dates: the Guardians 1286 to 1292

NHR

164

Place-dates of royal charters to 1296

John's short reign (1292-6) has left few acts of government. Although the nature of these acts indicates that he was concerned with all aspects of the realm's administration, their place-date distribution is very limited. He did attempt to exert control over the western seaboard, through the creation of sheriffdoms, but there is no evidence that he went there in person. The single act emanating from the south-west concerns the election to the bishopric of Whithorn, and three of the four documents place-dated to the north of Dundee relate to John's submission to Edward I in 1296; John, then, was not far-travelled in his pursuit of the day-to-day business of government. This was presumably as a result of the brevity of his reign, in the course of which he had little chance to travel widely. Not shown on the map, of course, are several acts place-dated in Newcastle upon Tyne and London, which relate to the king's troubled relationship with Edward I.

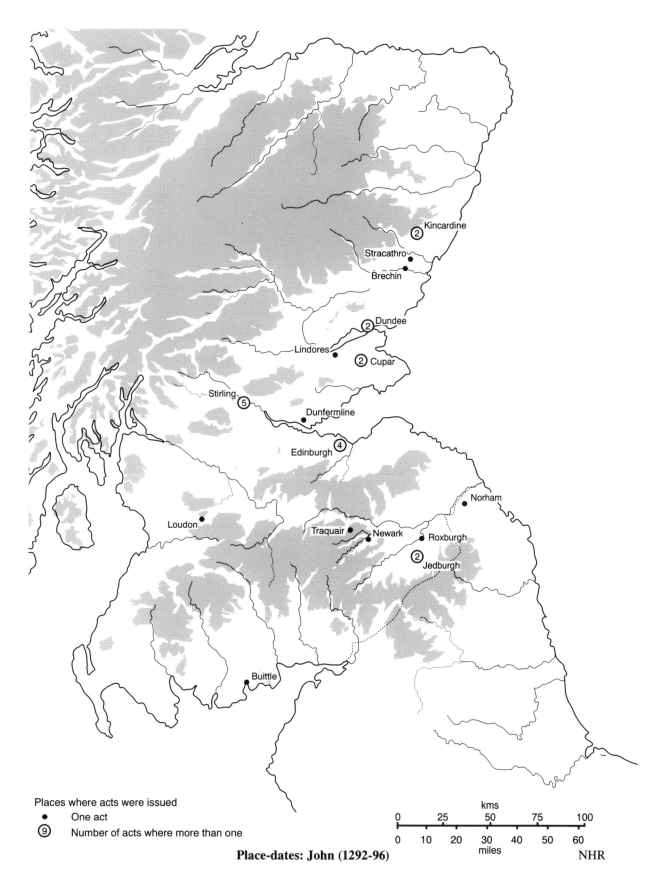

Places where acts were issued

- • One act
- ⑨ Number of acts where more than one

kms

0   25   50   75   100

0   10   20   30   40   50   60
miles

Place-dates: John (1292-96)

NHR

165

Place-dates of Robert I (1306-29)

Very few documents were issued by the king in this period when he had little control over Scotland south of the Forth. Some groups of documents, e.g. Scotlandwell 1313, Dundee 1313, probably represent councils or parliaments. Inchture and St Andrews were places where parliaments were held.

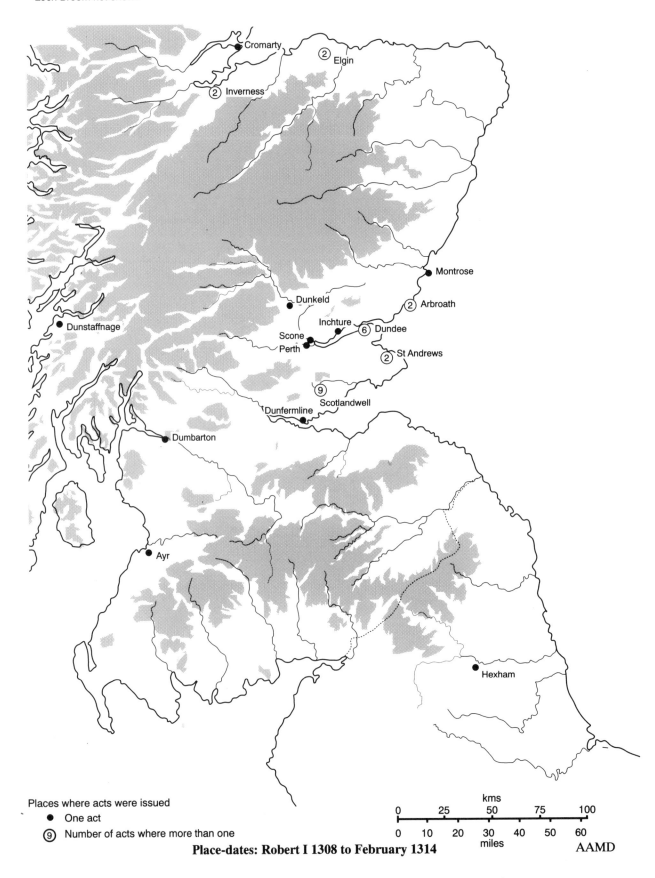

Loch Broom not shown

Places where acts were issued
- ● One act
- ⑨ Number of acts where more than one

Place-dates: Robert I 1308 to February 1314

AAMD

166

Place-dates of Robert I (1306-29)

This map covers the period between Bannockburn and the king's departure for Ireland. The Irish invasion was planned at an assembly at Ayr (1315) and in 1316 a parliament was held at Edinburgh, where many charters were issued. There is little trace of the campaigns of war except in the documents issued from the Tweed valley. The king moved round monasteries and other royal centres, never going north of the Mounth. The chancellor was the abbot of Arbroath which probably explains the large number dated there. Probably they do not represent the king's whereabouts.

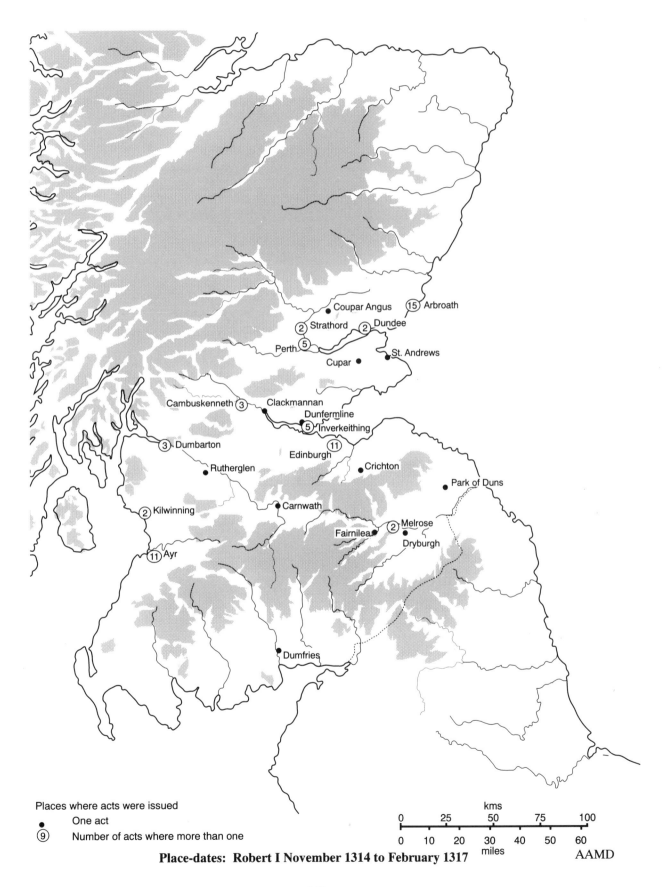

Places where acts were issued

- • One act
- ⑨ Number of acts where more than one

kms

0   25   50   75   100

0 10 20 30 40 50 60
miles

Place-dates: Robert I November 1314 to February 1317

AAMD

167

Place-dates of Robert I (1306-29)

Berwick fell in April 1318 and the king was much concerned with its defence until a two-year truce was made in December 1319. A parliament was held at Scone in December 1318 at which a group of acts is dated, while Arbroath dates probably represent the chancellor's (and not the king's) presence. The number of small places of issue and the scarcity of northern dates remains remarkable.

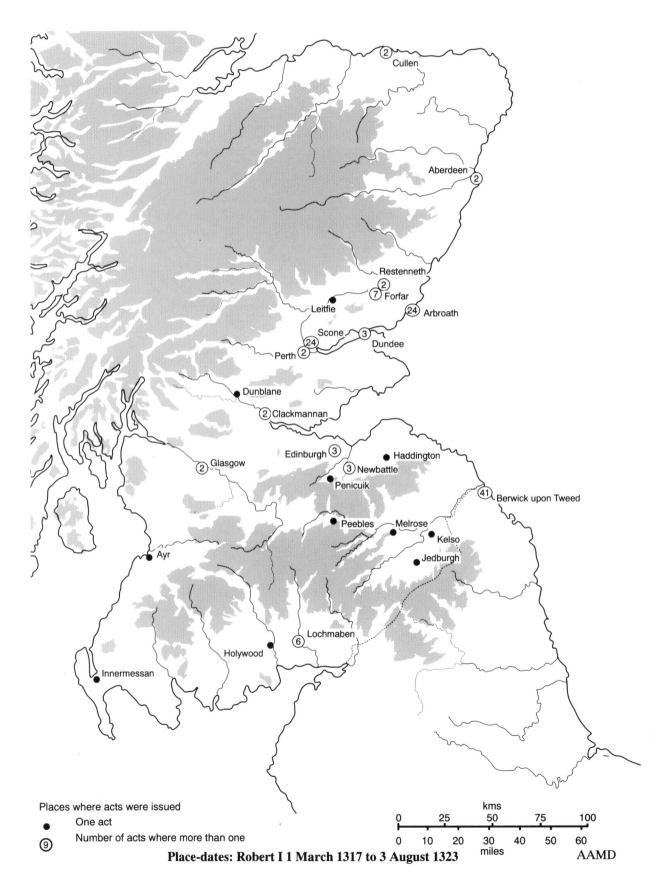

Places where acts were issued

● One act

⑨ Number of acts where more than one

Place-dates: Robert I 1 March 1317 to 3 August 1323

AAMD

Place-dates of Robert I (1306-29)

The period covered in this map is the time of the truce (1323 to 1327) and the campaign year of 1327 which scarcely shows at all. In 1325 a parliament was held at Scone and in 1326 at Cambuskenneth. In 1325 appears the first act dated at Cardross where a new manor house was built; when the king stayed there, some financial business seems to have centred on Glasgow. The smaller places were often hunting lodges.

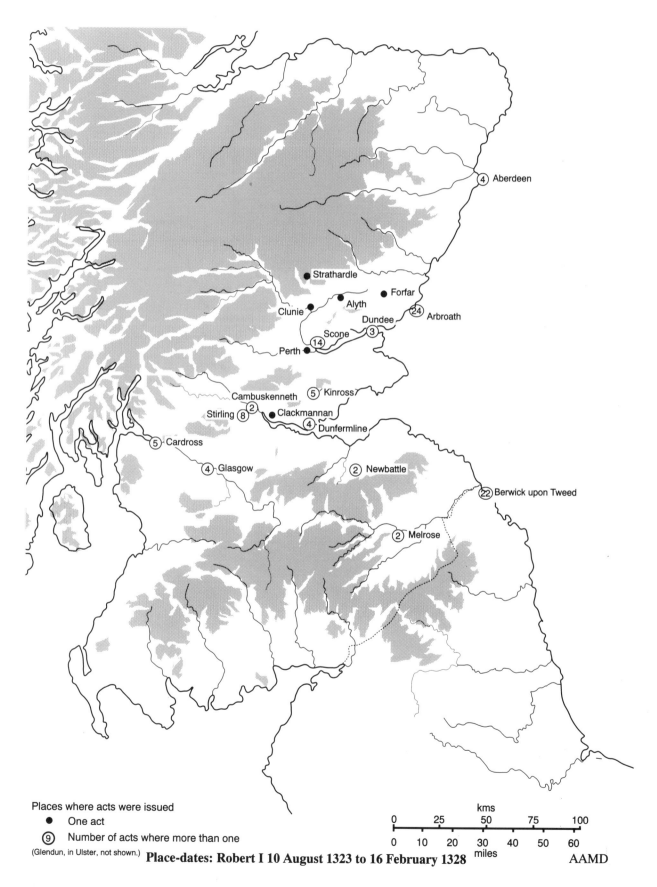

Places where acts were issued

● One act

⑨ Number of acts where more than one

(Glendun, in Ulster, not shown.)

Place-dates: Robert I 10 August 1323 to 16 February 1328

kms
0   25   50   75   100

0 10 20 30 40 50 60
miles

AAMD

Place-dates of Robert I (1306-29)

The changed distribution represents the king's illness including his pilgrimage by sea from Cardross to Whithorn. He was at Edinburgh for the March 1328 parliament but the other eastern places very probably represent the chancellor's or the chamberlain's whereabouts. The chancellor was no longer the abbot of Arbroath. The small inset is a composite of the preceding five maps. It shows the distribution of the places at which Robert I granted acts over his reign. Most of the places are in the low lying parts of Scotland.

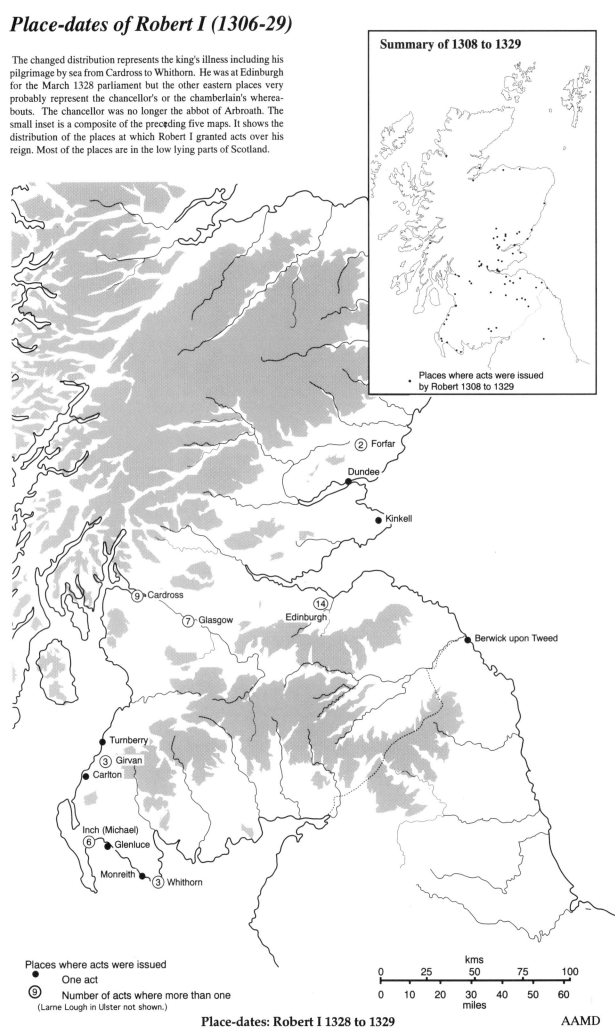

Summary of 1308 to 1329

Places where acts were issued by Robert 1308 to 1329

Forfar

Dundee

Kinkell

Cardross

Glasgow

Edinburgh

Berwick upon Tweed

Turnberry

Girvan

Carlton

Inch (Michael)

Glenluce

Monreith

Whithorn

Places where acts were issued
- One act
- ⑨ Number of acts where more than one

(Larne Lough in Ulster not shown.)

kms
0   25   50   75   100

0 10 20 30 40 50 60
miles

Place-dates: Robert I 1328 to 1329

AAMD

170

Place-dates: David II to James V

It is obvious that the patterns in this series of maps differ from each other. It is not so easy to be sure what these differences mean. An act was sealed by the king's clerks, but the date in the text may not be when and where this was actually done. Sometimes charters were issued under a warrant from the king. If so, it seems that they would normally bear the date of the warrant, which was probably when and where the king actually ordered the grant. Most royal grants, however, were formal, for example, confirmations of land transfers, which often did not involve the king at all. Such routine documents may well bear the actual date of issue; and it follows that their dates tell us nothing of the king's movements. Thus, the maps may reflect quite complex relationships between rulers and clerks, rather than the whereabouts of the king at any given time.

An example may illustrate the kind of questions that arise. In the second half of David's reign and under James I and II, acts issued at Edinburgh amount to around or even more than half all issued. Under some other rulers, particularly the governors (1406-24), there are proportionately far fewer. This may mean that David and the Jameses spent a lot of their time in Edinburgh or that Edinburgh was becoming the fixed seat of government. If Edinburgh was becoming the fixed seat of government, one may ask what happened under those rulers when the proportion of acts issued at Edinburgh falls; it may mean that the centre of government was elsewhere, perhaps less fixed; or that there was less routine government.

Some aspects of the distribution of acts may reveal territorial limitations in the structure of royal government. The almost complete absence of place-dates in the Highlands, certainly to the north and west of the Great Glen, and the small number issued in the Borders and the south-west, surely indicates that the kings in this period tended to concentrate their activities in the central Lowlands, Fife and Angus. Some variations seem personal. Robert II

(1371-90) and Robert III (1390-1406) issued more acts than anyone else in Renfrewshire and Ayrshire. The governors' acts bunch more in Fife. In both cases the distribution follows the ruler's personal lands. The Stewarts' territories were in Renfrewshire and Ayrshire; and the dukes of Albany had their main base in Fife.

But we must be cautious. Kings may go where they do not issue charters: James I certainly penetrated the Highlands though he issued no acts there, and the king's authority may be recognised well outside areas that he visits. Landowners in the Highlands and the Borders sometimes sought royal charters to support their titles, even if those charters were issued at Edinburgh or elsewhere in the Lowlands.

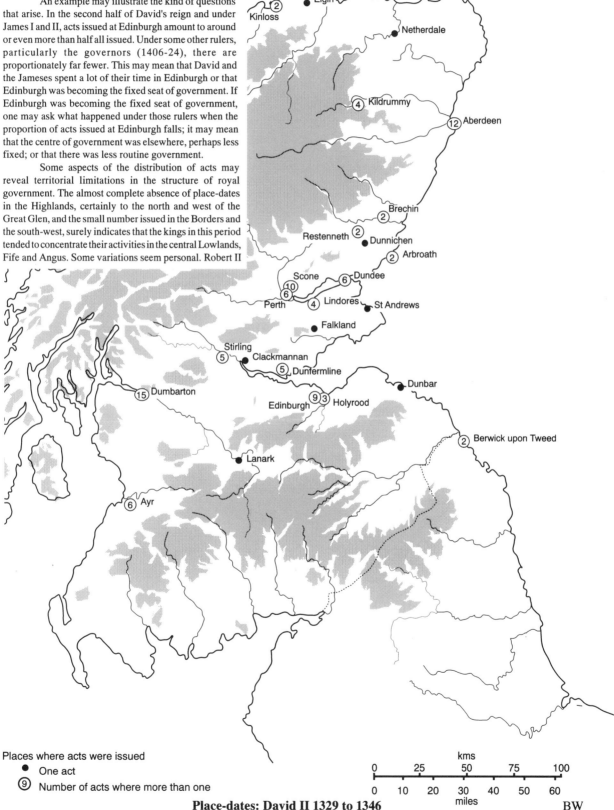

Places where acts were issued
- • One act
- ⑨ Number of acts where more than one

Place-dates: David II 1329 to 1346

BW

171

Place-dates: David II to James V

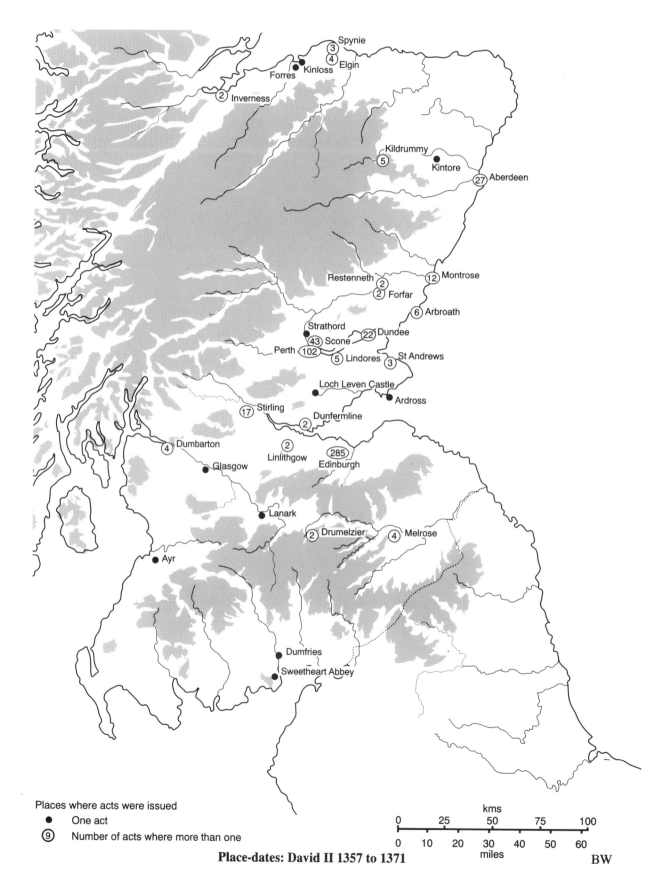

Places where acts were issued

● One act

⑨ Number of acts where more than one

kms
0 · 25 · 50 · 75 · 100

0 · 10 · 20 · 30 · 40 · 50 · 60
miles

Place-dates: David II 1357 to 1371

BW

Place-dates: David II to James V

Places where acts were issued

- ●   One act
- ⑨   Number of acts where more than one

Place-dates: Robert II (1371 - 90)

ALM

Place-dates: David II to James V

Logierait

Methven ⑫ Scone Dundee
㊲ Perth ● Strathtyrum

⑦ Cambuskenneth
Stirling ⑰ Dunfermline

Garvelane ● ㉘ Linlithgow
Finlaystone ③③ Dumbarton ㊻② Clerkington
Rothesay ⑥ ④ Renfrew Glasgow Edinburgh Holyrood

Ardneil ●
④ Irvine ● Lochgoin
⑥ Dundonald

Places where acts were issued
●   One act
⑨   Number of acts where more than one

kms
0   25   50   75   100

0   10   20   30   40   50   60
miles

Place-dates: Robert III April 1390 to April 1398

ALM

174

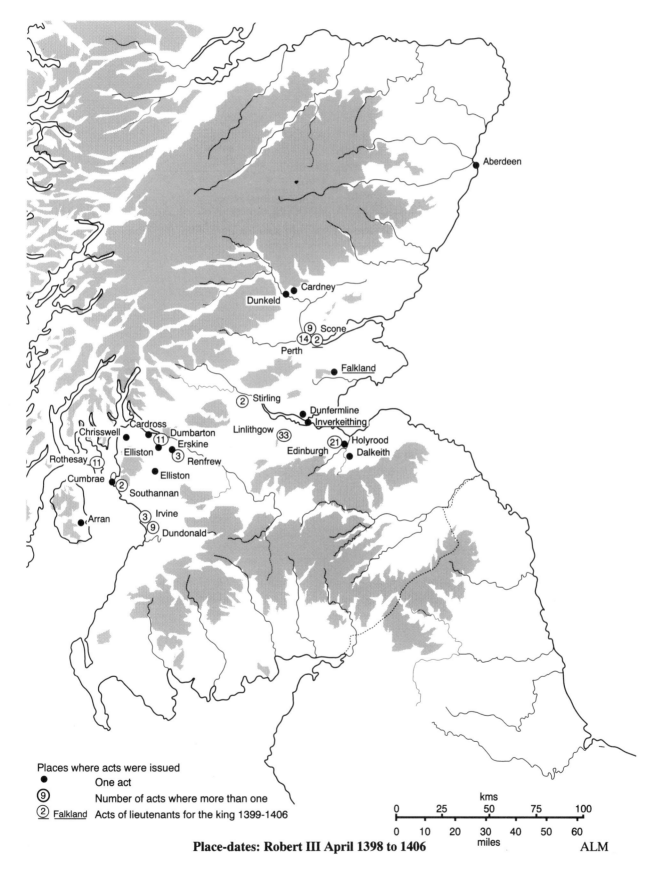

Places where acts were issued
- ●   One act
- ⑨   Number of acts where more than one
- ② Falkland   Acts of lieutenants for the king 1399-1406

Aberdeen

Cardney
Dunkeld

⑨ Scone
⑭②
Perth

Falkland

② Stirling
Dunfermline
Chrisswell Cardross Linlithgow Inverkeithing
Dumbarton ⑪ Erskine ③③
Elliston ③ Renfrew ㉑ Holyrood
Rothesay ⑪ Edinburgh Dalkeith
Cumbrae Elliston
② Southannan
Arran ③ Irvine
⑨ Dundonald

kms
0   25   50   75   100

0 10 20 30 40 50 60
miles

Place-dates: Robert III April 1398 to 1406

ALM

Place-dates: David II to James V

While James I was a captive in England from 1406 to 1424, the kingdom was ruled by governors who were the next in succession to the throne. As with the previous guardians between 1292 and 1296, the governors issued charters as a part of their administration of the realm. These acts are shown in the following maps.

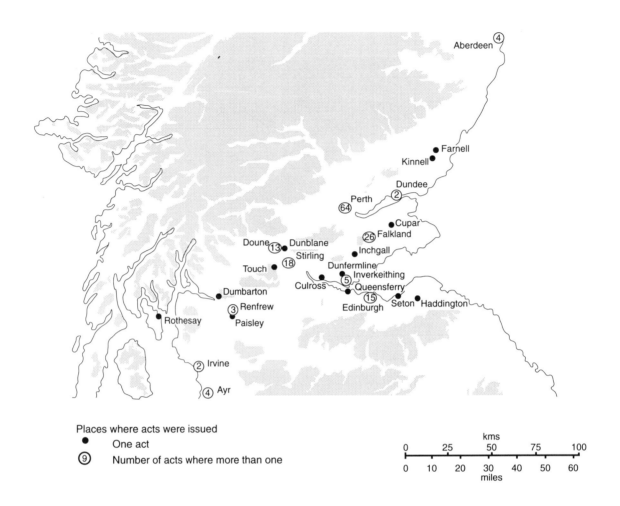

Places where acts were issued
- ● One act
- ⑨ Number of acts where more than one

Place-dates: Robert, duke of Albany, governor (1406-20)

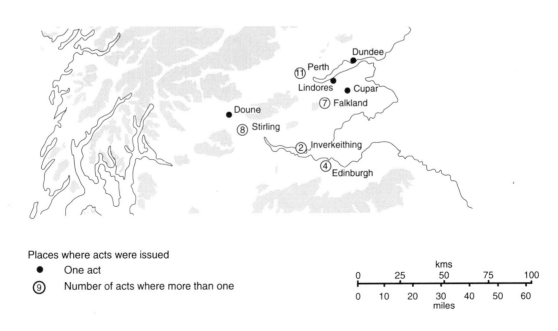

Places where acts were issued
- ● One act
- ⑨ Number of acts where more than one

Place-dates: Murdoch, duke of Albany, governor (1420-24)

ALM

176

Place-dates: David II to James V

④ Inverness

⑧ Aberdeen

● Brechin

● Auchterhouse

㊇ Perth

⑥ St Andrews

● Falkland

⑫ Stirling

● Dunfermline

Linlithgow ②

⑱⑥ ③
Edinburgh
Holyrood

● Dunstaffnage

● Melrose

● Ayr

● Durham

Places where acts were issued
● One act
⑨ Number of acts where more than one

kms
0   25   50   75   100

0 10 20 30 40 50 60
miles

Place-dates: James I 1424 to 1437

WWS

177

Place-dates: David II to James V

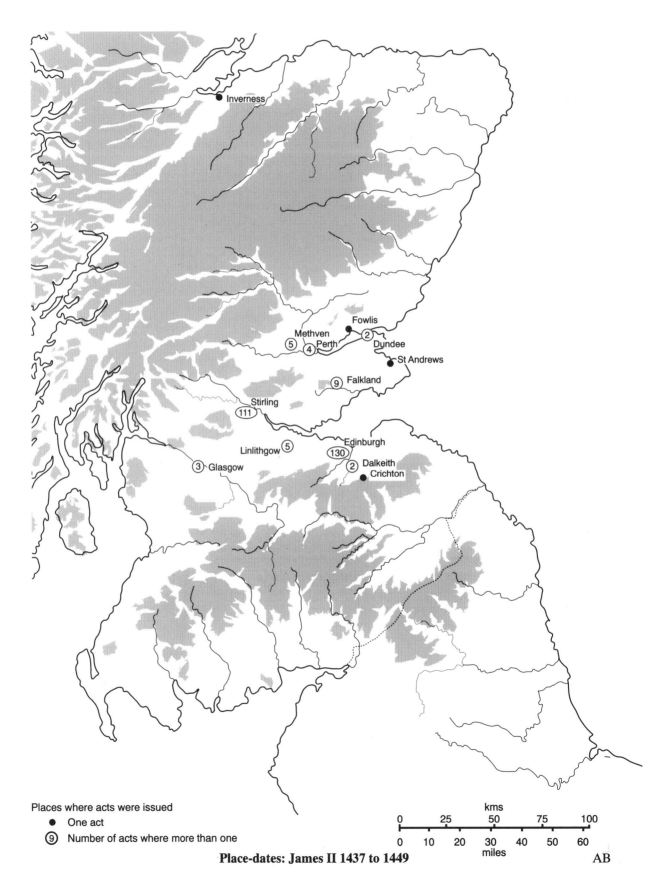

Inverness

Fowlis
Methven ⑤ ② Dundee
Perth ④ St Andrews
⑨ Falkland
Stirling
⑪⑪⑪ / 111

Linlithgow ⑤
Edinburgh
⑬⓪ / 130
③ Glasgow ② Dalkeith
Crichton

Places where acts were issued
- ● One act
- ⑨ Number of acts where more than one

kms
0   25   50   75   100

0   10   20   30   40   50   60
miles

Place-dates: James II 1437 to 1449

AB

178

Place-dates: David II to James V

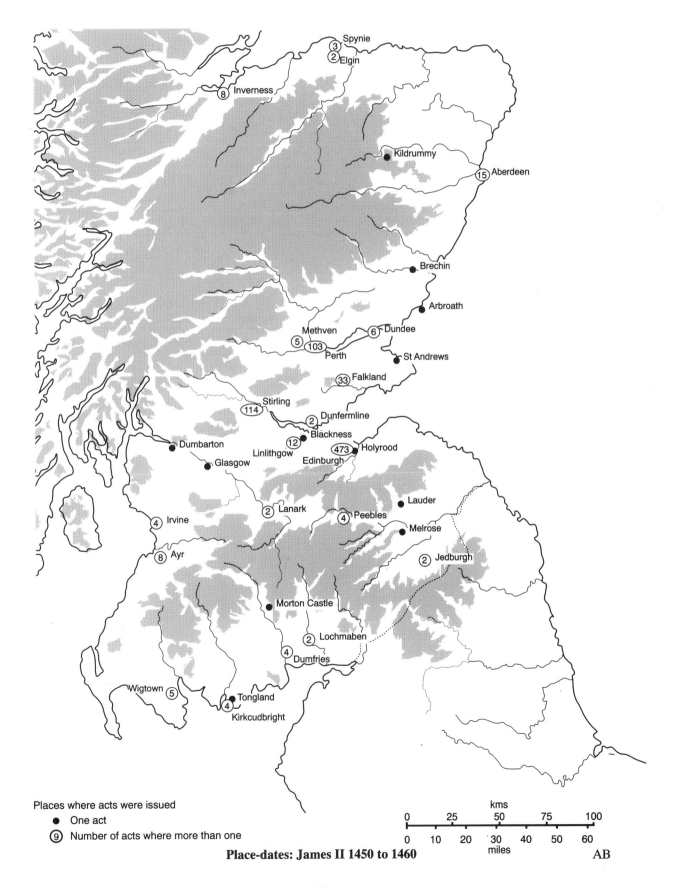

Spynie ③
Elgin ②
⑧ Inverness
● Kildrummy
⑮ Aberdeen
● Brechin
● Arbroath
Methven ⑥ Dundee
⑤ ⑩⑬
Perth
● St Andrews
㉝ Falkland
Stirling
⑭
Dunfermline
② Blackness
⑫
Linlithgow
Edinburgh ㊸ Holyrood
● Dumbarton
● Glasgow
● Lauder
② Lanark
④ Peebles
● Melrose
④ Irvine
② Jedburgh
⑧ Ayr
● Morton Castle
② Lochmaben
④ Dumfries
Wigtown ⑤
④ ● Tongland
Kirkcudbright

Places where acts were issued

● One act

⑨ Number of acts where more than one

kms
0   25   50   75   100

0   10   20   30   40   50   60
miles

Place-dates: James II 1450 to 1460

AB

179

Place-dates: David II to James V

The last three place-date maps cover the reigns of James III (1460-88), James IV (1488-1513) and James V (1513-42). The maps show respectively 12, 57 and 46 places where acts were issued: the durations of the reigns were about 28, 25 and 29 years. The frequency of the extant acts confirms the overwhelming preponderance of Edinburgh as the place of issue: these represent 98% of over 900 acts, 70% of over 2000 acts and 50% of nearly 3000 acts.

A striking fact is that during the period of James III's adult rule (November 1469 to May 1488), out of a total of 712 great seal documents which bear a place of issue, all but five emanate from Edinburgh. This static royal administration differs markedly from the much wider distribution of acts in the next two reigns. In all three reigns, the place where the biggest number of acts were granted was Stirling - respectively, 5%, 14% and 15%: in James V's reign the Falkland number reached 6.7%, and Linlithgow and St. Andrews had 4% but the number of acts issued in other places was minute in all three reigns.

(The map of the place-dates for James IV does not attempt to plot the detail of his Highland campaigns in the 1490s: and the English campaign of 1496 is the subject of an earlier map.)

Places where acts were issued
- ● One act
- ⑨ Number of acts where more than one

kms
0   25   50   75   100
0 10 20 30 40 50 60
miles

Place-dates: James III (1460 - 88)

NATM

Place-dates: David II to James V

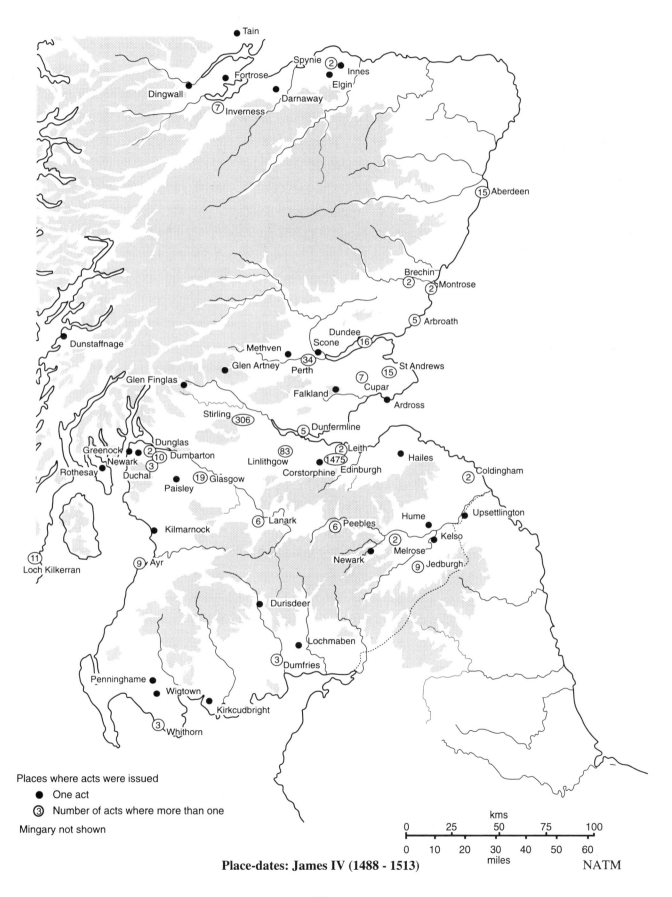

Tain

Spynie ②
Innes
Elgin
Fortrose
Dingwall
Darnaway
⑦ Inverness

⑮ Aberdeen

Brechin
②
② Montrose

⑤ Arbroath

Dundee
Methven   Scone ⑯
Glen Artney Perth
Dunstaffnage

⑦   ⑮ St Andrews
Cupar
Glen Finglas   Falkland
Ardross

Stirling ⑳⑥

⑤ Dunfermline

Dunglas
Greenock   ② ⑩ Dumbarton   ⑧③   ② Leith   Hailes
Newark   Linlithgow   ⑭⑦⑤   ② Coldingham
Rothesay   ③   Corstorphine Edinburgh
Duchal   ⑲ Glasgow   Upsettlington
Paisley   Hume
Kilmarnock   ⑥ Lanark   ⑥ Peebles   Kelso
⑪   ② Melrose
Loch Kilkerran   ⑨ Ayr   Newark   ⑨ Jedburgh

Durisdeer

Lochmaben

③ Dumfries

Penninghame
Wigtown
Kirkcudbright
③ Whithorn

Places where acts were issued
● One act
③ Number of acts where more than one

Mingary not shown

kms
0   25   50   75   100

0   10   20   30   40   50   60
miles

Place-dates: James IV (1488 - 1513)   NATM

181

Place-dates: David II to James V

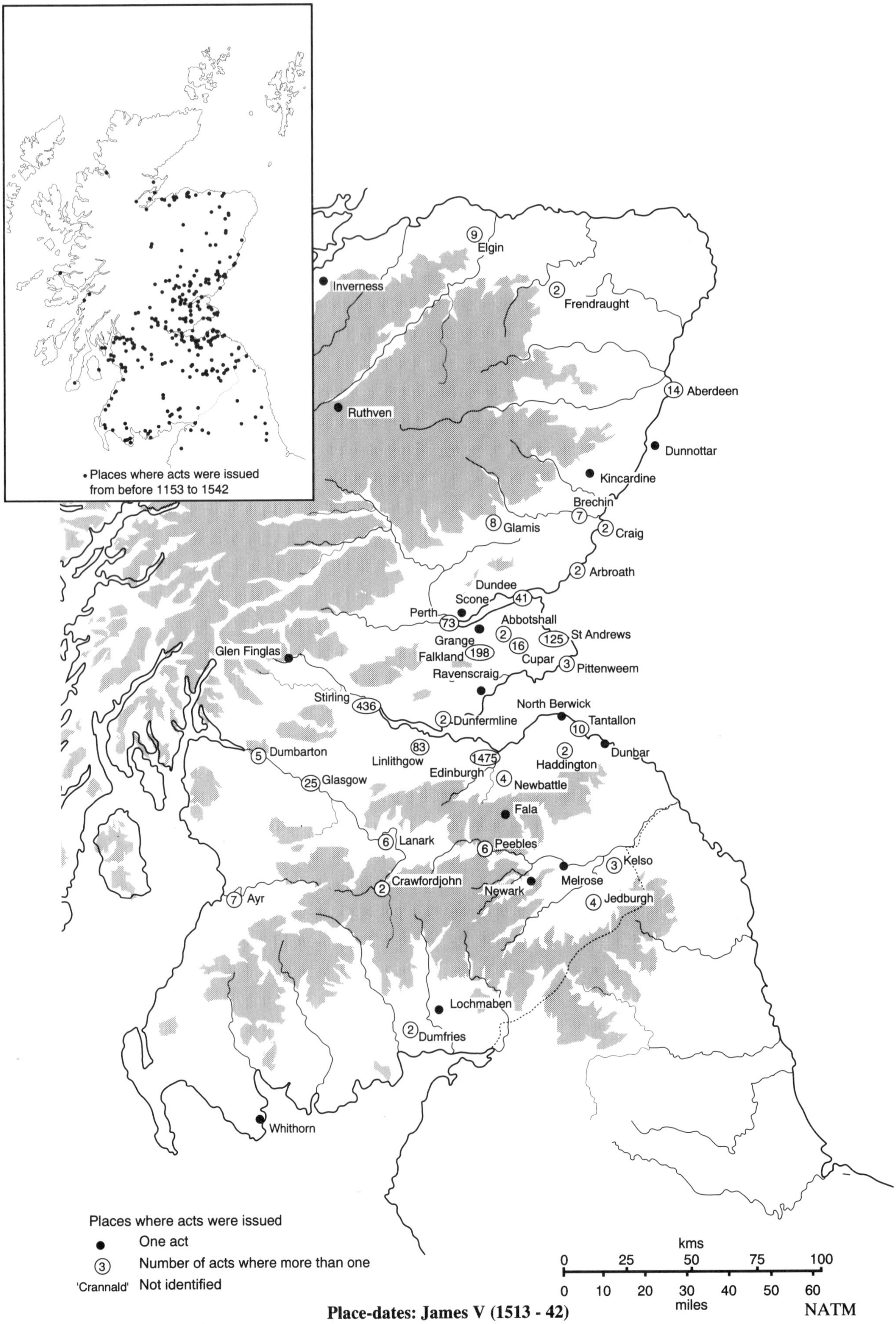

• Places where acts were issued from before 1153 to 1542
9 Elgin
Inverness
2 Frendraught
14 Aberdeen
Ruthven
Dunnottar
Kincardine
Brechin
7
8 Glamis
2 Craig
2 Arbroath
Dundee
Scone
41
Perth
73
Abbotshall
2
Grange
16
125 St Andrews
Falkland 198
Cupar
3 Pittenweem
Ravenscraig
Glen Finglas
Stirling 436
2 Dunfermline
North Berwick
10 Tantallon
Dunbar
83
Linlithgow
1475
Edinburgh
2 Haddington
4 Newbattle
5 Dumbarton
25 Glasgow
Fala
6 Lanark
6 Peebles
Melrose
3 Kelso
2 Crawfordjohn
Newark
4 Jedburgh
7 Ayr
Lochmaben
2 Dumfries
Whithorn
Places where acts were issued
● One act
③ Number of acts where more than one
'Crannald' Not identified
kms
0 25 50 75 100
0 10 20 30 40 50 60
miles

Place-dates: James V (1513 - 42) NATM

Earldoms and 'provincial lordships' 1124 to 1286

The first map is intended to indicate the maximum territorial extents of earldoms before 1286. It must be stressed that the territorial power and public authority enjoyed by earls were not invariably conterminous. Furthermore, with few exceptions (e.g. Atholl, Buchan, Lennox) the whole subject still requires detailed investigation; there is often a dearth of evidence contemporary with the period 1124-1286; and since the medieval earldoms both lost and gained territories, the territorial rights or claims recorded after 1286 may be misleading guides to earlier conditions. This map is therefore only a preliminary statement and by no means definitive. It excludes remoter lands (e.g. North Argyll held by the earls of Ross) that may or may not have been regarded as parts of earldoms. No attempt has been made to map Gowrie or Moray. Gowrie, called an earldom in twelfth-century sources, was held by the crown; Moray lapsed shortly after 1130 and was not revived until 1312. Where later records have been used, e.g. an extent of Fife (1293-4) and account rolls of Strathearn (1379-80, 1442-6) and Dunbar or March (1450-4), this is subject to the reservation noted above.

There were thirteen Scottish earldoms in 1286. Most had developed from the mormaerships (provincial governorships) of pre-feudal Scotland north of the Forth-Clyde line. Eight of the thirteen certainly existed by about 1150: Fife, Strathearn, Angus, Atholl, Mar, Buchan and Caithness in Scotland proper, and Dunbar in Lothian. The earldoms of Carrick, Lennox, Menteith and Ross are also mentioned before 1200. The only new earldom created in the thirteenth century was Sutherland (about 1235). Ross, suppressed in 1168, was revived in c. 1215.

Although royal control over the earldoms intensified, they retained importance as provincial governorships until the fourteenth century. But the strength of the earldom-province relationship must not be overstated. Pockets of Crown demesne, even seats of royal sheriffdoms, existed within earldoms. The earls of Fife clearly built up their earldom lands in stages, largely through royal favour from about 1150, and were never in fact allowed to possess the whole of Fife. Dunbar, strictly a 'non-provincial' earldom, included much but scarcely all of the Merse, and there is the especially striking case of Angus, whose territory was from early on fragmented and limited. Moreover, in the thirteenth century Mar (about 1225), Caithness (about 1240), and Menteith (1285) were all partitioned: in Caithness and Menteith, each earl's territory was reduced to half the original earldom lands. Even before 1286, therefore, some earldoms were evidently less impressive as administrative and territorial dignities than others.

In the twelfth century only native magnates had the rank of earls, but five earldoms were by 1286 in the hands of families of Anglo-continental descent. Buchan had passed by marriage to a junior branch of the Comyns, Menteith to a junior branch of the Stewarts, Angus to the Umfravilles, and Carrick to the Bruces. Sutherland remained under the lordship of the Flemish de Moravias (Murrays).

'Provincial lordships' is a modern term for large estates, similar to the earldoms, which were more or less coextensive with provinces or districts of the kingdom. Their lords, some of whom held earldoms as well, belonged to the uppermost reaches of noble society. But, as can be seen from the second map, 'provincial lordships' were not all of like dimensions, and a few appear to have been roughly the same size as, or even smaller than, certain self-contained estates

usually regarded as 'sub-provincial': e.g. Lauderdale bears comparison with Bothwell, Carnwath and Douglasdale, all within the wider division of Clydesdale. The assignment of estates to one category or the other can in fact be problematic. While efforts have been made to illustrate the extents of 'provincial lordships' as accurately as possible, those of a fair number are highly conjectural due to lack of full or easily accessible evidence. No attempt has been made to map Assynt, Glen Dochart or other units which ought to be considered, but about which information is virtually a complete blank before 1286.

From 1124 feudal colonisation helped to forge nineteen 'provincial lordships', at least some of which were actually ancient districts or lordships taken over and adapted as feudal holdings. All save Lauderdale lay in the 'outer zone' of the kingdom, where local administration based on sheriffdoms remained relatively undeveloped and the granting to trusted vassals of big tracts of territory, interspersed between the earldoms and other great lordships, was a key means of advancing royal power. By 1165 Anglo-continental families held seven provincial fiefs: Strathgryfe with Renfrew and Mearns (Stewart), Cunningham with Largs (Morville), Kyle Stewart or North Kyle, Annandale (Brus), Upper Eskdale with Ewesdale (Avenel), Liddesdale (Soules), and Lauderdale (Morville). North of the Forth, between about 1180 and about 1250 incoming lords acquired Garioch (earl of Huntingdon), Strathbogie (David son of Earl Duncan II of Fife), Strath Avon or Stratha'an (earl of Fife), Badenoch and Lochaber (Comyn), the Aird with Strathglass (Bisset), Sutherland (Murray), and Strathnaver (Murray of Duffus). The Stewarts, having secured Bute by c. 1200, controlled Cowal by the 1250s, and a junior branch of the family asserted dominance over Arran and Knapdale in the 1260s. Before 1286 Cunningham (1234), Lauderdale (1234), Garioch (1237), the Aird (about 1260), and Strathnaver (about. 1260) were all partitioned among coheiresses and began to play less important roles. Sutherland was erected into an earldom in about 1235.

Whereas each of these 'provincial lordship' was created for, or taken over by, a colonising family normally of Anglo-French descent, the map includes five others, all with pre-feudal origins, which were held by semi-independent native dynasties who gradually came under stronger central authority. Nithsdale (about 1185) and Galloway (1234-5) were ultimately broken up. In the far west, mainland (Scottish) and island (Norwegian to 1266) territories remained under the control of three families descended from Somerled Macgillebrigte (d. 1164): the Macdonalds of Islay, the Macdougalls of Lorn, and the Macruaries of Garmoran. The precise distribution of territories among them is uncertain. Morvern and Ardnamurchan have been linked with Islay or Garmoran, but may well have pertained to Lorn.

The map thus shows twenty-four 'provincial lordships', although Bute and Cowal can readily be associated with Strathgryfe, Arran with Knapdale, and Lochaber with Badenoch.

By combining the two previous maps, the third map underlines the formidably wide predominance of earldoms and 'provincial lordships' in earlier medieval Scotland. Study of the relative distribution of these great territorial units, detailed consideration of their relationship with the expanding network of royal sheriffdoms, and systematic study of the fluctuating composition of the aristocracy they supported, are all invaluable ways of throwing light on the making of the medieval kingdom.

KJS

Earldoms and 'provincial lordships' 1124 to 1286

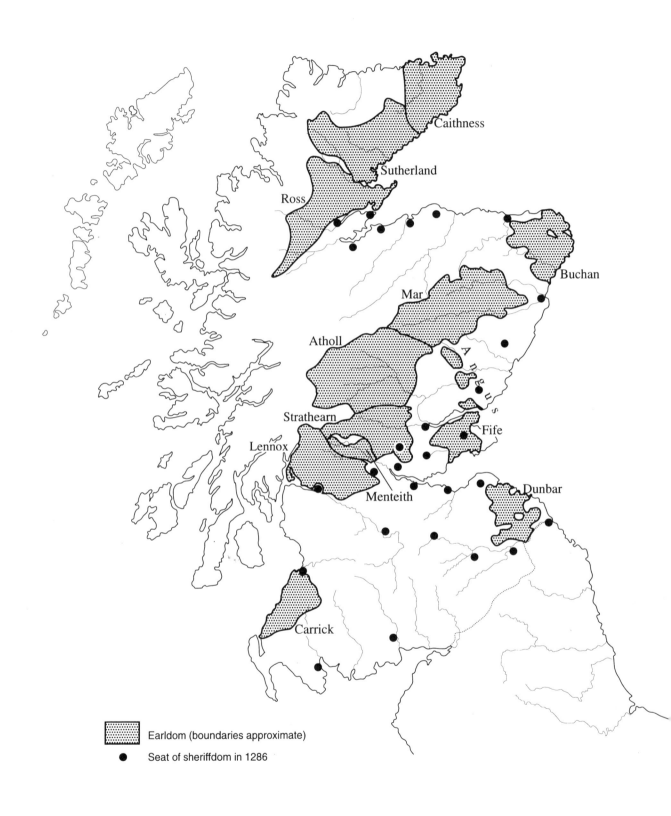

Caithness

Sutherland

Ross

Buchan

Mar

Atholl

Angus

Strathearn

Fife

Lennox

Menteith

Dunbar

Carrick

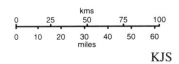

Earldom (boundaries approximate)

● Seat of sheriffdom in 1286

kms
0   25   50   75   100

0 10 20 30 40 50 60
miles

Earldoms 1124 to 1286

KJS

Earldoms and 'provincial lordships' 1124 to 1286

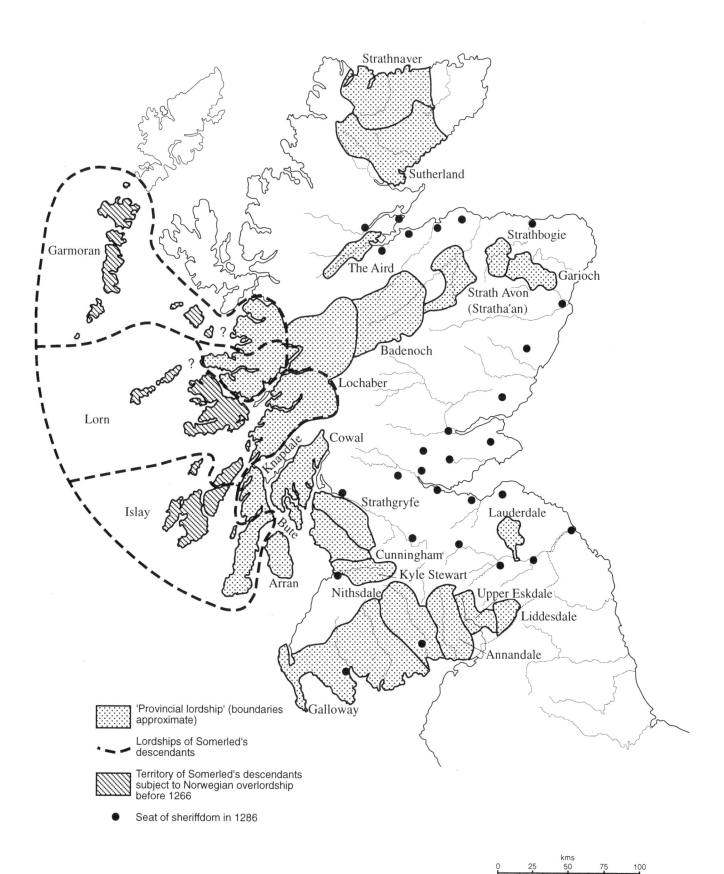

Strathnaver

Sutherland

Garmoran

Strathbogie

The Aird

Garioch

Strath Avon
(Stratha'an)

Badenoch

Lochaber

Lorn

Cowal

Knapdale

Strathgryfe

Lauderdale

Islay

Bute

Cunningham

Arran

Kyle Stewart

Nithsdale

Upper Eskdale

Liddesdale

Annandale

Galloway

'Provincial lordship' (boundaries approximate)

Lordships of Somerled's descendants

Territory of Somerled's descendants subject to Norwegian overlordship before 1266

Seat of sheriffdom in 1286

kms
0   25   50   75   100

0 10 20 30 40 50 60
miles

'Provincial lordships' 1124 to 1286

KJS

Earldoms and 'provincial lordships' 1124 to 1286

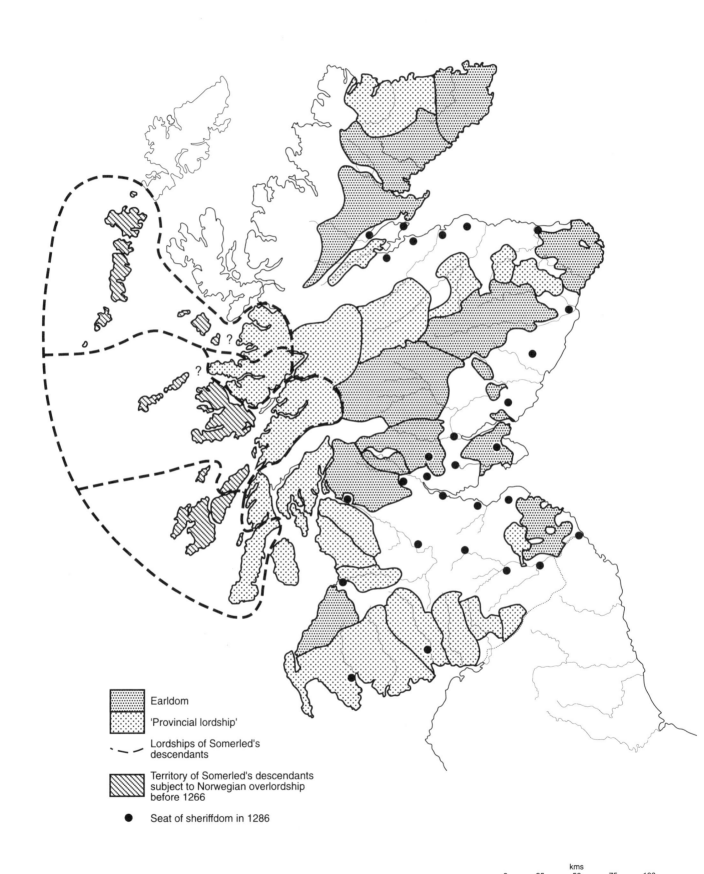

Earldom

'Provincial lordship'

Lordships of Somerled's descendants

Territory of Somerled's descendants subject to Norwegian overlordship before 1266

● Seat of sheriffdom in 1286

kms
0   25   50   75   100
0   10   20   30   40   50   60
miles

Earldoms and 'provincial lordships' 1124 to 1286

KJS

Shires and thanages

This and the next map show, respectively, the location of portions of royal and magnatial demesne to which record applied the descriptive or defining term 'shire' in the period from about 1100 to about 1350, and places associated in the same period with officers styled 'thanes' (*teinus, thaynus, toisech*, in some cases 'sheriff', *minister* or *prepositus*), most commonly by being called 'thanages' or 'thanedoms' (*teinagium, thanagium*). It will be seen that there is a considerable degree of correlation between the two. The key to an understanding of the two phenomena is the lordship enjoyed and exercised by the kings almost certainly to be traced back into prehistoric times. This lordship was exercised over districts conveniently controlled and administered from some principal centre of kingly authority (often originally a fortified centre, hill-fort, promontory-fort or the like), and it was realised in the form of renders in kind, cereals, animals and other foodstuffs, certain labour services (often of a specialised sort such as assistance with the lord's hunting), occasionally some money rents, and a variety of semi-predial, semi-administrative functions and services. Such lordship may be described as 'extensive', because very little land was retained to be exploited directly by the lord and very little use was made of year-round, servile or 'manorial' labour. Instead the population dwelled in dispersed settlements at varying distances from the centre, each settlement constituting an agrarian unit, pastoral or crop-growing or a mixture of the two, and some at least of the settlements specializing in a particular product such as oats, barley, cheese, geese, fish, honey, etc. On the other hand, an estate so organised would be limited to an area within which foodstuffs could be conveniently transported and tenants could travel - mostly, perhaps, on foot - to perform the necessary services. The Old English and Middle English term *scir, scire (shire)*, literally 'division', was used to describe or identify such estates in much of southern and eastern Scotland (as indeed in northern and midland England). It is not certain what earlier vernacular term was used in any of the Celtic languages, but it seems likely that some form of the word *cathair* or *caer* (loans from Latin *castrum, castra*)was applied to shires in early times.

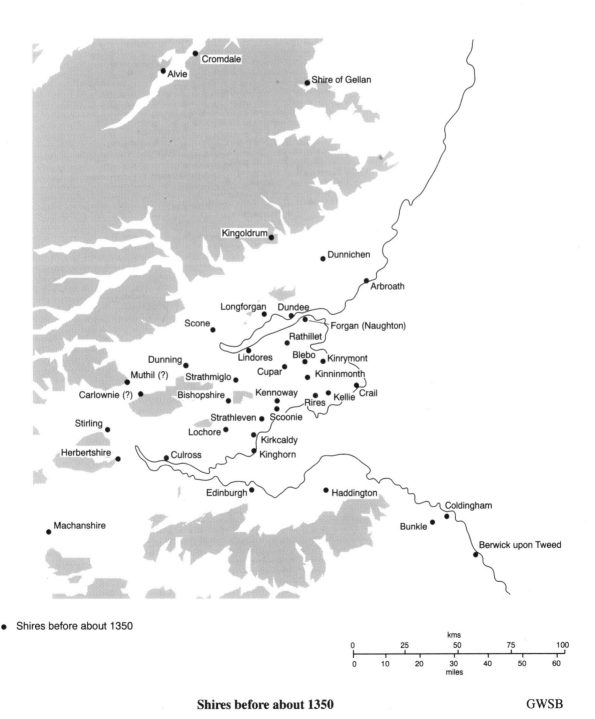

• Shires before about 1350

Shires before about 1350   GWSB

Shires and thanages

The characteristic officer responsible for administering the shire on behalf of kings, earls or bishops was known as a thane (Old English *þegn* 'one who serves'). In Tweedale, Teviotdale, Lothian and the Merse it appears that the typical ministerial class in the earlier twelfth century, intervening between the king and the greatest magnates on the one hand and the mass of the population on the other, was composed of thanes and then slightly less substantial and powerful companion officials known by the Scandinavian loan-word, drengs. In the south-eastern region references to individual thanes and thanages are rare, whereas in Scotland north of Forth it is commoner to find individual references than to thanes as a class. Owing to the comparative lack of documentary record for the south-west and the western highlands it would be rash to say positively that shire organisation and thanes or their equivalent were not normal features of those areas. Nevertheless, sufficient record material survives for the west from the period before 1350 to suggest that if royal lordship was organised there in a comparable way to that found in the east, then a somewhat different vocabulary was employed by which its details were habitually described. 'Shires' remained a living word in Scotland in the later middle ages. It could still be used in the old sense of a portion of a larger estate, as in Herbertshire, Machanshire and Bishopshire; but from the sixteenth century the word came increasingly to be used - as it had long been used in England - as synonymous with sheriffdom or county.

● Thanages recorded before about 1350

kms

| 0 | 25 | 50 | 75 | 100 |

| 0 | 10 | 20 | 30 | 40 | 50 | 60 |
miles

Thanages about 1350

GWSB

Breitheamh, breive, dempster and deemster

An important judicial officer in Celtic Scotland was the *breitheamh*, a Gaelic word meaning judge, Scotticised as 'breive' or 'dempster'. In Latin documents between about 1100 and about 1300 these officers are designated 'judex'. The map is based first on Professor G.W.S. Barrow's list of these Scottish *judices*, which suggests that they had a provincial jurisdiction. Further, however, tradition and documentary evidence from after 1400 tell how each of the islands within the Lordship of the Isles had its own judge under a chief judge - *the judex insularum* - who may have been based in Lewis. The Scottish judges had their counterparts in Ireland, Wales and, in particular, in the *briw* or deemster of Man, as the repositories of traditional law and custom. The map indicates those provinces to which documentary evidence shows *judices* were attached, indicating such provinces with capital lettering. Also shown (in italic lettering) are those other provinces within which *judices* were operative or with which they were traditionally associated. It should be noted that there is a close parallel with the geographical distribution of the toiseachdeor.

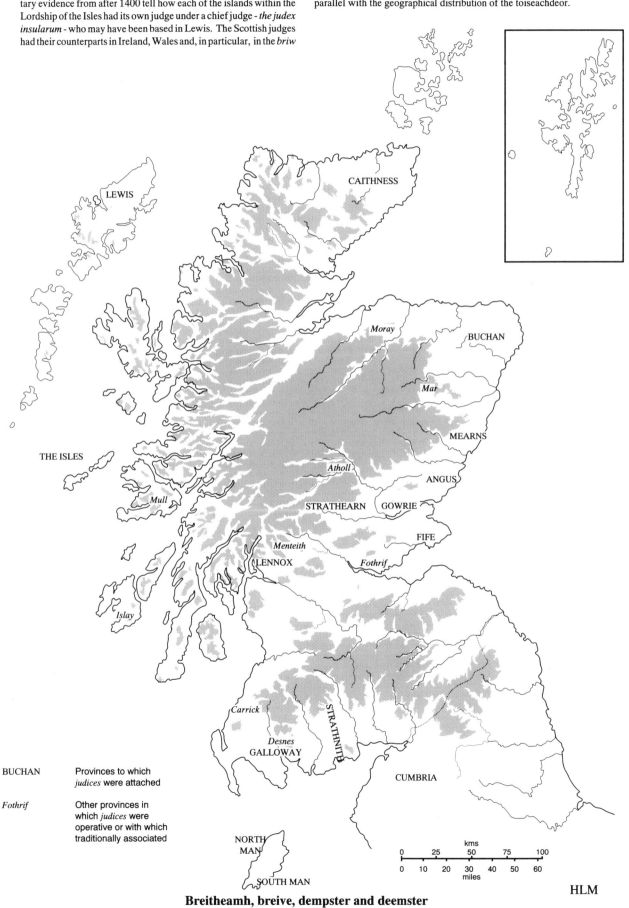

BUCHAN — Provinces to which *judices* were attached

Fothrif — Other provinces in which *judices* were operative or with which traditionally associated

kms
0 25 50 75 100
0 10 20 30 40 50 60
miles

HLM

Breitheamh, breive, dempster and deemster

Toiseachdeor

The toiseachdeor was an important officer of the law in Celtic times, although his precise function is unclear, as indeed is the etymology of his name. Like the *breitheamh* ('judex') and the mair, the toiseachdeor survived into the Middle Ages and beyond. He was often equated with the coroner, and in a number of cases there is clear continuity between earlier toiseachdeor and later coroner. The map plots references to the office, indicating the earliest date at which a particular toiseachdeor appears on the record. In every case, however, the office must have existed for many years - and probably many centuries - previous to the earliest surviving mention.

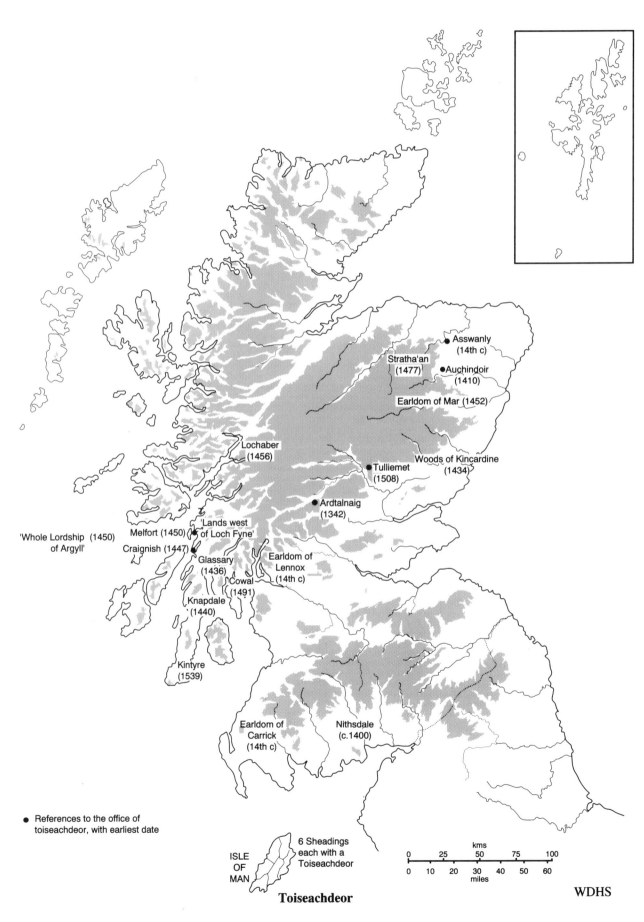

Asswanly (14th c)

Stratha'an (1477)

Auchindoir (1410)

Earldom of Mar (1452)

Lochaber (1456)

Woods of Kincardine (1434)

Tulliemet (1508)

Ardtalnaig (1342)

'Lands west of Loch Fyne'

Melfort (1450)

'Whole Lordship (1450) of Argyll'

Craignish (1447)

Glassary (1436)

Earldom of Lennox (14th c)

Cowal (1491)

Knapdale (1440)

Kintyre (1539)

Earldom of Carrick (14th c)

Nithsdale (c.1400)

● References to the office of toiseachdeor, with earliest date

ISLE OF MAN

6 Sheadings each with a Toiseachdeor

kms
0   25   50   75   100
0 10 20 30 40 50 60
miles

Toiseachdeor

WDHS

190

Comhdhail: 'popular' courts

The Gaelic word *comhdhail* (Old Irish *Comdal*), meaning 'assembly' or 'tryst', was evidently applied to popular courts of a local nature. In this sense it is recorded in the fourteenth century in the form *conthal* or *couthal*, referring to Angus and Mearns. It seems possible that this word is embodied in a number of place-names,

some surviving, some obsolete, occurring chiefly in north and eastern Scotland; and in some at least of these instances the name indicates a place where such local popular courts customarily met. A high proportion of these place-names, usually having the form Cothil, Cuthel, Cuttle, etc, are located in the vicinity of prehistoric cairns, tumuli and stone circles, i.e. the kind of site at which medieval courts are known from other evidence to have met.

1	Cuthill
1a	Cuthil
2	Cothall
3	Cothall
4	Glenquithle
5	Cuttyhill
6	Cuttlehill, Upper and Nether
7	Candle Stone
8	Cuttlecraigs
9	Cothill, Cothal
10	Cothill
11	Cothill
12	Cothill
13	Coldstone
14	Cuttieshillock
15	Quittlehead
16	Cuttieshillock, Cuttieswood, Ord of Cuttieshillock
17	Quithelhead
18	Quithel
19	Cothelhill
20	Cothill
21	Cuthile Harbour
22	Cuthlie
23	Culthill
24	Innercochill, Glen Cochill, Cochill Burn
25	Cuthil, Cuthilmuir
26	Coldrain
27	Cuttlehill
28	Cuthelton
29	Cuthill
30	Cuthill
31	Couthalley, Couthally, Cowthally

A	*Clach na Comhalaich*
B	*Cuthilfield*
C	*Cuthilbyrnie Hill*
D	*Cuttlebrae*
E	*Cuthill, Cothill*
F	*Candlehill*
G	*Cothiemuir Hill, The Cothiemuir*
H	*Cottilstane, Cot Hillock*
I	*Colsten Burn, Glen Colsten*
J	*Quitelhead*
K	*Cowthill*
L	*Cotthill, common moor of Cot Hill*
M	*Login Cuthel*
N	*Coledunes*
O	*Cuthill Furd*
P	*Candle Hill*
Q	*Cowthill, Cowill, Cuthley, Cuthill*
R	*Cothill*
S	*Cuttleburn*
T	*Cothil of Keithick*
U	*Cuthill wood of Craigmakerran*
V	*Cuthillsydes*
W	*Cutles, Easter & Wester*
X	*Cuthel, Cuthilmyre*
Y	*Cuthill*
Z	*Cutilhill, Cuidthilhill, Cuttlehill*
Aa	*Cuithilhall, Cuttlehall*
Bb	*Lie Cuthil*
Cc	*Cuthill, Cuthil Brae*
Dd	*Cuthil Brae*
Ee	*Cothill*
Ff	*Cuthill*
Gg	*Cothill*

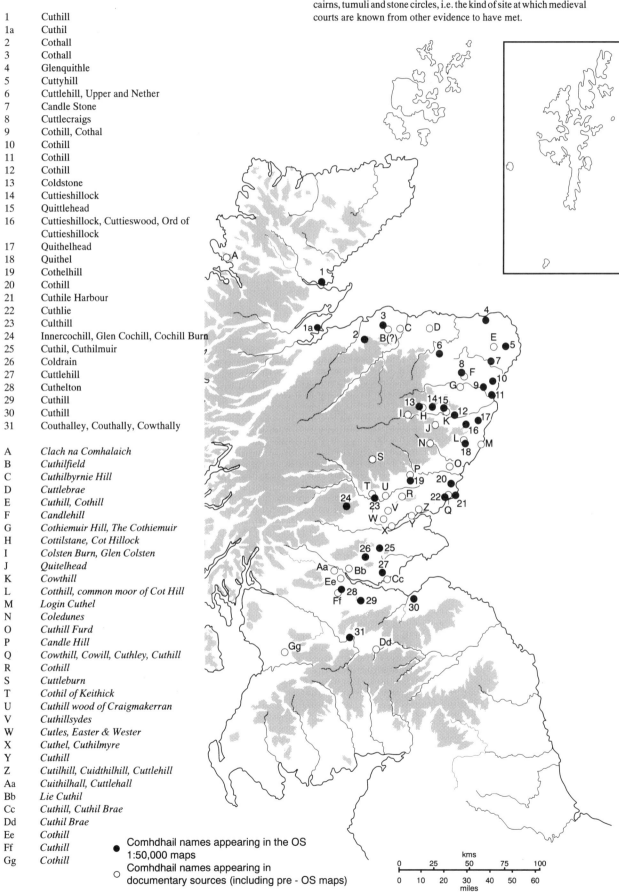

● Comhdhail names appearing in the OS 1:50,000 maps

○ Comhdhail names appearing in documentary sources (including pre - OS maps)

kms
0   25   50   75   100
0 10 20 30 40 50 60
miles

Comhdhail: popular courts in early medieval Scotland

GWSB

Sheriffdoms

The map shows those sheriffs and sheriffdoms for which there is documentary evidence before 1165, together with the approximate date of the earliest reference to them. There was a sheriff, probably connected with Roxburgh, before the accession of David I (1124-53). In his reign and that of Malcolm IV (1153-65) sheriffs were established at royal demesne centres in the south and east of Scotland. Their functions included the collection and distribution of revenues but there is no evidence of a sheriff court at this period. South of the Forth some sheriffs may be associated with royal castles and the enforcement of the obligation of castle-guard incumbent upon those holding land for knight service. The appearance of a sheriff of Lanark or Clydesdale in the reign of Malcolm IV coincides with the king's establishment of a group of Flemish settlers in the area. The sheriffs probably also had functions in connection with the king's burghs, especially north of the Forth at Perth, Crail, Dunfermline and perhaps Forfar. Although thus apparently linked with other twelfth-century developments, there are signs of continuity with the established institutions of the shire and thane. South of the Forth some early sheriffs had Anglian names and were connected with shires. The sheriff of Lothian who existed in the reign of David I may have been set over the shires of that province, with the emergence of sheriffs of Linlithgow, Edinburgh and possibly Haddington being perhaps later events. In the north, except at Perth and Crail, early sheriffs had Celtic names and at Scone and Forfar local thanes may have been elevated to the status of sheriff to compensate for the lack of comital authority in the provinces of Gowrie and Angus. Finally the absence of sheriffs from the earldoms and lordships of the north and west should be noted.

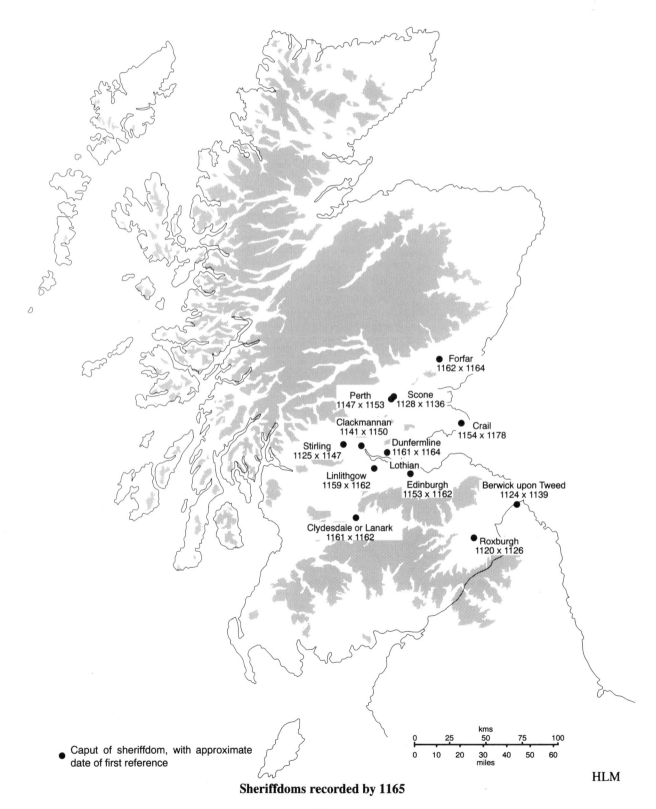

● Caput of sheriffdom, with approximate
date of first reference

Sheriffdoms recorded by 1165

HLM

192

Sheriffdoms

This map shows the expansion of the sheriffs in line with the development of the feudal settlement under William I (1165-1214). Early in his reign we find a sheriff of the province of Moray which by the beginning of the thirteenth century had apparently been divided into the sheriffdoms of Inverness and Invernairn. Probably by then, there were also sheriffs of Forres, Elgin, Banff and Aberdeen but no good documentary evidence of this survives. A single document refers to the sheriffs and bailies of Carrick, Galloway and Lennox in the 1190s and it is possible that there was a sheriff of Dumfries by this period. The sheriffs of Selkirk, Traquair and Mearns were all connected principally with areas of royal forest, the sheriff of Ayr with a new castle and burgh. Some sheriffdoms disappeared: Dunfermline (where the king's burgh was also abandoned) and Crail (in the possession of the king's mother until 1178) were both subsumed in the new sheriffdom of Fife by 1214. Lauder represents a baronial sheriffdom. The functions of the royal sheriff now clearly went beyond the administration of the king's affairs to the protection of the king's subjects - for example, by the recovery of fugitive serfs or the enforcement of teinds. There is evidence of a sheriff court. More and more the sheriffs were drawn from baronial families with Anglo-French origins who were major landowners in the sheriffdom. But the office was not yet hereditary in nature; the only sheriffship certainly heritable at this period was that of Selkirk, in the family of Sinton.

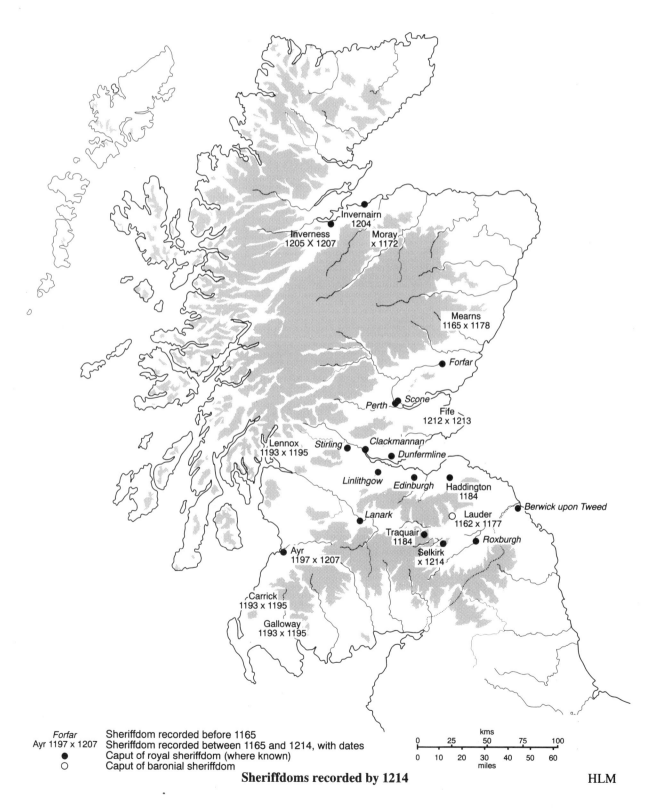

Forfar	Sheriffdom recorded before 1165
Ayr 1197 x 1207	Sheriffdom recorded between 1165 and 1214, with dates
●	Caput of royal sheriffdom (where known)
○	Caput of baronial sheriffdom

Sheriffdoms recorded by 1214

HLM

Sheriffdoms

Since it is likely that most if not all of the sheriffdoms of Dumfries, Aberdeen, Banff, Elgin and Forres were established before 1214, the map may give a misleading impression of expansion in the thirteenth century. Peebles was a development of the sheriffdom of Traquair, while Dumbarton may have evolved from the earlier sheriffdom of Lennox in association with the burgh established in 1222. Mearns became the sheriffdom of Kincardine with the erection of a royal castle there, probably by Alexander II (1214-49). Dumfries may have expanded to incorporate Galloway east of the Cree following the partition of the province in 1234, Wigtown being set up with castle and burgh at about the same time. Four new sheriffdoms - Auchterarder, Cromarty, Dingwall and Kinross - may have been elevated thanages. The sheriffdoms of Skye, Lorne and Kintyre were created by act of parliament in 1293, perhaps taking over from an earlier wardenship of the whole area.

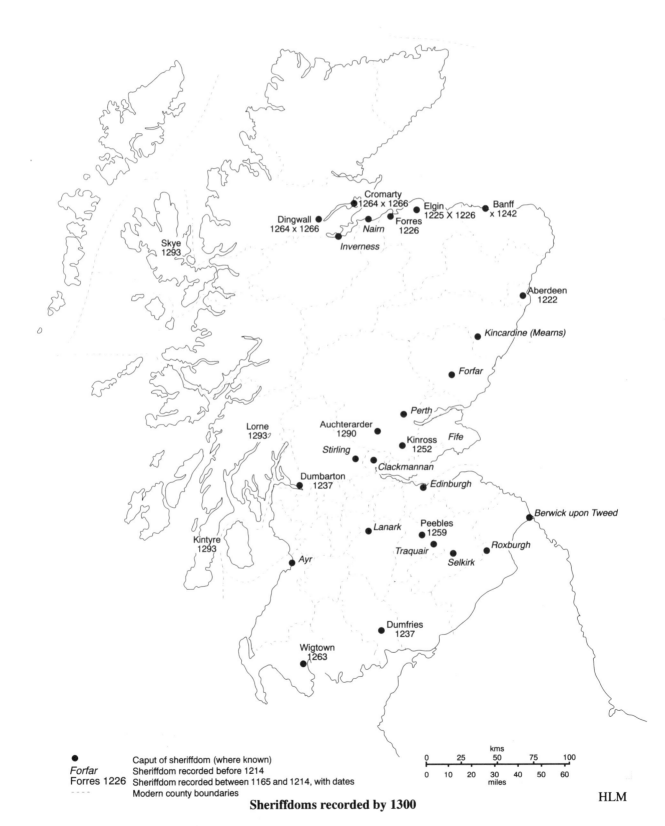

Cromarty
1264 x 1266

Elgin
1225 X 1226

Banff
x 1242

Dingwall
1264 x 1266

Forres
1226

Nairn

Skye
1293

Inverness

Aberdeen
1222

Kincardine (Mearns)

Forfar

Perth

Lorne
1293

Auchterarder
1290

Kinross
1252

Fife

Stirling

Clackmannan

Dumbarton
1237

Edinburgh

Berwick upon Tweed

Lanark

Peebles
1259

Roxburgh

Kintyre
1293

Traquair

Selkirk

Ayr

Dumfries
1237

Wigtown
1263

●   Caput of sheriffdom (where known)
Forfar   Sheriffdom recorded before 1214
Forres 1226   Sheriffdom recorded between 1165 and 1214, with dates
- - - -   Modern county boundaries

kms				
0	25	50	75	100

0	10	20	30	40	50	60
miles

Sheriffdoms recorded by 1300

HLM

Justice ayres in the thirteenth century

The justice or justiciar first appears in the twelfth century as a royal officer carrying out judicial and other functions. Normally there was more than one at a time; and each seems to have been asssigned a particular area of the kingdom in which to perform his duties. By early in the thirteenth century a twofold division of the justiciarship was established: Scotia in the north and Lothian in the south. There may also have been a justiciarship of Galloway in the late twelfth century, which was re-established in the mid-thirteenth century. By this period the administration of the justiciary was well settled.

Twice a year, in the spring and winter, the justiciar (normally a high-ranking layman) went on circuit or ayre through the sheriffdoms of his region, holding courts at the head burgh of each one. These courts exercised a wide jurisdiction and the income produced from the fines and other payments consequent upon this was accounted for to the exchequer by the sheriffs. From some surviving accounts of the 1260s it is possible to reconstruct the probable routes followed by the ayres of Scotia and Lothian and this is shown on the map. In Galloway the justiciary was subdivided into two parts defined by the River Urr rather than the two sheriffdoms of Dumfries and Wigtown.

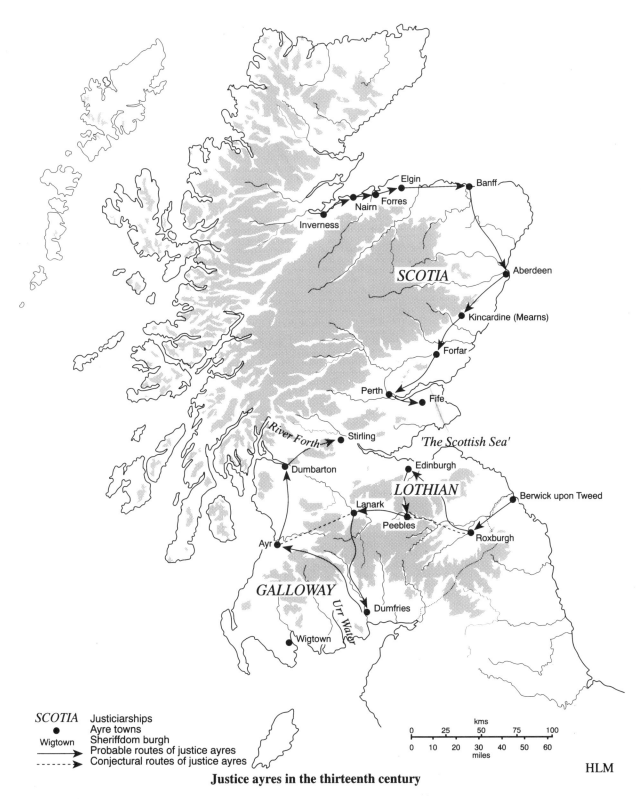

SCOTIA	Justiciarships
●	Ayre towns
Wigtown	Sheriffdom burgh
⟶	Probable routes of justice ayres
┈┈⟶	Conjectural routes of justice ayres

HLM

Justice ayres in the thirteenth century

195

Burghs to 1300

The preponderance of burghs in the east reflects the more rapid economic development of regions which had access by sea to the North Sea trading area. Towns grew up on overland livestock routes (Rutherglen, Peebles, Roxburgh), at important intersections of land and water-borne routes (Stirling, Perth), or at good river-mouth harbours (Berwick, Montrose, Aberdeen). A few places were given burgh privileges because they were important royal strongholds (Edinburgh, Stirling) or cult centre (Dunfermline). The two burghs in Moray are those most likely to represent a 'plantation' with castle to hold down a newly subdued province.

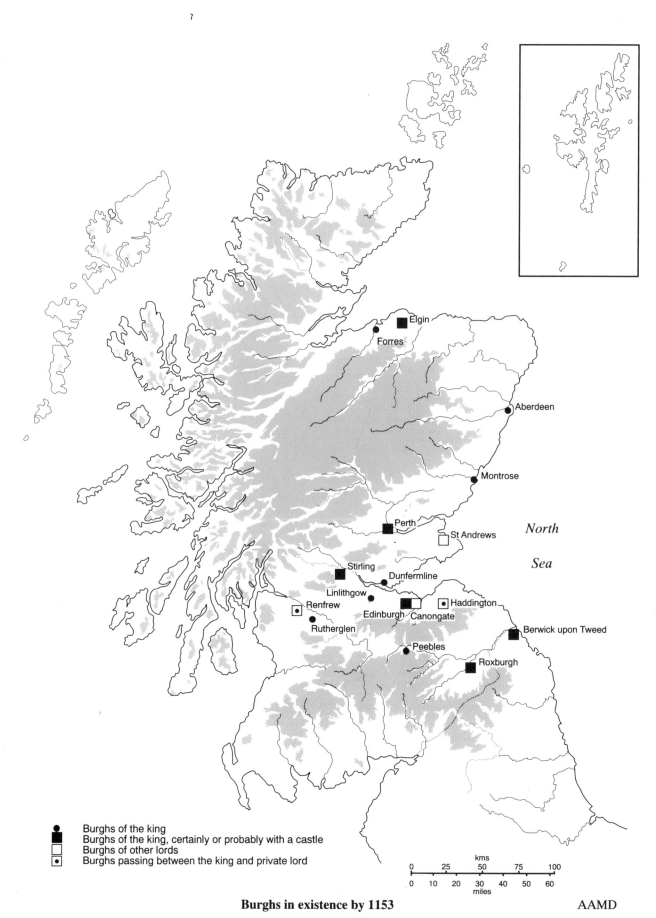

- ● Burghs of the king
- ■ Burghs of the king, certainly or probably with a castle
- ☐ Burghs of other lords
- ⊡ Burghs passing between the king and private lord

Burghs in existence by 1153

AAMD

Burghs to 1300

The most striking extension of burgh settlements is in Moray, where the town plans point to enclosed, fortified settlements with royal castles attached; Auldearn was destroyed by rebels and Nairn founded in its place. Berwick too was enclosed (because it was close to England) but only Perth had a town wall, and many burghs had only the flimsiest of enclosure for security at night. Inverness (unless it is older than we know) and Ayr are the only new ports of significance. The additional towns are for the most part regional trading centres, supplying the surrounding country with specialist trades and goods.

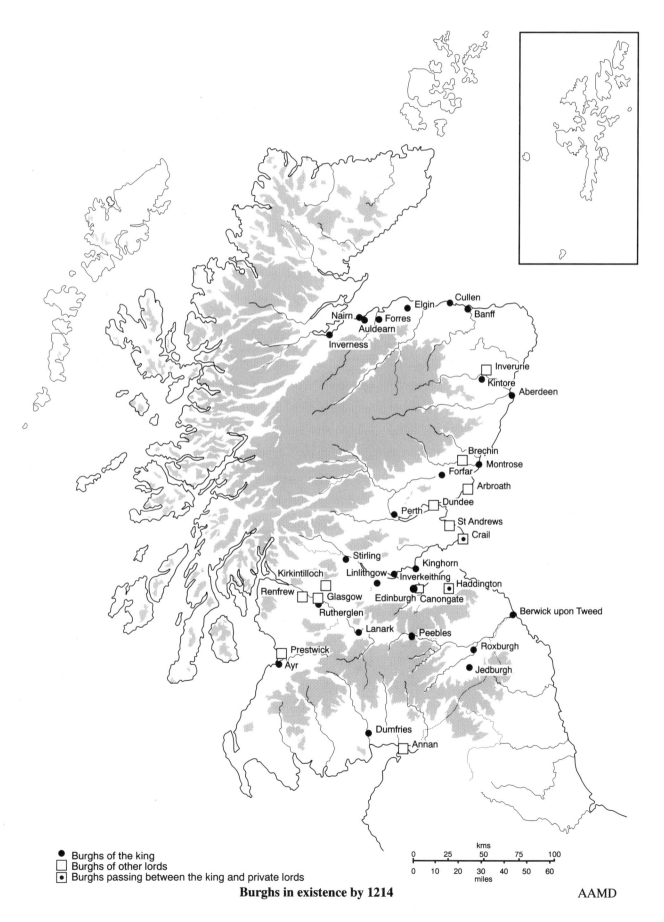

- ● Burghs of the king
- ☐ Burghs of other lords
- ☐● Burghs passing between the king and private lords

Burghs in existence by 1214

AAMD

197

Burghs to 1300

It is likely that Cromarty was established before 1214 ; Dingwall represents fairer control of Ross and Wigtown of Galloway, a lordship which was partitioned in 1235. In general the scarcity of new foundations in the thirteenth century is very remarkable, for while existing major ports (for example, Berwick) undoubtedly grew in size, the infrastructure of 'market towns' diffusing specialist wares through the country, did not increase in size, and places like, Girvan, Duns, Dalkeith, Kinross, had, it seems, no mercantile privileges.

● Burghs of the king
☐ Burghs of other lords
⊡ Burghs passing between the king and private lords

Burghs in existence by 1300

AAMD

Forests 1124 to 1286

A royal forest was a hunting reserve in which no-one could hunt without the king's permission. David I (1124-53) introduced royal forests to Scotland, having become acquainted with the idea in England as earl of Huntingdon. The first royal forests appear to have been created in the 1130s. Most of the royal forests on the map (which shows forests first recorded between 1121 abd 1286) were established by David: Ettrick (or Selkirk, as it was known to c.1300), Gala and Leader, Stirling and Clackmannan, Clunie, Birse, Banchory and Elgin, Forres and Inverness. These reserves covered large tracts of ground and in the ensuing centuries were gradually reduced in size. The boundaries of the forests shown on the map are approximate.

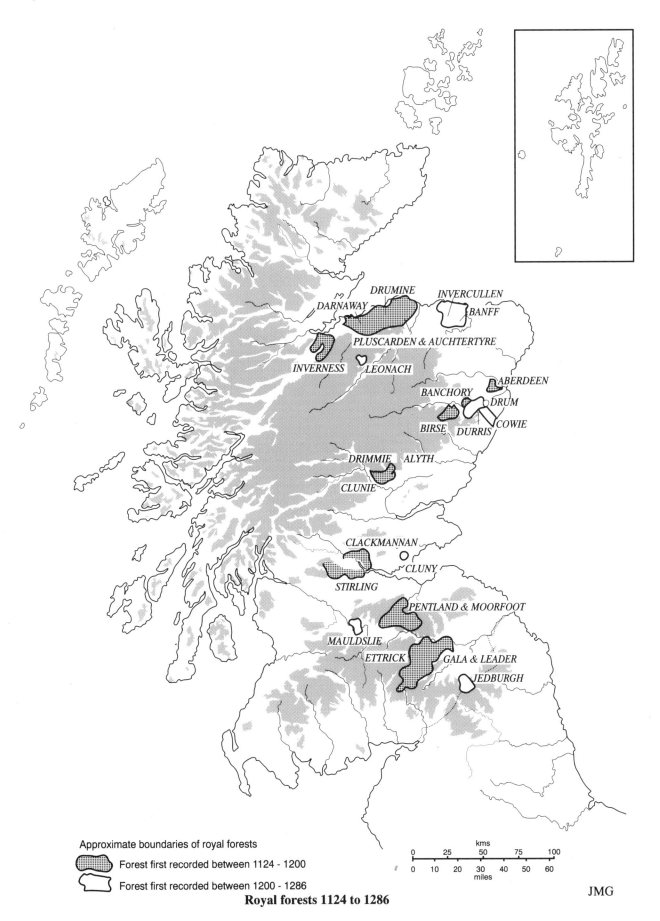

Approximate boundaries of royal forests

Forest first recorded between 1124 - 1200

Forest first recorded between 1200 - 1286

Royal forests 1124 to 1286

JMG

199

Forests 1124 to 1286

David I (1124-53) also initiated the forest grant which gave a baron forest rights enabling the beneficiary to have hunting reserves on his land and to hunt there without royal licence. In his forests the baron could exercise the same rights as the king in a royal forest. When such grants were made to ecclesiastical foundations, it was probably to ensure that their flocks of sheep were not disturbed by baronial hunting parties. In the early twelfth century several of these reserves were very large: Annandale, Eskdale, Renfrew and Cunninghame. By the thirteenth century forests created by royal grant were smaller and mainly in the north. The baron could grant concessions to his tenants or the church and had to face the problem of pressure on the other resources of the reserve. The map shows the baronial forests which were first recorded between 1124 and 1286. The boundaries shown are approximate.

Approximate boundaries of royal forests

Forest first recorded between 1124 - 1200

Forest first recorded between 1200 - 1286

ATHOLL Forest with no defined limit

Baronial forests 1124 to 1286

JMG

Baronies, lordships and earldoms in the early 15th century

The following six maps deal with Scottish baronies at the beginning of the fifteenth century (but only *lay* ones; ecclesiastical estates, which were usually held as baronies, are *not* included). 'Barony' did not then have its normal modern meaning of the lowest rank of the peerage (that derives from a different, English, usage). Instead, it was an estate held *in liberam baroniam*, with special 'baronial' powers exercised in the barony court; this disciplined the tenants, settled their disputes, heard such criminal cases as assault, theft, and accidental homicide (with convicted thieves being put to death), and enforced various kinds of national legislation. Baronies were thus significant local administrative units. Lords exercising baronial powers were known as barons. In twelfth- and thirteenth-century Scotland the terminology had been employed loosely: all tenants-in-chief of single knight's feus probably counted as barons, and their estates as baronies, which were seen as subdivisions of the sheriffdoms. But late medieval usage was more precise: from Robert I's reign on, baronies needed either specific creation or crown ratification of their existence (which was not automatic; a number of earlier 'baronies' lapsed). Now, when an estate was erected into or recognised as a 'free barony', it gained a more permanent status, and could survive as a geographical concept even if the baronial powers were not exercised, or if its lands had been divided or had escheated to the crown. A number of the baronies shown here were actually 'in abeyance', so to speak, in the early fifteenth century.

When exercised, baronial authority gave the lord considerable social status, plus considerable income from fines and forfeitures. Thus grants 'in free barony' became a significant feature of royal patronage (and not only royal: great magnates and ecclesiastical institutions also occasionally granted land *in liberam baroniam*). As a result, late medieval baronies proliferated, from some 2-300 in Robert I's reign to at least 400 by the early fifteenth century; and there were probably well over a thousand by the seventeenth century. Those seventeenth-century baronies, however, would be impossible to map: many were tiny individual pieces of land, many others combined properties scattered across numerous sheriffdoms. But that was the result of a trend beginning in the mid-fifteenth century, and around 1400 the territorial pattern is much clearer. Then, baronies did *not* contain lands in more than one sheriffdom. Also, in most cases they probably consisted of fairly compact and coherent blocks of land. Furthermore, many had the same names as parishes, and appear often to have covered much the same territory. Admittedly, baronies often contained lands in more than one parish, and parishes often contained several baronies. Nevertheless, by taking careful account of the relevant parish boundaries together with the location of the *caput*, an idea of the likely extent of each early fifteenth-century barony can be gained; this is done in in the first four maps.

The baronies are mapped by sheriffdoms. Each barony's *caput* is normally indicated by a circle, with a number referring to the numbered lists of baronies ②. Often, lines radiate outwards from the circles [⑦], to give a rough impression of the larger baronies' lands. Where there were two separate blocks in a barony, these are linked by a dotted line; where a barony consisted of more, scattered, portions, this has been shown by locating its *caput* with a cross [✕]; neither case is common. In the lists, each barony's name is accompanied by the name (in italics) of the medieval parish containing its *caput*, and if a barony included land in two or more parishes, this is indicated by + or ++; that helps to elucidate barony-parish relationships. An asterisk [*] before a barony's name shows that it was held of an earldom or provincial lordship. With baronies

in Berwickshire, however, account has been taken of the 1401 enactment that if an earldom came into crown hands, all baronies in it were to be detached and held directly of the crown; that was applied at once to the temporarily forfeited earldom of March. (This is one reason why the maps are dated about 1405, not about 1400.)

The first four maps also depict some 'superbaronies', the 'provincial' earldoms and lordships, which were invariably held *in liberam baroniam*. It should be stressed that the boundaries shown are often only conjectural and approximate. The earldoms are the thirteen old earldoms already mapped in the earlier section on 'Earldoms and "Provincial Lordships", 1124 to 1286', plus Moray (revived in 1312 and dating in the form shown here from 1372). The main changes since 1286 are the revival of Moray, the expansion of Ross, the virtual disappearance of Buchan (suppressed after 1308, but revived in token form in 1382), and the shrinkage of March. As for the "provincial lordships" mapped in the earlier section, most belonged to earls in the late Middle Ages, and ten - Annandale, Badenoch, Galloway, Garioch, Kyle Stewart, Lauderdale, Liddesdale, Lorn, Nithsdale and Skye - appear to have had a special status, indicated by the fact that their owners' titles took the form 'earl of A and lord of B'. Of the rest, the Stewarts' ancestral lordship of Renfrew, and Cunningham (granted to them by Robert I), may be considered to have had the same status; the new Lordship of the Isles accounts for Islay, Garmoran, Lochaber and Knapdale; and Strathbogie was to form the core of the later lordship of Gordon and earldom of Huntly. Thus there were thirteen likely 'provincial lordships' at the beginning of the fifteenth century; the others had lapsed.

The fifth map also deals with provincial earldoms and lordships, depicting them on a country-wide basis. It demonstrates how immensely important they still were in the early fifteenth century - but not for much longer, for during that century most of them came into the crown's hands, radically changing the country's territorial power structure. This map also indicates the lands of the new 'honorific' earldoms of Douglas (created 1358) and Crawford (created 1398); both consisted of scattered baronies and (in Douglas's case) lordships, and foreshadow the new earldoms of the later fifteenth century. In addition, the map shows the main Stewart possessions, which in 1404 were united into a great appanage for Robert III's heir, Prince James.

Finally, the sixth map is concerned with another type of 'superbarony', the regality. A grant of regality bestowed major extra powers: authority to deal with 'the pleas of the crown' (murder, rape, arson and violent robbery, which were normally reserved to the justiciar courts), and execute those found guilty; exclusive jurisdiction over the regality's tenants, so that any of them brought before another court could be 'repledged' to that of the regality; and freedom from interference by royal officers. Lords of regality thus had supreme control over their regalities, subject only to parliament and the king. Such major privileges were much more restricted than those of ordinary baronies. In the early fifteenth century there were only fifteen lords of regality, of whom several had powers confined to small areas. Others, however, held whole earldoms or provincial lordships in regality, and there were four particularly large complexes: the Stewart appanage (from 1404); the earldom of Douglas; the lands of the Douglas earl of Angus, including Liddesdale and Jedworth Forest; and the dozen baronies in southern Scotland held by James Douglas of Dalkeith, the richest lord in Scotland bar a few earls. Members of the house of Douglas thus had regality powers over a vast amount of territory. And, in general, it is striking how much of early fifteenth-century Scotland was withdrawn from the normal administrative structure because of the regalities.

AG

Baronies, lordships & earldoms

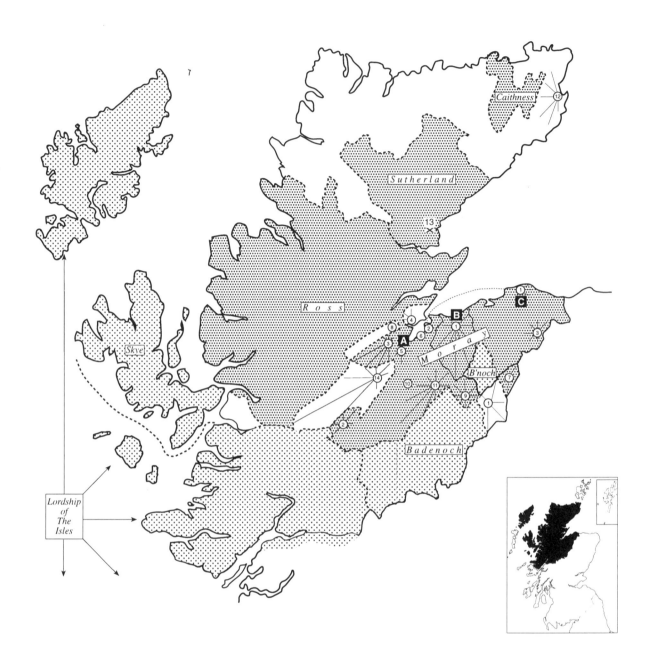

A: INVERNESS

1.	Abernethy	*(Abernethy)*
2.	*Abertarff	*(Abertarff)*
3.	*The Aird	*(Wardlaw +)*
4.	Avoch	*(Avoch)*
5.	*Bona	*(Bona)*
6.	*Brachlie	*(Brachlie)*
7.	*Cromdale	*(Cromdale)*
8.	Eddirdour	*(Killearnan)*
9.	*Glencairnie	*(Duthill)*
10.	*Kirdell	*(Daviot)*
11.	*Strath Dearn	*(Moy +)*
12.	Old Wick	*(Wick)*
13.	*Torboll	*(Dornoch)*
14.	Urquhart	*(Urquhart)*

B: NAIRN

1.	*Nairn	*(Invernairn ++)*

C: ELGIN

1.	*Duffus	*(Duffus)*
2.	*Petty	*(Petty)*
3.	*Rothes	*(Rothes)*

KEY TO ALL MAPS OF BARONIES ABOUT 1400

①	*Caput* of small barony (for numbers, see accompanying lists)
④	*Caput* of larger barony, with indication of likely extent of lands
13 ✕	*Caput* of barony consisting of scattered lands
C	*Caput* (usually) of sheriffdom or constabulary
- - - - -	Boundary of sheriffdom
⌒⌒	Approximate boundary of provincial earldom or lordship
Ross	Provincial earldom
Badenoch	Provincial lordship
·········	Linkages between detached parts of baronies, earldoms, sheriffdoms

Baronies about 1405, (1): northern Scotland
(sheriffdoms of Inverness, Nairn, Elgin)

AG

202

Baronies, lordships & earldoms

D: BANFF

1. Aberchirder (Aberchirder)
2. Boharm (Boharm)
3. Boyne (Inverboyndie)
4. Deskford (Deskford)
5. Findlater (Cullen)
6. Glendowachy (Gamrie)
7. Inverugie (Inverugie)
8. Mortlach (Mortlach)
9. Rothiemay (Rothiemay)
10. Strathalvah (Alvah)
11. Strathavon (Inveravon +)
12. Troup (Gamrie)
Unidentified: 'Kilsaurle'

E: ABERDEEN

1. Aberdour (Aberdour++)
2. Aboyne (Aboyne)
3. Aden (Deer)
4. Balgownie (Aberdeen St Machar)
5. Balhalgardy (Logie Durno ++)
6. Banchory-Devenick (Banchory-Devenick)
7. Belhelvie (Belhelvie)
8. Cluny (Cluny)
9. Coull & O'Neil (Coull, Kincardine O'Neil)
10. Cruden (Cruden)
11. Cushnie (Cushnie)
12. Drum (Dalmayock)
13. Drumblade (Drumblade)
14. Fedderate (Deer)
15. Findon (Banchory-Devenick)
16. Forbes (Forbes)
17. Formartine (Fyvie +)
18. Foveran (Foveran)
19. Frendraught (Forgue)
20. Kellie (Methlick ++)
21. Kingedward (Kingedward ++)
22. Kintore (Kintore)
23. *Leslie (Leslie)
24. Ludquharn (Longside ++)
25. Little Culter (Peterculter)
26. Midmar (Midmar)
27. Monycabbo (Aberdeen St Machar)
28. Murtle (Peterculter)
29. Philorth (Philorth)
30. Pitfodels (Banchory-Devenick)
31. Rattray (Crimond ++)
32. Rothienorman (Fyvie)
33. Shivas (Tarves)
34. Skene (Skene)
35. Slains (Slains)

F: KINCARDINE

1. Allardyce (Arbuthnot)
2. Balmaleedie (Aberlethnot/Marykirk)
3. Benholm (Benholm)
4. Cowie (Fetteresso)
5. Craigie (Ecclesgreig)
6. Dunottar (Dunottar)
7. Durris (Durris)
8. Glenbervie (Glenbervie)
9. Inverbervie (Kinneff)
10. Kincardine (Fordoun ++)
11. Kinneff (Kinneff)
12. Mondyness (Fordoun)
13. Newdosk (Newdosk)
14. Strachan (Strachan)
15. Thornton (Aberlethnott/Marykirk)
16. Tullibole (Banchory-Ternan)
17. Urie (Fetteresso)

G: FORFAR

1. Aberlemno (Aberlemno)
2. Ardler (Kettins)
3. Auchterhouse (Auchterhouse)
4. Auchtertyre (Newtyle)
5. Brechin (Brechin)
6. Clova (Clova)
7. Cortachy (Cortachy)
8. Craig & Glenisla (Inchbrayock/Craig, Glenisla)
9. Downie (Tannadice)
10. Dun (Dun)

(FORFAR, contd.)
11. Dundee (Dundee)
12. Earl's Ruthven (Ruthven)
13. Eassie (Eassie)
14. *Ethiebeaton (Monifieth)
15. Fern (Fern)
16. Fethies (Farnell)
17. Formal (Lintrathen)
18. Gask (Kettins)
19. Glamis (Glamis)
20. Guthrie (Guthrie)
21. Glenesk (Edzell)
22. Inverarity (Inverarity)
23. Inverlunan (Lunan)
24. Kellie (Abirlot)
25. Kettins (Kettins)
26. Kinblethmont (Inverkeillor)
27. Kinnaber (Montrose)
28. Kinnell (Kinnell)
29. Kinnetles (Kinnetles)
30. *Kirriemuir (Kirriemuir+)
31. Lintrathen (Lintrathen)
32. Logie (Logie Montrose)
33. Lour (Restennet)
34. Lundie (Lundie)
35. Nevay (Nevay)
36. Newtyle (Newtyle)
37. Ogilvie (Glamis)
38. Panbride (Panbride)
39. Panmure (Panbride)
40. Red Castle (Inverkeillor)
41. Reddie (Tannadice)
42. Rossie (Inchbrayock)
43. *Strathdichty (Mains/Strathdichty)
44. Tannadice (Tannadice)
45. Tealing (Tealing)
46. Turin (Rescobie)
Unidentified: 'Galloweald', 'Murlettre'

H: FIFE

1. Aberdour (Aberdour)
2. Ardross (Kilconquhar)
3. Ballenbreich (Flisk)
4. Carnock (Carnock)
5. Ceres (Ceres)
6. Cleish (Cleish)
7. Crail (Crail)
8. Crombie (Crombie)
9. Dysart (Dysart)
10. Fithkill (Leslie/Fithkill)
11. Glassmount (Kinghorn)
12. Inverkeithing (Inverkeithing)
13. Kellie (Carnbee/Kellie)
14. Kilbrakmont (Kilconquhar)
15. Kinghorn (Kinghorn ++)
16. Kinnear (Kilmany?)
17. Leuchars (Leuchars)
18. Lochore (Ballingry)
19. Naughton (Balmerino)
20. *Reres (Kilconquhar)
21. Rosyth (Rosyth)
22. *Scoonie (Scoonie)
Unidentified: 'Pitconnochie'

I: KINROSS

1. Lochleven

J: CLACKMANNAN

1. Alloa (Alloa)
2. Clackmannan (Clackmannan)
3. Tillycoultry (Tillycoultry)
4. Tullibody (Tullibody)
Unidentified: 'Schenbothy'

Baronies about 1405, (2): eastern Scotland
(sheriffdoms of Banff, Aberdeen, Kincardine, Forfar, Fife, Kinross, Clackmannan)

AG

Baronies, lordships & earldoms

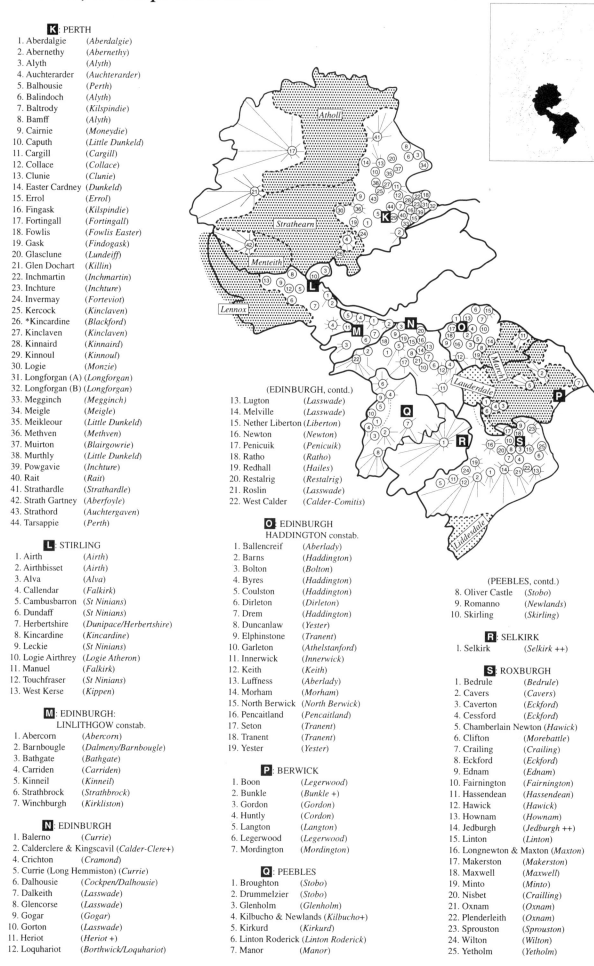

K: PERTH
1. Aberdalgie   (*Aberdalgie*)
2. Abernethy   (*Abernethy*)
3. Alyth   (*Alyth*)
4. Auchterarder   (*Auchterarder*)
5. Balhousie   (*Perth*)
6. Balindoch   (*Alyth*)
7. Baltrody   (*Kilspindie*)
8. Bamff   (*Alyth*)
9. Cairnie   (*Moneydie*)
10. Caputh   (*Little Dunkeld*)
11. Cargill   (*Cargill*)
12. Collace   (*Collace*)
13. Clunie   (*Clunie*)
14. Easter Cardney   (*Dunkeld*)
15. Errol   (*Errol*)
16. Fingask   (*Kilspindie*)
17. Fortingall   (*Fortingall*)
18. Fowlis   (*Fowlis Easter*)
19. Gask   (*Findogask*)
20. Glasclune   (*Lundeiff*)
21. Glen Dochart   (*Killin*)
22. Inchmartin   (*Inchmartin*)
23. Inchture   (*Inchture*)
24. Invermay   (*Forteviot*)
25. Kercock   (*Kinclaven*)
26. *Kincardine   (*Blackford*)
27. Kinclaven   (*Kinclaven*)
28. Kinnaird   (*Kinnaird*)
29. Kinnoul   (*Kinnoul*)
30. Logie   (*Monzie*)
31. Longforgan (A) (*Longforgan*)
32. Longforgan (B) (*Longforgan*)
33. Megginch   (*Megginch*)
34. Meigle   (*Meigle*)
35. Meikleour   (*Little Dunkeld*)
36. Methven   (*Methven*)
37. Muirton   (*Blairgowrie*)
38. Murthly   (*Little Dunkeld*)
39. Powgavie   (*Inchture*)
40. Rait   (*Rait*)
41. Strathardle   (*Strathardle*)
42. Strath Gartney   (*Aberfoyle*)
43. Strathord   (*Auchtergaven*)
44. Tarsappie   (*Perth*)

L: STIRLING
1. Airth   (*Airth*)
2. Airthbisset   (*Airth*)
3. Alva   (*Alva*)
4. Callendar   (*Falkirk*)
5. Cambusbarron   (*St Ninians*)
6. Dundaff   (*St Ninians*)
7. Herbertshire   (*Dunipace/Herbertshire*)
8. Kincardine   (*Kincardine*)
9. Leckie   (*St Ninians*)
10. Logie Airthrey   (*Logie Atheron*)
11. Manuel   (*Falkirk*)
12. Touchfraser   (*St Ninians*)
13. West Kerse   (*Kippen*)

M: EDINBURGH:
LINLITHGOW constab.
1. Abercorn   (*Abercorn*)
2. Barnbougle   (*Dalmeny/Barnbougle*)
3. Bathgate   (*Bathgate*)
4. Carriden   (*Carriden*)
5. Kinneil   (*Kinneil*)
6. Strathbrock   (*Strathbrock*)
7. Winchburgh   (*Kirkliston*)

N: EDINBURGH
1. Balerno   (*Currie*)
2. Calderclere & Kingscavil (*Calder-Clere+*)
4. Crichton   (*Cramond*)
5. Currie (Long Hemmiston) (*Currie*)
6. Dalhousie   (*Cockpen/Dalhousie*)
7. Dalkeith   (*Lasswade*)
8. Glencorse   (*Lasswade*)
9. Gogar   (*Gogar*)
10. Gorton   (*Lasswade*)
11. Heriot   (*Heriot +*)
12. Loquhariot   (*Borthwick/Loquhariot*)

(EDINBURGH, contd.)
13. Lugton   (*Lasswade*)
14. Melville   (*Lasswade*)
15. Nether Liberton (*Liberton*)
16. Newton   (*Newton*)
17. Penicuik   (*Penicuik*)
18. Ratho   (*Ratho*)
19. Redhall   (*Hailes*)
20. Restalrig   (*Restalrig*)
21. Roslin   (*Lasswade*)
22. West Calder   (*Calder-Comitis*)

O: EDINBURGH
HADDINGTON constab.
1. Ballencreif   (*Aberlady*)
2. Barns   (*Haddington*)
3. Bolton   (*Bolton*)
4. Byres   (*Haddington*)
5. Coulston   (*Haddington*)
6. Dirleton   (*Dirleton*)
7. Drem   (*Haddington*)
8. Duncanlaw   (*Yester*)
9. Elphinstone   (*Tranent*)
10. Garleton   (*Athelstanford*)
11. Innerwick   (*Innerwick*)
12. Keith   (*Keith*)
13. Luffness   (*Aberlady*)
14. Morham   (*Morham*)
15. North Berwick   (*North Berwick*)
16. Pencaitland   (*Pencaitland*)
17. Seton   (*Tranent*)
18. Tranent   (*Tranent*)
19. Yester   (*Yester*)

P: BERWICK
1. Boon   (*Legerwood*)
2. Bunkle   (*Bunkle +*)
3. Gordon   (*Gordon*)
4. Huntly   (*Cordon*)
5. Langton   (*Langton*)
6. Legerwood   (*Legerwood*)
7. Mordington   (*Mordington*)

Q: PEEBLES
1. Broughton   (*Stobo*)
2. Drummelzier   (*Stobo*)
3. Glenholm   (*Glenholm*)
4. Kilbucho & Newlands (*Kilbucho+*)
5. Kirkurd   (*Kirkurd*)
6. Linton Roderick (*Linton Roderick*)
7. Manor   (*Manor*)

(PEEBLES, contd.)
8. Oliver Castle   (*Stobo*)
9. Romanno   (*Newlands*)
10. Skirling   (*Skirling*)

R: SELKIRK
1. Selkirk   (*Selkirk ++*)

S: ROXBURGH
1. Bedrule   (*Bedrule*)
2. Cavers   (*Cavers*)
3. Caverton   (*Eckford*)
4. Cessford   (*Eckford*)
5. Chamberlain Newton (*Hawick*)
6. Clifton   (*Morebattle*)
7. Crailing   (*Crailing*)
8. Eckford   (*Eckford*)
9. Ednam   (*Ednam*)
10. Fairnington   (*Fairnington*)
11. Hassendean   (*Hassendean*)
12. Hawick   (*Hawick*)
13. Hownam   (*Hownam*)
14. Jedburgh   (*Jedburgh ++*)
15. Linton   (*Linton*)
16. Longnewton & Maxton (*Maxton*)
17. Makerston   (*Makerston*)
18. Maxwell   (*Maxwell*)
19. Minto   (*Minto*)
20. Nisbet   (*Crailling*)
21. Oxnam   (*Oxnam*)
22. Plenderleith   (*Oxnam*)
23. Sprouston   (*Sprouston*)
24. Wilton   (*Wilton*)
25. Yetholm   (*Yetholm*)

Baronies about 1405, (3): central and south-eastern Scotland
(sheriffdoms of Perth, Stirling, Edinburgh, Berwick, Peebles, Selkirk, Roxburgh)

AG

Baronies, lordships & earldoms

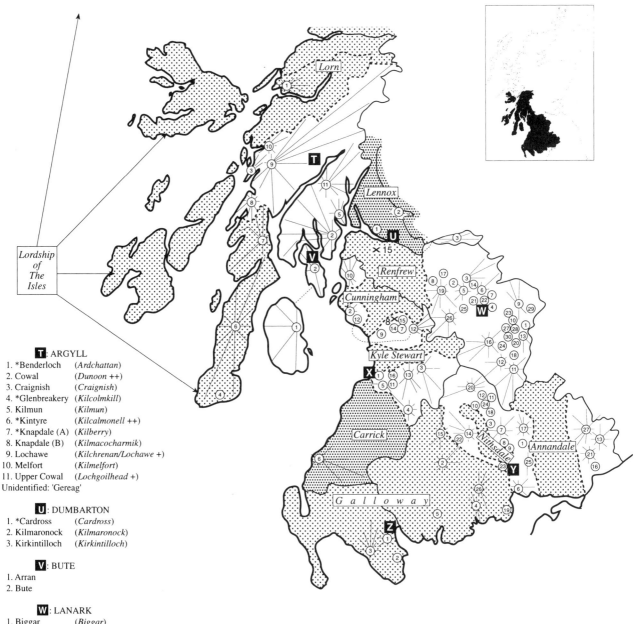

T: ARGYLL
1. *Benderloch   (*Ardchattan*)
2. Cowal   (*Dunoon* ++)
3. Craignish   (*Craignish*)
4. *Glenbreakery   (*Kilcolmkill*)
5. Kilmun   (*Kilmun*)
6. *Kintyre   (*Kilcalmonell* ++)
7. *Knapdale (A)   (*Kilberry*)
8. Knapdale (B)   (*Kilmacocharmik*)
9. Lochawe   (*Kilchrenan/Lochawe* +)
10. Melfort   (*Kilmelfort*)
11. Upper Cowal   (*Lochgoilhead* +)
Unidentified: 'Gereag'

U: DUMBARTON
1. *Cardross   (*Cardross*)
2. Kilmaronock   (*Kilmaronock*)
3. Kirkintilloch   (*Kirkintilloch*)

V: BUTE
1. Arran
2. Bute

W: LANARK
1. Biggar   (*Biggar*)
2. Blantyre   (*Blantyre*)
3. Bothwell   (*Bothwell*)
4. Braidwood   (*Carluke*)
5. Cadzow   (*Cadzow*)
6. Cambusnethan   (*Cambusnthan*)
7. Carluke   (*Carluke*)
8. Carmunnock   (*Carmunock*)
9. Carnwath   (*Carnwath* +)
10. Covington   (*Covington*)
11. Crawford   (*Crawford*)
12. Crawfordjohn   (*Crawfordjohn*)
13. Coulter   (*Culter*)
14. Dalziel   (*Dalziel*)
15. *Dennistoun   (*Kilmalcolm*)
16. Douglas   (*Douglas* +)
17. Drumsargard   (*Camuslang/Drumsargard*)
18. Hartside   (*Hartside*)
19. Kilbride   (*Kilbride*)
20. Lamington   (*Lamington*)
21. Machan   (*Machan*)
22. Mauldslie   (*Carluke*)
23. Pettinain   (*Pettinain*)
24. Roberton   (*Roberton*)
25. Stonehouse   (*Stonehouse*)
26. Strathaven   (*Strathaven*)
27. Symington   (*Symington*)
28. Thankerton   (*Thankerton*)
29. Walston   (*Walston*)
30. Wiston   (*Wiston*)

X: AYR
1. Alloway   (*Alloway*)
2. Ardrossan   (*Ardrossan*)
3. Cumnock   (*Cumnock*)
4. Dalmellington   (*Dalmellington*)
5. Dalrymple   (*Dalrymple*)
6. *Glenstinchar   (*Colmonell*)
7. Grougar   (*Kilmarnock*)
8. Kilmarnock   (*Kilmarnock*)
9. Kilmaurs   (*Kilmaurs*)
10. Largs   (*Largs*)
11. Lochmartnaham   (*Coylton*)
12. Loudon   (*Loudon* +)
13. Ochiltree   (*Ochiltree*)
14. Pokelly   (*Kilmarnock*)
15. Rowallan   (*Kilmarnock*)
16. Sundrum   (*Coylton*)

Y: DUMFRIES
1. Amisfield   (*Tinwald*)
2. *Balmaclellan   (*Balmaclellan*)
3. Barburgh   (*Dalgarno*)
4. *Buittle   (*Buittle*)
5. *Cally   (*Girthon*)
6. Carlaverock   (*Carlaverock*)
7. Closeburn   (*Closeburn*)
8. Dalswinton (A)   (*Kirkmahoe*)
9. Dalswinton (B)   (*Kirkmahoe*)

(DUMFRIES, contd.)
10. Drumlanrig   (*Durisdeer*)
11. Durisdeer   (*Durisdeer*)
12. Enoch   (*Durisdeer*)
13. Ewesdale   (*Ewes*)
14. Glencairn   (*Glencairn*)
15. *Glenken   (*Dalry*)
16. Kirkandrews   (*Kirkandrews*)
17. Kirkmichael   (*Kirkmichael*)
18. Morton   (*Morton*)
19. *Preston   (*Kirkbean*)
20. Sanquhar   (*Sanquhar*)
21. Staplegordon   (*Staplegordon*)
22. Snade   (*Glencairn*)
23. Terregles   (*Terregles*)
24. Tibbers   (*Durisdeer*)
25. Torthorwald   (*Torthorwald*)
26. *Urr   (*Urr*)
27. Westerkirk   (*Westerkirk*)
Unidentified: 'Malarnock', *'New Forest'

Z: WIGTOWN
1. *Carnesmole   (*Kirkinner/Carnesmole*)
2. *Cruggleton   (*Cruggleton*)
3. *Mochrum   (*Mochrum*)

Baronies about 1405, (4): south-western Scotland
(sheriffdoms of Argyll, Dumbarton, Bute, Lanark, Ayr, Dumfries, Wigtown)

AG

Baronies, lordships & earldoms

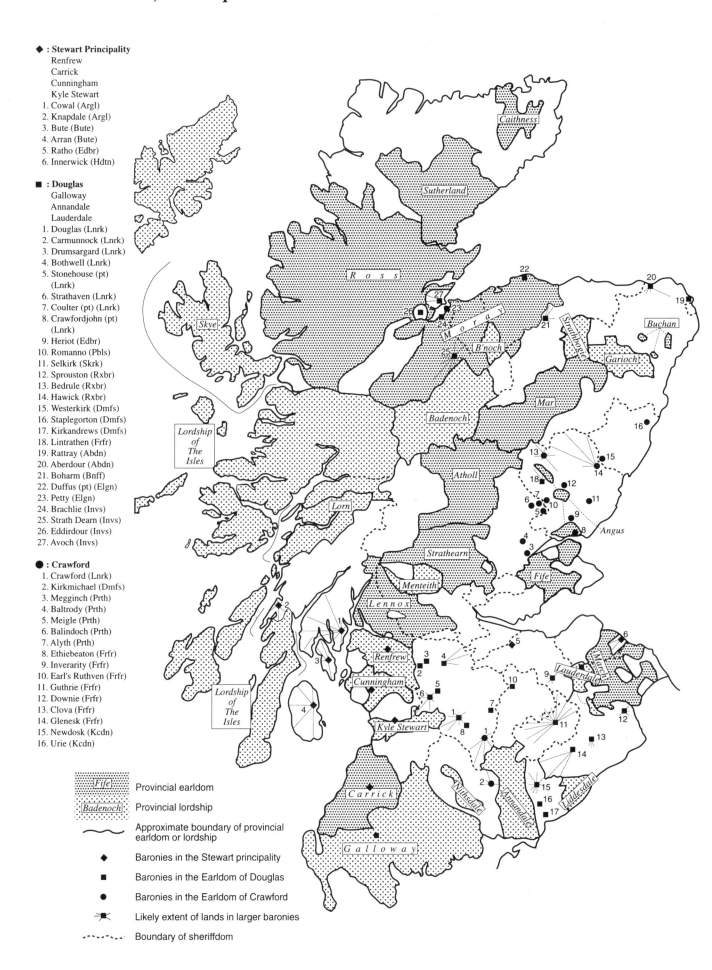

♦ : **Stewart Principality**
Renfrew
Carrick
Cunningham
Kyle Stewart
1. Cowal (Argl)
2. Knapdale (Argl)
3. Bute (Bute)
4. Arran (Bute)
5. Ratho (Edbr)
6. Innerwick (Hdtn)

■ : **Douglas**
Galloway
Annandale
Lauderdale
1. Douglas (Lnrk)
2. Carmunnock (Lnrk)
3. Drumsargard (Lnrk)
4. Bothwell (Lnrk)
5. Stonehouse (pt) (Lnrk)
6. Strathaven (Lnrk)
7. Coulter (pt) (Lnrk)
8. Crawfordjohn (pt) (Lnrk)
9. Heriot (Edbr)
10. Romanno (Pbls)
11. Selkirk (Skrk)
12. Sprouston (Rxbr)
13. Bedrule (Rxbr)
14. Hawick (Rxbr)
15. Westerkirk (Dmfs)
16. Staplegorton (Dmfs)
17. Kirkandrews (Dmfs)
18. Lintrathen (Frfr)
19. Rattray (Abdn)
20. Aberdour (Abdn)
21. Boharm (Bnff)
22. Duffus (pt) (Elgn)
23. Petty (Elgn)
24. Brachlie (Invs)
25. Strath Dearn (Invs)
26. Eddirdour (Invs)
27. Avoch (Invs)

● : **Crawford**
1. Crawford (Lnrk)
2. Kirkmichael (Dmfs)
3. Megginch (Prth)
4. Baltrody (Prth)
5. Meigle (Prth)
6. Balindoch (Prth)
7. Alyth (Prth)
8. Ethiebeaton (Frfr)
9. Inverarity (Frfr)
10. Earl's Ruthven (Frfr)
11. Guthrie (Frfr)
12. Downie (Frfr)
13. Clova (Frfr)
14. Glenesk (Frfr)
15. Newdosk (Kcdn)
16. Urie (Kcdn)

Fife   Provincial earldom

Badenoch   Provincial lordship

——   Approximate boundary of provincial earldom or lordship

♦   Baronies in the Stewart principality

■   Baronies in the Earldom of Douglas

●   Baronies in the Earldom of Crawford

✳   Likely extent of lands in larger baronies

–·–·–   Boundary of sheriffdom

Earldoms and lordships about 1405   AG

Baronies, lordships & earldoms

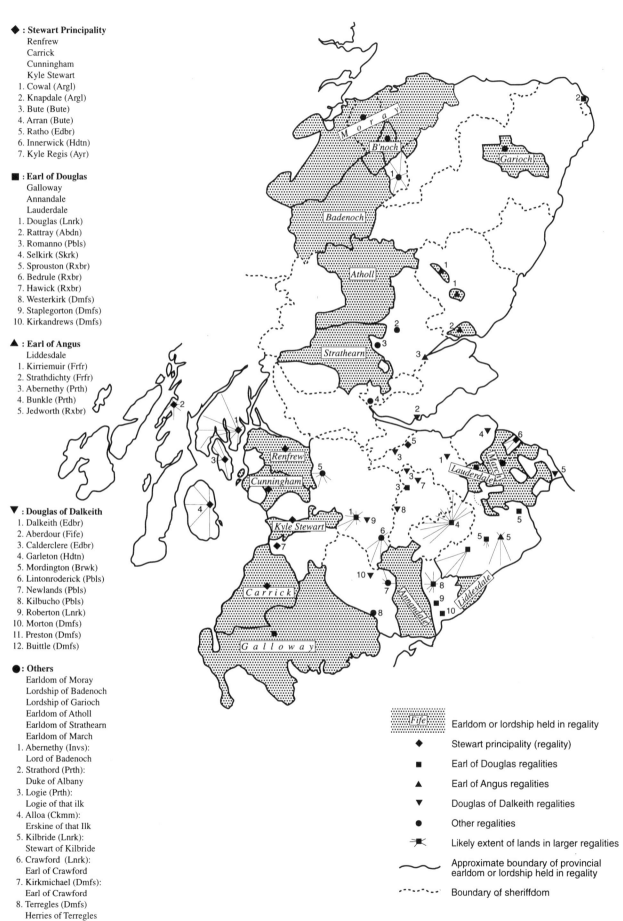

◆ : Stewart Principality
Renfrew
Carrick
Cunningham
Kyle Stewart
1. Cowal (Argl)
2. Knapdale (Argl)
3. Bute (Bute)
4. Arran (Bute)
5. Ratho (Edbr)
6. Innerwick (Hdtn)
7. Kyle Regis (Ayr)

■ : Earl of Douglas
Galloway
Annandale
Lauderdale
1. Douglas (Lnrk)
2. Rattray (Abdn)
3. Romanno (Pbls)
4. Selkirk (Skrk)
5. Sprouston (Rxbr)
6. Bedrule (Rxbr)
7. Hawick (Rxbr)
8. Westerkirk (Dmfs)
9. Staplegorton (Dmfs)
10. Kirkandrews (Dmfs)

▲ : Earl of Angus
Liddesdale
1. Kirriemuir (Frfr)
2. Strathdichty (Frfr)
3. Abernethy (Prth)
4. Bunkle (Prth)
5. Jedworth (Rxbr)

▼ : Douglas of Dalkeith
1. Dalkeith (Edbr)
2. Aberdour (Fife)
3. Calderclere (Edbr)
4. Garleton (Hdtn)
5. Mordington (Brwk)
6. Lintonroderick (Pbls)
7. Newlands (Pbls)
8. Kilbucho (Pbls)
9. Roberton (Lnrk)
10. Morton (Dmfs)
11. Preston (Dmfs)
12. Buittle (Dmfs)

● : Others
Earldom of Moray
Lordship of Badenoch
Lordship of Garioch
Earldom of Atholl
Earldom of Strathearn
Earldom of March
1. Abernethy (Invs):
    Lord of Badenoch
2. Strathord (Prth):
    Duke of Albany
3. Logie (Prth):
    Logie of that ilk
4. Alloa (Ckmm):
    Erskine of that Ilk
5. Kilbride (Lnrk):
    Stewart of Kilbride
6. Crawford (Lnrk):
    Earl of Crawford
7. Kirkmichael (Dmfs):
    Earl of Crawford
8. Terregles (Dmfs)
    Herries of Terregles

Fife Earldom or lordship held in regality

◆ Stewart principality (regality)

■ Earl of Douglas regalities

▲ Earl of Angus regalities

▼ Douglas of Dalkeith regalities

● Other regalities

⚹ Likely extent of lands in larger regalities

⁓ Approximate boundary of provincial earldom or lordship held in regality

·-----· Boundary of sheriffdom

Regalities about 1405   AG

Sheriffs, stewards and bailies

This sequence of maps shows first the relatively slight development of sheriffdoms in the later Middle Ages. The sheriffdom of Argyll emerges in the reign of Robert I (1306-29), Bute later in the fourteenth century. Renfrew was separated from Lanark about 1414. Linlithgow appears to have evolved from a constabulary of Edinburgh into an independent sheriffdom in the fifteenth century, while Elgin and Forres were merged. The first reference to a sheriffdom of Tarbert is in 1481. Not shown are those burghs which received grants of shrieval jurisdiction during the period. A significant development resulted from forfeitures of large regalities, which led to their administration coming under royal authority as stewartries distinct from neighbouring sheriffdoms - Menteith, Strathearn, Annandale and Kirkcudbright. The final point illustrated by the maps is the holders of the offices of sheriff, steward and bailie, based on the sets of sheriffs' accounts surviving for 1359, 1455 and 1501, supplemented from other sources.

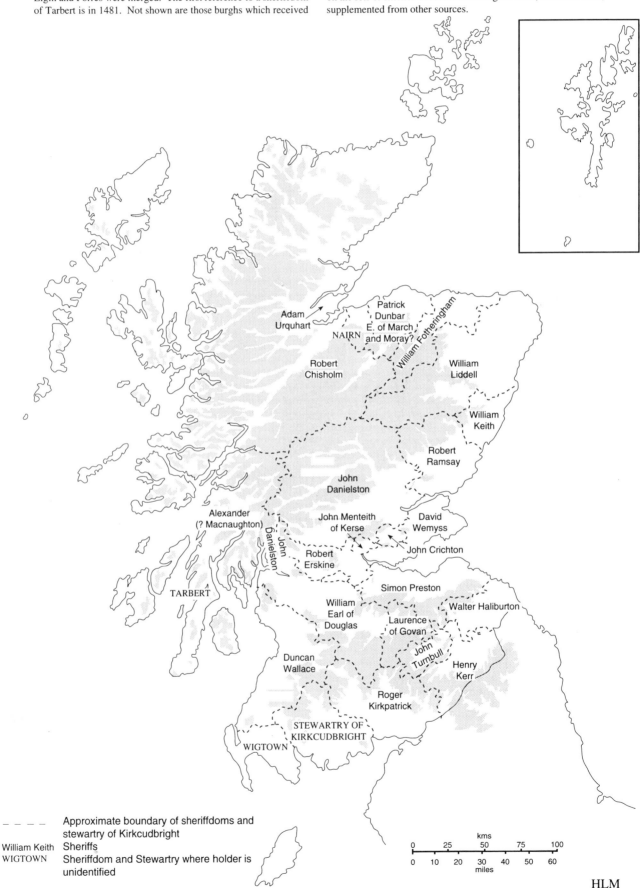

Adam Urquhart

Patrick Dunbar E. of March and Moray?

NAIRN

William Fotheringham

Robert Chisholm

William Liddell

William Keith

Robert Ramsay

John Danielston

Alexander (? Macnaughton)

John Danielston

John Menteith of Kerse

David Wemyss

John Crichton

Robert Erskine

Simon Preston

TARBERT

William Earl of Douglas

Laurence of Govan

Walter Haliburton

John Turnbull

Henry Kerr

Duncan Wallace

Roger Kirkpatrick

STEWARTRY OF KIRKCUDBRIGHT

WIGTOWN

- - - - Approximate boundary of sheriffdoms and stewartry of Kirkcudbright

William Keith Sheriffs

WIGTOWN Sheriffdom and Stewartry where holder is unidentified

kms
0 25 50 75 100
0 10 20 30 40 50 60
miles

HLM

Sheriffs, stewards and bailies about 1360

208

Sheriffs, stewards and bailies

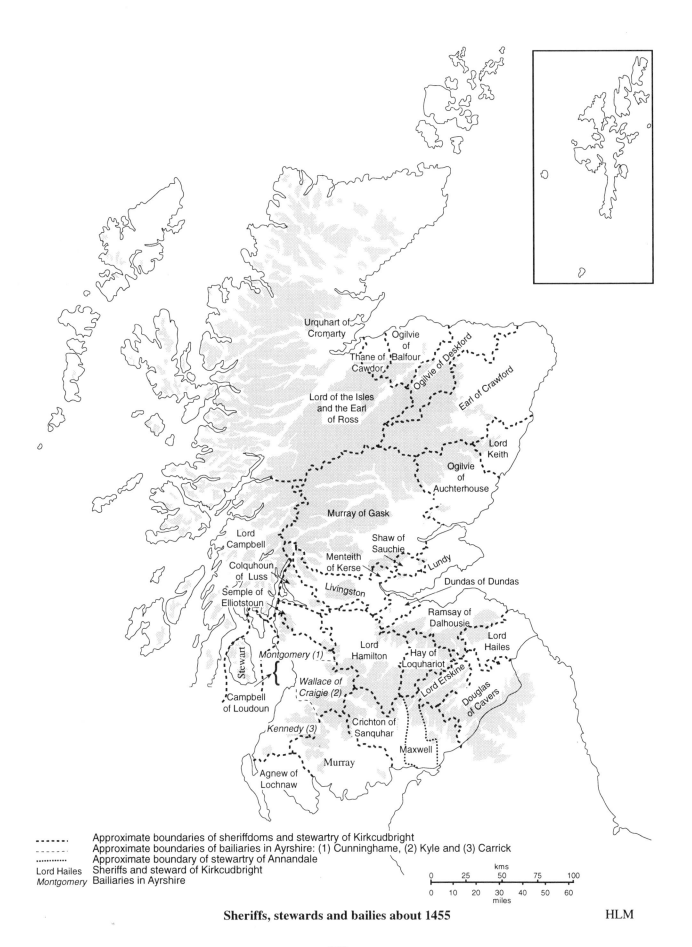

Urquhart of Cromarty

Ogilvie of Balfour

Thane of Cawdor

Ogilvie of Deskford

Earl of Crawford

Lord of the Isles and the Earl of Ross

Lord Keith

Ogilvie of Auchterhouse

Murray of Gask

Lord Campbell

Shaw of Sauchie

Colquhoun of Luss

Menteith of Kerse

Lundy

Semple of Elliotstoun

Livingston

Dundas of Dundas

Ramsay of Dalhousie

Lord Hailes

Montgomery (1)

Lord Hamilton

Hay of Loquhariot

Lord Erskine

Douglas of Cavers

Stewart

Wallace of Craigie (2)

Campbell of Loudoun

Kennedy (3)

Crichton of Sanquhar

Maxwell

Murray

Agnew of Lochnaw

-------- Approximate boundaries of sheriffdoms and stewartry of Kirkcudbright
- - - - - Approximate boundaries of bailiaries in Ayrshire: (1) Cunninghame, (2) Kyle and (3) Carrick
·········· Approximate boundary of stewartry of Annandale
Lord Hailes Sheriffs and steward of Kirkcudbright
Montgomery Bailiaries in Ayrshire

kms
0   25   50   75   100

0 10 20 30 40 50 60
miles

Sheriffs, stewards and bailies about 1455

HLM

Sheriffs, stewards and bailies

Urquhart of Cromarty
Thane of Cawdor
Earl of Huntly
Earl of Buchan
Earl of Crawford
Ogilvie of Bune
Keith Earl Marischal
Lord Gray
Lord Ruthven
Earl of Argyll
Lord Drummond (1)
Menteith of Kerse
Lundy of Balgownie
Edmonstone (2)
Earl of Lennox
Cunningham of Polmaise
Douglas of Lochleven
Hamilton
Semple of Elliotstoun
Earl of Bothwell
TARBERT
Earl of Bothwell
Lord Montgomery (1)
Stewart
Lord Hamilton
Hay of Yester
Lord Erskine
Douglas of Cavers
Campbell of Loudoun
Campbell of Craigie (2)
Lord Kennedy (3)
Crichton of Sanquhar
Lord Maxwell (3)
Agnew (Dunbar of Mochrum)
Earl of Bothwell

- - - - - -   Approximate boundaries of sheriffdoms and stewartry of Kirkcudbright
- - - - - -   Approximate boundaries of bailiaries in Ayrshire: (1) Cunninghame, (2) Kyle and (3) Carrick
············   Approximate boundary of stewartry of (1) Strathearn (2) Menteith (3) Annandale
Lord Hailes   Sheriffs and steward of Kirkcudbright
Montgomery   Bailiaries in Ayrshire

kms
0   25   50   75   100

0 10 20 30 40 50 60
miles

Sheriffs, stewards and bailies about 1501   HLM

Justice ayres in the fifteenth century

This map illustrates the circuits of the fifteenth-century justiciars as they may be deduced from a variety of sources. There is little change from the thirteenth century save that the justiciary of Galloway was not revived by Robert I (1306-20). Instead it was subsumed within the justiciary of Lothian, which was renamed the justiciary south of Forth at the end of David II's reign. The justiciary of Scotia had already become the justiciary north of Forth. Some of the ayre towns changed: Lauder replaced Berwick and Jedburgh Roxburgh, as a result of English occupation, while the ayre of Angus was held sometimes in Forfar, sometimes in Dundee. Some sheriffdoms do not seem to have received ayre visitations, notably Argyll, where local lieutenants were sometimes given justiciary powers. In theory, the ayres were still held twice a year and they were held more often than has usually been held by historians. The ayres were also supplemented by ad hoc commissions of justiciary.

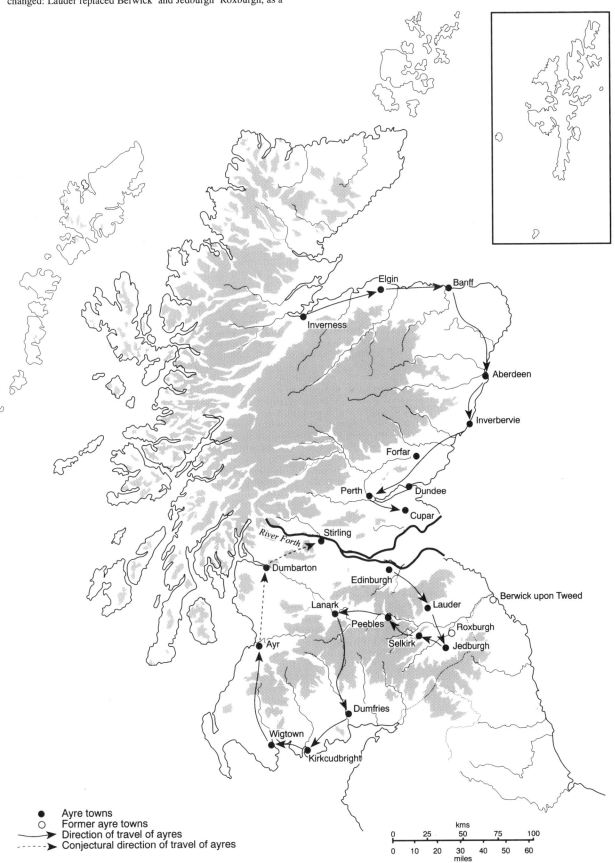

●	Ayre towns
○	Former ayre towns
——→	Direction of travel of ayres
- - -→	Conjectural direction of travel of ayres

Justice ayres in the fifteenth century

HLM

211

Burghs 1426 to 1550

The first burgh to receive a feu-farm (feu-ferme) charter was Berwick sometime in the second half of the thirteenth century. The grant had to be renewed twice subsequently after the burgh had been recovered from English control. Aberdeen was the first burgh to receive a feu-farm charter which remained permanently in force. This was in 1319; similar grants to other burghs soon followed so that by 1425 at least 22 burghs had feu-farm charters. The privilege enabled the burgesses to put any surplus revenue above the amount of the annual farm towards a 'common good' fund which could be used for community projects such as the repair or extension of town buildings. The importance of the charter should not be overestimated. Many burghs had long been leasing their revenues from the chamberlain on a fixed rent running for several years and some were still doing this in the early fifteenth century. Accordingly, the financial administration for supervision of the collection and spending of the burgh revenues was already in place. The main effect of the charters was to put this organisation on a more permanent footing, although they were probably also seen as a mark of status and indicate the crown's recognition of the burghs' increasing economic (and political?) inportance. All but three or four were granted after 1357 when the question of David II's ransom brought the burgesses to new prominence and parliamentary representation of the burghs became a permanent feature of central government. Although the charters were largely restricted to royal burghs the idea was copied by other burgh landlords with Dunfermline being granted feu-farm status in 1395.

Banff (1372)

Inverness (1370)

Aberdeen (1319)

Montrose (1370)

Forfar (1393)

Perth (1374) Dundee (1360)

Cupar (before 1426)

Crail (1393)

Stirling (1386) Dunfermline (1395)

Kinghorn (1329x1371)

Dumbarton (from 1384) Inverkeithing (1399)

Linlithgow (1388)

Renfrew (1397) Edinburgh (1329) Haddington (1388)

Rutherglen (1388)

Berwick (13th century)

Lanark (1393)

Irvine (from 1399) Peebles (from 1406)

Ayr (1400) Jedburgh (from 1406)

Dumfries (1395)

- ● Burghs with feu-farm charters
- ○ Burghs with long-term leases from the chamberlain

```
kms
0    25    50    75    100
0  10  20  30  40  50  60
        miles
```

Burghs with feu-farm status by 1426

EE

212

Burghs 1426 to 1550

Two important features were the rapid expansion in the number of
foundations compared with earlier centuries and the increasing
predominance numerically of burghs of barony, both ecclesiastical
and secular. The administration of such burghs was in line with that
of earlier burghs in that (i) they had no rural hinterland where they
might monopolise and control trade; (ii) they had no inherent right
to be represented in parliament and so were not liable for cess; and
(iii) they might not offically participate in overseas trade. Burghs of
barony however might be raised to the status of royal burghs (for
example, Pittenweem in 1541) and not all such burghs occupied a
lesser status . The five greater ecclesiastical burghs - St Andrews,
Glasgow, Brechin, Arbroath and Dunfermline - had the same trading
privileges as royal burghs. St Andrews and Brechin were represented in parliament by the end of the fifteenth century, as were the
others by 1579. In the course of the sixteenth century they also came
to be represented in the convention of royal burghs which protected
the privileges of the royal burghs. Membership of this body was
another distinction between the 'free' king's burghs and the 'unfree'
burghs of barony. Nevertheless, the burghs of barony were increasingly encroaching upon the former's privileges by the end of the
sixteenth century.

Kirkwall
(1486)

Tain (15?)

Fortrose
(1455)
Spynie
(1451)
Fordyce
(1499)
Kinloss
(1497)
Huntly
(1488)
Rayne
(1493)
Old Aberdeen
(1489)
Kingussie
(1464)
Torry (1495)

Belliehill (1500)
Kirriemuir (1459)
Glamis (1491)
Auchterhouse (1497)
Keithick (1492)

Abernethy (1459)
Falkland (1458)
Inveraray (1474)
Port of Menteith
(1467)
Leslie Green (1458)
Alloa (1497)
Culross (1490)
Kilmun
(1490)
Cramond
(1492)
Dunbar (1445)
Dunglass (1489)
Paisley
(1488)
Roslin
(1456)
Hamilton (1475)
Duns (1490)
Strathaven
(1450)
Carnwath (1451)
Newmilns
(1491)
Biggar
(1451)
Earlston (1489)
Douglas
(1464)
Newton Upon Ayr
(1446)
Sanquhar
(1484)
Torthorwald
(1473)
Lochmaben
(1440)
Ballinclach,
(1497)
Myreton (1477)
Whithorn
(1451)

• Burghs held of the crown

▲ Burghs of Barony (ecclesiastical)

⊡ Burghs of Barony

kms
0   25   50   75   100

0   10   20   30   40   50   60
miles

Burghs 1430 to 1500

EE

213

Burghs 1426 to 1550

1 Aberdour (West) 1501
2 Clatt
3 Fettercairn 1504
4 Merton 1504
5 Pencaitland 1505
6 Auchinleck 1507
7 Ruthwell 1508
8 Newburgh 1509 *de novo*
9 Cumnock 1509
10 Kildrummy 1509
11 Dysart 1501, 1549 *de novo*
12 Langton 1510
13 Strathmiglo 1510
14 Terregles or Herries 1510
15 Dalnagairn 1510
16 Mauchline 1510
17 Crawford 1511 (a 13 c burgh, re-erected burgh
    of barony)
18 Hawick 1511
19 Auldearn 1511
20 Dunning 1511
21 Wemyss or Wester Wemyss 1511
22 Kirkmichael or Kirkill or Kirkton or Tomlachan
    1511
23 Balnkilly 1511
24 Balnald 1511
25 Corshill - Over Inchgall 1511
26 Kincardine O'Neil 1511
27 Whithorn 1511 (till this date dependent on the
    prior and canons of Whithorn)
28 Turiff 1512
29 Largo 1513
30 Maybole 1516
31 Auchtermuchty 1517
32 Pittenweem 1526 *de novo*
33 Kirkintilloch 1526 (13 c burgh, re-erected
    burgh of barony)
34 Scrabster 1527
35 Dryburgh 1527
36 Kilmaurs 1527
37 Down or Doune 1528
38 Saltcoats 1529
39 Kincardine 1532 (erected *in liberum burgum*,
    but probably ancient burgh)
40 Findhorn or Seatown or Kinloss 1532
41 Annan 1532 (in 13 c dependent on the Bruce
    lords of Annandale)
42 Drummochy 1540
43 Dalkeith 1540 (early 15 c burgh, re-erected
    burgh of barony
44 Anstruther Wester 1541
45 Pittenweem 1541 (previously dependent on the
    prior of Pittenweem)
46 Burntisland 1541
47 Pitlessie 1541
48 Kinross 1541
49 Cowie 1541
50 Durris 1541
51 East Haven of Panmure 1541
52 Ballantrae 1541
53 Newbigging 1541
54 Tranent 1542
55 Arbuthnott 1543
56 Fraserburgh or Faithlie 1546
57 Hamilton 1549 (in 15 c a burgh of barony)
58 Portsoy 1550

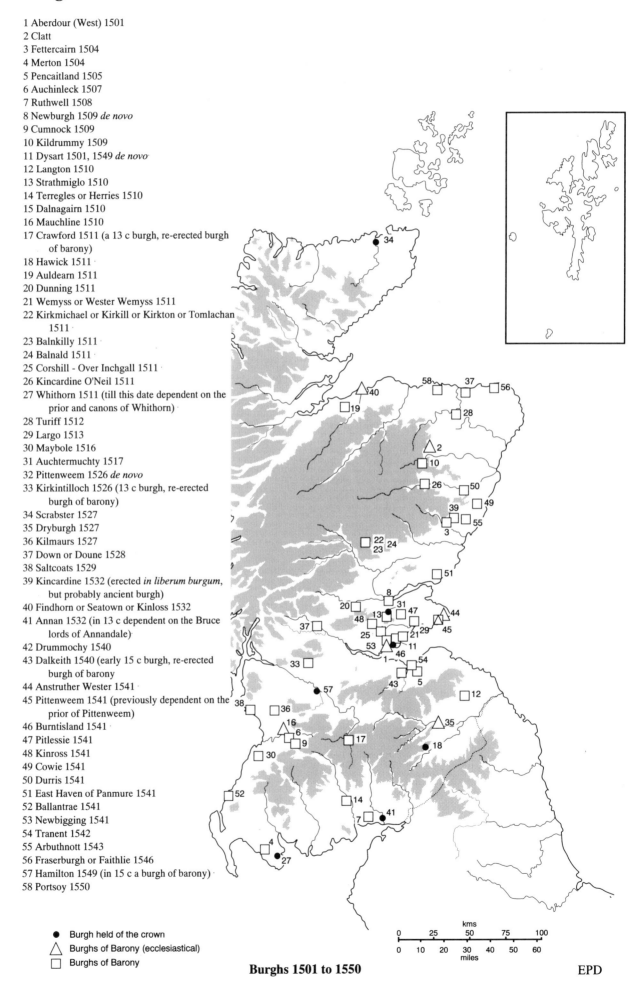

● Burgh held of the crown
△ Burghs of Barony (ecclesiastical)
□ Burghs of Barony

Burghs 1501 to 1550

EPD

Burghs 1426 to 1550

Gilds are found throughout medieval western European as socio-religious groups which developed in towns as economic organisations involved in mercantile pursuits. The emergence of burghs in Scotland was often tightly linked with gilds merchant, although it cannot be concluded with certainty that all early burghs possessed them. The early gild merchant could reflect the self-expression of the burgh, and gild members (as able members of society rather than as gild members) took an increasingly dominant role in the organisation of the burgh and admission of burgesses. The intermingling of the function of burgh and gild lasted into the fifteenth and sixteenth centuries in smaller burghs and was most apparent in the gild's control of the town's commercial activities (e.g. pricing of basic commodities, fining forestallers and regraters, monopolisation of dealing in staple goods, hides, furs, skins, wool and woolfells, overseeing the cloth and leather industries, controlling overseas trade). Gild members were the wealthier burgesses, entrance being by right of inheritance, or for service to the town or gild, or by the intercession of the crown or other influential person, or by payment. Early burgh laws and charters exclude weavers, fleshers, dyers and fullers from gild membership, but in practice craftsmen were accepted into the gild's fraternity. As formal craft organisations emerged in the larger burghs in the late fifteenth and sixteenth centuries, a certain exclusiveness and social stratification manifested itself in economic tension between groups, but in the smaller burghs the gild merchant maintained its role as an organisation of men, whether merchants or craftsmen, who dealt in merchandise.

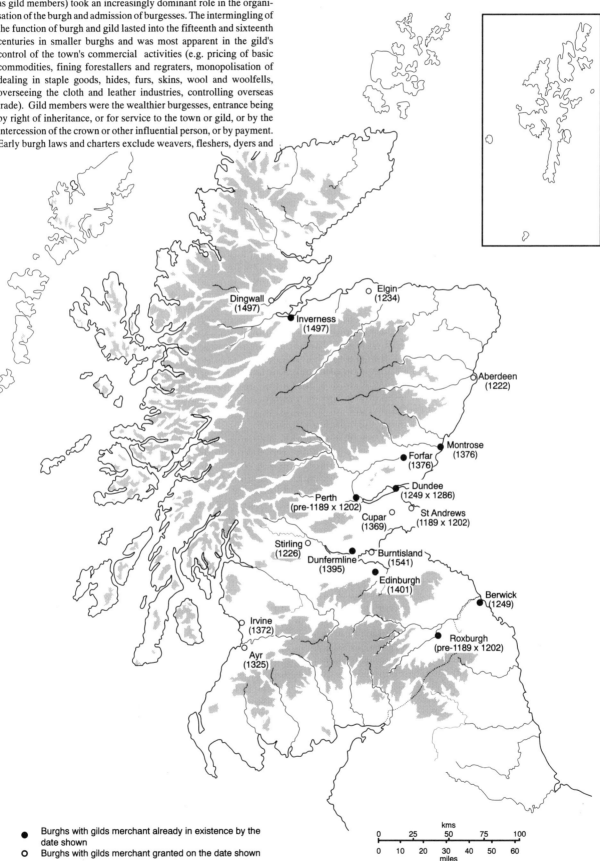

● Burghs with gilds merchant already in existence by the date shown
○ Burghs with gilds merchant granted on the date shown

kms
0 25 50 75 100
0 10 20 30 40 50 60
miles

Burghs with gilds merchant by 1550

EPD

215

Forests 1286 to 1513

Several royal forests survived into the later Middle Ages, but many were subdivided or alienated. Few new royal forests appeared in the fourteenth century. In the fifteenth century more reserves appear in the Highland area than previously as game was more plentiful there and there was less detrimental economic activity. A cluster of reserves appeared in the southern central Highlands, where Glenfinglas was a favoured royal lodge, and royal forests spread in the Don and Dee valleys

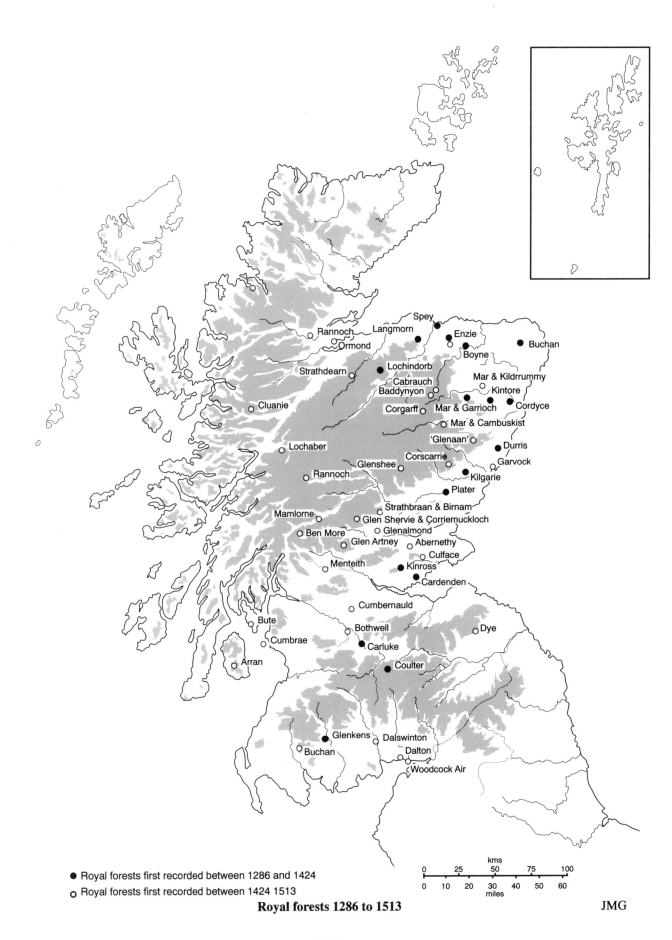

● Royal forests first recorded between 1286 and 1424
○ Royal forests first recorded between 1424 1513

kms

| 0 | 25 | 50 | 75 | 100 |

| 0 | 10 | 20 | 30 | 40 | 50 | 60 |

miles

Royal forests 1286 to 1513

JMG

216

Forests 1286 to 1513

The fourteenth century saw a decline in the popularity of the forest grant. Instead there was a preference for the hunting park within which it was easier to control game than in the unenclosed forest. Several of the larger reserves appear to have died out. The later fifteenth century witnessed a resurgence of the forest grants, especially in the north. It was no longer the preservation of game but the protection of the vert for which such grants were valued, reflecting a shortage of timber and the changing position of hunting rights generally.

- ● Baronial forests first recorded between 1286 and 1424
- ○ Baronial forests first recorded between 1424 and 1513

Baronial forests 1286 to 1513

JMG

Forests 1286 to 1513

In his forests the king controlled the vert as well as the game. The vert, which comprised whatever vegetation there was in the forest, was reserved for the harbouring and nourishment of the game. The king could licence others to use the forest resources, sometimes free of charge but more frequently for payment of tolls such as pannage for grazing pigs or herbage and foggage for other animals. Controlling economic pressures to graze and plough within the reserve led to severe difficulties, for example in Ettrick Forest, where by the fifteenth century the whole of the reserve was divided into steads or holdings. A special system of wards, officials and courts was developed to try to control the use of the vert and venison (greater game), but finally James IV (1488-1513) gave up the struggle. The rents of Ettrick were far too valuable to lose and feu-ferming was introduced between 1506 and 1510.

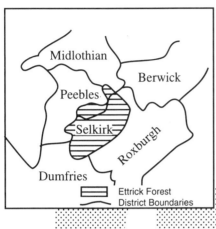

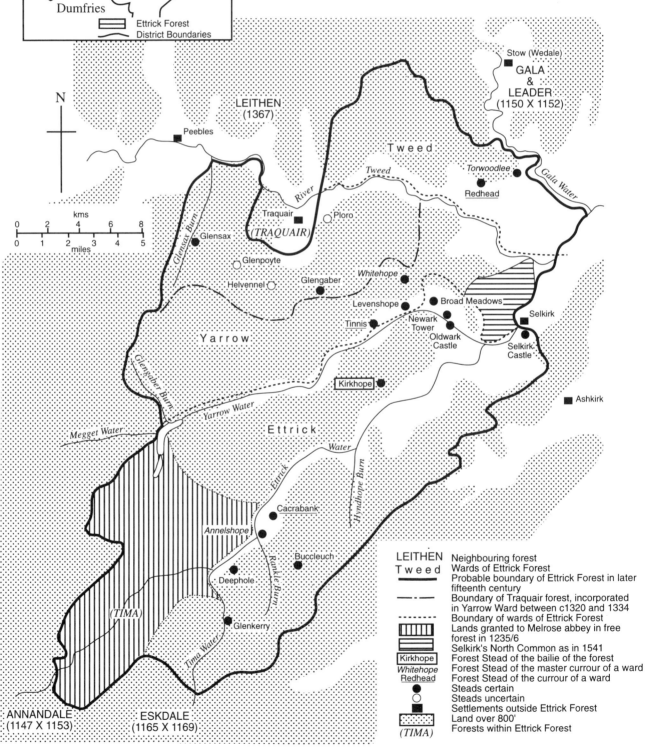

Ettrick Forest

JMG

The Session

In the first three-quarters of the fifteenth century, the main central civil court was parliament, which usually nominated committees of auditors to hear causes whilst and whenever the parliament was sitting. On several occasions between 1457 and 1472 the estates chose further groups of lords to hold judicial sittings - 'the session' - in regional centres, between parliaments. Thereafter, when parliament was not sitting, civil causes were dealt with centrally only by the king's council. By 1496 the council had superseded the parliamentary committees as the main central civil tribunal, the direct antecedent of the college of justice and the court of session.

From some time in the 1470s until 1488 the council held judicial sittings only in Edinburgh, but in James IV's reign, and especially in the 1490s, the council heard causes in the provinces, following the ayres, or sitting wherever the king's court happened to be at the time.

After 1500 that practice became less common, and the council's regular Edinburgh sessions were organised to deal with cases from specific parts of the country in turn. In 1503 an extensive table of causes was drawn up based on a five part division of the kingdom.

Later groupings of sheriffdoms had greater geographical coherence, but the composition, and the time allocated to each grouping, varied from one diet to another. Subsequently, the districts became larger and fewer, and the time allocated to each correspondingly longer.

After 1590 the system of districts fell into desuetude: the whole country was then treated as a unity and the court dealt with cases according to priority of calling. On the other hand, the central criminal court has always gone on circuit, and to this day still does.

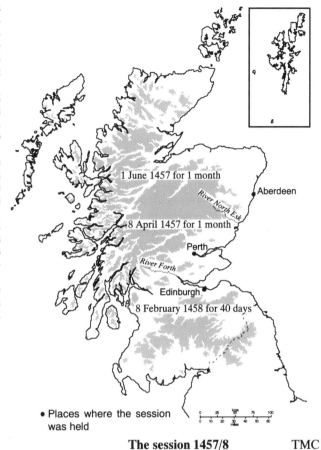

1 June 1457 for 1 month

• Aberdeen

8 April 1457 for 1 month

Perth

River North Esk

River Forth

Edinburgh

8 February 1458 for 40 days

• Places where the session was held

The session 1457/8   TMC

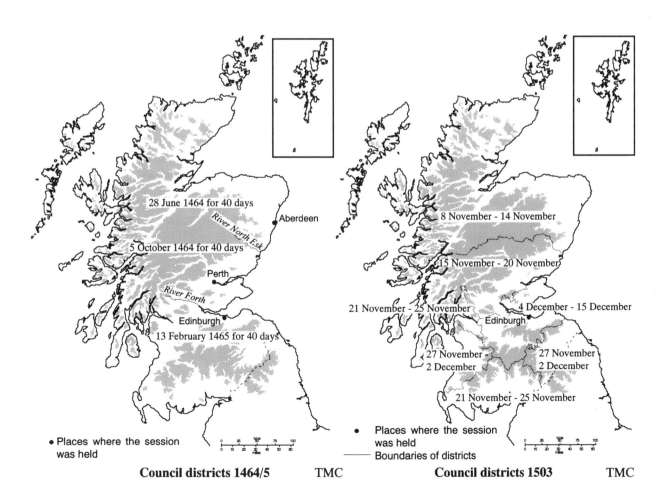

28 June 1464 for 40 days

• Aberdeen

River North Esk

5 October 1464 for 40 days

Perth

River Forth

Edinburgh

13 February 1465 for 40 days

• Places where the session was held

Council districts 1464/5   TMC

8 November - 14 November

15 November - 20 November

21 November - 25 November

4 December - 15 December

Edinburgh

27 November - 2 December

27 November - 2 December

21 November - 25 November

• Places where the session was held
—— Boundaries of districts

Council districts 1503   TMC

219

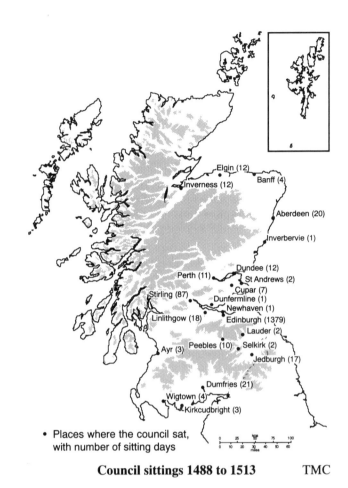

- Places where the council sat,
  with number of sitting days

Council sittings 1488 to 1513   TMC

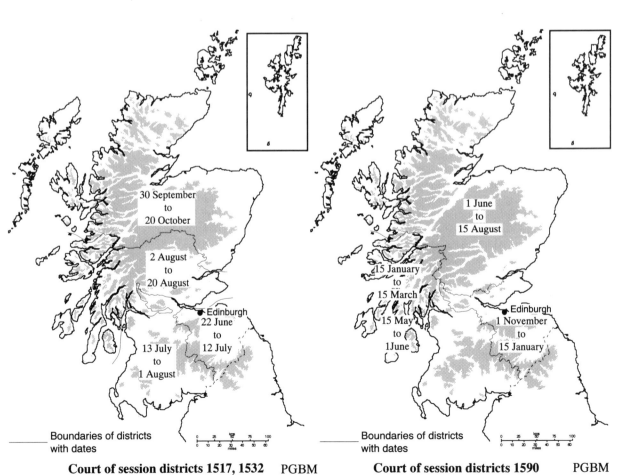

Boundaries of districts
with dates

Court of session districts 1517, 1532   PGBM

Boundaries of districts
with dates

Court of session districts 1590   PGBM

Lords of erection

Generally, the holder of an ecclessiastical benefice had only a life interest in that benefice. This was the case with regularly appointed bishops, abbots and parsons; and it was also the case with those who, whether they were churchment or laymen, were commendators or *oeconomi* for life of the benefice. After the Reformation grants of benefices *in commendam* were made by the crown, and they were made increasingly to laymen: but these grants remained for life only. In 1587 an act of parliament annexed to the crown (with certain exceptions) all lands, lordships and other rights which had formerly pertained to ecclesiastical persons; and others were annexed later. The crown used its position as proprietor of these lands to *erect* former ecclesiastical property (mostly monastic lands) into temporal lordships which were indistinguishable from lay tenures. The map shows the foundations which were thus created: some others were merely secularised.

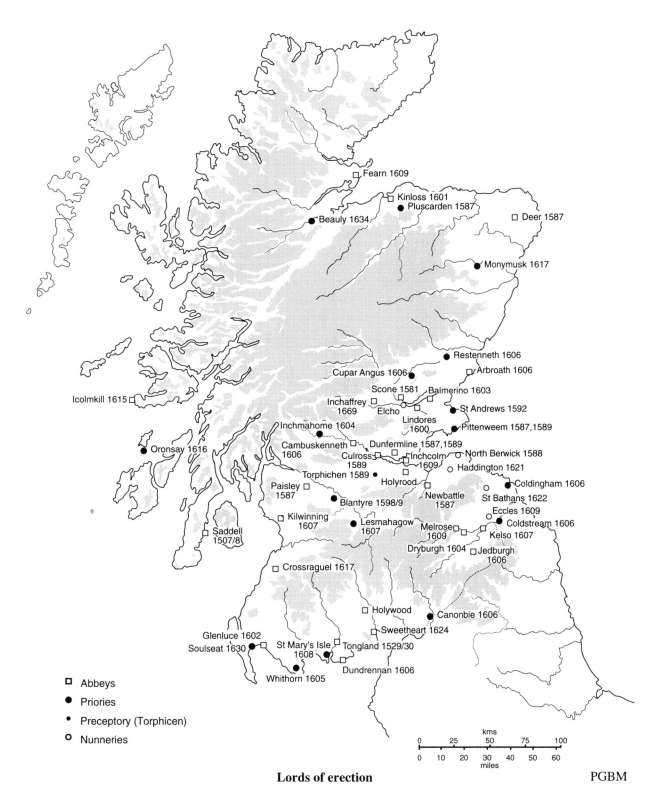

☐ Abbeys

● Priories

• Preceptory (Torphicen)

○ Nunneries

Lords of erection

PGBM

Justices of the peace 1587 to 1663

In England from the Middle Ages, the justice of the peace had constituted a significant element in local administration and justice. In Scotland, on the other hand, the office was only introduced tentatively in 1587; and more extensive and more elaborate commisions were made in 1610 and 1663. The Cromwellian period had enhanced the status of the justices; after the Restoration and more so after the Union, the jurisdiction of the justices increased.

Their primary function was the keeping of the peace; but they also acquired power to enforce regulations in relation to vagabonds, the poor, forestallers and regraters, wages and the like. The county of Edinburgh arrogated to itself a civil jurisdiction in small claims up to £40 Scots (£3:6:8d or £3.33 sterling). Their administrative duties were ultimately taken over by central and local government.

The three maps show the numbers of commissioners designated for each shire in the years 1587, 1610 and 1663. The commissions of 1610 and 1663 included as *ex officio* commissioners, privy councillors and lords of session; and the commission of 1610 also included as *ex officio* commissioners the magistrates of the burghs and towns within the county. Cromarty (but not Ross) appears in the commissions of 1587 and 1610; and Ross (but not Cromarty) appears in the commission of 1663.

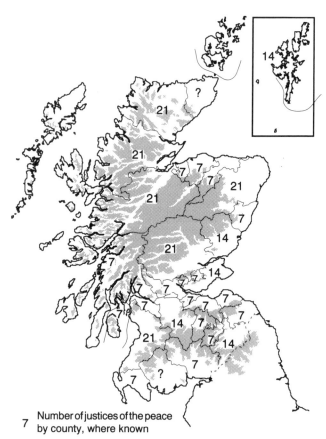

7 Number of justices of the peace by county, where known

Justices of the peace 1587

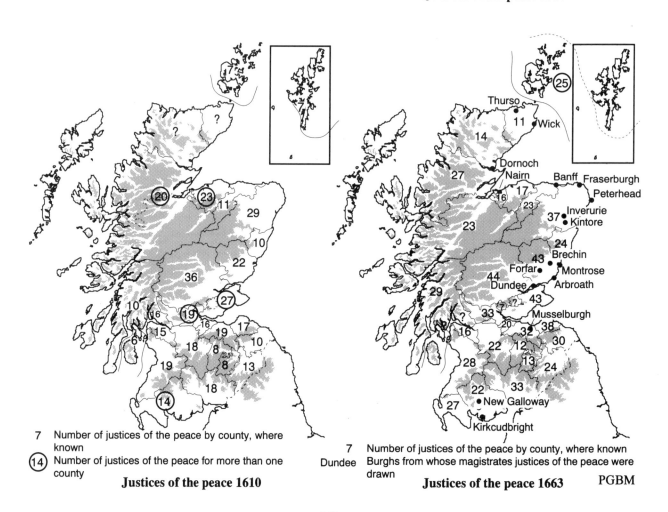

7 Number of justices of the peace by county, where known

(14) Number of justices of the peace for more than one county

Justices of the peace 1610

7 Number of justices of the peace by county, where known

Dundee Burghs from whose magistrates justices of the peace were drawn

Justices of the peace 1663   PGBM

Circuit courts 1672

From 1514 to 1628 the office of justice general of all Scotland was held by the earls of Argyll. After 1628, the office was surrendered to the Crown but under reservation to the Campbell family of the justiciary of Argyll and the Isles which was held by the Campbells until the abolition of the heritable jurisdictions in 1748

In 1672, after various attempts to grapple with the administration of criminal justice outside Edinburgh, the former system of appointing justice deputes was brought to an end; and instead, the justice general, the justice clerk and five lords of session (who were already remunerated in respect of their civil judgeships) were charged with jurisdiction in criminal causes. Two of these 'lords commissioners of justiciary' were appointed to keep courts at the circuit towns which are shown on the map. In general, each circuit court dealt with the crimes which had been committed within the counties within the circuit. Later, the circuits came to be referred to by the points of the compass, north, south, west and home; and the circuits were modified to meet the changes in population and the incidence of crime.

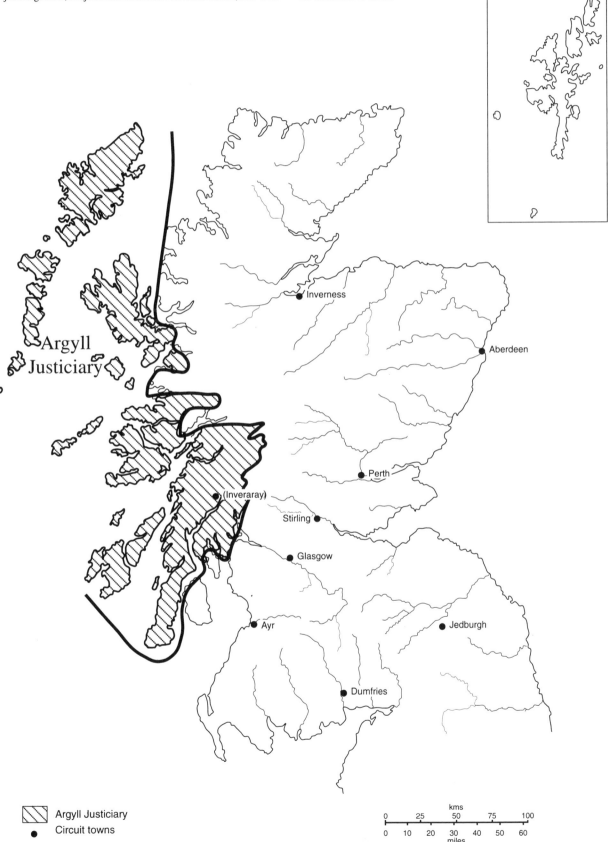

Argyll Justiciary

Circuit towns

kms

0   25   50   75   100

0   10   20   30   40   50   60
miles

Circuit courts 1672

PGBM

Parliament 1660 to 1707

The Scottish parliament of the Restoration consisted of the lords, the bishops (from 1662 to 1689) and the representatives of the shires and the burghs. The bishops had been restored to their rights in 1662. Earlier, in 1633, the new bishopric of Edinburgh had been created: it consisted of that part of the archbishopric of St. Andrews which lay to the south of the Firth of Forth.

The maps, which show the distribution of the members of parliament before the Union, are based on the sederunts of 1662 and 1706. After 1707, the Scots were accorded a smaller number of seats in the united parliament of Great Britain. Thus, in the House of Lords, there were only sixteen Scottish peers and they were elected by the whole body of Scottish peers. This system lasted in substance until the Peerage Act 1963 which permitted all Scottish peers to sit and vote in the House of Lords.

Isles   Bishoprics

●   Episcopal sees

■   Archiepiscopal sees

Parliament: the bishops 1662 to 1689

PGBM

Parliament 1660 to 1707

The map shows the location of the seats of the various lords who appear in the sederunt of 1706, with the addition of the chancellor, the earl of Seafield. Some seats cannot be identified and some lords had no Scottish seat (Islay, Dunmore, Bellenden, Abercorn, Delorain and Selkirk). Notable absentees from the sederunt of 1706 include the dukes of Douglas and Gordon and the earls of Aberdeen, Aboyne, Airlie, Breadalbane, Carnwath, Linlithgow, Melville, Moray, Nithsdale, Seaforth and Southesk.

Lord	Seat
1 Caithness	Haimer
2 Sutherland	Dunrobin
3 Cromartie	Tarbat House
4 Duffus	Duffus Castle
5 Seafield	Cullen House
6 Findlater	Cullen House
7 Oliphant	Pittendreigh
8 Saltoun	Philorth House
9 Banff	Forglen House
10 Forbes	Castle Forbes
11 Fraser	Castle Fraser
12 Kintore	Keith Hall
13 Erroll	Slains
14 Atholl	Blair Atholl
15 Forfar	Bothwell Castle
16 Marischal	Dunnottar Castle
17 Strathmore	Glamis Castle
18 Northesk	Ethie Castle
19 Gray	Gray House
20 Kinnaird	Drimmie House
21 Stormont	Scone Palace
22 Dupplin	Dupplin Castle
23 Balmerino	Balmerino
24 Rollo	Duncrub Park
25 Crawford	Struthers
26 Argyll	Inveraray Castle
27 Montrose	Buchanan Castle
28 Mar	Alloa House
29 Rothes	Leslie
30 Leven	Balgonie Castle
31 Balcarres	Balcarres House
32 Kincardine	Broomhall
33 Hopetoun	Hopetoun House
34 Torphichen	Calder House
35 Roseberry	Barnbougle
36 Morton	Dalmahoy
37 Lothian	Newbattle Abbey
38 Cranston	Cranston
39 Dalhousie	Dalhousie Castle
40 Elibank	Ballencreiff
41 Blantyre	Lennoxlove
42 Haddington	Tyninghame House
43 Belhaven	Biel House
44 Bute	Mount Stuart
45 Glasgow	Kelburn Castle
46 Sempill	Sempill Castle
47 Ross	Hawkhead
48 Elphinstone	Elphinstone Tower
49 Kilsyth	Kilsyth Castle
50 Hamilton	Hamilton Palace
51 Hyndford	Carmichael House
52 Tweeddale	Yester Castle
53 Garnock	Kilbirnie Castle

Lord	Seat
54 Glencairn	Kilmaurs
55 Eglinton	Eglinton Castle
56 Kilmarnock	Kilmarnock House
57 Loudon	Loudon Castle
58 Wemyss	Wemyss Castle
59 Lauderdale	Thirlstane Castle
60 Marchmont	Polwarth
61 Colville	Ochiltree Castle
62 Buchan	Cardross House
63 Roxburghe	Floors House
64 Bargany	Bargany
65 Queensberry	Drumlanrig Castle
66 Stair	Castle Kennedy
67 Wigtown	Cumbernauld House
68 Galloway	Glasserton House
69 Annandale	Lochwood

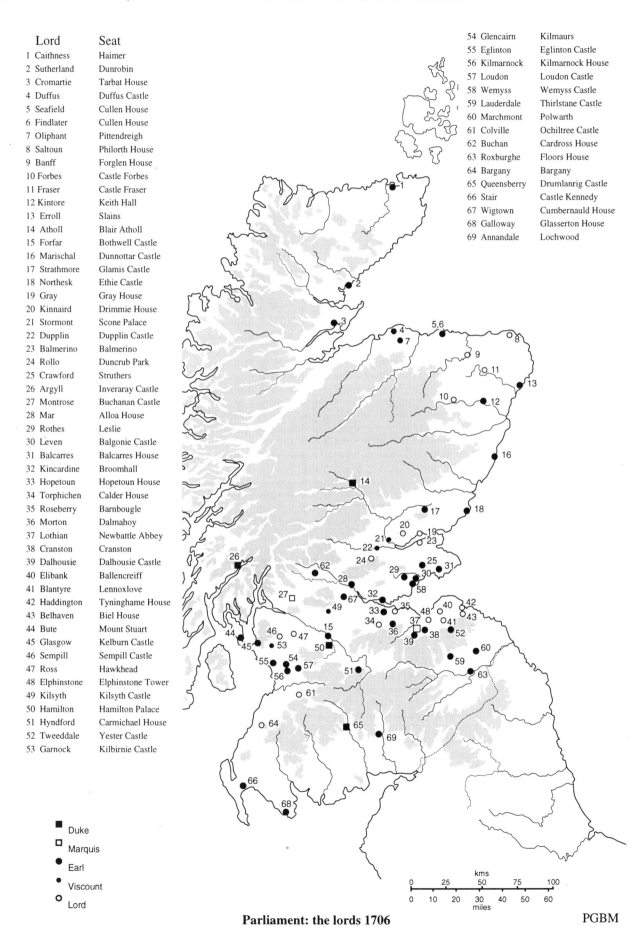

■ Duke
□ Marquis
● Earl
• Viscount
○ Lord

Parliament: the lords 1706

PGBM

225

Parliament 1660 to 1707

In the pre-Union parliament, each shire was represented by one to four members - depending upon the importance of the shire. By 1681 the number of shires had been stabilised as 33. The constabulary of Haddington and the stewartry of Kircudbright were regarded as the equivalent of shires. The information shown on the map is taken from the sederunt of 1706: there, Sutherland appears without any representative against it; and Kinross has been omitted.

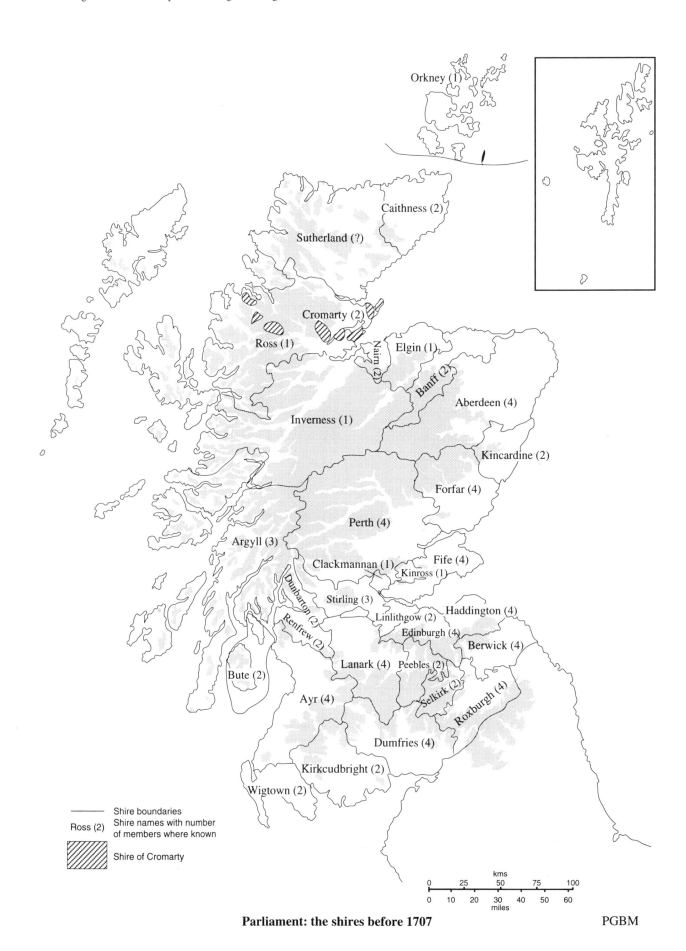

Orkney (1)

Caithness (2)

Sutherland (?)

Cromarty (2)

Ross (1)

Nairn (2)

Elgin (1)

Banff (2)

Aberdeen (4)

Inverness (1)

Kincardine (2)

Forfar (4)

Perth (4)

Argyll (3)

Clackmannan (1)

Kinross (1)

Fife (4)

Stirling (3)

Dunbarton (2)

Renfrew (2)

Linlithgow (2)

Haddington (4)

Edinburgh (4)

Berwick (4)

Bute (2)

Lanark (4) Peebles (2)

Selkirk (2)

Roxburgh (4)

Ayr (4)

Dumfries (4)

Kirkcudbright (2)

Wigtown (2)

—— Shire boundaries

Ross (2) Shire names with number of members where known

Shire of Cromarty

kms
0   25   50   75   100
0 10 20 30 40 50 60
miles

Parliament: the shires before 1707

PGBM

Parliament 1660 to 1707

In the British House of Commons there were to be forty-five Scottish members. The Scottish parliament settled the distribution of the members among the shires and burghs in such a way that thirty of the shires had one member each; and the remaining six shires were made into three groups of three: in each group the election was made in one shire after another

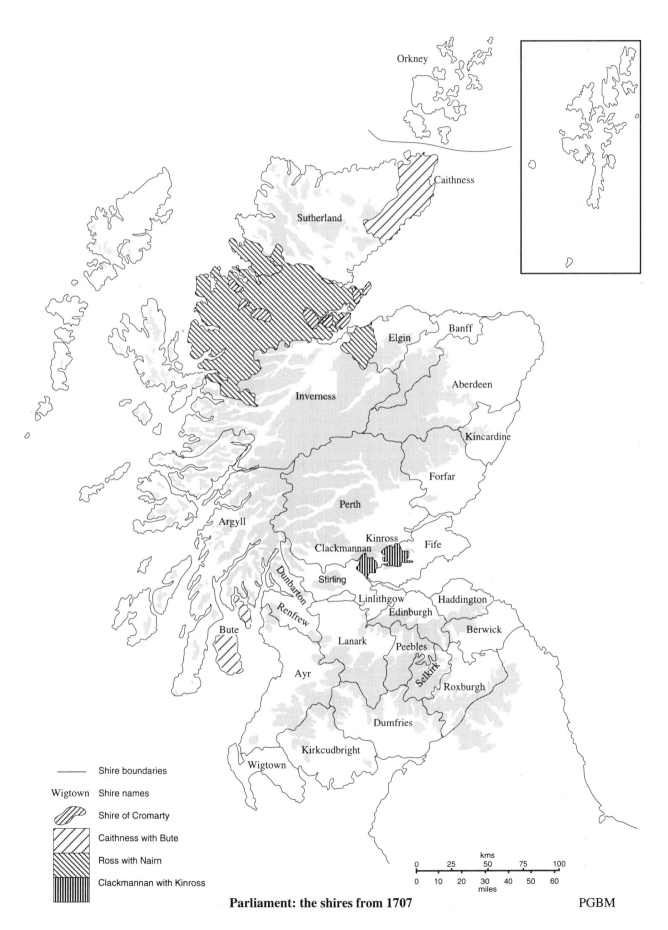

Orkney

Caithness

Sutherland

Banff

Elgin

Aberdeen

Inverness

Kincardine

Forfar

Perth

Kinross

Clackmannan

Fife

Argyll

Stirling

Dunbarton

Linlithgow

Haddington

Edinburgh

Renfrew

Berwick

Bute

Lanark

Peebles

Selkirk

Ayr

Roxburgh

Dumfries

Kirkcudbright

Wigtown

————— Shire boundaries

Wigtown   Shire names

Shire of Cromarty

Caithness with Bute

Ross with Nairn

Clackmannan with Kinross

kms
0   25   50   75   100

0 10 20 30 40 50 60
miles

Parliament: the shires from 1707

PGBM

227

Parliament 1660 to 1707

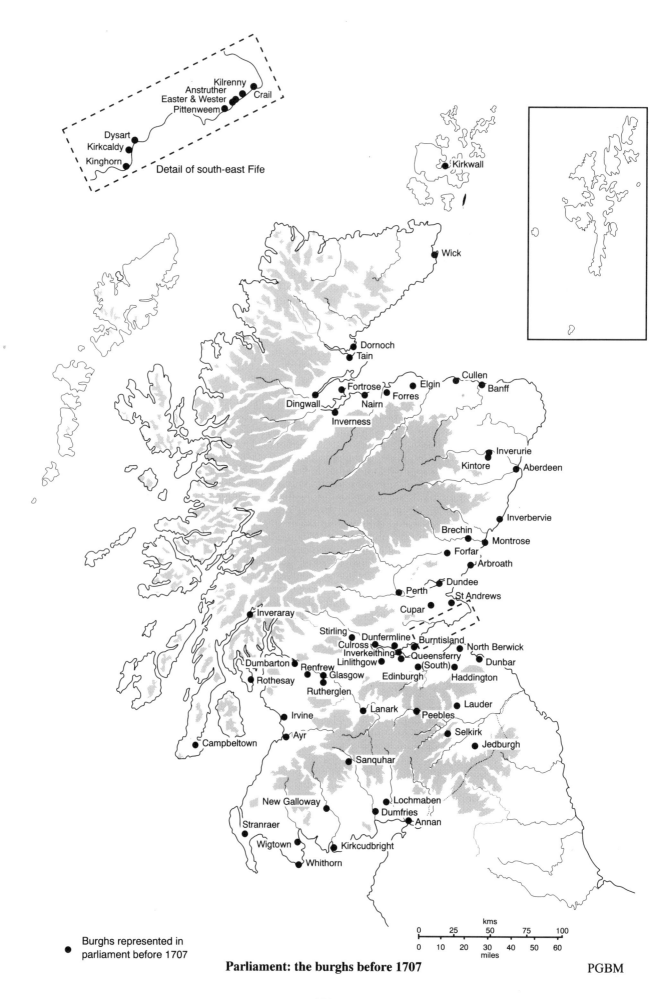

Detail of south-east Fife

Kilrenny
Anstruther
Easter & Wester
Pittenweem
Crail

Dysart
Kirkcaldy
Kinghorn

Kirkwall

Wick

Dornoch
Tain

Cullen
Fortrose
Elgin
Banff
Nairn
Forres
Dingwall
Inverness

Inverurie
Kintore
Aberdeen

Inverbervie
Brechin
Montrose
Forfar
Arbroath
Dundee
Perth
St Andrews
Cupar

Inveraray

Stirling
Dunfermline
Burntisland
Culross
North Berwick
Inverkeithing
Queensferry
Dunbar
Linlithgow
(South)
Dumbarton
Renfrew
Rothesay
Glasgow
Edinburgh
Haddington
Rutherglen
Lauder
Lanark
Peebles
Irvine
Selkirk
Campbeltown
Ayr
Jedburgh
Sanquhar

New Galloway
Lochmaben
Stranraer
Dumfries
Annan
Wigtown
Kirkcudbright
Whithorn

• Burghs represented in
  parliament before 1707

kms
0   25   50   75   100
0 10 20 30 40 50 60
miles

Parliament: the burghs before 1707

PGBM

Parliament 1660 to 1707

The Scottish parliament distributed the Scottish burgh seats in the united parliament of Great Britain. Edinburgh had one member; and the rest of the burghs were organised in groups of either four or five, and each group had one member. This arrangement lasted until the Representation of the People (Scotland) Act 1832 which redistributed the seats in a different way so as to give better reflection of the changes in population which had taken place since the Union.

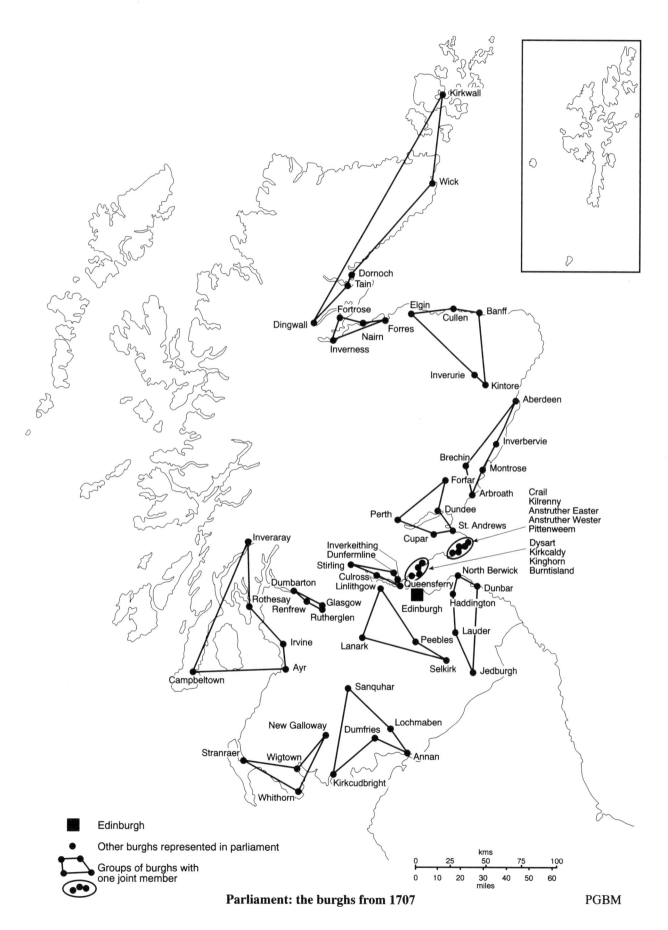

Kirkwall

Wick

Dornoch
Tain

Fortrose
Dingwall
Nairn   Forres
Inverness

Elgin
Cullen   Banff

Inverurie

Kintore

Aberdeen

Inverbervie

Brechin
Montrose

Forfar
Arbroath

Perth   Dundee

St. Andrews

Cupar

Crail
Kilrenny
Anstruther Easter
Anstruther Wester
Pittenweem

Dysart
Kirkcaldy
Kinghorn
Burntisland

Inverkeithing
Dunfermline
Stirling
Culross
Linlithgow
Queensferry
North Berwick
Dunbar
Edinburgh
Haddington

Inveraray

Dumbarton
Rothesay
Renfrew
Glasgow
Rutherglen

Irvine

Ayr

Campbeltown

Lanark
Peebles
Selkirk
Lauder
Jedburgh

Sanquhar

New Galloway
Dumfries
Lochmaben

Stranraer
Wigtown
Annan

Whithorn
Kirkcudbright

■ Edinburgh

● Other burghs represented in parliament

Groups of burghs with one joint member

Parliament: the burghs from 1707

PGBM

kms
0   25   50   75   100

0   10   20   30   40   50   60
miles

229

Economic development

Burghs

Scottish burghal status was divided into three types: royal, ecclesiastical and baronial, depending on whether the overlord was the king, an abbot or bishop or a magnate. The earliest burghs were founded by the king, but soon the Crown allowed others to found their own burghs. The first ecclesiastical burghs of which we have records are St Andrews (1140 x 1153) and Canongate (1143 x 1147). Prestwick (1165 x 1173) was the first to be founded as a baronial burgh. Between 1430 and 1530 there was an escalation in the number of burgh foundations compared with earlier centuries. Perhaps more significant was the increasing number of burghs of barony, whether ecclesiastical or secular. Such 'unfree' burghs were not granted rural hinterlands where they might monopolise or control trade; they had no inherent right to be represented in parliament, but consequently were not liable for cess (except in so far as they contributed as part of a shrieval levy), and they might not, officially, participate in overseas trade. These burghs might be raised to royal status, as was Pittenweem (founded in 1525), in 1541. The five greater ecclesiastical burghs - St Andrews, Glasgow, Brechin, Arbroath and Dunfermline - not only enjoyed the same trading privileges as royal burghs, but also paid taxation and were represented in the Convention of Royal Burghs.

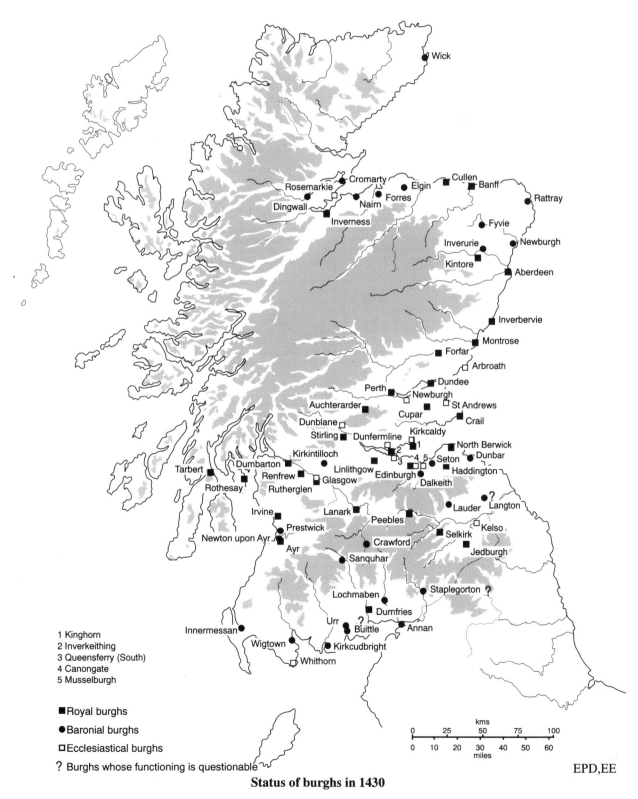

1 Kinghorn
2 Inverkeithing
3 Queensferry (South)
4 Canongate
5 Musselburgh

■ Royal burghs
● Baronial burghs
□ Ecclesiastical burghs
? Burghs whose functioning is questionable

EPD,EE

Status of burghs in 1430

231

Burghs

Some burghs changed their status over time. Royal burghs, such as Jedburgh and Wigtown, were granted by the king to baronial overlords. Burghs might also change status with a change in status of their overlord. Irvine, a baronial burgh, became royal when its Stewart overlord succeeded to the crown in 1371.

Until the fifteenth century, status was not an issue of vital importance for burghs, as rights and privileges were based on the antiquity of the burgh's charters. Several non-royal burghs, such as St Andrews, North Berwick and Dunbar, participated in trade and were taxed by the Crown in the fourteenth century along with the royal burghs. The first hint of a differentiation probably developed in the later fourteenth century with the regular representation of some burghs, mostly royal, in parliament. The first reference to a 'royal burgh' came in the foundation charter of Rothesay in 1401. In the same year, the charter for Dalkeith referred to it as 'baronial'. By the early fifteenth century, non-royal began to outnumber royal burghs, and status had become a more important issue.

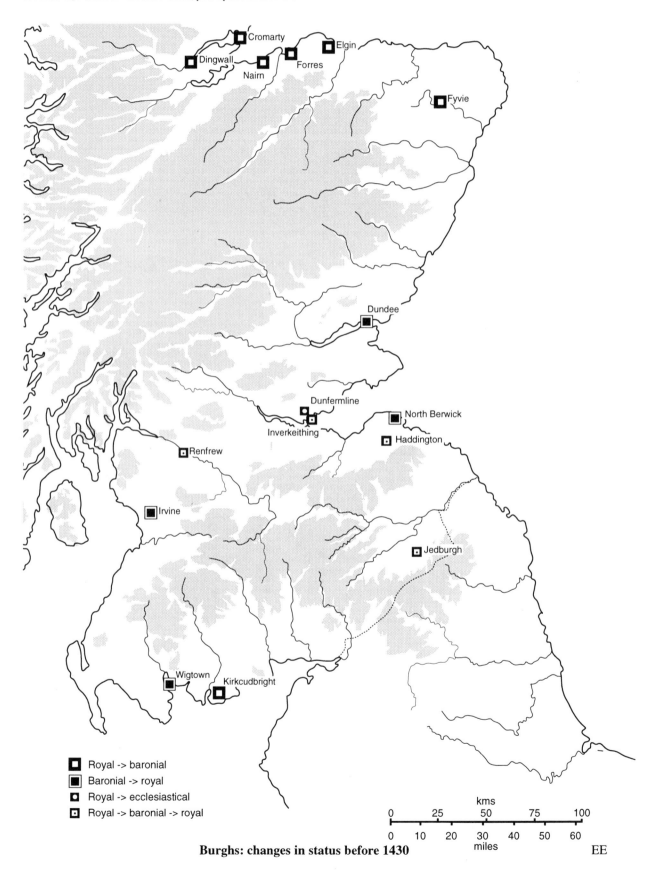

■ Royal -> baronial
■ Baronial -> royal
□ Royal -> ecclesiastical
□ Royal -> baronial -> royal

kms

0   25   50   75   100

0   10   20   30   40   50   60
miles

Burghs: changes in status before 1430

EE

232

Royal burghs and burghs of barony

There were comparatively few royal burghs founded in the sixteenth and seventeenth centuries - a total of 21 between 1560 and 1707 but only two of these came after 1650. The period 1450-1707 saw, however, the erection of 350 burghs of barony and regality; 121 of them were founded 1561-1660 and a further 110 between 1661-1707. It has been suggested that as many as 140 of these, including many of the post-1660 foundations, were non-viable.

The case of Perthshire is a useful example. In 1692, the pre-1560 foundations (both royal and baronial) accounted for 51% of inland trade; those founded between 1600 and 1660 accounted for 29% more; the large number of post-1660 foundations, including licensed market centres outside burghs, handled only 16% and nearly half of this was accounted for by Crieff.

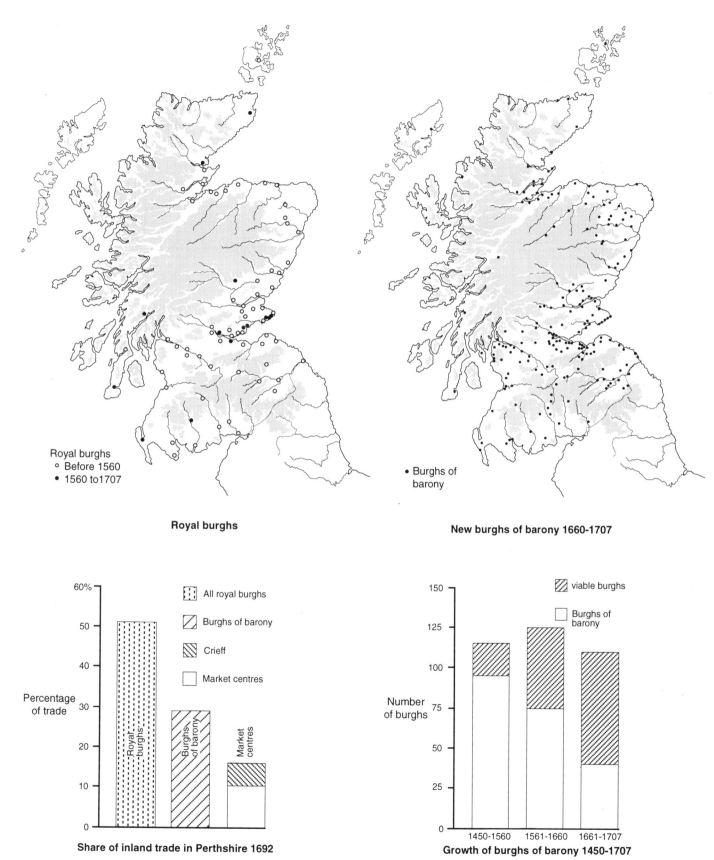

Royal burghs
○ Before 1560
● 1560 to 1707

Royal burghs

● Burghs of barony

New burghs of barony 1660-1707

Share of inland trade in Perthshire 1692

All royal burghs
Burghs of barony
Crieff
Market centres

Percentage of trade

Growth of burghs of barony 1450-1707

viable burghs
Burghs of barony

Number of burghs

1450-1560   1561-1660   1661-1707

Royal burghs and burghs of barony to 1707

ML

Burgh trading liberties

Aberdeen was granted the sheriffdom as its trading liberty by Alexander II without prejudice to the rights of other burghs such as Kintore and Fyvie. By 1400, however, Aberdeen was apparently claiming jurisdiction over baronial burghs like Fyvie and similarly over tanners at Inverurie, although inhabitants of Kintore were still customarily sent to the sheriff.

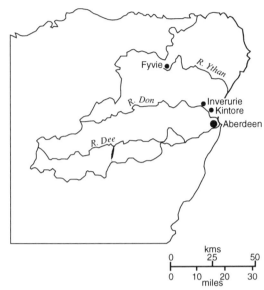

Burgh trading liberties: Aberdeen

Ayr's earliest charter of 1203 x 1207 named five places, roughly outlining the boundaries of Ayrshire, for collection of toll on market goods. The southern extent of the liberty is a matter of controversy: if 'Lochtalpin' is placed at Dalmellington, the area included only Cunningham and Kyle; if identified at Laicht, it included Carrick, which is more likely as it is Ayr that later claimed jurisdiction over Maybole. By the fourteenth century, Ayr's liberty had been eroded to the north by the privileges of Irvine, confirmed in 1372 as extending over Cunningham and Largs.

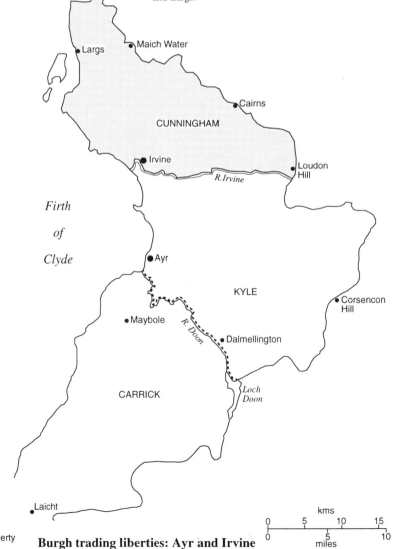

Burgh trading liberties: Ayr and Irvine

EE

Burgh trading liberties

In 1363, David II confirmed to the four regality burghs of Dunferm-line - Dunfermline, Kirkcaldy, Musselburgh and Queensferry - the sole right to trade within the regality. Although this did not make clear whether the regality was made up into four separate areas of monopoly, the burgh records of Dunfermline and Kirkcaldy indicate that their commercial hinterlands lay to the north of the Forth and were distinct. The grant of 1363 affected the liberty of Inverkeithing, which had been defined as early as the reign of William the Lion as between the waters of the Devon and Leven, and further confirmed in 1399 as such and lying to the south of 'the large standing stone beyond the mill of Ellhorth' (Milnathort); its north-east boundary marked that of Cupar.

Enforcement of trading boundaries in such a patchwork of jurisdictions was never wholly effective. In 1488, Dunfermline rebuffed Kirkcaldy's claim to sole right to trade in Goatmilk by appealing to the feudal superior, the abbot of Dunfermline; yet by 1583 Kirkcaldy claimed both it and Kinglassie from Dunfermline. By the sixteenth century, Inverkeithing's rights over Culross, the extent of the parish of Kinghorn, the petty customs at Dysart and the customs of the St Luke's fair at Kinross were all disputed; the erection of Burntisland and Culross into royal burghs in 1586 and 1592 further threatened Inverkeithing's liberty.

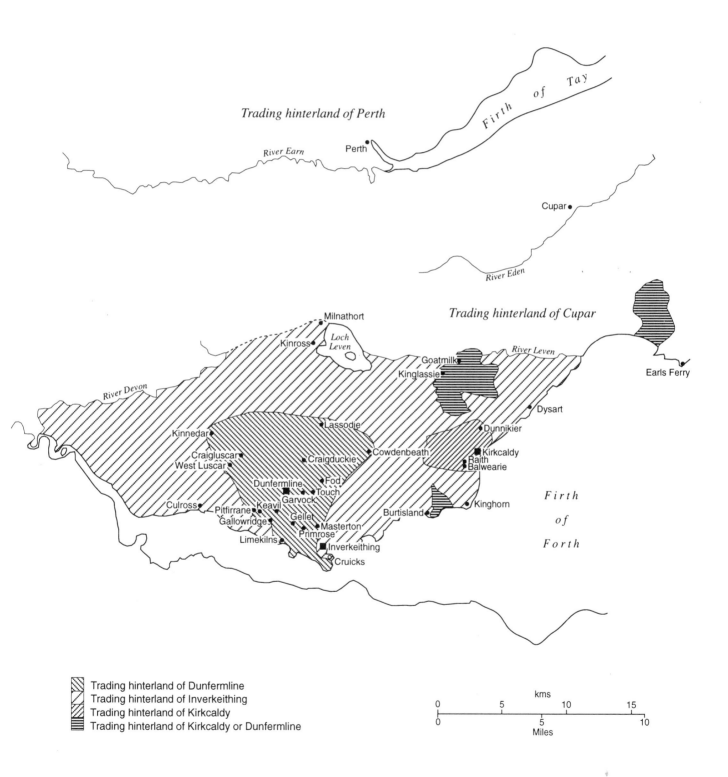

Trading hinterland of Perth

Trading hinterland of Cupar

Trading hinterland of Dunfermline
Trading hinterland of Inverkeithing
Trading hinterland of Kirkcaldy
Trading hinterland of Kirkcaldy or Dunfermline

Burgh trading liberties: Dunfermline, Kirkcaldy and Inverkeithing about 1500   EPD

Burgesses' landed interest

During the fourteenth century it became increasingly common for wealthier burgesses - like Adam Forrester of Edinburgh, who was prominent in crown service, or the Perth families of Mercer and Spens, who acquired lands along Loch Lomond through marriage to a Campbell heiress - to acquire lands outwith their burghs. Country estates provided produce, rents and status. They could be acquired through marriage or as a reward for service to church, Crown or a magnate as well as being a means to invest surplus capital. Some families severed their connections with their burgh of origin but this generally took a number of generations; most continued to participate in burgh life. This practice was made easier by the fact that most country estates belonging to burgesses were situated relatively close to their burghs.

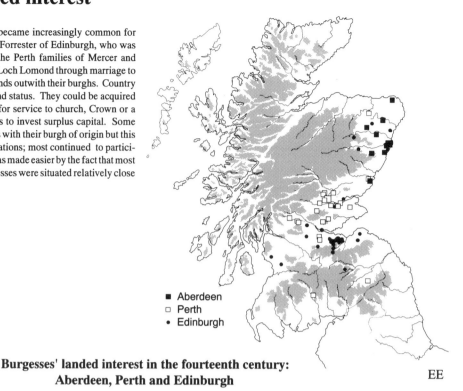

■ Aberdeen
□ Perth
• Edinburgh

Burgesses' landed interest in the fourteenth century: Aberdeen, Perth and Edinburgh

EE

The early seventeenth century saw a boom in the acquiring by wadset of rural property by Edinburgh merchants as collateral for lending money to nobles and lairds throughout Scotland. Almost half of the 300 wealthiest merchants of the capital accepted the mortgage of rural property, under terms of reversion usually of two, seven or nineteen years. None abandoned mercantile activities to become either property speculators or country lairds. In a period of rising grain prices, the wadsetters were more interested in collecting the rentals and produce rather than establishing themselves on estates, more than 40% of which were beyond the immediate vicinity of Edinburgh. Yet the areas involved included some of the most fertile in the country. William Dick, wealthiest of Edinburgh's merchant princes, had properties extending from Ayrshire to Caithness and

purchased a six-year tack of Orkney in 1636 for £35,730 per annum. But many, like Dick, were badly hit by the crises of the 1640s and 1650s; the Edinburgh money market, as a result, was far less interested in investing in rural property in the second half of the century.

Amongst the nobles and lairds involved were the Kerrs, Homes and Maitlands in the Borders; the Erskines and Hamiltons in central Scotland; the Bruces and Wardlaws in Fife; the Sinclairs and Urquharts, as well as the earl of Caithness and the Earl Marischal, north of the Tay; the earl of Eglinton, Lord Herries and the Stewarts in the south-west; and the earl of Morton along with representatives of almost every prominent family in Lothian.

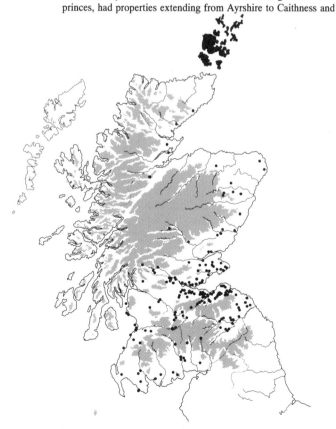

Distribution of Edinburgh burgesses' landed interest in the seventeenth century

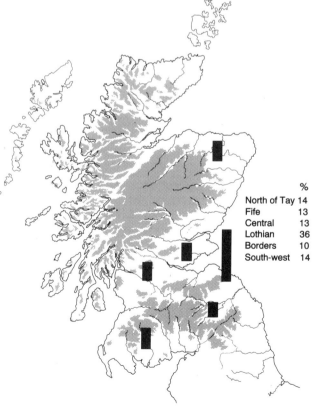

	%
North of Tay	14
Fife	13
Central	13
Lothian	36
Borders	10
South-west	14

Percentage distribution of Edinburgh burgesses' landed interest in the seventeenth century, by region

JB

Trade: wool producing monasteries

The handbook of the Italian merchant, Francesco Balducci Pegolotti, which was composed about 1400, contains two lists of prices of wool from various Scottish monasteries: the first list gives prices of three types of graded wool from eight monasteries (all of which except Dunfermline were Cistercian); the second gives seven houses which sold unsorted wool at an average of 9-10.5 merks a sack. The concentration of these wool producing monasteries (based on Professor Duncan's identification of them) in the east and the south-east is striking. It underlines the predominance of east coast burghs in overseas trade. Berwick, and by the fourteenth century, Edinburgh were well placed to export wool which went mostly to Flanders; the ungraded wool came from their hinterlands. Although Glenluce and Dundrennan may have sent wool to Ireland, Pegolotti's prices suggest that their wool was of the best quality and perhaps worth transporting to the east.

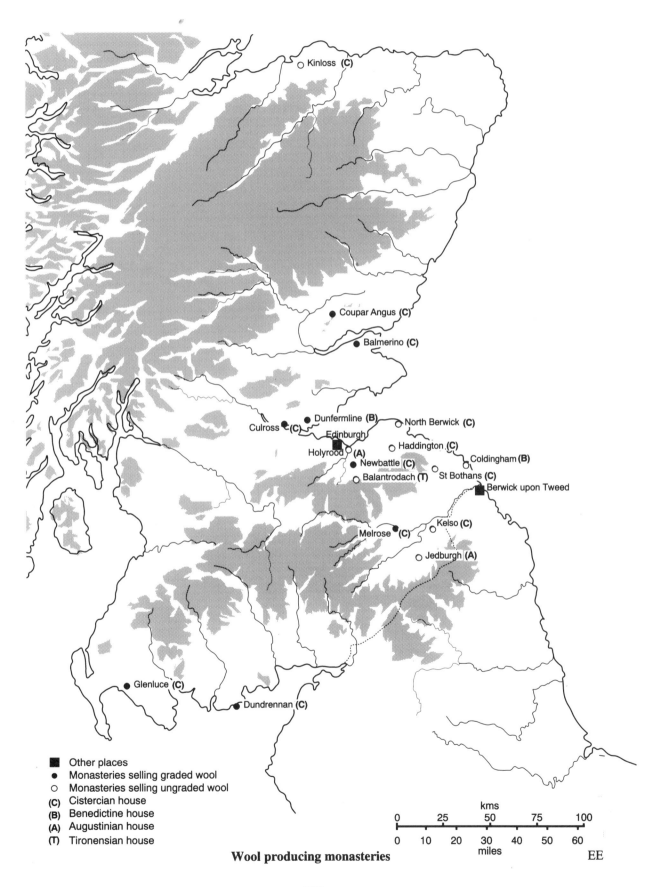

Kinloss (C)

Coupar Angus (C)

Balmerino (C)

Culross (C)   Dunfermline (B)   North Berwick (C)

Edinburgh

Holyrood (A)   Haddington (C)   Coldingham (B)

Newbattle (C)

Balantrodach (T)   St Bothans (C)

Berwick upon Tweed

Kelso (C)

Melrose (C)

Jedburgh (A)

Glenluce (C)

Dundrennan (C)

■ Other places
● Monasteries selling graded wool
○ Monasteries selling ungraded wool
(C) Cistercian house
(B) Benedictine house
(A) Augustinian house
(T) Tironensian house

kms
0   25   50   75   100

0   10   20   30   40   50   60
miles

Wool producing monasteries

EE

237

Overseas trade: the Middle Ages to the sixteenth century

In the twelfth and thirteenth centuries the Scottish economy was transformed by an unprecedented upsurge in economic activity that occurred throughout western Europe. The rapid expansion of international trade brought a great influx of foreign traders into Scotland, mainly in search of wool, skins (cowhides, sheepskins, wild animal pelts) and fish. The creation of burghs was a spin-off from this, geared to the regulation of trading activity and to the collection of tolls on commercial traffic. Scotland became, after England, the most important wool producer in Europe and this wool was mainly exported to Flanders and Artois. The herring and cod fisheries were remarkably prolific and the trade in woolfells and cowhides was also important.

Until the late thirteenth century only what later became known as the Petty Customs were levied: tolls on imports, exports and internal traffic. But, apart from tariff rates, no record of these has survived. By the fourteenth century they had become accepted as an integral part of the burghs' own revenues(see below, Burgh farms). This change was probably precipitated by the introduction of what later became known as the Great Customs: on wool, hides and woolfells, which had been levied in England since 1275. The rates of duty were far higher than the Petty Customs and, although their extent was limited, they immediately became a most valuable source of royal revenue. The earliest surviving series are for the period between 1327 and 1333. There are a few stray returns for the 1340s, and a more or less continuous run from 1361 until 1599.

Until the Wars of Independence there was an almost continuous expansion of the Scottish economy and it seems likely that by the 1290s Scotland was, relative to England, substantially more prosperous and also, perhaps, more so than it has been ever since (see below, Taxation in medieval Scotland). The country was divided into three economic regions, each with a major entrepot: Berwick south of the Forth, Perth in central Scotland and Aberdeen beyond the Mounth. Southern Scotland was always the richest part of the country. The earliest surviving customs accounts show that receipts from southern Scotland were slightly higher than those from the other two regions combined, with the central and northern regions almost equal. This disparity was to widen inexorably as the Scottish economy contracted throughout the fourteenth and fifteenth centuries. By the 1420s the proportion of southern receipts had risen to over two-thirds of the national total and by the 1530s to nearly three-quarters.

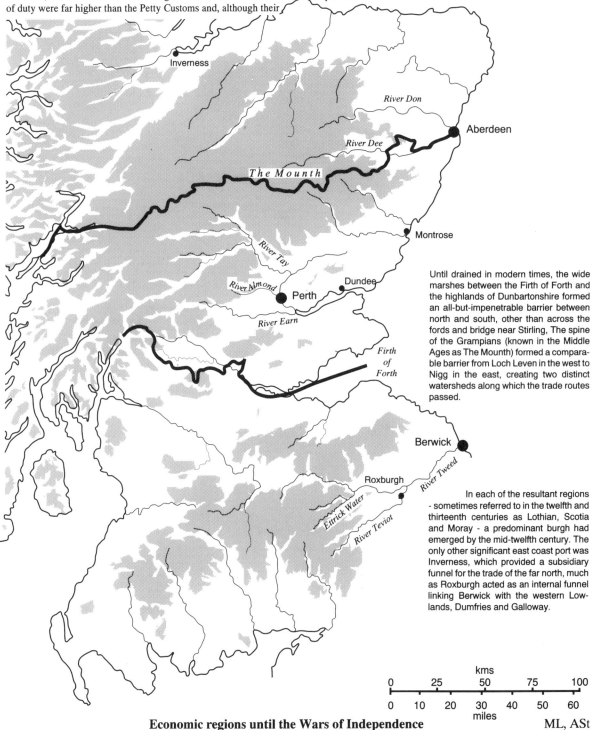

Until drained in modern times, the wide marshes between the Firth of Forth and the highlands of Dunbartonshire formed an all-but-impenetrable barrier between north and south, other than across the fords and bridge near Stirling, The spine of the Grampians (known in the Middle Ages as The Mounth) formed a comparable barrier from Loch Leven in the west to Nigg in the east, creating two distinct watersheds along which the trade routes passed.

In each of the resultant regions - sometimes referred to in the twelfth and thirteenth centuries as Lothian, Scotia and Moray - a predominant burgh had emerged by the mid-twelfth century. The only other significant east coast port was Inverness, which provided a subsidiary funnel for the trade of the far north, much as Roxburgh acted as an internal funnel linking Berwick with the western Lowlands, Dumfries and Galloway.

Economic regions until the Wars of Independence

ML, ASt

Overseas trade: the Middle Ages to the sixteenth century

The Wars of Independence transformed both the economic situation of the country and the relative ranking of the Scottish burghs. Perth lost its precedence in central Scotland and thereafter had to share power with Dundee, whose coastal position was better suited to the larger ships of the late Middle Ages. By the acquisition of subservient ports (at Leith, Blackness and Aberlady), Edinburgh, Linlithgow and Haddington each secured part of Berwick's former trade; as did other, smaller burghs. By the 1320s Edinburgh had already taken part of Berwick's trade. It was therefore well placed to take the largest share of the remainder when Berwick fell to the English in 1333. In the course of the fifteenth century Edinburgh pushed aside all its rivals and by the 1470s controlled over half the Scottish export trade; by the 1530s it controlled two thirds and was the only port of consequence south of the Forth (see below, Burghs' shares of customs). By then the former regional structure of the country had effectively been transformed and Edinburgh had become an economic centre for the entire country (see below, Taxation of burghs 1535 to 1705). It was this economic power base that made Edinburgh the natural capital of Scotland .

Before the Wars of Independence Scotland had developed a diverse international trade, attracting merchants from Norway, England, Western Germany, the Low Countries, northern France, Brittany, Gascony, Spain and Italy. In the fourteenth century links with most of these became tenuous. Few foreign merchants visited Scotland and Scottish traffic was mainly directed to Flanders. By the 1290s Bruges was already the principal centre of Scottish overseas trade. Probably in the reign of Robert I (1306-29) the primacy of trade links with Bruges was formally recognised by establishing it as the Scottish Staple - to which all wool, hides and woolfells exported by Scottish merchants had to be sent (unless special dispensation had been given). With a few short intervals, the Scottish Staple remained there until 1477. Since wool, hides and woolfells were directed by law to Bruges, and the Scottish sea fisheries had almost disappeared during the fourteenth century, the wherewithal for trade with other lands was greatly diminished. Cheap cloth, salmon, (other) skins and salt were the main exports to other countries. Much of the salmon was exported to England in times of peace, and by the late fourteenth century there was a flourishing east coast trade with the Baltic ports of Danzig and Stralsund (see below, Overseas trade in the seventeenth century) and

with Normandy. On the west coast there was a modest trade with Ireland, Brittany and the Biscay ports.

There was a serious trade deficit from the fourteenth century onwards. The Scots became dependent on the importation of manufactures and many raw materials, mainly via Bruges, and often on grain from the Baltic, Normandy and, occasionally, from England. The price of wool declined throughout the fourteenth century and demand dropped catastrophically at its end. The trade in hides and woolfells also declined. In order to boost customs revenues James I (1406-37) greatly expanded the list of exports subject to duty, a process completed by James III (1460-88). The customs accounts from then on give a fuller picture of the extent of Scottish exports. They confirm a downward spiral of Scottish trade until the 1470s, when the sea fisheries were revived on a limited scale. It was not until the last quarter of the sixteenth century that there was a marked and prolonged expansion of Scottish trade.

As trade with Flanders declined there was increasing pressure to open or expand alternative markets, a process greatly helped by abandonment of the Bruges Staple. After a period without a staple port from 1477 to 1508, the small port of Veere on the island of Walcheren (see below, Ports of departure to Veere) became the designated distribution point (a looser form of staple) for the major commercial centres in the Low Countries and nominally maintained this role, with a few short intervals, until 1799. Trade with the Low Countries continued to decline until the late sixteenth century. This loss was mainly made good by a great expansion in trade with France, particularly with Dieppe (see below, Destination of ships from Leith), stimulated by privileged access to the French market; and, to a lesser extent, in trade with the Baltic (see below, Trade with northern Europe). For much of the sixteenth century France was Scotland's principal overseas market. In the later sixteenth and early seventeenth centuries the main growth areas were the Baltic and Scandinavia (see below, Overseas trade in the seventeenth century). Each market had different demands and the changing pattern of Scottish exports is a reflection of this. The trade in wool became insignificant in the sixteenth century, while the trade in cloth, fish and possibly skins greatly expanded; and with the rapid expansion of Baltic trade late in the sixteenth century salt and coal exports also burgeoned.

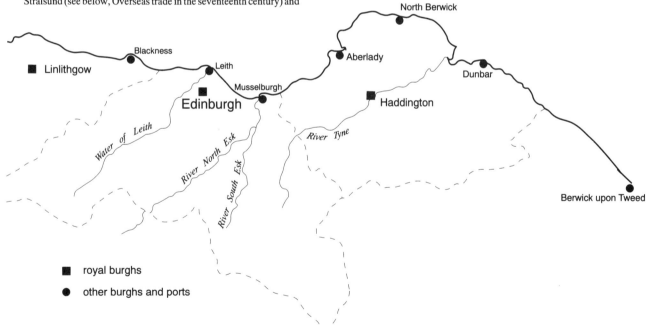

Before the Wars of Independence almost all of southern Scotland's international trade had passed through Berwick. Its loss, from 1296 to 1318 and again from 1333 onwards, necessitated the development of alternative ports. Several minor harbours had long existed in the Lothians, which had acted as transit points for inter-regional trade and for the shipment of goods to and from Berwick; but, Berwick apart, there was no major coastal burgh south of the Firth of Forth. The inland

burghs of Edinburgh, Linlithgow and Haddington jealously guarded their privileges as the administrative centres of the sheriffdom of Edinburgh and its subsidiary constabularies (later Midlothian, West Lothian and East Lothian). Each effectively seized control of their nearest harbours. Leith became the out-port for Edinburgh. Linlithgow secured the small harbour at Blackness, 4 miles to the northeast. Haddington secured a less satisfactory tidal harbour, 5 miles to the north-west, at Aberlady.

Position of Edinburgh after the Wars of Independence

ML, ASt

Distance of main European ports from Leith, in miles

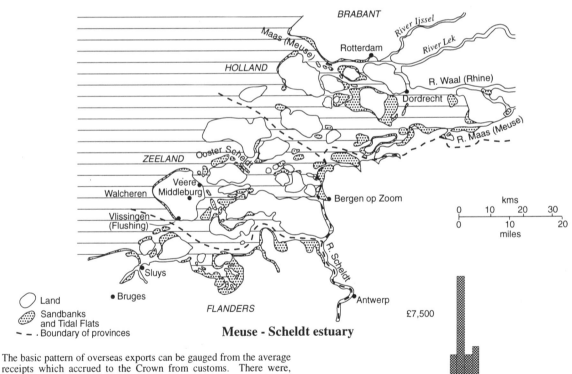

Land
Sandbanks and Tidal Flats
Boundary of provinces

Meuse - Scheldt estuary

The basic pattern of overseas exports can be gauged from the average receipts which accrued to the Crown from customs. There were, however, various changes in rates of duty which partly mask some of the real underlying patterns: between 1357 and 1368 rates on wool, hides and fells were quadrupled, so that on the exports in the 1360s was in real terms 30 per cent lower than in the period 1327-33. There were, however, minor surges in the 1370s and 1420s and again in the last years of the reign of James V (1513-42), although it was not until the last quarter of the sixteenth century that real recovery from the prolonged slump which had lasted since the 1290s took place. The number of taxable commodities increased from three (wool, woolfells and hides) to ten in 1424, although regular returns from some of the new commodities were not made until later. Various increases were also subsequently made in the rates on some commodities, such as salmon and coal. All rates were substantially raised in 1597 as the Crown's response to the new boom in overseas trade.

Overseas trade: annual average customs receipts

ML

Overseas trade: the Middle Ages to the sixteenth century

The long slump in Scotland's overseas trade, which began with the Wars of Independence and continued until the last quarter of the sixteenth century, with short-lived upswings in the 1360s and 1370s, 1420s and 1430s, and the late 1530s, is revealed by the receipts for those exported commodities which paid custom to the crown. The steepest and irrecoverable decline lay in what was Scotland's most important export for much of the medieval period - raw wool. The recovery after the 1570s lay in a revival of the fisheries and the finding of new markets for cloth, sheep and lamb skins, salt and coal. Custom was levied only on three commodities until the 1420s, when James I extended it to a further sixteen. Many of the newly taxed commodities never produced significant customs returns; but the returns on others were spectacular, providing a first indication of what may long have been major exports. Most of the new duties temporarily lapsed after the death of James I. The later maps showing customs on exports from 1327 to 1599 explain the various weights and measures.

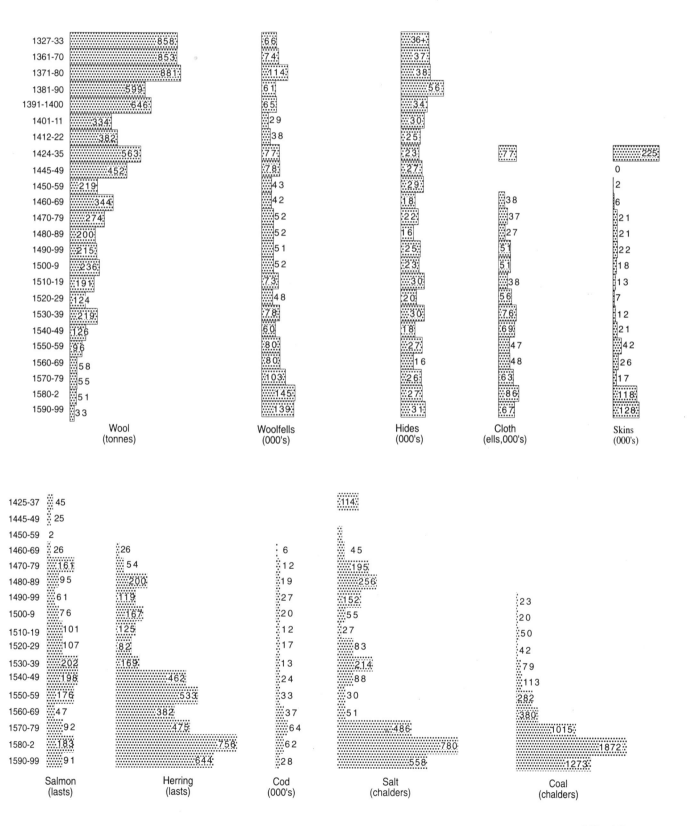

Annual average exports, all Scotland 1327 to 1599

ML, ASt

Overseas trade: the Middle Ages to the sixteenth century

By the time of the earliest surviving customs data the Scottish economy was already in a state of transition, precipitated by the Wars of Independence. Berwick, Aberdeen and Perth (in that order) had earlier been the major exporting burghs. Until 1333 it seemed probable that Berwick and Aberdeen would remain pre-eminent, although Dundee had overtaken Perth and Edinburgh had become an irritating rival to Berwick. The second Wars of Independence transformed the situation by eliminating Berwick, providing new opportunities for numerous minor burghs, notably Linlithgow and Haddington, but Edinburgh was the main beneficiary. Wool was much the most important export throughout the period, but in those burghs funnelling the trade of the Highlands and the west cowhides were also an important factor.

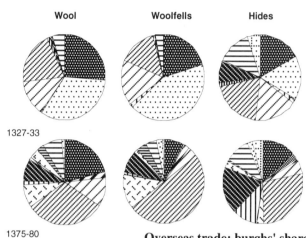

1327-33

1375-80

Overseas trade: burghs' share of customs: fourteenth century

There was a marked slump in the wool trade at the end of the fourteenth century and only a temporary recovery thereafter, under James I. The wool trade was increasingly concentrated in Lothian and, by the later fifteenth century, mainly in Edinburgh. Edinburgh was consolidating its position as the economic capital of Scotland; while Aberdeen, Dundee, Perth and, most spectacularly, Linlithgow all declined. Aberdeen compensated to some extent by an increase in salmon exporting, and Dundee by developing its cloth trade.

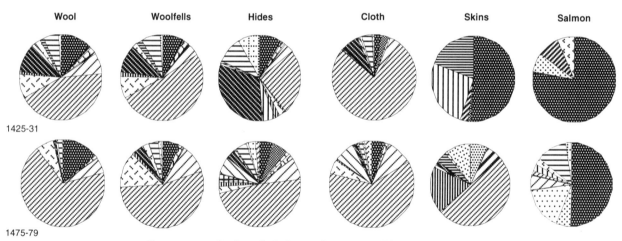

1425-31

1475-79

Overseas trade: burghs' share of customs: fifteenth century

The sixteenth century saw the continuing consolidation of Edinburgh in most sectors of the export trade, at its greatest in wool, cloth, hides and woolfells. As a result both of this and the continuing stagnation of overseas trade until the late 1570s (despite a brief surge in the last years of James V's reign), there was a sharp decline in the trading activities of a number of towns, like Haddington and Linlithgow, and decay in the case of others such as Perth and Stirling. The increase in overseas markets for the fisheries , however,

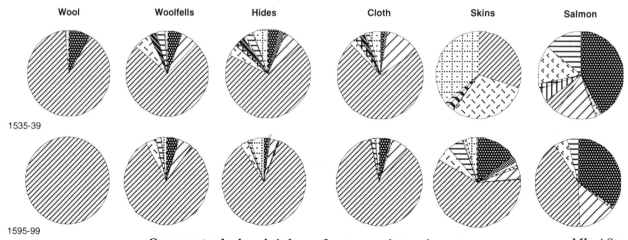

1535-39

1595-99

Overseas trade: burghs' share of customs: sixteenth century

ML, ASt

242

Overseas trade: the Middle Ages to the sixteenth century

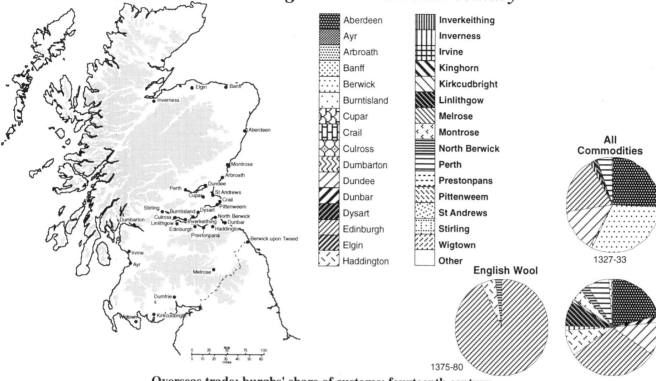

All Commodities

English Wool

1327-33

1375-80

Overseas trade: burghs' share of customs: fourteenth century

Many further commodities were subjected to duty by James I, of which cloth, shorn sheepskins, salmon and lambskins (in that order) were initially the most important - the duty on shorn sheepskins and lambskin was introduced in the 1430s but after James I's death was levied only on aliens. The sea fisheries remained insignificant until the 1470s but thereafter the Forth and Clyde ports took on a new lease of life, although on the east coast a high proportion of catches was exported through Edinburgh.

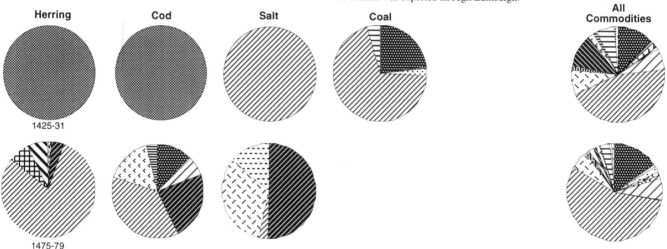

Herring   Cod   Salt   Coal   All Commodities

1425-31

1475-79

Overseas trade: burghs' share of customs: fifteenth century

did stimulate exports from ports like Dundee, Perth and Montrose; this rise, especially in salmon exports, benefited Aberdeen (which did not custom salmon exported by burgesses until the late 1530s) and Inverness (where returns for the 1590s are not extant) more than is suggested here, but the most dramatic increase was in the ports of south-east Fife.

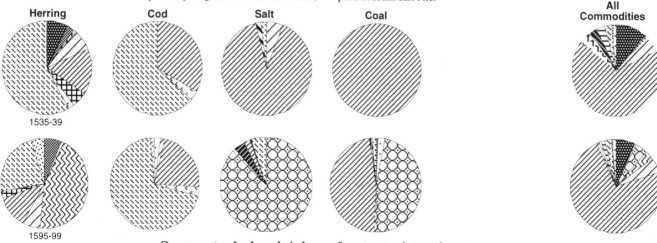

Herring   Cod   Salt   Coal   All Commodities

1535-39

1595-99

Overseas trade: burghs' share of customs: sixteenth century

ML, ASt

Restructuring urban economies in the later Middle Ages

The long slump in Scottish overseas trade throughout the late medieval period, together with the increasing concentration in Edinburgh of sectors of that trade, forced a certain restructuring of the export geared area of the economy of many towns. The following series of maps, drawn from customs data, compares the receipts for exported commodities as percentages of total receipts over six sample periods between the 1320s and 1590s. The overall profile of Scottish overseas trade is also given as a comparative benchmark. Some caution needs to be exercised in using the results over-literally, as custom was applied at different rates on different commodities and these also changed over time - custom for most of the period was at its highest on wool whose importance will thus tend to be over-emphasized in the profile of individual towns and at its lowest on fish (except for salmon), salt and coal.

Aberdeen, the one major burgh to hold on to a significant share of the wool trade throughout the fourteenth and fifteenth centuries, was nevertheless increasingly dependent on the salmon trade from the 1470s, and to a greater extent than the graph suggests because Aberdeen burgesses escaped paying duty on salmon until the late fifteenth century. The sixteenth century saw a sharp increase in its export of woollen cloth and, to a lesser extent, of fells. The complete collapse of Inverness's wool trade by the 1420s had, by contrast, left it reliant on hides but a sharp decline by the 1470s in that sector had encouraged a large dependence on the salmon trade. In Banff the pattern was apparently simpler, the decline in wool bringing about a growing dependence in the fifteenth century on salmon.

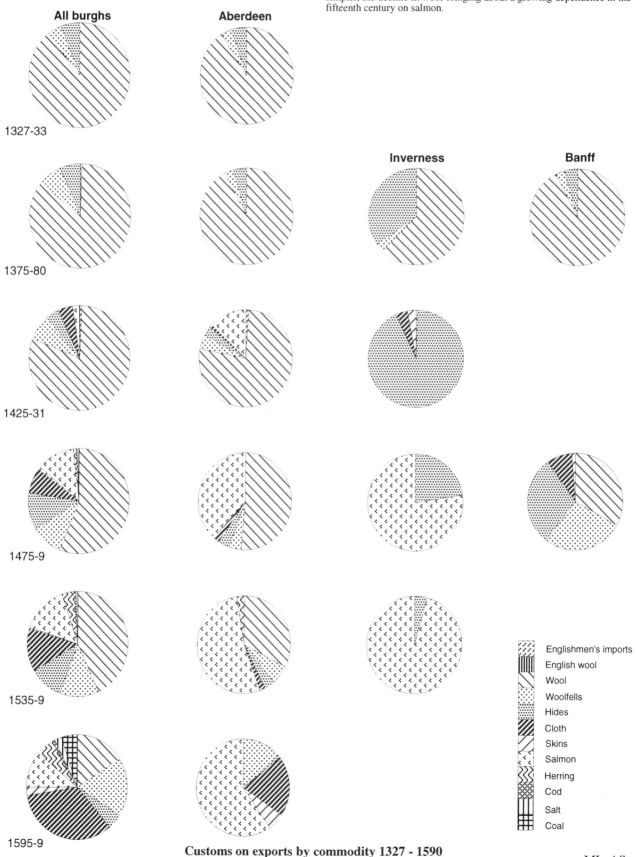

Customs on exports by commodity 1327 - 1590

ML, ASt

244

Restructuring urban economies in the later Middle Ages

The volatile effects of the shifts in overseas trade markets is well demonstrated by the shifts in the economy of Perth, which by the 1550s claimed to be a 'craft town'. Its development in wool, though delayed until well into the fifteenth century, was matched by growing dependence on fells and hides; but the severe slippage in its share of the growing market in hides in the sixteenth century was compensated only by an increasing dependence on fisheries and cloth manufacture. The port of Dundee had a similar, shifting profile, though the difference, not revealed here, was that it managed to hold on to its levels of exports whereas in Perth, whose share of overseas trade halved between the 1420s and 1470s, decay accompanied restructuring. In the port of Montrose, diversification first out of wool and latterly out of fells and hides into salmon, brought new prosperity in the sixteenth century; Montrose pioneered the re-establishment of cod fisheries in the fifteenth century, but by the sixteenth century it had here given way to the Forth ports. There seems also to have been wholesale restructuring in both Cupar and St Andrews but, unlike the other Tay towns, their stake in the salmon trade was small and their overall share of overseas trade much more modest.

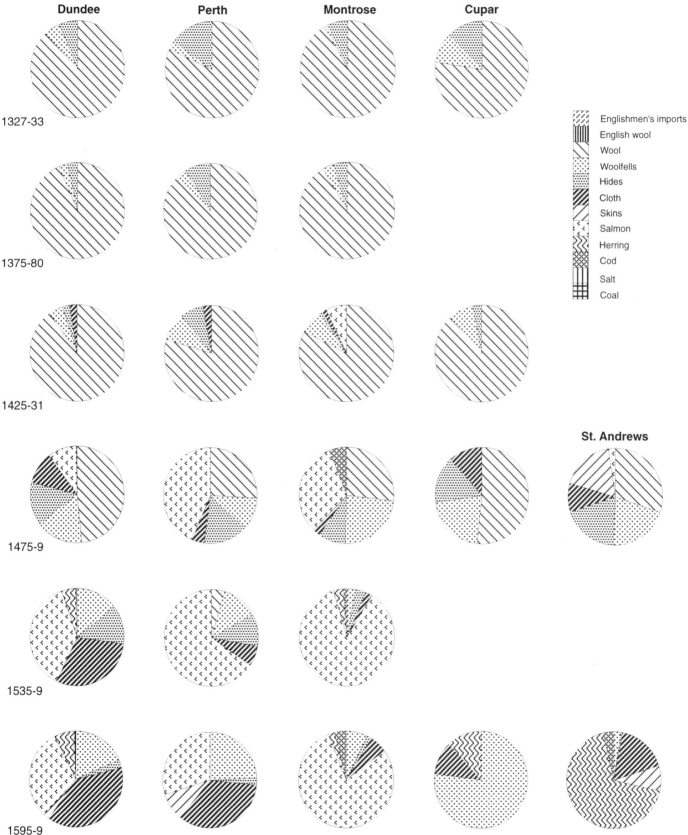

Dundee **Perth** **Montrose** **Cupar** **St. Andrews**

1327-33

1375-80

1425-31

1475-9

1535-9

1595-9

Englishmen's imports
English wool
Wool
Woolfells
Hides
Cloth
Skins
Salmon
Herring
Cod
Salt
Coal

Customs on exports by commodity 1327 - 1590

ML, ASt

Restructuring urban economies in the later Middle Ages

Edinburgh's gradual consolidation of a majority share of the major exported commodities, though clear from these figures, is understated; the capital had by the sixteenth century a uniquely wide industrial and trading base which affected the structure of towns both in the Forth basin and much further afield. The dependence of Linlithgow on the trade in hides and fells, when combined with the data showing the steep decline of these sectors in the fifteenth century, reveals a town in serious decay, unable to diversify into more lucrative areas and increasingly reliant on its position as a royal centre. Stirling, with a similarly shaped economy but a more modest exporting base in the fourteenth and fifteenth centuries, survived into the sixteenth century better. Haddington, an important wool centre until the end of the fifteenth century, saw its nascent cloth industry collapse during the English invasions of the 1540s, leaving a narrowly based economy, dependent on hides, fells and skins, in serious decline.

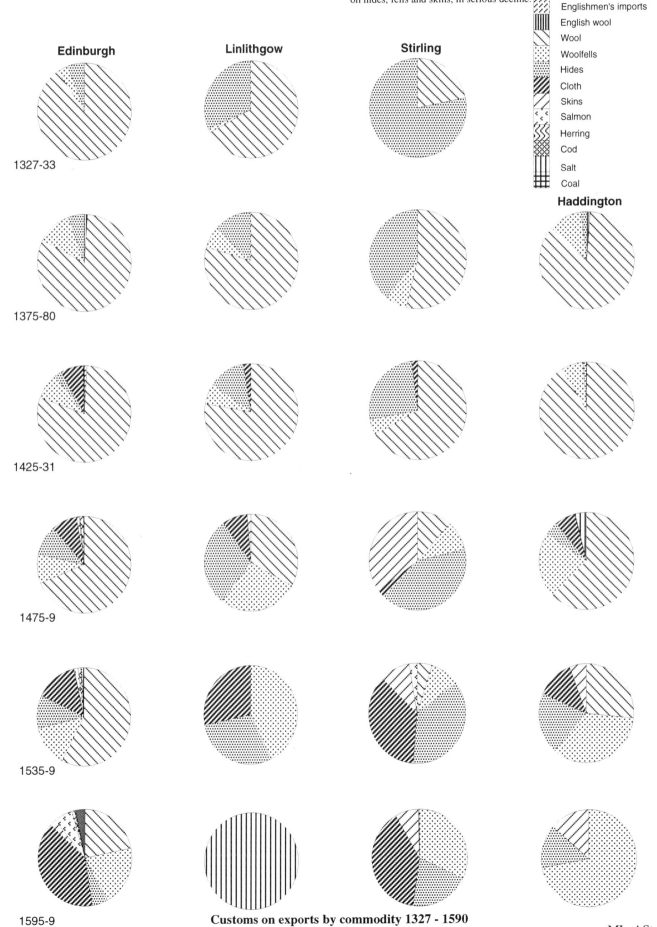

Edinburgh — Linlithgow — Stirling — Haddington

1327-33 · 1375-80 · 1425-31 · 1475-9 · 1535-9 · 1595-9

Legend: Englishmen's imports · English wool · Wool · Woolfells · Hides · Cloth · Skins · Salmon · Herring · Cod · Salt · Coal

Customs on exports by commodity 1327 - 1590

ML, ASt

Restructuring urban economies in the later Middle Ages

The dependence of west-coast ports on wool seems always to have been much slighter, but a significant cloth industry, with its markets in Brittany, Bordeaux and La Rochelle, is evident in Ayr and Dumbarton in the fifteenth and sixteenth centuries and Irvine in the sixteenth, as well as in Kirkcudbright and Wigtown, which are not shown, in the fifteenth.

All three of the ports shown developed an interest in the export of hides which fell away sharply - after 1470 in the case of Ayr and Irvine, but not until the late 1550s in the case of Dumbarton. By the second half of the sixteenth century, all three were largely dependent on the herring industry, which had been revived in the 1480s.

Customs on exports by commodity 1327 - 1590

247

ML, ASt

Foreign traffic and bullion exports 1331 to 1333

In 1330 duty was introduced on English-owned goods at a rate of 4d in the £ (1.67), perhaps as a belated reaction to the £20,000 indemnity paid to England between 1328 and 1330 as a 'contribution for peace'. In 1331 duty was also introduced on bullion exports, at a rate of 12d in the £ (5%), because of an adverse trade balance and fears about a loss of coinage. Both of these new duties were initially levied along with the Petty Customs and returns were made by the burgh authorities rather than by customs officials (see below, Burgh farms). Returns for 1331 have therefore survived from Haddington, Banff and Inverness, which did not at that time submit customs accounts to the Exchequer. For some reason, the new duty on bullion exports

seems not to have been levied at Scotland's principal port, Berwick. Collection practices also seemed to have varied at other burghs.

Berwick had much the largest volume of English traffic, but a total value of £1,270 over two years is perhaps lower than might have been expected. There seem to have been little English trade and few bullion exports through Perth; most such traffic passed through Dundee. Surprisingly, as important in the central region was Inverkeithing, which seems have focused almost exclusively on English trade and may almost have acted as an English factory. The returns from Inverkeithing were higher than those from either Edinburgh or Aberdeen, which were the only other major returning burghs.

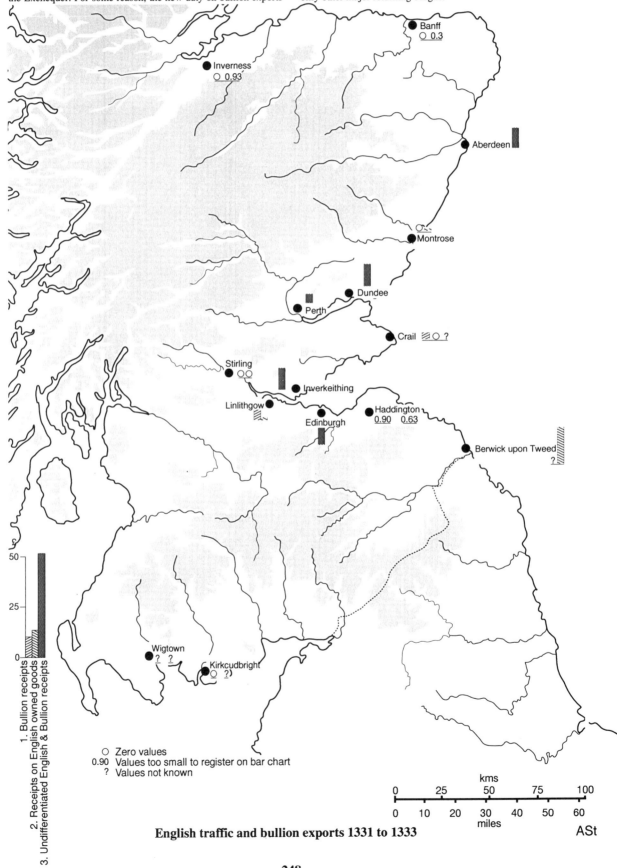

○ Zero values
0.90 Values too small to register on bar chart
? Values not known

1. Bullion receipts
2. Receipts on English owned goods
3. Undifferentiated English & Bullion receipts

kms

miles

English traffic and bullion exports 1331 to 1333

ASt

Foreign traffic and bullion exports 1331 to 1333

Double duty was levied at most Scottish ports between 1331 and 1333 on wool, hides and woolfells exported by aliens (although, sadly, not at Berwick). At burghs other than Berwick, foreign merchants accounted for only about 15% of wool exported and 14% of woolfells and hides. As the maps indicate, the spread of alien activity was very uneven. Aberdeen, Dundee and Inverkeithing were the main centres of alien merchants' activity. For some reason, Inverkeithing seems to have been a focal point for English trade and an amazing 93 % of its customs receipts came from the new duties (the double duty on aliens' exports and the duties on English-owned goods and bullion exports).

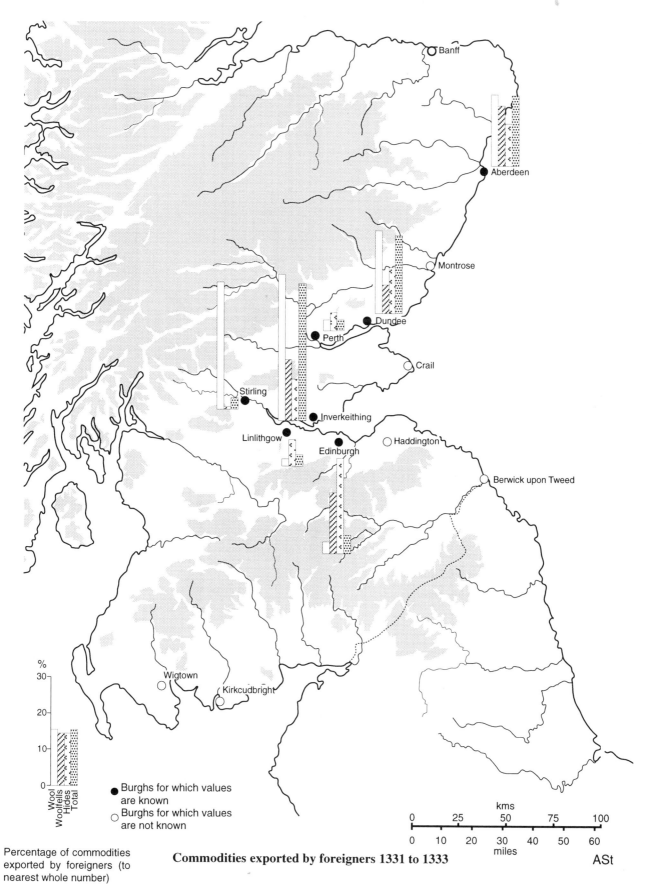

Burghs for which values are known
Burghs for which values are not known

Percentage of commodities exported by foreigners (to nearest whole number)

Commodities exported by foreigners 1331 to 1333

ASt

Overseas trade: the Middle Ages to the sixteenth century

The exchequer returns only give a partial picture of Scotland's export trade in the fourteenth century because the "Great Custom" was levied only on wool, hides and woolfells. Rates of duty were initially fairly low, but were quadrupled between 1358 and 1368 to help pay the ransom of David II. James I added cloth, fish, salt and skins to the list of dutiable exports: while reducing the duty on wool by 19%, James III completed the process by making all exports subject to duty, although he failed to dislodge certain exemptions after the death of James I.

Despite these later additions total customs receipts drifted down, and their value was further eroded by inflation. The principal source of royal income in the fourteenth century, customs revenue had been far exceeded by income from Crown lands by the late fifteenth century. For much of the sixteenth century the customs at many ports were farmed, often for years at a time. Only in the latter years of James V's reign and after 1574 was this practice reversed. In both instances customs receipts markedly increased thereafter.

The late recapture of Berwick (1318) and its subsequent loss in 1333 transformed the economic map of southern Scotland. The most important Scottish burgh of the twelfth and thirteenth centuries, Berwick's former trade was divided between various burghs: principally Edinburgh, Linlithgow and Haddington % of customs in the 1320s, 32% in the 1370s, 45% in the 1420s, 55% in the 1470s, 67% in the 1530s and 75% in the 1590s.

The other regional centres of thirteenth-century Scotland had been Aberdeen and Perth. Aberdeen retained its place but Perth fell behind Dundee. In the fourteenth and fifteenth centuries Edinburgh, Aberdeen, Dundee and Perth were regarded on the continent as the 'four great towns' of Scotland. But Edinburgh's pre-eminence was increasing and by the sixteenth century it had become the economic focal point of the entire country.

The customs returns provide our clearest indicator of relative growth, decline and restructuring. The series of maps which follow illustrate the different patterns of each sector of the export trade and the shifting share of each held by the exporting burghs.

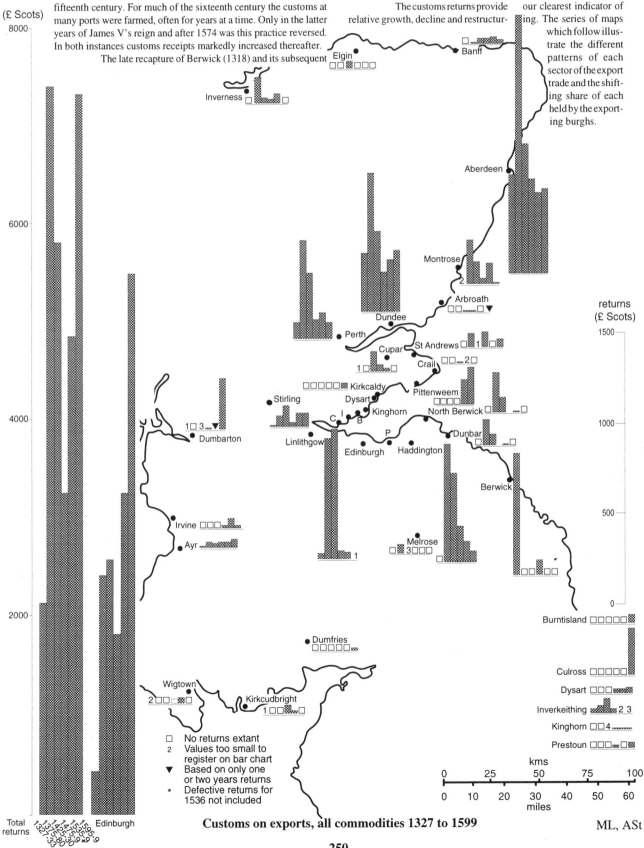

			No returns extant
2			Values too small to register on bar chart
▼			Based on only one or two years returns
*			Defective returns for 1536 not included

Customs on exports, all commodities 1327 to 1599

ML, ASt

Overseas trade: the Middle Ages to the sixteenth century

Rapid expansion of the wool trade had played a vital part in the economic revolution of the twelfth and thirteenth centuries. Even after the introduction of duty on many other commodities, the duty on wool continued to account for over two-thirds of customs receipts until the late fifteenth century - this despite a worsening slump in wool exports from the end of the fourteenth century onwards. But the wool trade was increasingly concentrated upon Edinburgh, to the detriment of the other Scottish burghs. Edinburgh accounted for 70 % of wool exports by the 1470s and 90 % by the 1530s.

The market for Scottish wool was in Flanders and northern France, with Bruges acting as the Scottish staple for most of the period between the 1320s and the 1470s, much as Calais acted as the English wool staple. Prices fell sharply from the middle of the fourteenth century onwards and demand contracted along with the Flemish cloth industry. An alternative market was established in Normandy in the late fifteenth century but this did not adequately compensate. To encourage cloth manufacture, wool exports were restricted in the sixteenth century and periodically banned under James VI.

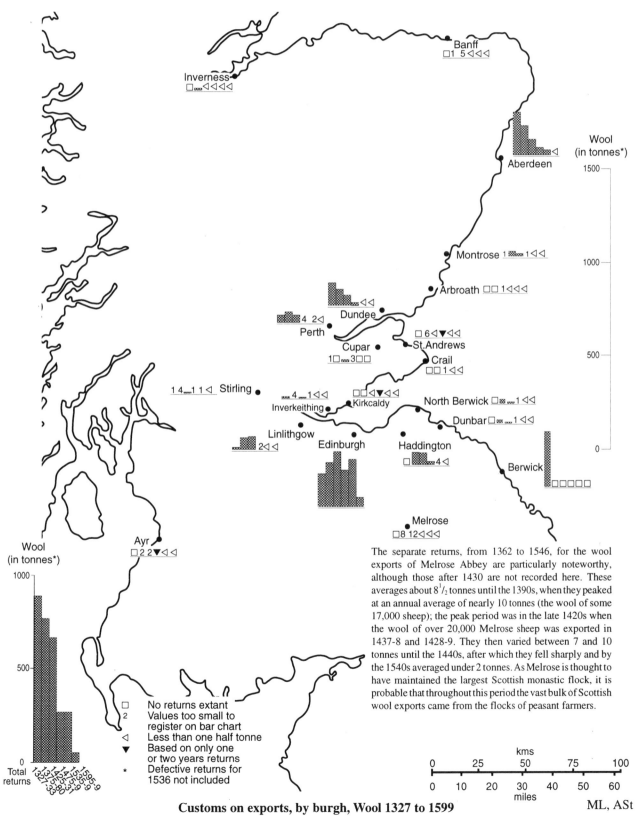

The separate returns, from 1362 to 1546, for the wool exports of Melrose Abbey are particularly noteworthy, although those after 1430 are not recorded here. These averages about $8\frac{1}{2}$ tonnes until the 1390s, when they peaked at an annual average of nearly 10 tonnes (the wool of some 17,000 sheep); the peak period was in the late 1420s when the wool of over 20,000 Melrose sheep was exported in 1437-8 and 1428-9. They then varied between 7 and 10 tonnes until the 1440s, after which they fell sharply and by the 1540s averaged under 2 tonnes. As Melrose is thought to have maintained the largest Scottish monastic flock, it is probable that throughout this period the vast bulk of Scottish wool exports came from the flocks of peasant farmers.

Customs on exports, by burgh, Wool 1327 to 1599

ML, ASt

251

Overseas trade: the Middle Ages to the sixteenth century

Woolfells, like wool, were exported mainly to Flanders and often together, as shown by the *The Ledger of Andrew Halyburton*, a Scottish merchant and factor based in the Netherlands in the late fifteenth century. Yet the patterns, both of general export levels and of levels for individual towns, often varied significantly from those in the wool trade. Southern Scotland traditionally dominated the trade in woolfells even more than in wool, with over 70% of the trade in all but a couple of decades between the mid-fourteenth and early sixteenth centuries. Central Scotland had about 20% of the trade in woolfells, and northern Scotland under 10%. As in wool, northern

Scotland's trade in woolfells was always monopolised by Aberdeen,

Unlike wool, the volume of fells increased markedly in sixteenth century, reaching 18% of all customs receipts by the 1590s; and the capital largely benefited, holding 80% of the trade by the 1590s. With Linlithgow, the drop in fells came at much the same time as with wool; Haddington and Aberdeen compensated a little for their loss of wool exports with a reasonably steady share of the market in fells. In the cases of Dundee and Stirling, volume was actually rising quite sharply by the late sixteenth century.

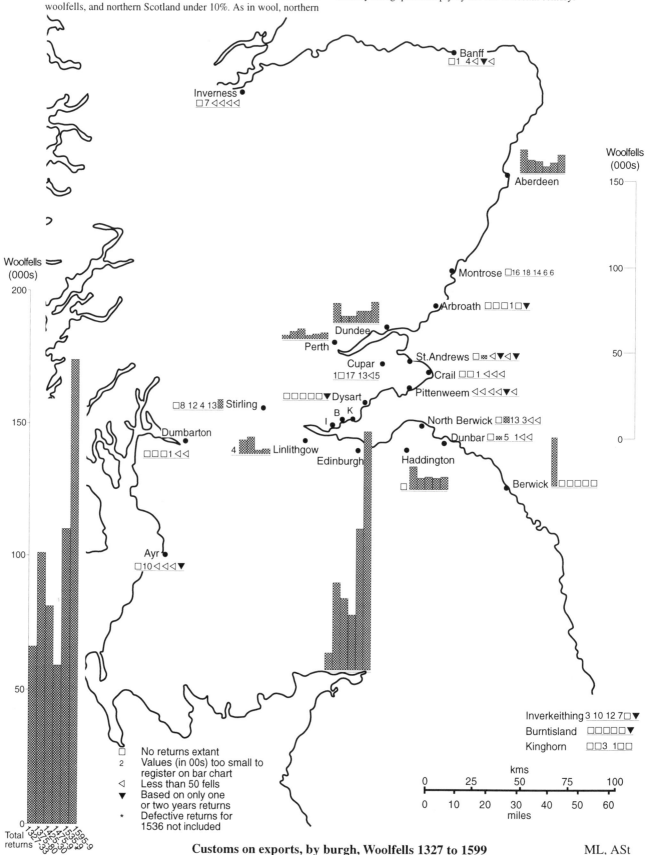

Customs on exports, by burgh, Woolfells 1327 to 1599

ML, ASt

Overseas trade: the Middle Ages to the sixteenth century

Until the introduction of hardy sheep breeds in the late eighteenth century, it was cattle rather than sheep that were to be found in the poorer upland regions. The main cowhide exporting burghs were those that provided market centres for the Highlands and the more westerly districts of the southern uplands. The main overseas markets for hides were in the Low Countries, northern France and latterly the Baltic, so there was surprisingly little trade in hides through the west-coast ports.

If the battleground amongst the Scottish burghs had been for wool in the late fourteenth and early fifteenth centuries, it lay in hides and woolfells in the mid-fifteenth century. In the 1420s, 45% of exports in hides was held by a group of middle-ranking-towns including Inverness, Linlithgow and Stirling. Edinburgh, by contrast, held just 25%, as it did as late as the 1460s. By that time other medium-sized towns like Ayr and Kirkcudbright had also claimed 15% of the trade. A decisive shift is, however, shown in the figures for the 1470s: Edinburgh claimed 48% and would by the end

of the century have 66%, and 85% by the 1590s. The share of the five middle-ranking towns dropped to 20% in the 1470s and fell still further thereafter. But evidence from Inverness is thin from the late fifteenth century onwards, because its customs were usually farmed. Also, no returns made were before 1358 because the earldom of Moray was exempted.

By 1500, when hides had become second only to wool in terms of receipts to the Crown, the main market for the trade lay in France rather than the Low Countries. By the 1570s, when about 3,000 dacres (or 30,000 hides) were exported each year, the Baltic was probably the major market for both hides and skins.

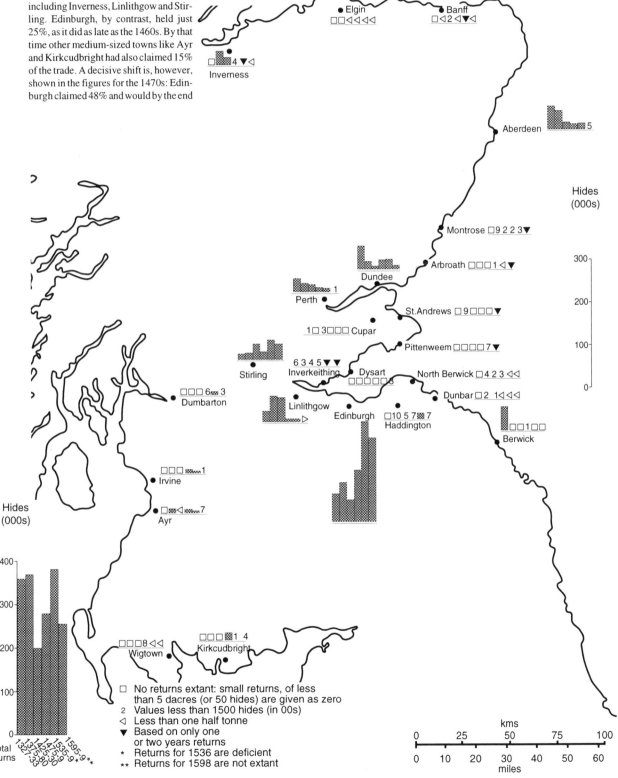

□ No returns extant: small returns, of less than 5 dacres (or 50 hides) are given as zero
2 Values less than 1500 hides (in 00s)
◁ Less than one half tonne
▼ Based on only one or two years returns
* Returns for 1536 are deficient
** Returns for 1598 are not extant

Customs on exports, by burgh, Hides 1327 to 1599

ML, ASt

253

Overseas trade: the Middle Ages to the sixteenth century

A huge variety of animal skins was exported, ranging from rabbit to goat and otter, but the main groups were lambskins and shorn sheepskins. Duty was introduced on wild animal pelts in 1424 and on lambskins and shorn sheepskins in 1434. The recorded volume of wild animal pelts exported was always low, but huge quantities of lambskins and shorn sheepskins were exported in the short period between the introduction of the new duties and the death of James I in 1437.

Duty on all these skins lapsed after James I's death and was not reintroduced until the 1450s. For whatever reason, customs duties on lambskins and shorn sheepskins seem to have been particularly unpopular until the late 1570s; whereupon lambskins in particular reappear as major exports. In the intervening period, while duty was apparently levied on wild animal pelts, duty on lambskins and shorn sheepskins seems only to have been collected from foreign merchants. Even so, the customs returns on these skins were far greater than on wild animal pelts, most of which may simply have evaded duty.

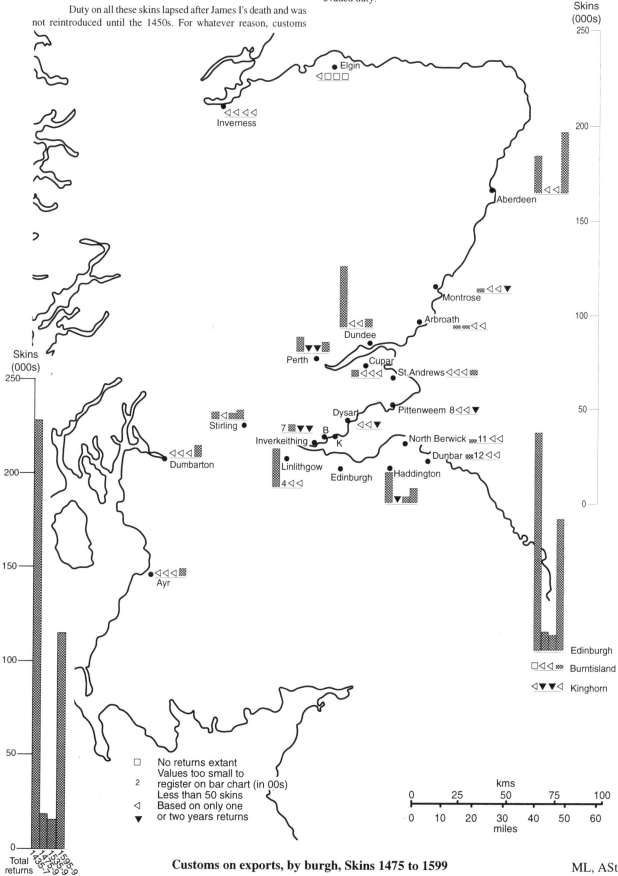

Customs on exports, by burgh, Skins 1475 to 1599

ML, ASt

254

Overseas trade: the Middle Ages to the sixteenth century

Woollen cloth had been a major constituent of Berwick's booming economy in the twelfth and thirteenth centuries but the extent of exports is unknown. The manufacture of cloth ceased to be significant in burgh affairs. In the fourteenth century it may largely have been produced in the countryside. Cloth found its main export market amongst the urban poor of Flanders and latterly in the Baltic. Duty was introduced in 1425 but accounted for less than 10% of customs receipts until the sixteenth century. There was a dramatic rise in levels of customed exports from the 1520s, peaking at over 175,000 ells in 1541-2. Thereafter war with England and the Holy Roman Empire, followed by the Reformation, brought about a slump which lasted until the 1570s. Although the rate of duty on cloth was nominally 2s in £ Scots, in practice it became fossilised in most burghs at a rate of 1d an ell until well into the sixteenth century. Before the death of James V it had been increased to $2\frac{1}{4}$d, which probably was then a tenth of the average value. That in turn became the fossilised rate until James VI increased the duty to 1s an ell in 1598. As a result, by the end of the sixteenth century cloth accounted for no less than 34% of all customs receipts.

The bulk of recorded cloth exports was located in Edinburgh throughout this period: 75% in the 1420s, 65% in the 1470s and over 80% by the 1530s. Yet a cloth industry was significant in some other towns: Kirkcudbright and Wigtown, exporting cloth to Brittany and the Biscay ports, held a 20% share in the 1430s and a 13% share in the 1470s.

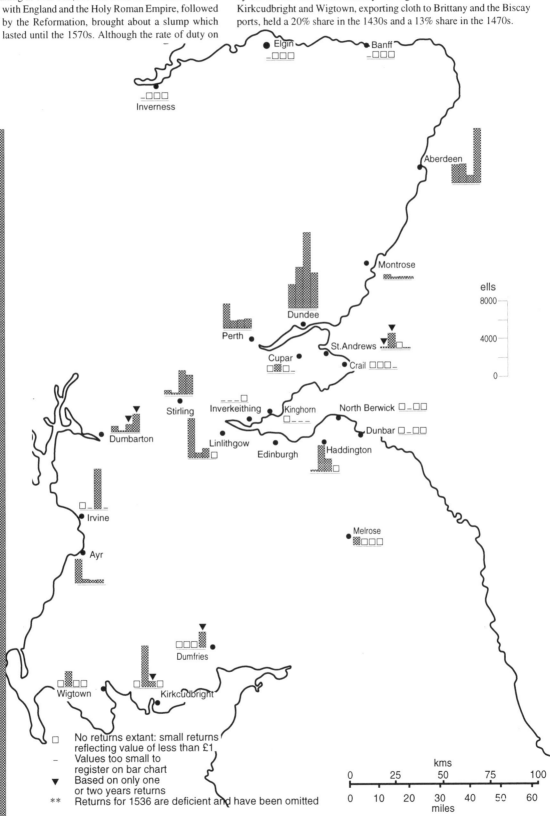

	No returns extant: small returns reflecting value of less than £1
–	Values too small to register on bar chart
▼	Based on only one or two years returns
**	Returns for 1536 are deficient and have been omitted

Customs on exports, main burghs, Cloth 1425 to 1599

ML, ASt

Overseas trade: the Middle Ages to the sixteenth century

Evidence on salmon exports before duty was introduced in the 1425 is slight. The market for salmon in Flanders was never strong and under James I most seems to have been exported to England. Salmon long remained Scotland's main export to England, although in the later fifteenth century and the sixteenth century most was exported to France. Aberdeen was always the main exporting port.

Salmon exports rapidly increased as direct trade links with France expanded from the 1470s onwards. Salmon accounted for less than 3% of customs receipts in the 1420s but rose to over 10% in the 1470s and stood at nearly 14% by the 1530s. Exports peaked at over 500 lasts p.a. in the last years of James V. But diminishing trade with France and a vast increase in the rate of duty, from 4s or 5s per barrel under James V to 37s 6d by 1597, greatly reduced the size of the market (if not the rate of return to the crown which collected £1,923 from salmon, almost 17% of total receipts, in 1598). For much of the period, although not the years in this series, the total volume of salmon exports cannot be accurately assessed because Aberdeen burgesses were exempted from paying duty and the customs at certain burghs, especially along the Moray firth, were usually farmed after 1485.

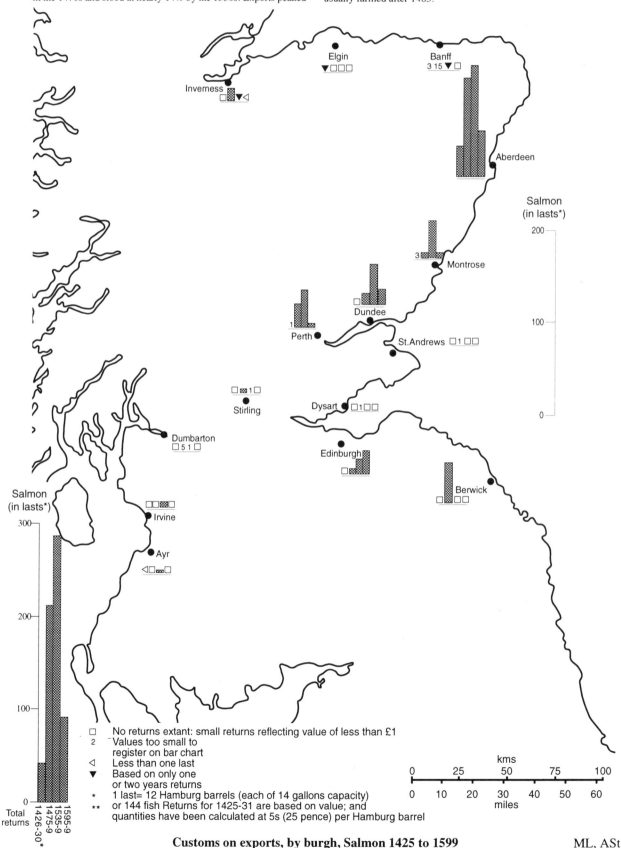

Customs on exports, by burgh, Salmon 1425 to 1599

ML, ASt

Overseas trade: the Middle Ages to the sixteenth century

Herring had been fished in great quantities in the twelfth and thirteenth centuries, but during the Wars of Independence the sea fisheries seem to have collapsed. One theory is that the herring shoals migrated in the fourteenth century to the mouth of the Baltic; another possibility is that the Scots were forced to abandon the fisheries because of frequent English attacks. The Dutch revived the North Sea fisheries in the mid-fifteenth century but, although duty was levied from the 1420s, Scottish customs returns are insignificant until the 1470s. Duty was, however, doubled from 6d to 12d a barrel early in the 1480s; by then herring had become the main growth area of the export trade with large cargoes being sent to France and Brittany from both Forth and west-coast ports. Exports rarely exceeded 200 lasts a year, however, until 1535; by the end of the sixteenth century they were often over 800 lasts. By then the main ports were Dumbarton (for which returns however exist only for three of the years 1595-9) and those around Pittenweem.

Markets for herring lay mainly in France and, after 1590, in the Baltic, which by the 1620s was receiving over 600 lasts (or 7 million fish) a year from Scotland. The herring industry was the only one of the three fisheries to sustain its growth throughout the sixteenth century and its net value probably exceeded that of salmon (in 1611-14 their annual yields were estimated at £100,000 and £50,000 (but see below Customs receipts 1595 to 1599); its profit to the Crown was always more modest than that from salmon.

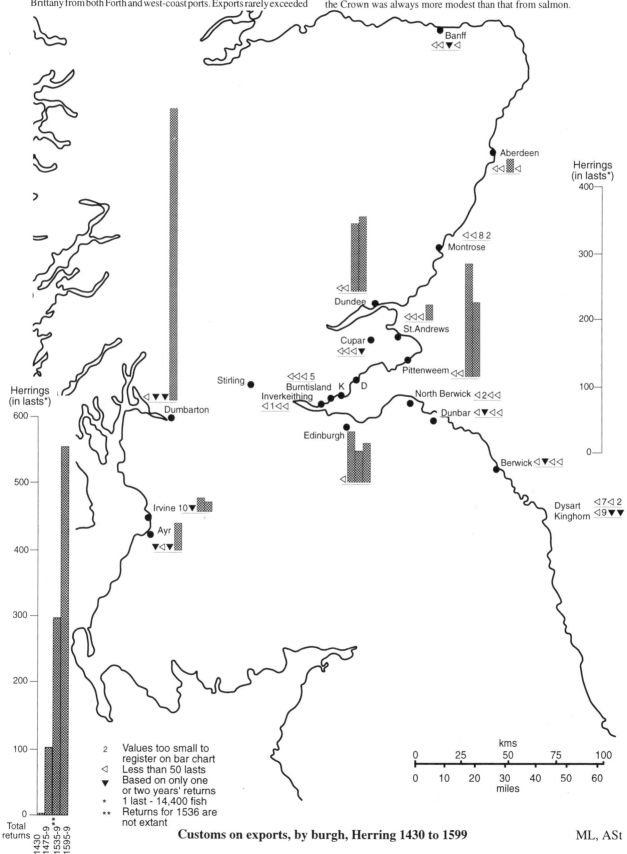

Customs on exports, by burgh, Herring 1430 to 1599

ML, ASt

257

Overseas trade: the Middle Ages to the sixteenth century

Cod, like herring, had been fished in large quantities in the twelfth and thirteenth centuries. Such was the reputation of Aberdeen as a producer that cod was known as Aberdaan in its main market in Flanders. Aberdeens seem also to have been common in England. The revival of the fisheries after a long period of slump came only in the late 1460s (there is only one entry, of 25 dozen fish out of Ayr, for the whole of the period 1425-31). The revival was, however, much more modest than that in herring or salmon: it peaked in the 1570s when 55,000 fish a year were exported. The profit to the Crown from cod exports, despite a rise in the rate levied from 20d to 40d per thousand over the period surveyed, was small: 0.7% in 1504-5 and only 0.4% even in its peak year of 1574.

The main ports by the 1530s were the group around Pittenweem, Anstruther, St Monance and Crail, which paid over 50% of customs; by the 1570s they paid 90%. Other major exporters were Edinburgh and Montrose, as shown on the map, but also Banff, which is not shown, as its brief 25% share of the trade came in the 1540s. A curious absentee from this list was Aberdeen, which preferred by this period to concentrate on the more lucrative trade in salmon.

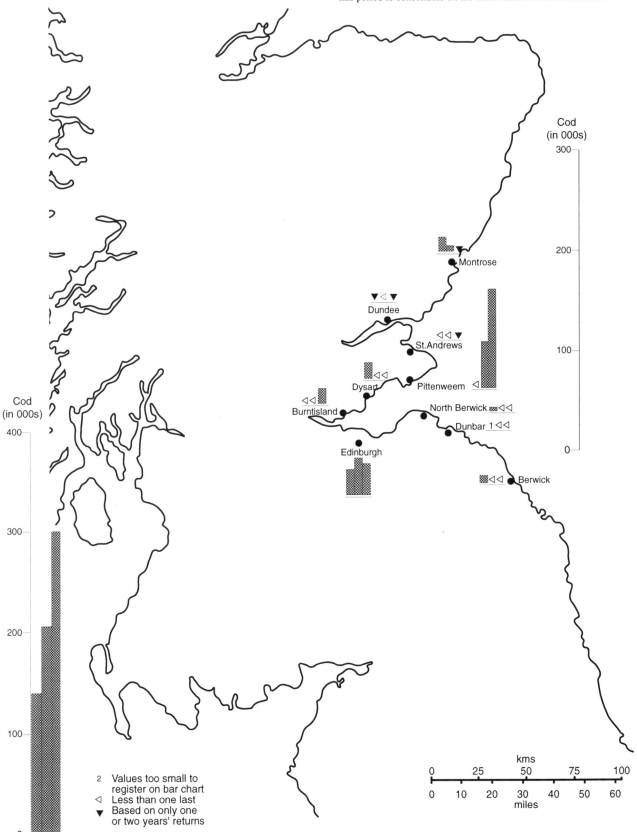

Customs on exports, by burgh, Cod 1475 to 1599

ML, ASt

Overseas trade: the Middle Ages to the sixteenth century

Coastal salt-pans are recorded in Scottish charters from the twelfth century onwards. Most were linked with coal-mines, salt being produced by boiling sea-water in large metal vessels. Customs duty on salt was introduced in 1429. Almost all the salt exported seems to have come from salt-pans owned by collieries. The salt from Edinburgh and Haddington came from the pans at Prestoun (hence Prestonpans), which were linked to the colliery at Tranent; similarly, the salt from Dysart and Culross was produced there at pans owned by adjacent collieries. Customs returns for salt, unlike those for coal, begin from the point at which they were devised but salt exports were volatile, peaking at 448 chalders in 1479 and 627 in 1486 but falling below 100 chalders in all but two of the thirty years after 1497. Here, however, the returns may be misleading for Dysart, which held a 73% share of exports in the 1490s, and ceased to send returns between 1506 and 1541 when its customs were farmed. Exports, as with coal, increased dramatically from 1574, coinciding with a rise in the price of salt from the Bay of Biscay; the bulk of exports in the 1570s were funnelled through Prestonpans, which held a 70% share. Returns for Culross do not begin until 1580 but by the 1590s it produced 89% of all Scottish salt exported. Throughout the period, almost all the salt exports went to Scandinavia and the Baltic, mainly to Danzig.

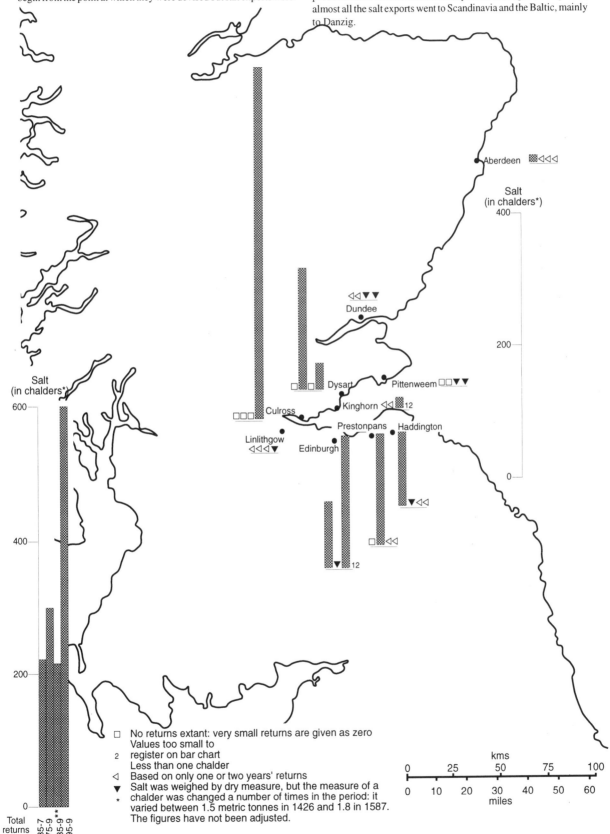

□ No returns extant: very small returns are given as zero
Values too small to
2 register on bar chart
Less than one chalder
◁ Based on only one or two years' returns
▼ Salt was weighed by dry measure, but the measure of a
* chalder was changed a number of times in the period: it
varied between 1.5 metric tonnes in 1426 and 1.8 in 1587.
The figures have not been adjusted.

Customs on exports by burgh, Salt 1435 to 1599

ML, ASt

Overseas trade: the Middle Ages to the sixteenth century

Customs returns for coal are recorded only from 1488, at a rate of 16d per chalder, but were insignificant in terms of revenue until the 1530s. Rates were raised in 1575 to 35d or 37d and were raised a further seven times between then and 1599, when they stood at 56d; this reflected a dramatic rise in output and a fourfold increase in exports in the thirty years after 1565-9, when they stood at an average of 282 chalders per year. Much of the coal mined at Culross must have gone into the manufacture of salt, but its coal exports (whose returns begin only in 1580) were by the 1590s equal in value though less in tonnage to those exported out of Leith, Edinburgh; uniquely, Culross coal was customed at various rates between 51d and 117d, reflecting its high quality. The main customers for coal were Dutch, although much of it was taken, in Dutch ships, to the Baltic as well as to the Netherlands. Exports from west-coast ports reached 20% of the total exports in 1576 but were generally more modest.

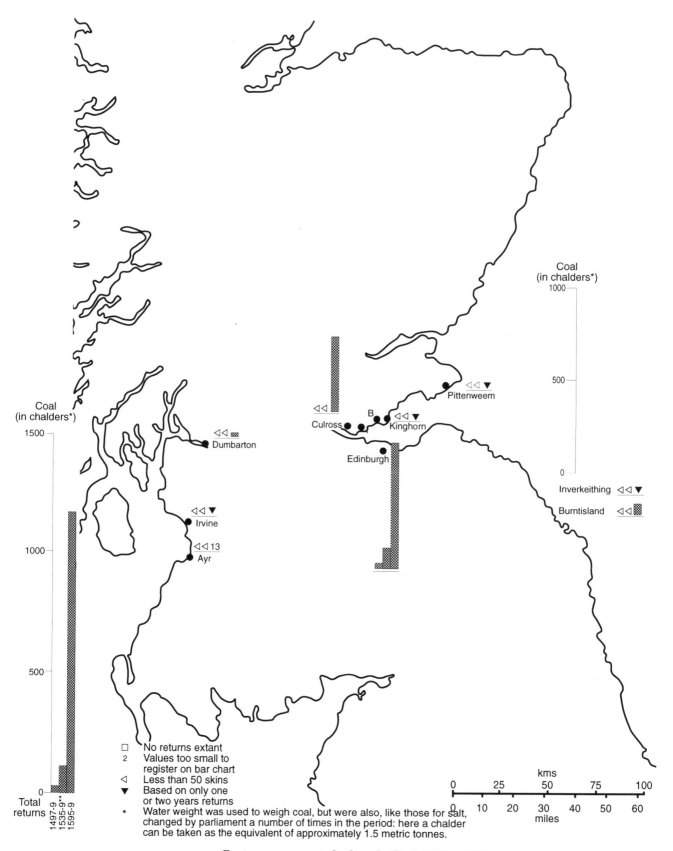

Coal
(in chalders*)

Coal
(in chalders*)

Coal
(in chalders*)

1000

500

0

Inverkeithing ◁◁ ▼

Burntisland ◁◁ ▨

◁◁ ▨
Dumbarton

◁◁
Culross

B

◁◁ ▼
Kinghorn

◁◁ ▼
Pittenweem

Edinburgh

1500

1000

500

0

◁◁ ▼
Irvine

◁◁ 13
Ayr

Total
returns

1497-9
1535-9**
1595-9

☐ No returns extant
2 Values too small to register on bar chart
◁ Less than 50 skins
▼ Based on only one or two years returns
* Water weight was used to weigh coal, but were also, like those for salt, changed by parliament a number of times in the period: here a chalder can be taken as the equivalent of approximately 1.5 metric tonnes.

kms
0   25   50   75   100

0 10 20 30 40 50 60
miles

Customs on exports by burgh, Coal 1425 to 1599

ML, ASt

Destinations of shipping from Leith, 1510 to 1513

The Leith port books for 1510-11 and 1512-13 are among the earliest surviving Scottish port books. Unlike the customs accounts, the port books include the particulars of the cargoes sent by named merchants on each ship leaving Leith for foreign destinations. From 1508 Veere was the compulsory entry port (or staple) for Scottish shipping visiting the Low Countries; cargoes were mainly of wool, woolfells and cloth, though some hides, skins and miscellaneous other goods were also sent. Most were probably destined for sale in the growing commercial centres of Antwerp and Bergen op Zoom

The cargoes for French ports were similar though the proportion of hides was somewhat larger. In addition, large amounts of salmon, cod and herring were also sent to Normandy. An expatriate Scottish community had lived in Dieppe since the later fifteenth century and, although there was no official Scottish staple in France, Dieppe clearly attracted the bulk of Leith's French trade, at least between 1510 and 1513.

Despite growing political tension after 1509 and piracy committed by both sides, a few ships continued to trade with England. Their cargoes, however, in which salmon predominated, were small. The low level of Baltic-bound vessels perhaps also reflects the dangerous political situation in the Baltic. The Scots were allied to the Danes in their war against Sweden and several Hanseatic towns, led by Lübeck, though Danzig endeavoured to remain neutral. The Danzig-bound vessels were laden primarily with lambskins. Cloth and coal were sent to Copenhagen, but the three Stralsund-bound ships were virtually empty.

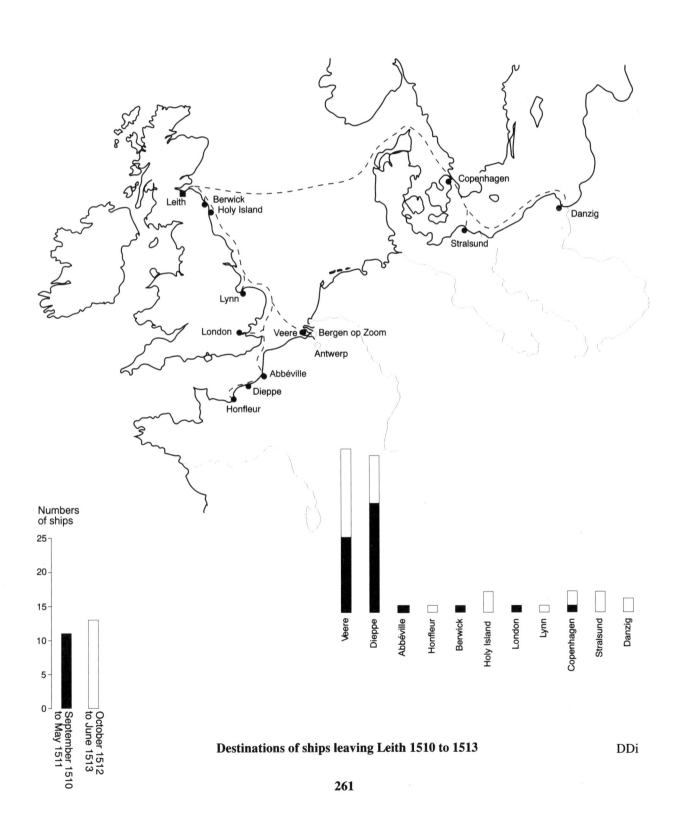

Destinations of ships leaving Leith 1510 to 1513

DDi

Trade with northern Europe: Scottish ports

By the later thirteenth century merchants from western Germany were visiting Scotland. Little is known about their trade, though they probably shipped wool, woolfleeces and hides to the Low Countries. Although Germans traded in Scotland throughout the Wars of Independence, they appear to have been displaced by Scottish merchants from the 1330s. With the opening of the Sound to shipping in the 1380s, direct contact between Scotland and the Baltic became possible. Skins, hides, cheap cloth and salt were exported to the Baltic and became the principal ingredients of the *Krämerwaren* sold by Scottish pedlars in the eastern Baltic from the later fifteenth century. By then, Bremen and Hamburg merchants were visiting Shetland in search of fish, in contravention of ordinances made by the kings of Norway which also applied to Orkney. As trade expanded in the sixteenth century, skins continued to dominate exports to the Baltic, though herring, coal and salt, sent from the Forth burghs, increased in importance. Some cloth was still exported and, from the 1580s, wool was sent to Sweden. Despite periodic slumps in their relative importance, all these commodities were shipped to the Baltic in the seventeenth century. In addition, Norway particularly began to import Scottish grain.

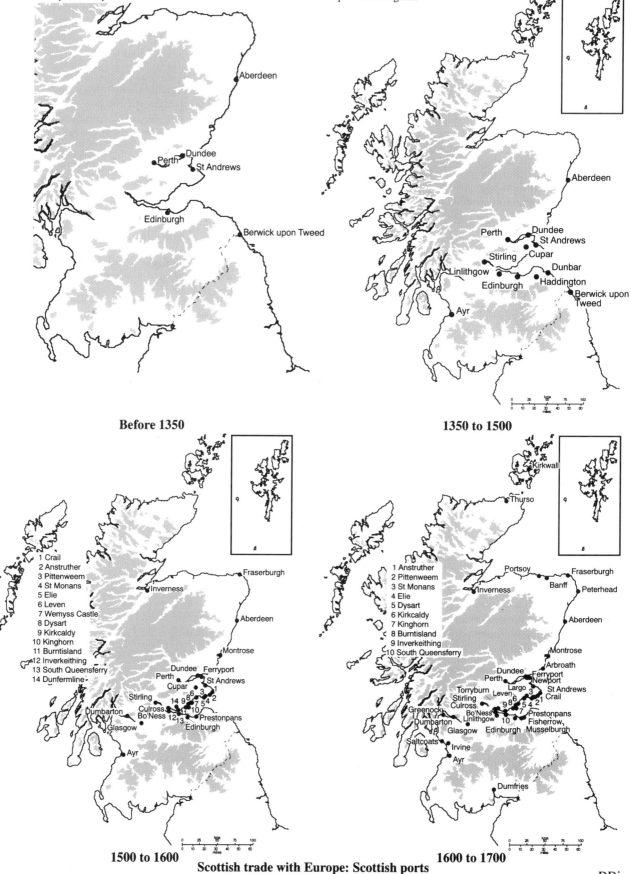

Before 1350

1350 to 1500

1500 to 1600

1600 to 1700

Scottish trade with Europe: Scottish ports

DDi

Scottish emigration to the Baltic

The large-scale emigration of Scots to northern Europe began in the later Middle Ages. Some emigrants were students heading for the universities of Cologne and Louvain. From the sixteenth century a few also attended the new universities in the Baltic region. Other emigrants were established merchants who settled in the coastal ports. Latterly, some also made for the inland towns. From the later sixteenth century considerable numbers of Scots served in Polish, Russian, Scandinavian and German armies. Most emigrants, however, were pedlars who sought a living selling cheap merchandise to the poorer sections of society. Complaints against such activities were common in the Danzig area from the later fifteenth century. As the numbers of Scottish pedlars multiplied in the later sixteenth and early seventeenth centuries, attempts to restrict their activities also grew. Scots have been traced to over 400 localities in Poland alone. Eventually, however, the emigrants were assimilated into Baltic society. The reasons for Scottish emigration are complex but to many Scots the opportunities for economic advancement, particularly in the prevalent atmosphere of religious toleration in Poland, were greater than at home.

● Centres of emigration before 1500
○ Selected centres of emigration after 1500
□ University towns

Öregrund
Uppsala
Västeras
Köping
Enköping
Karlstad
Arboga
Stockholm
Örebr
Tors-wa'lla
Söbertälje
Nyköping
Vadstema
Linköbing
Nylöse (Göteborg)
Aalborg
Växjö
Kalmar
Memel (Klaipeda)
Angelholm
Halsingborg
Elsinore (Helsingor)
Landskrona
Kristianstad
Slangerup
Copenhagen
Ahus
Roskilde
Lund
Malmö
Ystad
Tilsit (Sovetsk)
Falsterbo
Wladyslawow (Kudirkos)
Colberg (Kolobrzeg)
Stralsund
Rügen
Königsberg (Kaliningrad)
Barth
Greifswald
Danzig (Gdansk)
Wolgast
Belgard (Bralogard)
Lübeck
Rostock
Demmin
Anklam
Schwerin
Plau
Stettin (Szczecin)
Falkenberg (Zlocieniee)
Thorn (Torun)
Frankfurt
Plozk (Plock)
Helmstedt
Schwiebus (Swiebodzin)
Posen (Posnan)
Zullichau (Sulechow)
Warsaw (Warszawa)
Wittenberg
Kalisch (Kalisz)
Leipzig
Sieradz
Lubin
Meissen
Belzyce
Breslau (Wroclaw)
Zamosc
Hirschberg (Jelenia Go'ra)
Sandomir (Sandomierz)
Annaberg (Gora SW. Anny)
Cracow
Tarnow
Jaroslav Lemberg (Lovov)
Wieliczka
Przemyslo
Jaslo
Krossen (Kroso)

Memel (Klaipeda)
Heydekrug (Silute)
Tilsit (Sovetsk)
Wischwill (Viesvile)
Neukirch (Timiryazevo)
Ragnit (Neman)
Putzig (Jedrzejowo)
Fischhausen (Pimorsk)
Königsberg (Kaliningrad)
Tapiau (Gvardeysk)
Insterburg (Chernyákhovsk)
Stalluponen (Nesterov)
Lochstadt
Pillau (Battifsk)
Wehlau (Znamensk)
Lauenburgh (Lebork)
Zinten (Korneyo)
Muhlhausen (Gvardeyskoye)
Stolp (Stupsk)
Braunsberg (Braniewo)
Domnau (Domnovo)
Nordenburg (Krylovo)
Goldap (Gotdap)
Danzig (Gdanzk)
Frauenburg (Frombork)
Schippenbeil (Sepopol)
Angerburg (Wegorzewo)
Praust (Pruscz Gdanski)
Elbing (Elblag)
Mehlsack (Pieniezno)
Bartenstein (Bartoszyce)
Barten (Barciany)
Drengfurth (Srokowo)
Butow (Bytow)
Hohenstein (Pszczotki)
Berent (Koscierzyna)
Wormditt (Orneta)
Rastenburg (Ketrzyn)
Oletzko
Schoneck (Skarszewy)
Dirschau (Tczew)
Pr-holland (Pastek)
Arnsdorf (Lubomino)
Rummelsburg (Miastko)
Marienburg (Malbork)
Christburg (Dzierzgon)
Guttstadt (Dobre Hiasto)
Mewe (Gnicw)
Stuhm (Stzum)
Pr-mark (Przezmark)
Sensburg (Mragowo)
Lyck (Etk)
Riesenburg (Prabuty)
Konitz (Chojnice)
Neuenburg (Nowe)
Marienwerder (Kwidzyn)
Johannisburg (Pisz)
Jastrow (Jastrowic)
Tuchel (Tuchela)
Graudenz (Grudziadz)
Hohenstein (Olsztynek)
Ortelsburg (Szczytno)
Deutsch-krone (Walcz)
Lobsens (Lobzenica)
Kuln (Chelmno)
Neumark (Nw. Miasto Lubawskie)
Neidenburg (Nidzica)
Schneidemuhl (Pila)
Exin (Kcynia)
Bromberg (Bydgoszcz)
Strasburg (Brodnica)
Thorn (Torun)

Scottish emigration to the Baltic before and after 1500

263

DDi

Trade with northern Europe: Baltic ports

Because of the paucity of records, it is difficult to map Scotland's commercial connections with northern Europe before 1350. There was some trade with Norway, probably in fish, though this perhaps declined in the fourteenth century due to the Hanseatic League's virtual monopoly of Norwegian commerce. From the later thirteenth century, merchants from western and northern Germany also visited Scotland. During the Wars of Independence they supplied Scotland with arms and victuals from the Low Countries and, ironically, from England also.

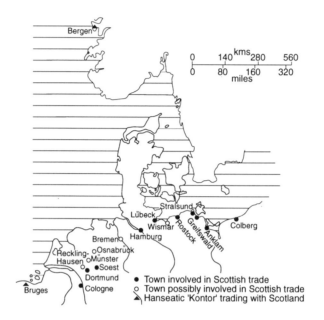

Before 1350

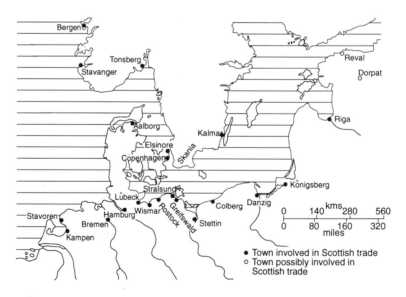

From 1350 to 1500

Scottish trade with Europe: Baltic ports to 1500

DDi

Trade with northern Europe: Baltic ports

Soon afterwards, direct trade with western Germany ceased, although Rhenish wine continued to be imported via the Low Countries. Contacts with northern Germany continued, but remained generally limited. Beer was probable the most important import from this region. Scots also began to visit the Skaian herring fairs. By the later fourteenth century, merchants from the eastern Baltic were trading in Scotland, bringing flax, hemp, sylvan products and grain. This trade remained important throughout the period, although grain shipments declined from the mid-seventeenth century. Norwegian trade revived from the later fifteenth century, but timber and tar were now the principal commodities sent westward. From the later sixteenth century, these products were also imported from Sweden, although metals (particularly iron) were the chief Swedish exports to Scotland. Trade with Denmark developed before that with Sweden, but was generally less significant.

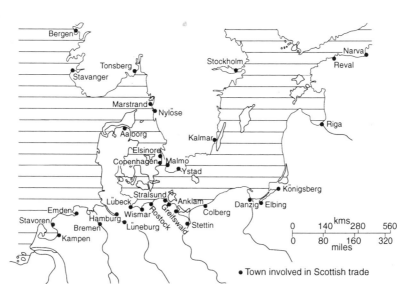

From 1500 to 1600

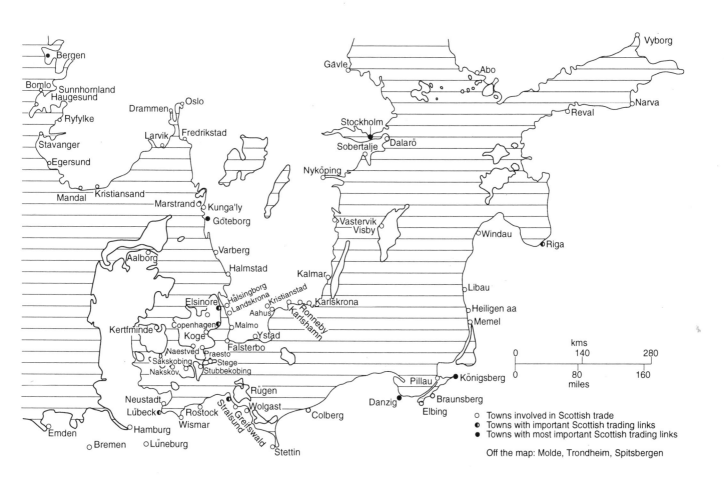

Scottish trade with Europe: Baltic ports 1500 to 1700

DDi

265

Scottish trade in the seventeenth century

By the 1590s, the components making up the Scottish export trade were little different from a century earlier but their relative importance had altered markedly, as the statistics for customs receipts for 1595-9 clearly show. Wool, once the mainstay and most lucrative part of the trade, had shrunk to less than 16 per cent of customs revenue, whereas cloth, a modest component in the 1460s and even in the 1530s, now accounted for a third and the duty on it was sharply increased in the revision of customs dues made in 1597. The recovery of the fisheries, which had begun in the 1470s, continued until the 1650s or 1660s with duty on salmon, the most lucrative sector, also increased in 1597. The export of hides, skins and woolfells to their traditional markets in the Baltic and Netherlands, continued at healthy levels, at least until the 1640s. Salt and coal, although they had still a relatively low duty, begi n to figure prominently in the returns, but would by the 1620s reach far greater heights.

The regular *Exchequer Rolls* series, which permits a systematic analysis of Scotland's exports from the 1370s, ends in 1599. There are only a few port books or local shipping lists for the early seventeenth century, and a Report drawn up by the Cromwellian administration in 1656 until more systematic evidence for both exports and imports becomes available in the 1680s. There is, however, a remarkable survey drawn up in 1614, which largely confirms the patterns of the customs receipts of the 1590s. Entitled 'The wirris and commodities that are shipped and transported further of this kingdom yearly by sea', it estimated the total annual value of all goods shipped out of Scotland between 1611 and 1614 as £736,986 Scots.

By 1700, hides and skins which accounted for a quarter of the 1590s customs revenue and a third of the 1614 survey, would have shrunk drastically; fish, especially herring, worth a fifth of visible exports in 1614, would expand until the 1680s but then contract sharply. Exports of coal, worth 3% by the reckoning of 1614, when about 16,000 tons were produced a year, doubled by the 1680s but then fell away; the fall of the overseas markets for salt, worth appreciably more than coal in 1614, was earlier, in the 1650s and 1660s, and more spectacular. Grain, brought by sea from the north and north-east to the Forth in increasing quantities, began to be exported from 1610 onwards but its overseas markets began to dry up from the 1690s. The two major growth sectors of the export trade in the seventeenth century were in linen and cattle, but both, unlike traditional Scottish exports, were focused on a single market - in England, and much linen followed cattle overland on the drove roads rather than by sea.

Along with the shift in the balance of commodities exported went a drastic change in the directions taken by foreign trade. The 1620s and 1630s saw record levels of traditional exports like hides and skins, mostly still sent to traditional markets such as the Netherlands and the Baltic. But already trade was spreading outwards, from the Dutch staple port of Veere: grain and coal were largely sent to Rotterdam and the widening range of imports came from a series of Dutch ports, including Amsterdam. Increasing numbers of ships came laden with timber and iron, from Norway and Sweden. The beginnings of a new trade with Spain and America, mostly out of west-coast ports, can be seen after 1660. The means of tracing these changes are diverse and a single indicator - whether numbers of ships or custom paid on commodities - may be misleading if used in isolation; the size of ships varied greatly, as did the amount of duty levied on different commodities.

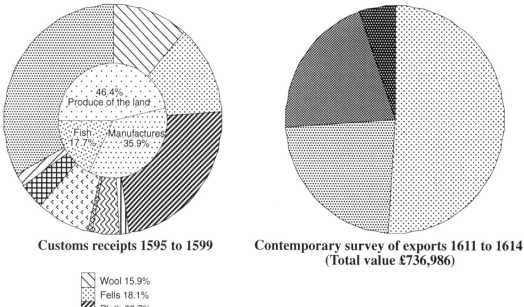

Customs receipts 1595 to 1599

Contemporary survey of exports 1611 to 1614
(Total value £736,986)

Wool 15.9%
Fells 18.1%
Cloth 33.7%
Salt 2.2 %
Herring 5.6%
Cod 0.9%
Salmon 11.2%
Coal 5.2%
Skins 2.5%
Hides 4.7%

Produce of the land 50.9% (£375,085)
Manufactures 23.0% (£169,097)
Fish 20.8% (£153,354)
Re-exports 5.3% (£39,047)

The survey of 1611-14 is useful in giving, for the first time, the real values of exports as distinct from customs revenue in which certain commodities which attracted a high duty (such as wool and salmon) are given greater weighting than those with low duty (such a as coal, salt and hides). It fell into four parts: most valuable were the commodities that yield yearly, ranging from wheat, barley and malt to wool, hides, skins and coal. Next most valuable were manufactures, and the discrepancy between their value given here and in the customs returns of the 1590s is that, as the 1614 survey noted, much linen cloth and yarn was 'daily' carried overland into England. Although duty on salmon had been sharply increased in 1597, exports of herring brought in twice as much; but sales of deep sea fish were insignificant. Re-exports were as yet largely made up of wax from the Baltic and some timber from Norway; dealing in English cloth and wool, which would figure controversially in Anglo-Scots relations by 1700, was still modest.

ML

Scottish trade in the seventeenth century

The make-up of the four categories is shown in the following pie-charts.

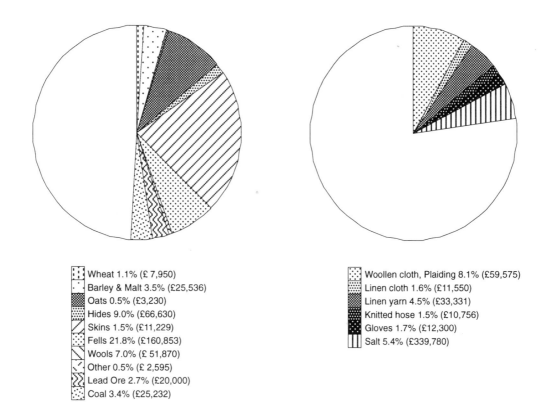

Wheat 1.1% (£ 7,950)
Barley & Malt 3.5% (£25,536)
Oats 0.5% (£3,230)
Hides 9.0% (£66,630)
Skins 1.5% (£11,229)
Fells 21.8% (£160,853)
Wools 7.0% (£ 51,870)
Other 0.5% (£ 2,595)
Lead Ore 2.7% (£20,000)
Coal 3.4% (£25,232)

Exports of produce of the land 1611 to 1614
(Total value £375,125)

Woollen cloth, Plaiding 8.1% (£59,575)
Linen cloth 1.6% (£11,550)
Linen yarn 4.5% (£33,331)
Knitted hose 1.5% (£10,756)
Gloves 1.7% (£12,300)
Salt 5.4% (£339,780)

Export of manufactures 1611 to 1614
(Total value £169,097)

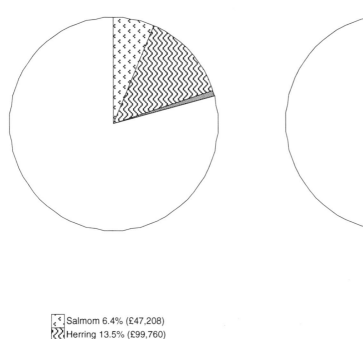

Salmom 6.4% (£47,208)
Herring 13.5% (£99,760)
Other 0.9%
Fish 79.2%, & Oil (£6,387)

Exports of fish 1611 to 1614
(Total value £153, 355)

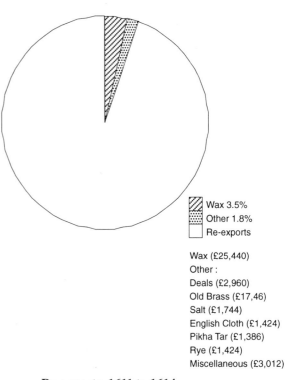

Wax 3.5%
Other 1.8%
Re-exports

Wax (£25,440)
Other :
Deals (£2,960)
Old Brass (£17,46)
Salt (£1,744)
English Cloth (£1,424)
Pikha Tar (£1,386)
Rye (£1,424)
Miscellaneous (£3,012)

Re-exports 1611 to 1614
(Total value £39,047)

Contemporary survey of exports, 1611 to 1614

ML

Scottish trade in the seventeenth century

The Scottish staple port in the Low Countries was first established at Bruges in the fourteenth century. It had a complicated subsequent history, alternating between Bruges and the Walcheren town of Middelburg, until it finally settled in the small port of Veere, at the westernmost tip of the Scheldt estuary, in 1540. 'Staple' goods - such as wool, hides, skins, and fish - were supposed to be shipped through the staple port, under the supervision of a resident Scottish factor. There are, despite its importance, only occasional lists of Scottish shipping at Veere, unlike the systematic records shown earlier for the Sound.

The list of 1561, giving all ships which paid anchorage dues at Veere during that period, demonstrates the increasing grip which Edinburgh/Leith had built up since 1400 over the bulk of the export trade in staple goods. It is likely that Kinghorn, whose tax assessment was linked to Edinburgh's, was also being used as a base by merchants from the capital. Other east-coast ports probably shipped more goods, to Leith for export from there rather than exported them direct.

By the 1620s the picture, revealed by payments made over a fifteen-month period in 1626 - 7 to the Scots kirk in Veere, had changed considerably. Most of the vessels from the Forth were small colliers, plying out of Dysart and Kirkcaldy; many of them were bound for Middelburg or Flushing, both also on the island of Walcheren. Cargoes from Leith and Dundee were of staple goods or mixed, including coal. Exports were being shipped in large quantities to other Dutch ports like Amsterdam and Rotterdam, which also held a large share of the imports sent to Scotland.

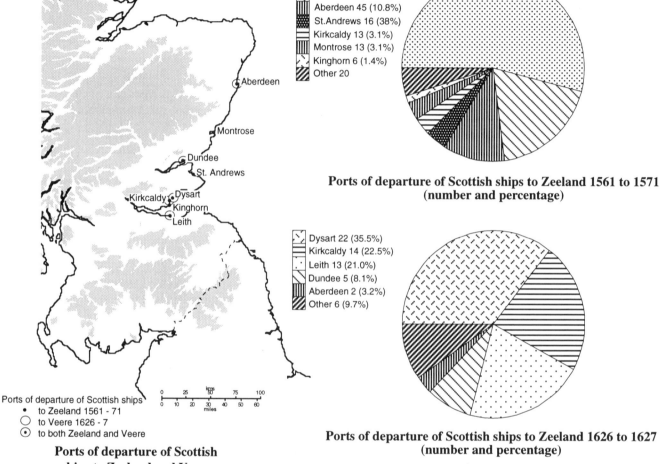

Edinburgh 225 (54.0%)
Dundee 79 (19.0%)
Aberdeen 45 (10.8%)
St.Andrews 16 (38%)
Kirkcaldy 13 (3.1%)
Montrose 13 (3.1%)
Kinghorn 6 (1.4%)
Other 20

**Ports of departure of Scottish ships to Zeeland 1561 to 1571
(number and percentage)**

Dysart 22 (35.5%)
Kirkcaldy 14 (22.5%)
Leith 13 (21.0%)
Dundee 5 (8.1%)
Aberdeen 2 (3.2%)
Other 6 (9.7%)

**Ports of departure of Scottish ships to Zeeland 1626 to 1627
(number and percentage)**

Ports of departure of Scottish ships
• to Zeeland 1561 - 71
○ to Veere 1626 - 7
◉ to both Zeeland and Veere

**Ports of departure of Scottish
ships to Zeeland and Veere**

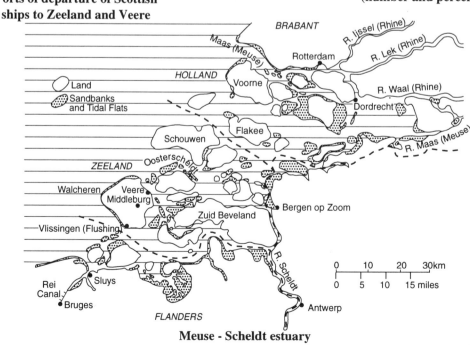

Meuse - Scheldt estuary

ML

Scottish trade in the seventeenth century

These following statistics are based on local Aberdeen shore accounts and Dundee shipping lists. For neither port is there a continuous sequence of accounts. The Dundee lists include only incoming ships; the Aberdeen figures also include outward-bound vessels. The origin of 9.9% of the former and 24.3% of the latter are unknown and have been omitted from the charts. The Dundee lists do not include Scottish arrivals, except from the Northern Isles.

Aberdeen's trade was dominated by shipping from other Scottish ports but much of this, particularly from Leith, carried foreign goods. Salt came from La Rochelle and Fife, wine from Bordeaux, and apples, onions and other miscellaneous goods from northern France and the Low Countries. Beer was imported from England and the Baltic, while Sweden, conspicuously absent from the Aberdeen figures, supplied iron.

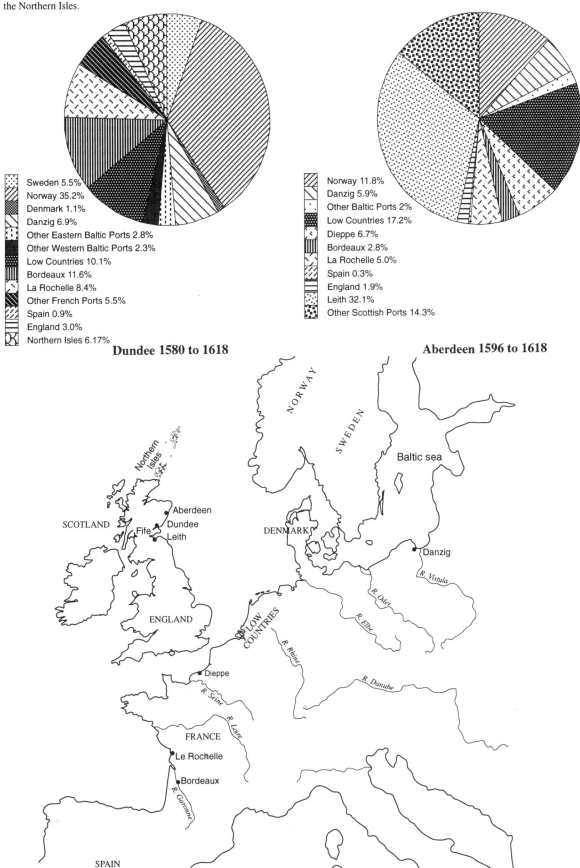

Sweden 5.5%
Norway 35.2%
Denmark 1.1%
Danzig 6.9%
Other Eastern Baltic Ports 2.8%
Other Western Baltic Ports 2.3%
Low Countries 10.1%
Bordeaux 11.6%
La Rochelle 8.4%
Other French Ports 5.5%
Spain 0.9%
England 3.0%
Northern Isles 6.17%

Dundee 1580 to 1618

Norway 11.8%
Danzig 5.9%
Other Baltic Ports 2%
Low Countries 17.2%
Dieppe 6.7%
Bordeaux 2.8%
La Rochelle 5.0%
Spain 0.3%
England 1.9%
Leith 32.1%
Other Scottish Ports 14.3%

Aberdeen 1596 to 1618

Destination of exports, Dundee and Aberdeen, 1580 to 1618

DDi

269

Scottish trade in the seventeenth century

Although the printed *Exchequer Rolls* series ends in 1599, the continuing dominant role played by Edinburgh, which by the 1590s paid 72% of all customs on exports, is revealed in port books which survive for a few years of the early seventeenth century. Export lists survive for Leith for 1611-12 and 1626-8; imports lists exist for 1621-3 and 1636-9. The traditional two-fold pattern of Scottish foreign trade continued, with both parts largely dominated by Edinburgh merchants: hides, fells, skins, coal and fish from all parts of Scotland flowed out, at record levels, and luxury goods and raw materials entered, in increasing volume.

In the trade boom of the 1620s and 1630s, traditional exports reached unprecedented levels. London increased markedly in importance, although the staple port of Veere still figured as the main destination for exports. Cloth and herring were still exported to Baltic ports like Königsberg. Plaiding, herring and fells were sent to Dieppe, but also to Newhaven, La Rochelle and elsewhere in France. The figures for trade with France in 1626-8 are usually low, caused by the hostilities with England.

Dutch and French ports provided a rich variety of luxury goods, ranging from cloth, spices and paper to glassware, but the wine ships from Bordeaux, important enough to be kept in a separate register, are not reflected in the figures given here. In the Baltic, grain, dyes, iron and wax were purchased. Cloth, shipped from London, was the main import from England. Scandinavia, and especially Norway, provided raw materials like timber, pitch and tar, and iron. The map shows all the ports with which Leith traded in the period, both exporting and importing.

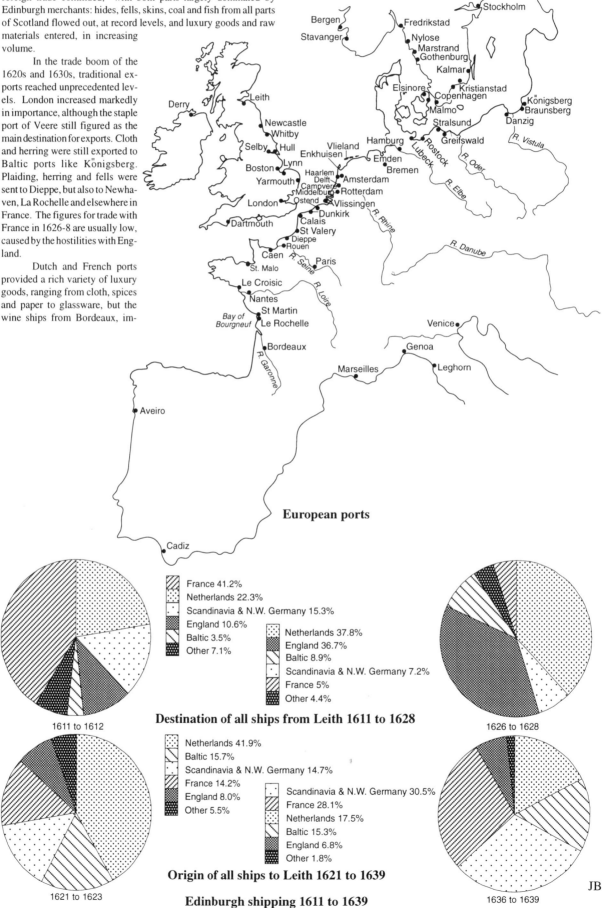

European ports

France 41.2%
Netherlands 22.3%
Scandinavia & N.W. Germany 15.3%
England 10.6%
Baltic 3.5%
Other 7.1%

Netherlands 37.8%
England 36.7%
Baltic 8.9%
Scandinavia & N.W. Germany 7.2%
France 5%
Other 4.4%

1611 to 1612

Destination of all ships from Leith 1611 to 1628

1626 to 1628

Netherlands 41.9%
Baltic 15.7%
Scandinavia & N.W. Germany 14.7%
France 14.2%
England 8.0%
Other 5.5%

Scandinavia & N.W. Germany 30.5%
France 28.1%
Netherlands 17.5%
Baltic 15.3%
England 6.8%
Other 1.8%

1621 to 1623

Origin of all ships to Leith 1621 to 1639

Edinburgh shipping 1611 to 1639

1636 to 1639

JB

270

Scottish trade in the seventeenth century

The figures represented on the map show the percentage of imports, as measured by custom duties, shipped from the main foreign ports by Edinburgh's 300-strong merchant elite. These merchants paid £8,593 or 30.5% of all Leith customs in the period. The ports or areas shown accounted for over 91% of customs paid on imports. As well as the standard range of luxury manufactures and raw materials from London, the Netherlands and elsewhere, many of the ships from the Baltic during the harvest failures in Scotland of the mid-1620s carried grain. The figures do not, however, include imports of French wine, chiefly from Bordeaux, the most lucrative source of revenue and customed separately.

Levels of customs can also be compared with numbers of ships, as given in the table below. The same ports accounted for 91% of ships entering Leith but there are significant discrepancies between the two sets of figures, caused by the different rates of duty on various imported commodities: only a modest number of ships, for example, arrived from London but they accounted for over 20% of all custom paid because most carried high-duty cloth.

There are differences, too, in the patterns of ships plying to and from Leith. The twin bar charts are based on the 331 ships which left Leith 1621 to 3 carrying cargoes for this group of merchants and the 118 which arrived 1626 to 8. The staple port of Veere, for example, held a greater share of exports from Leith than of imports sent there, which increasingly came from other Dutch ports. Counting all ships, 107 arrived from Amsterdam and Rotterdam in 1621 to 3 and 109 from Veere. But on ships carrying cargoes for Edinburgh's elite merchants, who had begun to specialize in certain commodities, 65 came from Rotterdam or Amsterdam and 59 from Veere, even if those from the staple port did pay more duty.

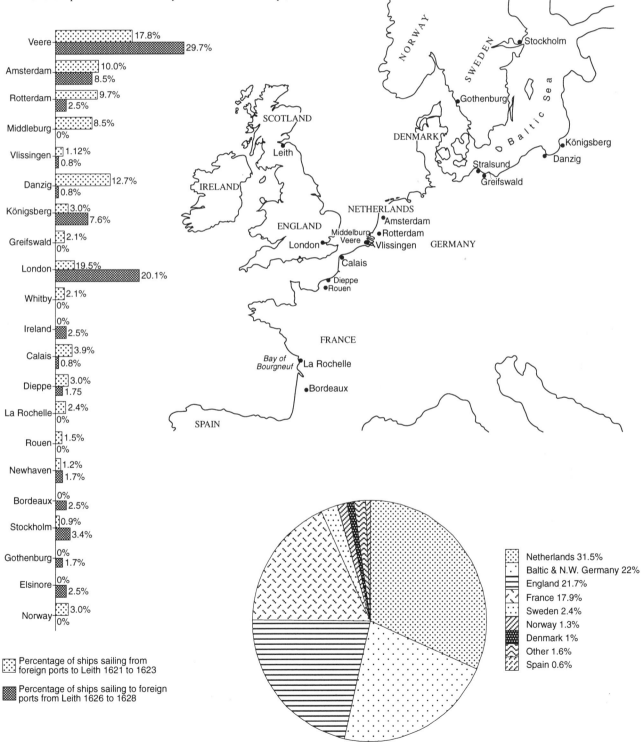

Imports into Leith 1621 to 1623

Customs paid on imports (excluding wine) 1621 to 1623   JB

Scottish trade in the seventeenth century

The 'Compt of Edward Little of Shore Dues collected at Leith' (Edinburgh City Archive) is the only early seventeenth-century list detailing coastal shipping arriving at Leith. The list gives only the name of the vessel and its master, its point of embarkation and a brief description of its cargo. A total of 249 ships arrived between November 1638 and November 1639, although 90% docked between March and November. Their cargoes were largely of grain or cured herring, emphasising Edinburgh's importance not just as a market place but as an entrepôt for exports of staple goods abroad from much of Scotland.

Most of the 155 ships embarking between Inverness and North Berwick carried grain, underlining the role of ports in Moray, Aberdeenshire and Fife as collection points for agricultural produce. The large number from Montrose and Dunbar reflect their function as both fish and grain markets. The twelve from Orkney probably carried the produce of William Dick, who held the islands in wadset and regularly exported

their produce to Holland. The surprisingly small returns from the important ports of Dundee and Aberdeen are probably explained by a deficiency in the source material. But the smallness of the overall number of coastal vessels arriving at the most important port in Scotland may indicate that trade had already begun to be seriously affected by the political crisis of the Wars of the Covenant.

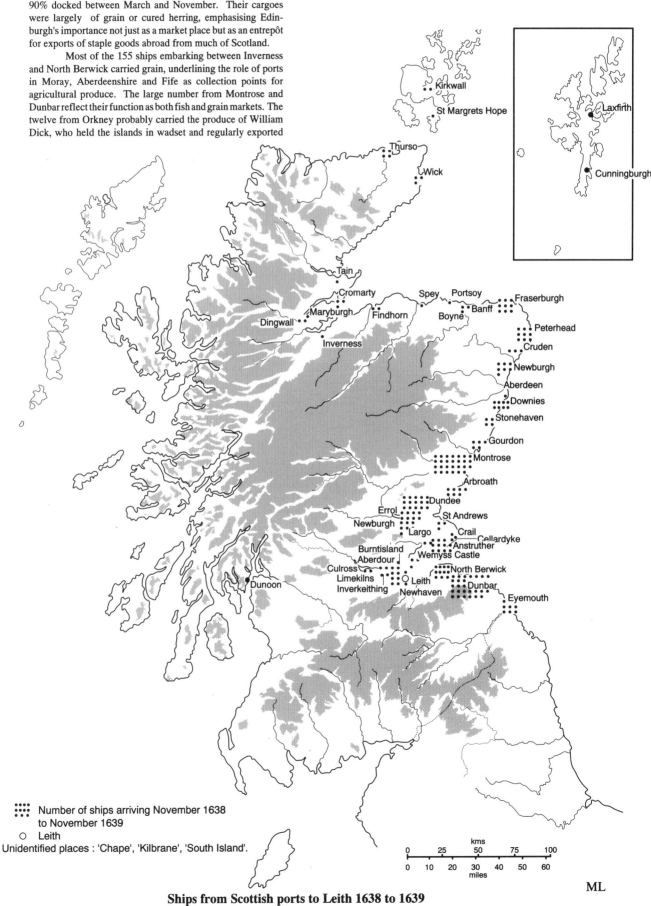

Number of ships arriving November 1638 to November 1639

○ Leith

Unidentified places : 'Chape', 'Kilbrane', 'South Island'.

kms
0   25   50   75   100
0 10 20 30 40 50 60
miles

ML

Ships from Scottish ports to Leith 1638 to 1639

Scottish trade in the seventeenth century

In 1656 a Cromwellian official, Thomas Tucker, drew up a Report reorganising the collection of customs and excise duties. It envisaged the creation of eight administrative districts or 'precincts', each with its head port where a collector would be based. An excise had already been introduced by the Scottish parliament in 1644, which placed dues on the sale and import (where appropriate) of all ale, beer and whisky, as well as on imported wine, tobacco and textiles; but Tucker's scheme involved harmonization with the English system of tunnage and poundage. The result was complex and over-firm conclusions should not be drawn from the data, which is based on revenue over a three-month period in 1655-6; imports were subject to customs dues and often to excise as well, but levels of dues varied greatly, high for example on wine and foreign salt but low on timber.

The combined returns, though complicated, do reflect, as do the burgh tax rolls, a marked rise of Glasgow, which had begun to use the road via Kilsyth to Bo'ness, now said to be 'the chief port' after Leith, as an entry to east-coast based overseas trade. Yet the Bo'ness precinct also catered for Stirling's trade, the coal and salt of Culross and Limekilns and some cloth from Perth and its returns should not be claimed wholly or even largely for Glasgow. The most striking difference between the customs for 1655-6 and those for the 1590s is the sharp fall of Leith, from 73% to under 40%. Its dominant postion as an entrepôt had slipped drastically since the 1630s and certain exported commodities, especially coal and salt, were now shipped direct, also helping to lift the Bo'ness returns.

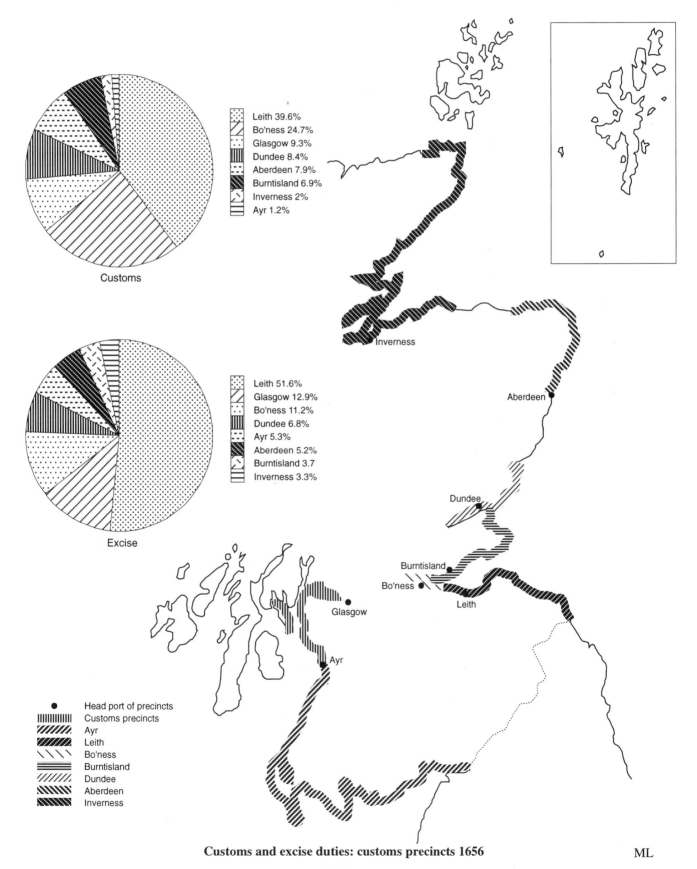

Customs

Leith	39.6%
Bo'ness	24.7%
Glasgow	9.3%
Dundee	8.4%
Aberdeen	7.9%
Burntisland	6.9%
Inverness	2%
Ayr	1.2%

Excise

Leith	51.6%
Glasgow	12.9%
Bo'ness	11.2%
Dundee	6.8%
Ayr	5.3%
Aberdeen	5.2%
Burntisland	3.7
Inverness	3.3%

● Head port of precincts
Customs precincts
Ayr
Leith
Bo'ness
Burntisland
Dundee
Aberdeen
Inverness

Customs and excise duties: customs precincts 1656

ML

Scottish trade in the seventeenth century

As part of his Report of 1656, the Cromwellian customs official, Thomas Tucker, listed the number of home-owned ships, often together with their tonnages, in Scottish ports. The small number (215 'ships of burden' were counted twelve years later) reflects the losses inflicted by the Wars of the Covenant. The size of sea-going ships ranged from 250 to about 50 tons; although open boats of 6 tons plied between Norway and Orkney, most smaller vessels were engaged in the coastal trade and probably many plied between their home port and Leith; the small barques, carrying coal, salt, fish and other such cargoes, varied between 30 and 3 or 4 tons. The list is at its vaguest in describing shipping on the south side of the Forth, such as at Newhaven and Prestonpans, where, it said, 'any small vessels' picked up salt. It does not itemize either fishing boats or the flat-bottomed barges, which, for example, carried goods up the shallower part of the Forth to Stirling; the number of 'twelve or fourteen' given

for Leith seems low for a port in which a tax roll of 1647 recorded over 140 skippers. Only three sea-going vessels at Leith had tonnages recorded - each of 250 tons. The number and size of vessels does, however, give a good indication of the kind of trade carried on in each port for which there are fuller details. It also reflects the shallow or awkward draught of most Scottish harbours - the reason for the construction of Port Glasgow ten years later.

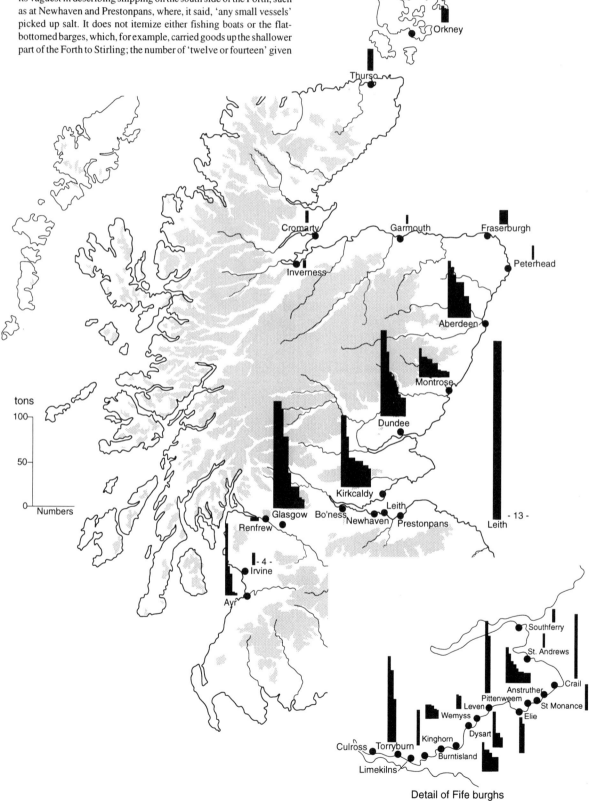

Numbers and tonnage of Scottish shipping 1656

ML

274

Scottish trade in the seventeenth century

The Register of the State and Condition of Every Burgh within the Kingdom of Scotland of 1692 gives the answers made to various questions posed by the Convention of Royal Burghs about burghs' finances, trade and condition. One question related to the number of 'ships, barques, boats and ferry boats' belonging to them. Not all burghs answered directly; others, like Dysart, South Queensferry or Glasgow (which did not itemize its eight small lighters), did so only vaguely; and five of the remotest burghs were not visited. Some, like Perth, related a sorry tale, including the loss of three ships since 1679. *The Register* lists 109 ships, averaging 67 tons burden. Leith had 29 ships, totalling 1,700 tons; Glasgow had 23, totalling 1,200 tons. A comparison with the list of 1656 partly reflects the changing nature of Scotland's overseas trade and, for example, underscores the sharp drop in activity, (revealed also in the Sound Toll registers and the burgh tax rolls in many of the small Fife ports, like Anstruther which complained of 'no ships, no merchants, no trade'). The report also gives details of ferry boats and fishing boats (usually for herring, like the 17 at Dunbar, 20 at Crail, 19 at Rothesay and 24 belonging to Renfrew) but these have been excluded.

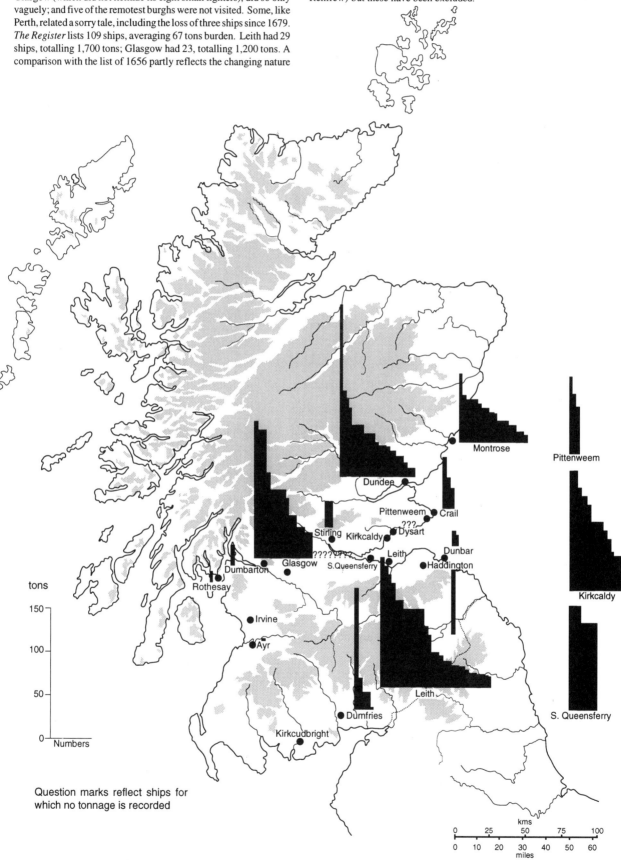

tons

Question marks reflect ships for which no tonnage is recorded

Numbers and tonnage of Scottish shipping 1692

ML

275

Scottish trade in the seventeenth century

Thomas Tucker's reorganisation of customs administration in 1656 was continued and extended after the Restoration. By the 1680s there were over twenty 'precincts', each with its head port where customs were collected: their approximate boundaries are given here, with details of imports, drawn from T C. Smout, *Scottish Trade on the Eve of Union* (1963), for the main ports only. The precincts included five along the Border, made necessary by the re-imposition of an English customs barrier after 1660. Deals (sawn fir planks) and iron came from Norway and Sweden respectively, mostly into east-coast ports; madder, a dyestuff, from the Netherlands; most leather, by contrast, came from England, either by sea into the Clyde or overland.

Wine, by contrast, came largely from France, dried fruit from the wholesale markets of the Netherlands, hops from England or Flanders; cooking pots, brassware kettles and the like from north-west Germany and Sweden as well as from England and the Netherlands. The quantities of luxury consumables coming into Leith confirms it as an entrepôt for other Scottish ports and the capital as a centre of conspicuous consumption; but the disproportionate amount of madder and pots entering Bo'ness was far more than local needs merited and must have been transported overland to the west and south-west.

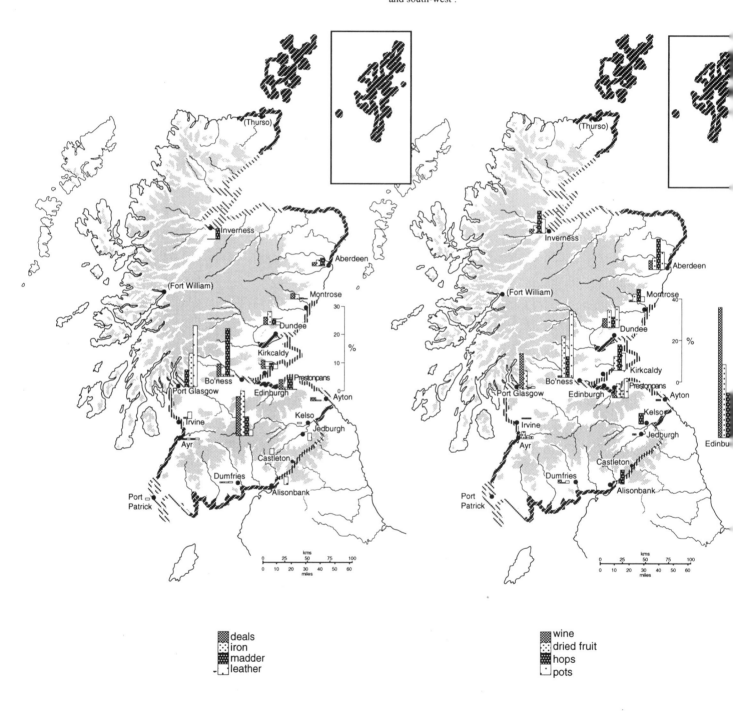

deals
iron
madder
leather

wine
dried fruit
hops
pots

Imports of deals, iron, madder and leather by ports 1686 to 1696

Imports of French wine, dried fruit, hops and pots by ports 1686 to 1696

ML

276

Scottish trade in the seventeenth century

The following series of maps, drawn from statistics in T.C. Smout's, *Scottish Trade on the Eve of Union, 1660-1707 (1963)* are based on the returns of customs books, of arrivals and departures of laden ships, for the various precincts. They do not deal with the considerable, but mostly small-scale trade with Ireland, nor with the exports from the Dumfries precinct, where the books of departures do not survive. They deal in numbers of ships, which could vary considerably in size depending both on distance travelled and commodity carried and do not necessarily reflect the value, especially of imports.

Measured by ships alone, by far the most important ports, both for arrivals and departures, lay in the Forth estuary, though no longer, as earlier in the century, Leith alone. The pattern of trade did, however, vary considerably, not only in terms of geographical point of embarkation or destination, but also between the import and export trades. Twice as many ships arrived carrying imports into Leith as departed from it with exports. Far fewer ships went to Norway than arrived from there; yet as many left Montrose for Norway with grain as arrived with its timber.

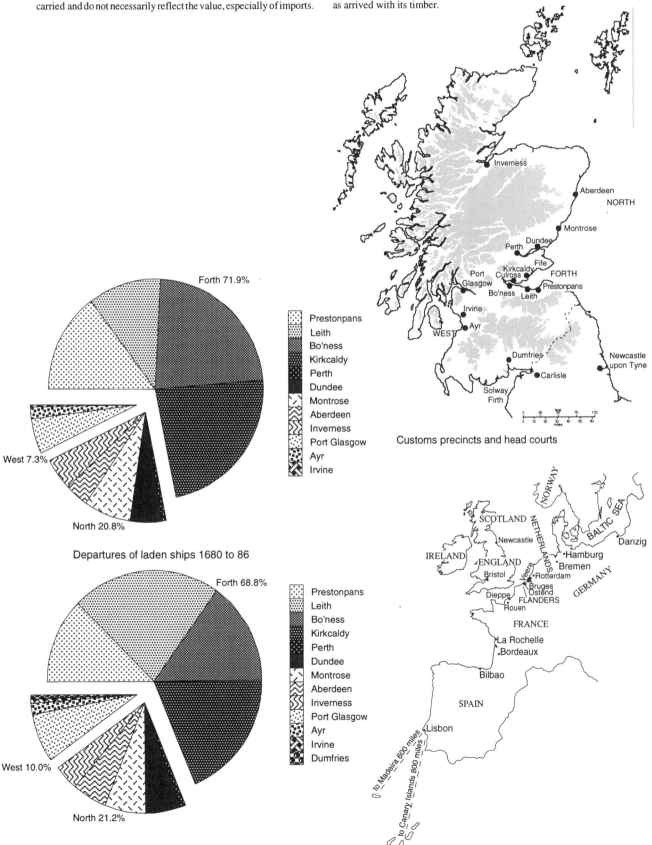

Customs precincts and head courts

Departures of laden ships 1680 to 86

Arrivals of laden ships 1680 to 86

Exports and imports 1680 to 1686

ML

Scottish trade in the seventeenth century

Trade with the Baltic, which had long been an importer of cheap cloth, hides and skins from Scotland (taking 200,00 skins a year in the early seventeenth century, some 40% of total exports), declined sharply after 1660, averaging only 93,000 a year. The 1690s would, however, see a revival in the Baltic trade, especially in fish. One of the major shifts in the Scottish economy in the seventeenth century lay in the export of grain and Norway was one of the chief markets for it, explaining why half of all ships bound for there came from the Tay. But the fall in Norway's demand for Scottish salt after 1660 underlines the relatively modest number leaving from the Forth. Most of the cargoes to N.W. Germany were of coal, from the collieries of the Forth.

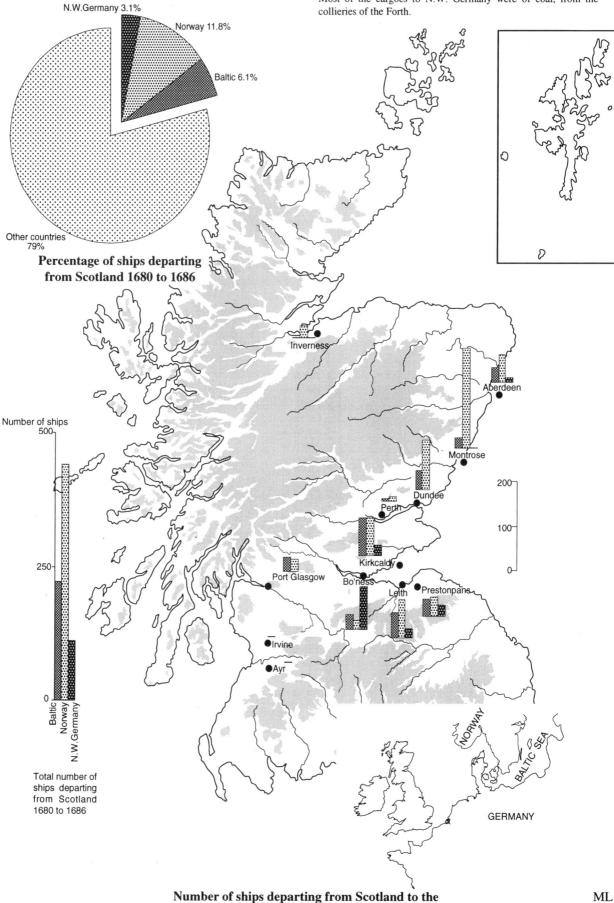

N.W.Germany 3.1%

Norway 11.8%

Baltic 6.1%

Other countries 79%

Percentage of ships departing from Scotland 1680 to 1686

Number of ships

Total number of ships departing from Scotland 1680 to 1686

Number of ships departing from Scotland to the Baltic, Norway and North-West Germany 1680 to 1686, by burgh

ML

Scottish trade in the seventeenth century

Exports from the southern Baltic, of flax, hemp, some linseed and miscellaneous goods, like brass, pots, glass and beer (but no longer of grain and rye, as in the 1620s, mostly from Danzig and Königsberg, came largely into east-coast ports. In contrast, about a third of the iron and copper, which made up the bulk of Sweden's exports, came to the Clyde. By far the highest proportion of ships arriving from the north (almost three out of every ten) came from Norway: in some precincts, like Montrose and Prestonpans, they accounted for as many as 50 to 60% of all arrivals. After 1660 timber ships became a commoner sight on the Upper and Lower Clyde. Almost all of them carried timber, usually in the form of deals, which averaged 360,000 pieces a year but attracted a low customs duty; some also had pitch and tar. Imports from Hamburg and Bremen, confined mostly to east-coast ports, were diverse and much slighter, although N.W. Germany did have a Scottish factor in the 1690s.

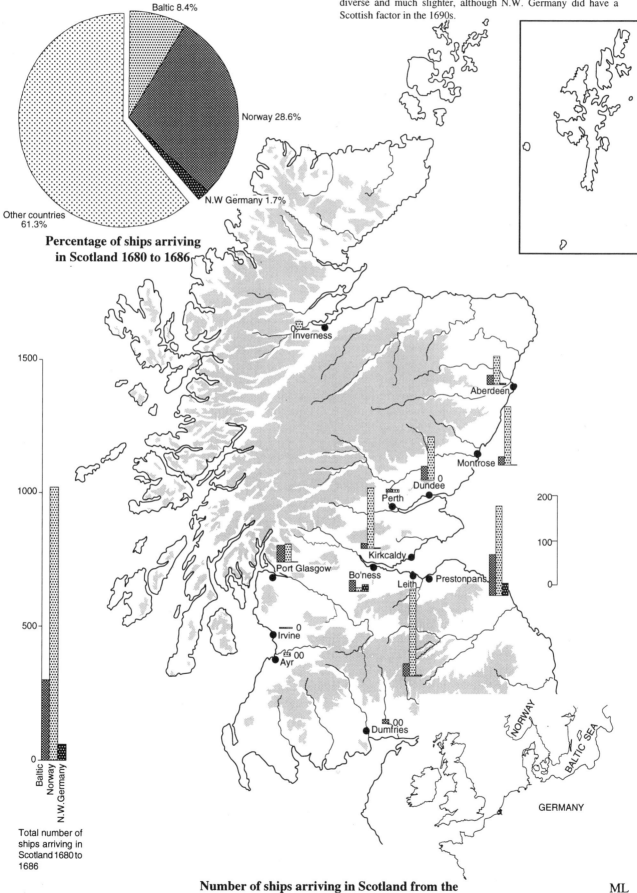

Percentage of ships arriving in Scotland 1680 to 1686

Total number of ships arriving in Scotland 1680 to 1686

Number of ships arriving in Scotland from the Baltic, Norway and North-West Germany 1680 to 1686, by burgh

ML

279

Scottish trade in the seventeenth century

Most of the staple exports to the Netherlands - hides, cloth, and plaiding - continued to go from traditional east-coast ports like Leith, but their volume fell sharply, especially after 1685. Coal, from the ports of Bo'ness, Culross and Kirkcaldy, mostly went to Rotterdam until demand for it there collapsed in the 1670s and 1680s; the still large number of cargoes shown here were probably trans-shipped from there to Flanders. Some coal also went to Normandy, but the bulk of exports to France was made up of fish from the Clyde and the Forth and woollen and linen cloth from the west country - until 1689-90 when a ban on imports of herring and cloth and punitive tariffs on coal imposed by the French government sharply reduced trade, with severe consequences, especially for the Forth ports.

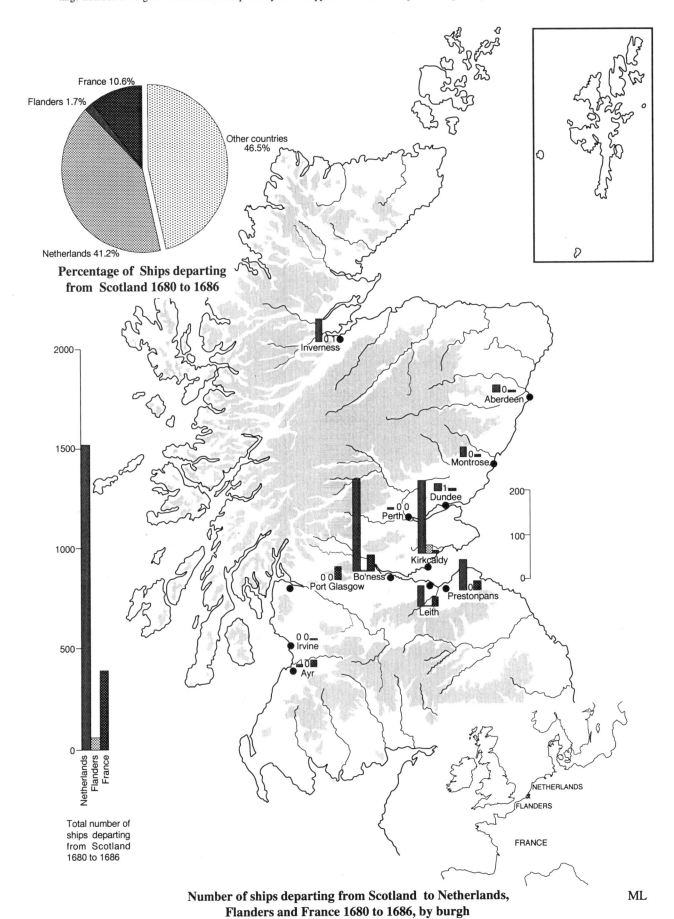

Percentage of Ships departing from Scotland 1680 to 1686

Total number of ships departing from Scotland 1680 to 1686

Number of ships departing from Scotland to Netherlands, Flanders and France 1680 to 1686, by burgh

ML

Scottish trade in the seventeenth century

The pattern of trade with the Netherlands had been changing since at least the 1620s with a drift, especially of imports, away from the staple port of Veere; by the 1680s it sent only 7% of the ships from the Netherlands to Scotland, and Rotterdam 85%. But over 80% of these imports still arrived in the Forth and almost all the rest between there and Aberdeen. Dutch imports were huge in their variety - textiles, fancy foodstuffs, dyestuffs, seeds, manufactures - and mostly easily transported overland, from Bo'ness to Glasgow and western burghs. Flanders' trade, mostly from Bruges or Ostend to Fife, was very modest by comparison although it prospered during the Dutch Wars of 1665-7 and 1672-4.

French imports - of wine and brandy from Bordeaux, salt from La Rochelle and manufactured goods from Normandy ports like Dieppe and Rouen - were of high value in relation to their bulk and the figure of 10% of ships carrying them may understate their significance. 35% of French cargoes went to Leith and 20% to Glasgow - a quite different pattern from Dutch imports, explained both by the southerly position of their ports of departure and local needs. 63% of wine went to Leith and 17% to Glasgow; French salt was more important to the Clyde, which had far fewer native salt pans than the Forth.

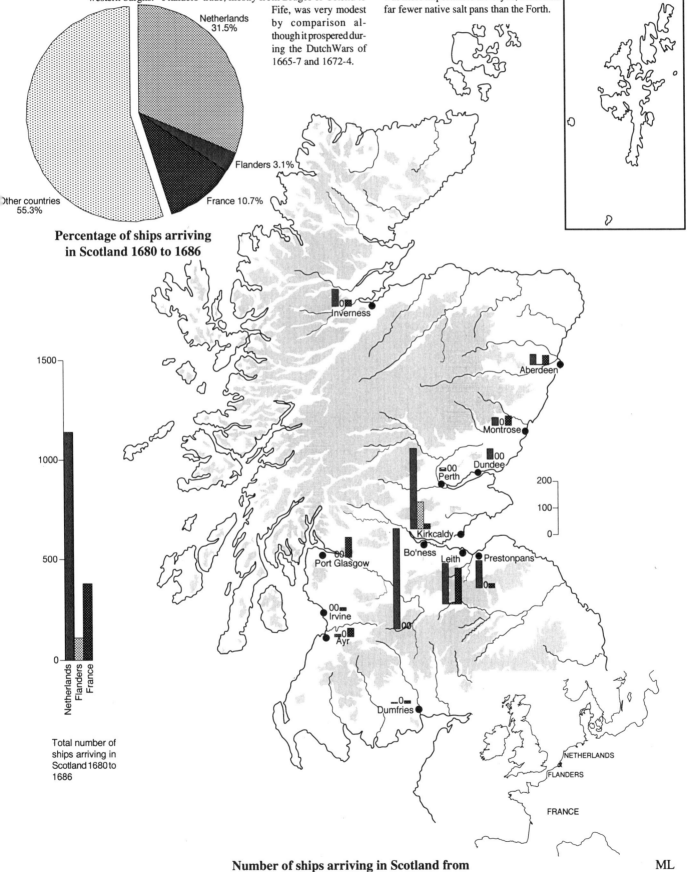

Percentage of ships arriving in Scotland 1680 to 1686

Netherlands 31.5%

Other countries 55.3%

Flanders 3.1%

France 10.7%

Total number of ships arriving in Scotland 1680 to 1686

Number of ships arriving in Scotland from Netherlands, Flanders and France 1680 to 1686, by burgh

ML

281

Scottish trade in the seventeenth century

Linen cloth accounted for at least a third and, at times, two-thirds of the value of all exports to England. But cattle, driven overland mostly through Carlisle (and not shown here), was probably the most consistently valuable single export to England and must have seriously reduced the amount of hides exported there and elsewhere by sea. The map does not, however, reflect the large number of small, open boats plying southwards across the Solway with hides and other staple wares. Other skins continued to be shipped, especially to London, which in peak years received as many as the Baltic. Neither herring nor salmon figured greatly amongst exports to England and barriers were successfully raised against cheaper Scottish grain, salt and coal after the Restoration, although the large number of ships leaving Prestonpans and Bo'ness were small colliers.

Exports to Spain were slight and those to America, confined largely to west-coast ports, were mixed - including indentured servants as well as coal, linen and woollen cloth - but as yet modest in both value and quantitiy

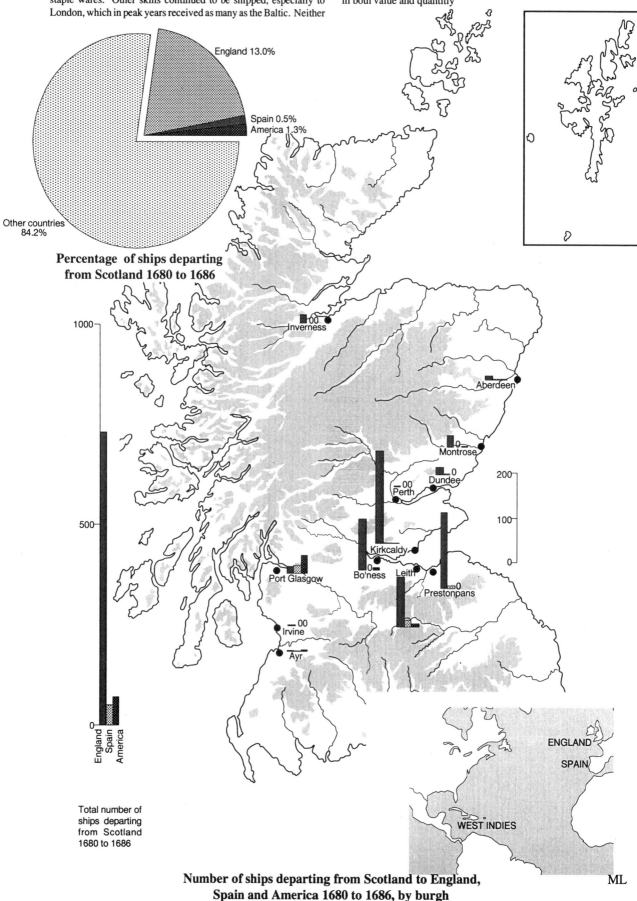

Percentage of ships departing
from Scotland 1680 to 1686

Total number of
ships departing
from Scotland
1680 to 1686

**Number of ships departing from Scotland to England,
Spain and America 1680 to 1686, by burgh**

ML

Scottish trade in the seventeenth century

Imports from England came overland by drove roads; in small, open boats over the Solway (which have not been reflected here in the returns for Dumfries); and by coasters, which made up 13% of all foreign arrivals. 78% of the sea-borne imports went to the Forth. Most - over 60% by value - came from London, and the bulk of the rest from east-coast ports from Newcastle southwards. English imports resembled Dutch in variety and nature: almost a half were manufactured goods, especially textiles, despite heavy duties and outrights bans imposed on them.

Trade with Spain dated only from the later sixteenth century but imports - of both wine and salt - would increase sharply during the 1690s as a result of England's war with France. By the 1690s ships from Madeira and the Canaries came regularly to the Clyde. Imports from America - mostly either sugar from the West Indies or tobacco from Virginia and Maryland - came exclusively to the west coast and mostly to Glasgow, which by the 1680s saw six or seven cargoes a year. Some tobacco also came from entrepot ports like Bristol, Lisbon and Bilbao.

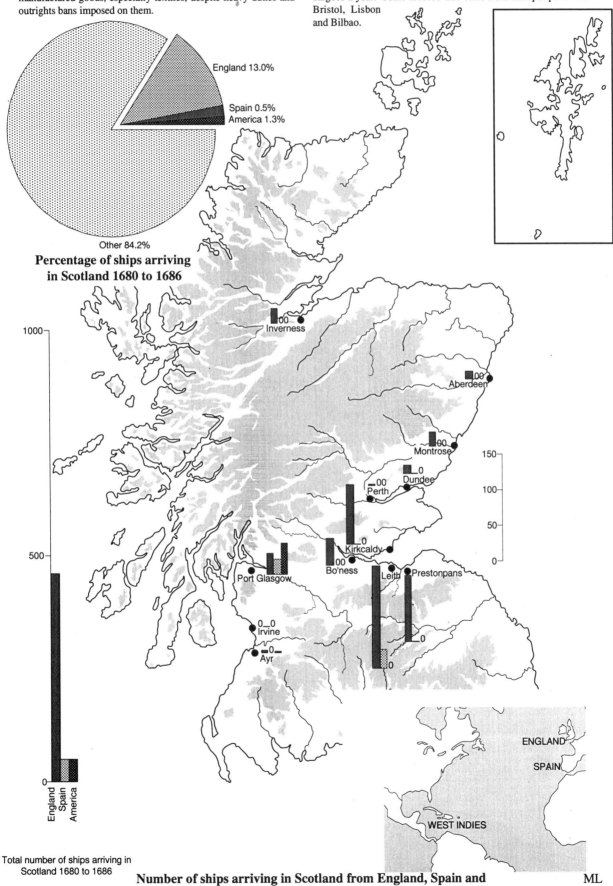

Percentage of ships arriving in Scotland 1680 to 1686

England 13.0%
Spain 0.5%
America 1.3%
Other 84.2%

Total number of ships arriving in Scotland 1680 to 1686

Number of ships arriving in Scotland from England, Spain and America 1680 to 1686, by burgh

ML

Medieval land assessment

There were various units of land assessment in early medieval Scotland; the principal were the davach, ounceland, pennyland and ploughgate. Davach is derived from the Gaelic *dabhach* 'a large tub or vat'; it probably represents the amount of land in respect of which a large vat of grain was paid as a render. Strictly a measure of arable land, probably in the region of 200 acres, davachs were situated in the most fertile locations of those parts of the country where they are found. It was commonly named and was a tangible, permanent unit whose shape was largely determined by natural boundaries. There was no significant difference between the davach in the north-east

and the west. The ounceland was simply the davach by another name and was presumably the term applied to a unit of land which paid a tax in money or produce to the value of one ounce of silver. The pennyland also belonged to the davach/ounceland system of land assessment. It represented the amount of land which paid tax to the value of one silver penny In the west Highlands and Islands the ounceland or davach comprised twenty pennylands. Pennylands were also grouped in twenties in the south-west, where place-name evidence indicates that the davach was once in use. In the Northern Isles and Caithness, there were eighteen pennylands in one ounceland.

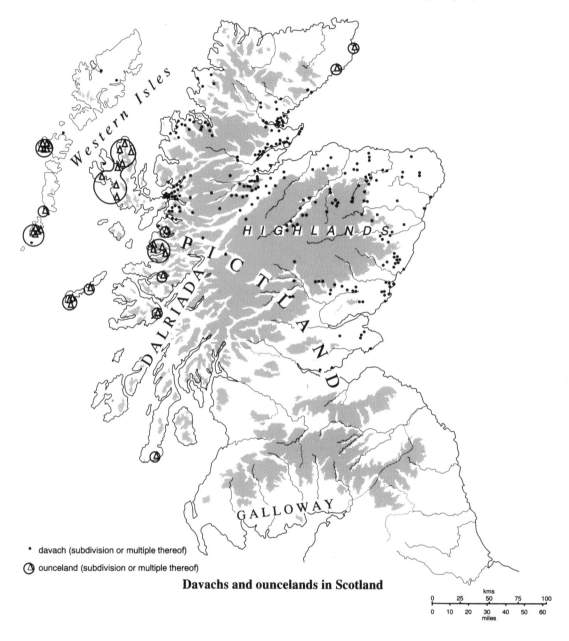

- • davach (subdivision or multiple thereof)
- △ ounceland (subdivision or multiple thereof)

Davachs and ouncelands in Scotland

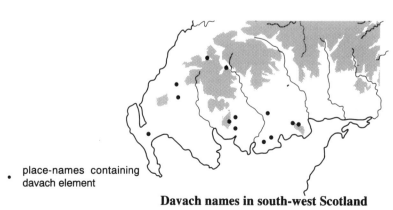

- • place-names containing davach element

Davach names in south-west Scotland

AE

Medieval land assessment

These units served an important fiscal role as the basis on which military service (*forinsecum servitium*) and taxes were assessed. The origins of the system may be traced back to the house system of seventh-century Dalriada as recorded in *Senchus fer nAlban*. The geographical distribution of the units is explicable in terms of population movements and settlement patterns during the Dark Ages - of Scots to Pictland, Scandinavians to the Western Isles, Northern Isles and Caithness, and Gallgaidhil to Galloway. Not part of the same system but fulfilling a similar function was the ploughgate, normally what a plough-team could handle in one year - usually about 104 acres of arable land.

kms
0   25   50   75   100
0 10 20 30 40 50 60
miles

kms
0   25   50   75   100
0 10 20 30 40 50 60
miles

Pennylands in Scotland before 1600

Ploughgates in Scotland before 1600

AE

Medieval rural settlement

The documentary evidence for medieval rural settlement tends to be vague or allusive. As yet, field work has not made good this deficiency. A growing number of possible medieval sites have been surveyed, but few have been excavated or dated accurately. Moreover, where sites have been excavated, as at Lix (Perthshire), it has emphasised rather than resolved the problems involved. To a degree, pre-improvement estate plans drawn up during the eighteenth century support some inferences about earlier forms, but their facile use can attach a false stability to settlement morphology. Such difficulties must make any generalisations provisional.

With this proviso firmly in mind, we may tentatively assert that the commonest form of settlement was the small ferm-toun, an irregular cluster of farmsteads, outbuildings and kailyards occupied by the co- or joint-tenants who shared possession of the toun. The small scale of such settlement (generally 2 to 6 tenants) can be ascribed to the fragmented nature of good-quality, undrained arable soil and to a process whereby growing ferm-touns tended to fission into smaller units. Its random plan can be attributed to the absence of a formally-designated area for the farmsteads and to their part construction out of perishable raw materials like wattle and turf. As in medieval England, the ordinary peasant dwelling needed regular replacement and, over time, shifted between different positions and alignments. Although the most widespread form of rural settlement, small, irregular touns were not the only one. The layout of some pre-improvement estate plans discloses a greater semblance of order, perhaps by being arranged on a one- or two-row basis or around a simple, open courtyard. Possibly these more orderly plans were associated with the wider adoption of stone-built housing and more efficient farming over the seventeenth century. However, we cannot exclude the possibility that some had medieval antecedents. Scattered references to tofts from the twelfth century onwards bear this out. In theory, tofts were allotments specifically set aside for the farmsteads of a toun, an area of private space. They imposed a stable and, usually, an orderly framework of bounds around the farmsteads of the toun and *ipso facto* limitations on their movement. Toft systems were laid out on a one- or two-row basis and even on either side of a green (for example Midlem in Roxburghshire). There are also descriptions of 'full' or 'half' tofts as if there was a calculation to their size, whilst the possession of others was clearly seen as betokening the possession of a particular holding, but the extent to which their size or sequence of allocation was linked to that of holdings has still to be demonstrated. Indeed, whilst we find touns in which each landholder was required, as on the Coupar Angus Abbey estate, to 'set his bygyn apon his awin toft', there are hints that this was not the case everywhere. The landholders who shared a ferm-toun faced the choice of either dividing their portions into separate, consolidated holdings or laying them out in the form of intermixed strips (or runrig). Although the first of these options was used to a limited extent, runrig was the more widely-adopted

strategy, illustrated here at Auchencraw and one that invariably forced tenants into a degree of cooperation over husbandry.

Prior to the improving movement, the toun economy was organised around areas of intensive cropping or infield, of alternate grass and arable husbandry or outfield and common grazings. The precise cropping of infield and outfield varied from one region to another. Generally speaking, infields in the more fertile east and south-east might carry a crop of wheat as well as the staple grains of oats and bere plus a crop of peas or beans, whereas those of the north and west were subjected to a monotonous cycle of oats and barley. The main differences in outfield cropping practice lay in the proportion cropped and the duration of each cropping cycle, with touns to the north and north-west developing the more exploitive system. Rights of access to common grazing were contingent on possession of a holding, with the amount of stock grazed by each landholder being carefully stented. Where pasture was abundant, the more distant grazings were exploited through a shieling system. There is ample evidence that shieling systems were initially developed in areas like Lammermuir as well as throughout the Highlands. However, with the development of the monastic economy, hill pasture in the southern uplands was used to support a more independent pastoral economy. Outwardly, infield, outfield and common grazing represent different sectors of farm activity. However, they possess a further dimension of meaning. *Ab origine*, infield formed that part of the medieval township which was assessed as arable and measured in terms of standard tenemental units such as merklands or husbandlands, whilst outfield represented a later expansion, perhaps as late as the fifteenth or sixteenth century, into the surrounding waste. The temporary cropping of outfield can be attributed to the fact that the only manure which it received was that provided by the tathing of livestock during the summer prior to its cultivation, so that its limited reserves of fertility declined until, after three or four years of cropping, it was abandoned to grass again.

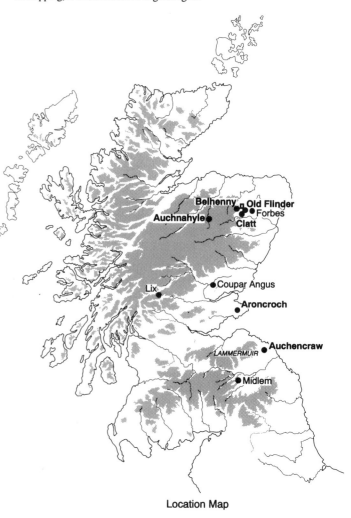

Location Map

RAD

286

Medieval rural settlement

These and the following maps are all based on eighteenth-century estate plans held in the Scottish Record Office.

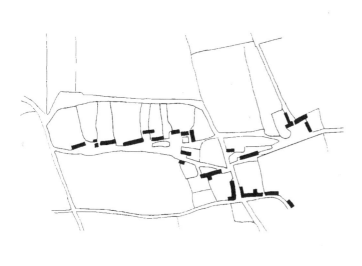

Aroncroch, Fife, 1786

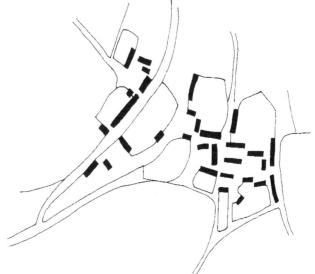

Belhenny, Aberdeenshire, 1776

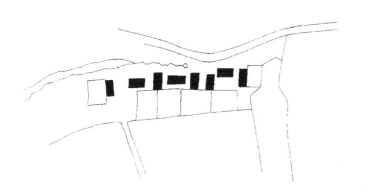

■ Buildings

Old Flinder, Aberdeenshire, 1762

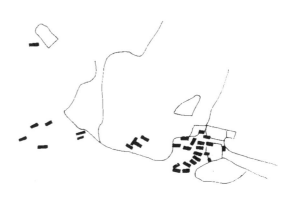

Auchnahyle, Banffshire, 1773

Medieval rural settlement from later estate plans

RAD

Medieval rural settlement

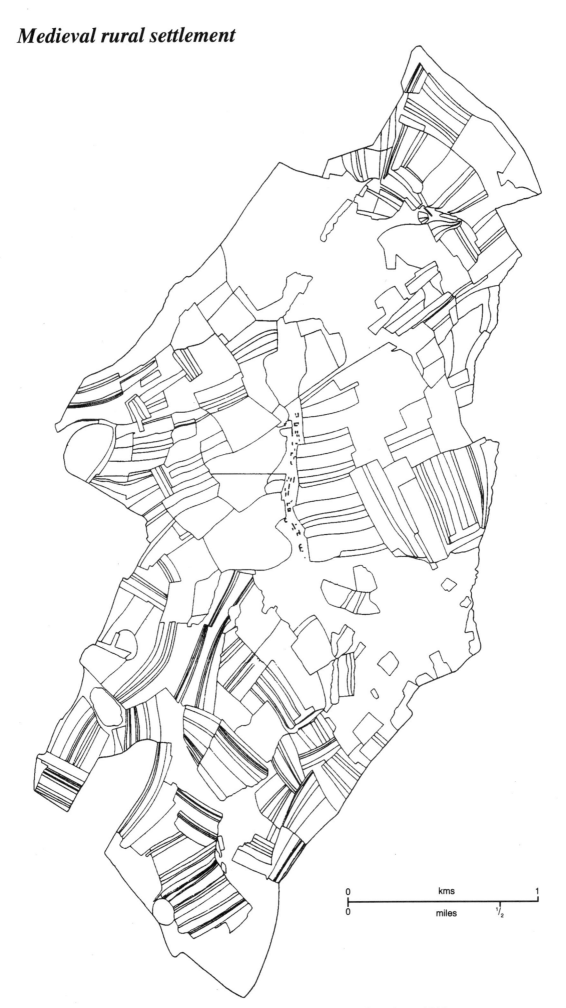

Runrig lands of Auchencraw, Berwickshire, about 1713

RAD

Blairdinny

Greenmoss

West Tayloch

East Tayloch

Stoneyfield

Towie

Braeside

Bankhead

Percylieu

Infield

Outfield

Common grazing

Medieval township economy: the lands of Forbes, parish of Clatt, about 1771

RAD

Feuing of Church lands in the sixteenth century

The feuing of church lands - whereby bishops, abbots, commendators and other benefice holders, instead of leasing their lands for a year or years (or for life or lives) in return for a rent, granted a feu in perpetuity in return for a single lump sum (or grassum) and a perpetual but fixed annual feu duty - can be traced from the fifteenth century. But the granting of feus reached a peak in the years 1550 to 1570. The great volume of feus in these years had a far-reaching effect in turning many tenants into owner-occupiers - particularly since church lands were generally the most fertile.

At first glance, these transactions did not offend against the rule that they must not diminish the patrimony of the church; but with the rapid depreciation of the coinage, the real value of the fixed feu-duty also fell, benefiting the feuars. The map and charts shows the extent to which feus of church lands were granted to sitting tenants.

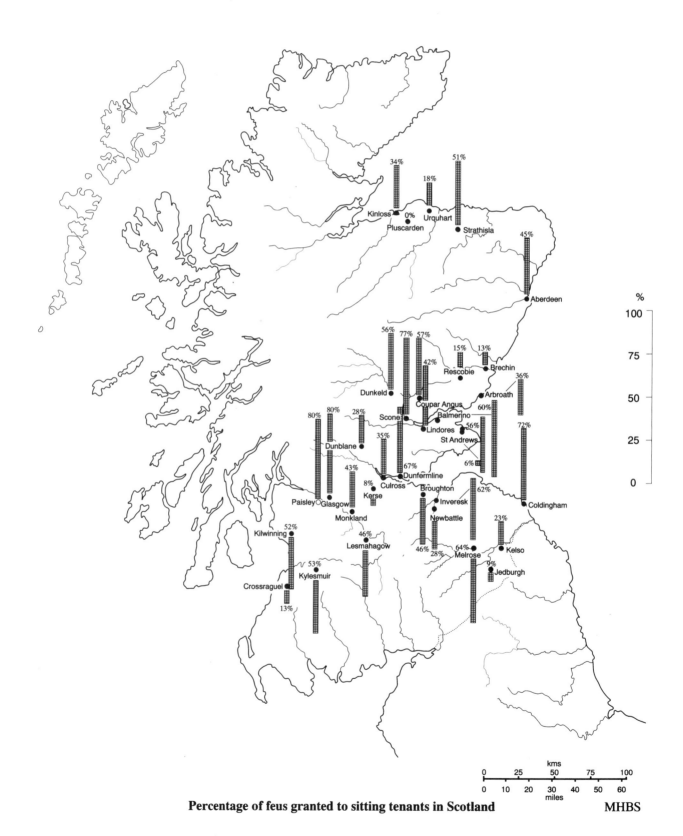

Percentage of feus granted to sitting tenants in Scotland

MHBS

Feuing of Church lands in the sixteenth century

The map illustrates the pattern of feuing in a particular barony, that of Strathisla in Banffshire belonging to the abbey of Kinloss which was itself situated in Morayshire. Strathisla lay in the fertile valley of the river Isla and its tributaries the Aultmore and Paithnick burns, even the lower slopes of Knock and Lurg Hill being under cultivation. The land was cultivated by numerous tenants on the fixed runrig pattern. At the centre of the barony stood the tower of Strathisla, the administrative headquarters, and the parish church of Keith, a mensal kirk of the bishop of Moray.

The feu charters of Kinloss abbey as a whole span the period from the paternalist government of Abbot Thomas Chrystal to the commendatorship of Edward Bruce. The abbey was erected into a temporal lordship in favour of Edward Bruce, by charters of 1601 and 1608. One hundred out of the 104 extant charters were granted by Walter Reid, who was abbot in 1553-83. By the mid-seventeenth century, the area was peppered with the small tower houses of the bonnet lairds of Strathisla.

Distribution of feuars

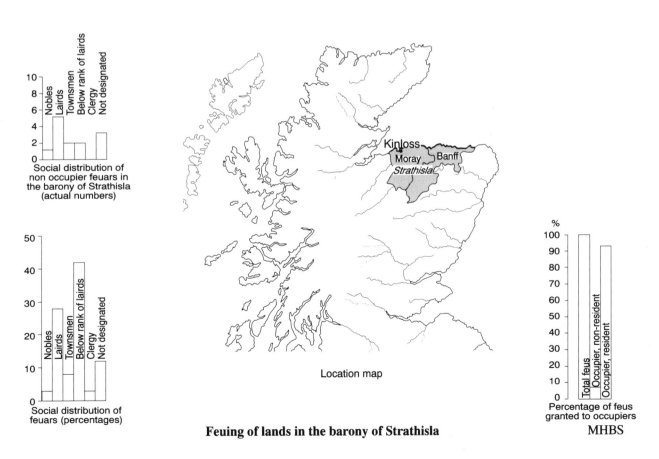

Location map

Feuing of lands in the barony of Strathisla

MHBS

291

Customary succession in leases

The surviving rentals of Coupar Angus Abbey cover the years from 1464 to 1516 and from 1539 to about 1560. The gap is an unfortunate one because since there was clearly a move towards longer leases in the intervening period; this was the policy of Abbot Donald Campbell who feued the lands in the 1550s, thus making permanent the trend towards stability of possession. The use of patronymics on the abbey lands during the earlier period makes it impossible to give round figures in connection with customary inheritance, but it is safe to say that on most of the farmtouns several families are found in possession for two to three generations, and in some cases more.

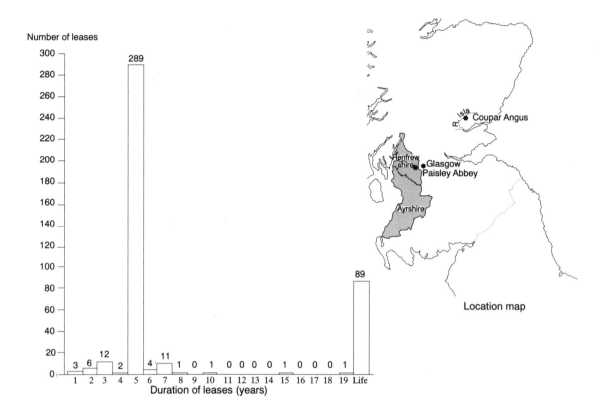

Pattern of 418 leases in the lands of Coupar Angus Abbey 1464 - 1516

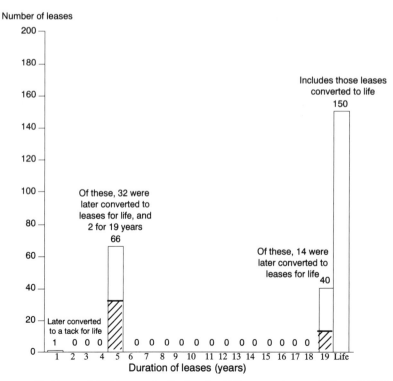

Pattern of 257 leases in the lands of Coupar Angus Abbey 1539 to about 1560

MHBS

292

Customary succession in leases

Important though it was, and reaching a peak in the 1540s and 1550s, feuing spread only gradually on church lands: significant feuing did not appear in Glasgow until the early 1580s. Thus, many families remained tenants for much of the sixteenth century.

The most common forms of customary tenure were the lease granted for years or for life and the special case of the rental (life lease) which was renewed on the death of the tenant in favour of his kin. Rentalling was most common in southern Scotland where it had long existed in lands as far apart as Newbattle, Melrose, Glasgow, Paisley and Kilwinning. Even with tacks, including short tacks, it was customary to renew them in favour of the tenant or his family. Continuity of possession, while not universally guaranteed, would seem to be the norm in many parts of the country, in both lay and ecclesiastical lands. In practice these tenants had the right of succes-

sion to their holdings but unlike freeholders and feuars they did not have a heritable title. In late medieval Scotland, the claim to customary inheritance by tenants was called the 'kindness' of the holding, the right to succeed because the new tenant was kindly ('kin') to the previous tenant.

When a rentaller died leaving a wife and children, the widow enjoyed the lands for her lifetime only; but the children were entitled to be rentalled; and the widow had no power to put in any person in the rental. Further, in Glasgow, even if the deceased tenant had alone been rentalled, his widow was entitled to the lands for her lifetime by the privilege of St Mungo's widow. The graphs show the breakdown of the customary sucession in leases in the lands of the abbey of Paisley in Renfrewshire and Ayrshire and in the lands of the barony of Glasgow.

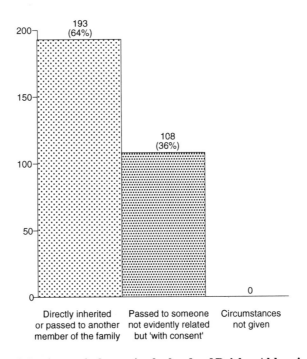

Customary inheritance in leases in the lands of Paisley Abbey in Renfrewshire and Ayrshire, 1526 to 1555

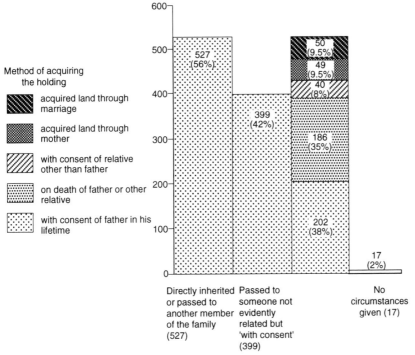

Customary inheritance in leases in the barony of Glasgow, about 1509 to 1570

MHBS

293

Enclosures

Location map

John Adair's maps of the Lothians show that in that area, where enclosure was relatively advanced, few complexes exceeded about 250-300 acres (approximately 101-121 hectares). However, in such an area, where estates were relatively small and closely spaced, enclosure even on this modest scale could have profound impact on the rural landscape. We are fortunate in having Adair's surveys for parts of eastern Scotland for the last decade of the seventeenth century. These surveys are acknowledged to show settlement with reasonable accuracy. Thus they probably represent a fairly good picture of the state of enclosure. The actual extent of the enclosed lands may have been slight in relation to landscape, but when their areas are calculated as accurately as is possible from the scale of the map, which is not entirely precise, they do not seem unduly out of proportion in relation to other evidence. The map represents the distribution and approximate size of the enclosures as shown by Adair.

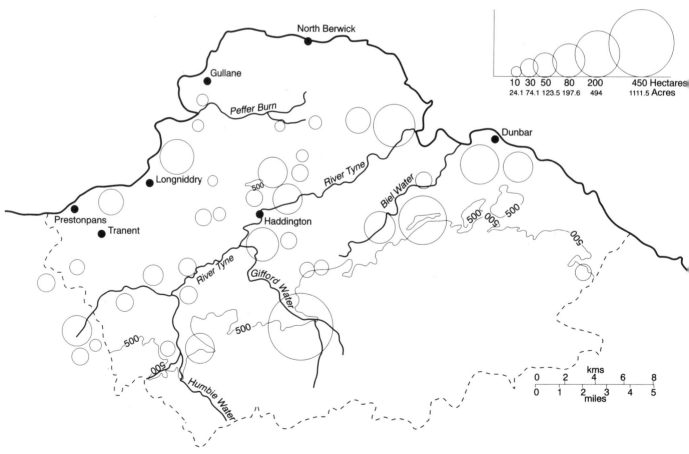

Enclosures in East Lothian in the seventeenth century

IDW

294

Markets and fairs outside burghs

Between 1550 and 1660, 143 market centres were licensed, followed by a further 346 between 1660 and 1707 (see above, Royal burghs and burghs of barony). But the post-Restoration foundations were often different in being granted a licence to hold a regular market or a fair without being given the status of a burgh. There were, it has been estimated, about 50 non-burghal centres before 1660 but a further 136 were authorised by parliament 1660 and 1707, many in areas remote from existing burghs. These post-1660 foundations were also rather different in their distribution, reaching into the Highlands and larger islands of the Inner Hebrides. By 1707, only 18% of the mainland of Scotland was more than fifteen miles from an authorised market centre, whether situated in a burgh or outside.

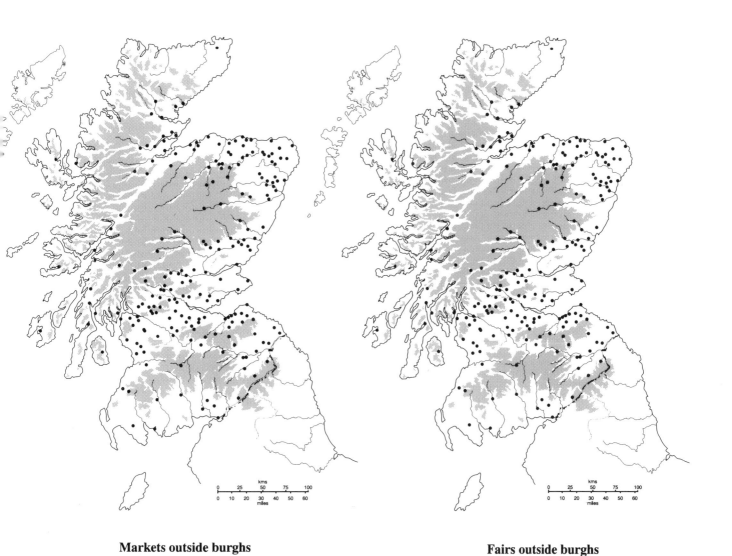

Markets outside burghs

Fairs outside burghs

IDW

295

Employment

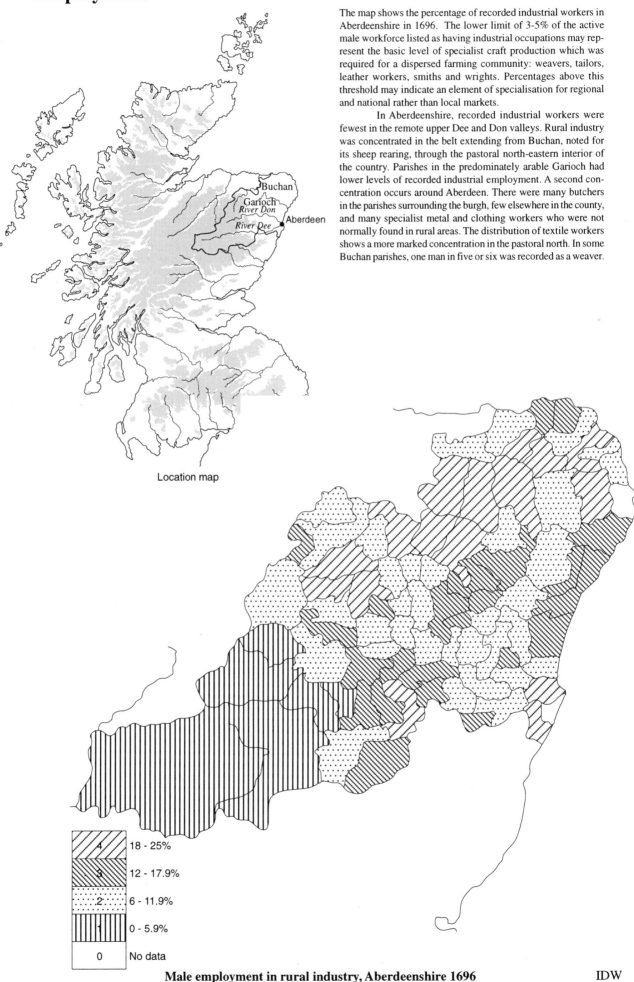

The map shows the percentage of recorded industrial workers in Aberdeenshire in 1696. The lower limit of 3-5% of the active male workforce listed as having industrial occupations may represent the basic level of specialist craft production which was required for a dispersed farming community: weavers, tailors, leather workers, smiths and wrights. Percentages above this threshold may indicate an element of specialisation for regional and national rather than local markets.

In Aberdeenshire, recorded industrial workers were fewest in the remote upper Dee and Don valleys. Rural industry was concentrated in the belt extending from Buchan, noted for its sheep rearing, through the pastoral north-eastern interior of the country. Parishes in the predominately arable Garioch had lower levels of recorded industrial employment. A second concentration occurs around Aberdeen. There were many butchers in the parishes surrounding the burgh, few elsewhere in the county, and many specialist metal and clothing workers who were not normally found in rural areas. The distribution of textile workers shows a more marked concentration in the pastoral north. In some Buchan parishes, one man in five or six was recorded as a weaver.

Location map

4 18 - 25%

3 12 - 17.9%

2 6 - 11.9%

1 0 - 5.9%

0 No data

Male employment in rural industry, Aberdeenshire 1696

IDW

Growth of manufactories, 1590 to 1707

There was an appreciable growth, especially after 1660, of 'manufactories'. The details here, from a convenient list in G. Marshall, *Presbyteries and Profits* (1980), which derives from the printed records, mostly of parliament and privy council, almost certainly understates the real number. Yet they hardly amounted to, as was once claimed, ' an industrial revival' . Their growth should be considered along with other developments of the seventeenth-century economy such as the growth of burghs of barony; the flight of some crafts, especially in Edinburgh, to the suburbs to secure cheaper costs and wage rates; the increasing range of merchant investment of capital in non-mercantile areas and the growing sophistication of business partnerships made on joint-stock lines, which dates from the 1620s rather than the 1690s; and the repeated government intervention in the economy, seen in the acts in 1641, 1661 and 1681 to encourage woollen manufactures. The projects in paper, glass, hardware, soap and sugar were new but much of the investment in wool, textiles and leather, unlike the famous cloth manufactory at Newmills near Haddington, was probably only an extension of long-established patterns of putting-out to rural industry. Most manufactories were small-scale and, except for those in sugar, hardly profitable. They did not, as they were intended to, make Scotland self-sufficient in these products. Their concentration around Edinburgh (which had at least nine before 1650) and, after 1660, in Glasgow reflects the predominance of investment by burgesses of these two towns and neighbouring lairds in these ventures.

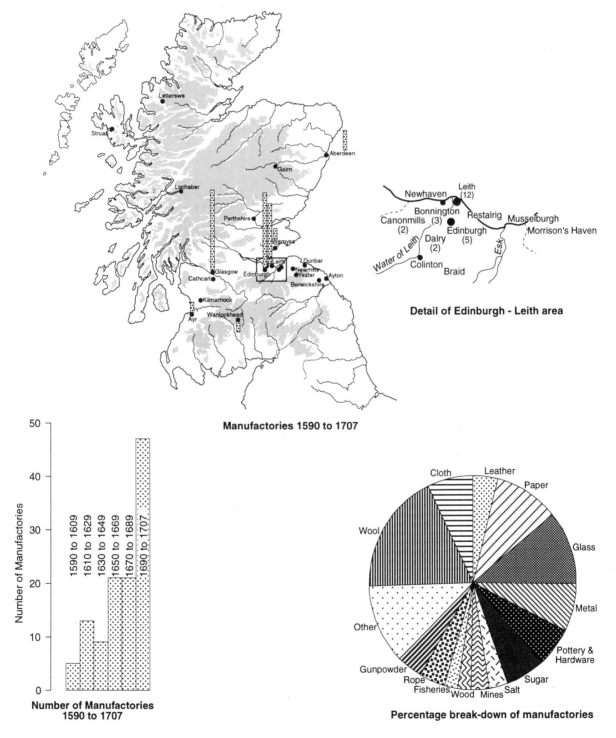

Detail of Edinburgh - Leith area

Manufactories 1590 to 1707

**Number of Manufactories
1590 to 1707**

Percentage break-down of manufactories

Growth of manufactories 1590 to 1707

IDW

Taxation in medieval Scotland

The Old Extent of benefices (parish revenues, also known as spiritualities) is preserved in a diocesan list presented to the Scottish parliament in 1366. It is also to be found in four ecclesiastical registers, which record both summary totals for all the mainland Scottish dioceses and valuations of individual parishes in the dioceses of St Andrews, Brechin and Aberdeen. All are copies of lost originals that had been drawn up for a tax of 4d in the merk (a fortieth) and subsequently used to calculate taxes of 5d and 6d in the merk. The only recorded tax of a fortieth - of all revenues and saleable goods - was ordered by Pope Innocent III in 1199 for the relief of the Holy Land. It was the first ecclesiastical income tax and was levied in England and France in 1201, the same year that a papal legate is known to have visited Scotland. Taxes of both 5d and 6d in the merk were agreed by the Scottish Church in 1267; over the intervening period papal taxes known to have been collected in Scotland were twentieths. Internal evidence therefore suggests that the Old Extent of benefices may date from 1201 and is certainly earlier than 1267.

As teinds - in theory the tenth part of the produce of land or labour - constituted the main element of benefices, this map provides an invaluable indication of the geographical distribution of wealth and population throughout Scotland. Regrettably, the only detail to have survived is from the wealthy eastern dioceses. The overall value per square mile of Aberdeen (£0.71) was greatly diminished by the poor Highland deanery of Mar. Similar variations would have occurred in most dioceses, particularly Glasgow and Moray. The distortion is reversed in the case of Dunkeld, where the value per square mile of its Highland core is unduly enhanced by a large number of wealthy and distant Lowland parishes (diocesan 'peculiars' in church law). No comparable data survive for the Western or Northern Isles, then in the ecclesiastical province of Nidaros (Norway).

The Old Extent of benefices remained the basis for papal taxation of spiritualities until the 1270s, when a new collector - Baiamondo di Vezza - was instructed to draw up fresh assessments of both spiritualities and temporalities (ecclesiastical estates). Although some accounts and assessments from 'Bagimond's Roll' survive, they are incomplete and cannot readily be mapped. This and the following assessment (see below, Nicholas IV tithe) were intensely unpopular. In the fourteenth century the Old Extent was reintroduced for the taxation of benefices.

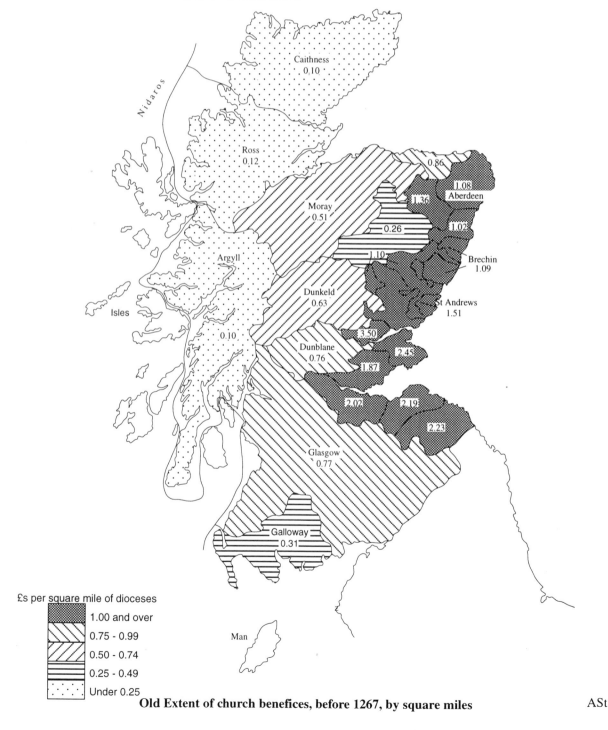

Old Extent of church benefices, before 1267, by square miles

ASt

Taxation in medieval Scotland

Direct taxation was rare in medieval Scotland. In the main the crown was expected to support itself from its own revenues. In the twelfth century occasional taxation was agreed between the king, clergy, barons and burghs on the basis of a lump sum from each estate; each probably divided up by agreement amongst themselves. This was the system readopted on the rare occasions that taxation was levied in the later fifteenth and early sixteenth centuries. Apart from taxation of the clergy, almost nothing is known about taxation in the thirteenth century. But from fourteenth-century references it is apparent that, as in England, taxes based on the detailed assessment of saleable goods and revenues supplanted the older system of tallage in the thirteenth century. After a period of fossilisation around old assessments, a national system of income assessment was reintroduced to pay for the ransom of David II.

The earliest surviving assessments of lay and ecclesiastical estates are known from summaries by sheriffdom that were presented to the Scottish parliament in 1366, when they were compared with current valuations. Tax legislation of the 1320s states that the assessment of estates then in use dated from the reign of Alexander III (1249-1286). For most areas, surviving summary tax returns of the 1320s are broadly consistent with the old valuations recorded in 1366. But returns from the border sheriffdoms, which by the 1360s were partly occupied by the English, were much higher. These higher valuations are reflected in the map below. Various other changes may also be inferred.

The sheriff of Inverness was responsible for tax collection throughout northern Scotland. His jurisdiction had earlier also extended to the Hebrides, but in 1366 the mainland and Inner Hebridean estates of the Lord of the Isles were separately recorded within Argyll. Argyll seems to have had a very loosely defined status. In 1366 it is recorded as a series of fiefs, which may earlier have been divided between other sheriffdoms. Various estates of the 'Lord Steward of Scotland' were listed separately within Argyll. His principal Lowland estate, the barony of Renfrew, seems to have been included within the sheriffdom of Dunbarton, although previously part of Lanarkshire.

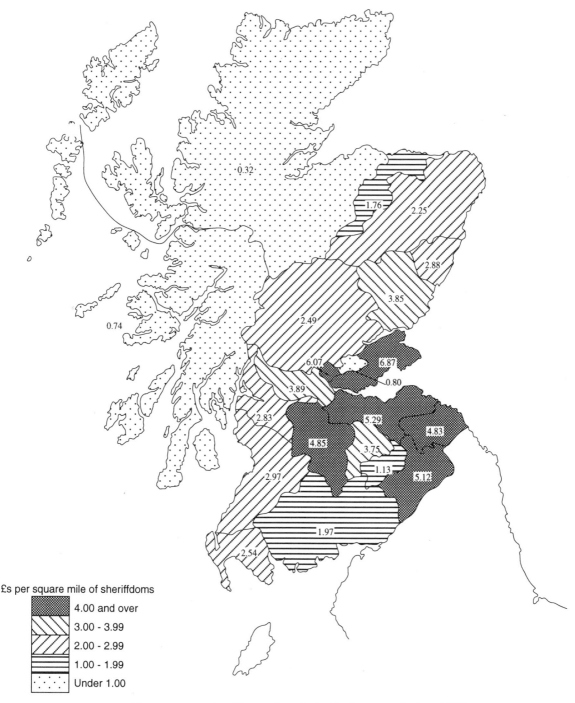

£s per square mile of sheriffdoms

- 4.00 and over
- 3.00 - 3.99
- 2.00 - 2.99
- 1.00 - 1.99
- Under 1.00

Tax assessments of lay and ecclesiastical estates, before 1286

ASt

Taxation in medieval Scotland

In 1290 Pope Nicholas IV ordered new assessments of ecclesiastical income to be made throughout western Christendom and tithes to be levied for six years towards the cost of a crusade. The assessments were prepared between the autumn of 1291 and the spring of 1292, on the basis of sworn statements by the clergy of the value of all ecclesiastical revenues and saleable goods. The military orders, leper hospitals and clerical incomes of 6 merks (£4) or less were exempt. The first tithe was levied in 1292.

As an inducement to take up the cross, Pope Nicholas granted all receipts from the British Isles to King Edward I of England. The Scottish record survives, among documents of Bishop Halton of Carlisle, the chief collector for Scotland, in a summary account of diocesan assessments and receipts. Although still part of the ecclesiastical province of Nidaros (Norway), Halton also collected tithes in the diocese of Sodor (the Hebrides, the islands in the Firth of Clyde and the Isle of Man). On the Isle of Man tithes were collected for all six years of the tax, thus providing separate evidence for the valuation of Man; whereas in the rest of Scotland the tithe was levied only for the first four years, because of the breakdown in Anglo-Scottish relations towards the end of 1295 and the subsequent wars.

A detailed assessment of benefices and other ecclesiastical revenues in the archdeaconry of Lothian (excluding the appropriated benefices and estates of the bishop of St Andrews) survives among the records of Coldingham Priory. This provides the one point of reference with the Old Extent of benefices and shows an average increase in the value of Lothian benefices of some 56%: an increase of 65 % in the deanery of Linlithgow, 69% in the deanery of Haddington and 38% in the deanery of Merse. It also provides evidence of the ratio of spiritualities (benefices) to temporalities (ecclesiastical estates) and indicates that in Lothian 64.5% of recorded ecclesiastical income was derived from benefices, almost

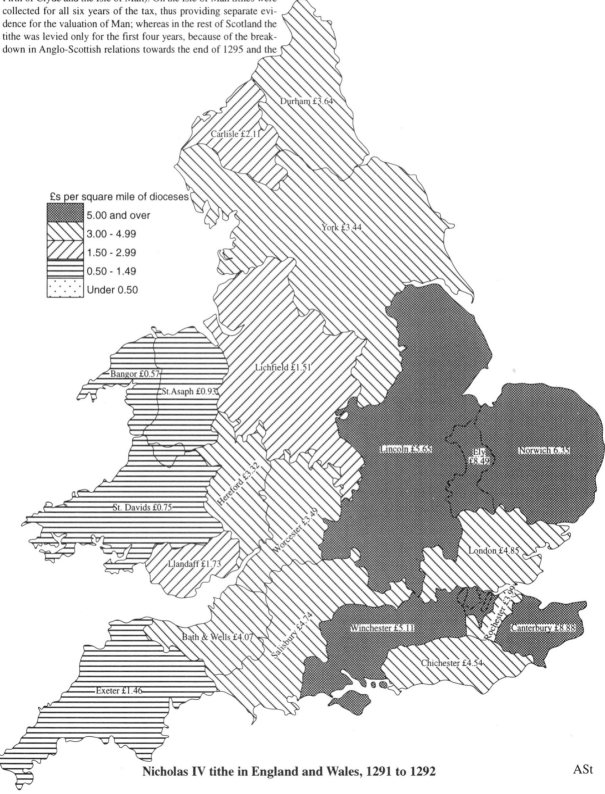

£s per square mile of dioceses

- 5.00 and over
- 3.00 - 4.99
- 1.50 - 2.99
- 0.50 - 1.49
- Under 0.50

Durham £3.64
Carlisle £2.11
York £3.44
Lichfield £1.51
Bangor £0.57
St.Asaph £0.93
Lincoln £5.65
Ely £3.49
Norwich 6.35
Hereford £3.32
St. Davids £0.75
Worcester £3.49
London £4.85
Llandaff £1.73
Salisbury £4.74
Winchester £5.11
Rochester £3.90
Canterbury £8.88
Chichester £4.54
Bath & Wells £4.07
Exeter £1.46

Nicholas IV tithe in England and Wales, 1291 to 1292

ASt

Taxation in medieval Scotland

identical to the English and Welsh average of 64.4%. Compared with most other parts of Scotland, there was a large concentration of religious houses in and around the archdeaconry of Lothian, which suggests that the disproportionate scale of Scottish monastic estates is a myth; unlike the appropriation of benefices, which accounted for almost half the monastic assessment and at least 60% of parishes.

Comparison with the English and Welsh assessments indicates a national average of £4.04 per square mile in England, £1.34 per square mile in Scotland and £0.90 per square mile in Wales. As might be expected, the Western Isles and the north and west Highlands were much the poorest areas recorded in the Nicholas IV assessment, followed by the Welsh dioceses, Galloway, the Isle of Man, Devon and Cornwall. More surprising is the relative poverty of the north-western Midlands. In all these English and Welsh dioceses (other than Llandaff) ecclesiastical estates accounted for a quarter or less of the assessment. By contrast, in the richest English dioceses (apart from Lincoln and Norwich) ecclesiastical estates accounted for nearly half the assessment, well over half in the case of Ely. Remarkably, mile for mile, St Andrews was apparently wealthier than all but a handful of English dioceses. The evidence

from Lothian suggests that this was not disproportionately due to temporal revenues, although later evidence indicates that the concentration of ecclesiastical estates was significantly greater in the archdeaconry of St Andrews (see below, Taxed income, 1365 to 1373).

It has often been suggested that in Scotland the Nicholas IV assessment was excessively high. At nearly a fifth of the English total its scale is remarkable - double the ratio of GDP today. But recent numismatic research and analysis of Coldingham estate records tend to support its conclusions.

The 'Taxation of Pope Nicholas' was rapidly abandoned in Scotland but in England and Wales, despite initial protests about its severity, it remained the basis for ecclesiastical taxation until the Reformation.

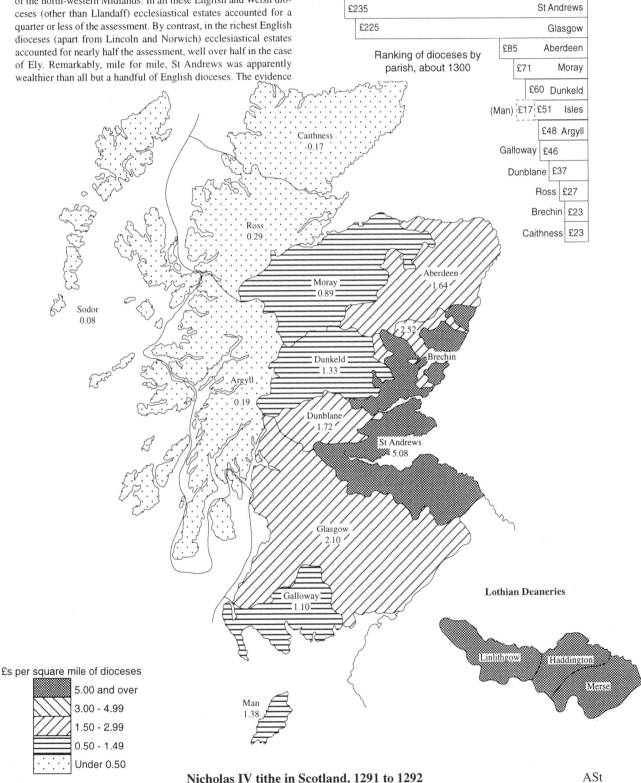

Ranking of dioceses by parish, about 1300

£235	St Andrews
£225	Glasgow
£85	Aberdeen
£71	Moray
£60	Dunkeld
(Man) £17 £51	Isles
£48	Argyll
Galloway £46	
Dunblane £37	
Ross £27	
Brechin £23	
Caithness £23	

£s per square mile of dioceses

- 5.00 and over
- 3.00 - 4.99
- 1.50 - 2.99
- 0.50 - 1.49
- Under 0.50

Nicholas IV tithe in Scotland, 1291 to 1292   ASt

301

Taxation in medieval Scotland

To help raise the ransom of David II, the Scottish Parliament enacted in 1357 that annual revaluations be made of all revenues: benefices, rents, goods, crops, livestock and all other possessions. All classes were to be assessed and taxed. The only items to be exempted from taxation, but not assessment, were white sheep, domestic horses, oxen and household utensils. Taxes were levied every year from 1358 to 1360. There was then a break until 1365, apart from annual tithes of Church income that had been granted by the Pope.

In 1366, with the English government threatening hostilities if the ransom was not discharged within four years, a major review became necessary. In May 1366, it was ordered that all old and new assessments of lay and ecclesiastical lands and revenues were to be collected and presented to parliament. Parliament met at Scone in July to consider the position and agreed that further assessments be made of the goods of burgesses and husbandmen (tenant farmers) - these later assessments have not survived. When the true value of all goods throughout the kingdom was known, it was enacted that a general contribution be levied.

Full comparison with the Old Extent (see above) was not possible in 1366. A reduction of 21% had been made in the Old Extent of

benefices for the diocese of Glasgow, because Annandale and many parishes in the deaneries of Eskdale and Teviotdale were 'subject to the king of England'. For the same reason, in the deanery of Merse many parishes had been revalued by estimate, for comparative purposes, and Berwick had been excluded. Comparison with tax returns of the 1320s indicates that at least 73% (by value) of estates in the sheriffdom of Berwick were under English occupation, 67% of those in both Roxburgh and Selkirk, and 31% in Dumfries. These reductions have been reflected in the valuations per square mile in the remaining maps of this series. A further problem was that in Argyll the Lord of the Isles, the 'Lord Steward of Scotland' and John of Lorn had prevented the making of any assessment of their estates: the old extent of these lands was presented but not their current value. Resistance in Argyll is likely to have been matched in the sheriffdom of Inverness, where the earl of Ross was in rebellion and where the Lord of the Isles also had extensive estates; as there is no qualification in the 1366 record of Inverness, it may be that here too revaluations had been made by estimate.

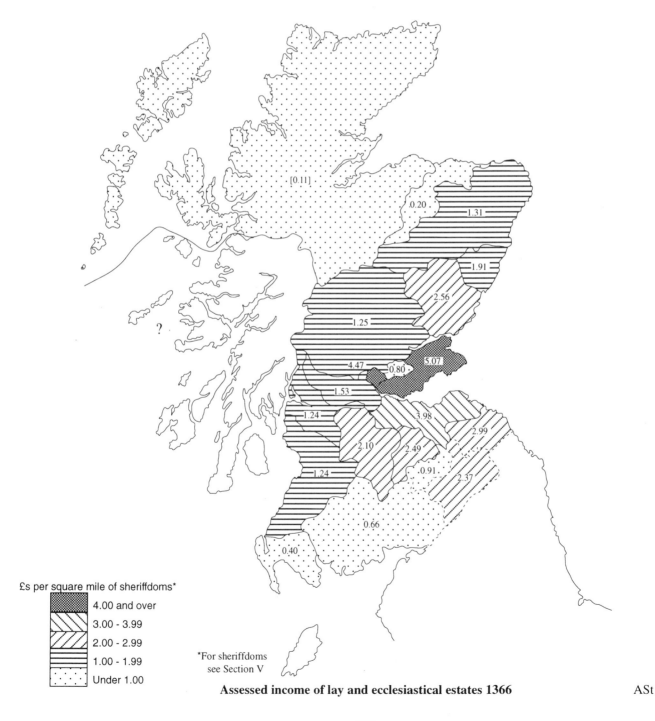

£s per square mile of sheriffdoms*

- 4.00 and over
- 3.00 - 3.99
- 2.00 - 2.99
- 1.00 - 1.99
- Under 1.00

*For sheriffdoms
see Section V

Assessed income of lay and ecclesiastical estates 1366

ASt

Taxation in medieval Scotland

Taken at face value, average income from lay and ecclesiastical estates had declined by 49% since the reign of Alexander III and income from benefices by 37% since the date of the Old Extent (before 1267, possibly 1201). As there is no discernible reduction in the 1320s, most or all of this decline had occurred later. The principal cause must have been depopulation as a result of the Black Death in 1349-50 and the Grey Death in 1361-2, leading to reductions in rent and the abandonment of marginal land. Climatic deterioration may also have been a significant factor. So too may have been the trebling of export duty on wool, hides and woolfells in 1358. This provided an additional return to the Exchequer of nearly £3,000 in 1365-6, almost 13% of the total recorded value of lay and ecclesiastical estates, although much of the impact would have been borne by the peasantry, which was always a major producer (see below, Taxed income).

There is a pronounced gradient in the reduction of estate values from west to east and from north to south (see above, Tax assessments of lay and ecclesiastical estates, before 1286). The reduction was least in the eastern Lowland sheriffdoms of Edinburgh, Fife, Clackmannan, Peebles, Forfar and Kincardine (down by between 25% and 34%); with Roxburgh, Lanark, Berwick and Stirling, these had been the richest areas in the thirteenth-century assessment. Doubtless, destabilisation exacerbated the reduction in Berwick (40% less), Roxburgh (54% less) and Selkirk (47% less). Lanark and Stirling seem to have been affected by their relative height and more westerly position (down by 57% and 61%). The west-coast Lowland sheriffdoms had declined by between 56% (Dunbarton and Renfrew) and 67% (Dumfries), with Wigtown down by 84%. In the Highlands, the Argyll estates that had been re-assessed were 78% lower, the valuation of Inverness was 65 % lower, and Perth was 50% lower. Banff had declined by 88%, a suspiciously high figure when compared with later tax returns (see below, Taxed income). Aberdeen had declined by 42%.

The pattern of decline in the assessment of benefices has many similarities, although it is less pronounced (see above, Old Extent of church benefices, before 1267). The assessment confirms that the wealthiest, most densely populated part of the country remained the eastern Lowlands, which had declined least; while the Highlands and Galloway had declined most. The reported income of benefices in the diocese of Caithness had declined by 70%, in both Moray and Galloway by 61%, in Argyll by 53% and in Dunkeld by 50%. There is much less variation between Dunblane (38%), Glasgow (37%) and St Andrews (34%). The decline was least in Brechin (27%), Ross (23%) and Aberdeen (9%). The figure for Ross looks surprising but seems to be borne out by later tax returns, which must always have been heavily skewed towards the lowlands of Easter Ross and the Black Isle (see below, Taxed income); whereas £0.65 per square mile for Aberdeen was far higher than can be justified by later returns and may result from a transcriptional error.

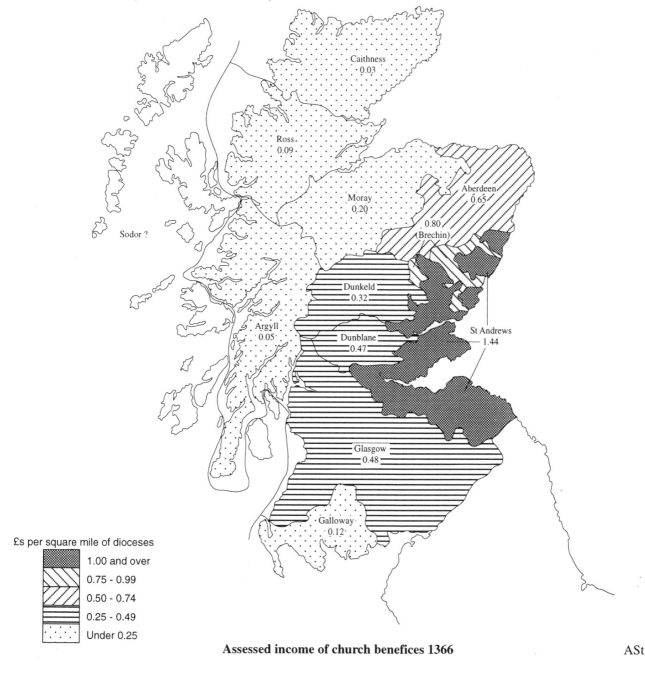

£s per square mile of dioceses

▓▓▓	1.00 and over
⧄	0.75 - 0.99
⟋	0.50 - 0.74
☰	0.25 - 0.49
⋰	Under 0.25

Assessed income of church benefices 1366

ASt

Taxation in medieval Scotland

Preserved among the exchequer rolls are summaries of receipts from the taxes levied as contributions towards David II's ransom. The nature of the returns differs significantly from the 1366 assessments in that taxes were collected by the sheriffs from lay freeholders and their tenants and by diocesan officials from the clergy and their tenants.

It is unclear whether the structure of the 1366 assessments had been primarily dictated by the preoccupations of the Scottish parliament or by the nature of the earlier assessments (which had related to aids payable by tenants holding lands in fee from the crown and to dues on spiritualities owed to the papacy). The former seems more probable. The prelates and barons must have been deeply worried about a steep decline in their income. They sought to spread the tax burden and to highlight their predicament to the king by comparing the latest available assessments with the earlier standards.

The figures mapped below are derived from the highest recorded return from each source. The returns cover six years: 1365, 1366, 1368, 1369, 1370 and 1373. In 1365 the burghs compounded to pay a fixed sum and other groups were taxed at a rate of 1s in the pound (a twentieth), which was the general rate in 1366 and 1370. In 1368 the burghs again compounded to pay a fixed sum and the

tax rate for other groups was set at 6d in the pound (a fortieth). The rate for all groups in 1369 was 3d in the pound (an eightieth). While in 1373 the clergy and their tenants were taxed at a rate of 6d in the pound and other groups at 1s in the pound.

Most sheriffdoms and dioceses contributed in all years, but their returns fluctuated greatly in value and contributions from many sources seem to have been forthcoming only in certain years. In lands controlled by the earl of Ross and in the dioceses of Caithness and Sodor no taxes may have been collected in the years from 1365 onwards. In the diocese of Argyll tax returns were made only in 1365 and 1373; modest returns from the sheriffdom of Argyll were made in 1365 and 1369, but the lordship of the Isles submitted no return until 1373 and it is probable that was also the case on the Argyll estates of the Steward (by 1373 King Robert II). In the south, returns from the sheriffdoms of Edinburgh, Berwick, Selkirk and Wigtown were irregular and fluctuated wildly. The fluctuations in Midlothian are particularly surprising, and the few returns from East Lothian are too low to be credible.

Because no detailed accounts have survived, it is impossible to gauge the thoroughness of the tax collectors or to establish whether all classes of society were included (there were large substrata in town and country below burgesses and husbandmen, the lowest classes specifically mentioned in the 1366 legislation). The best that can be said is that the summary assessments and returns from 1365 to 1373 provide the most comprehensive statistical representation available of medieval Scottish society.

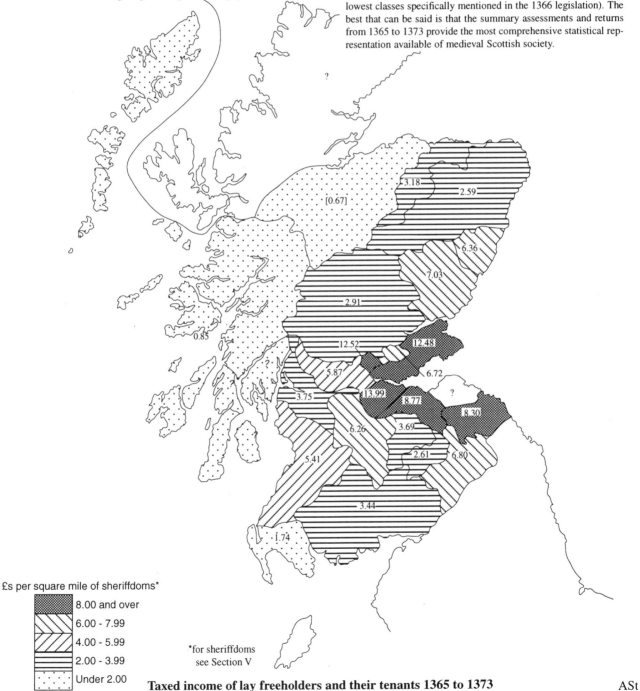

£s per square mile of sheriffdoms*

- 8.00 and over
- 6.00 - 7.99
- 4.00 - 5.99
- 2.00 - 3.99
- Under 2.00

*for sheriffdoms
see Section V

Taxed income of lay freeholders and their tenants 1365 to 1373

ASt

Taxation in medieval Scotland

As the assessments of 1366 and the tax returns of 1365 to 1373 were constructed on different bases, the value of church income from benefices (spiritualities) can be directly gauged, but not church income from ecclesiastical estates (temporalities). Similarly, it is impossible to gauge directly the relative values of lay and ecclesiastical estates. But a rough estimate may be made of the relative scale of ecclesiastical benefices to temporalities in each diocese. The average division across Scotland, on the basis of the highest tax returns, was 43% spiritualities to 57% temporalities (the combined income of the church and its tenants from ecclesiastical estates - unlike the Nicholas IV data, which related only to church income). The large land holdings seem to have been in Galloway (86% of taxed income - where the church accounted for nearly 40% of the highest combined clerical and lay returns from Wigtownshire), Glasgow (68%), Brechin (67%), Dunkeld (65%) and Moray (64%). St Andrews was closer to the national average, at 58%, than any other diocese - probably well below average in the archdeaconry of Lothian, where many of the largest ecclesiastical estates were under English occupation, and well above average in the archdeaconry of St Andrews. In relative terms, the smallest land holdings seem to have been in Dunblane (31%), Aberdeen (39%), Argyll (44%) and Ross (47%).

There were also wide variations across Scotland in the ratio of freeholders' to tenants' income. The position is distorted by the inclusion of church income in the 1366 assessment of estates but its exclusion from the sheriffs' tax returns. Yet the general trends are clear. In the west (and probably the north) landowners' income formed a much smaller proportion of the total returns than in the east. Excluding Argyll and Inverness, where the comparative coverage is unclear, the sum of the highest returns from the sheriffdoms was 67% greater than the 1366 assessment of lay and ecclesiastical estates. At one extreme were Banff and Kinross, where the highest sheriffdom returns were 94% greater than the estates' assessment; at the other was Peebles, where they were only 33% greater. More typical of a regional trend are: in the south-west and west-central, Dumfries (81%), Ayr and Wigtown (both 77%), Stirling (74%), Dunbarton and Renfrew (67%), Lanark (66%) and Clackmannan (65%); in the borders, Berwick, Roxburgh and Selkirk (all about 65%); in the east and east-central, Edinburgh (c.60%), Fife (59%), Perth (57%), Forfar (64%), Kincardine (an atypical 70%) and Aberdeen (49%).

Comparison of the highest returns with the thirteenth-century estate assessments suggests that proportionate values per square mile had fallen most in the sheriffdoms of Wigtown, Peebles, Lanark, Roxburgh, Perth, Aberdeen, Dunbarton and Renfrew (all areas with much high and marginal land); that they had appreciated most in Kinross, Clackmannan and Kincardine (where rents and services may always have been relatively light), and were little altered elsewhere. This suggests that a significant part of the apparent reduction between the thirteenth-century and 1366 estate assessments may indeed be due to falling rents and services. But the pattern varied greatly across the country: transfer of income seems to have been most marked in the west, Banff and Kincardine; least apparent in Lothian, Fife, Peebles, Perth and Aberdeen.

Taxed income of the church and its tenants 1365 to 1373

ASt

305

Burgh farms

A major factor in the creation of the burghs was their potential as a source of monetary revenue. This derived from rents on burgh properties, petty customs levied on goods entering or leaving the burgh, charges on stalls set up in the burgh market, and fines on those breaking the burgh laws. But these revenues were expensive and difficult to administer, so it became common practice for the crown to lease or farm (also spelled ferm) the collection of some or all of a burgh's revenues for a fixed sum agreed in advance. Often the lease would be only for a year but sometimes it was for several years.

Berwick was the first burgh, perhaps by 1231, to obtain an agreement from the crown to farm its revenues in perpetuity or feu for the sum of 500 marks a year. Whether other burghs did so in the thirteenth century is unknown. The Wars of Independence wrought terrible damage on the Scottish burghs - the charters of most were destroyed - and it is likely that the value of many burgh farms was sharply reduced. The value of Berwick's farm was reassessed at 400 marks in 1320, two years after its recapture from the English. Aberdeen obtained its feufarm from the crown in 1319, at an annual rate of 300 marks. Edinburgh followed in 1329 with a feufarm fixed at 52 marks. From the perspective of Edinburgh's later development, this seems extraordinarily low, but Edinburgh's prosperity grew out of Berwick's loss.

In thirteenth-century and early fourteenth-century Scotland there was one major urban centre in each of the three economic regions into which the country was divided: Berwick in southern Scotland south of the Forth and Clyde, Perth in central Scotland, and Aberdeen north of the Grampians (beyond the Mounth). These had acted both as the principal craft centres of their regions (hence the scale of their burgh farms), and as entrepôts for inter-regional and international trade. By the 1320s the old order was breaking down. As the disparity between their export trade and burgh farms indicates, both Edinburgh and Dundee had become important entrepôts without a corresponding growth as craft centres.

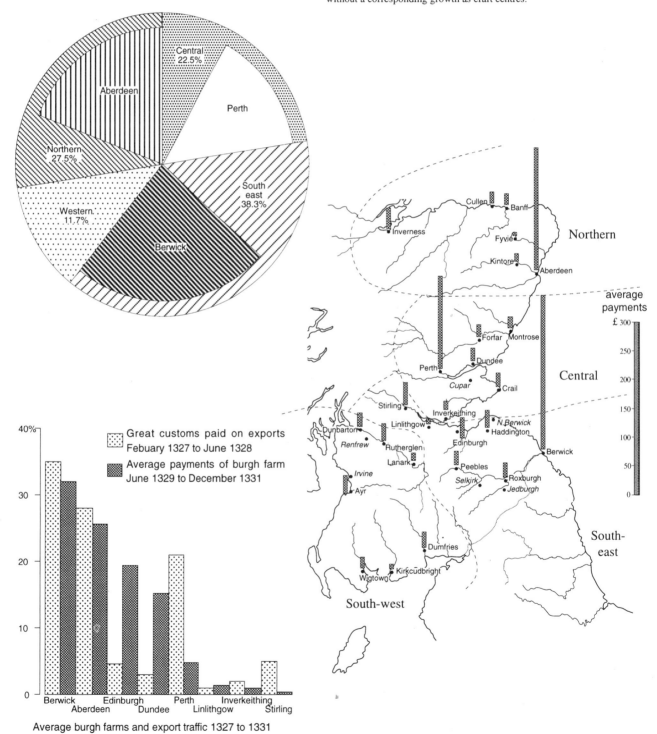

Average burgh farms and export traffic 1327 to 1331

Average payments of burgh farms 1327 to 1331

ASt

Burgh farms

Perth possibly had a feufarm of 240 marks under Robert I, but its prosperity was wrecked by the English occupation of the 1330s, which, in lesser degree, so damaged most of the Scottish burghs. Perth did not farm its revenues again until 1375, and then for a feu of only 120 marks. Apart from the already established feufarms of Aberdeen and Edinburgh, the farms of all burghs other than Banff and Inverness tumbled and never recovered to their earliest recorded levels. This is as clear an indication as it is possible to find of an absolute decline in both size and prosperity.

War and plague combined to produce a long period of stagnation. Feufarms became increasingly common. Dundee was fixed in Inverness and Montrose followed in the end of the fourteenth century almost all the burghs making regular returns to the Exchequer were operating feufarms.

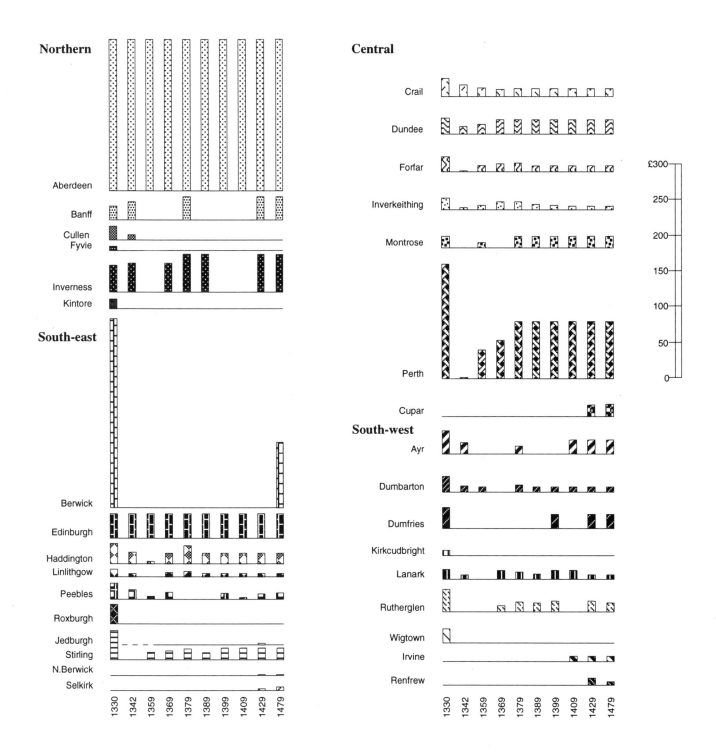

Burgh farms for ten separate years between 1330 and 1479

ASt

Taxation of burghs

Unlike the sheriffdoms and dioceses, the changing circumstances of the burghs cannot be gauged from the taxation record (but see above, Burgh farms). The tax returns of the 1360s and 1370s therefore provide a unique insight into the relative wealth and size of the burghs. They confirm the overwhelming predominance and number of the east-coast burghs. Other evidence may indicate that even the greatest burghs were very small, but they were nonetheless powerful. The townsfolk of Edinburgh were as wealthy as all the barons, clergy and peasantry of Midlothian combined; while those of Aberdeen possessed about a third of the income of their rural hinterland. But these were exceptions: most of the burghs were very poor and were, presumably, minute; many contributed only in 1366 and may

have been included in the sheriffdom and diocesan returns in other years. Apart from Lanark, which had inherited Roxburgh's fair as a result of the English occupation, only those burghs with substantial overseas trade were of much consequence.

Comparison between the tax returns and the 1366 assessments provides a rough indication of the distribution of income throughout Scottish society, as shown in the two pie charts below. The peasantry contributed 54% of the total and the burghs 16% . The division between the clergy and lay freeholders is less clear. Assuming that the average division of income between freeholders and tenants was the same, the clergy contributed about 12% of the total (8.5% from benefices) and lay freeholders about 18%.

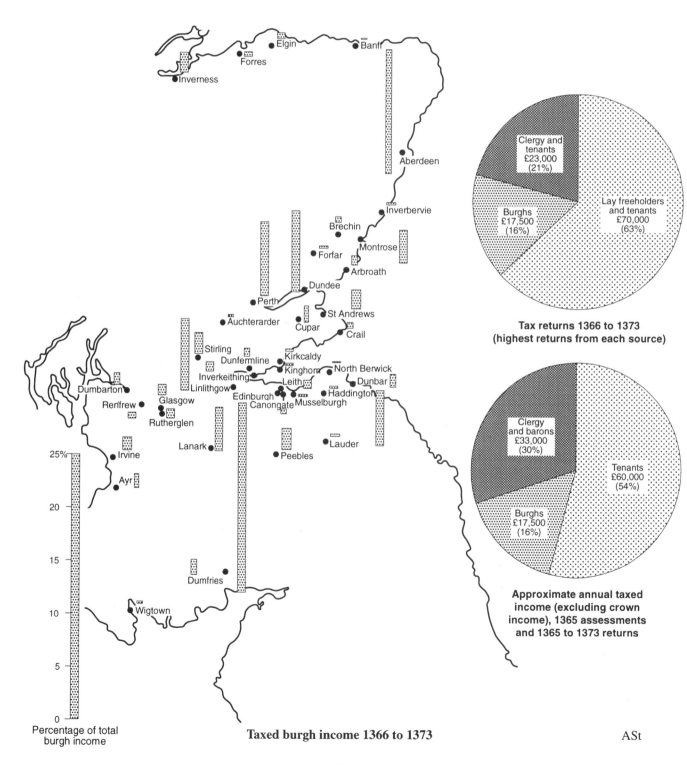

**Tax returns 1366 to 1373
(highest returns from each source)**

**Approximate annual taxed
income (excluding crown
income), 1365 assessments
and 1365 to 1373 returns**

Percentage of total
burgh income

Taxed burgh income 1366 to 1373

ASt

Taxation of burghs

One fractional return of a tax on the burghs exists before 1535 - for 'the burghs beyond Forth' in 1485. This map shows the percentage assessments on these northern towns in 1485 and 1535. There are significant differences, which reflect the volatile economic fortunes of late medieval towns and the contrasting structure of the two regions encompassed: two burghs disappeared from the list of Tay towns in 1535 and two were added to those in the north-east, but the overall assessment saw a movement of 5% in favour of the Tay towns. Assessments on the ports of Montrose and Arbroath increased sharply, while that on St Andrews fell. The sharpest falls, however, lay along the Moray Firth, where only Elgin had its assessment raised.

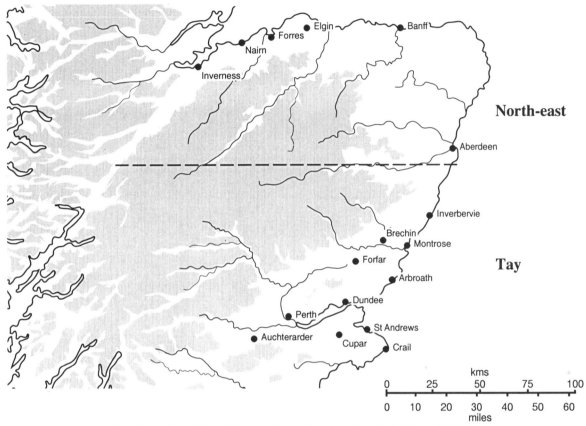

North-east and Tayside burghs paying taxation in 1485 and 1535

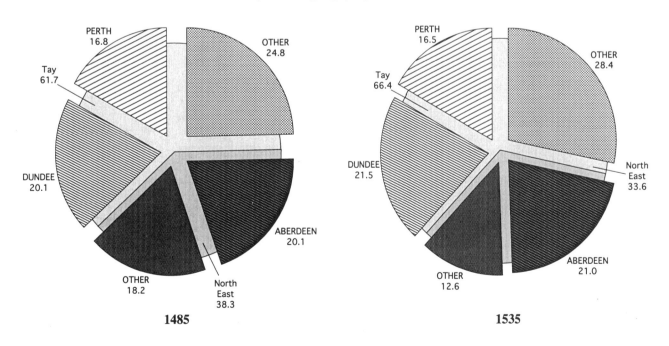

Tax assessments on north-east and Tayside regions in 1485 and 1535

ML

Taxation of burghs

The regular series of tax rolls levied on the royal burghs begins only in 1535. Assessments took account of a number of different factors, reflecting burgh income and the extent of burgh lands as well as shares of overseas and inland trade. These percentage assessments can usefully be compared with those based on customs, which give a measurement of overseas trade alone.

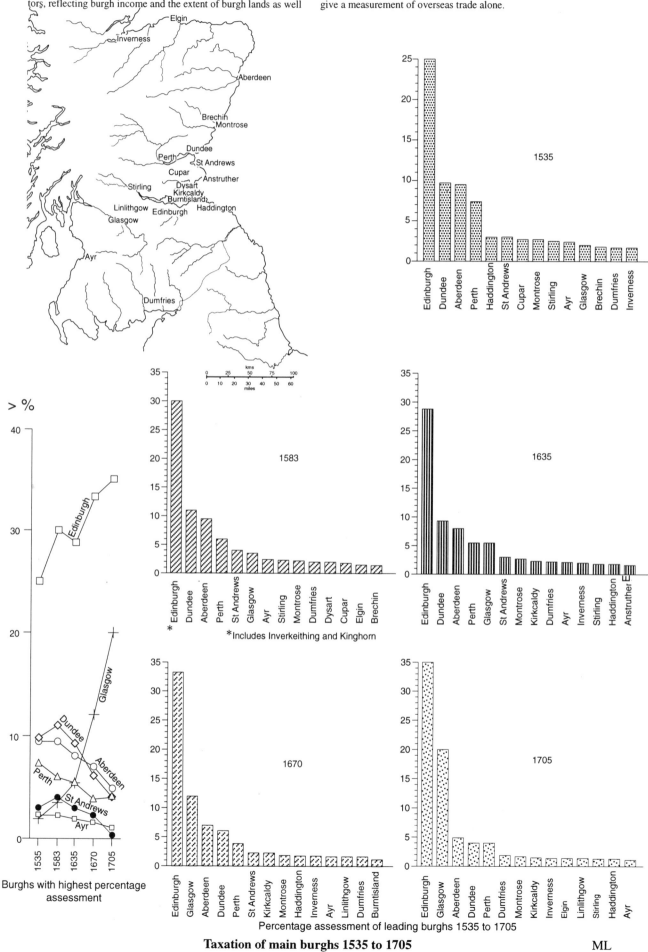

Burghs with highest percentage assessment

*Includes Inverkeithing and Kinghorn

Percentage assessment of leading burghs 1535 to 1705

Taxation of main burghs 1535 to 1705

ML

Taxation of burghs

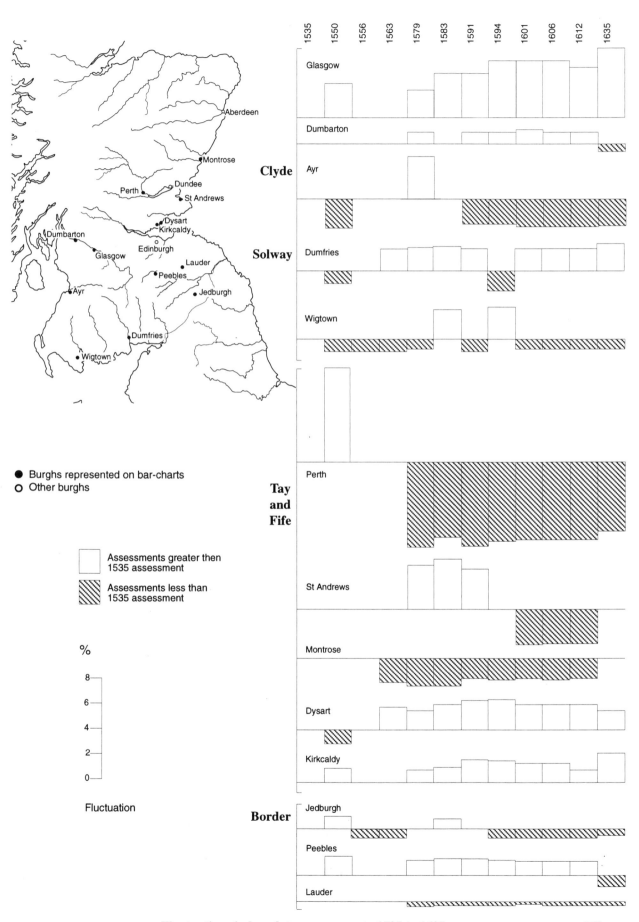

Fluctuations in burgh tax assessments 1535 to 1635

ML

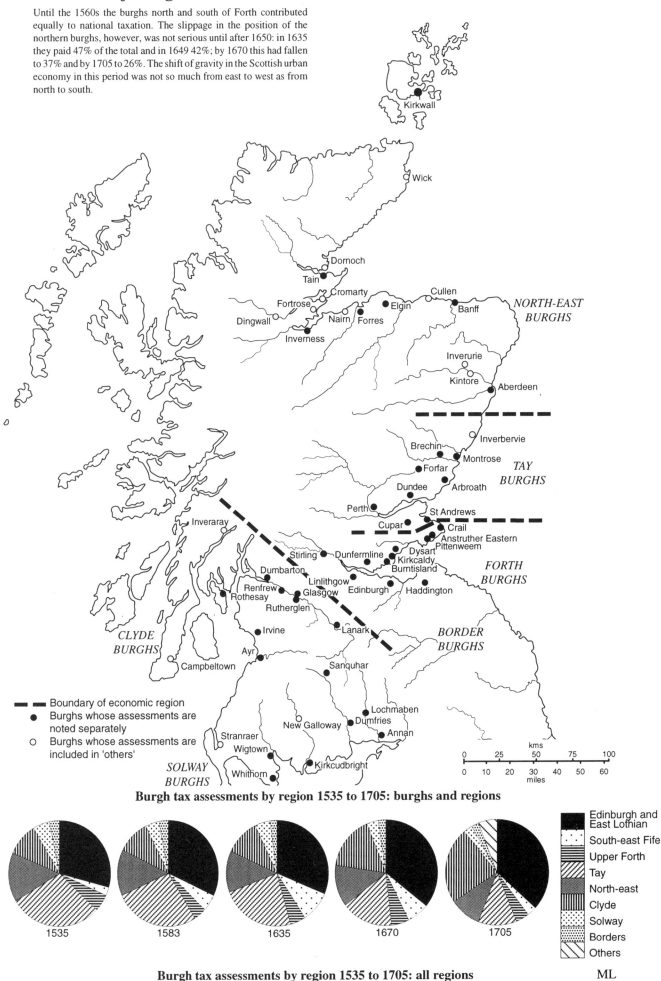

Taxation of burghs

Until the 1560s the burghs north and south of Forth contributed equally to national taxation. The slippage in the position of the northern burghs, however, was not serious until after 1650: in 1635 they paid 47% of the total and in 1649 42%; by 1670 this had fallen to 37% and by 1705 to 26%. The shift of gravity in the Scottish urban economy in this period was not so much from east to west as from north to south.

Kirkwall

Wick

NORTH-EAST BURGHS

Dornoch
Tain
Cromarty   Cullen
Fortrose   Elgin   Banff
Dingwall   Nairn Forres
Inverness

Inverurie
Kintore   Aberdeen

Inverbervie

Brechin
Montrose   *TAY BURGHS*
Forfar
Dundee   Arbroath
Perth   St Andrews
Cupar   Crail
Anstruther Eastern
Pittenweem

Inveraray

Stirling   Dunfermline   Dysart
Kirkcaldy   *FORTH BURGHS*
Dumbarton   Burntisland
Linlithgow
Renfrew   Glasgow   Edinburgh   Haddington
Rothesay
Rutherglen

Irvine   Lanark   *BORDER BURGHS*

Ayr
Campbeltown   Sanquhar

CLYDE BURGHS

Lochmaben
New Galloway   Dumfries
Stranraer   Annan
Wigtown
Whithorn   Kirkcudbright

SOLWAY BURGHS

- - - Boundary of economic region
● Burghs whose assessments are noted separately
○ Burghs whose assessments are included in 'others'

kms
0   25   50   75   100
0 10 20 30 40 50 60
miles

Burgh tax assessments by region 1535 to 1705: burghs and regions

1535   1583   1635   1670   1705

■ Edinburgh and East Lothian
▤ South-east Fife
▤ Upper Forth
▨ Tay
▨ North-east
▥ Clyde
▦ Solway
▧ Borders
▨ Others

Burgh tax assessments by region 1535 to 1705: all regions

ML

312

Taxation of burghs

Edinburgh dominated the Forth Basin, with all the old, established burghs like Haddington, Linlithgow and Stirling progressively slipping against it. The rise, particularly between 1590 and 1650, of a number of small Fife ports, whose size belied the level of their trading activity, is one of the most notable features of the tax rolls; but their sharp fall after 1680 was equally spectacular.

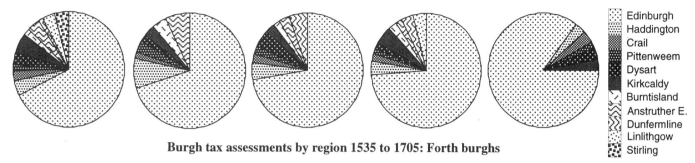

Burgh tax assessments by region 1535 to 1705: Forth burghs

Legend: Edinburgh, Haddington, Crail, Pittenweem, Dysart, Kirkcaldy, Burntisland, Anstruther E., Dunfermline, Linlithgow, Stirling

A different perspective on the fortunes of provincial centres - like Aberdeen, Dundee, Perth and Glasgow- emerges when they are considered, within their own regions. Although Aberdeen was slipping in terms of both real and percentage share of Scotland's overseas trade in the later sixteenth century, its tax assessments were relatively stable because it was consolidating its position as the unrivalled market centre for the whole of the north-east. No other burgh ever accounted for more than 15% of the region's taxation.

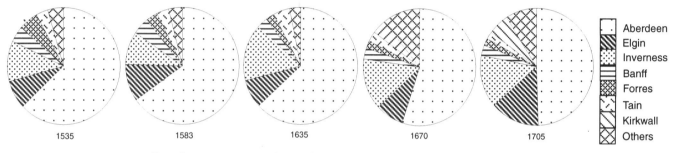

1535   1583   1635   1670   1705

Burgh tax assessment by region 1535 to 1705: North-east burghs

Legend: Aberdeen, Elgin, Inverness, Banff, Forres, Tain, Kirkwall, Others

Amongst the Tay burghs, Dundee and Perth stood out as rival regional centres, together accounting for between 58% and 66% of taxation in the period. Their progress over the period, however, was sharply divergent, as was that of what were otherwise the two largest ports, St Andrews and Montrose.

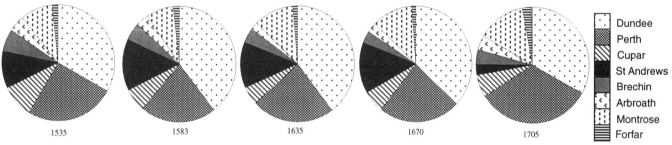

1535   1583   1635   1670   1705

Burgh tax assessments by region 1535 to 1705: Tay burghs

Legend: Dundee, Perth, Cupar, St Andrews, Brechin, Arbroath, Montrose, Forfar

The marked rise of Glasgow, described as the most spectacular of the patterns in the seventeenth-century tax rolls, stemmed largely, at least until 1635, from its success in funnelling regional as well as local trade through itself. Its activity in overseas trade was more modest.

The two other major regional centres - Ayr and Dumfries - began to slip against Glasgow after the 1580s; both languished after 1650. The decay of the other Solway towns from the 1580s onwards, however, was real as well as relative.

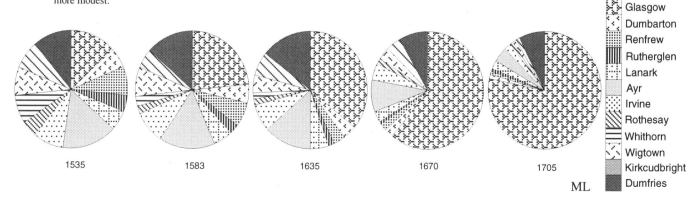

1535   1583   1635   1670   1705

Legend: Glasgow, Dumbarton, Renfrew, Rutherglen, Lanark, Ayr, Irvine, Rothesay, Whithorn, Wigtown, Kirkcudbright, Dumfries

ML

Assessments on burghs 1587

In 1587 the crown levied an unusual tax on the burghs, to make up for the loss it had sustained by farming out the customs since 1583; it reflected the income made by each burgh from trade. This customs tax can be compared with the assessments made in a conventional tax levied a month earlier, which reflected a broader set of criteria, including burgh income and lands, and inland trade as well as exports overseas.

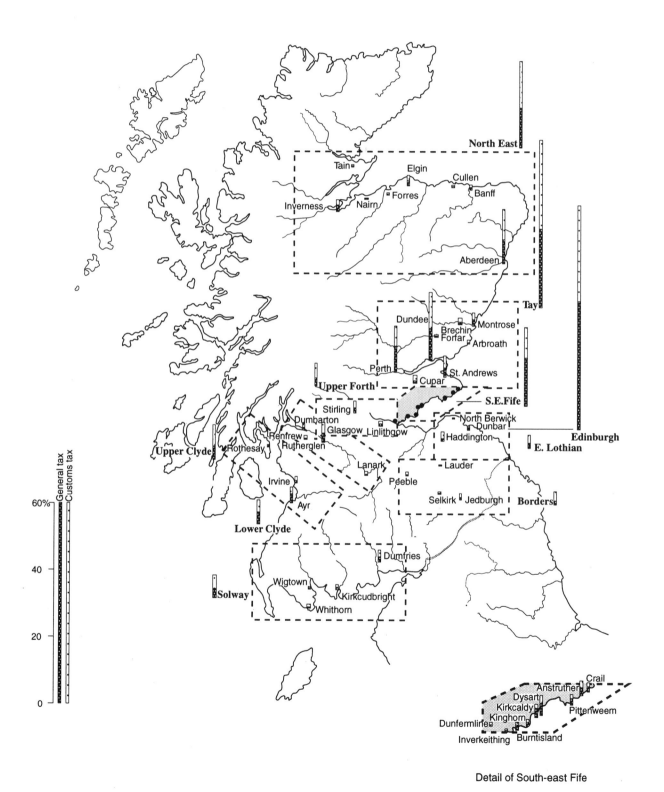

Detail of South-east Fife

Tax and customs assessments 1587

ML

Assessments on burghs 1587

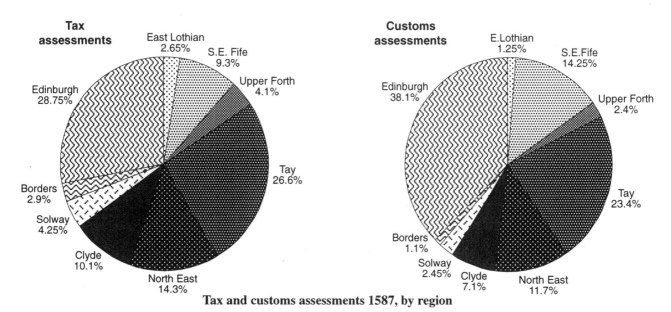

Tax and customs assessments 1587, by region

Every region paid less in customs tax, except for Edinburgh, which had alone accounted for 61% of custom paid 1581-3, and south-east Fife, where every port paid more. All the towns or ports of the Borders, Solway, Upper Clyde (including Glasgow) and the Upper Forth (except for Inverkeithing) paid less. Ayr was the only west-coast port with a large enough stake in the export trade for its assessment to rise. Of the Tay towns, only Perth and Montrose paid more; and in the north-east a trio of Inverness, Elgin and Banff, which probably stemmed from their trade in salmon. Some entries for ports - like North Berwick, Nairn, Irvine, Whithorn and Wigtown - are markedly lower in the customs tax and they may have relied on coastal rather than overseas trade. Yet no burgh was rendered exempt in the customs tax, even if some, like Tain and Forfar, had their assessments cut to a nominal fraction: every royal burgh, whether port or inland town, provincial or local market centre, depended to some extent on the export trade in staple commodities - wool, skins, hides, cloth, fish, salt or coal.

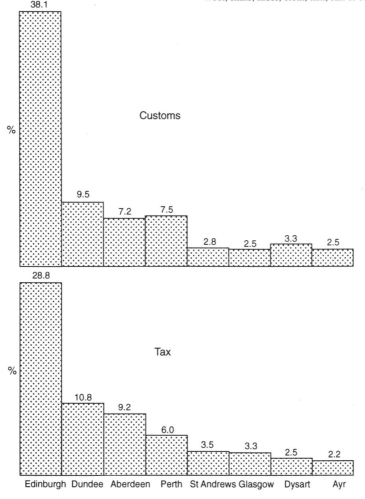

Tax and Customs assessments on leading burghs 1587, as a percentage of total assessments on all burghs

ML

Burgh tax assessments: Aberdeen and Edinburgh

Tax rolls are, at best, only a crude indicator of the overall size of urban populations. Scottish burghs were lightly taxed by comparison with their English counterparts: Aberdeen, the second or third largest town in Scotland, had only 445 taxpayers in 1448, which would have put it below such small English towns as Wells, Bridgnorth or Barking with taxpaying populations of about 900, yet coming fortieth or below in the league table of towns paying the lay subsidy of 1377. So comparisons with English towns on this basis are unsound, as are attempts to use English multipliers to produce an overall population figure for Scottish towns. But comparisons of numbers of taxpayers can be used to give a rough indication of the growth of a burgh or to compare the different sizes of towns - Aberdeen had 445 taxpayers in 1448, 553 in 1608 and 569 in 1637; Edinburgh had 1,245 in 1583, 1,152 in 1605 and 1,548 in 1637.

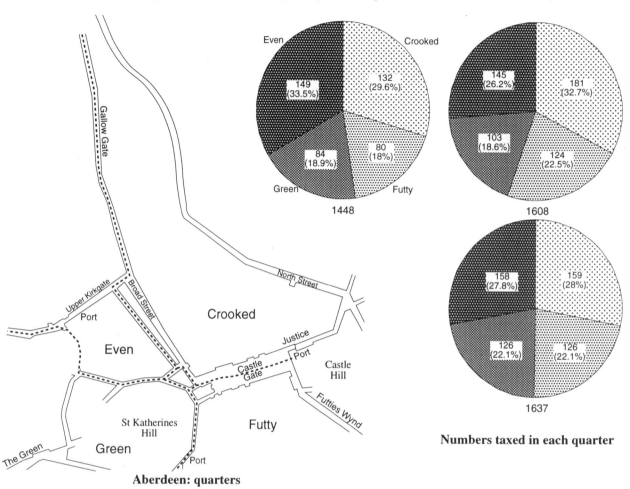

Aberdeen: quarters

Numbers taxed in each quarter

Tax rolls may also be used, as here, to compare the economic structure both of different towns and of different parts of a town. The pyramid of wealth for Aberdeen is quite differently shaped from that for Edinburgh, reflecting Aberdeen's proportionately smaller number of craftsmen and Edinburgh's greater extremes of wealth and poverty. Aberdeen, like most Scottish towns, did not have a genuine poor quarter but there was a greater concentration of craftsmen in the Green; the top 10% of taxpayers owned 38% of wealth.

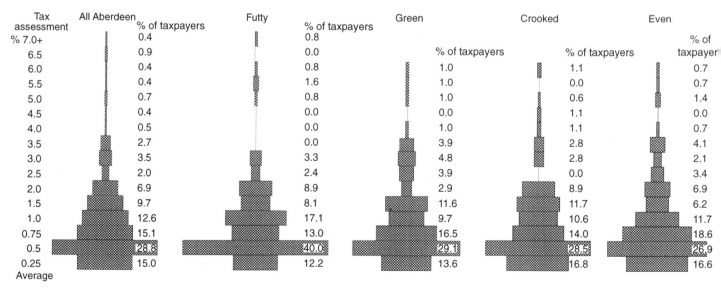

Tax assessment %	All Aberdeen % of taxpayers	Futty % of taxpayers	Green % of taxpayers	Crooked % of taxpayers	Even % of taxpayers
7.0+	0.4	0.8			
6.5	0.9	0.0			
6.0	0.4	0.8	1.0	1.1	0.7
5.5	0.4	1.6	1.0	0.0	0.7
5.0	0.7	0.8	1.0	0.6	1.4
4.5	0.4	0.0	0.0	1.1	0.0
4.0	0.5	0.0	1.0	1.1	0.7
3.5	2.7	0.0	3.9	2.8	4.1
3.0	3.5	3.3	4.8	2.8	2.1
2.5	2.0	2.4	3.9	0.0	3.4
2.0	6.9	8.9	2.9	8.9	6.9
1.5	9.7	8.1	11.6	11.7	6.2
1.0	12.6	17.1	9.7	10.6	11.7
0.75	15.1	13.0	16.5	14.0	18.6
0.5	28.8	40.0	29.1	28.5	26.9
0.25	15.0	12.2	13.6	16.8	16.6
Average					

Aberdeen : quarters

Social structure of burgh tax assessments, Aberdeen 1608

ML

Burgh tax assessments: Aberdeen and Edinburgh

In Edinburgh the crafts until 1583 paid a fixed 20% of taxation and their distinctive structure was not unlike that of the poorest of the burgh's quarters, the south-east. Their own pyramid also reflects the numbers within the new craft aristocracy, of tailors, goldsmiths and the like. Yet for Edinburgh tax statistics are distinctly misleading because lawyers escaped taxation. A measure of their wealth can be gleaned from an unusual contribution list of 1565 which included 31 of them; by the time of the poll tax of 1694 the lawyers paid more than all the burgh's merchants and craftsmen put together.

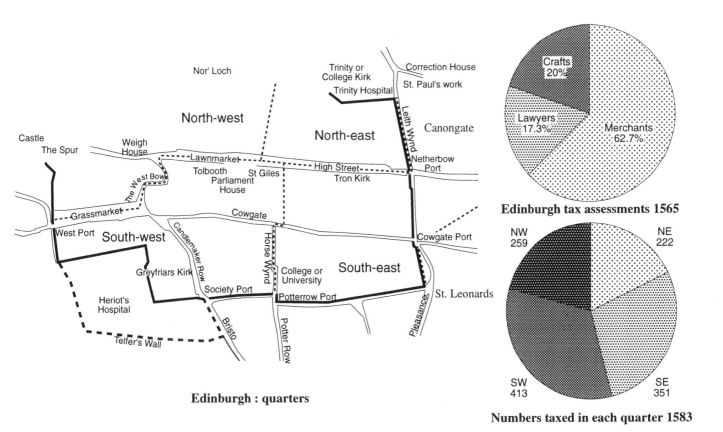

Edinburgh : quarters

Edinburgh tax assessments 1565

Numbers taxed in each quarter 1583

In the capital the top 10% owned a remarkable 56% of the burgh's wealth. Here, there was a much sharper contrast between the four quarters: the north-west, which included the north side of the Lawnmarket, had a marked concentration of wealth within it; the south-east, below and to the east of St. Giles', had already by far the largest numbers as well as the greatest proportion of poor. The two southern quarters would be the area which would experience the largest increases in population over the next fifty years and in 1635 have some of the lowest average rents.

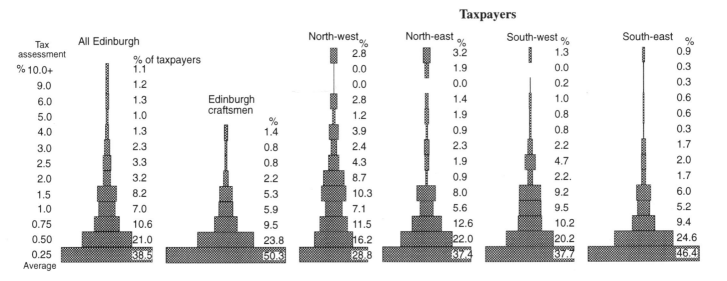

Social structure of burgh tax assessments, Edinburgh 1583

ML

Valued rents of burghs 1639

Conventional tax assessments, which reflect a number of different indicators of burgh performance and income, are not an accurate guide to urban populations. A valued rent roll of 1639 is likely to be a better guide to size, at least of medium-sized and smaller towns. It suggests that, for example, Elgin, Inverness, Lauder and Rothesay were all rather larger than their tax assessments suggest. Correspondingly, many ports (as might be expected) were much smaller than their assessments indicate, but (less expectedly) so were local market centres like Banff, Brechin and Lanark. The Glasgow rental figure suggests an earlier and greater rise, at least of population: a total of £23,644 falls in line with the estimate of a visitor of 1636 who thought it had between 6,000 and 7,000 adult communicants, suggesting a population of 10,000-12,000.

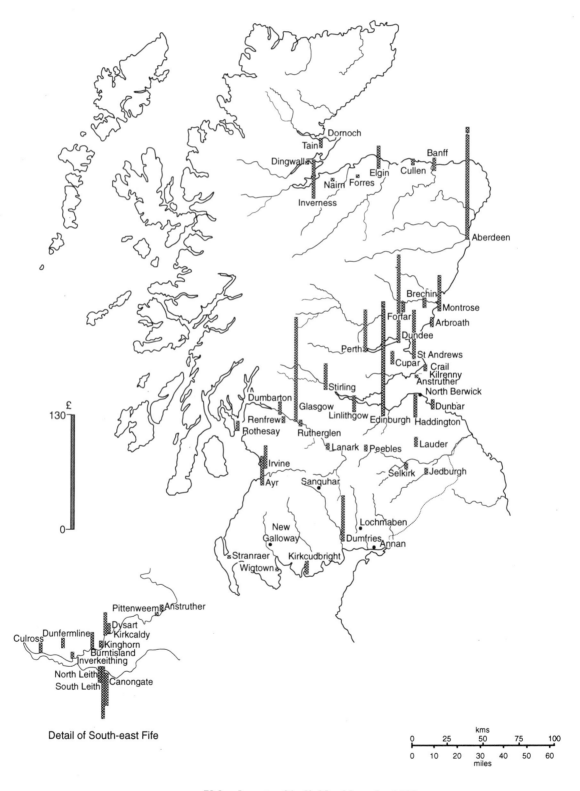

Detail of South-east Fife

Valued rents of individual burghs 1639

ML

Valued rents of burghs 1639

The valued rents of 1639 can be compared with the conventional tax assessments made in 1635. As might be expected, small but highly active ports, like Wigtown (but not Dunbar) and all those of south-east Fife, were taxed more highly than they were rated for rents. The same was true of small but bustling market towns like Jedburgh,

Selkirk, Cupar and Lanark. The most intriguing contrast is for Glasgow, rated well above Dundee and Perth, but still in 1635 only taxed on a par with Perth; this suggests that its rise in the seventeenth century was initially triggered mainly by population growth, which after 1650 would come to be matched by economic expansion on all fronts.

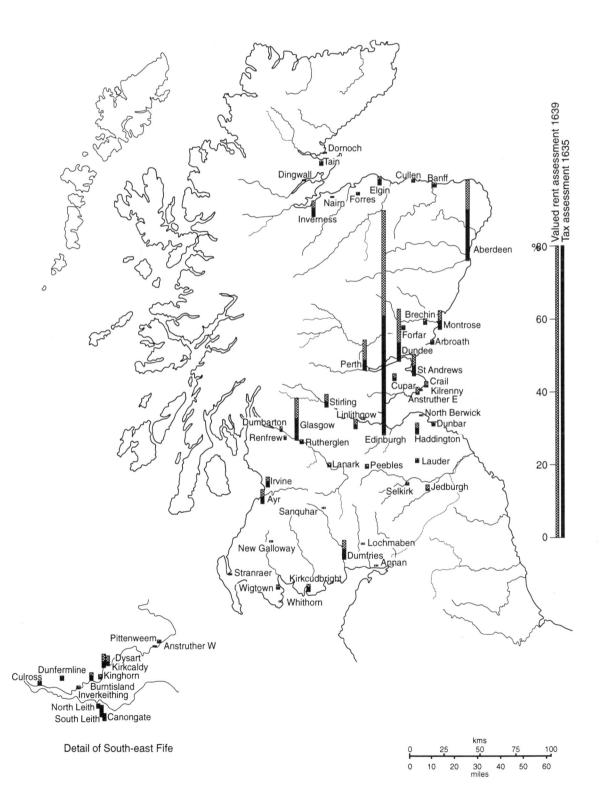

Detail of South-east Fife

Valued rents of 1639 and conventional tax assessments of 1635

ML

Valued rents of burghs 1639

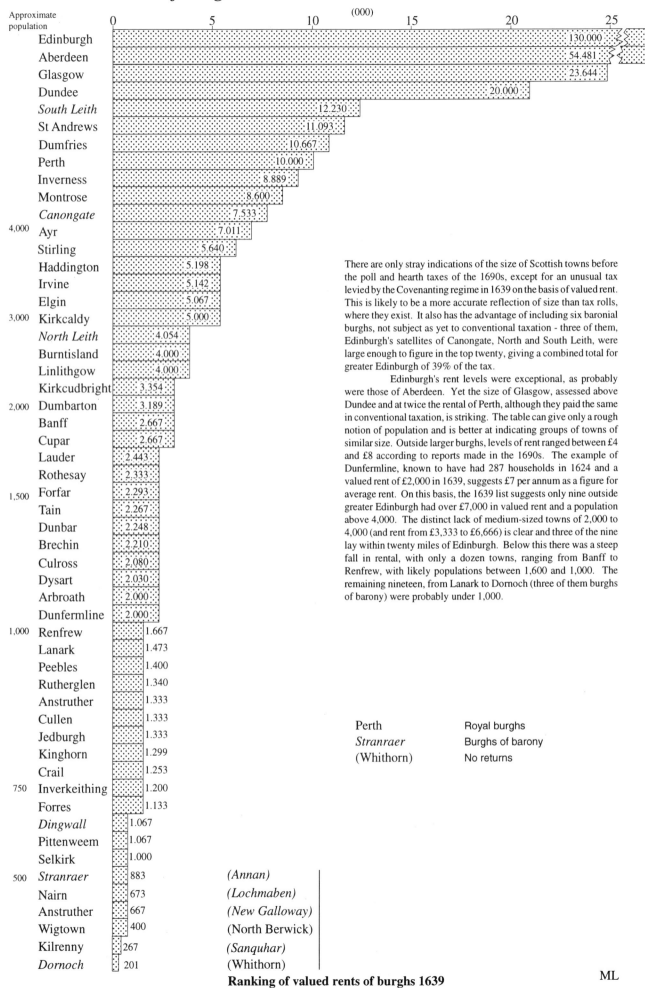

Approximate population	Burgh	Value
	Edinburgh	130.000
	Aberdeen	54.481
	Glasgow	23.644
	Dundee	20.000
	South Leith	12.230
	St Andrews	11.093
	Dumfries	10.667
	Perth	10.000
	Inverness	8.889
	Montrose	8.600
	Canongate	7.533
4,000	Ayr	7.011
	Stirling	5.640
	Haddington	5.198
	Irvine	5.142
	Elgin	5.067
3,000	Kirkcaldy	5.000
	North Leith	4.054
	Burntisland	4.000
	Linlithgow	4.000
	Kirkcudbright	3.354
2,000	Dumbarton	3.189
	Banff	2.667
	Cupar	2.667
	Lauder	2.443
	Rothesay	2.333
1,500	Forfar	2.293
	Tain	2.267
	Dunbar	2.248
	Brechin	2.210
	Culross	2.080
	Dysart	2.030
	Arbroath	2.000
	Dunfermline	2.000
1,000	Renfrew	1.667
	Lanark	1.473
	Peebles	1.400
	Rutherglen	1.340
	Anstruther	1.333
	Cullen	1.333
	Jedburgh	1.333
	Kinghorn	1.299
	Crail	1.253
750	Inverkeithing	1.200
	Forres	1.133
	Dingwall	1.067
	Pittenweem	1.067
	Selkirk	1.000
500	*Stranraer*	883
	Nairn	673
	Anstruther	667
	Wigtown	400
	Kilrenny	267
	Dornoch	201

There are only stray indications of the size of Scottish towns before the poll and hearth taxes of the 1690s, except for an unusual tax levied by the Covenanting regime in 1639 on the basis of valued rent. This is likely to be a more accurate reflection of size than tax rolls, where they exist. It also has the advantage of including six baronial burghs, not subject as yet to conventional taxation - three of them, Edinburgh's satellites of Canongate, North and South Leith, were large enough to figure in the top twenty, giving a combined total for greater Edinburgh of 39% of the tax.

Edinburgh's rent levels were exceptional, as probably were those of Aberdeen. Yet the size of Glasgow, assessed above Dundee and at twice the rental of Perth, although they paid the same in conventional taxation, is striking. The table can give only a rough notion of population and is better at indicating groups of towns of similar size. Outside larger burghs, levels of rent ranged between £4 and £8 according to reports made in the 1690s. The example of Dunfermline, known to have had 287 households in 1624 and a valued rent of £2,000 in 1639, suggests £7 per annum as a figure for average rent. On this basis, the 1639 list suggests only nine outside greater Edinburgh had over £7,000 in valued rent and a population above 4,000. The distinct lack of medium-sized towns of 2,000 to 4,000 (and rent from £3,333 to £6,666) is clear and three of the nine lay within twenty miles of Edinburgh. Below this there was a steep fall in rental, with only a dozen towns, ranging from Banff to Renfrew, with likely populations between 1,600 and 1,000. The remaining nineteen, from Lanark to Dornoch (three of them burghs of barony) were probably under 1,000.

	(Annan)	
	(Lochmaben)	
	(New Galloway)	
	(North Berwick)	
	(Sanquhar)	
	(Whithorn)	

Perth	Royal burghs
Stranraer	Burghs of barony
(Whithorn)	No returns

Ranking of valued rents of burghs 1639

ML

320

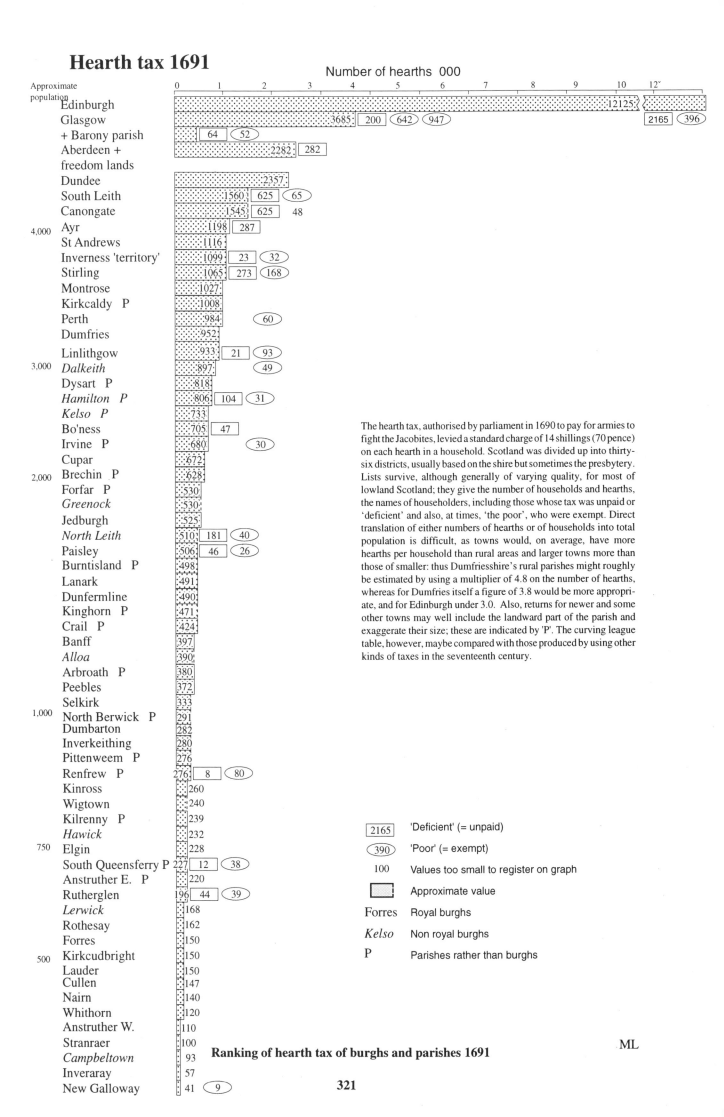

Hearth tax 1691

Number of hearths 000

Approximate population

Burgh/Parish	Hearths	'Deficient'	'Poor'
Edinburgh	12125		
Glasgow	3685	200, 2165	642, 947, 396
+ Barony parish	64		52
Aberdeen + freedom lands	2282	282	
Dundee	2357		
South Leith	1560	625	65
Canongate	1545	625	48
Ayr	1198	287	
St Andrews	1116		
Inverness 'territory'	1099	23	32
Stirling	1065	273	168
Montrose	1027		
Kirkcaldy P	1008		
Perth	984		60
Dumfries	952		
Linlithgow	933	21	93
Dalkeith	897		49
Dysart P	818		
Hamilton P	806	104	31
Kelso P	733		
Bo'ness	705	47	
Irvine P	680		30
Cupar	672		
Brechin P	628		
Forfar P	530		
Greenock	530		
Jedburgh	525		
North Leith	510	181	40
Paisley	506	46	26
Burntisland P	498		
Lanark	491		
Dunfermline	490		
Kinghorn P	471		
Crail P	424		
Banff	397		
Alloa	390		
Arbroath P	380		
Peebles	372		
Selkirk	333		
North Berwick P	291		
Dumbarton	282		
Inverkeithing	280		
Pittenweem P	276		
Renfrew P	276	8	80
Kinross	260		
Wigtown	240		
Kilrenny P	239		
Hawick	232		
Elgin	228		
South Queensferry P	227	12	38
Anstruther E. P	220		
Rutherglen	196	44	39
Lerwick	168		
Rothesay	162		
Forres	150		
Kirkcudbright	150		
Lauder	150		
Cullen	147		
Nairn	140		
Whithorn	120		
Anstruther W.	110		
Stranraer	100		
Campbeltown	93		
Inveraray	57		
New Galloway	41		9

The hearth tax, authorised by parliament in 1690 to pay for armies to fight the Jacobites, levied a standard charge of 14 shillings (70 pence) on each hearth in a household. Scotland was divided up into thirty-six districts, usually based on the shire but sometimes the presbytery. Lists survive, although generally of varying quality, for most of lowland Scotland; they give the number of households and hearths, the names of householders, including those whose tax was unpaid or 'deficient' and also, at times, 'the poor', who were exempt. Direct translation of either numbers of hearths or of households into total population is difficult, as towns would, on average, have more hearths per household than rural areas and larger towns more than those of smaller: thus Dumfriesshire's rural parishes might roughly be estimated by using a multiplier of 4.8 on the number of hearths, whereas for Dumfries itself a figure of 3.8 would be more appropriate, and for Edinburgh under 3.0. Also, returns for newer and some other towns may well include the landward part of the parish and exaggerate their size; these are indicated by 'P'. The curving league table, however, maybe compared with those produced by using other kinds of taxes in the seventeenth century.

Legend:

2165 'Deficient' (= unpaid)

390 'Poor' (= exempt)

100 Values too small to register on graph

▭ Approximate value

Forres Royal burghs

Kelso Non royal burghs

P Parishes rather than burghs

Ranking of hearth tax of burghs and parishes 1691

ML

321

Hearth tax 1691

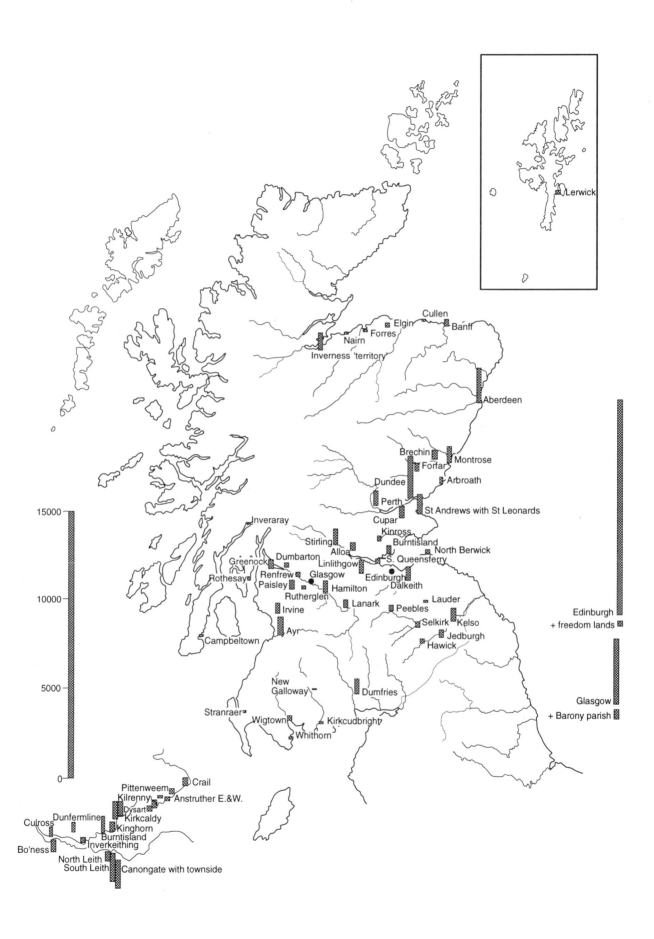

Number of paid hearths 1691

ML

Hearth tax 1691

The hearth tax can also be used to analyse the structure of urban society. The proportion of single hearths may be used to compare the numbers living in single-hearth houses in different towns, or between different parts of the same town. The differences in the upper layers of the pyramid of wealth would be indicated by variations in the proportion of multiple hearths.

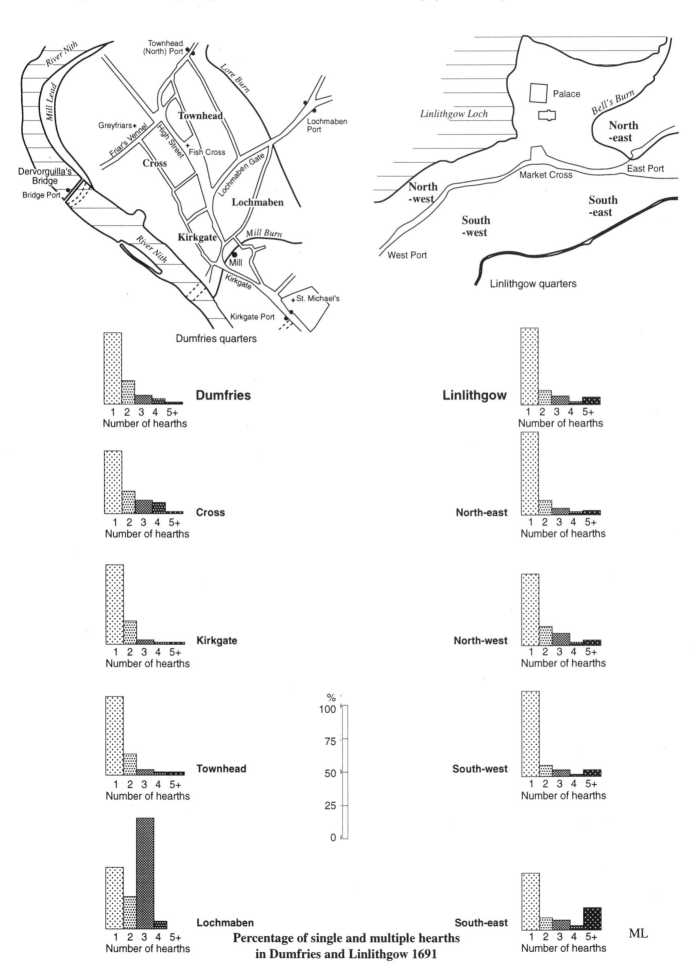

Percentage of single and multiple hearths in Dumfries and Linlithgow 1691

ML

Poll tax 1694

The 1694 poll tax was imposed by act of Parliament on 29 May 1693 in order to raise money for the armed forces and Edinburgh Town Council decreed on 15 August 1694 that all householders were required to 'give up their names, qualities, degrees and value of their estates with a full and true list under their hand of their whole servants apprentices and residents within their families ...'. This information was required in order to determine the tax due from each household, but had the added virtue of providing a detailed account of Edinburgh's taxable households. Overall, the poll tax data, though incomplete, provide the only available information on household structure and distribution in late seventeenth-century Edinburgh. The main features of note are that large multi-generation households were not common, and household composition varied from the inner to the outer areas of the town, notwithstanding the compact geographical nature of pre-New Town Edinburgh.

Although the unknown, but probably large number of 'poor' were exempt and despite the eroded condition of several lists, the poll tax provides a valuable survey of both overall population and individual household structure. The lists for 'greater' Edinburgh comprise the seven inner parishes - College Kirk, Greyfriars, Lady Yester, New Kirk, Old Kirk, Tolbooth, Tron - together with Canongate, North and South Leith and the sprawling West Kirk parish. In all, some 20,600 inhabitants are detailed, from 5,514 households. The Figure below shows population by parish. Some 13,612 (66%) of the inhabitants were crowded into the 7 inner parishes, emphasising the congested nature of old town life.

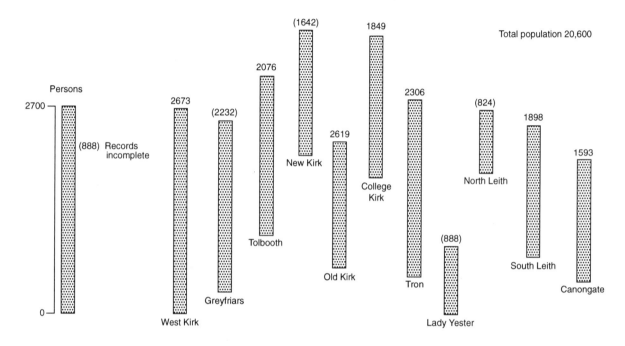

Population of Edinburgh from poll tax, by parish

The bar-charts below indicates the number of households in each parish and average household size. The average for those households known to be complete is included for the inner parishes (the regulations did not require children in some taxation categories to be listed), although some households were mainly in the central parishes, with fewer in the more rural outskirts.

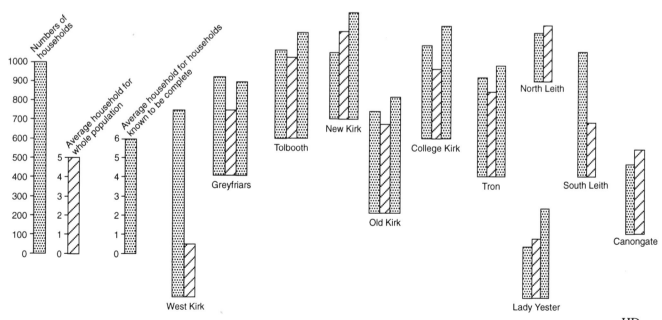

Number of households and average size households in Edinburgh 1694

HD

Poll tax 1694

The bar-charts illustrate household structure, which varied markedly in the different parishes. The highest percentages of children and servants were in the central parishes, while over 60% of the West Kirk households consisted of married couples only, compared with 30% in New Kirk and an overall average of 40%. The percentages of 'others', that is, lodgers and resident kin, although small, were also higher in the inner areas.

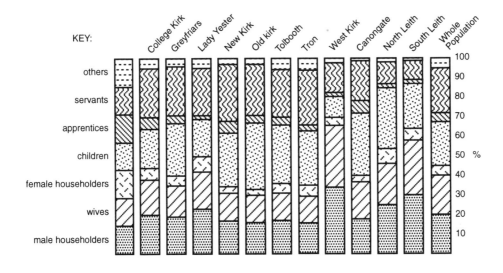

Distribution of members of households 1694

The bar-charts give household statistics for five parishes, across the urban-rural range. The percentages for A,B,C and D relate to characteristics of larger households, and show a fairly consistent pattern, with the more socially and occupationally diverse New and Old Kirk parishes generally boasting higher numbers. Conversely, section E is a complete reversal, as households without servants were a feature of the outer, poorer areas. Canongate parish displays an intermediate structure, falling between the more complex inner area and the semi-rural West Kirk parish.

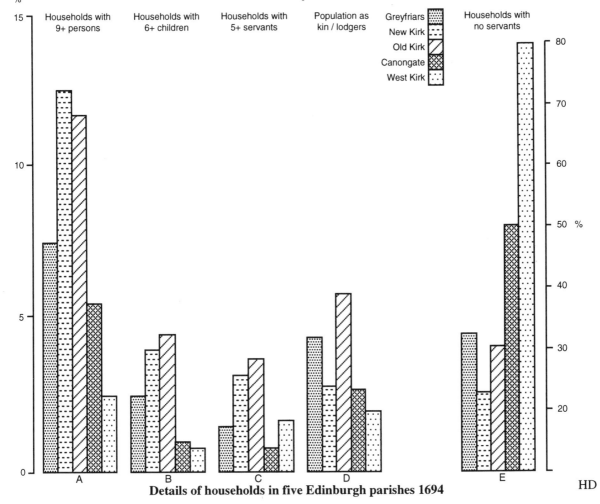

Details of households in five Edinburgh parishes 1694

HD

Prices and wages

The fiars 'struck' each Candlemas by the sheriff courts provide an unparallelled series of seventeenth- and eighteenth-century grain prices. Established by a jury of landowners, farmers and merchants, these referred to, and took the date of, the preceding year's crop. Their purpose was to regulate the settlement of debts, the conversion of rents in kind to cash, and the discharge of any other payments based upon that crop.

Surviving fiars seldom pre-date the 1620s, although isolated examples from a number of counties show that they were being struck as early as the mid-sixteenth century. Only for Fife is there to be found anything approaching an unbroken series charting the movement of grain prices during the second half of the sixteenth century.

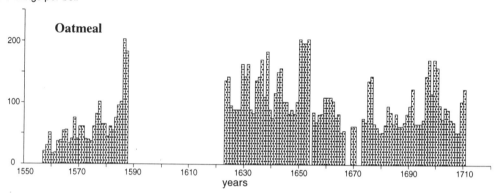

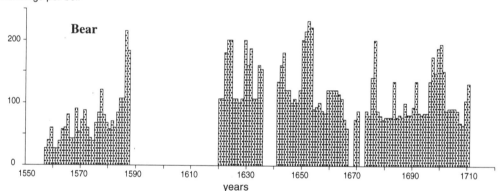

Fiars for oatmeal and bear, Fife

Carefully regulated markets were one of the earliest features of Scottish burgh organisation. The quality and price of a great many goods and services were subject to intermittent legislation as burgh officials strove to protect jealously guarded privileges and counter the medieval crimes of forestalling and regrating.

Wheat bread, ale and tallow were of particular concern and were subject to annual price statutes for much of the sixteenth and seventeenth centuries. These ostensibly set prices on the basis of the cost of the raw materials from which they were made; a process most explicit in the case of wheat bread. Tables were produced allowing burgh officials, after having established the price at which wheat was commonly sold, to read off the price at which wheat bread should be sold. Such tables were in use as early as the twelfth century and find counterparts in England and Ireland. The same principle was used to fix the price of ale and, in Aberdeen at least, was probably also used to set the price of tallow.

It is for Edinburgh and Glasgow that the most complete series are available. Predating the emergence of regular fiars prices, these burgh statutes are invaluable as the only major price series covering the sixteenth-century price revolution. They do, however, demand some care as it is uncertain how strictly they were adhered to or to what extent they were subject to political influence.

AGi

Prices and wages

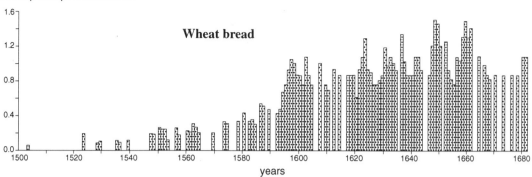

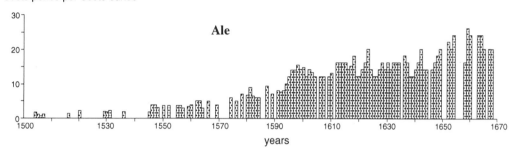

Statute prices, Edinburgh town council, 1500 to 1700

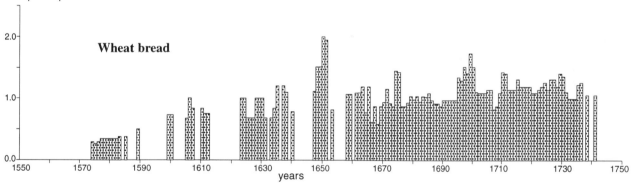

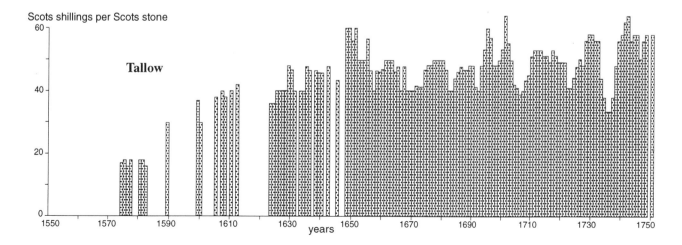

Statute prices, Glasgow town council, 1550 to 1750

AGi

Prices and wages

As individual building projects were generally of short duration, it is only in accounts of the crown and the principal Scottish burghs that long-term series of labourers' wage-rates are to be found. These accounts vary greatly in quality and attempting to determine an 'annual wage-rate' is fraught with difficulties. Whether or not food and/or drink was provided and the nature of the work being undertaken could both affect level of wages.

The guiding principle has been to determine the maximum wage-rate commonly paid during the summer season to labourers who received nothing extra in the way of food. The only problem with this method is that during the late sixteenth and early seven-

teenth centuries it appears that wages were increased, first by additional payments for drink and for specific tasks and only later as an increase in basic wage-rates. Thus although the general trend is unquestionable, its precise timing may reflect the method by which these annual wage-rates have been determined.

The Edinburgh series is based upon accounts of the Town Council and of the Masters of Work relative to Edinburgh. The Aberdeen series is based upon wage rates recorded in the Kirk and Bridge Work Accounts as well as the annual wage-maxima set by the Town Council throughout much of the second half of the seventeenth century.

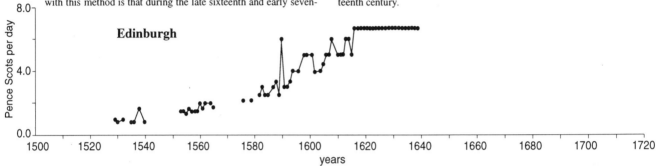

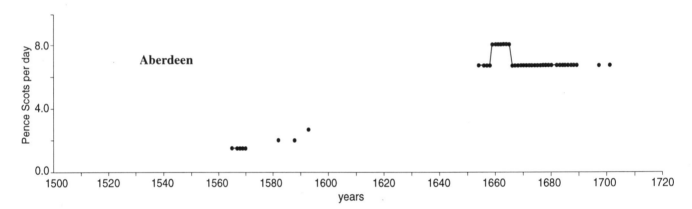

Wage rates of Scottish urban day-labourers

Successive Scottish administrations found coinage debasement to be a useful and most profitable source of revenue. A fiscal device enhancing the face value of a coin far above its intrinsic value, this policy led to the issue of coins with a progressively lower silver or gold content. Thus Scottish coins struck in 1601 contained but a

fifth of the silver or gold used in coins of the same value issued at the end of the fifteenth century - a depreciation which far outstripped that experienced in England. Concentrated in the second half of the sixteenth century, the debasement of the Scottish coinage coincides with, and is clearly relevant to, the contemporary rise in wages and prices, shown in the preceding charts.

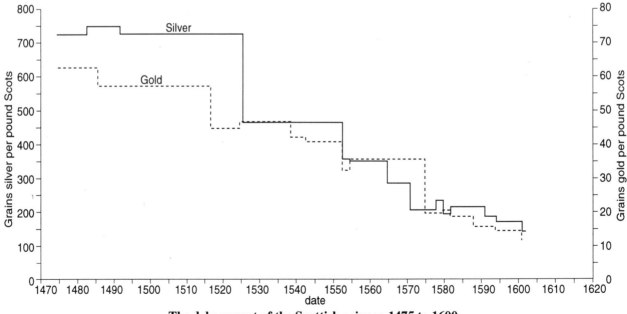

The debasement of the Scottish coinage 1475 to 1600

AGi

The church

Early Christianity

The distinctive memorial stones of Galloway and the Borders, many with inscriptions and clearly akin to those of Wales, show that from the fifth century an episcopally organised church spread through southern Scotland, though doubtless much disrupted by Anglian settlements from the sixth century, a disruption which may explain why the memorial stones (and Ecles names) have an upland distribution, the early Anglian settlement being stronger on the coast and in the Tweed Valley. Nonetheless when the Angles became Christian after 633 they supported monasteries at Coldingham and Melrose and a see at Abercorn, whose Celtic names suggest that they took over British religious establishments there. The low Latin word for a church, Eclesia, entered British as Ecles and also entered Pictish. It has left a scatter of place-names which suggest British influence on early Christianity in southern Pictland.

The spread of Christianity in the period of Anglian expansion may be documented by cemeteries containing graves without grave-goods, oriented east-west, the bodies extended and enclosed in rough stone coffins. One such cemetery is associated with a memorial stone (Kirkliston south of Abercorn), but in general the dates of burials are inferred not proved. The extension of Christianity from Lothian to Fife which the distribution suggests agrees with one scrap of literary evidence: a visit by Cuthbert from Northumbria to the Picts in Fife.

Other sculpture of early date, including, some of Anglian character, is difficult to date, but is generally later than the British memorial stones. Such other sculpture is indicated on the map only for the southern area (including Dunbartonshire). The equivalent northern sculpture, and the main index of Pictish Christianity must be the Class II symbol stones with their elaborate relief crosses (see Pictish Monuments). There is little evidence to support Bede's claim that St Columba converted the northern Picts, and early Columban monasteries in Pictland (if any) cannot be named.

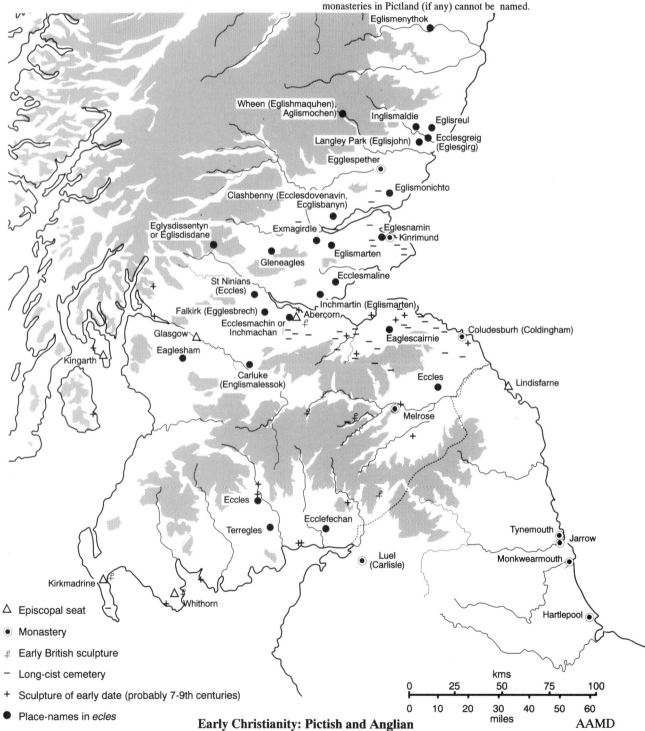

△ Episcopal seat

◉ Monastery

ℓ Early British sculpture

— Long-cist cemetery

+ Sculpture of early date (probably 7-9th centuries)

● Place-names in *ecles*

Early Christianity: Pictish and Anglian

AAMD

330

Early Christianity

The pilgrimage of Columba to Iona in 563 extended Irish church discipline and fervour to Scotland. Columba had a number of smaller monasteries on Tiree beside Lochawe, and an important one on Hinba (unidentified). He also founded Durrow in Offaly County in Ireland. In 633 Iona monks's went to Lindisfarne, whence Christianity spread through much of England. When Lindisfarne chose in 663 to follow the practices of 'St Peter' and reject those of Columba, the dissenters returned to Iona and thence to Inishbofin and Mayo in western Ireland and from these places new missions to Frisia and elsewhere on the Continent emerged.

But there were other, less well recorded Irish pilgrimages, of St Maelrubha to Applecross, of St Moluag to Lismore and of St Donnan to Eigg, the last a hermitage (probably like the remains on Eileach an Naoimh) but later an anchoritical monastery. The spread of Christianity from Ireland can be measured by the monasteries these men founded.

Another measure may be the distribution of simple incised crosses on stones often in graveyards, which seem to mark Christian burials in areas influenced by Irish Christianity. The concentration in mid-Argyll and the Inner Hebrides is to be expected, but there is no literary evidence of Irish influence to lead us to expect those in Galloway and Man. The scattered far northern examples fit with the tradition of Irish peregrinating monks who left their traces in names like Pabbay (Priest's Isle). Such Norse names must have ousted any earlier Gaelic name.

The complementary distribution-map for names containing cill 'church' or ⌀ 'churchyard' shows remarkable similarity of distribution. The far north has none, having been overlaid by Norse names. There is a sprinkling of cill names up the Great Glen in Ross and in Fife, and the former is perhaps one of the few pieces of evidence that Columban missionary effort was effective among the northern Picts. It is thought that cill names were formed before 800.

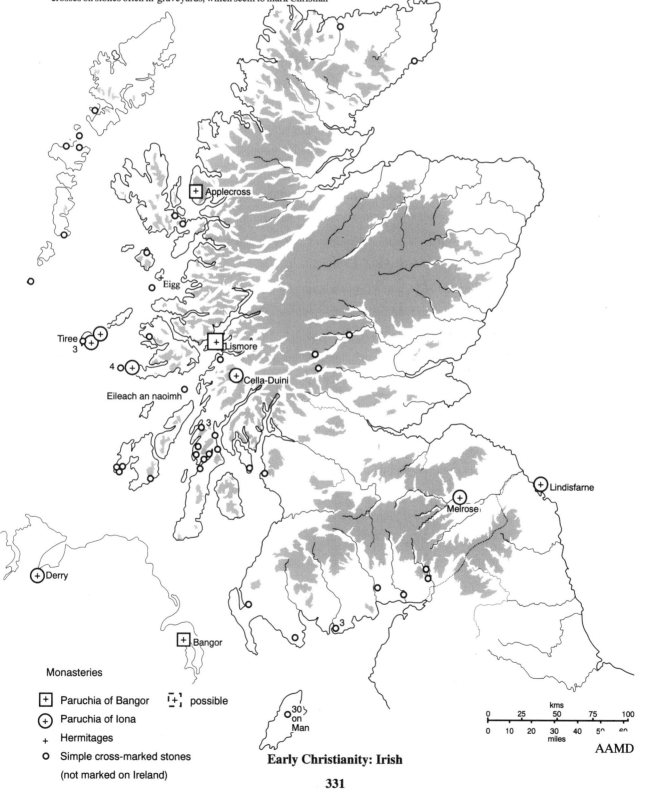

Applecross

Eigg

Tiree
3

4

Lismore

Cella-Duini

Eileach an naoimh

3

Lindisfarne

Melrose

Derry

Bangor

30
on
Man

kms
0   25   50   75   100

0 10 20 30 40 50 60
miles

AAMD

Early Christianity: Irish

Early Christianity

'Annat' comes from a Latin word itself a shortening of *antiquitas*, antiquity and seems to have been borrowed into Irish to mean the mother-church of a paruchia (that is a group of scattered monastic houses acknowledging a particular head). In Scotland where it is much more frequent than in Ireland, the distribution shows that it does not have this meaning. It is found in a few cases associated with an old graveyard, once with traces of a church building. Very rarely these Annat sites have a known dedication. Most Annats however are within one or two kilometres of, but not at, a church site, and it has been suggested that they represent the old (or former site of the) church.

Although the word is Gaelic, it is thinly represented in Argyll, and it has been suggested that therefore it is later than the early phase of Christianising; it could represent dislocation caused by the Viking raids and settlements. This fits the Western Isles distribution, but not the eastern examples. Annat might therefore represent a very early graveyard, perhaps pre-Christian, abandoned gradually when an early church site was established, and in that case would belong to the seventh or eighth centuries.

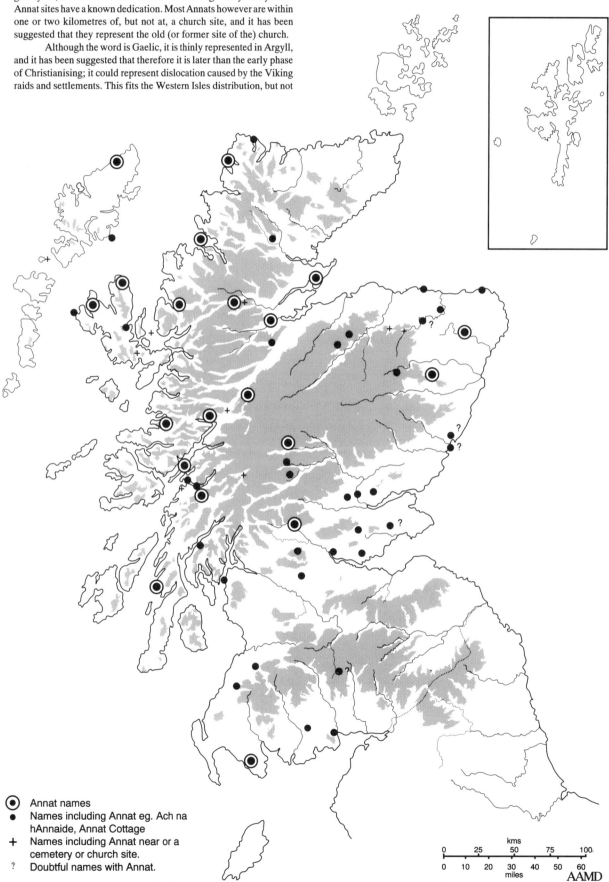

⊙	Annat names
●	Names including Annat eg. Ach na hAnnaide, Annat Cottage
+	Names including Annat near or a cemetery or church site.
?	Doubtful names with Annat.

Early Christianity: place-names containing *annat* in Scotland

AAMD

The post-Viking church

This map shows centres for which there is documentary evidence, often from a much later period, of the existence of a community of clerics with characteristics which suggest that they existed before the twelfth century. Some are Culdees and probably monastic; others have abbots and may have been monastic. Then there are thirteenth-century families which claim the title 'abbot of X', from which we may deduce that the abbot of a community elsewhere possessed X as his endowment (e.g. Edzell, a possession of the abbot of Brechin). The large parishes in southern Scotland mapped here are probably only a haphazard selection, mentioned in written records, of those which existed by this date; these were minsters or small colleges of clerics, and something similar to them existed at Deer, Clova, Methven, Dunblane and doubtless elsewhere north of the Forth.

The post-Viking church: major centres before 1100

AAMD

The post-Viking Church

Sculptured stones in southern Scotland in the post-Viking period (which may be seen as complementary to the Class II and Class III sculptured stones in the Pictish area indicated above are as difficult to date as is earlier sculpture. This map represents most of the known sculptures probably datable about 850 to about 1200 found in southern Scotland i.e. within Strathclyde and Lothian to the south of the boundary with Dalriada to the north-west and Pictland to the north-east. (Sculptures in northern England are not shown.) Some are found at old ecclesiastical centres such as Abercorn, Aberlady, Hoddom and show the influence of Anglian sculpture as well as later forms, notably hog-backed sepulchral stones. The finest collection of these hog-backed post-Viking sculptures is at Govan.

The concentrations suggest that there are flourishing ecclesiastical centres on Bute, on the lower Clyde, in Galloway and in Nithsdale, most probably at Kingarth, Glasgow, Whithorn and Hoddom respectively - though Glasgow itself has only recently (1994) produced an early cross head, not mapped here. However these sculptures are predominantly sepulchral and their fewness in the east probably shows a different fashion in commemoration of the dead rather than a less-developed ecclesiastical organisation. In the Tweed valley at the Hirsel near Coldstream have been found the only remains of an early proprietary church known in Scotland.

● Sculpture
+ Proprietary church

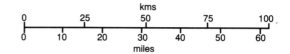

kms

| 0 | | 25 | | 50 | | 75 | | 100 |

miles

The post-Viking Church: sculptured stones in southern Scotland   AAMD

The post-Viking church

By the time of Malcolm III (1055-93) there were a number of territorial bishoprics in the Scottish church, and each bishop would have his own church with one or two clergy there. But the evidence for the existence of all except St Andrews is from the twelfth century or even later. There was a bishop in Strathearn, but we are not sure that his seat was at Dunblane. Similarly there was a bishop in Skye, but his seat at Snizort is uncertain. This bishop appears to have replaced earlier bishops associated with Iona; it is not known how he related to the bishop of Man, whose seat was possibly at Maughold on the east coast, but from about 1000, perhaps, on St Patrick's Isle, Peel off the west coast. There is a gap in the known succession of bishops at Whithorn after the early ninth century until the 1220s. In addition to the bishops shown there may have been a bishop for Moray with a seat near Elgin. And finally the bishop at Chester-le-Street (Durham from 995) who possessed the relics of St Cuthbert had not abandoned his claim to be pastor in Lothian and Tweeddale even though these districts had effectively passed to the bishops of St Andrews and Glasgow respectively.

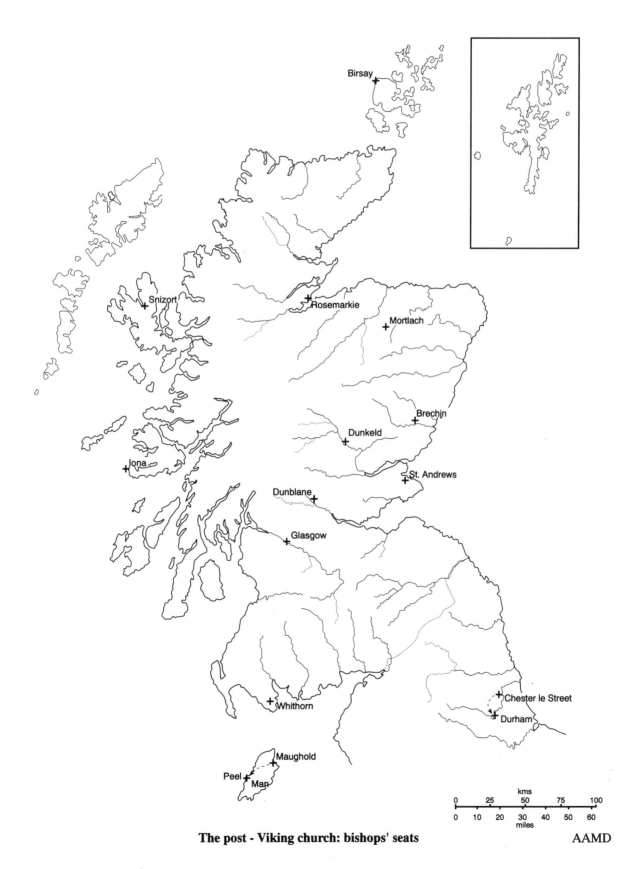

The post - Viking church: bishops' seats

AAMD

Ecclesiastical organisation about 1300

The date about 1300 has been chosen for this general map and for the maps showing the parishes of each diocese because as a result of the collection of taxes from the clergy ordered by popes in 1274 and 1291 records survive which provide the earliest known (if incomplete) description of the divisions of the Scottish church. Since the twelfth century a continuous series of bishops can be traced in the thirteen dioceses which by then had come to be permanently established within the area covered by modern Scotland. Ten of these on the mainland formed what was recognised by the papacy as the *ecclesia Scoticana*, forming a distinct unit directly under Rome, the equivalent for most purposes of an ecclesiastical province , but most unusually without any one of the ten bishops recognised as the superior of the others as archbishop and metropolitan. The three outlying dioceses each had a different status. Galloway was part of the kingdom of Scotland and was treated as part of the Scottish church for papal taxation purposes; but its bishops at this date recognised the superior metropolitan authority of the archbishop of York, and were to do so until 1355. Sodor had been part of the kingdom of Norway until 1266, and had since the mid-twelfth century recognised the archbishop of Trondheim as metropolitan. It now lay within the kingdom of Scotland, and like Galloway was taxed with the Scottish church, though its bishops still took some part in Norwegian affairs. Orkney was quite different. It was in no sense part of Scotland; it was still part of the Norwegian kingdom and of the Trondheim church province.

The boundaries of all these dioceses had become clear-cut and unchanging in the course of the twelfth century. This had necessarily followed the enforcement by royal authority of the payment of teind, which had led first to the definition of parish boundaries and then to diocesan boundaries. But no contemporary evidence survives which makes it possible to map these boundaries with exactitude. No doubt many boundaries followed obvious natural features on the ground, and very many of them remained the same throughout the centuries, so that a large proportion of post-Reformation boundaries indicated in maps of later date below may well have been the same as they had been about 1300. But here the boundaries are only roughly delineated for lack of specific evidence. Rather more exactitude is found in the detailed maps of each diocese at this date which follow.

Unlike England where dioceses were invariably named after the place where the bishop had his seat (that is his see), more than half of these dioceses were usually named after a pre-existent

secular unit of lordship or provincial government. This applied to Orkney and Sodor in the Norwegian kingdom, to Caithness, Ross, Moray, Argyll and Galloway (though in the last two cases the names of the cathedral sites Lismore and Whithorn were sometimes applied to the dioceses also). In the northern dioceses at any rate bishops had found it useful or necessary to move their sees within their dioceses. The see of Orkney was moved from Birsay to Kirkwall in the mid-twelfth century. About the same time the see of Caithness was being established probably at Halkirk initially; but it was moved south to Dornoch in the 1230s as part of a deliberate policy of associating this diocese more with Scotland than with Orkney. In the early twelfth century too the see at Mortlach which had apparently served much of the area to the south of the Moray Firth was moved to a site near the new royal castle and administrative centre at Aberdeen. The bishopric of Moray emerges about the same time, but had no settled see for perhaps a hundred years; instead the bishop resided at any of Birnie, Kinneddar or Spynie at his choice, and only in the 1220s did royal endowment make possible the building of a cathedral at the royal administrative centre at Elgin. The move of the see of Ross from Rosemarkie to Fortrose in the early thirteenth century was simply to a new site within the same parish.

The old episcopal seats of Glasgow, St Andrews, Dunblane, Dunkeld and Brechin had retained respect and authority. The first two were the centres of the wealthiest and most influential of the Scottish bishops, with their dioceses in each case by this date were sub-divided into two archdeaconries. (Orkney was probably similarly divided, but all the other bishoprics supported only one archdeacon.) While the diocese of Glasgow was a coherent geographical area with a simple boundary, the other four in this group were notable for the complexity of their inter- relationships. Probably as a result of centuries-old loyalties dating back to missionary days, each of these bishops retained authority over parishes which were geographically detached from the main area of the diocese - indeed in the case of Brechin the whole diocese comprised parishes scattered throughout St Andrews diocese. The details can be studied in the parish maps which follow; here only the rough boundary between St Andrews on the one hand and Dunblane and Dunkeld on the other is shown. No attempt is made to delineate the boundaries of the Brechin parishes; but the convenient heading ' St Andrews with Brechin' must not be taken to suggest that the bishop of Brechin was in any way subordinate to the bishop of St Andrews. Administratively and juridically (if not economically) they were equals.

Ecclesiastical organisation about 1520

The kingdom of Scotland had by 1520 been consolidated within its modern boundaries, with Orkney and Shetland ceded by Norway in 1469 and Berwick finally lost to England and to Durham diocese in 1482. There had been changes in the three outlying dioceses. No bishop of Galloway after 1355 tendered his obedience to the archbishop of York, except during the Great Schism of the Papacy (1378-1419) when rival popes supported by Scotland and England respectively appointed rival bishops. In 1430 James I ordered that Galloway was to be regarded as a Scottish diocese. The effect of the Schism on Sodor diocese was more drastic; from 1387 onwards Peel cathedral and the Isle of Man were occupied by a series of bishops of Man loyal to England, while the northern part of this scattered diocese came to be permanently separated as the distinct Scottish diocese of The Isles, with the see certainly in the mid-fifteenth century at the old centre at Snizort on Skye (though it is not clear it was still there about 1520). These two dioceses of Galloway and The Isles gradually detached themselves under papal protection from meaningful obedience to York or Trondheim. Then came the association of Orkney with Scotland and a time for formal changes. In

1472 the bishop of St Andrews was promoted archbishop with metropolitan authority over the other twelve bishops of the Scottish kingdom of that date. Political unity now matched ecclesiastical unity.

But this clear-cut situation did not last long. Some bishops were restive about it from the start. Then in 1492 the bishop of Glasgow was also raised to the rank of archbishop with metropolitan status (though not with the extra status of primate which had been granted in 1487 to St Andrews). At first Glasgow was given four subordinate dioceses (Argyll, Galloway, Dunblane and Dunkeld) while St Andrews retained the rest; but Dunblane was transferred back to St Andrews in 1500 and Dunkeld likewise by 1515. This therefore was the situation in about 1520. The two archbishops were constantly jockeying for position, so providing a basic disunity in the Scottish church. Nonetheless between 1536 and 1559 the archbishop of St Andrews was to be able to use his powers as primate to assemble a number of provincial councils at which all thirteen dioceses of the kingdom were represented. The Scottish church was in a real sense still one despite its appearance on the map.

DERW

(Birsay) ○
Kirkwall ○
Orkney

Shetland

*TRONDHEIM
(NIDAROS)*

(Halkirk?)

Caithness

○ Dornoch

Ross

Fortrose ○

(Kinnedar)
Elgin ○ (Spynie)
○
(Birnie)
Mortlach ○

Moray

Aberdeen

Aberdeen ○

Sodor

Argyll

○ Lismore

Dunkeld

Dunkeld ○

Brechin ○

*St Andrews
with
Brechin*

St Andrews ●

Dunblane

Dunblane ○

Glasgow ○

Glasgow

St Andrews

Lothian

Berwick ●

ARMAGH

Glasgow

Teviotdale

Galloway

Whithorn ●

YORK

ARMAGH Province
Glasgow Diocese
Teviotdale Archdeaconry
Whithorn Cathedral City
(Birnie) Earlier Cathedral
━━━━━ Boundary of Province
━ ･ ━ ･ ━ Boundary of Diocese
━ ━ ━ ━ Boundary of Archdeaconry

○ Peel (Isle Of Man)

kms
0   25   50   75   100
0 10 20 30 40 50 60
miles

The Scottish church about 1300

DERW

337

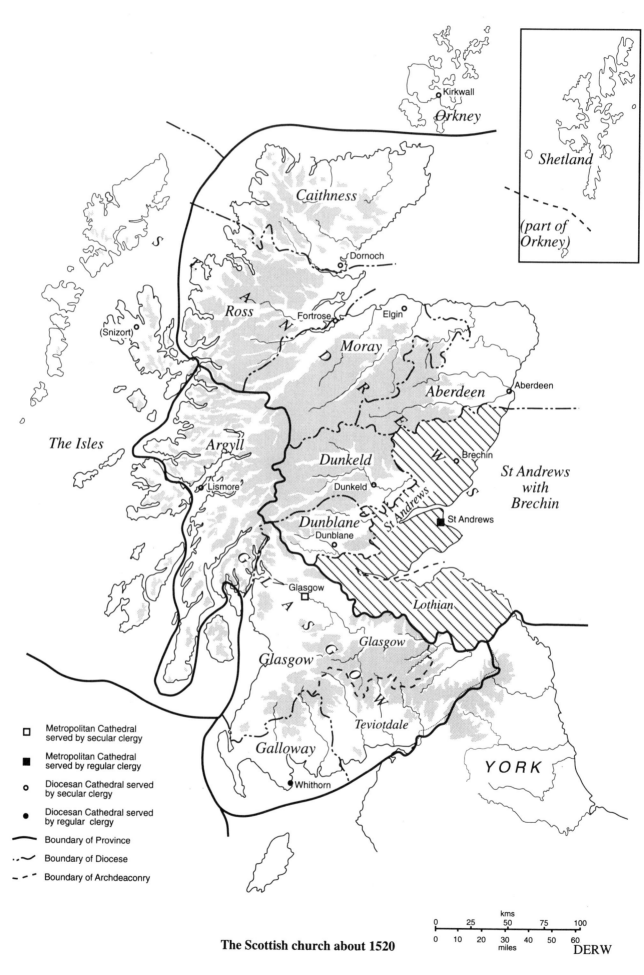

Ecclesiastical organisation

Orkney

Kirkwall

Shetland

(part of Orkney)

Caithness

Dornoch

Ross

Elgin

Fortrose

Moray

(Snizort)

Aberdeen

Aberdeen

The Isles

Argyll

Brechin

Dunkeld

St Andrews
with
Brechin

Lismore

Dunkeld

St Andrews

Dunblane

Dunblane

St Andrews

Glasgow

Glasgow

Lothian

Glasgow

Glasgow

Teviotdale

Galloway

YORK

Whithorn

□ Metropolitan Cathedral
served by secular clergy

■ Metropolitan Cathedral
served by regular clergy

○ Diocesan Cathedral served
by secular clergy

● Diocesan Cathedral served
by regular clergy

— Boundary of Province

·-·-·- Boundary of Diocese

--- Boundary of Archdeaconry

The Scottish church about 1520

kms
0   25   50   75   100

0   10   20   30   40   50   60
miles

DERW

The church in north-western Europe

The map of the ecclesiastical provinces of north-western Europe puts the two Scottish provinces in their European context. Across Europe there was a significant disparity of size in the provinces which arose for historical reasons. Many of the European provinces are very much larger than the Scottish ones; but in Italy (not shown) - particularly in the Papal States and in Naples - there was a great concentration of much smaller provinces.

Ecclesiastical provinces in north-western Europe in the fifteenth century

Some of the monastic and other orders - such as the Benedictines and the Franciscans - took their names from their founder. Others took their name from the places where they had originated or with which they had been associated. The map plots these European centres with, in some cases, their dates of foundation.

It appears that there was no distinct order of Thiron, but that the Tironensian observance was an off-shoot of the Benedictine order.

The names of the orders or congration, with their place of origin are:

Arrouaisian	Arrouaise
Carthusian	Chartreuse
Cistercian	Cîteaux
Cluniac	Cluny
Premonstratensian	Prémontré
Tironensian	Thiron
Valliscaulian	Val des Choux

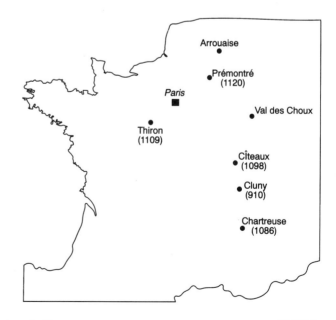

Monastic centres in Europe

PGBM

339

Monastic orders

Monasticism which followed in the footstep of the first Christian missionaries was apparently first introduced into Scotland in the fifth century, but by the mid-eleventh century communities survived at best at Iona and possibly Turriff; elsewhere so-called monasteries approximated more closely to minsters consisting of secular clerks. The arrival in Scotland of the Saxon princess, Margaret, who in 1068-9 married Malcolm III (1057-93) paved the way for the introduction of monasticism of the medieval type. To this end before 1089, Lanfranc, archbishop of Canterbury, at Queen Margaret's request, sent three Benedictine monks to Dunfermline where they established a priory. By this step the queen inaugurated a policy of encouraging the establishment of monastic orders, a course of action which was to be developed by her three sons, Edgar, Alexander and David, who ruled between 1097 and 1153. During these years Augustinian canons, Tironensian and Cistercian monks, inspired directly or indirectly by reformed orders in France, joined the Benedictines. In addition to royal foundations, the Augustinian priory of St Andrews (1144) was established by the bishop of that see; and a house of Premonstratensians was founded at Dryburgh (1150) by Hugh de Morville. Royal generosity, however, endowed the earliest Scottish nunnery at Berwick upon Tweed (before 1153) and also introduced

the military orders, the knights Templars and the Hospitallers. David's foundations were widely distributed from the Borders to the Moray firth, from Lothian to Galloway.

Succeeding rulers and magnates followed David's example and the existing orders continued to expand. Many foundations of these orders took place in outlying parts of the kingdom though the influence of local potentates. Successive lords of Galloway established Premonstratensians at Soulseat (by 1161) (and perhaps Whithorn by 1175) as well as at Tongland and Cistercians at Glenluce (1191- 2), while the Benedictine nunnery at Lincluden (by 1174) is said to have been founded by Uchtred, son of Fergus of Galloway. Again the Benedictine abbey (by 1203) and the Augustinian nunnery (by 1208) of Iona and the Cistercian house of Saddell in Kintyre had as their founder Reginald son of Somerled, lord of the Isles. Walter Fitzalan brought Cluniacs initially to Renfrew and then, to Paisley by 1169. Equally significantly the order of the Val des Choux (vallis Caulium) was introduced in 1230 and established by the kinq at Pluscarden (1230-1). Contemporaneously two other Valliscaulian houses - Ardchattan and Beauly - were founded in isolated regions in the north and west of Scotland.

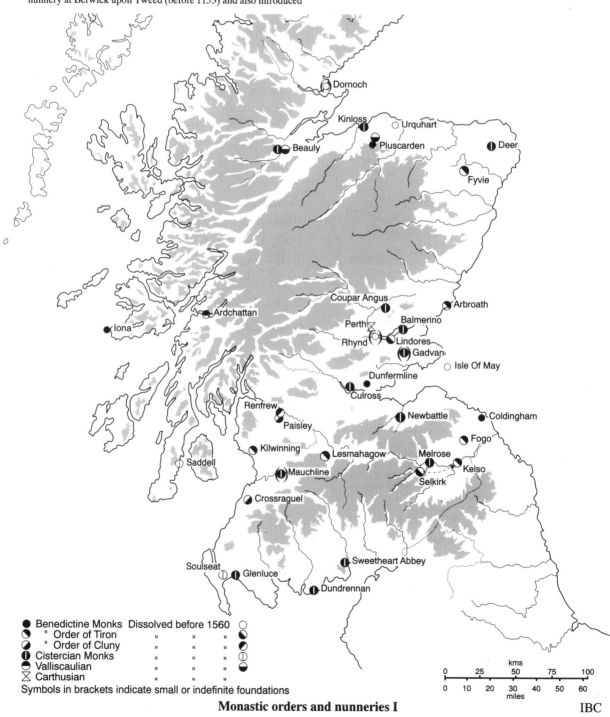

		Benedictine Monks	Dissolved before 1560	
		" Order of Tiron	" " "	
		" Order of Cluny	" " "	
		Cistercian Monks	" " "	
		Valliscaulian	" " "	
		Carthusian	" " "	

Symbols in brackets indicate small or indefinite foundations

Monastic orders and nunneries I

IBC

Monastic orders

In another innovatory move, the Trinitarians (sometimes misleadingly described as Red friars) were placed (1240-8) at Berwick and Dunbar. By this period, however, the age of major monastic foundations was almost over and effectively ended with the endowment in 1273 of the abbey at Sweetheart by Dervorguilla Balliol. If the Carthusians do not appear until 1429, only one or two smaller houses were otherwise still to be founded.

The geographical distribution of these monasteries was uneven. Although they spread into the Hebrides, the great majority were situated in central and southern Scotland. Of the larger houses a number were located in Lothian and the proximity of the border, which was advantageous for economic development in time of peace, but precarious in days of war and invasion. These hazards were however surmountable, and the religious houses remained in reasonable shape until the end of the fifteenth century. By then, however, other forces were at work: for headships were increasingly bestowed upon members of the secular clergy who only entered the order after appointment; even this formality was widely ignored, and the opportunities for appointing secular commendators for life was

facilitated by the indult of 1487 which allowed the crown within a period of eight months to recommend candidates for papal provision, a faculty which was formally recognised as nomination. Thereafter, secularisation of monastic revenues continued apace; even without the Reformation many religious houses, of which only a handful retained their choir monks at their head, might have followed the small number which had been dissolved in the fifteenth and early sixteenth centuries and eventually disappeared. The events of 1559-60 not only hastened this process, but ensured its completeness. When the Reformation came, the commendators remained, but any pretensions to monastic status mattered little; and their virtual possession of monastic property counted for much as religious communities slowly died out. The annexation of the monasteries to the Crown in 1587, a quarter of a century after they had ceased to function, came as a belated measure, and its effect was restricted by the fact that by this date most of the monastic possessions had been alienated beyond recall. Only the formal erection of the monasteries in to temporal lordships remained to be achieved.

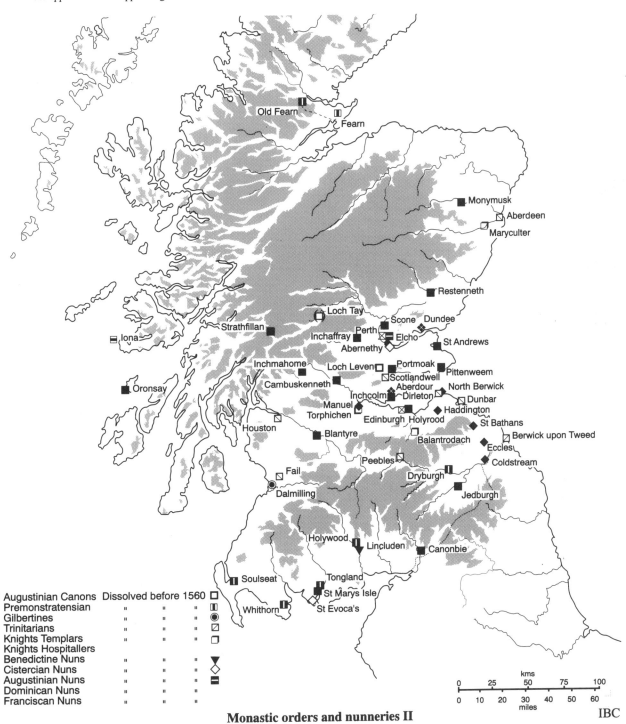

Monastic orders and nunneries II

IBC

Friaries

Virtually half of Scotland's friaries, representing five orders, were founded in the last seventy years of the thirteenth century, the century which saw both the founding of the orders of friars and their remarkable growth. After the first era of enthusiasm, it seems, the fourteenth century saw very few foundations (some caution is necessary because many dates of foundation are not known). In the fifteenth century there seems to have been a renewed interest, just over half the new houses being accounted for by the reformed version of the Franciscans, the Observants, encouraged by royal patronage. The small number of foundations of any order after 1500 suggests that enthusiasm was waning.

The aim of the friars was to preach, and therefore friaries were almost always in centres of population - hence the concentration in the central belt and in the eastern coastal strip as far north as Inverness. With the exception of Kingussie, the Highlands and Islands had none. But this does not mean that individual friars were not seen in these areas, for they were highly mobile. Dominicans can be traced in the Hebrides in the thirteenth century, and served as bishops of Argyll for more than a century from 1264 onwards.

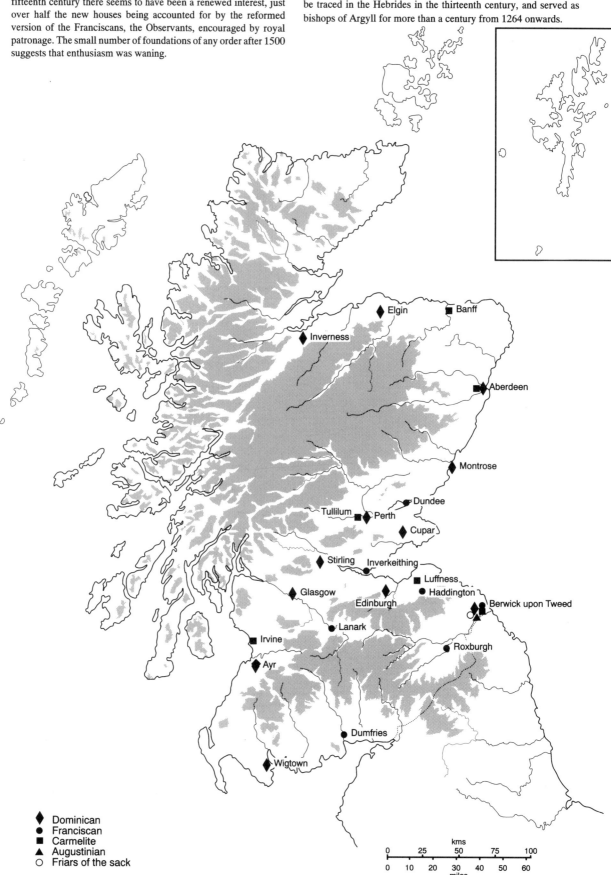

♦ Dominican
● Franciscan
■ Carmelite
▲ Augustinian
○ Friars of the sack

Friaries founded in the thirteenth and fourteenth centuries

NFS

342

Friaries

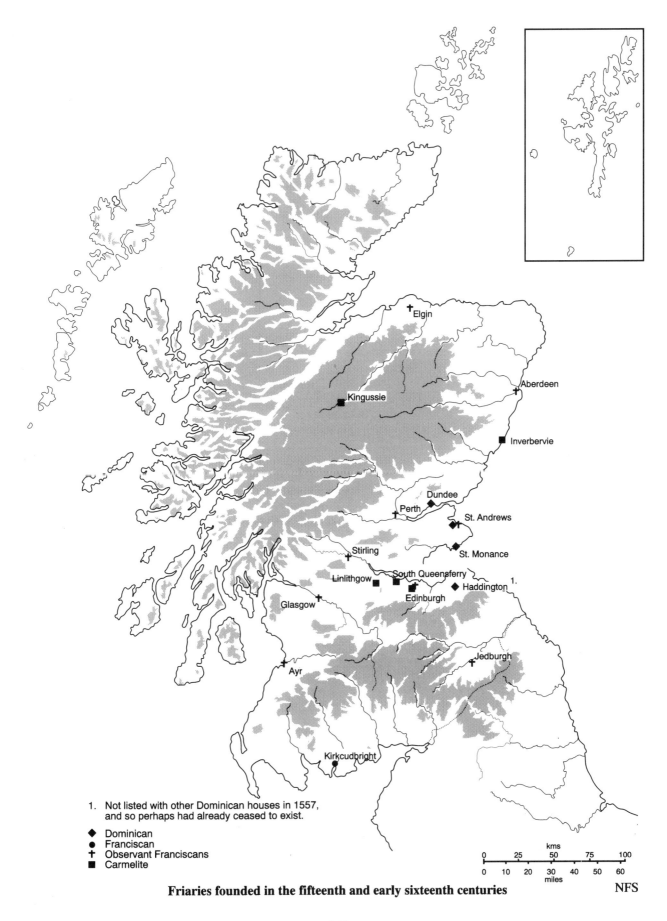

1. Not listed with other Dominican houses in 1557,
   and so perhaps had already ceased to exist.

◆ Dominican
● Franciscan
✝ Observant Franciscans
■ Carmelite

Friaries founded in the fifteenth and early sixteenth centuries

NFS

Hospitals

Few hospital foundations can be precisely dated, and so the first four maps are based on the first recorded date. The fifth map seeks to identify both hospitals which lasted for a reasonable after 1560 (some have been excluded on the grounds that survival after 1560 was very brief), and those which were new foundations. Temporary foundations for outbreaks of plague have been omitted.

The first map shows that, in general terms, Scotland was well provided with hospitals. There were some sixty by 1300, though they were heavily concentrated in the central belt, Lothian, Fife and the Borders. The absence of hospitals in the Highlands and Islands might be due to a different social system or simple lack of evidence; but even the eastern coastal strip north of the Inverness area apparently lacked hospitals, and Galloway is surprisingly empty. Berwick was well provided with hospitals, but it was a major town, and different hospitals served different needs, such as those of the poor, the sick, lepers and travellers.

The second map shows that the fourteenth century added relatively few hospitals, though it is not certain whether this reflects our lack of knowledge or is genuine evidence of fewer foundations. These hospitals seem largely to reinforce existing provision, except that Helmsdale and St Magnus extend it northwards.

The next map seems to show that there was a greater interest in new foundations in the fifteenth century than in the fourteenth, though even in the fifteenth century precise dates of foundation are few. The fourth map shows a surprising number of hospitals first referred to in the sixty years before the Reformation, some of them certainly sixteenth-century foundations. Neither the fifteenth century nor the sixteenth saw any significant change in the geographical distribution of hospitals.

The last map is different in purpose, and attempts to show which hospitals survived, often under the control of town councils, and which were new foundations between 1560 and 1707. This is a subject which requires further investigation: there are many uncertainties and problems, and this map is offered in the knowledge that it is likely to be very incomplete. Apart from Kirkwall, the hospitals of this period also do not extend the geographical area of provision.

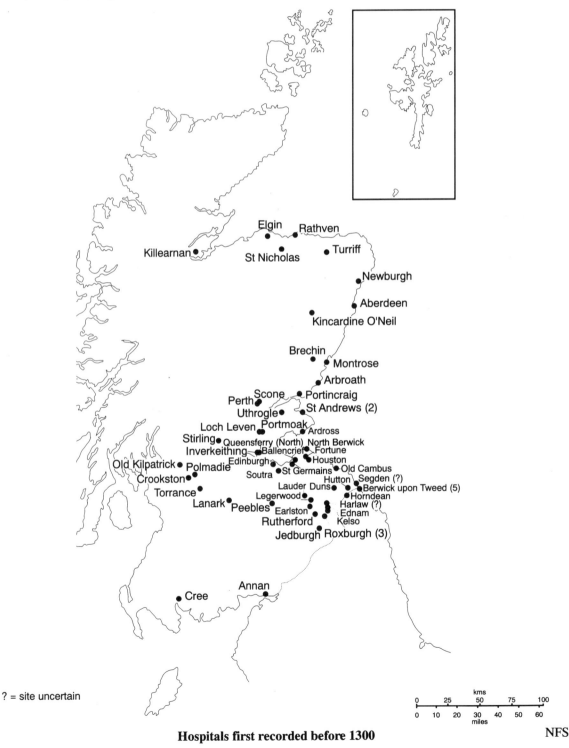

? = site uncertain

Hospitals first recorded before 1300

NFS

344

Hospitals

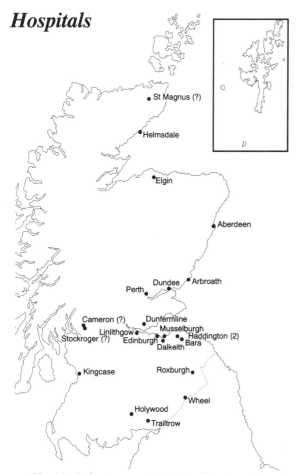

Hospitals first recorded in the fourteenth century

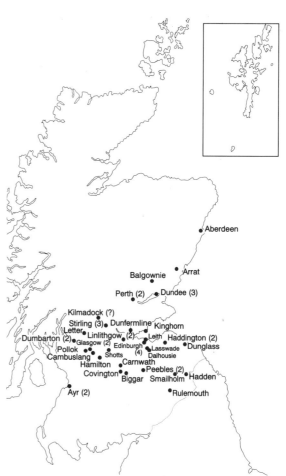

Hospitals first recorded in the fifteenth century

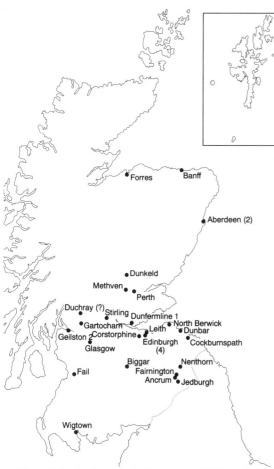

Hospitals first recorded between 1500 and 1560

1 References occur only post 1560, but since it was dedicated to
a saint, it seems to be pre-Reformation. It may well be much earlier
in date than the 16th century.
2 First mentioned in 1563

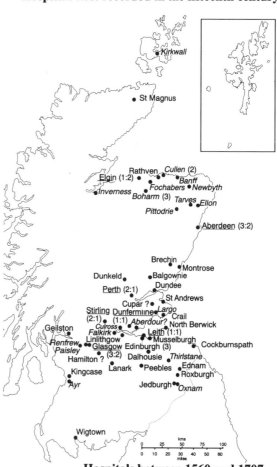

Hospitals between 1560 and 1707

Wigtown	Known to have been in existence post-1560 (number in brackets if more than one)
Ayr	Founded between 1560 and 1707 (number in brackets if more than one)
<u>Glasgow</u>	Place with both old and new foundations (number in brackets) in existence in the eighteenth century;
?	date of foundation unknown, but possibly pre-1707

NFS

Collegiate churches

By the late thirteenth century most of the Scottish cathedrals had been provided with a chapter (*capitulum*) in the form of a self-governing corporate body of clergy under a dean. The map shows the sites of forty-six other churches where in the late Middle Ages similar corporate groups of from thee to more than thirty clergy came to be established with similar corporate rights. Each group was said to form a college (*collegium*) - hence the term collegiate church usually under the presidency of a provost (*prepositus*), a term which implied responsibility for financial management.

Three of these colleges were founded before 1400 by the re-allocation of old endowments; at least twelve followed before 1450 and another eleven by 1500. In l501 came the grandest of all, the new Chapel Royal in Stirling Castle, followed by nearly twenty more foundations until as late as the 1540s. The main function of these communities was the saying of masses perpetually for departed souls to assist their progress through purgatory. But there were four rather different colleges within the universities of St Andrew and Aberdeen, where the endowments were provided to support masters and student teachers studying there.

About two-thirds of these communities were founded in rural areas in chapels additional to the parish churches. The rest were intended to enhance the services offered in the large burgh churches, often as an expression of civic pride. The founders were most often laymen from the king down to wealthy burgesses, all seeking to provide for their own salvation. But the theological revolt at the Reformation against masses for the dead quite suddenly outmoded these institutions, and new uses had to be found for their endowments.

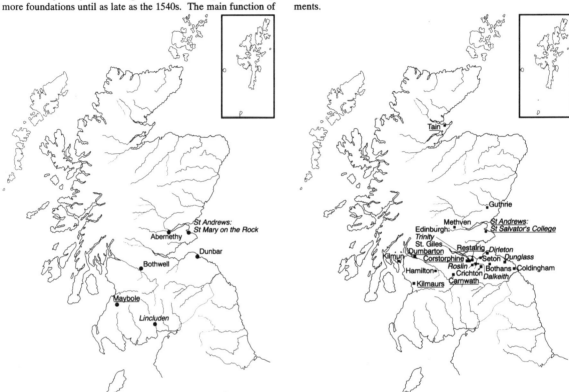

Collegiate churches founded before 1400

Collegiate churches founded between 1400 and 1500

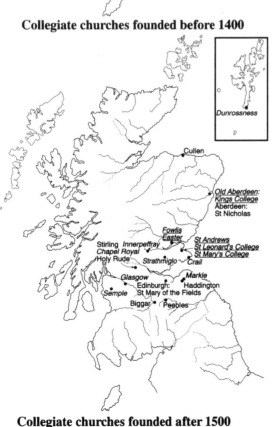

Collegiate churches founded after 1500

Abernethy	Parish churches which acquired collegiate character
Carnwath	Collegiate bodies formed in chapels in or near parish churches but separately organised
Dalkeith	Collegiate churches at some distance from parish churches
Aberdeen: King's College	Colleges within universities

DERW

Parish churches about 1300

This series of maps presents an attempt to identify the sites of every parish church in Scotland, Orkney and Shetland in about 1300. This date has been chose mainly for the same reason given above for selecting it as the date to show the boundaries of ecclesiastical organisation. The existence of perhaps two-thirds of the total is demonstrated by the mention of these parishes as paying papal taxes in the decades just before 1300; but the relevant records (the most famous of which goes by the name of 'Bagimond's Roll') are incomplete. There are at least minor gaps for every diocese, and no records at all survive for the dioceses of Argyll, Sodor and Orkney, nor for the half of Glasgow diocese comprising the Archdeaconry of Glasgow. For Moray, Aberdeen, St Andrews and Brechin these financial records can be supplemented by parish valuation lists which survive in several monastic cartularies from a rather earlier thirteenth-century date. Where precise evidence of this contemporary kind does not exist, it is a question of reading back from late records. This usually demands some reasonable guesswork, and it is not pretended that the existence of every parish mapped here can definitely be proved. But in every case there is reasonable certainty.

Parish boundaries are not attempted for reasons explained above; instead the attempt has been made to identify the oldest-known site of the parish church in each case. The boundaries which have been drawn are schematic rather than precise, indicating the limits of each diocese, of the archdeaconries within St Andrews, Glasgow and Orkney dioceses, and of the subordinate deaneries (groups of parishes under the authority of one of the parish clergy as dean of Christianity) within the archdeaconries. There is certain contemporary evidence for these last administrative and jurisdictional units in the dioceses of Galloway, Glasgow, St Andrews, Aberdeen and Moray by this date, and it is usually clear which parishes belonged to each. Exceptionally we know that deaneries existed in Argyll diocese, but no allocation of parishes to deaneries is available.

By 1300 it appears that the whole country had come to be divided in parishes. This had been a gradual process over the previous two centuries; now each defined area was the spiritual responsibility of the benefice-holder, who could be an individual parish priest as rector or parson, or alternatively a religious corporation such as a monastery or cathedral chapter (in which case the parish was said to have been appropriated to the use of such a corporation - as is shown in later maps). In either situation the liturgical and pastoral work might be performed by priests who were deputies of the official benefice-holder, whether with the status of vicar or of chaplain. The parish was now the basic unit of ecclesiastical administration, finance and discipline. In large parishes subordinate chapels were often built for the convenience of parishioners; but everyone owed an over-riding duty to the parish church itself. Hence the interest in identifying the sites of these churches. Many lessons for local history can be learned from their geographical distribution; there must be a specific reason behind the siting of each one.

It is not surprising that arrangement in the Norwegian dioceses of Orkney and Sodor were rather different. Parishes had been developed there over the same period as in Scotland, but there are indications that, in accordance with the practice of the Norwegian church to which both dioceses then belonged, the area of a parochial cure was the 'priest's district' (*prestegjeld*)- rather than the 'parish' (*sokn*). While some such districts might contain no more than a single parish church, most comprised two or three and some as many as four 'head churches'; and these groupings could change from one period to another in Shetland at any rate. The system has been clearly identified in Orkney diocese (which was to remain part of Norway until 1468-9), and it has been suggested that a similar arrangement (albeit less convincingly) lies behind the distribution of churches in Sodor diocese, which had been part of Scotland only since 1266. In the lists of churches for these two dioceses therefore various definite or possible groupings are indicated by brackets.

In all these lists a distinction is made between the names of unappropriated churches in roman type and the names of appropriated churches in italic type. In some cases the evidence about the situation in 1300 is inferential rather than certain, and caution has guided editorial practice. More churches may in fact have been appropriated by this date than is now indicated; but at least a conservative view of how far this process had gone by this date is now available. Place-names are given in modern forms whenever the 1300 form is clearly recognisable; they are left in some contemporary form within quotes where this is not possible; and where the name has been completely changed (often because the site of the church has been moved within the parish bounds) a modern equivalent form is also provided.

Parish churches about 1300

Diocese of St Andrews (with diocese of Brechin) ignoring enclaves
Archdeaconries of St Andrews and Lothian
Deaneries
Other dioceses
• Parish churches

Parish churches about 1300: diocese of St Andrews

DERW

Parish churches about 1300

Archdeaconry of St Andrews

Mearns Deanery

1. Nigg
2. Durris
3. Fetteresso
4. Dunnottar
5. Fordoun
6. Arbuthnott
7. Kinneff
8. Newdosk
9. Fettercairn
10. Conveth (now Laurencekirk)
11. Garvock
12. Benholm
13. Aberluthnot (now Marykirk)
14. Ecclesgreig (now St Cyrus)

Angus Deanery

15. Dalbog
16. Edzell
17. Dunlappie
18. Logie
19. Dun
20. Lintrathen
21. Airlie
22. Kirriemuir
23. Restenneth and Forfar
24. Rescobie
25. Tannadice
26. Aberlemno
27. Aldbar
28. Kinnell
29. Inverkeilor
30. Inverlunan
31. Dunninald
32. Inchbraoch (now Craig)
33. Kettins
34. Newtyle
35. Nevay
36. Eassie
37. Glamis
38. Kinnettles
39. Meathie Lour
40. Inverarity
41. Idvies (now Kirkden)
42. Arbirlot
43. Arbroath and Ethie
44. Lundie
45. Liff
46. Invergowrie
47. Logie Dundee (now Lochee)
48. Strathdighty Martin (now Strathmartine)
49. Strathdighty Comitis (now Mains)
50. Murroes
51. Monifieth
52. Barry

Gowrie Deanery

53. Blair (now Blairgowrie)
54. Luncarty
55. Cambusmichael
56. Collace
57. Fowlis
58. Methven
59. Scone
60. Kinnoull
61. Perth
62. Forteviot
63. Pottie (now Dunbarney)
64. Rhynd
65. Kinfauns
66. Kilspindie
67. Rait
68. Errol
69. Inchture
70. Rossinclerach (now Rossie)
71. Forgan (now Longforgan)
72. Benvie

Fife Deanery

73. Flisk
74. Creich
75. Kilmany
76. Logie Murdoch
77. Forgan
78. Leuchars
79. Lindores (or Abdie)
80. Dunbog
81. Collessie
82. Monimail
83. Auchtermoonzie (now Moonzie)
84. Dairsie
85. Cupar
86. Tarvit
87. Ceres
88. Kemback
89. St Andrews
90. Dunino
91. Kennoway
92. Scoonie
93. Largo
94. Newburn
95. Kilconquhar
96. Abercrombie (now St Monance)
97. Kellie (now Carnbee)
98. Anstruther
99. Kilrenny
100. Crail

Fothrif Deanery

101. Arngask
102. Auchtermuchty
103. Kilgour
104. Lathrisk
105. Cults
106. Forthar (now Kirkforthar)
107. Muckhart
108. Cleish
109. Kinross
110. Portmoak
111. Auchterderran
112. Kinglassie
113. Markinch
114. Clackmannan
115. Torry (now Torryburn)
116. Carnock
117. Dunfermline
118. Inverkeithing
119. Parva Kinghorn
120. Magna Kinghorn
121. Kirkcaldy
122. Dysart
123. Wemyss
124. Methil

Archdeaconry of Lothian

Linlithgow Deanery

1. Stirling
2. Kirkton
3. Airth
4. Dunipace
5. Larbert
6. Bothkenner
7. Falkirk
8. Slamannan
9. Kinneil
10. Carriden
11. Linlithgow
12. Binny
13. Ecclesmachan
14. Auldcathie
15. Liston (now Kirkliston)
16. Dalmeny
17. Gogar
18. Bathgate
19. Strathbrock (now Uphall)
20. Ratho
21. Livingston
22. Calder Comitis (now West Calder)
23. Calder Clere (now East Calder)
24. Newton (now Kirknewton)
25. Kinleith (now Currie)
26. Hailes (now Colinton)
27. St Cuthbert under the Castle
28. Restalrig
29. St Giles of Edinburgh
30. St Mary in the Fields
31. Duddingston
32. Woolmet (now Newton)
33. Melville
34. Lasswade
35. Pentland
36. Penicuik

Haddington Deanery

37. Mount Lothian
38. Clerkington (now Temple)
39. Carrington
40. Loquhariot (now Borthwick)
41. Cockpen
42. Masterton (now Newbattle)
43. Crichton
44. Cranston
45. Heriot
46. Soutra
47. Fala
48. Keith Marischal
49. Keith Humbie (now Humbie)
50. Ormiston
51. Pencaitland
52. Saltoun
53. Bolton
54. Bothans (now Yester)
55. Bara
56. Morham
57. Garvald
58. Musselburgh
59. Tranent
60. Seton
61. Haddington
62. Athelstaneford
63. Linton (now Prestonkirk)
64. Gullane
65. North Berwick
66. Auldhame
67. Hamer (now Whitekirk)
68. Tyninghame
69. Dunbar
70. Innerwick
71. Oldhamstocks

Merse Deanery

72. Channelkirk
73. Cranshaws
74. Ellem (now Ellemford)
75. St Bathans (now Abbey St Bathans)
76. Old Cambus
77. Coldingham
78. Hallyburton
79. Greenlaw
80. Fogo
81. Polwarth
82. Langton
83. Duns
84. Edrom
85. Chirnside
86. Simprim
87. Swinton
88. Whitsome
89. Hilton
90. Hutton
91. Foulden
92. Mordington
93. Lamberton
94. Wedale (now Stow)
95. Lauder
96. Gordon
97. Legerwood
98. Earlston
99. Mertoun
100. Smailholm
101. Makerstoun
102. Nenthorn
103. Stichill
104. Ednam
105. Hume
106. Eccles
107. Lennel (now Coldstream)
108. Upsettlington (now Ladykirk)
109. Horndean
110. Fishwick
111. Berwick

Parish churches about 1300

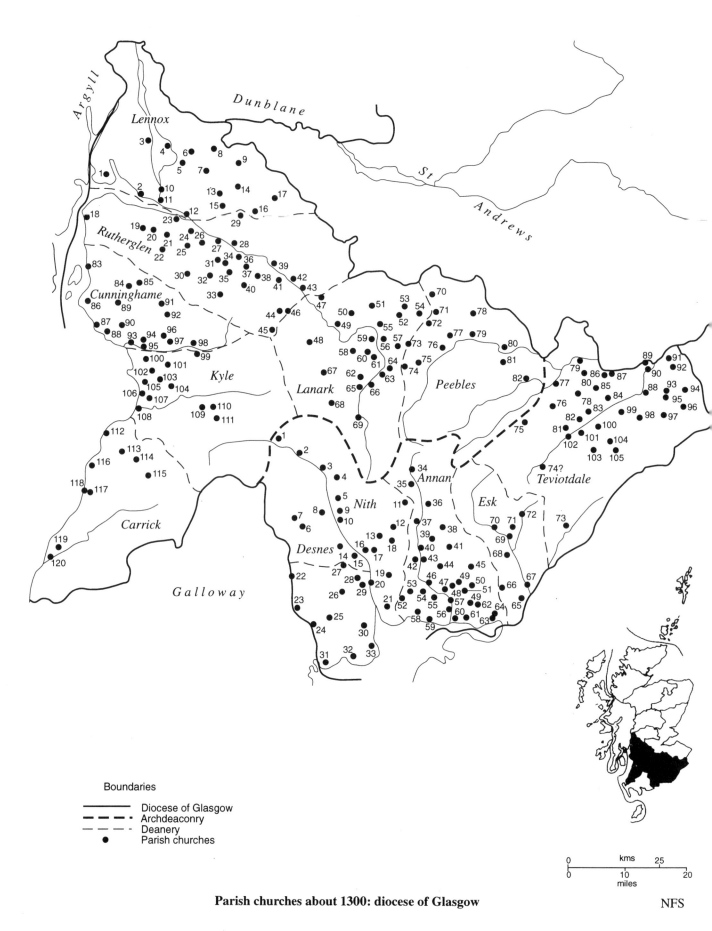

Boundaries

——————— Diocese of Glasgow
— — — Archdeaconry
– – – Deanery
● Parish churches

kms 0 25

miles 0 10 20

Parish churches about 1300: diocese of Glasgow

NFS

Parish churches about 1300

Archdeaconry of Glasgow

Lennox Deanery

I Neveth (now Rosneath)
2 Cardross
3 Luss
4 Inchcailloch (now Inchcailloch or Buchanan)
5 Kilmaronock
6 Drymen
7 Killearn
8 Balfron
9 Fintry
10 Bonhill
11 Dumbarton
12 *Kilpatrick*
13 *Strathblane*
14 *Campsie*
15 Baldernock
16 *Kirkintilloch*
17 Monyabroch (now Kilsyth)

Rutherglen Deanery

18 *Inverkip*
19 *Kilmacolm*
20 *Killallan*
21 *Houston*
22 *Kilbarchan*
23 *Erskine*
24 *Inchinnan*

25 *Paisley*
26 *Renfrew*
27 *Govan*
28 *Glasgow Cathedral*
29 *Cadder*
30 Neilson
31 Eastwood
32 Mearns
33 *Eaglesham*[1]
34 *Cathcart*
35 *Carmunnock*
36 Rutherglen
37 Drumsargad (now Cambuslang)
38 *Blantyre*
39 Bothwell
40 Kilbride (now East Kilbride)
41 Cadzow (now Hamilton)
42 *Dalziel*
43 *Cambusnethan*
44 Glasford
45 Strathaven

Lanark Deanery

46 Stonehouse
47 Eglismalescok (now Carluke)
48 *Lesmahagow*
49 Lanark

50 *Carstairs*
51 *Carnwarth*
52 *Walston*
53 *Dunsyre*
54 Dolphinton
55 Libberton
56 Quothquan
57 Biggar
58 Carmichael
59 Covington
60 *Thankerton (or Tinto)*
61 *Symington*
62 *Wiston*
63 Lamington
64 Culter
65 *Roberton*
66 Hartside[1] (or Wandel)
67 Douglas
68 *Crawfordjohn*
69 Crawford

Peebles Deanery

70 *Linton Roderick (now West Linton)*
71 Newlands
72 Orde (or Horde now Kirkurd)
73 Skirling

74 Kilbucho
75 Glenholm
76 *Stobo*
77 *Lyne*[2]
78 *Eddleston*
79 *Peebles*
80 *Innerleithen*
81 *Traquair*
82 Forest Kirk (now Yarrow)

Cunninghame Deanery

83 *Largs*
84 *Kilbirnie*[1]
85 *Beith*
86 *Kilbride*[1] (now West Kilbride)
87 *Ardrossan*
88 Stevenston
89 Dalry
90 Kilwinning
91 *Dunlop*[1]
92 *Stewarton*[1]
93 Irvine
94 *Perceton*[1]
95 *Dreghorn*[1]
96 *Kilmaurs*
97 Kilmarnock
98 *Loudoun*

Kyle Deanery

99 *Galston*[1]
100 Dundonald
101 Craigie
102 Symington
103 *Barnwell*[1]
104 Tarbolton
105 Prestwick Monachorum (now Monkton)
106 Prestwick Burgh
107 St Quivox (or Sanquhar)
108 Ayr
109 Ochiltree
110 Auchinleck
111 Cumnock[1]

Carrick Deanery

112 *Kirkbride*
113 *Maybole*
114 *Kirkmichael*
115 *Straiton*
116 *Kirkoswald*
117 *Dalquharran (now Dailly)*
118 *Girvan*
119 *Colmonell*
120 *Kirkcudbright Invertig*[1] (now Ballantrae)

Archdeaconry of Teviotdale

Nith Deanery

I *Kirkconnel*
2 Sanquhar
3 Kirkbride
4 Durisdeer
5 *Morton*
6 Glencairn
7 *Tynron*
8 Penpont
9 *Dalgarnock*
10 Closeburn
11 Dumgree
12 Garvald
13 Kirkmichael
14 *Dunscore*
15 *Holywood (Dercongal)*
16 Kirkmahoe
17 Tinwald
18 *Trailflat*
19 Torthorwald
20 *Dumfries*
21 *Kirkblain* (now Caerlaverock)

Desnes Deanery

22 *Blaiket*

23 Kirkpartick Durham
24 *Urr*
25 *Kirkgunzeon*[2]
26 *Lochrutton*
27 Kirkpatrick Cro (now Irongray)
28 *Terregles*
29 Troqueer
30 *Loch Kindar (now New Abbey)*
31 Colvend
32 Southwick
33 *Kirkbean*

Annan Deanery

34 Moffat
35 Kirkpatrick-Juxta
36 Wamphray
37 Johnstone
38 Hutton (Magna)
39 *Sibbaldbie*
40 Jardine (or Applegarth)
41 Corrie
42 *Lochmaben*
43 *Dryfesdale*
44 Tundergarth

45 *Carruthers*
46 Castlemilk (now St Mungo)
47 Hoddom
48 Ecclefechan
49 Middlebie
50 Kirkconnell
51 Pennersaughs
52 Mouswald
53 Dalton Parva
54 Dalton Magna
55 Trailtrow
56 *Brydekirk*
57 Luce
58 Ruthwell
59 *Cummertrees*
60 Annan
61 Dornock
62 *Kirkpatrick-Fleming*
63 *Raynpatrick (now Redkirk)*
64 *Gretna*

Esk Deanery

65 *Kirkandrews*
66 Morton
67 Canonbie

(or Liddel)
68 *Wauchope*
69 *Staplegordon*
70 Westerkirk
71 Ewesdale St Cuthbert
72 Ewesdale St Martin (or Ewes Duris)

Teviotdale Deanery

73 *Castleton*
74 Cavers Magna
75 Rankleburn (now Buccleuch)
76 *Ashkirk*
77 *Selkirk Abbatis and Selkirk Regis*
78 Lilliesleaf
79 *Melrose*
80 *Bowden*
81 *Wilton*
82 *Hassendean*
83 Minto
84 *Ancrum*
85 *Longnewton*
86 *Lessudden*

(now St Boswells)
87 Maxton
88 *Eckford*
89 *Roxburgh, Old* *Roxburgh, Holy Sepulchre?* *Roxburgh, St James*
90 *Maxwell*
91 *Sprouston*
92 *Lempitlaw*
93 Linton
94 Yetholm and Yetholm Parva?
95 *Morebattle*
96 *Mow*
97 *Hownam*
98 *Oxnam*
99 *Jedburgh*
100 Bedrule
101 Cavers Parva (now Kirkton)
102 Hawick
103 *Hobkirk (or Rule)*
104 *Abbotrule*
105 Southdean

1   These churches are likely to have been erected by about 1300, but the evidence is inferential rather than clear.

2   These churches may still have been non-parochial chapels about 1300, but certainly became parish churches soon afterwards.

Parish churches about 1300: diocese of Glasgow   NFS

Parish churches about 1300

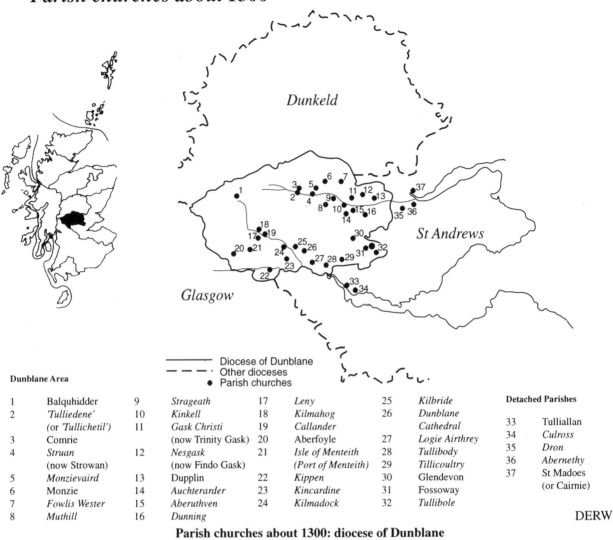

DERW

Parish churches about 1300: diocese of Dunblane

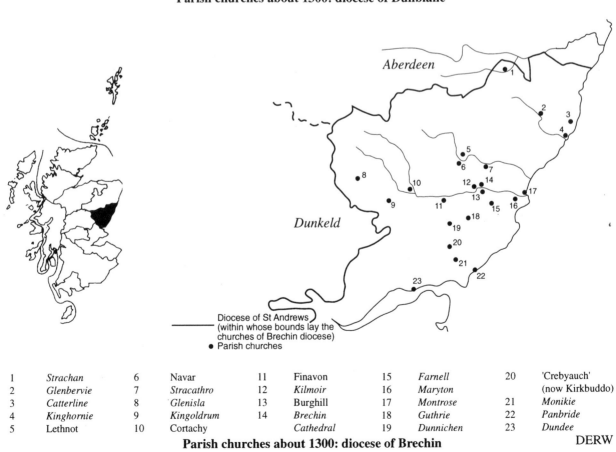

Parish churches about 1300: diocese of Brechin

DERW

Parish churches about 1300

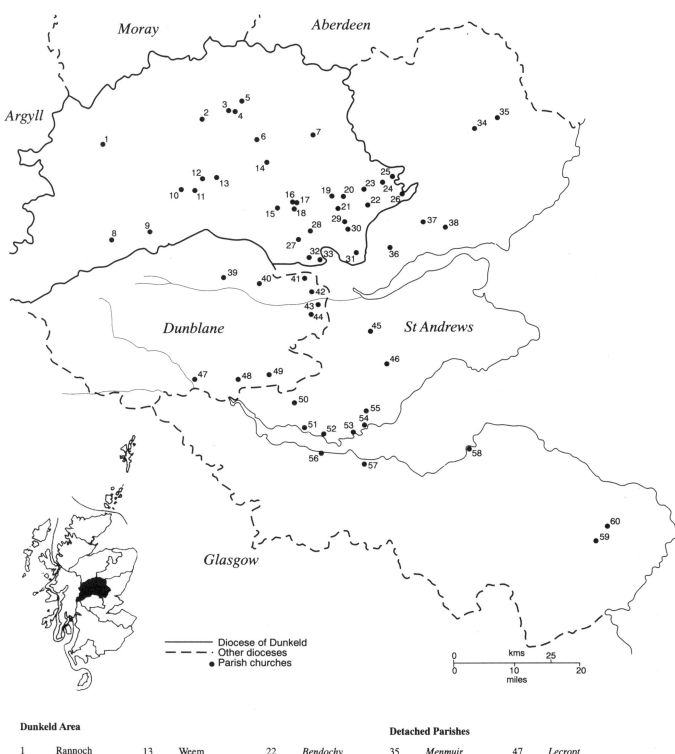

Parish churches about 1300: diocese of Dunkeld   DERW

Parish churches about 1300

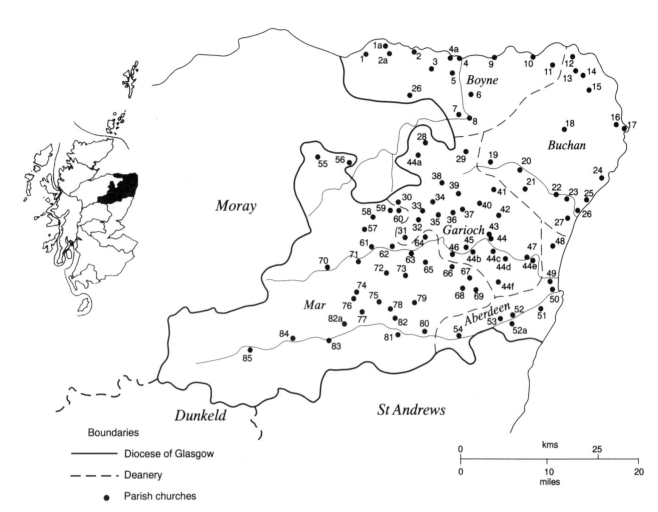

Boundaries

—— Diocese of Glasgow

– – – Deanery

• Parish churches

	Boyne Deanery							

Boyne Deanery

1	Rathven
1a	'Farskane'
2	*Fordyce*
2a	*Cullen*
2b	*Ordiquhill*
3	'Monbrey'
4	*Banff*
4a	*Inverboyndie*
5	Alvah
6	King Edward
7	Forglen
8	Turriff
9	*Gamrie*
10	Aberdour
11	*Tyrie*

Buchan Deanery

12	Philorth
13	Rathen
14	Lonmay
15	*Crimond* (or *Rattray*)
16	*Longley* (or *Inverugie*)
17	*Peterugie* (now Peterhead)
18	*Deer*
19	*Fyvie*
20	Methlick
21	*Tarves*
22	Ellon
23	Logie Buchan
24	*Cruden*
25	Slains
26	Forvie
27	Foveran

Garioch Deanery

28	*Forgue*
29	*Auchterless*
30	*Kennethmont*
31	Tullynessle
32	*Leslie*
33	*Rathmuriel* (now Christ's Kirk)
34	*Insch*
35	*Premnay*
36	*Oyne*
37	*Logie Durno*
38	*Culsalmond*
39	*Rayne*
40	*Daviot*
41	*Bethelnie*
42	*Bourtie*
43	*Inverurie*
44	Kinkell
44a	Dumblade
44b	Kemnay
44c	Kintore
44e	Dyce
44f	Skene
45	*Fetternear*
46	Monymusk
47	*Fintray*

Aberdeen Deanery

48	*Belhelvie*
49	*Aberdeen Cathedral*
50	Aberdeen St Nicholas
51	*Banchory-Devenick*
52	*Culter* (now Peterculter)
52a	*Templars' Chapel* (now Maryculter)
53	Dalmaik (now Drumoak)
54	*Banchory-Ternan*

Mar Deanery

55	*Mortlach*
56	*Dumeath*
57	*Clova*
58	Auchindoir
59	Kearn
60	*Clatt*
61	Kildrummy
62	Forbes
63	*Alford*
64	*Keig*
65	Tough
66	*Cluny*
67	*Kinnernie*
68	*Midmar*
69	*Echt*
70	Invernochty (now Strathdon)
71	*Kinbattoch* (now Towie)
72	Cushnie
73	*Leochel*
74	*Migvie*
75	*Tarland*
76	Coldstone
77	*Logie Mar* (or *Logie Ruthven*)
78	*Coull*
79	*Lumphanan*
80	*Kincardine O'Neil*
81	*Birse*
82	*Aboyne*
82a	*Tullich*
83	*Glenmuick*
84	Crathie
85	*Kindrochit* (now Braemar)

Parish churches about 1300: diocese of Aberdeen　　　　　　**DERW**

Parish churches about 1300

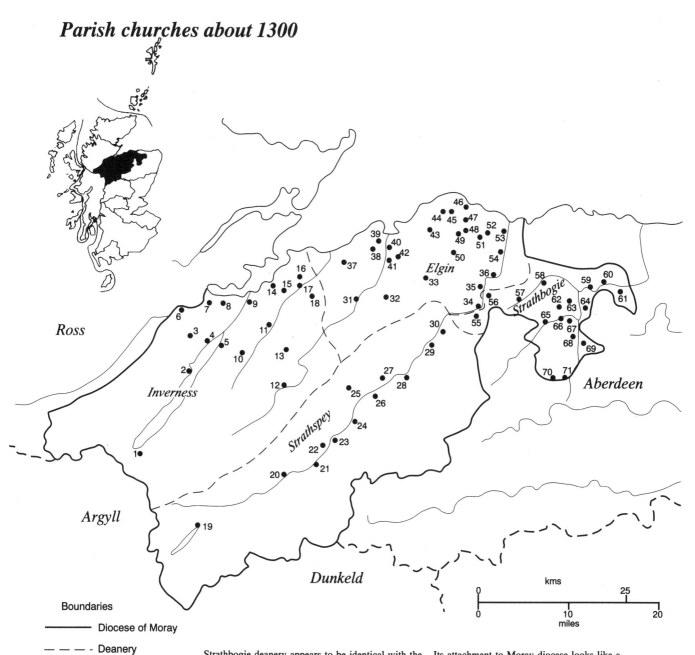

Boundaries

———— Diocese of Moray

— — — - Deanery

● Parish churches

Strathbogie deanery appears to be identical with the lordship of Strathbogie created by David I in the mid-twelfth century for a younger son of the earl of Fife.

Its attachment to Moray diocese looks like a deliberate act of policy, now that nearby Mortlach was no longer an episcopal centre

Inverness Deanery		15	Dalcross	29	*Advie*	44	*Duffus*	60	*Aberchirder*
		16	*Brackley*	30	*Inveravon*	45	*Ogston*		(now *Marnoch*)
1	*Abertarff*	17	*Croy*			46	*Kinneddar*	61	*Inverkeithny*
2	*Urquhart*	18	*Ewan*	**Elgin Deanery**		47	*Spynie*	62	*Botary*
3	*Convinth*		(or *Barevan*			48	Elgin Cathedral	63	*Ruthven*
4	Abriachan		now *Cawdor*)	31	*'Fothervays'*	49	*Elgin St Giles*	64	*Kinnoir*
	(now *Bona*)				(now *Ardclach*)	50	*Birnie*	65	Glass
5	*Dores*	**Strathspey Deanery**		32	*Logie Fythenach*	51	*Lhanbryde*	66	*Drumdelgie*
6	*Kiltarlity*				(now *Edinkillie*)	52	*Urquhart*	67	*Dunbennan*
7	*Wardlaw*	19	*Logie Kenny*	33	*Dallas*	53	*Essle*	68	*Edendiack*
	(now *Kirkhill*)		(now *Laggan*)	34	*Elchies*	54	*Dipple*	69	*Grantully*
8	*'Ferneway'*	20	*Kingussie*	35	*Rothes*				(now *Gartly*)
9	*Inverness*	21	*Insh*	36	*Dundurcus*	**Strathbogie Deanery**		70	*Essie*
10	Lundechty	22	Alvie	37	*Auldearn*			71	*Rhynie*
	(now *Dunlichity*)	23	*Rothiemurcus*	38	*Dyke*	55	*Aberlour*		
11	*Daviot*	24	Kincardine	39	*Moy*	56	*Arndilly*		
12	*Dalarossie*	25	*Duthil*	40	*Forres*		(now *Boharm*)		
13	*Lunnin*	26	*Abernethy*	41	*Altyre*	57	*Botriphnie*		
	(now *Moy*)	27	*Inverallan*	42	*Rafford*	58	*Keith*		
14	*Petty*	28	*Cromdale*	43	*Alves*	59	*Rothiemay*		

Parish churches about 1300: diocese of Moray

DERW, MA

355

Parish churches about 1300

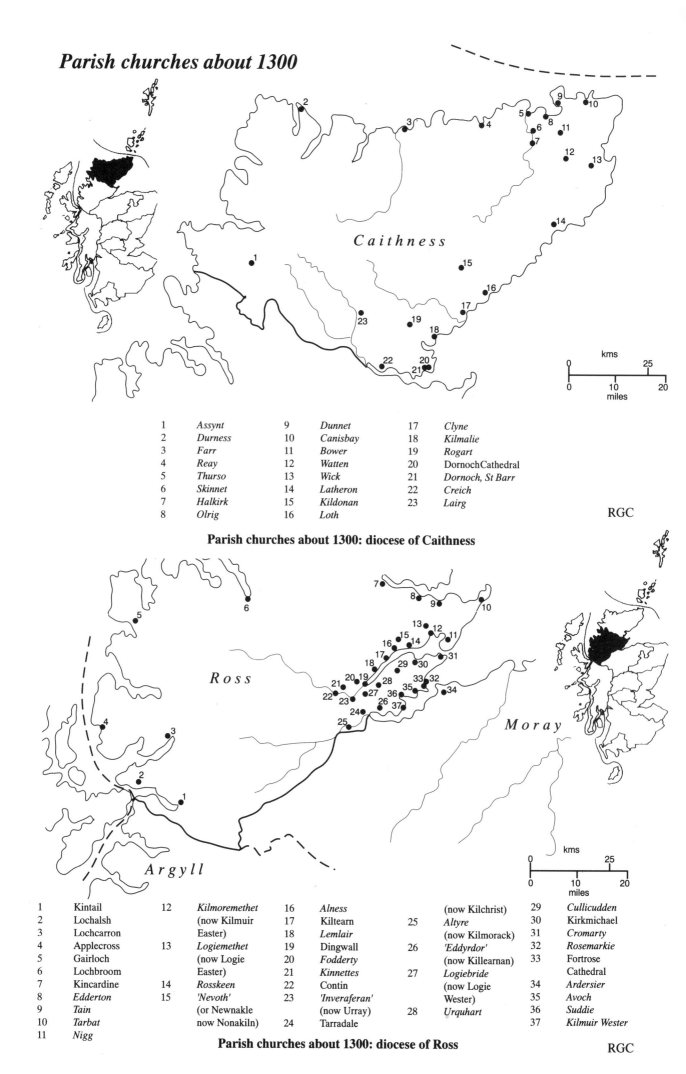

Caithness

1	Assynt	9	Dunnet	17	Clyne
2	Durness	10	Canisbay	18	Kilmalie
3	Farr	11	Bower	19	Rogart
4	Reay	12	Watten	20	Dornoch Cathedral
5	Thurso	13	Wick	21	Dornoch, St Barr
6	Skinnet	14	Latheron	22	Creich
7	Halkirk	15	Kildonan	23	Lairg
8	Olrig	16	Loth		

RGC

Parish churches about 1300: diocese of Caithness

Ross   *Moray*   *Argyll*

1	Kintail	12	Kilmoremethet (now Kilmuir Easter)	16	Alness		(now Kilchrist)	29	Cullicudden
2	Lochalsh			17	Kiltearn	25	Altyre (now Kilmorack)	30	Kirkmichael
3	Lochcarron			18	Lemlair			31	Cromarty
4	Applecross	13	Logiemethet (now Logie Easter)	19	Dingwall	26	'Eddyrdor' (now Killearnan)	32	Rosemarkie
5	Gairloch			20	Fodderty			33	Fortrose Cathedral
6	Lochbroom			21	Kinnettes	27	Logiebride (now Logie Wester)		
7	Kincardine	14	Rosskeen	22	Contin			34	Ardersier
8	Edderton	15	'Nevoth' (or Newnakle now Nonakiln)	23	'Inveraferan' (now Urray)	28	Urquhart	35	Avoch
9	Tain			24	Tarradale			36	Suddie
10	Tarbat							37	Kilmuir Wester
11	Nigg								

Parish churches about 1300: diocese of Ross

RGC

356

Parish churches about 1300

Rhinns Deanery

1 *Kirkcolm*
2 Leswalt
3 *Inch*
4 *Soulseat*
5 *Glenluce*
6 Stoneykirk
7 Clayshant
8 Toskerton
   (or Kirkmadrine)
9 Kirkmaiden

Farines Deanery

10 Mochrum
11 Longcastle
12 Kirkmaiden
13 Glasserton
14 *Whithorn Cathedral*
15 Cruggleton
16 *Sorbie*
17 *Kirkmadrine*
    (or Egerness)
18 Carnesmole
    (or Kirkinner)
19 Wigtown
20 Penninghame
21 'Awengalceway'
    (now Minnigaff)

Desnes Deanery

22 *Kirkmabreck*
23 Kirkdale
24 *Anwoth*
25 *Girthon*
26 Kirkandrews
    (or Purton)
27 *Borgue*
28 Senwick
29 Kirkchrist
30 *Twynholm*
31 *Tongland*
32 *Kirkcudbright*
33 *Galtway*
34 *Dunrod*
35 *Rerrick*
36 *Barncrosh*
37 *Kirkcormack*
38 Gelston
39 Buittle
40 *Kelton*
41 Crossmichael

Glenken Deanery

42 *Balmaghie*
43 Parton
44 Kells
45 'Trevercarcou'
    (now Balmaclellan)
46 Dalry

Parish churches about 1300: diocese of Galloway   RO

Parish churches about 1300

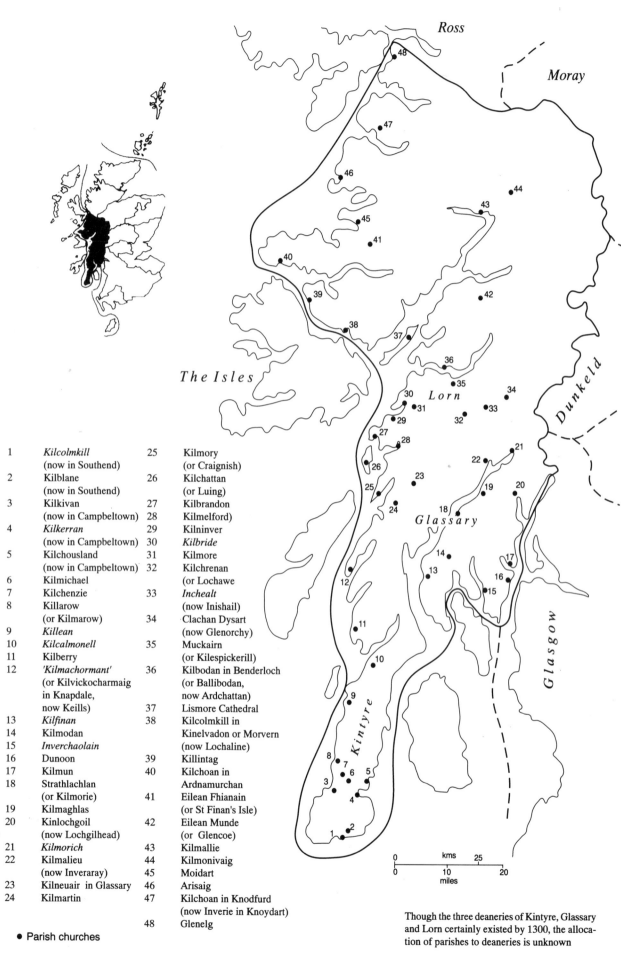

Ross

Moray

The Isles

Lorn

Dunkeld

Glassary

Glasgow

Kintyre

1	*Kilcolmkill*	25	Kilmory
	(now in Southend)		(or Craignish)
2	Kilblane	26	Kilchattan
	(now in Southend)		(or Luing)
3	Kilkivan	27	Kilbrandon
	(now in Campbeltown)	28	Kilmelford
4	*Kilkerran*	29	Kilninver
	(now in Campbeltown)	30	*Kilbride*
5	Kilchousland	31	Kilmore
	(now in Campbeltown)	32	Kilchrenan
6	Kilmichael		(or Lochawe
7	Kilchenzie	33	*Inchealt*
8	Killarow		(now Inishail)
	(or Kilmarow)	34	Clachan Dysart
9	*Killean*		(now Glenorchy)
10	*Kilcalmonell*	35	Muckairn
11	Kilberry		(or Kilespickerill)
12	'Kilmachormant'	36	Kilbodan in Benderloch
	(or Kilvickocharmaig		(or Ballibodan,
	in Knapdale,		now Ardchattan)
	now Keills)	37	Lismore Cathedral
13	*Kilfinan*	38	Kilcolmkill in
14	Kilmodan		Kinelvadon or Morvern
15	*Inverchaolain*		(now Lochaline)
16	Dunoon	39	Killintag
17	Kilmun	40	Kilchoan in
18	Strathlachlan		Ardnamurchan
	(or Kilmorie)	41	Eilean Fhianain
19	Kilmaghlas		(or St Finan's Isle)
20	Kinlochgoil	42	Eilean Munde
	(now Lochgilhead)		(or Glencoe)
21	*Kilmorich*	43	Kilmallie
22	Kilmalieu	44	Kilmonivaig
	(now Inveraray)	45	Moidart
23	Kilneuair in Glassary	46	Arisaig
24	Kilmartin	47	Kilchoan in Knodfurd
			(now Inverie in Knoydart)
		48	Glenelg

● Parish churches

kms 25
0   10   20
miles

Though the three deaneries of Kintyre, Glassary
and Lorn certainly existed by 1300, the allocation of parishes to deaneries is unknown

Parish churches about 1300: diocese of Argyll

IF

358

Parish churches about 1300

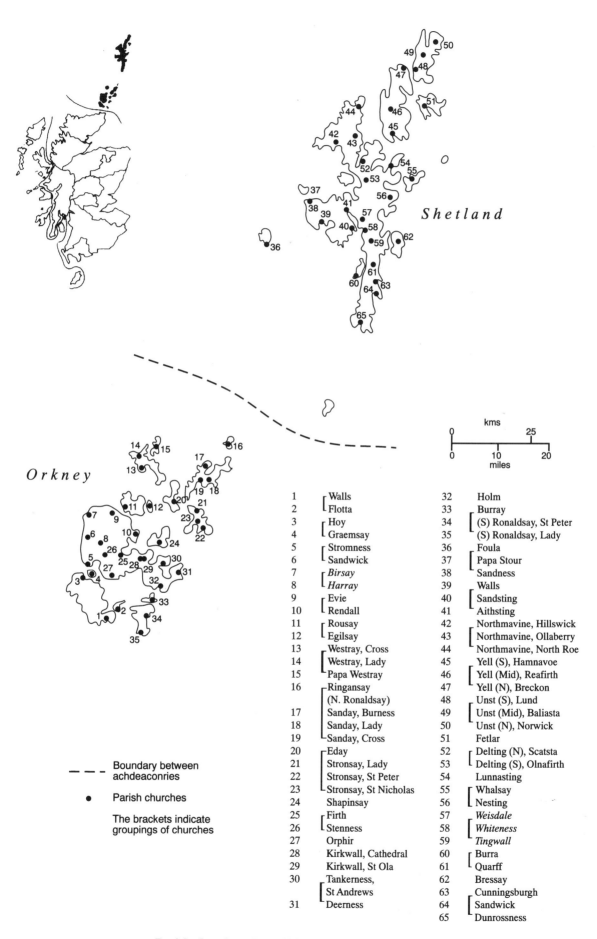

1	Walls	32	Holm
2	Flotta	33	Burray
3	Hoy	34	(S) Ronaldsay, St Peter
4	Graemsay	35	(S) Ronaldsay, Lady
5	Stromness	36	Foula
6	Sandwick	37	Papa Stour
7	*Birsay*	38	Sandness
8	*Harray*	39	Walls
9	Evie	40	Sandsting
10	Rendall	41	Aithsting
11	Rousay	42	Northmavine, Hillswick
12	Egilsay	43	Northmavine, Ollaberry
13	Westray, Cross	44	Northmavine, North Roe
14	Westray, Lady	45	Yell (S), Hamnavoe
15	Papa Westray	46	Yell (Mid), Reafirth
16	Ringansay (N. Ronaldsay)	47	Yell (N), Breckon
		48	Unst (S), Lund
17	Sanday, Burness	49	Unst (Mid), Baliasta
18	Sanday, Lady	50	Unst (N), Norwick
19	Sanday, Cross	51	Fetlar
20	Eday	52	Delting (N), Scatsta
21	Stronsay, Lady	53	Delting (S), Olnafirth
22	Stronsay, St Peter	54	Lunnasting
23	Stronsay, St Nicholas	55	Whalsay
24	Shapinsay	56	Nesting
25	Firth	57	*Weisdale*
26	Stenness	58	*Whiteness*
27	Orphir	59	*Tingwall*
28	Kirkwall, Cathedral	60	Burra
29	Kirkwall, St Ola	61	Quarff
30	Tankerness, St Andrews	62	Bressay
		63	Cunningsburgh
31	Deerness	64	Sandwick
		65	Dunrossness

Boundary between achdeaconries — – –

● Parish churches

The brackets indicate groupings of churches

Parish churches about 1300: diocese of Orkney

RGC

Parish churches about 1300

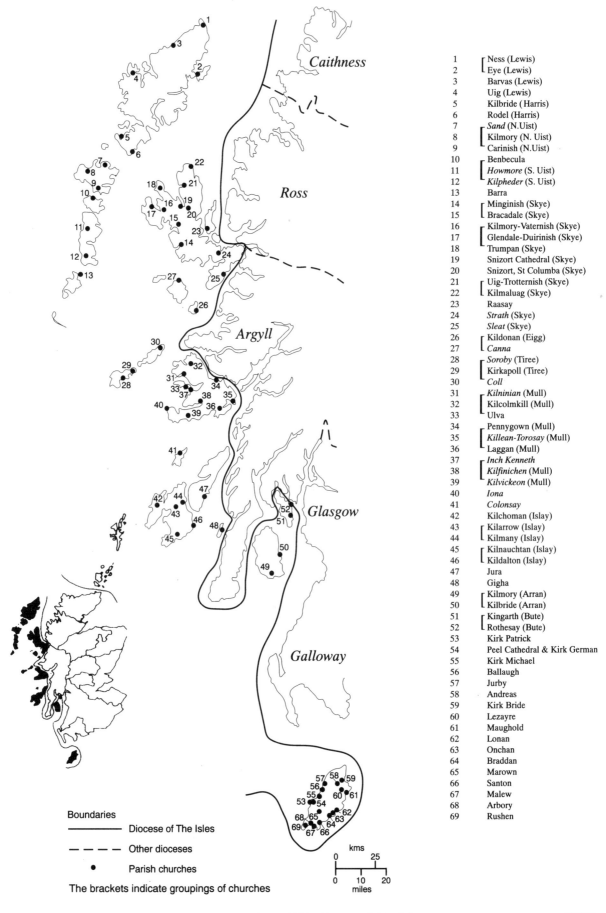

1 [Ness (Lewis)
2 [Eye (Lewis)
3 Barvas (Lewis)
4 Uig (Lewis)
5 Kilbride (Harris)
6 Rodel (Harris)
7 [*Sand* (N.Uist)
8 [Kilmory (N. Uist)
9 Carinish (N.Uist)
10 [Benbecula
11 [*Howmore* (S. Uist)
12 [*Kilpheder* (S. Uist)
13 Barra
14 [Minginish (Skye)
15 [Bracadale (Skye)
16 [Kilmory-Vaternish (Skye)
17 [Glendale-Duirinish (Skye)
18 Trumpan (Skye)
19 Snizort Cathedral (Skye)
20 Snizort, St Columba (Skye)
21 [Uig-Trotternish (Skye)
22 [Kilmaluag (Skye)
23 Raasay
24 *Strath* (Skye)
25 *Sleat* (Skye)
26 [Kildonan (Eigg)
27 [*Canna*
28 [*Soroby* (Tiree)
29 [Kirkapoll (Tiree)
30 *Coll*
31 [*Kilninian* (Mull)
32 [Kilcolmkill (Mull)
33 Ulva
34 [Pennygown (Mull)
35 [*Killean-Torosay* (Mull)
36 Laggan (Mull)
37 [*Inch Kenneth*
38 [*Kilfinichen* (Mull)
39 *Kilvickeon* (Mull)
40 *Iona*
41 *Colonsay*
42 Kilchoman (Islay)
43 [Kilarrow (Islay)
44 [Kilmany (Islay)
45 [Kilnauchtan (Islay)
46 [Kildalton (Islay)
47 Jura
48 Gigha
49 [Kilmory (Arran)
50 [Kilbride (Arran)
51 [Kingarth (Bute)
52 [Rothesay (Bute)
53 Kirk Patrick
54 Peel Cathedral & Kirk German
55 Kirk Michael
56 Ballaugh
57 Jurby
58 Andreas
59 Kirk Bride
60 Lezayre
61 Maughold
62 Lonan
63 Onchan
64 Braddan
65 Marown
66 Santon
67 Malew
68 Arbory
69 Rushen

Boundaries

—————— Diocese of The Isles

– – – – – Other dioceses

• Parish churches

The brackets indicate groupings of churches

kms
0   25
0   10   20
miles

Parish churches about 1300: diocese of The Isles

RGC

Lands and churches of the see of St Andrews

The bishops of St Andrews were the lords of a far-flung and extensive demesne. By the early thirteenth century their lands had a total value of £1,000, making them amongst the wealthiest magnates in Scotland.

At least some of the bishop's domain had come into their possession in Celtic times, many of the sites being ancient monastic centres or connected with important saints such as Ternan (Arbuthnott) and Cuthbert (Stow). These early lands almost certainly included the lands within the Boar's Raik (*Cursus Apri*), the ancient *parochia* of St Andrews, as well as Monymusk, Keig, Loch Leven, Stow in Wedale, Tyninghame and Broxmouth. Other early possessions probably included Ellon, Nigg, the kirkton of Arbuthnott, Inchbraoch and the Abthane of Kinghorn. The vast majority of the bishop's remaining lands came by endowment during the twelfth-century reorganisation of the diocese along the customary lines of the western church. Other lands were lost, or granted to other religious corporations, such as the abbeys of Lindores and Arbroath. Around St Andrews itself there was considerable rearrangement of lands and rights between the bishop, the culdees and the chapter of Augustinian canons founded by bishop Robert.

The 'Norman' bishops of the twelfth century also created a system of secular administration for their lands. Under Bishop Robert (1127-59) a chamberlain was introduced to take overall charge of the bishop's estates. By the end of the twelfth century two seneschals appear, acting under the chamberlain and in charge of the bishop's estates north and south of the Forth; in the early thirteenth century a third one was introduced so that the three were in charge of, respectively, Lothian, Fife and Fothrif, and the scattered estates north of the Tay. Under these seneschals were local bailies who usually operated from an episcopal residence, although by 1300 in some areas (such as Tyninghame) the office of bailie had become hereditary with local families.

Some of the eight episcopal residences recorded by the early fourteenth century had been in existence since the twelfth century (St Andrews castle and some others in east Fife, such as Inchmurdo), although the majority first appear in record in the thirteenth century. William Lamberton (1297-1328) is said to have built the residences at Muckhart, Stow and Kirkliston.

The bishops had mensal and patronage rights in churches. The former meant that a stipendiary priest could be assigned to the church and the payments in kind due from the church were paid to the bishop's *mensa* (table, or household). In the latter case the bishop had the right to present to the living. This was a favourite way of maintaining episcopal servants such as archdeacons and officials.

1	Culsalmond	43	Tarvit
2	Ellon	44	Moonzie
3	Monkeigie	45	Kilmany
	(now Keithhall)	46	Dairsie
4	Kinkell	47	Kemback
5	Keig	48	St Andrews
6	Monymusk		Castle
7	Dyce	49	Dunino
8	Nigg	50	Inchmurdo
9	Craighton	51	Kilrenny
10	Durris	52	Pitcorthie
11	Banchory	53	Kilconquhar
12	Arbuthnott	54	Muircambus
13	Kinneff	55	Scoonie
14	Benholm	56	Methil
15	Dalbog	57	Dysart
16	Newdosk	58	Abthane of
17	Fettercairn		Kinghorn
18	Aberluthnot	59	Muckhart
19	Logie	60	Pitgober
20	Inchbraoch		
21	Aldbar		
22	Rescobie		
23	Kinnell		
24	Kinnettles		
25	Meathie		
26	Idvies		
27	Inverarity		
28	Blairgowrie		
29	Nevay		
30	Kettins		
31	Luncarty	61	Torry
32	Collace	62	Ecclesmachan
33	Kilspindie	63	Kirkliston
34	Rossie	64	Ratho
35	Strathmartine	65	Kinleith
36	Balmuir		(now Currie)
37	Pourie	66	Lasswade
38	Forteviot	67	Gullane
39	Loch Leven	68	Bass Rock
	(or Bishopshire)	69	Tyninghame
40	Kirkforthar	70	Broxmouth
41	Monimail	71	Stow in Wedale
42	Cults	72	Nenthorn

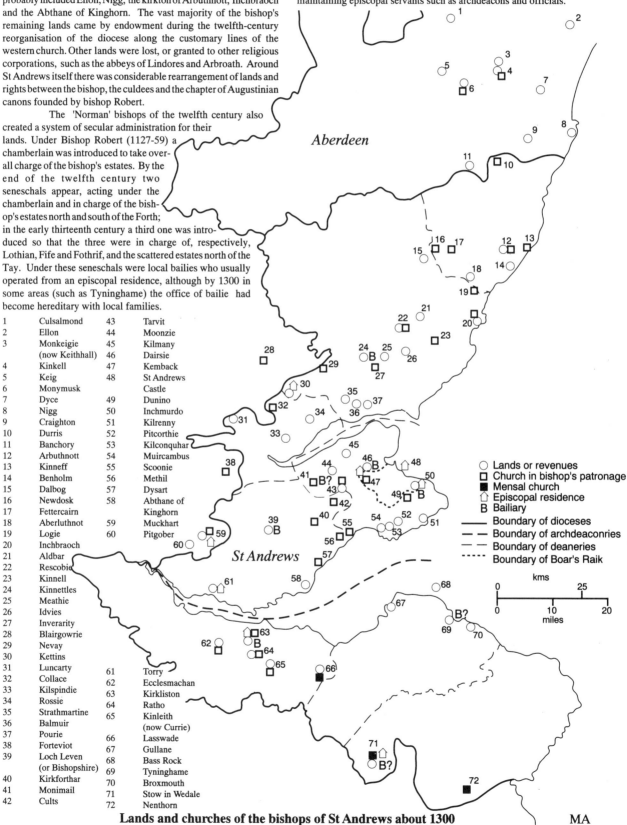

Aberdeen

St Andrews

○ Lands or revenues
□ Church in bishop's patronage
■ Mensal church
⌂ Episcopal residence
B Bailiary
— Boundary of dioceses
– – Boundary of archdeaconries
— — Boundary of deaneries
···· Boundary of Boar's Raik

kms
0   10   25
0   10   20
miles

Lands and churches of the bishops of St Andrews about 1300   MA

Lands and churches of the see of St Andrews

The *Cursus Apri*, or Boar's Raik, was the territory immediately surrounding St Andrews, probably corresponding with the modern parishes of St Andrews and St Leonards, Cameron, Dunino, Ceres and Kemback. The origin of the name is obscure, perhaps deriving from an especially memorable boar hunt or referring to a totemic symbol of the local tribe or ruling family. According to the various twelfth-century legends describing the arrival of the relics of St Andrew in Scotland, the *Cursus Apri* was the territory granted to the church of the apostle.

This may well be the case, for despite being dispersed and alienated during the long interregnum following the death of Bishop Fothad II in 1093, these same lands were nevertheless used to form the basis of the endowment of the Augustinian priory in 1144. At the same time, moreover, they were specifically stated not to belong to the office of the bishop. Those lands which the bishops of St Andrews did hold within the Boar's Raik therefore may have come to them by right of their implied status as inheritors of the Celtic abbots. The isolated episcopal estate and residence at Inchmurdo probably represents part of this ancient endowment; even today the parish boundary crosses the Kenly Water to include the site of the 'palace'. Certainly the bishop's lands were not central to the Boar's Raik in the way the chapter's lands were.

Throughout the later twelfth century and the thirteenth there were a number of agreements over lands and rights in the Boar's Raik between the bishop, the priory, the archdeacon of St Andrews, and the Culdees (who formed the collegiate corporation of the church of St Mary of the Rock by the middle of the thirteenth century). As a result of these agreements the archdeacon came to hold a compact bloc of territory to the north of St Andrews, centred on Strathtyrum, and the Culdees held substantial groups of lands to the east and south of the city. An inquest of 1309 found that there were three baronies within the Boar's Raik: the bishop's, the Priory's and the Culdees', and that the latter two were subject to the bishop's authority.

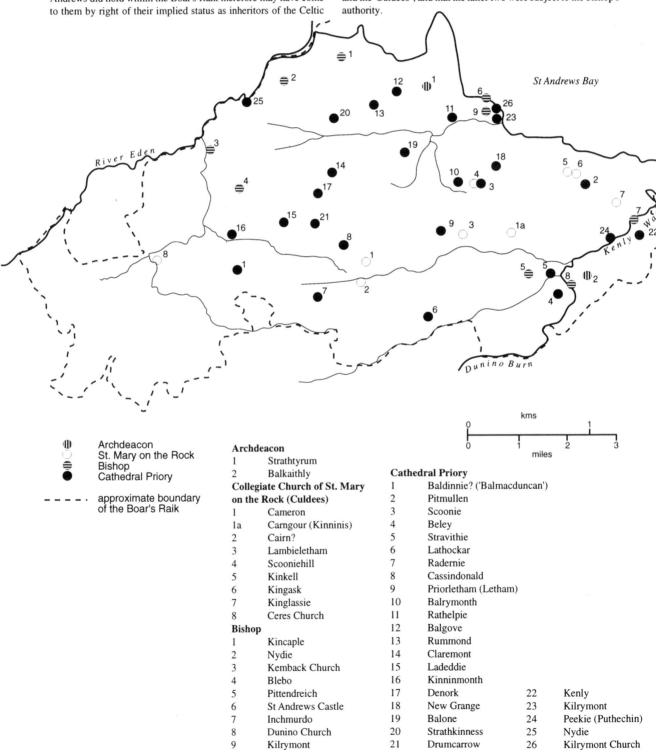

	Archdeacon
⦀	Archdeacon
○	St. Mary on the Rock
≋	Bishop
●	Cathedral Priory

- - - - approximate boundary
of the Boar's Raik

Archdeacon

| 1 | Strathtyrum |
| 2 | Balkaithly |

Collegiate Church of St. Mary on the Rock (Culdees)

1	Cameron
1a	Carngour (Kinninis)
2	Cairn?
3	Lambieletham
4	Scooniehill
5	Kinkell
6	Kingask
7	Kinglassie
8	Ceres Church

Bishop

1	Kincaple
2	Nydie
3	Kemback Church
4	Blebo
5	Pittendreich
6	St Andrews Castle
7	Inchmurdo
8	Dunino Church
9	Kilrymont

Cathedral Priory

1	Baldinnie? ('Balmacduncan')		
2	Pitmullen		
3	Scoonie		
4	Beley		
5	Stravithie		
6	Lathockar		
7	Radernie		
8	Cassindonald		
9	Priorletham (Letham)		
10	Balrymonth		
11	Rathelpie		
12	Balgove		
13	Rummond		
14	Claremont		
15	Ladeddie		
16	Kinninmonth		
17	Denork	22	Kenly
18	New Grange	23	Kilrymont
19	Balone	24	Peekie (Puthechin)
20	Strathkinness	25	Nydie
21	Drumcarrow	26	Kilrymont Church

The Boar's Raik

MA

Lands and churches of Kelso Abbey

The Tironensian abbey of Kelso had some scattered properties, but there were two main *foci* - Kelso itself and its dependent priory of Lesmahagow. More remote holdings are to be explained by the position of the lands of the donor - e.g. a toft in Inverkeithing from Malcolm IV and one in Renfrew from Walter, son of Alan, the Steward. Besides arable and pasture, there were shielings in the Lammermuirs, granges, fishing rights (e.g. on the Tweed), a salt-pan at New Abbey, peataries, mills and brewhouses. The abbey's lands produced rents and services. The surviving records provide little evidence of Kelso's part in the wool trade, apart from references to sheep, but Berwick must have been the main port of export for the abbey's wool, at least until its sack in 1296; the abbey had properties and revenues in Berwick, and the husbandmen of Redden did carting service to it.

Kelso had the distinction of holding the largest number of appropriated churches in Scotland. They lay mainly in the dioceses of St Andrews and Glasgow, but also in those of Aberdeen and Moray. The two *foci* of Kelso and Lesmahagow, though less obvious in this respect, are still evident on the map.

A rental drawn up for an Abbot Richard is usually ascribed to the abbot of that name who held office in the 1280s and 1290s. By then the abbey seems largely to have given up direct exploitation, preferring cash to labour services. A problem posed by the rental is that it apparently does not include all the abbey's lands. The group of properties in Lanarkshire, plus Kilmaurs and Auchinleck in Ayrshire, may have been administered by Lesmahagow Priory and there may have been some rationalisation, because many of the places omitted had only one piece of land belonging to the abbey. It is difficult, however, to explain the omission of Innerwick with its revenue, two pastures and two other pieces of land, or of Bothwell (Lothian) where Kelso still held land in the early fourteenth century. The rental survives only in a copy which contains lacunae, and so it is possible that some properties have been omitted.

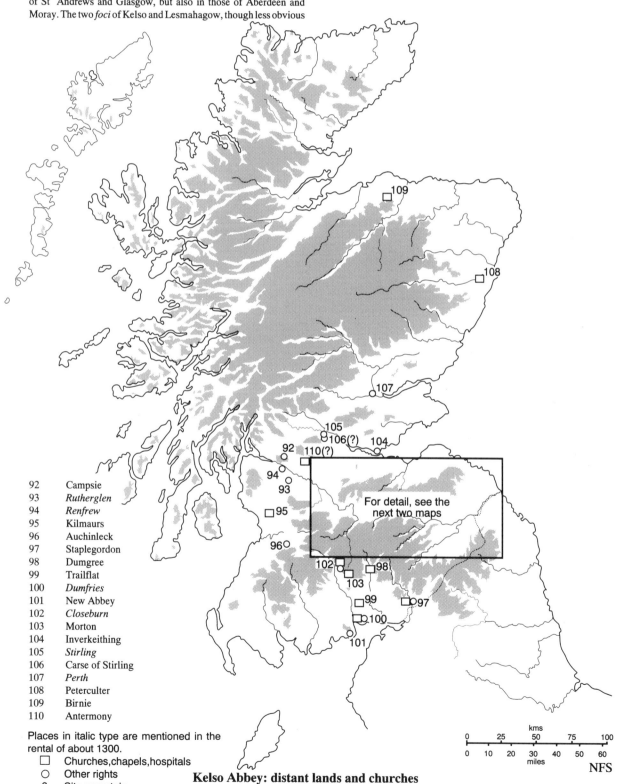

92	Campsie
93	*Rutherglen*
94	*Renfrew*
95	Kilmaurs
96	Auchinleck
97	Staplegordon
98	Dumgree
99	Trailflat
100	*Dumfries*
101	New Abbey
102	*Closeburn*
103	Morton
104	Inverkeithing
105	*Stirling*
106	Carse of Stirling
107	*Perth*
108	Peterculter
109	Birnie
110	Antermony

Places in italic type are mentioned in the rental of about 1300.

☐   Churches, chapels, hospitals
○   Other rights
?   Site uncertain

Kelso Abbey: distant lands and churches

NFS

Lands and churches of Kelso Abbey

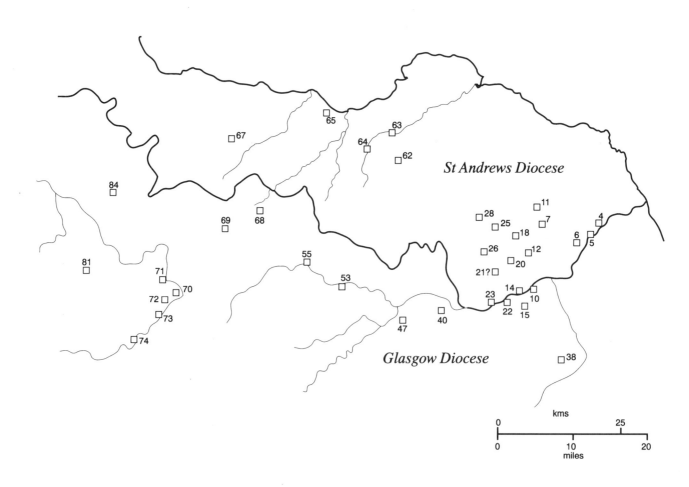

St Andrews Diocese

Glasgow Diocese

kms
0   25
0   10   20
miles

4	*Horndean**	22	*Roxburgh**	64	Cranstoun Riddel*
5	*Upsettlington**	23	*Makerstoun**	65	Duddingston*
6	*Simprim**	25	Hallyburton*	67	Calder Clere*
7	*Fogo**	26	Gordon*		(now East Calder)
10	*Sprouston**	28	*Wedderlie**	68	West Linton*
11	*Langton**	38	*Mow**	69	Dunsyre
12	*Lambden**	40	*Bowden**	70	Symington
14	Kelso*	47	*Selkirk**	71	Thankerton
15	Maxwell	53	*Innerleithen**	72	Wiston
18	*Greenlaw**	55	Peebles*	73	Roberton
20	*Hume**	62	*Humbie**	74	Crawfordjohn
21	Nenthorn	63	Pencaitland*	81	Lesmahagow*
				84	Cambusnethan*

Places in italic are mentioned in the rental of about 1300

⸻ Diocesan boundary

*   Other rights in addition

Kelso Abbey: churches, chapels and hospitals

NFS

Lands and churches of Kelso Abbey

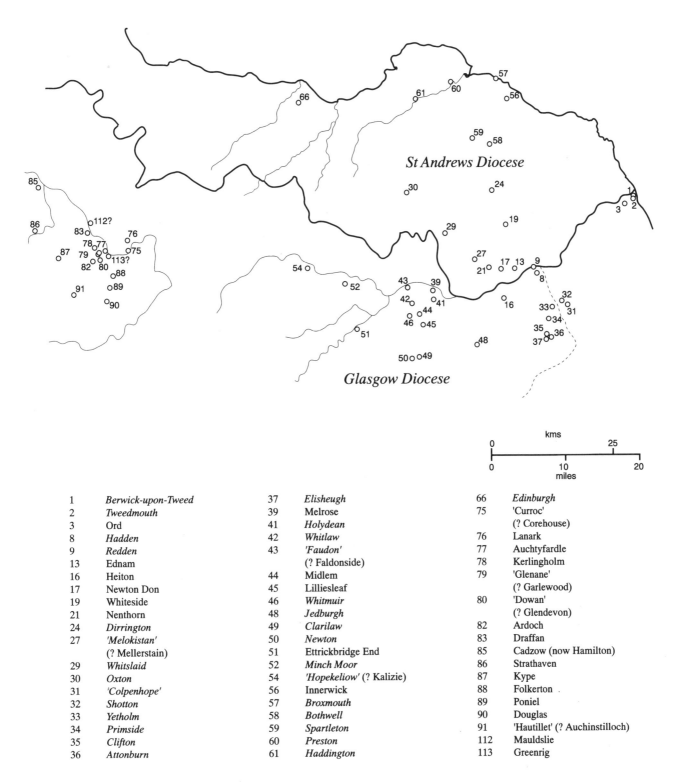

1	Berwick-upon-Tweed	37	Elisheugh	66	Edinburgh
2	Tweedmouth	39	Melrose	75	'Curroc'
3	Ord	41	Holydean		(? Corehouse)
8	Hadden	42	Whitlaw	76	Lanark
9	Redden	43	'Faudon'	77	Auchtyfardle
13	Ednam		(? Faldonside)	78	Kerlingholm
16	Heiton	44	Midlem	79	'Glenane'
17	Newton Don	45	Lilliesleaf		(? Garlewood)
19	Whiteside	46	Whitmuir	80	'Dowan'
21	Nenthorn	48	Jedburgh		(? Glendevon)
24	Dirrington	49	Clarilaw	82	Ardoch
27	'Melokistan'	50	Newton	83	Draffan
	(? Mellerstain)	51	Ettrickbridge End	85	Cadzow (now Hamilton)
29	Whitslaid	52	Minch Moor	86	Strathaven
30	Oxton	54	'Hopekeliow' (? Kalizie)	87	Kype
31	'Colpenhope'	56	Innerwick	88	Folkerton
32	Shotton	57	Broxmouth	89	Poniel
33	Yetholm	58	Bothwell	90	Douglas
34	Primside	59	Spartleton	91	'Hautillet' (? Auchinstilloch)
35	Clifton	60	Preston	112	Mauldslie
36	Attonburn	61	Haddington	113	Greenrig

Places in italic are mentioned in the rental of about 1300

——— Diocesan boundary

Kelso Abbey: other rights   NFS

Appropriations of some parish churches by 1560

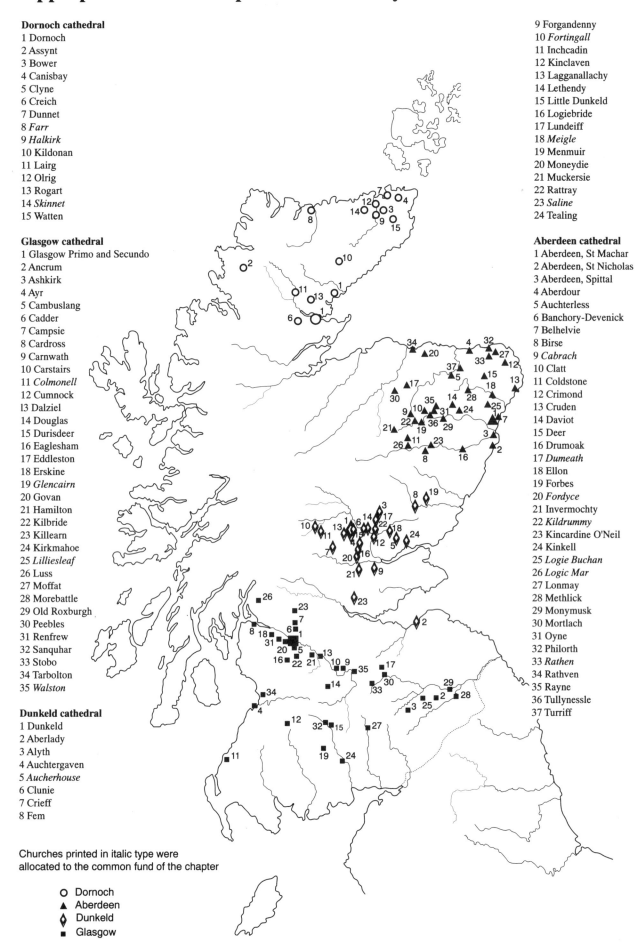

Dornoch cathedral
1 Dornoch
2 Assynt
3 Bower
4 Canisbay
5 Clyne
6 Creich
7 Dunnet
8 *Farr*
9 *Halkirk*
10 Kildonan
11 Lairg
12 Olrig
13 Rogart
14 *Skinnet*
15 Watten

Glasgow cathedral
1 Glasgow Primo and Secundo
2 Ancrum
3 Ashkirk
4 Ayr
5 Cambuslang
6 Cadder
7 Campsie
8 Cardross
9 Carnwath
10 Carstairs
11 *Colmonell*
12 Cumnock
13 Dalziel
14 Douglas
15 Durisdeer
16 Eaglesham
17 Eddleston
18 Erskine
19 *Glencairn*
20 Govan
21 Hamilton
22 Kilbride
23 Killearn
24 Kirkmahoe
25 *Lilliesleaf*
26 Luss
27 Moffat
28 Morebattle
29 Old Roxburgh
30 Peebles
31 Renfrew
32 Sanquhar
33 Stobo
34 Tarbolton
35 *Walston*

Dunkeld cathedral
1 Dunkeld
2 Aberlady
3 Alyth
4 Auchtergaven
5 *Aucherhouse*
6 Clunie
7 Crieff
8 Fern

9 Forgandenny
10 *Fortingall*
11 Inchcadin
12 Kinclaven
13 Lagganallachy
14 Lethendy
15 Little Dunkeld
16 Logiebride
17 Lundeiff
18 *Meigle*
19 Menmuir
20 Moneydie
21 Muckersie
22 Rattray
23 *Saline*
24 Tealing

Aberdeen cathedral
1 Aberdeen, St Machar
2 Aberdeen, St Nicholas
3 Aberdeen, Spittal
4 Aberdour
5 Auchterless
6 Banchory-Devenick
7 Belhelvie
8 Birse
9 *Cabrach*
10 Clatt
11 Coldstone
12 Crimond
13 Cruden
14 Daviot
15 Deer
16 Drumoak
17 *Dumeath*
18 Ellon
19 Forbes
20 *Fordyce*
21 Invermochty
22 *Kildrummy*
23 Kincardine O'Neil
24 Kinkell
25 *Logie Buchan*
26 *Logic Mar*
27 Lonmay
28 Methlick
29 Monymusk
30 Mortlach
31 Oyne
32 Philorth
33 *Rathen*
34 Rathven
35 Rayne
36 Tullynessle
37 Turriff

Churches printed in italic type were
allocated to the common fund of the chapter

○ Dornoch
▲ Aberdeen
◊ Dunkeld
■ Glasgow

Appropriations of parish churches by 1560: cathedrals of Dornoch, Aberdeen, Dunkeld and Glasgow IBC

Appropriations of some parish churches by 1560

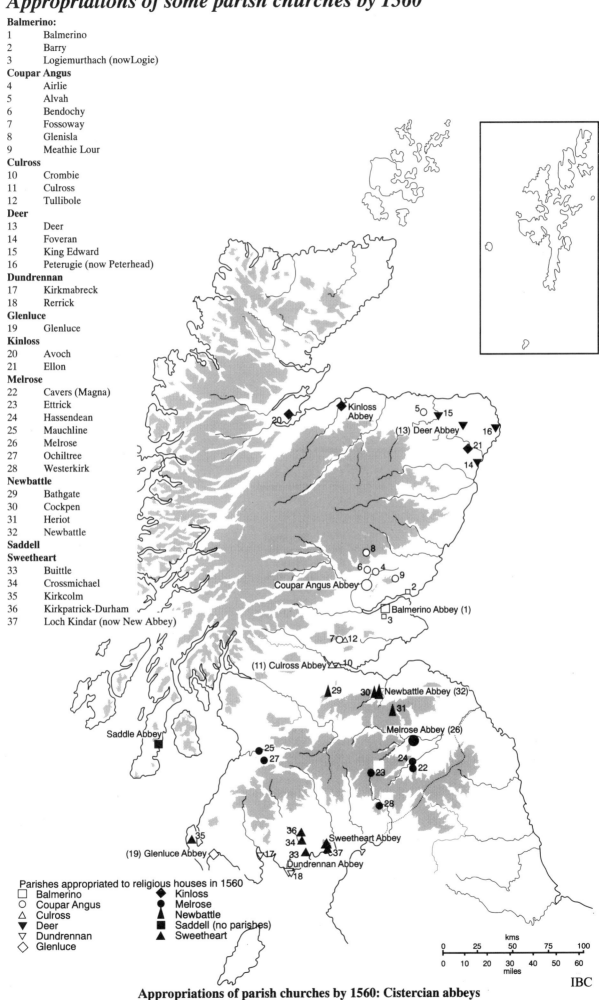

Balmerino:
1 Balmerino
2 Barry
3 Logiemurthach (nowLogie)

Coupar Angus
4 Airlie
5 Alvah
6 Bendochy
7 Fossoway
8 Glenisla
9 Meathie Lour

Culross
10 Crombie
11 Culross
12 Tullibole

Deer
13 Deer
14 Foveran
15 King Edward
16 Peterugie (now Peterhead)

Dundrennan
17 Kirkmabreck
18 Rerrick

Glenluce
19 Glenluce

Kinloss
20 Avoch
21 Ellon

Melrose
22 Cavers (Magna)
23 Ettrick
24 Hassendean
25 Mauchline
26 Melrose
27 Ochiltree
28 Westerkirk

Newbattle
29 Bathgate
30 Cockpen
31 Heriot
32 Newbattle

Saddell

Sweetheart
33 Buittle
34 Crossmichael
35 Kirkcolm
36 Kirkpatrick-Durham
37 Loch Kindar (now New Abbey)

Parishes appropriated to religious houses in 1560

☐ Balmerino   ◆ Kinloss
○ Coupar Angus ● Melrose
△ Culross   ▲ Newbattle
▼ Deer   ■ Saddell (no parishes)
▽ Dundrennan   ▲ Sweetheart
◇ Glenluce

Appropriations of parish churches by 1560: Cistercian abbeys

IBC

367

Appropriations of some parish churches by 1560

The creation of a parochial organisation during the course of the twelfth and thirteenth centuries provided the means of maintaining an endowed priest in every parish, but this was never intended to be its sole purpose. Others had equal claim to the teinds, and from their inception these revenues were regarded as a means of endowing other religious institutions besides the parish. Initially it was religious houses founded after the twelfth-century reforms that received churches; and eventually by 1560 no Scottish religious house of consequence (with the exception of friaries) lacked such an endowment, although the number of annexed parishes varied considerably. The Cistercians, who initially resisted the holding of parochial revenues, totalled only thirty-seven churches between their eleven houses. The largest single holders of parish churches were the Tironensian royal foundations such as Arbroath with thirty-four churches, closely followed by the Cluniac house at Paisley which owed most of its twenty-eight churches to the generosity of its founder, Walter Fitzalan. The holdings of these two houses, with the almost as large endowments of the Augustinian abbey of Holyrood which held twenty-five churches, illustrate the geographically compactness of most annexations. However distance in itself was no barrier to appropriation, although inaccessibility involved difficulty in the collection of teinds - a factor which Holyrood, with its remote churches in Galloway, seems to have partially solved by serving such churches by its own canons.

Parochial revenues were also used to support cathedral churches. At St Andrews and Whithorn there were communities of regular clergy supported by parish churches in the same way as the abbeys. In the other dioceses, commencing at Glasgow in the mid-twelfth century, it became common for the cathedral chapters to be made up of secular clergy. These bodies of ecclesiastics, known individually as canons, were assigned separate prebendal allowances, the revenues of which were normally derived from appropriated parish churches, which in turn gave their names to the prebends which they supported. New churches were constantly being added over the centuries, and by the Reformation Glasgow cathedral, closely followed by Aberdeen, possessed thirty-one and thirty prebends endowed with churches respectively, while Dunkeld with twenty such prebends came not far behind. Other cathedral chapters were much smaller; the chapter at Dornoch for example possessed only twelve such prebends. Not all appropriated churches were, however, allocated to individual canons, for others formed the basis of a common fund, the revenues of which were allocated among members of the chapter as a means of encouraging residence.

The basis of funding remained parochial revenues. This precedent in monasteries and cathedrals was followed in the erection of collegiate church and academic colleges from the mid-fourteenth century to the Reformation, by which period 86% of the parish churches of Scotland had been appropriated, bringing problems of service which were only partly assuaged by vicarage settlements, which sought to provide tenure and with less success an adequate stipend for the parochial incumbent who consequently was often unfitted for his duties. If laxity of service, rather than appropriation, was the principal canker within the medieval church, the system undoubtedly played a significant part in the deterioration of the structural organisation of the Scottish church.

Arbroath Abbey		Paisley Abbey		Holyrood Abbey	
1	Aberchirder	1	Auchinleck	1	Airth
2	Abernethy	2	Carmunnock	2	Balmaghie
3	Arbirlot	3	Cathcart	3	Bara
4	Banchory-Ternan	4	Craigie	4	Bolton
5	Banff	5	Cumbrae	5	Canongate
6	Bethelnie	6	Dundonald	6	Carriden
7	Coull	7	Eastwood	7	Corstorphine
8	Dunbog	8	Houston	8	Crawford (-Douglas)
9	Dunnichen	9	Innerwick	9	Dalgarnock
10	Ethie	10	Inverkip	10	Dunrod
11	Fetterangus	11	Kilbarchan	11	Falkirk
12	Forgue	12	Kilcalmonell	12	Kelton
13	Fyvie	13	Kilfinan	13	Kinghorn Easter
14	Gamrie	14	Killallan		(now Kinghorn)
15	Garvock	15	Kilmacolm	14	Kinneil
16	Glamis	16	Kilpatrick	15	Kirkcormack
17	Inverboyndie	17	Largs	16	Kirkcudbright
18	Inverkeilor	18	Legerwood	17	Liberton
19	Inverness	19	Lochwinnoch	18	Livingston
20	Inverugie	20	Mearns	19	Melginch
	(now St. Fergus)	21	Monkton		(now St. Martins)
21	Kinnernie	22	Neilston	20	Mount Lothian
22	Kingoldrum	23	Paisley	21	St. Cuthbert under
23	Kirriemuir	24	Prestwick		the Castle
24	Lunan	25	Riccarton	22	Tranent
25	Mains	26	Rosneath	23	Twynholm
26	Monifieth	27	Rutherglen	24	Urr
27	Monikie	28	St. Quivox	25	Hamer (now
28	Murroes				Whitekirk)
29	Newtyle				
30	Nigg				
31	Panbride				
32	Ruthven				
33	St. Vigeans				
34	Tarves				

Appropriations of parish churches by 1560: abbeys of Arbroath, Paisley and Holyrood

Appropriations of some parish churches by 1560

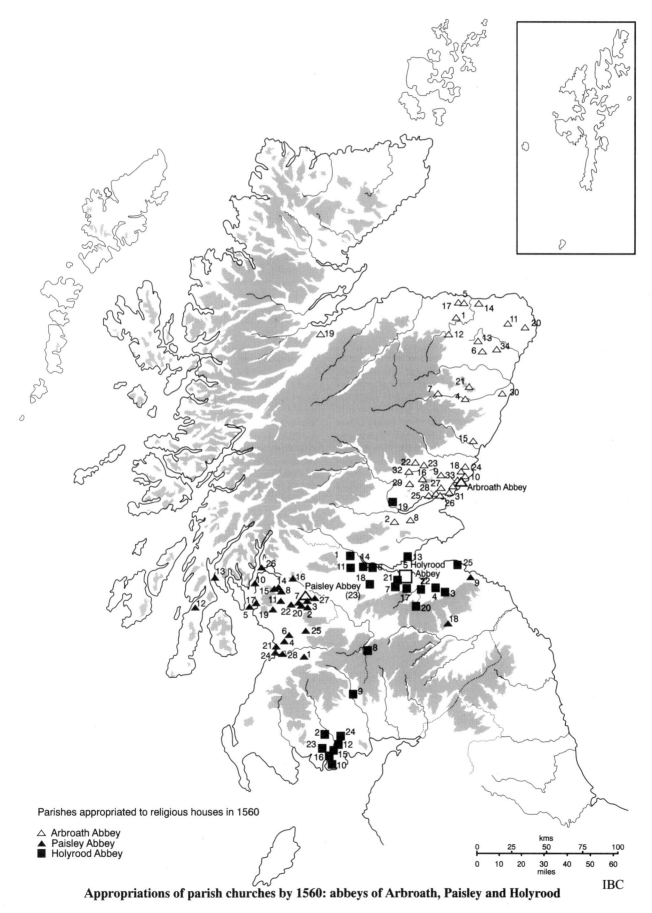

Parishes appropriated to religious houses in 1560

△ Arbroath Abbey
▲ Paisley Abbey
■ Holyrood Abbey

kms
| 0 | 25 | 50 | 75 | 100 |

| 0 | 10 | 20 | 30 | 40 | 50 | 60 |
miles

IBC

Appropriations of parish churches by 1560: abbeys of Arbroath, Paisley and Holyrood

Church plans from about 1120 to 1560

Church planning

A study of the ways in which the designers of Scottish ecclesiastical buildings responded to the needs of their patrons in the lay-out of the churches they built is of value both in assessing the influences at work on our ecclesiastical architecture, and in determining the relationships between individual buildings. Although the most ambitious varieties of planning employed elsewhere in north-western Europe were not reflected in Scotland and, indeed, a clear majority of our lesser churches were never of more than unaugmented rectangular form. A considerable range of plan types may still be observed. A preliminary attempt is here made broadly to categorise those churches of which the plan is known, or ascertainable with reasonable confidence.

Greater churches

The first plans of many of the great abbeys and cathedrals which began to rise from the 1120s onwards, as the momentum of new foundations gathered strength, are no longer known. But the surviving evidence indicates that it was to English sources that Scottish patrons were initially looking - albeit continental inspiration lay behind many of these sources. At Dunfermline and Kirkwall the original form of the aisled choirs with apsidal east ends suggests reference to such as Durham, and ultimately to Normandy, whilst the exotic double cross plan of Kelso may have come from eastern England, although the English masons possibly derived their own inspiration for such plans from the Rhineland.

As the twelfth century progresses and the evidence becomes more complete, the preponderant influence of northern England becomes more apparent. (In the western Highlands the earlier tradition of dependence on Ireland continued, although Ireland itself was by then at least partly under the tutelage of western England.) As in England, a growing preference for some form of rectangular eastern termination, rather than a curved apse, may be seen to emerge. Starting with St Andrews in the 1160s a type of plan with a square-ended presbytery projecting beyond an aisled choir came to be widely employed; possibly first developed at Southwell Minister before 1114 as a variant on the apse echelon arrangement, such plans were to be as popular in northern England - at Lanercost for example - as in lowland Scotland. At about the same time a simpler plan form, almost certainly originally evolved in Burgundy to meet the austere requirements of the Cistercian order, also came to be widely current in Scotland, not for Cistercian churches alone, but almost equally amongst several of the orders responsive to Cistercian thought. This form, which had no structurally distinct choir, but only a square presbytery flanked by transepts with eastern chapels, was almost certainly imported to Scotland from north Yorkshire, an area with a high concentration of Cistercian houses, where the missionary house of Rievaulx was one of the earlier English embodiments of the type.

One of the additional attractions of this Cistercian type for other orders was doubtlessly its relative cheapness, and it was probably a similar urge towards economy which led to a wide-spread preference for churches with extended aisle-less choirs, either directly adjoining the nave, or separated from it by transepts. One of the first churches to have had such a plan must have been Coldingham, where the foundations discovered below the existing late twelfth-century choir are of this form, and variants on such plans were to be employed throughout the rest of the Middle Ages.

Nevertheless, a number of more complex types were also adopted to meet the changing liturgical requirements of the later twelfth and thirteenth centuries. Extended choirs flanked to their full length by aisles - a markedly English type perhaps first employed at Winchester St Cross before becoming a firm favourite in the north at such as Jervaulx - were added to several buildings, including Kirkwall. In some cases, such as Dunfermline and perhaps also Whithorn, the southern English preference for softening the verticality of such choirs by providing a lower eastern chapel was reflected. At Glasgow the mid-thirteenth-century choir was provided with an eastern ambulatory with a row of chapels beyond, an arrangement possibly first developed in England, and later in Burgundy, to meet the Cistercian need for additional altars within a simple framework. It was used at Dore in Herefordshire and a variant was employed in North Yorkshire at Byland. It has recently been suggested that the plan may have been first used in Scotland at Cistercian Newbattle, an attractive idea despite the ambiguity of the excavated plan.

The tendency of Scottish patrons and masons to move out of the northern English architectural ambience after the Wars of Independence is less evident in planning than it is in architectural details. Many of the established plan types continued to be used with only minor changes to indicate their later date, although fewer buildings were laid out on the great scale common in earlier centuries, as lay patronage of the religious houses diminished. It is perhaps in only two aspects of planning that Scotland may be seen to mark its greater artistic independence in the later Middle Ages: the use of polygonal apses to choirs or even transeptal chapels, and the tendency to add laterally projecting chapels either irregularly or in a more fully articulated transeptal relationship with the main body. The first suggests a new direct European guidance in architecture; the second is essentially a native response to the need to accommodate growing numbers of altars for particular cults or for chantry purposes, and in at least one case - Restalrig - the additions were of strikingly idiosyncratic form.

RF

Church plans from about 1120 to 1560

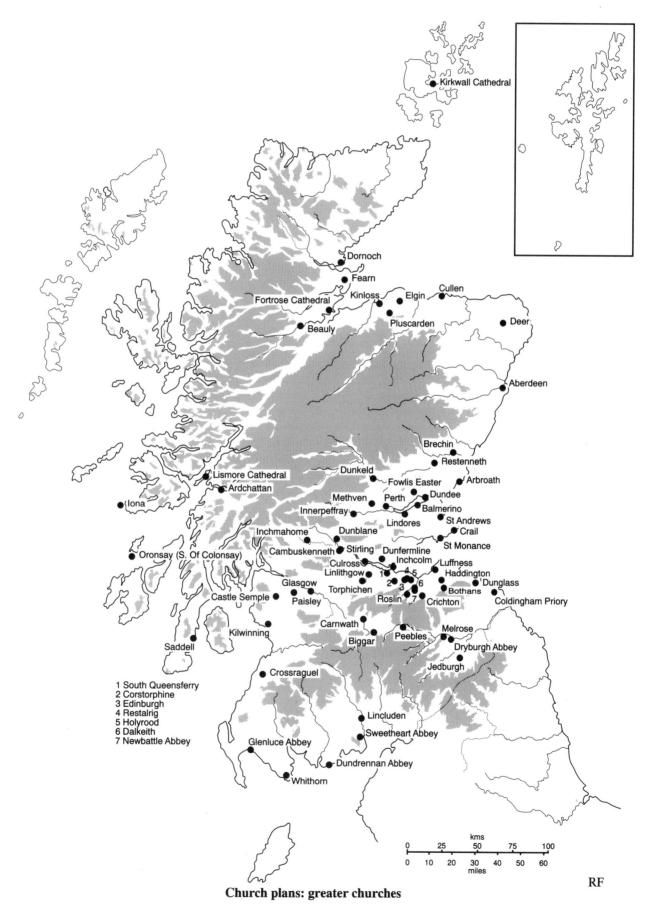

Kirkwall Cathedral

Dornoch
Fearn
Kinloss
Cullen
Elgin
Fortrose Cathedral
Pluscarden
Beauly
Deer

Aberdeen

Brechin
Restenneth
Dunkeld
Fowlis Easter
Arbroath
Lismore Cathedral
Ardchattan
Methven
Perth
Dundee
Innerpeffray
Balmerino
Iona
Lindores
St Andrews
Inchmahome
Dunblane
Crail
St Monance
Oronsay (S. Of Colonsay)
Cambuskenneth
Stirling
Dunfermline
Culross
Inchcolm
Luffness
1
Haddington
Linlithgow
4 5
Glasgow
2 3
Dunglass
Torphichen
6
Bothans
Roslin
7
Coldingham Priory
Castle Semple
Paisley
Crichton
Kilwinning
Carnwath
Melrose
Saddell
Biggar
Peebles
Dryburgh Abbey
Crossraguel
Jedburgh

1 South Queensferry
2 Corstorphine
3 Edinburgh
4 Restalrig
5 Holyrood
6 Dalkeith
7 Newbattle Abbey

Lincluden
Glenluce Abbey
Sweetheart Abbey
Dundrennan Abbey
Whithorn

kms
0   25   50   75   100
0   10   20   30   40   50   60
miles

Church plans: greater churches

RF

371

Church plans from about 1120 to 1560

1 Aisle-less choir and aisle-less nave

Aberdeen Franciscan Church
Elgin Franciscan Church
Fowlis Easter Collegiate Church
Innerpeffray Collegiate Church
*Lismore Cathedral
Restenneth Priory
St Andrews St Leonard's Collegiate Church
Glasgow Dominican Church
Linlithgow Carmelite Church
Luffness Carmelite Church

2 Choir and nave with asymmetrically projecting chapels or aisles

Beauly Priory
Corstorphine Collegiate Church
Crichton Collegiate Church
Cullen Collegiate Church
Fearn Abbey
*Fortrose Cathedral
Inchmahome Priory
Iona Abbey
Iona Nunnery
Lincluden Collegiate Church
Oronsay Priory
Peebles Trinitarian Church
South Queensferry Carmelite Church
Carnwath Collegiate Church
Methven Collegiate Church
Restalrig Collegiate Church
St Andrews Dominican Church

3 Aisle-less choir and symmetrically aisled nave

Crail Collegiate Church
*Dunblane Cathedral
Dunkeld Cathedral
Brechin Cathedral

4 Aisle-less choir with transepts

Bothans (Yester) Collegiate Church
*Dornoch Cathedral
Dunglass Collegiate Church
Inchcolm Abbey
Paisley Abbey
Saddell Abbey
St Andrews St Mary on the Rock Collegiate Church
Torphican Preceptory
Aberdeen Cathedral
St. Monance Dominican Church

5 Aisle-less choir and transepts with eastern chapels

Ardchattan Priory
Balmerino Abbey
Cambuskenneth Abbey
Coldingham Priory
Culross Abbey
Dundrennan Abbey
*Glenluce Abbey
Iona Abbey
Kinloss Abbey

Lindores Abbey
Pluscarden Priory
Sweetheart Abbey
Deer Abbey
Kilwinning Abbey

6 Symmetrically aisled choir beyond which rectangular presbytery projects

*Arbroath Abbey
Dryburgh Abbey
Elgin Cathedral
Jedburgh Abbey
Melrose Abbey
St Andrews Cathedral

7 Choir with full-length symmetrical aisles

Edinburgh St Giles Collegiate Church
*Haddington Collegiate Church
Holyrood Abbey
Kirkwall Cathedral
Perth Parish Church
Dundee Parish Church?
St Andrews Parish Church?

8 Choir with full-length symmetrical aisles and lower eastern chapel

*Dunfermline Abbey
Whithorn Cathedral?

9 Choir with full-length symmetrical aisles, easter ambulatory and chapels

*Glasgow Cathedral
Roslin Collegiate Church
Newbattle Abbey?

10 Aisle-less choir and aisle-less nave with eastern polygonal apse

Aberdeen King's Collegiate Church
Castle Semple Collegiate Church
Crossraguel Abbey
*St Andrews St Salvator's Collegiate Church

11 Aisle-less choir with transepts and with eastern polygonal apse

Biggar Collegiate Church
Dalkeith Collegiate Church
*Seton Collegiate Church

12 Choir with full-length symmetrical aisles and with eastern polygonal apse

Edinburgh Trinity Collegiate Church
Linlithgow Parish Church
Stirling Holy Rude Collegiate Church
*Aberdeen St Nicholas' Collegiate Church

The asterisks identify the plans nos. 1-12

Church plans: greater churches

RF

Church plans from about 1120 to 1560

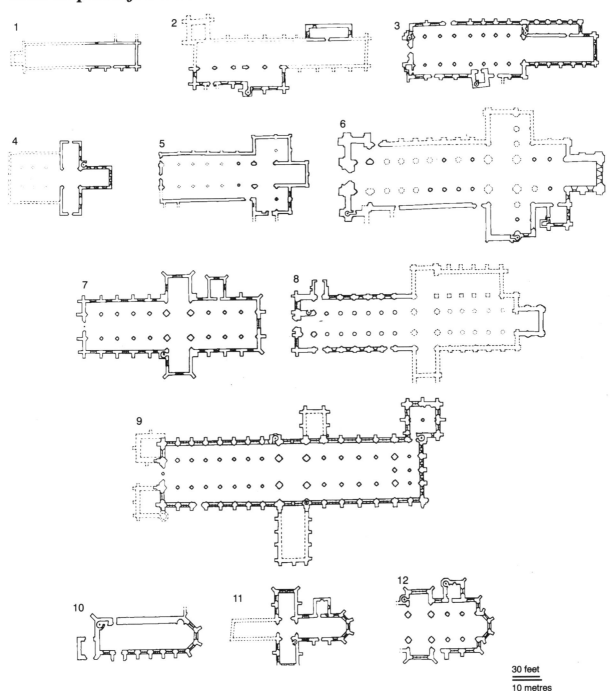

1. Aisle-less choir and aisle-less nave (Lismore Cathedral)

2. Choir and nave with asymmetrically projecting chapels or aisles (Fortrose Cathedral)

3. Aisle-less choir and symmetrically aisled nave (Dunblane Cathedral)

4. Aisle-less choir with transepts (Dornoch Cathedral)

5. Aisle-less choir and transepts with eastern chapels (Glenluce Abbey)

6. Symmetrically aisled choir beyond which rectangular presbytery projects (Arbroath Abbey)

7. Choir with full length symmetrical aisles (Haddington Collegiate Church)

8. Choir with full length symmetrical aisles and lower eastern chapel (Dunfermline Abbey)

9. Choir with full length symmetrical aisles, eastern ambulatory and chapels (Glasgow Cathedral)

10. Aisle-less choir and aisle-less nave with eastern polygonal apse (St Andrews St Salvator's Collegiate Church)

11. Aisle-less choir with transepts and eastern polygonal apse (Seton Collegiate Church)

12. Choir with full-length symmetrical aisles and with eastern polygonal apse (Edinburgh Trinity Collegiate Church)

Church plans: greater churches   RF

Church plans from about 1120 to 1560

Lesser churches

Throughout the Middle Ages a clear majority of lesser churches were of rectangular plan, with no structural distinction between choir and nave. Whilst such simplicity might be combined with enrichment of architectural detail, it does give an indication of the relative impoverishment of the parochial network within the Scottish church. However, there were periods when the parishes attracted the increased generosity of patronage which made complex planning more widely possible. The most significant of these were the centuries between about 1120 and 1220 and between about 1450 and 1550; the former corresponds roughly with the phase of greatest momentum in the establishment of the Scottish parishes, and the latter with the growing disenchantment with the great religious institutions which fostered a more personal expression of religious devotion.

In the first of these periods it is again clear that patrons in the lowland areas looked to England for architectural guidance. The careful articulation of nave and choir as an expression of the twin functions of a church was widely seen across the border, as were more sophisticated variants with a western bell tower or an eastern apse. But in the peripheral regions other sources may have been sought: whilst there are English parallels for the round church at Orphir or the cylindrical tower of Egilsay - both in Orkney - it seems possible that the builders were looking further afield. Most of these early parish churches or chapels were without flanking aisles, although the proliferation of cults and the emergence of a richer liturgy led to some of the burghs providing themselves with partly aisled churches from the later twelfth century onwards, as at Aberdeen or Crail.

By the fifteenth century Scotland can no longer be viewed as part of an extended northern English architectural province. Whilst the clearest evidence for this is in architectural details, it is at least partly evident in certain aspects of planning. As in the greater churches the increasing use of polygonal apses from the mid-century onwards, for example, points to European influence, whilst the tendency to add lateral chapels represents the Scottish solution to a universal problem.

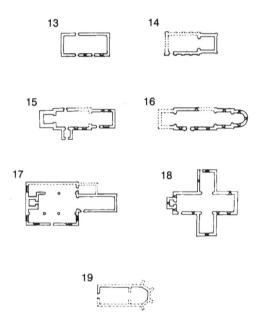

13	Unaugmented rectangular plan (Auchindoir)
14	Simple two-cell plan (Duddingston)
15	Simple two-cell plan augmented by western tower (Stobo)
16	Simple plan with semi-circular apse to choir (Dalmeny)
17	Plan augmented by chapels or aisles (Muthill)
18	Plan with more or less regular transeptal chapels (Tullibardine)
19	Plan with polygonal apse to choir (Culross, St. Mungo's)

30 feet

10 metres

Church plans: lesser churches   RF

Church plans from about 1120 to 1560

13 Unaugmented rectangular plan

(too numerous to be depicted on map: example *Auchindoir)

14 Simple two-cell plan

Bailivanish
Birnie
Buittle
Clow
Crosskirk
Cruggleton
*Duddingston
Dunrod
Eilean Mor
Gullane
Haddington St Martin's
Inchmarnock
Keith
Kilmahew
Kirkaby
Largs
Linton
Lundawick
Meal
Ness
Noss
Norwick
Old Cambus
Pierowall
Preston
Rothesay
Bute St Blane's
Sand
Smailholm
Uyea
Westside
Wyre
Deer?
Dron?
Kirkmaiden?
Legerwood?
Linton(Roxburgh)?

15 Simple two-cell plan augented by western tower

Dunning
Egilsay
Eynhallow
Southdean
*Stobo
Uphall
Kirkliston
Lasswade
Monymusk
St Andrews St Rule's (initial state)?

16 Simple plan with semi-circular apse to choir

Birsay (Brough)
Borthwick
Bunkle
*Dalmeny
Edinburgh St Margaret's (Castle)
Leuchars
Orphir
St Ninian's Isle
Thurso
Tyninghame

17 Plan augmented by chapels or aisles

Aberdour Airth
Airth
Alyth
Arbuthnott
Burntisland
Culross
Cupar
Douglas
Dysart
Eoropie
Guthrie
Hoddom
Kilconquhar
Killean
Kinghorn
Kirkbride
Kirkcaldy
*Muthill
Pencaitland
St Vigeans
Straiton
Dalry
Lanark
Rutherglen

18 Plan with more or less regular transeptal chapels

Cullingsburgh
Rodel
*Tullibardine
Whitekirk

19 Plan with polygonal apse to choir

*Culross St Mungo's
Glasgow St Nicholas' Hospital
Ladykirk
Midcalder
Terregles

The asterisks identify the plans nos. 13-19

Church plans: lesser churches

RF

375

Church plans from about 1120 to 1560

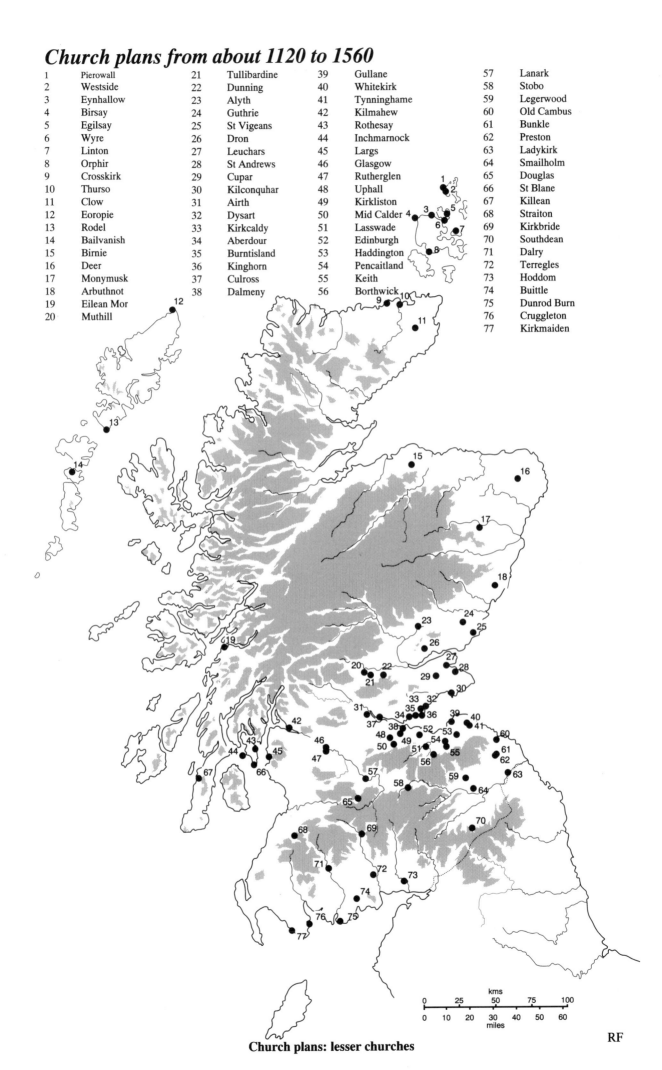

1	Pierowall	21	Tullibardine	39	Gullane	57	Lanark
2	Westside	22	Dunning	40	Whitekirk	58	Stobo
3	Eynhallow	23	Alyth	41	Tynninghame	59	Legerwood
4	Birsay	24	Guthrie	42	Kilmahew	60	Old Cambus
5	Egilsay	25	St Vigeans	43	Rothesay	61	Bunkle
6	Wyre	26	Dron	44	Inchmarnock	62	Preston
7	Linton	27	Leuchars	45	Largs	63	Ladykirk
8	Orphir	28	St Andrews	46	Glasgow	64	Smailholm
9	Crosskirk	29	Cupar	47	Rutherglen	65	Douglas
10	Thurso	30	Kilconquhar	48	Uphall	66	St Blane
11	Clow	31	Airth	49	Kirkliston	67	Killean
12	Eoropie	32	Dysart	50	Mid Calder	68	Straiton
13	Rodel	33	Kirkcaldy	51	Lasswade	69	Kirkbride
14	Bailvanish	34	Aberdour	52	Edinburgh	70	Southdean
15	Birnie	35	Burntisland	53	Haddington	71	Dalry
16	Deer	36	Kinghorn	54	Pencaitland	72	Terregles
17	Monymusk	37	Culross	55	Keith	73	Hoddom
18	Arbuthnot	38	Dalmeny	56	Borthwick	74	Buittle
19	Eilean Mor					75	Dunrod Burn
20	Muthill					76	Cruggleton
						77	Kirkmaiden

Church plans: lesser churches

RF

376

Shrines, hermitages and pilgrimages

The shrines marked on the first map are the places where the relics or tombs of saints, mainly the national saints of Scotland, were located according to the beliefs of the fifteenth century. By then some relics, particularly pastoral staffs of the 'Celtic' saints, had passed into secular hands (usually those of a hereditary 'dewar') and such relics, which were often itinerant, are not denoted on the map.

Going on pilgrimage was a popular pastime in medieval Scotland. Abroad the most popular destinations were Rome, Compostella, Amiens and, for the adventurous few, the Holy Land. In Scotland major centres of pilgrimage were Tain, St Andrews, Dunfermline, Glasgow and Whithorn, but short local pilgrimages were even more popular. Indulgences were widely available and by the mid-fifteenth century could be obtained at most monasteries, cathedrals, collegiate, burgh and even parish churches. Bridge building was often begun or encouraged by the clergy, and chapels for the use of pilgrims and travellers were frequently sited near these bridges, for example, on the Tay at Perth, the Forth at Stirling and on the Tweed near Peebles. Where there was no bridge the pilgrims went by ferry, the most famous being the Queensferry for pilgrims crossing the Forth to Dunfermline and St Andrews. The most important local centres are shown on the second map but the map cannot conveniently show every ecclesiastical centre (along with a multitude of holy wells and crosses) that drew its quota of pilgrims.

There is very little evidence on Scottish hermitages. Those represented on the first map appear in a variety of source material ranging in date from the twelfth to the seventeenth centuries, which rarely gives any indication of the precise location of the hermitages mentioned. However, enough evidence has survived to suggest that hermits carried out much the same roles in Scotland as they did elsewhere. Besides providing shelter for pilgrims and other travellers they tended shrines (as at Musselburgh), manned ferries (as at Ardclach on the Findhorn), and apparently found another more unusual function in Scotland as coast-watchers (as at Seacliff and presumably other coastal sites).

Popular belief in the efficacy of the shrines did not immediately die with the Reformation. In 1581 parliament had still to legislate against 'the dregges of Idolatrie, that remanis in divers pairtes of the realme, be using of pilgrimage to sum chappellis, wellis, croces, and sic uther monumentis of Idolatrie'.

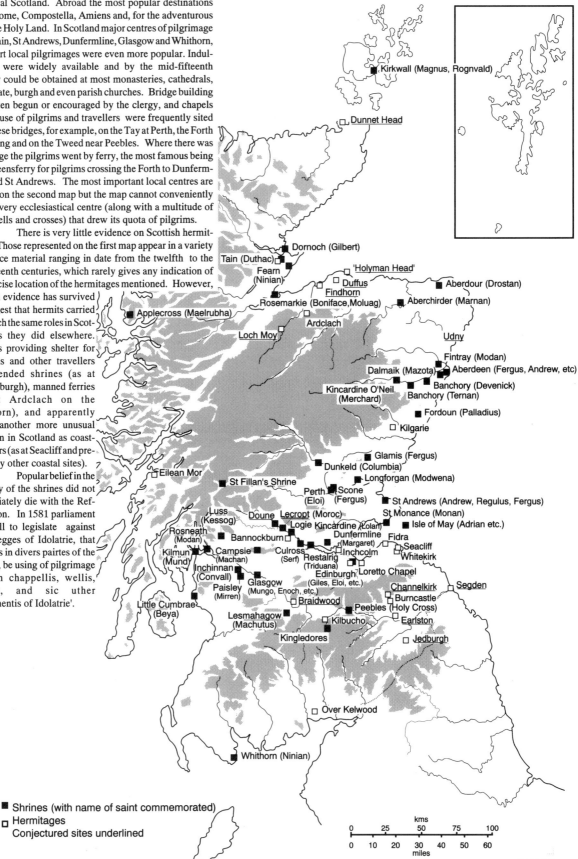

Shrines (with name of saint commemorated)
Hermitages
Conjectured sites underlined

Shrines and hermitages from about 1100 to 1560

JDG,IB

Shrines, hermitages and pilgrimages

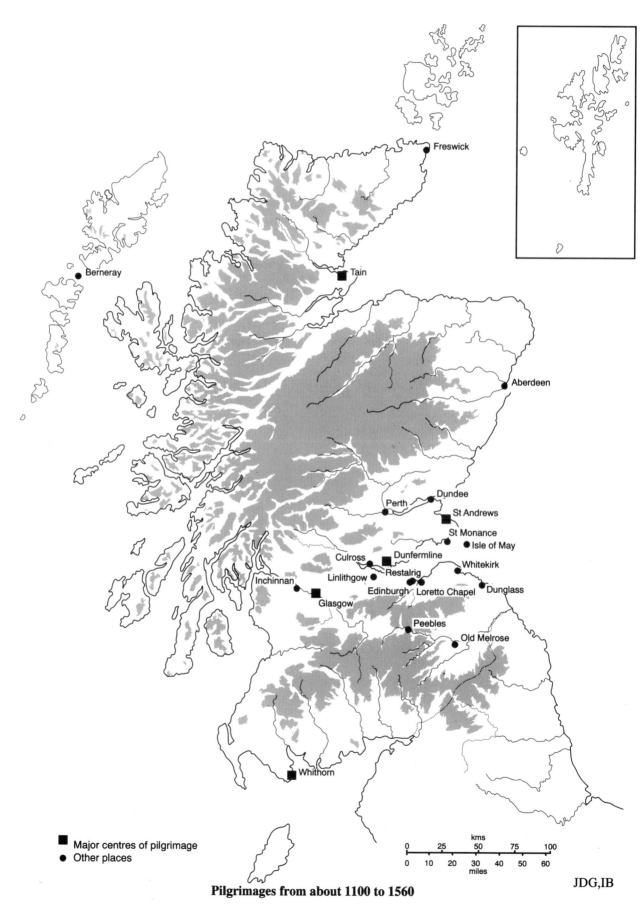

Major centres of pilgrimage
Other places

Pilgrimages from about 1100 to 1560

JDG,IB

Courts spiritual

The church in pre-Reformation Scotland exercised jurisdiction over almost every aspect of human affairs; and the ecclesiastical or spiritual courts were among the most important in the land. The bishop and other ecclesiastical office-holders had jurisdiction as part of their office. The bishop seldom exercised his jurisdiction in person but generally delegated it to a judge known as the official, who had power over the whole or a territorially limited part of the diocese. Thus, in the diocese of St Andrews there was in addition to the official of St Andrews an official of Lothian. Sometimes the bishop chose to grant jurisdiction to a commissary whose commission could be coextensive with the diocese or territorially limited. Officials might also delegate the whole or part of their jurisdiction to commissaries. In the diocese of Dunkeld the five parishes south of the Forth were the territory of the commissary 'south of Forth.' There were also commissaries of peculiar jurisdictions which pertained to an institution like Kelso Abbey, Lesmahagow, or to a cathedral prebend. This explains, to some extent, the number of commissariats within the diocese of Glasgow, such as Hamilton, Kilbride, Campsie, Carnwath, Manor, Stobo, Cardross, Douglas, Renfrew.

Orkney 1461
Kirkwall

Shetland 1545

Caithness 1398
+Dornoch

Ross 1451
+Elgin
+Fortrose
Moray 1233

Aberdeen 1175 x 1199 +Aberdeen

Brechin 1202 x 1214
Brechin +

Dunkeld 1203 x 1210
+Dunkeld

+Lismore
Mull 1422

Isles or
Sodor 1235x41

Argyll 1240
Dunblane 1266
Stirling
Chapel Royal
1511
Lochawe & *Cowal* 1410
+Glasgow
Bute & *Arran* 1502

St Andrews 1194
+St Andrews
Lothian 1392
Glasgow 1175x1189

Dumfries 1494
Galloway 1209x1222
Farines & *Rhinns* 1552
+Whithorn

Man 1219

Orkney — Officials with jurisdiction coextensive with the diocese
Shetland — Officials with territorially limited jurisdiction
+ — Episcopal sees
1219 — Date of first known evidence for the office

kms
0 25 50 75 100
0 10 20 30 40 50 60
miles

Pre-Reformation officials

DBS

Courts spiritual

Orkney 1504

Caithness 1522

Ross 1451

Inverness 1522 *Moray* 1464

Aberdeen
1446

Dunkeld   *Brechin* 1493
1467

Tullilum 1513

Dunblane 1474   *St Andrews* 1447

Stirling 1545

Cardross 1512 • *Campsie* 1506

Renfrew 1556 • Monkland 1555 Lothian 1456
Glasgow 1486 • Currie
Bute &   Hamilton 1513• Carnwath 1543 South of Forth
Arran Kilbride 1513• 1527 Manor 1511 1505 x11
1541   Lesmahagow• Stobo 1433 Kelso 1550
1513   Douglas
1516   Teviotdale 1492

Nithsdale 1459

Galloway Desnes &
1506   Glenken 1467
Farines
1501

Orkney Commissaries with jurisdiction
coextensive with the diocese
Stirling Commissaries with territorially
limited jurisdiction
•   Seat of commissary, where known
1447   Date of first known evidence for the office

kms
0   25   50   75   100

0   10   20   30   40   50   60
miles

Pre-Reformation commissaries   DBS

380

Courts spiritual

The abolition of the jurisdiction of the church courts by the Scottish parliament on 24 August 1560 created a judicial vacuum. For over three years the citizens did not know to which court to apply for the remedies which had formerly been sought in the courts spiritual. There is evidence of resort being made to kirk sessions, sheriff courts, the lords of council and session, and the privy council. Partly to alleviate this and partly to obtain revenue from the "quot silver" (the fee exacted for the confirmation of executors of deceased persons) so that the salaries of the lords of council and session might be augmented, a new system of spiritual courts, known as the commissary courts, was established in 1564. Inferior commissary courts were set up throughout the country to deal with spiritual cases, mainly the confirmation of executors, and the exaction of quots, and the commissary court of Edinburgh was given in addition to this ordinary jurisdiction within its area exclusive jurisdiction over the whole of Scotland in cases of divorce and nullity of marriage. The Edinburgh court, which was manned by four commissaries, was given the right to determine not only appeals from the inferior commissaries, but also from the decisions of pre-Reformation ecclesiastical judges; and it had the exclusive right to confirm the executors of Scots citizens who died abroad.

The records as to inferior commissaries are far from complete: it is difficult to determine the date at which the various commissariats were erected, and it appears that some pre-Reformation commissaries remained in, or were continued in, office. It will be seen from the maps that the new commissariats were generally set up in places where either an official or commissary had sat before the Reformation. The last commissariat to be established was Peebles in 1609. In the period between 1564 and 1609 there are references to commissariats such as Jedburgh, Melrose and Stobo, but none of these survived into the seventeenth century. By 1609 there were twenty-one inferior courts and the commissary court of Edinburgh. All of these continued until their jurisdiction was transferred to the Court of Session and the sheriff courts in the course of the nineteenth century.

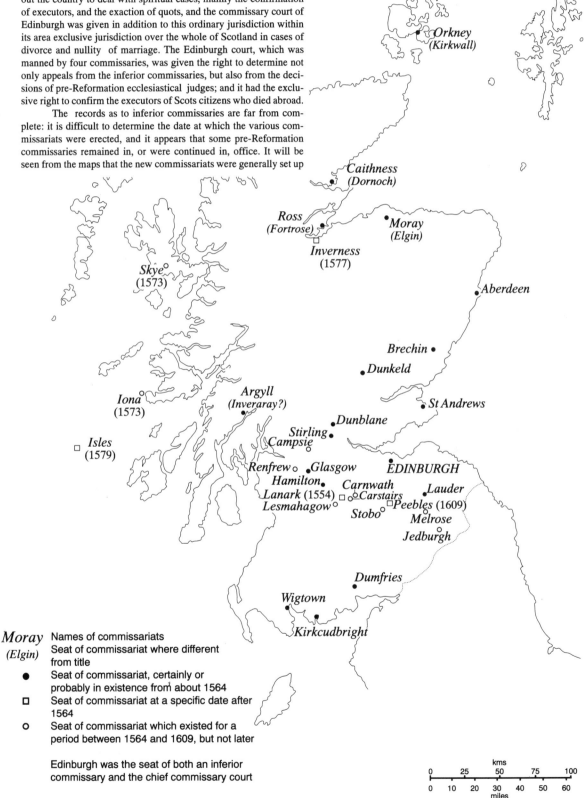

Moray
(Elgin)   Names of commissariats
Seat of commissariat where different from title

●   Seat of commissariat, certainly or probably in existence from about 1564

□   Seat of commissariat at a specific date after 1564

o   Seat of commissariat which existed for a period between 1564 and 1609, but not later

Edinburgh was the seat of both an inferior commissary and the chief commissary court

Post-Reformation commissaries

DBS

Ecclesiastical organisation: early post-Reformation

The reformers' resolution in 1560 to discard the entire edifice of medieval ecclesiastical organisation by substituting a new mode of government through councils, modelled on the early church, was effected with remarkable promptitude. The first Book of Discipline spoke eloquently of the spiritual, educational and social needs of congregations made up of the inhabitants of each parish, of which there were about one thousand in the country. Yet this emphasis was never permitted to obscure the needs of the wider church or negate the advice forthcoming from neighbouring ministers; and by 1560 direction from the centre was forthcoming in the general assembly which linked the network of local congregations.

Regional reorganisation followed when the authors of the Book of Discipline put their proposals first to a general assembly in December 1560 and then to the secular authorities in January and February 1561. Supervision of congregations and ministers was entrusted to superintendent ministers, charged essentially with the task of caring for Christian communities and extending the work of evangelism throughout the districts assigned to their charge. They were expected to work along with a court made up of the kirk session of their main town of residence, and they remained responsible to a provincial synod meeting twice a year. Their ten provinces were given boundaries drawn on a basis at variance with the thirteen old pre-Reformation dioceses whose uneven size and erratic boundaries were rejected by the reformers as a hindrance to effective supervision. The curious mixture of place-names and territorial names allocated as titles to the new provinces may reflect discrepancies in the composition of the Book of Discipline as it underwent revision and expansion during 1560. There was nothing indeterminate, however, about the towns which were to be the new regional centres for the kirk—except in Argyll, where no decision was forthcoming. Only six of the former diocesan seats were to be used, and reliance was placed elsewhere on burghs more closely associated with the main routes of communication. Singularly scant regard was paid to the interests of the three bishops who conformed to the Reformation and undertook service—Gordon of Galloway, Stewart of Caithness, and Bothwell of Orkney.

From 1561 onwards elections for the superintendents were held. Spottiswoode was appointed to Edinburgh in March, and Winram to St Andrews in April. Willock was chosen for Glasgow by September, Erskine of Dun was formally admitted to Brechin early in 1567 and Carswell was subsequently found at work as superintendent in Argyll. Spottiswoode remained parish minister of Mid Calder, and shared his time between there and Edinburgh where he had his court. Erskine seems to have found his home at Dun a convenient base for his work, though no doubt he was expected to work with the kirk session at Brechin on any disciplinary cases affecting his province. Carswell made Carnassarie Castle his centre of administration, but was presumably obliged to act with some kirk session in his province when holding court.

Shortage of finance and a lack of political initiative effectively ended the prospect of further appointment beyond these five. The general assembly therefore resorted to its own strategy of appointing ministers to act as commissioners of provinces. They held office for short, if renewable, terms before returning to their parish ministries. The three conforming bishops received commissions, as did other ministers selected by the assembly, to act as temporary overseers. The provincial boundaries were frequently adjusted during the 1560s to take account of local needs, especially from 1567 when superintendents and commissioners became the recognised agents for receiving presentations to benefices. By about that date this system of supervision by nine commissioners and five superintendents extended over most of the country, with only parts of the border country deprived of regular visitations.

The financial compromise worked out between Crown and kirk at Leith in 1572 introduced a novel dimension, in that ministers appointed to bishoprics (as a means of gaining access to the revenues) were expected at least to share the duties of oversight with the existing superintendents and commissioners, even if they never wholly superseded their work. The old diocesan organisation was now revived, with all the handicaps that this implied, and the assorted supervisors were expected to act within it. In the end the difficulties experienced in trying to revitalise this ancient machinery were resolved in 1576 with the eclipse of the bishops from any distinctive role in ecclesiastical administration. This followed the assembly's decision to scrap the old dioceses and substitute in their place two dozen or so smaller, more manageable districts (not mapped), each entrusted to a commissioner or visitor answerable to the assembly.

This renewed emphasis on smaller districts received a further stimulus with the assembly's approval of the Second Book of Discipline's programme. It decided in 1581 to establish thirteen model presbyteries in the main towns of the lowlands. These were clusters of neighbouring churches to form a common eldership with responsibility for supervising the welfare of congregations in the district. They were built on groupings of rural parishes around a nearby town which was the centre for meetings of ministers for the exercise of interpreting the scripture. Such occasions naturally led to the exchange of news and views, and had already been used sometimes for the transaction of administrative business. Now the two activities of prophesying and attending to the shared business of neighbouring kirks coalesced in the 'eldership' or presbytery.

Both privy council and assembly worked together in 1581 to dismantle the old dioceses in favour of a scheme for eighteen new dioceses or provinces, excluding Argyll and the Isles, which were intended to contain over fifty presbyteries within them. As the plans took effect some modifications ensued (as for example in the case of Stirling presbytery). But the experiment was soon eclipsed in 1584 when a government under the earl of Arran with more conservative instincts outlawed presbyteries in favour of a return to episcopal oversight. After Arran's fall from power, the assembly in 1586 assented to a scheme designed to reconcile King James' preference for bishops with the kirk's attachment to presbyteries. The king retained his right to appoint ministers to bishoprics but the duty of visitation was not to lie with them, but rather with ministers who had obtained from the assembly temporary commissions to act as visitors of provinces which were not co-terminous with the old dioceses. No less than 985 churches (excluding Argyll and the Isles) were listed and arranged in twenty-two new provinces so that presbyteries could be re-established. These provinces were: Shetland (32 churches), Orkney (39), Caithness (13), Sutherland (9), Ross (63) Moray (52), Banff (35), Aberdeen (70), Angus and Mearns (88), Perth (36), Dunkeld (30), Dunblane (20), Stirling (23), Fife (62), West Lothian (16), Edinburgh (34), Haddington (54), Merse, Teviotdale and Tweeddale (74), Clydesdale, Renfrew and Lennox (76), Cunninghame, Kyle and Carrick (46), Galloway (45), and Dumfries (68). The assembly did its best to undermine any role for the bishops in ecclesiastical administration and as a consequence an essentially presbyterian system prevailed in the years between 1586 and 1592, when parliament affirmed the role and jurisdiction of presbyteries and other courts of the church.

The general assembly had its origin in a gathering of Protestants who convened in the capital in July 1560. The occasion was a service of worship and thanksgiving in St Giles kirk for the recent Protestant victory and the treaty of Edinburgh, sealed on 8 July. After worship some business was transacted, to arrange for the approval of some appointments to the reformed ministry. The 'Reformation parliament' opened on 10 July, and it was to be a characteristic of some future assemblies also that a meeting was arranged so that parliament might conveniently be lobbied on the kirk's behalf.

Some assemblies were called at other times and in other places from those to which parliament was called. They tended to meet twice-yearly, which was more frequently than parliaments or even conventions of estates. They claimed to meet by Christ's authority and retained until 1584 the right to appoint their own meeting place and time for convening, though from 1586 onward they were usually summoned by royal proclamation. The great majority of meetings were held in Edinburgh; but warfare or other considerations might force a venue elsewhere as at Stirling, Leith, St Andrews and Perth in 1571-2. King James' determination to manipulate the assembly to his own advantage led him to assert a right to determine where and when it was to meet. In later years he exploited this tactical advantage to the full. He favoured less militant northern towns as meeting-places, and was ready at short notice to prorogue or change its meeting-place. Such were the strenuous efforts at managing his later assemblies summoned between 1605 and 1618 that the opposition considered the meetings 'unfree' and 'pretended', and so declined to recognise them as valid assemblies.

After 1618 James refused to summon further general assemblies and Charles I followed his father's action. Only with the covenanting crisis was it possible to hold assemblies again. The Glasgow assembly of 1638 met with the king's assent, but continued its sitting in defiance of the king's commissioner. Aberdeen was selected by Charles for the assembly that met in 1640 in the forlorn hope that royalism in the area would influence the assembly's proceedings. Though assemblies were held at St Andrews in 1641, 1642 and 1651, most assemblies between 1643 and 1653 were located in Edinburgh. This was the pattern that was to be re-established in 1690 after the Revolution when general assemblies, placed in abeyance since 1653 (when Cromwell prevented further meetings), were permitted to reconvene.

JK

Ecclesiastical organisation: early post-Reformation

The boundaries of parishes which controlled the fluctuating boundaries of higher units of ecclesiastical organisation between 1560 and 1707 were themselves subject to changes as some parishes were divided and others united. But for convenience the boundaries of parishes in the early eighteenth century are used as the base for many of the maps here. As in any case parish boundaries can be established and shown only in broad outline in maps of this scale, it should be appreciated that the boundaries of the higher units of organisation at different dates after 1560 are generally indicative rather than exact.

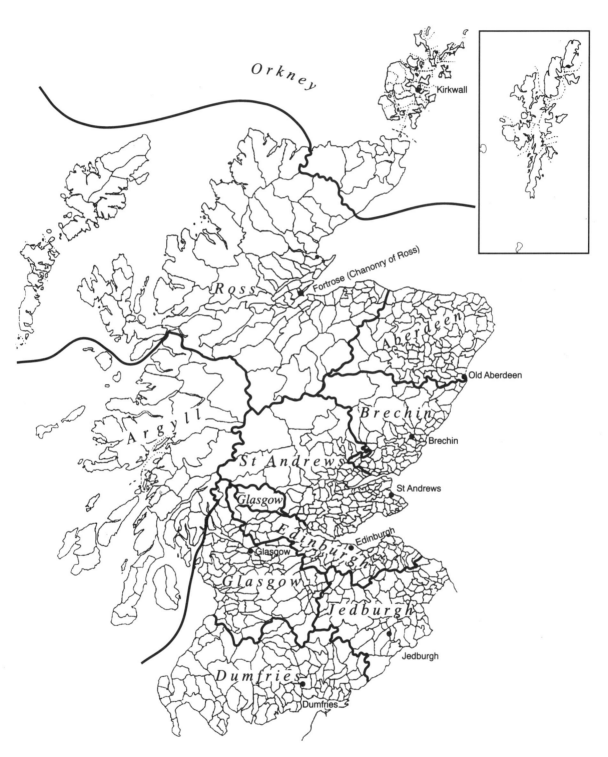

Places marked are the proposed sites of the residences of the superintendents

No seat was
designated for
province of Argyll

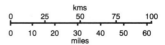

Proposed provinces for superintendents 1560 to 1561

JK

Ecclesiastical organisation: early post-Reformation

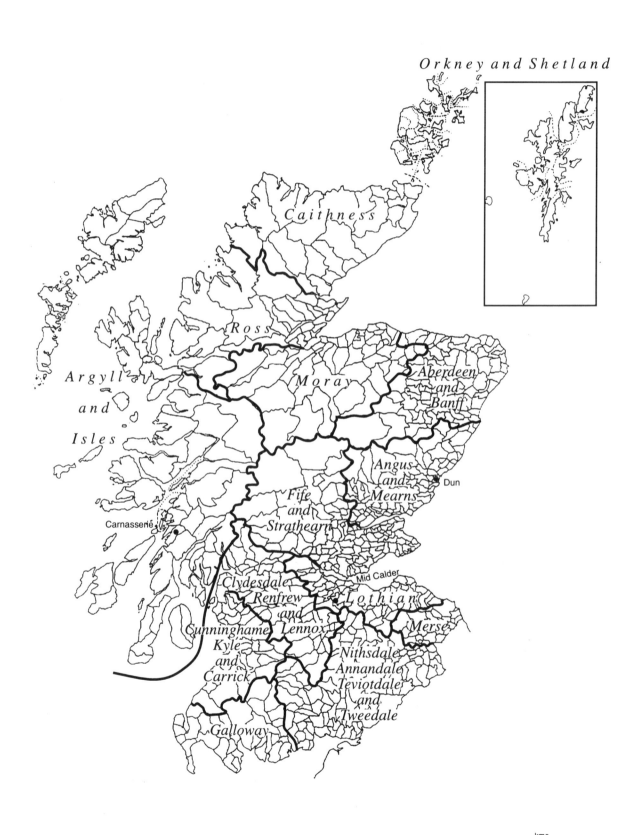

Orkney and Shetland

Caithness

Ross

Argyll
and
Isles

Moray

Aberdeen
and
Banff

Angus
and
Mearns

● Dun

Fife
and
Strathearn

Carnasserie ●

Clydesdale

Mid Calder

Renfrew
and
Lennox

Lothian

Cunninghame

Merse

Kyle
and
Carrick

Nithsdale
Annandale
Teviotdale
and
Tweedale

Galloway

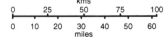

Provinces of superintendents and commissioners about 1567   JK

Ecclesiastical organisation: early post-Reformation

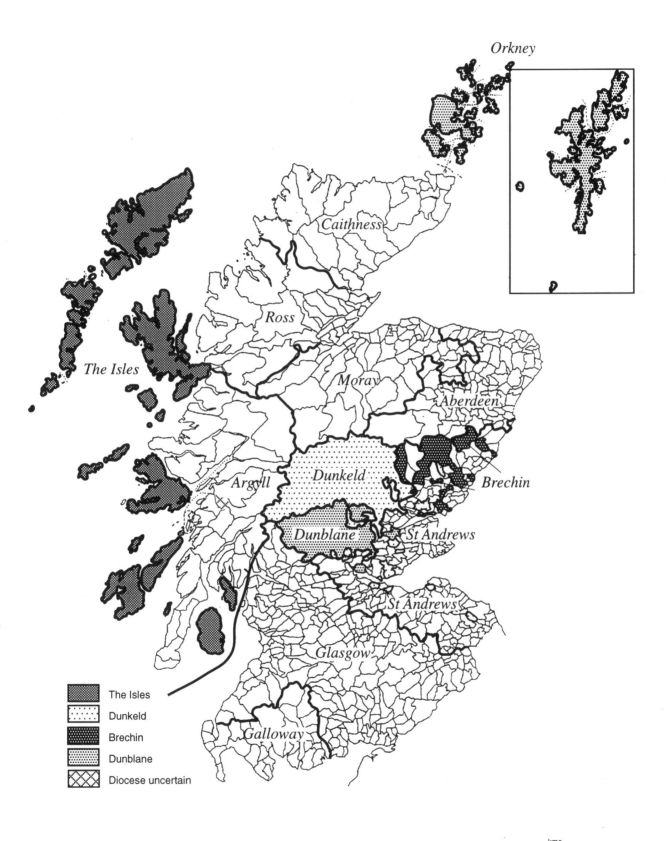

Orkney

Caithness

Ross

The Isles

Moray

Aberdeen

Argyll

Dunkeld

Brechin

Dunblane

St Andrews

St Andrews

Glasgow

Galloway

The Isles
Dunkeld
Brechin
Dunblane
Diocese uncertain

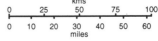

Diocesan structure as renewed 1572

JK

Ecclesiastical organisation: early post-Reformation

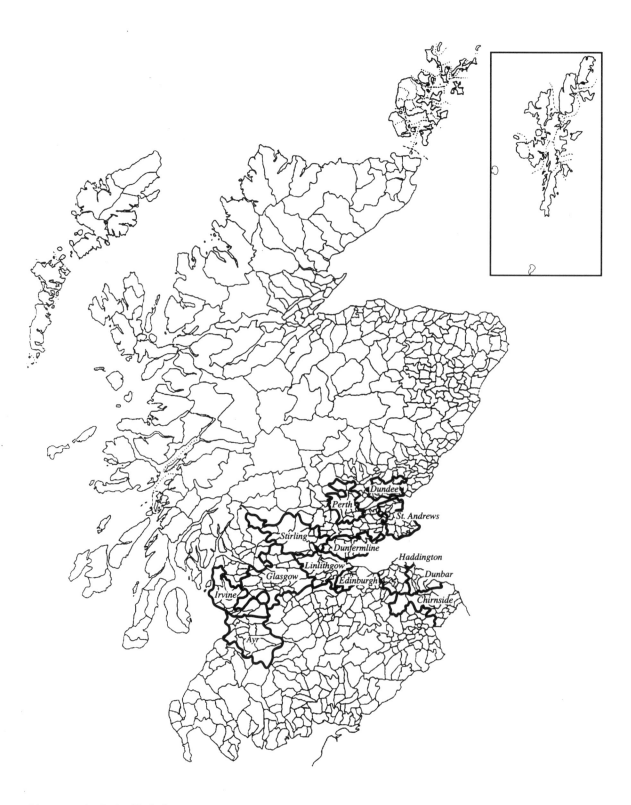

It is not certain whether Eaglesham
belonged to Irvine or Glasgow
presbytery, and Denny to Stirling or
Linlithgow presbytery.

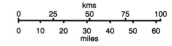

Thirteen model presbyteries 1581

JK

Ecclesiastical organisation: early post-Reformation

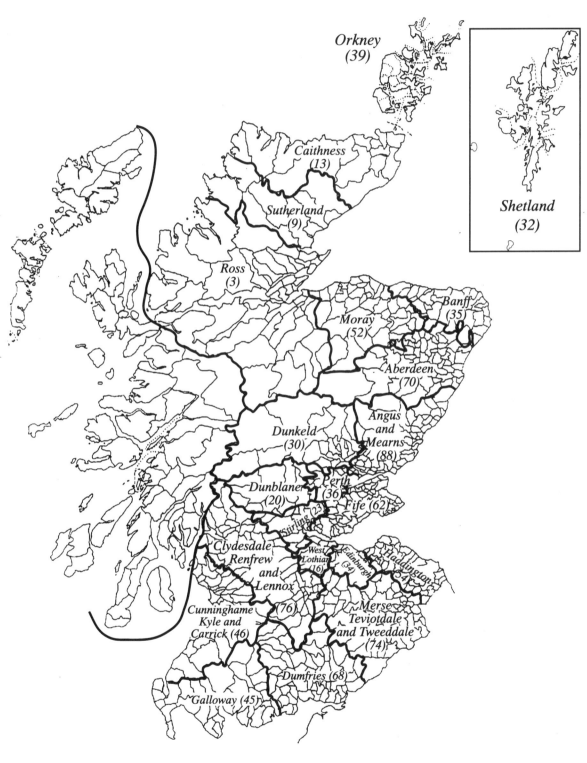

Orkney
(39)

Caithness
(13)

Sutherland
(9)

Shetland
(32)

Ross
(3)

Banff
(35)

Moray
(52)

Aberdeen
(70)

Dunkeld
(30)

Angus
and
Mearns
(88)

Dunblane
(20)

Perth
(36)

Stirling (23)

Fife (62)

Clydesdale
Renfrew
and
Lennox

West
Lothian
(16)

Edinburgh
(34)

Haddington
(34)

Cunninghame
Kyle and
Carrick (46)

(76)

Merse
Teviotdale
and Tweeddale
(74)

Dumfries (68)

Galloway (45)

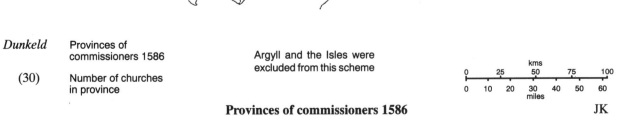

Dunkeld Provinces of
commissioners 1586

(30) Number of churches
in province

Argyll and the Isles were
excluded from this scheme

kms
0   25   50   75   100

0   10   20   30   40   50   60
miles

Provinces of commissioners 1586

JK

387

Ecclesiastical organisation: early post-Reformation

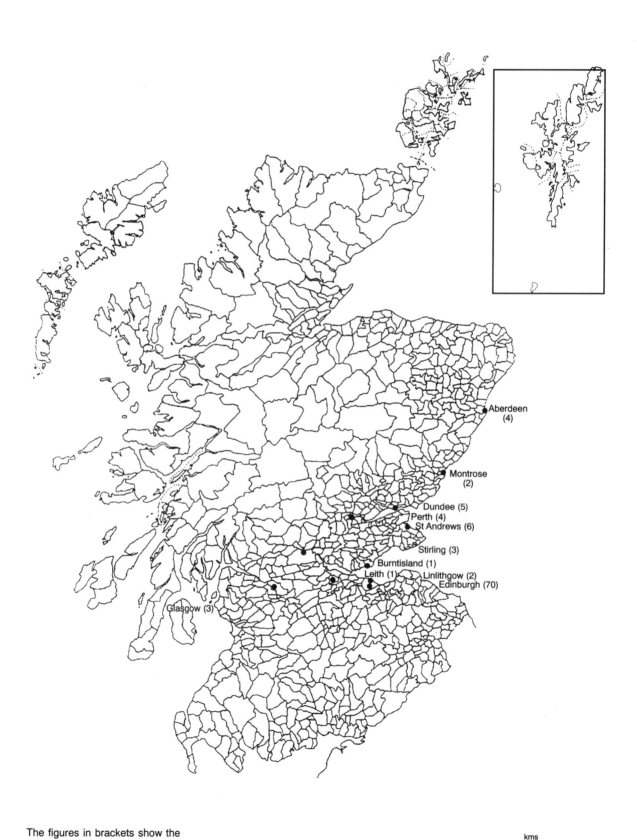

The figures in brackets show the
number of meetings in each place

General assemblies and conventions of the kirk 1560 to 1653

JK

Ecclesiastical organisation: the early seventeenth century

As part of the process by which James gradually restored the authority of bishops, the thirteen ancient dioceses as fleetingly restored in 1572 were by 1610 once more the recognised units of regional oversight. Synods were still held twice-yearly, but now with bounds coterminous with diocesan boundaries (though St Andrews had two synods for north and south of the Forth, and Glasgow apparently had three, meeting at Glasgow, Irvine and Peebles) and with the bishops as constant moderators.

At the same time the king accepted the continuing utility of presbyteries as indispensable units of administration. The royal chancery accepted them as an appropriate agency for examining and admitting candidates presented to benefices in the king's patronage; and the exchequer also followed the practice of listing ministers' stipends not according to dioceses but in the form of presbyterial districts. The number of presbyteries continued to grow, and by the early seventeenth century they were operating with varying efficiency throughout the country.

The coexistence of presbyteries with the diocesan structure for oversight and administration led to some anomalies, for presbyterial boundaries could not readily be accommodated to suit diocesan requirements. Most parishes in Perth presbytery, for example, lay within the diocese of St Andrews, but half a dozen parishes lay within Dunkeld, and four within Dunblane diocese. To add to the air of inconsistency, the moderator of the presbytery was the bishop of Dunkeld, who was also minister of St Madoes parish belonging to Dunblane diocese The archbishop of St Andrews, who kept in close touch with the presbytery through correspondence, supervised admissions to churches in his diocese, but often devolved the duties of ordination and admission to the presbytery and its bishop-moderator, whereas the bishop of Dunkeld took charge of admitting a minister to parishes like Forgandenny and Redgorton which lay within his diocese though in Perth presbytery.

This confusing administrative pattern in 1607 paved the way for the period of full episcopal ascendancy, 1610-38; and by 1633 a fourteenth diocese, Edinburgh, was created out of that portion of St Andrews diocese south of the Forth. Presbyteries continued without a break to play their role under episcopal guidance. The fully developed system as expressed in the canons of 1636 fulfilled the ideal of the bishop in presbytery, in which effective power and initiative lay with the bishop, and presbyteries acted as his executive agents.

The Glasgow assembly of 1638 abolished bishops, and the old dioceses were once again discarded as units of oversight and visitation. The country was divided instead into fifteen provinces, each of which was to be governed by a twice-yearly synod or provincial assembly and within their own districts by the constituent presbyteries assigned to each province. The plan was to establish no fewer than 67 presbyteries each with its elected moderator; and by the early 1640s as many as 64 are known to have been active. Only in Argyll and the Isles were the plans of 1638 partly frustrated. Elsewhere the presbyterian structure was resumed with vigour, and despite the distraction of civil war further presbyteries were to be added (such as Biggar in 1644). The aim of 1638 to return to the earlier presbyterial model was achieved in all essentials.

JK

Ecclesiastical organisation: the early seventeenth century

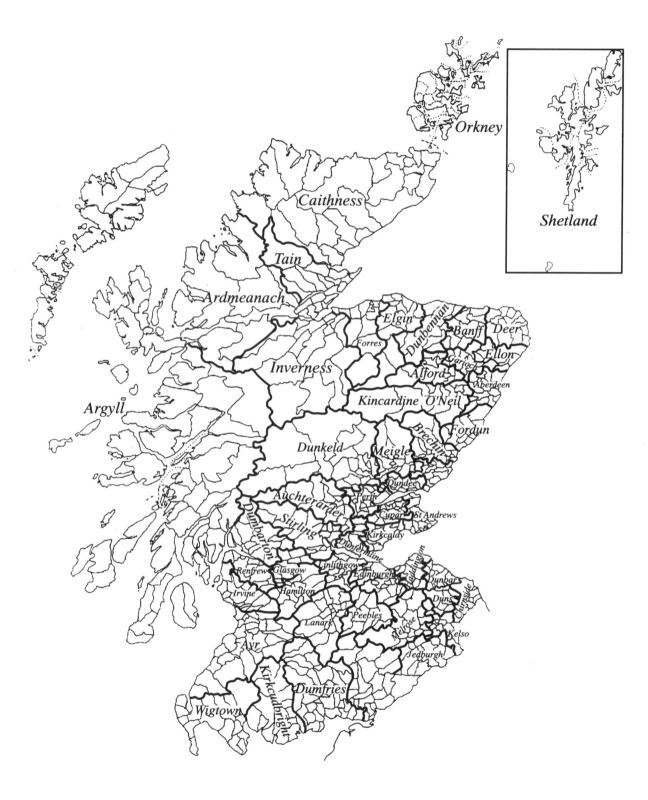

Orkney

Shetland

Caithness

Tain

Ardmeanach

Elgin

Forres

Dunbennan

Banff

Deer

Inverness

Carioch

Ellon

Alford

Aberdeen

Kincardine O'Neil

Argyll

Dunkeld

Brechin

Fordun

Meigle

Dundee

Auchterarder

Perth

Cupar

St Andrews

Dumbarton

Stirling

Kirkcaldy

Dunfermline

Renfrew

Glasgow

Linlithgow

Edinburgh

Haddington

Dunbar

Irvine

Hamilton

Duns

Churnside

Peebles

Melrose

Kelso

Lanark

Jedburgh

Ayr

Kirkcudbright

Dumfries

Wigtown

Records happen to survive which prove the existence of 49
presbyteries in 1607. At least one more presbytery is known to have
existed in the Western Isles, but no detailed records are available
to show what was happening in either Argyll or the Isles in general.
Another presbytery appears to have existed in the south between
Dumfries and Jedburgh presbyteries, where a block of parishes is
not mentioned in the record.

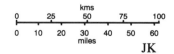

kms
0   25   50   75   100
0 10 20 30 40 50 60
miles

Presbyteries 1607

JK

Ecclesiastical organisation: the early seventeenth century

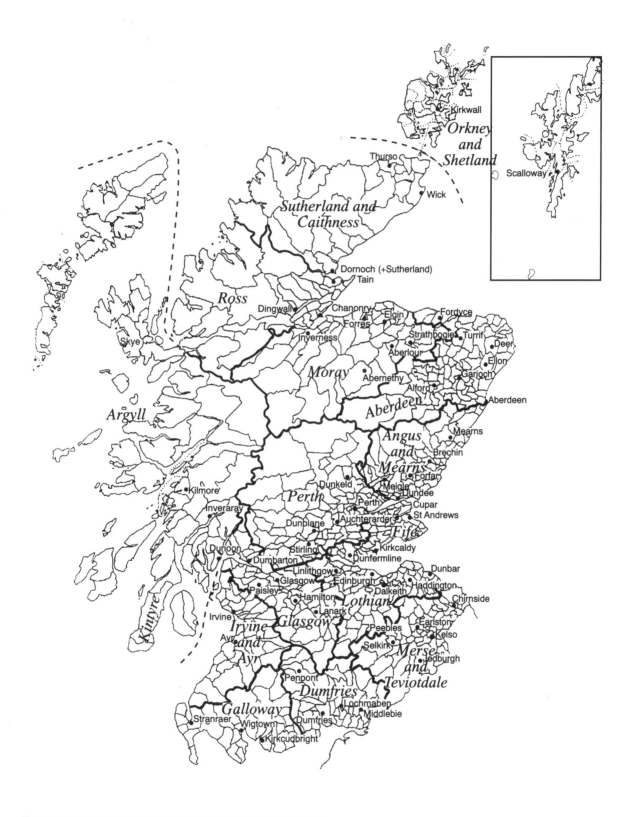

The general assembly records of 1642 and 1643 show how far the plans enacted in 1638 for re-erecting a Presbyterian polity had progressed by then. The expected separate province of the Isles had not materialised; and by 1644 at latest the province of Ayr and Irvine had been detached from Glasgow

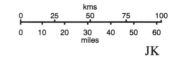

Provinces and seats of presbyteries 1642 to 1643

JK

Covenanter dominance

Open defiance of Charles I's religious policies first appeared in the disturbances in Edinburgh churches against the new Prayer Book on 23 July 1637. The opposition movement then turned to organising itself through supplications or petitions against the Book. The first group of these supplications, the four presented to the privy council on 23 August, were inspired by David Dickson, minister of Irvine. In the month that followed preparing supplications became widespread in Ayrshire and Fife, and on 20 September, 69 were delivered to the council, one being a general supplication signed by nobles and others who had gathered in Edinburgh. Of the 68 local petitions, 47 survive (originals or copies), and these are plotted on this map along with the August supplications, and Edinburgh's, which were presented on 26 September . The majority are unsigned, and the definitions of those submitting them varies greatly. The 42 issued in the names of parishes and/or burghs mention various combinations of elders, sessions, gentlemen, heritors, feuars, congregations, parishioners, ministers (in 14 cases) and, in the case of royal burghs, magistrates, councils and communities as being the parties involved in supplicating. It is, however, possible that many of the petitions exaggerate the extent of local support behind them. Some may have been presented before being approved - that of the burgh of Stirling was not approved by the burgh council until 25 September - but as many of the surviving petitions are undated, it may be that some were not presented until some days after 20 September.

The supplications were presented at a very early stage in the development of what was soon to become the covenanting movement, but already Fife and Ayrshire have clearly emerged as the heartlands of support that they were to remain during the years that the covenanters ruled Scotland. Strong support was also to emerge in other areas of southern and central Scotland, and in some parts of the north; but the map clearly indicates that it was ministers and laymen in these two shires who set the example of organised local opposition for other areas to follow.

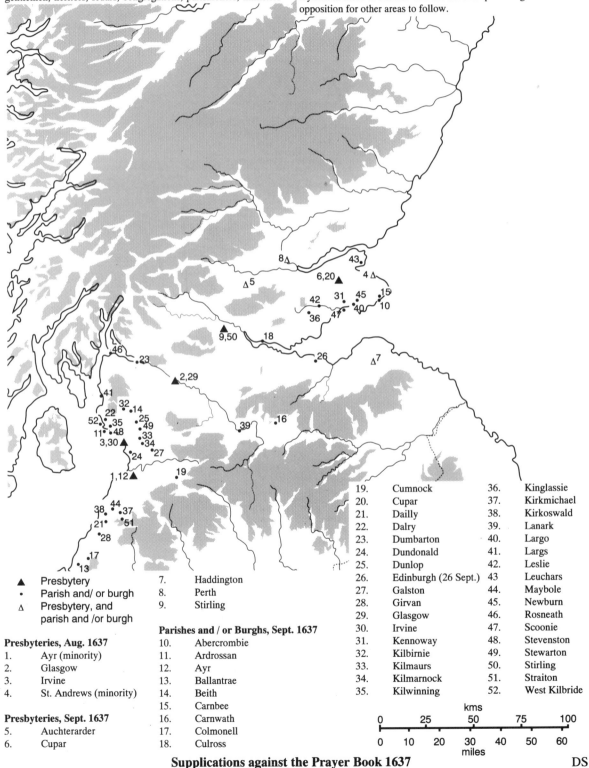

▲	Presbytery	7.	Haddington
•	Parish and/ or burgh	8.	Perth
△	Presbytery, and parish and /or burgh	9.	Stirling

Presbyteries, Aug. 1637

1. Ayr (minority)
2. Glasgow
3. Irvine
4. St. Andrews (minority)

Presbyteries, Sept. 1637

5. Auchterarder
6. Cupar

Parishes and / or Burghs, Sept. 1637

10. Abercrombie
11. Ardrossan
12. Ayr
13. Ballantrae
14. Beith
15. Carnbee
16. Carnwath
17. Colmonell
18. Culross
19. Cumnock
20. Cupar
21. Dailly
22. Dalry
23. Dumbarton
24. Dundonald
25. Dunlop
26. Edinburgh (26 Sept.)
27. Galston
28. Girvan
29. Glasgow
30. Irvine
31. Kennoway
32. Kilbirnie
33. Kilmaurs
34. Kilmarnock
35. Kilwinning
36. Kinglassie
37. Kirkmichael
38. Kirkoswald
39. Lanark
40. Largo
41. Largs
42. Leslie
43. Leuchars
44. Maybole
45. Newburn
46. Rosneath
47. Scoonie
48. Stevenston
49. Stewarton
50. Stirling
51. Straiton
52. West Kilbride

kms

0	25	50	75	100

0	10	20	30	40	50	60
miles

Supplications against the Prayer Book 1637

DS

Covenanter dominance

In the Glasgow Assembly (21 November to 20 December 1638) the covenanters overthrew the royal control over the church built up by James VI and Charles I. Archbishops and bishops were abolished and a presbyterian system of government established, innovations in forms of worship and in doctrine also being rejected.

Elections to the assembly were organised by the covenanters, who laid down that membership should consist of three ministers and one elder from each presbytery, one burgess from each royal burgh (two from Edinburgh), and a representative of each university.

This map indicates the number of members (if any) sent by each presbytery who attended throughout. Others withdrew on the orders of the king's commissioner, or were commissioned but evidently did not attend; in yet other cases the member's commission was rejected.

No attempt has been made to indicate cases in which commissions were rejected because they did not conform to the rules laid down for representation (the university of Glasgow's commission to four members instead of one, Rothesay's attempt to constitute a separate presbytery, the commission to a second elder from Orkney).

The facts that so few commissions were rejected, that only two of the members thus rejected were excluded as opponents of the covenanters and that so few withdrew on Hamilton's orders, all indicate the success the covenanters had had in dominating elections - either through genuine support or, in some areas, through intimidation and other malpractices. The almost total lack of members from the Highlands, except for Argyll and the eastern fringes, reflects the lack of organisation of the church in much of the north and west; and the limited representation of the north-east reflects the distribution of presbyteries and royal burghs as much as lack of enthusiasm for the Covenant.

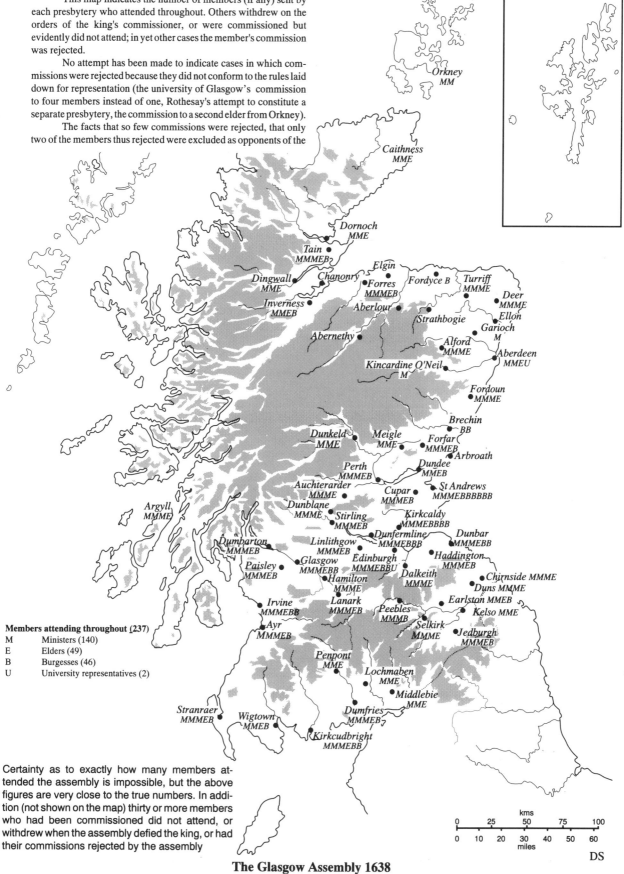

Members attending throughout (237)

M   Ministers (140)
E   Elders (49)
B   Burgesses (46)
U   University representatives (2)

Certainty as to exactly how many members attended the assembly is impossible, but the above figures are very close to the true numbers. In addition (not shown on the map) thirty or more members who had been commissioned did not attend, or withdrew when the assembly defied the king, or had their commissions rejected by the assembly

The Glasgow Assembly 1638

Covenanter dominance

In the wake of a political and ecclesiastical revolution the Covenanters between 1638 and 1651 purged their episcopalian and other opponents among the ministry of the kirk. As a crude index of the growth of persecution and bitterness 236 depositions are plotted on this map to show their chronological and geographical pattern. This is a minimum figure based on the surviving evidence. Perhaps as many as 10% of these depositions may have been for reasons other than persecution (such as immorality or inadequacy), yet interesting patterns emerge.

The years 1638-40 saw systematic deposition in the south of opponents of the Covenanters (78 depositions, 52 in 1639). It was most severe where there was majority support for the Covenanters but also a substantial minority opposed to them - Edinburgh, St Andrews, Glasgow and Ayr. There was little taste for deposing colleagues in the north, and when purging came there later (if at all), it was on the initiative of the general assembly rather than of the local courts. There was a lull during 1641-3 with only 15 scattered depositions. More systematic purging came during 1644-7, mainly of ministers who showed support for, or more commonly insufficient active hostility to, royalist revolts (8 depositions). Finally in 1648-51 purging became more intense than ever before (105 cases, 52 in

1649) as the extremist Kirk Party regime purged the more moderate ministers who had supported the Engagers' invasion of England in 1648, and also those in the far north who had failed to denounce Montrose's landing in 1650. Then as bitter fighting of factions followed among the Kirk Party in the face of moderate and royalist revival, in 1651 for the first time ministers (3) were deposed for being too extreme rather than too moderate, as the majority faction of Revolutions sought to subdue their Protester opponents.

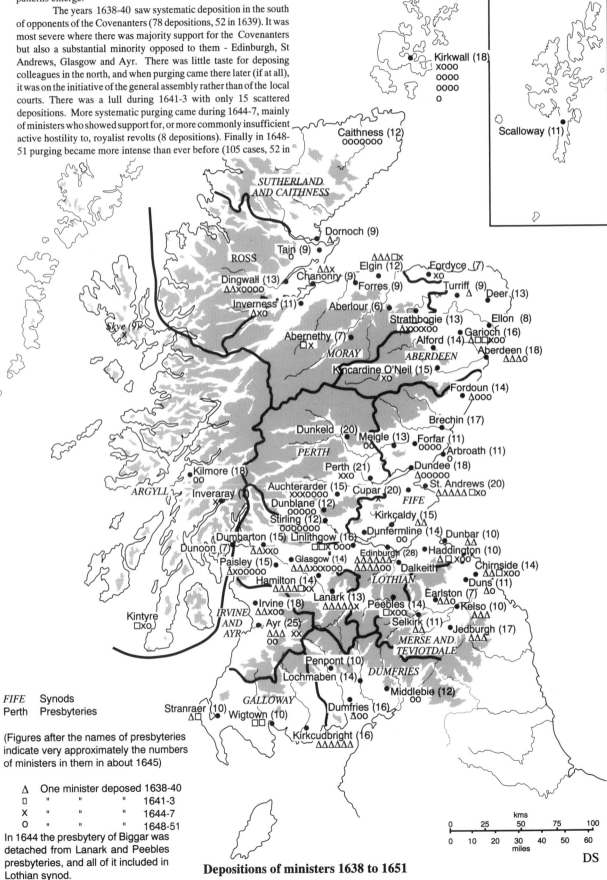

FIFE Synods
Perth Presbyteries

(Figures after the names of presbyteries indicate very approximately the numbers of ministers in them in about 1645)

Δ   One minister deposed 1638-40
□   "   "   "   1641-3
x   "   "   "   1644-7
o   "   "   "   1648-51

In 1644 the presbytery of Biggar was detached from Lanark and Peebles presbyteries, and all of it included in Lothian synod.

Depositions of ministers 1638 to 1651

DS

394

The Restoration to the Revolution

During the Restoration period 1661-89 episcopacy and the ancient dioceses were restored. Presbyteries continued to meet (though shorn of their elders), but the provincial synods of the presbyterian polity disappeared. For the purpose of historical investigation and comparison, however, it is useful to analyse evidence from this period area by area corresponding to the regions of the earlier and later presbyterian synods, rather than the confused and ephemeral dioceses. The boundaries shown on the maps of this period here have therefore only a hypothetical existence. They are based on those of the early eighteenth century on.

Attempts to enforce the Restoration Church Settlement of 1661 which re-established episcopacy resulted in the state's handling of 383 cases of nonconformity involving 809 illegal conventicles. The map which depicts the regional distribution and intensity of conventicling prosecutions according to the meetings' locations as cited in the privy council records therefore reflects not only official interest in suppressing conventicles but the geographic diversity of the activity itself.

Certain areas came under more intense official scrutiny. While traditional areas of protestant radicalism such as the synod of Glasgow and Ayr in the south-west contained a substantial number (117 cases) of the conventicles detected, the majority were found on the east coast in the synods of Fife (189) and in Lothian and Tweeddale (194). Conversely, little or no conventicling activity was reported in the more conservative north, most notably beyond the Moray Firth. Of all the conventicles cited in the council records, 64 have no location specified.

But the intensity of prosecutions in particular regions was not predicated on the indigenous religiosity of the area alone. Certainly, the presence of sympathetic heritors in a strong, covenanting region like the south-west could offer some protection to the non-indulged clergy from the central authorities; however, their influence could be circumscribed if they lacked sufficient political clout with the court and council officials or in the face of competing interests with town councils and bishops in regions containing royal burghs or episcopal sees.

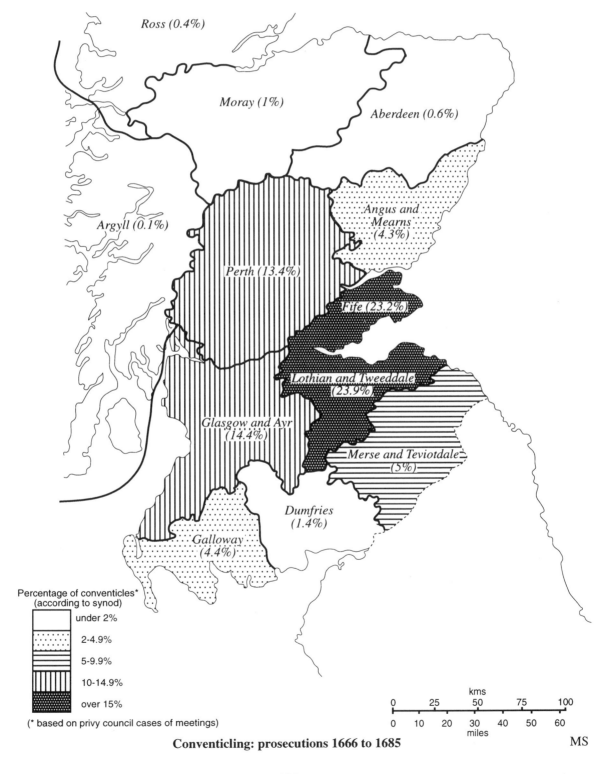

Percentage of conventicles*
(according to synod)

☐ under 2%

▫ 2-4.9%

▤ 5-9.9%

▥ 10-14.9%

▓ over 15%

(* based on privy council cases of meetings)

Conventicling: prosecutions 1666 to 1685

MS

The Restoration to the Revolution

Official interest in the apprehension and conviction of conventiclers resulted in the citation of 1901 individuals by the privy council between 1666 and 1685. But the pattern of these prosecutions was neither regular nor static. There was a considerable fluctuation in the rate of conventiclers prosecuted in each synod over the four periods specified as well as a significant change in the national pattern with respect to the regional distribution of the prosecutions.

Irregular and haphazard policing of the problem which varied widely across the country plus periodic firm action in 1670, 1674, 1677, 1680 and 1683 account for much of these differences.

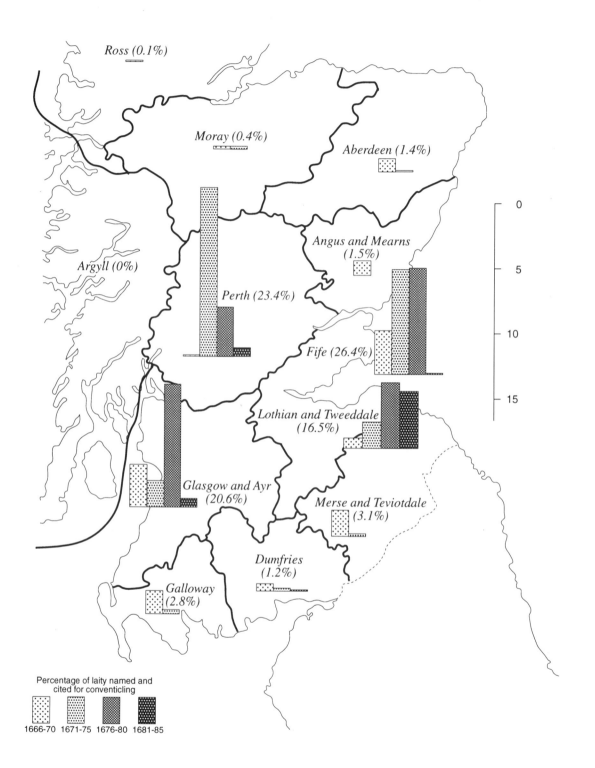

Percentage of laity named and cited for conventicling

1666-70 1671-75 1676-80 1681-85

1. Figures in brackets refer to the cumulative percentage of prosecuted conventiclers in each synod, 1666-85.

2. The privy council named and cited only one person for conventicling before 1666 and none after 1685.

3. In 2.9% of the cases, no location is specified.

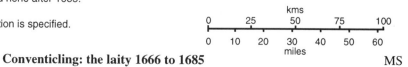

Conventicling: the laity 1666 to 1685

MS

The Restoration to the Revolution

Between 1666 and 1685 the privy council processed 541 cases of illegal preaching which involved the citation - often multiple - of 159 ministers; that is, almost one-fifth of the Scottish clergy. Although a significant proportion (17.4%) of the radical ministry were from the west coast, a similar number came from the south of Scotland (17.1%) and 40% were from the eastern synods of Fife and Lothian and Tweeddale. Moreover, the rate of ministerial prosecutions while numerically variable was proportionally consistent over the four periods specified: for example, Lothian and Tweeddale had the highest rate of prosecutions compared to the other synods throughout the Restoration.

Official interest in the suppression of conventicle preaching intensified during the latter half of the 1670s when two-thirds of the total number of ministers accused during the whole period were charged. This suggests that the government crackdown on the activities of the non-indulged clergy was a major contributing factor to the outbreak of the rebellion in 1679.

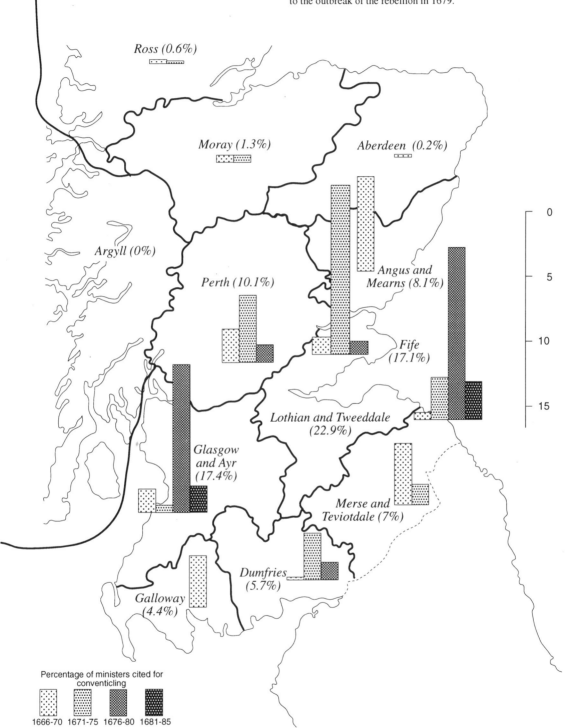

Percentage of ministers cited for conventicling

1666-70 1671-75 1676-80 1681-85

1. Figures in brackets refer to the cumulative percentage of ministers cited in each synod, 1666-85.

2. The privy council cited only 4 ministers for conventicle preaching prior to 1666 and none after 1685.

3. In 5.3% of the cases, no location is specified.

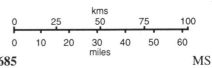

Conventicling: the clergy 1666 to 1685

MS

The Restoration to the Revolution

With the Indulgences of 1669, 1672 and 1678, the Caroline government gave outed ministers the opportunity to return to their clerical duties under certain licensing conditions which included the common provisions that they refrain from conventicling, recognise the church hierarchy, and receive collation from their diocesan bishop. By December of 1679, 149 ministers had accepted one of the pardons - in1669 43, in 1672 91, and in 1678 15 - and had been settled in 115 vacant parishes, many of which had been formerly occupied by the newly indulged incumbent. While the majority of the indulged clergy (63%) were from the western synod of Glasgow and Ayr, a significant number were from other regions of the country including 11% from the eastern synods of Fife and Lothian and Tweeddale; 14% from the border synods of Merse and Teviotdale, Dumfries, and Galloway; and 12% from the northern synods of Angus and Mearns, Argyll, and Perth.

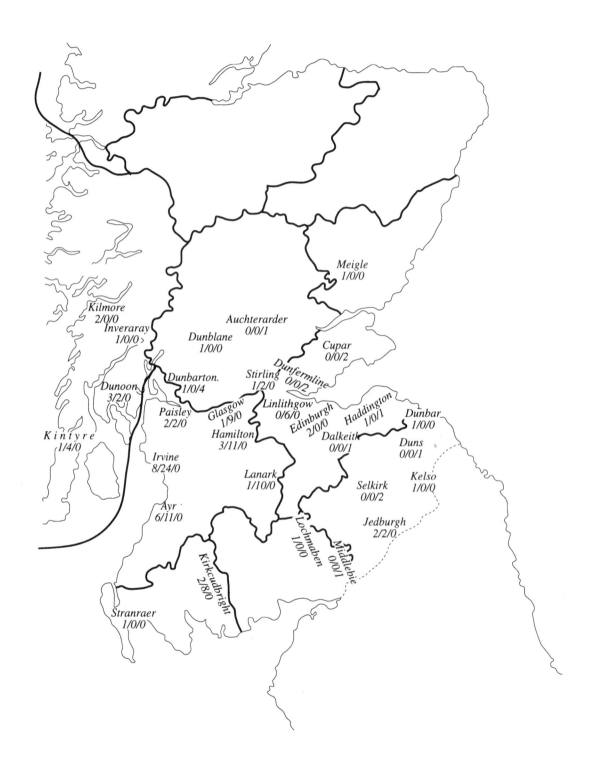

In each presbytery the number of ministers who accepted the indulgences of 1669, 1672 and 1678 respectively is shown e.g. Irvine 8/24/0. None of the other presbyteries had any indulged ministers.

The Caroline indulgences of 1669, 1672 and 1678

MS

398

The Restoration to the Revolution

For the presbyterian clergy, the proclamation of toleration in 1687 offered an equitable solution to the problem of nonconformity by enabling both conventicle preachers and the government to modify their respective approaches to the controversial question of Erastianism. On the one hand, the ministers accepted a degree of state authority in church matters by agreeing to make public announcements of their worship services as required by law. On the other hand, by dispensing with the practice of licensing ministers, the state in effect recognised prayer meetings held outwith the established church.

How successful this compromise was may be judged by the number of ministers who complied with the proclamation and advertised their prayer meetings. Between 9 October 1687 and 12 July 1688, 48 presbyterian ministers announced their intentions to preach at 72 different services which were held in a variety of locations including barns, private houses and special meeting halls. Of the 72 prayer meetings formally announced, the overwhelming majority were located in central Scotland with almost one third (24) held in the synod of Fife alone. Although one meeting has no specific location recorded, the remaining 47 meetings were concentrated in four other synods: Glasgow and Ayr (15); Lothian and Tweeddale (12); Angus and Mearns (11); and Perth (9).

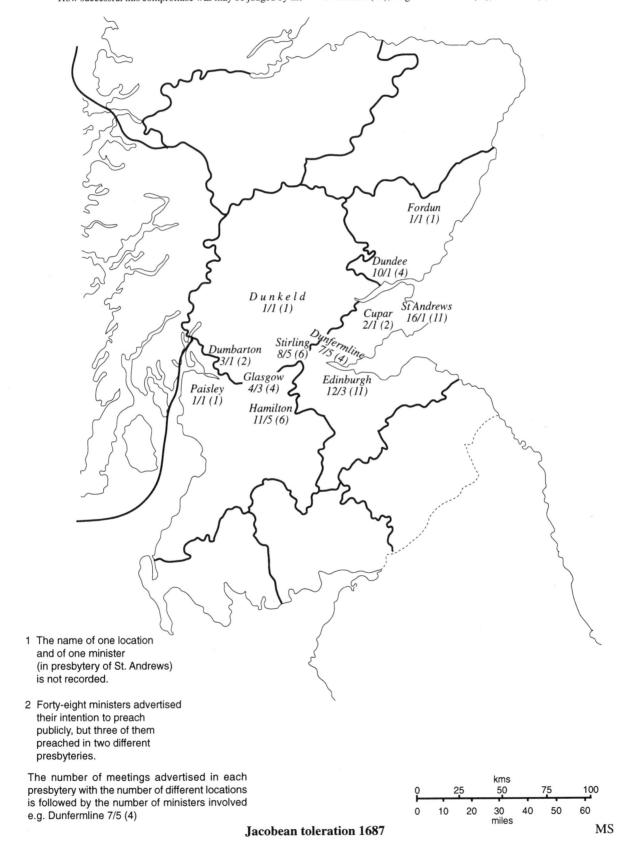

Fordun
1/1 (1)

Dundee
10/1 (4)

Dunkeld
1/1 (1)

Cupar
2/1 (2)

St Andrews
16/1 (11)

Stirling
8/5 (6)

Dunfermline
7/5 (4)

Dumbarton
3/1 (2)

Glasgow
4/3 (4)

Edinburgh
12/3 (11)

Paisley
1/1 (1)

Hamilton
11/5 (6)

1 The name of one location
and of one minister
(in presbytery of St. Andrews)
is not recorded.

2 Forty-eight ministers advertised
their intention to preach
publicly, but three of them
preached in two different
presbyteries.

The number of meetings advertised in each
presbytery with the number of different locations
is followed by the number of ministers involved
e.g. Dunfermline 7/5 (4)

kms
0   25   50   75   100

0   10   20   30   40   50   60
miles

Jacobean toleration 1687   MS

The Restoration to the Revolution

Charles II's ambivalent promise in 1660 to 'protect and preserve the government of the Church of Scotland, as it is settled by law, without violation', was followed in 1662 by parliamentary legislation restoring episcopacy. At the same time legislation was directed at the covenants, which were declared unlawful, and at conventicles, which were already a problem in areas where opponents of the religious settlement declined to attend their parish churches and worshipped privately, sometimes in groups on the hillsides. Particular danger lurked in one statute which required ministers admitted to charges after the abolition of patronage in 1649 to seek presentation from the patron and collation from the bishop. This scheme was considered by Middleton and like-minded politicians as a wonderful opportunity to purge the church of a small number of malcontents and extremists who would be caught in the net. In many parts of the country ministers and congregations acquiesced or accepted the proposals; but in the south-west a much higher proportion of ministers than had been anticipated refused to comply with legislation which forced them to recognise both episcopacy and lay patronage. As a consequence they were driven from their charges. Frequently too, congregations followed their 'outed' ministers and met secretly for worship. It has been reckoned that some 274 ministers were deprived from the parishes shown in the map, the bulk of them in 1662, but some also in the 1670s and 1680s. Of these 135 were located in the synod areas of Glasgow, Ayr, Dumfries and Galloway. North of the Tay (and even north of the Forth) less difficulty was experienced in securing conformity with the enactments.

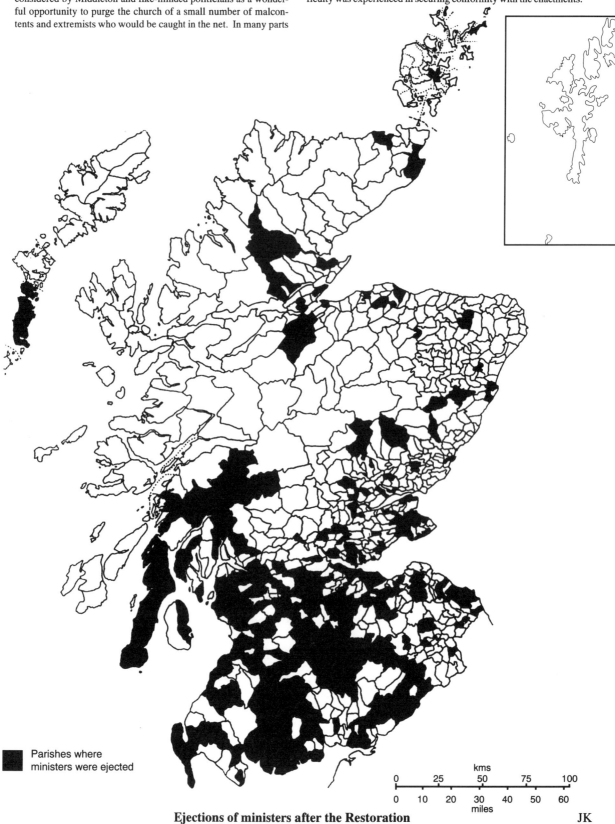

■ Parishes where ministers were ejected

kms
0   25   50   75   100

0 10 20 30 40 50 60
miles

Ejections of ministers after the Restoration   JK

The Restoration to the Revolution

At the Revolution, parliament abolished episcopal government in July 1689, and in June 1690 restored presbyterian government on the comparatively mild model of the 'Golden Act' of 1592. One effect of this was to avoid the awkward issue of the covenants, an omission which gave offence to many; yet most presbyterians accepted the settlement.

Earlier in April 1689 ministers throughout the country had been charged to read from their pulpits a proclamation appointing prayers to be said for William and Mary. Those who declined were reported to the privy council, and a substantial number of dismissals followed. At the same time action was taken to restore to their parishes some sixty ministers who had been 'outed' in 1662, and particularly in the south-west the Cameronians and others forcibly ejected over a hundred 'king's curates' i.e. ministers who had been introduced to vacant charges during the purges of the Restoration period.

The general assembly late in 1690 established two commissions of ministers and elders for visitation (one for lands north of the Tay, the other for the south) to purge the church of what were now regarded as undesirable elements. These commissions overplayed their hand when dealing with ministers of episcopal sympathies, who were victimised and deposed, though the strength of support for episcopacy in the north-east sometimes frustrated efforts at removing incumbents. But for the most part such ministers could expect little sympathy; and non-jurors, by declining to recognise William and Mary, cut themselves off from the national church to form their own small communion outside the establishment. Between 1689 and about 1702 some 664 ministers either left or were driven out of the parishes indicated on the map at a time when there were just over 900 parishes in all.

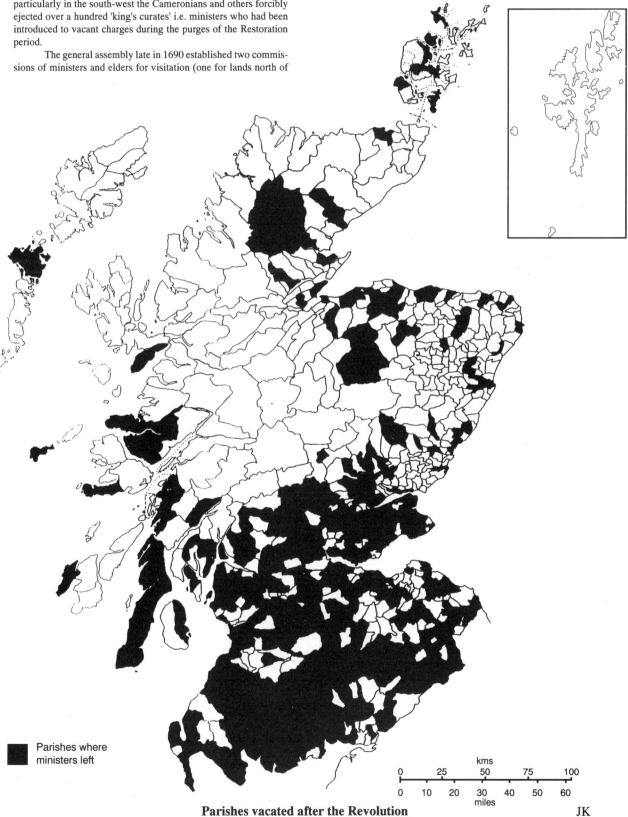

■ Parishes where ministers left

kms
0   25   50   75   100

0 10 20 30 40 50 60
miles

Parishes vacated after the Revolution

JK

Ecclesiastical organisation: the early eighteenth century

The maps in this section aim to present the situation about 1707 as the closing date for this Atlas. That year does not mark any particular ecclesiastical event or development.

The medieval inheritance of the parochial system had been adopted by the reformers after 1560 as a convenient network of territorial units. Over the next 150 years various commissions were appointed by parliament to make boundary adjustments where change of circumstances made it desirable to unite small parishes and divide large ones. By the early eighteenth century the country with around 1000 parishes had a parochial system that was still thought capable of meeting the needs of society, before the pressures of industrialisation demanded reappraisal and more drastic action. With a population standing, perhaps, at less than a million, a parish on average might possess rather less than 1000 souls, say between one and two hundred families and their servants. Most burghs, of course, were larger centres of population, but were usu-ally served still by a single parish. Edinburgh was an exception with six parishes by this date; Glasgow too had more than one parish, and other large burghs had more than one charge within the single parish.

The contrast between the large parishes in the Highlands and the compact ones along the eastern coast and in the central lowlands is a commentary not just on the disparity in resources and manpower in these areas, but also on the relative fertility of the land which sustained the population. In the earlier eighteenth century over two-thirds of the people of Scotland lived outside the Highlands and Islands. That the one-third of the population who lived in these areas was served by perhaps one-seventh of the country's parish ministers could hardly be considered adequate; but it is unreasonable to deny the difficulties which wild and mountainous terrain presented in communicating the gospel, or for that matter, anything else.

Parishes in the early eighteenth century

JK

Ecclesiastical organisation: the early eighteenth century

Following the re-establishment of Presbyterian government in 1690, the old diocesan structure was allowed to lapse and synods once again became 'provincial synods' with elected moderators. Presbyteries too resumed the practice of electing a moderator for a limited term. The broad model, insofar as it was practicable, was clearly the covenanters' polity of the 1640s. Changes were made from time to time, particularly in the northern areas where a short-age of ministers caused practical difficulties for presbyteries. Some presbyteries were united for a time, and then some were separated again after a short interval. The maps show the organisation as it was in 1707, with thirteen synods and sixty-one presbyteries. Despite its formidable problems in the Highlands, the established kirk sought to extend and intensify its operations across the country as a whole.

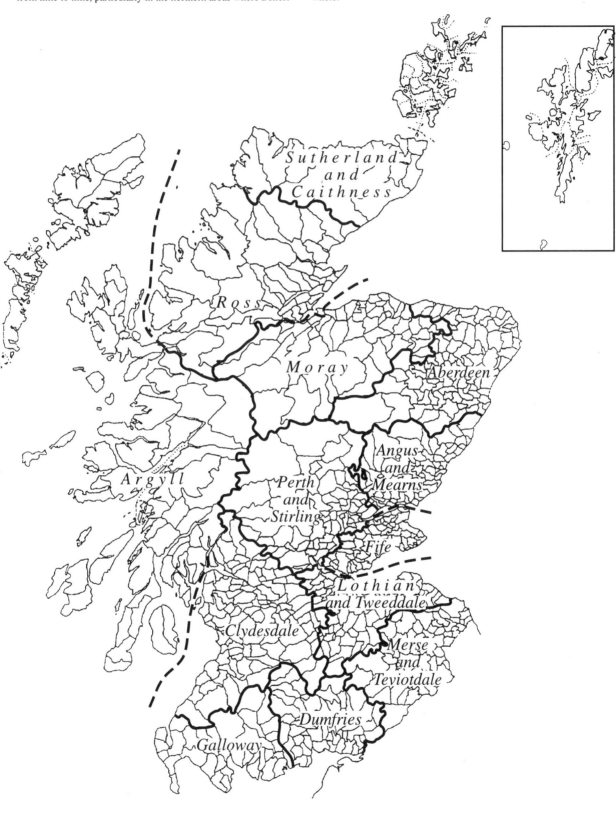

Synods in the early eighteenth century

JK

403

Ecclesiastical organisation: the early eighteenth century

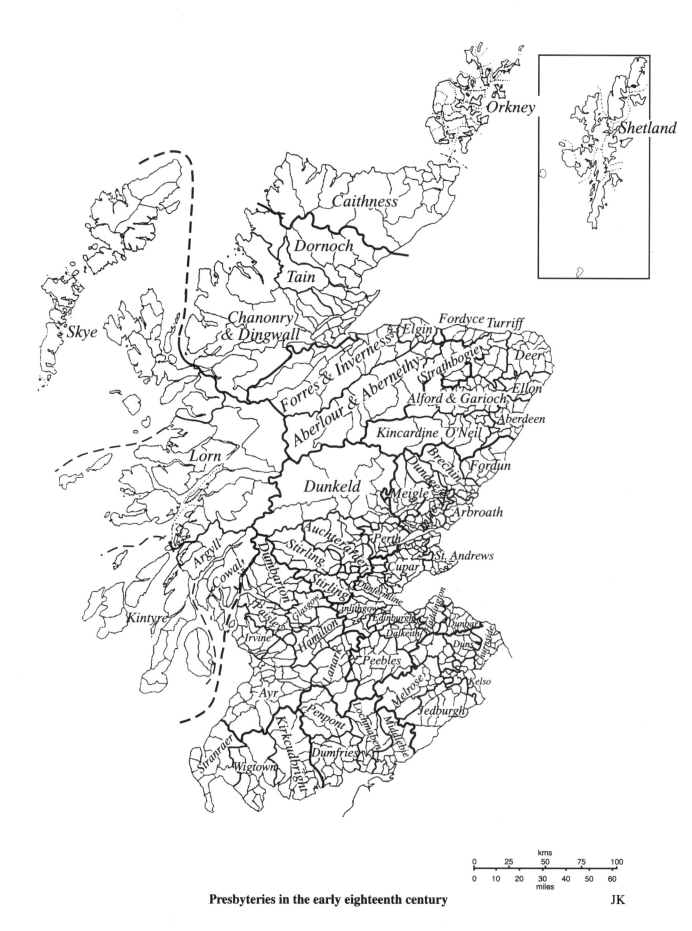

Presbyteries in the early eighteenth century

JK

Poor relief

Somewhat over a quarter of the parishes of Scotland have left kirk session registers covering the period of the famine of the 1690s. From these and other records it can be seen that forty-three parishes carried through a decision to implement the poor law statues and raise funds in one way or another from the heritors. This map shows the distribution of these parishes by shire. The assessed parishes are shown as a percentage of the parishes of all shires from where three or more kirk session registers survive. Those shires with no registers, or less than three are shown as leaving inadequate documentation even in the instance of Selkirkshire where the only surviving register is of an assessed parish.

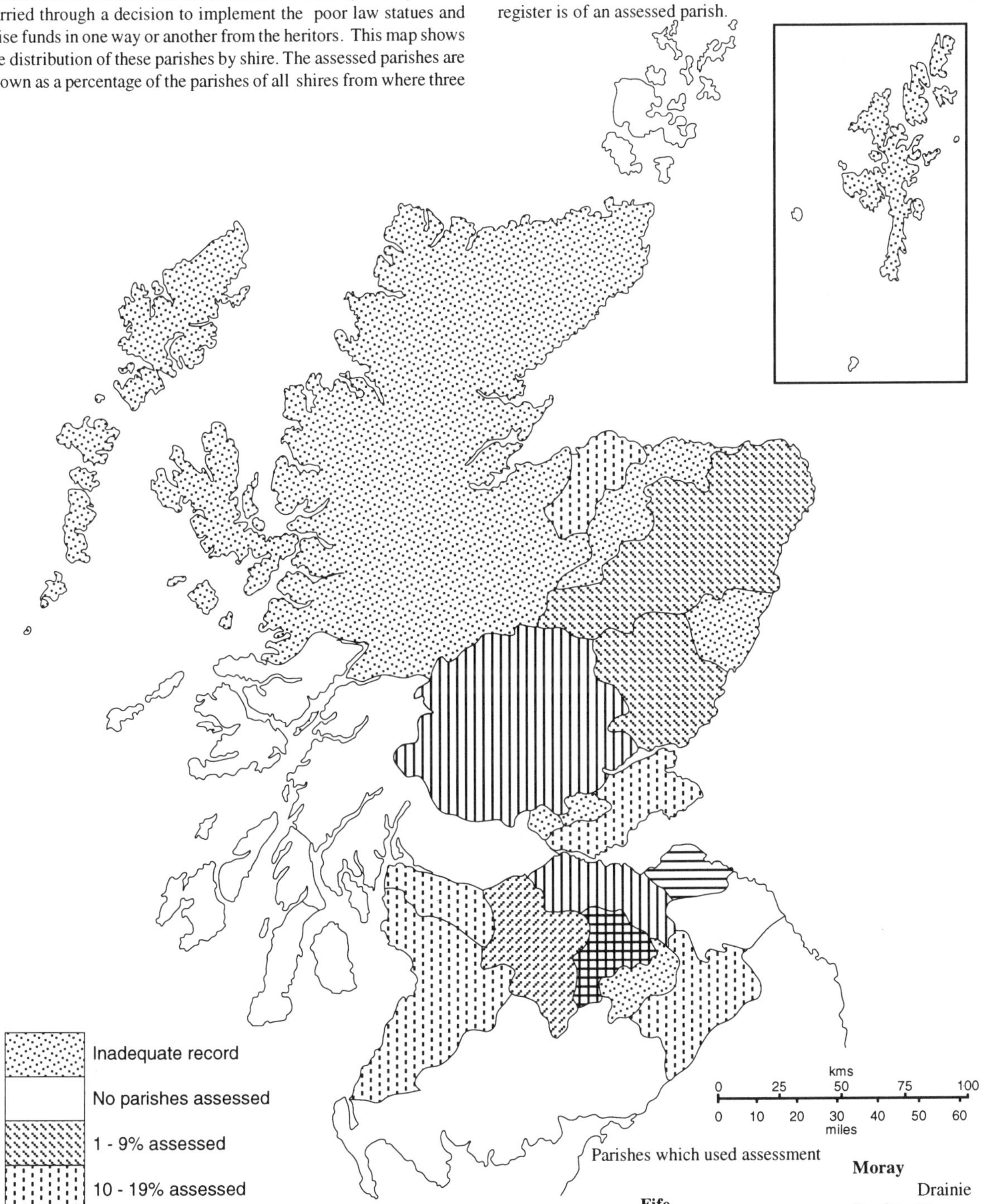

Inadequate record

No parishes assessed

1 - 9% assessed

10 - 19% assessed

20 - 29% assessed

30 - 39% assessed

40 - 49% assessed

over 50% assessed

kms
0   25   50   75   100
0 10 20 30 40 50 60
miles

Parishes which used assessment

Aberdeenshire
Longside
Angus
Kettins
Ayrshire
Kilmaurs
Kilwinning
East Lothian
Garvald
Haddington
North Berwick
Ormiston
Prestonkirk
Saltoun
Spott
Tyninghame
Whitekirk

Fife
Forgan
Kennoway
Kilconquhar
Kingsbarns
Lanarkshire
Carstairs
Douglas
Lesmahagow
Pettinain
Midlothian
Colinton
Corstorphine
Cramond
Crichton
Currie
Lasswade
Stow
Temple

Moray
Drainie
Peebleshire
Eddleston
Manor
Perthshire
Blackford
Logie
Longforgan
Monzie
Perth
Tibbermuir
Renfrewshire
Greenock
Roxburghshire
Ashkirk
Selkirkshire
Galashiels
West Lothian
Carriden
Uphall

Poor relief 1695 to 1707

RM

405

Roman Catholic recusancy

The term 'recusancy' has been taken to mean non-attendance at the communion and other Reformed services, which was liable to be accompanied by attendance at mass and other sacraments held according to Roman Catholic rite, as well as general adherence to Roman Catholic belief and observance. In spite of an uncompromising concept of one visible church, parliamentary ratification of the Reformed articles of faith and a rigorous penal code, there was little serious persecution in post-Reformation Scotland. Examination of contemporary records suggests that Catholicism, although by no means dead, gave few signs that it was an organised force at any time likely to challenge the Reformed establishment.

The map illustrates the survival of indigenous Catholicism, on the wane by the 1570s partly for want of priests, and the resurgence later in the century which was largely due to the external reinforcement of Jesuits and other missionaries from abroad and the internal protection of the politically-minded 'Catholic party'. Throughout the period the amount of reported recusancy was a reflection of the politico-religious climate; the doubtful constitutionality and initially poor endowment of the Reformed church; Catholic worship at the queen's court; increased cooperation between church and state after Mary's deposition in 1567; the 'test act' of 1573 which was followed by deprivation of non-conforming benefice-holders; the growth of presbyteries in the 1580s and watchfulness of the church authorities, as exemplified by the report to the general assembly of February 1588; the activities of the Jesuits in the last decade and at the turn of the century, at a time when James VI for political reasons was inclined to adopt a tolerant attitude to influential, known Catholics.

Geographically, recusancy reflects the protection of Catholic families, particularly in the north-east, south-west and in parts of the Lothians. At the same time, delay in the provision of a minister in every parish created trouble-spots of recusancy in some areas, such as the Borders. The one attempt to erect Roman Catholic worship publicly, at Easter 1563, took place in the south-west. It was stage-managed by Archbishop John Hamilton of St Andrews assisted by personnel of two conservative monastic communities (Paisley of which he was the commendator and Crossraguel) the beneficed clergy of some of the churches appropriated to them, and the earl of Cassillis with some of his kinsmen and dependents. The Jesuits were active mainly in those areas protected by the earl of Huntly (i.e. Aberdeenshire, Moray and Sutherland), in parts of the Lothians under the patronage of Lord Seton, and in and around Dumfries with the support of Lord Maxwell and the abbot of New Abbey. There is only a little surviving evidence of reported recusancy in the west Highlands and the Islands prior to 1603.

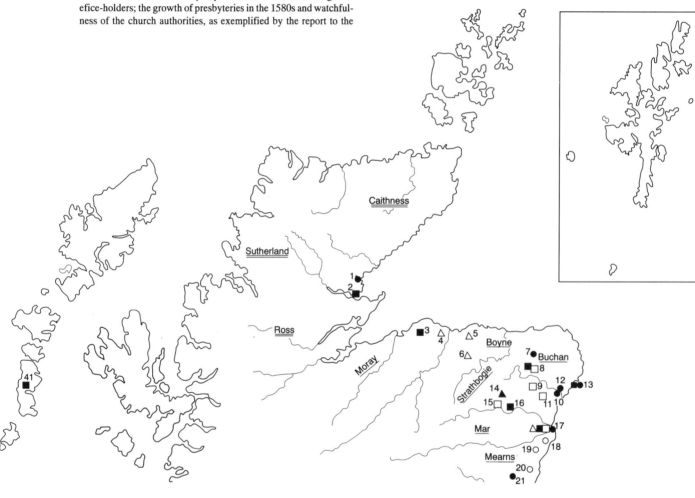

Mearns ○	Areas and places mentioned in the report on recusancy of 1587/8
Moray ●	Areas and places of Jesuit activity in 1580s and 1590s
<u>Caithness</u>	Areas mentioned in the report on recusancy of 1588 and of Jesuit activity in 1580s and 1590s
■	Celebration of or attendance at mass or other sacraments according to Roman Catholic rite
□	General nonconformity and adherence to Catholic belief and observance
▲	Places associated with clergy cited before the privy council, 1569
△	Places associated with the benefices of those deprived for failure to subscribe the Articles of Faith 1573

Roman Catholic recusancy 1560 to 1603

MHBS

Roman Catholic recusancy

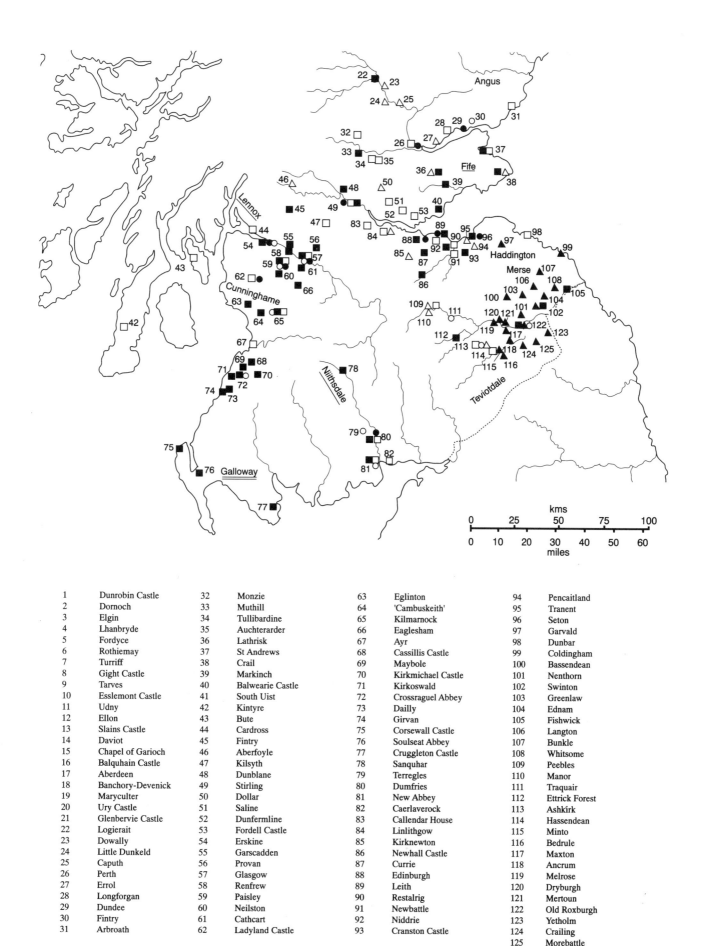

1	Dunrobin Castle	32	Monzie	63	Eglinton	94	Pencaitland
2	Dornoch	33	Muthill	64	'Cambuskeith'	95	Tranent
3	Elgin	34	Tullibardine	65	Kilmarnock	96	Seton
4	Lhanbryde	35	Auchterarder	66	Eaglesham	97	Garvald
5	Fordyce	36	Lathrisk	67	Ayr	98	Dunbar
6	Rothiemay	37	St Andrews	68	Cassillis Castle	99	Coldingham
7	Turriff	38	Crail	69	Maybole	100	Bassendean
8	Gight Castle	39	Markinch	70	Kirkmichael Castle	101	Nenthorn
9	Tarves	40	Balwearie Castle	71	Kirkoswald	102	Swinton
10	Esslemont Castle	41	South Uist	72	Crossraguel Abbey	103	Greenlaw
11	Udny	42	Kintyre	73	Dailly	104	Ednam
12	Ellon	43	Bute	74	Girvan	105	Fishwick
13	Slains Castle	44	Cardross	75	Corsewall Castle	106	Langton
14	Daviot	45	Fintry	76	Soulseat Abbey	107	Bunkle
15	Chapel of Garioch	46	Aberfoyle	77	Cruggleton Castle	108	Whitsome
16	Balquhain Castle	47	Kilsyth	78	Sanquhar	109	Peebles
17	Aberdeen	48	Dunblane	79	Terregles	110	Manor
18	Banchory-Devenick	49	Stirling	80	Dumfries	111	Traquair
19	Maryculter	50	Dollar	81	New Abbey	112	Ettrick Forest
20	Ury Castle	51	Saline	82	Caerlaverock	113	Ashkirk
21	Glenbervie Castle	52	Dunfermline	83	Callendar House	114	Hassendean
22	Logierait	53	Fordell Castle	84	Linlithgow	115	Minto
23	Dowally	54	Erskine	85	Kirknewton	116	Bedrule
24	Little Dunkeld	55	Garscadden	86	Newhall Castle	117	Maxton
25	Caputh	56	Provan	87	Currie	118	Ancrum
26	Perth	57	Glasgow	88	Edinburgh	119	Melrose
27	Errol	58	Renfrew	89	Leith	120	Dryburgh
28	Longforgan	59	Paisley	90	Restalrig	121	Mertoun
29	Dundee	60	Neilston	91	Newbattle	122	Old Roxburgh
30	Fintry	61	Cathcart	92	Niddrie	123	Yetholm
31	Arbroath	62	Ladyland Castle	93	Cranston Castle	124	Crailing
						125	Morebattle

Roman Catholic recusancy 1560 to 1603

MHBS

Roman Catholic recusancy

The prospects for Catholicism as a living faith within Scottish communities were transformed radically, if gradually, following the reinvigoration of the Scottish mission from the second decade of the seventeenth century. The ground rules for the work of conversion in the Lowlands were laid down from 1617 by the Jesuits who targeted landed families, particularly those with heritable jurisdictions able to protect priests and encourage apostasy within their territorial spheres of influence. Leading catholic families were encouraged to intermarry both to consolidate their faith and bridge their geographic isolation. From 1622 oversight of all regular and secular clergy on the Scottish mission was exercised by the Sacred College of Propaganda at Rome. Despite chronic underfunding by Propaganda and rivalries among the clergy, recusancy thrived within geographic pockets in the south-west as well as the north-east, continuing on an upward spiral until 1685. By then Catholicism in the Lowlands though still based on households where mass was celebrated privately and irregularly had spread from the country seats of nobles to those of gentry, and from their town-houses to the tenements of burgesses.

In the Highlands and Islands the neglect of organised religion allied to relative spiritual deprivation since the Reformation had offered the greatest prospects for the entrenchment of Catholicism as the faith of whole communities. Although Jesuits and secular priests made strenuous efforts to maintain a minimal presence, the dearth of native Gaelic speakers led to Irish priests providing the main impetus for the work of conversion - most notably the Franciscans, whose pioneering mission from 1619 was resumed after a gap of twenty-two years in 1668. In the meantime the Vincentian mission which commenced in 1651 and occasional sorties by Dominicans helped ensure that Catholicism was revived within whole communities. Unlike the Lowlands, recusancy within the Highland and Islands can be identified with clan affiliations, not just landed households. However the optimistic accounting of thousands of conversions in the course of these Irish missionary endeavours cannot be dissociated from their desperate need to attract funding from Propaganda. In fact priests serving in the Highlands and Islands at any one time rarely numbered more than six; and the numbers serving together on the Scottish Mission as a whole prior to 1685 usually fluctuated between twelve and twenty.

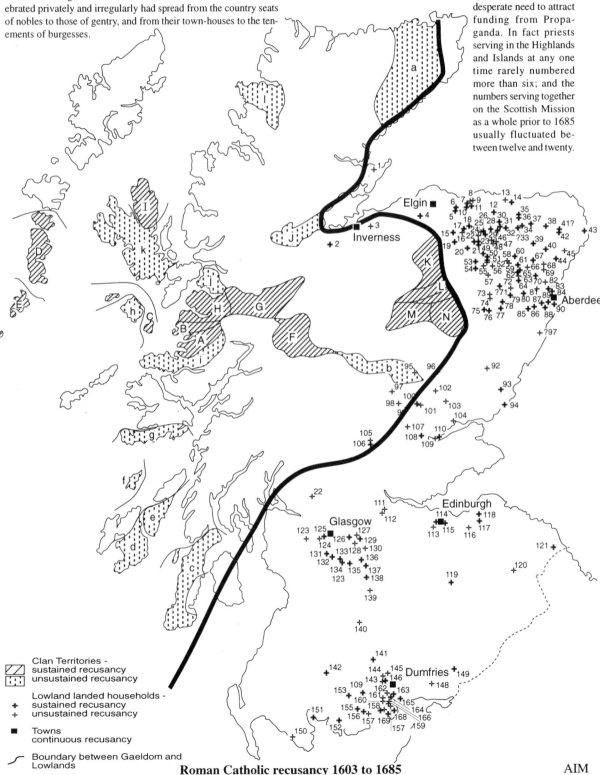

Roman Catholic recusancy 1603 to 1685

Clan Territories -
/// sustained recusancy
:::: unsustained recusancy

Lowland landed households -
+ sustained recusancy
+ unsustained recusancy

■ Towns
continuous recusancy

⌒ Boundary between Gaeldom and
Lowlands

AIM

Roman Catholic recusancy

Lowland landed households-sustained recusancy dating from initial citation

2	Dochfour,1667	34	Delgatie, 1625	76	Drumgesk, 1629	125	Haggs, 1679		
4	'Tulliquode',1653	35	'Blacktoun', 1628	77	Beltie, 1630	126	'Braidsholme', 1683		
5	Huntly*, 1604	36	'Artamford'. 1643	78	Learney, 1653	129	Lauchope, 1683		
6	'Swelton', 1653	37	Auchry, 1620	79	Corsindae, 1607	131	Bogton, 1683		
7	Arradoul, 1650	38	Fedderate, 1661	80	Skene, 1672	132	Sheilds, 1683		
10	Farnachty, 1622	39	Gight, 1607	83	Grandhome, 1661	133	Shawtonhill, 1683		
11	Letterfourie	40	Schivas, 1637	84	Balgownie, 1628	134	Chapelton, 1683		
12	Park, 1666	41	'Knockmylne', 1629 ?	85	Drum, 1640	135	Sempill*, 1606		
14	Banff*,1631	42	Crichie, 1671	86	Craigton, 1629	136	Woodside, 1683		
15	'Murefauld', 1661	43	'Cairnfield', 1681	87	Hilton, 1627	137	Craignethan, 1683		
17	Auchindachy, 1628	44	'Bridgeford', 1661	88	Blairs, 1628	138	'Whiteside', 1683		
18	'Clasterm', 1653	49	Culdrain, 1638	89	Pitfodels, 1644	141	Barjarg, 1684		
19	Auchindown, 1607	50	Cults, 1663	90	Tullos, 1653	146	Herries*. 1606		
20	Baldorney, 1685	51	Kirkhill, 1663	93	Wester Braikie, 1649	149	Wauchope, 1627		
21	Wellheads, 1647	53	Lesmoir, 1639	94	'Newgrange', 1624	151	Bagbie, 1634		
22	Cairnborrow, 1628	54	Craig, 1624	96	Clintlaw, 1653	152	'Nunton', 1665		
23	Artloch, 1649	60	Warthill, 1685	100	Craigie, 1610	153	Parton, 1647		
26	Littlemill, 1628	61	Pitcaple, 1628	106	Perth*, 1685	154	Barncailzie, 1684		
27	Cormalet, 1628	62	Braco, 1668	108	Kinnoul*, 1650	155	Breoch, 1664		
28	Rothiemay, 1653	64	Fetternear, 1653	110	'Gormock', 1669	156	'Brakenside', 1667		
29	Auchingoul, 1684	65	Balquhain, 1685	114	Coates, 1669	158	Auchenskeoch, 1628		
30	Auchintoul, 1669	67	Meldrum, 1639	115	Niddrie, 1653	163	Conheath, 1620		
31	Frendraught*, 1632	70	Concraig, 1607	117	Clerkington, 1685	164	Kirkconnell, 1627		
32	Oliphant*, 1652	71	Kirkton, 1685 ?	118	Garleton, 1671	165	Nithsdale*, 1606		
33	'Dunkinty' 1629 ?	75	Aboyne*, 1656	119	Traquair*, 1667	168	Kirkhouse, 1684		
				121	Mordington*, 1641	169	Torrorie, 1684		

Lowland landed households- unsustained recusancy dating from final citation

1	Cromarty, 1631	58	Newton, 1621	101	Gourdie, 1607	130	Cambusnethan, 1627
3	Cawdor, 1631	59	'Rayniston', 1629	102	Balwhyrne, 1670		
8	'Fetterletter', 1631	63	Keithny, 1629	103	Drumkilbo, 1640	139	Douglas*, 1653
9	'Edinville', 1631	66	Bourtie, 1628	104	Gray*, 1653	140	Carco, 1660
13	Whitehills, 1622	68	Udny, 1639	105	Alichmore, 1639	142	Garroch, 1622
16	Tombreck, 1630	69	Tillygreig, 1628	107	Coldrochie, 1649	143	'Mains', 1628
24	'Terrisoule'. 1628	72	Cluny, 1633	109	Errol*, 1672	144	Gribton, 1632
25	'Drumquhill', 1651	73	Craigievar, 1608	111	West Kerse, 1629	145	Cowhill, 1627
45	Auchleuchries, 1655	74	Camphill, 1648	112	Middlerig, 1629	147	Almagill, 1627
46	Lessendrum, 1629	81	Caskieben, 1669	113	'Redhall', 1653	148	Middlebie, 1628
47	Monellie, 1668	82	Goval, 1656	116	Winton*, 1658	150	Monreith, 1628
48	Troupsmill, 1629	91	'Carrone', 1607 ?	120	Home*, 1606	157	Kirkennan, 1667
52	Mosstown, 1667	92	Balnamoon, 1627	122	Drumquhassle, 1624	159	Lochhill, 1634
55	Forbes*, 1606	95	Ashintully, 1639	123	Abercorn*, 1653	160	Kinharvie, 1632
56	New Leslie, 1630	97	Kinnaird, 1607	124	Cowglen, 1615	161	Troston, 1627
57	Terpersie, 1667	98	Inver, 1641	127	Monkland, 1615	162	Mabie, 1643
		99	Murthly, 1615	128	Carfin, 1657	166	'Arkiebus', 1627
						167	Corbelly, 1627

Towns with a continuous history of recusancy dating from initial citation

Aberdeen , 1605   Dumfries, 1605   Elgin, 1623

Edinburgh, 1605   Glasgow, 1607   Inverness, 1653

Clan territories   (i) sustained recusancy dating from initial mission

A	Moidart, 1624
B	Arisaig and South Morar, 1625
C	Eigg and Canna, 1625
D	Benbecula, South Uist and Eriskay, 1625
E	Barra, 1626
F	Braes of Lochaber, 1636
G	Glengarry, 1651
H	Knoydart and North Morar, 1651
I	Trotternish, 1652
J	Strathfarrer, Strathglass and the Aird, 1669
K	Inveravon and Glenlivet, 1652
L	Strathavon and Strathdon, 1630
M	Braemar, 1660
N	Upper Deeside, 1632

Names within quotes do not appear on the modern Ordnance Survey map; they lay within the same parish as the place plotted on the map.

A query indicates that the identification of the place-name is probable rather than definite.

An asterisk indicates the name of a noble family whose principal residence was at the place indicated (though it may have had a different name).

(ii) unsustained recusancy dating duration

a	Caithness and East Sutherland, 1619-37
b	Blair Atholl, 1636-46
c	Kintyre and Gigha, 1619-47
d	Islay, 1624-47
e	Jura, 1624-37
f	Colonsay, 1624-39
g	Ross of Mull, 1624-47
h	Rum and Muck, 1625-37
i	Ardnamurchan and Sunart, 1625-53
j	Glenelg, 1624-37
k	Skye, 1624-37
l	Assynt, 1624-37

AIM

Roman Catholic recusancy

Recusancy after 1650 was marked by a distinct increase in the number of apostates from Protestantism. Although the toleration conceded in 1687 lasted barely two years and was sandwiched between anti-popish riots in Edinburgh, the brief reign of James VII afforded Catholics the opportunity to worship publicly and propagate their faith free from harassment by the kirk. Holyroodhouse became the centre of Catholicism in Scotland, with a chapel run by the secular clergy, a Jesuit college and a printing press for devotional tracts and liturgical books. Although the deposition of James VII in 1683 obliged the Scottish Mission to resume its covert and underfunded posture, the king's refusal to sacrifice his faith for his throne stiffened the resolve of the recusants not to be reconciled to Protestantism in the Highlands and Islands; moreover, despite a continuing shortage of Gaelic-speaking priests there was a pronounced drift towards Catholicism in the wake of the Revolution Settlement.

Catholicism was given a unifying national focus in 1694 when the appointment of Thomas Nicholson as vicar-apostolic brought the Scottish Mission under the episcopal jurisdiction of the first native bishop since the demise of the last of the pre-Reformation hierarchy ninety-one years earlier. (The canonical authority exercised by prefects-apostolic since 1653 had been confined to secular clergy in the Lowlands.) Although Nicholson did not take up his duties in Scotland until 1696 and another five years were to elapse before the Jesuits made a formal and complete submission to his authority, the proved standing of the Scottish Mission in the eyes of Propaganda ensured that the number of serving priests rose steadily above thirty by 1707. Yet despite the radical transformation of Catholicism into a community-based faith by the early eighteenth century, recusancy remained a minority pursuit between 1603 and 1707. Professed papists probably amount to no more than 2% of the total population in this period.

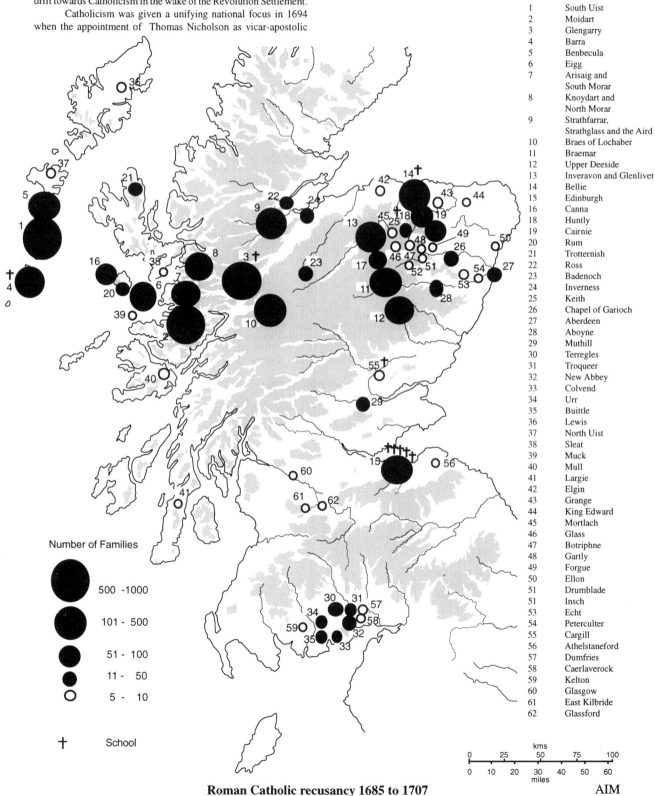

1	South Uist
2	Moidart
3	Glengarry
4	Barra
5	Benbecula
6	Eigg
7	Arisaig and South Morar
8	Knoydart and North Morar
9	Strathfarrar, Strathglass and the Aird
10	Braes of Lochaber
11	Braemar
12	Upper Deeside
13	Inveravon and Glenlivet
14	Bellie
15	Edinburgh
16	Canna
17	Huntly
18	Cairnie
19	Rum
20	Trotternish
21	Ross
22	Badenoch
23	Inverness
24	Keith
25	Chapel of Garioch
26	Aberdeen
27	Aboyne
28	Muthill
29	Terregles
30	Troqueer
31	New Abbey
32	Colvend
33	Urr
34	Buittle
35	Lewis
36	North Uist
37	Sleat
38	Muck
39	Mull
40	Largie
41	Elgin
42	Grange
43	King Edward
44	Mortlach
45	Glass
46	Botriphne
47	Gartly
48	Forgue
49	Ellon
50	Drumblade
51	Insch
51	Echt
53	Peterculter
54	Cargill
55	Athelstaneford
56	Dumfries
57	Caerlaverock
58	Kelton
59	Glasgow
60	East Kilbride
61	Glassford
62	

Number of Families

- 500 -1000
- 101 - 500
- 51 - 100
- 11 - 50
- 5 - 10

✝ School

kms
0   25   50   75   100
0 10 20 30 40 50 60
miles

Roman Catholic recusancy 1685 to 1707

AIM

Social and cultural

Landholding in the mid-twelfth century

The map is a snapshot of the leading landholding families, including the royal house, about the end of David I's reign and the beginning of that of Malcolm IV (1153-65). It shows that the native 'pre-feudal' landowners still dominated the overall pattern of lordship even in that part of the realm (largely non-Highland) for which adequate evidence exists. Nevertheless, across much of south-eastern Scotland and here and there in the Clyde valley and in Fife and Gowrie, incoming feudally tenured families had taken hold strongly.

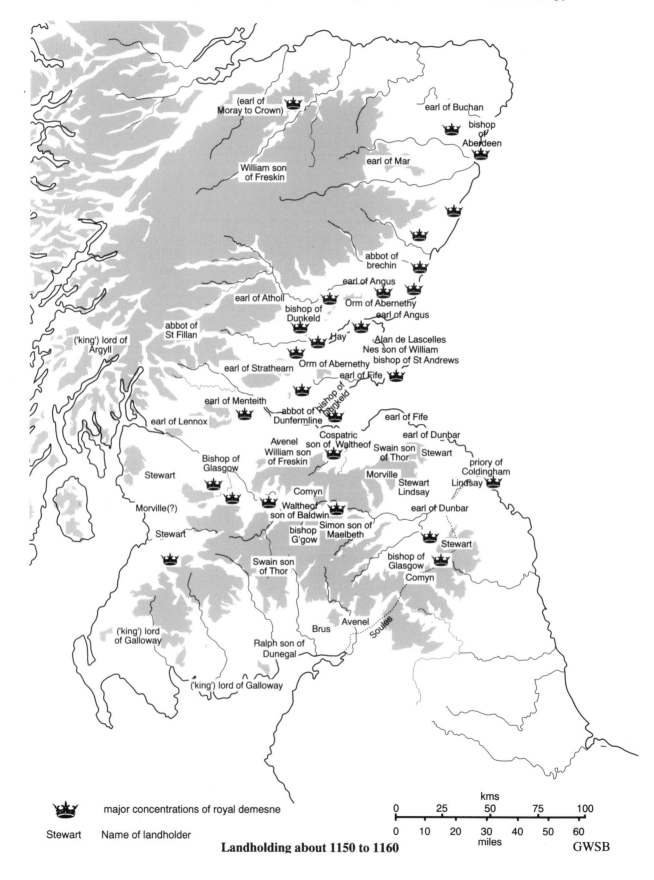

major concentrations of royal demesne

Stewart   Name of landholder

Landholding about 1150 to 1160

GWSB

The growth of military feudalism

This map and that showing landholding are mutually complementary. The shading is designed to show the intensity and in simplified form the character of feudalisation, involving the creation of knights' fees and other military holdings, between the beginning of the twelfth century and the later part of the reign of Alexander II (1214-49). The contrast between small unit knights' fees and larger units probably reflects an earlier social and economic arrangement.

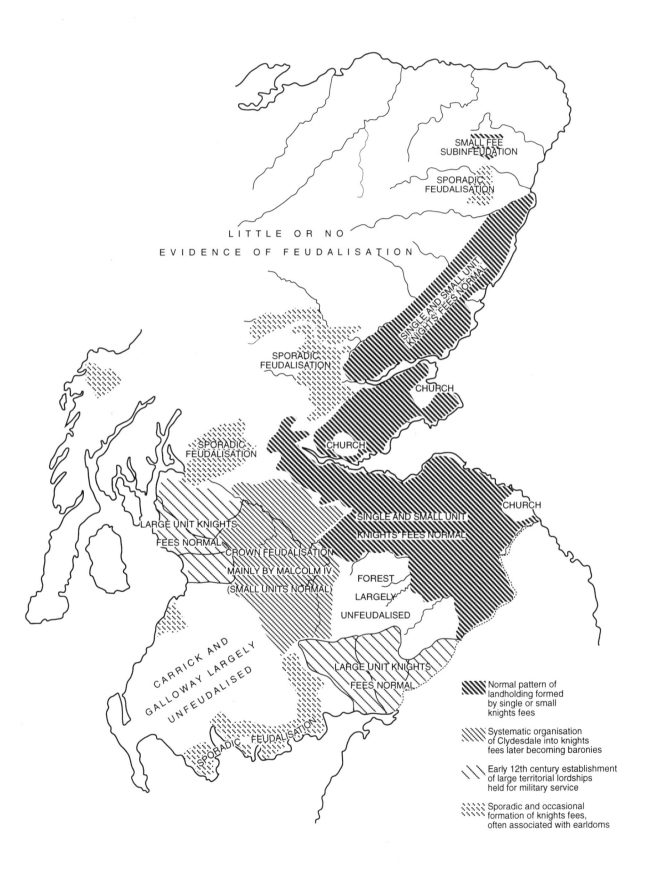

SMALL FEE SUBINFEUDATION

SPORADIC FEUDALISATION

LITTLE OR NO EVIDENCE OF FEUDALISATION

SPORADIC FEUDALISATION

SINGLE AND SMALL UNIT KNIGHTS' FEES NORMAL

CHURCH

SPORADIC FEUDALISATION

CHURCH

LARGE UNIT KNIGHTS FEES NORMAL

CROWN FEUDALISATION MAINLY BY MALCOLM IV (SMALL UNITS NORMAL)

SINGLE AND SMALL UNIT KNIGHTS' FEES NORMAL

CHURCH

FOREST LARGELY UNFEUDALISED

CARRICK AND GALLOWAY LARGELY UNFEUDALISED

LARGE UNIT KNIGHTS FEES NORMAL

SPORADIC FEUDALISATION

Normal pattern of landholding formed by single or small knights fees

Systematic organisation of Clydesdale into knights fees later becoming baronies

Early 12th century establishment of large territorial lordships held for military service

Sporadic and occasional formation of knights fees, often associated with earldoms

The growth of military feudalism from about 1100 to about 1240

GWSB

Perambulations

The creation of new estates, the bestowal of old estates upon new families, often to be held by feudal tenure, and above all the endowment of monastic houses with lands previously in royal or magnatial lordship, stimulated the formal definition of marches or boundaries in the twelfth and thirteenth centuries. Perambulations, as the process was known, might often be in response to an explicit royal command (by brieve of perambulation) and the results could be registered in the royal archives. The use of many natural, and a few man-made features to serve as boundary-markers and lines makes the surviving perambulation records an enormously valuable source for the topography and human geography of medieval Scotland.

The maps show boundary features which figure in thirteenth century perambulations of: (a) the upper Clydesdale estate of Crawford Lindsay, feudalised from the late twelfth century; (b) the marches between Dunfermline Abbey's hunting reserve of Outh on the one hand and the estates of neighbouring lairds, e.g. of Cult, Cleish and Crambeth (Dowhill) on the other; and (c) the old royal shire or thanage of Kingoldrum in the Braes of Angus, granted to Arbroath Abbey in 1178.

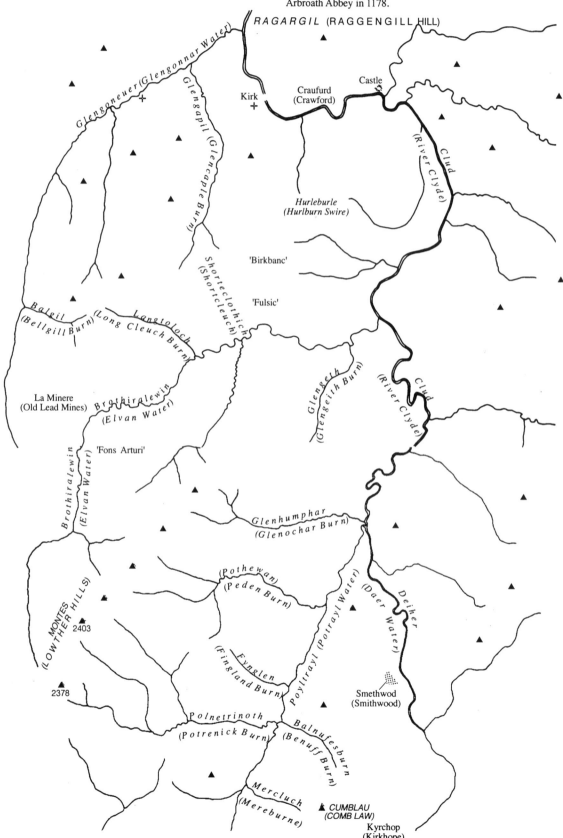

Perambulations: Crawford twelfth to thirteenth centuries   GWSB

Perambulations

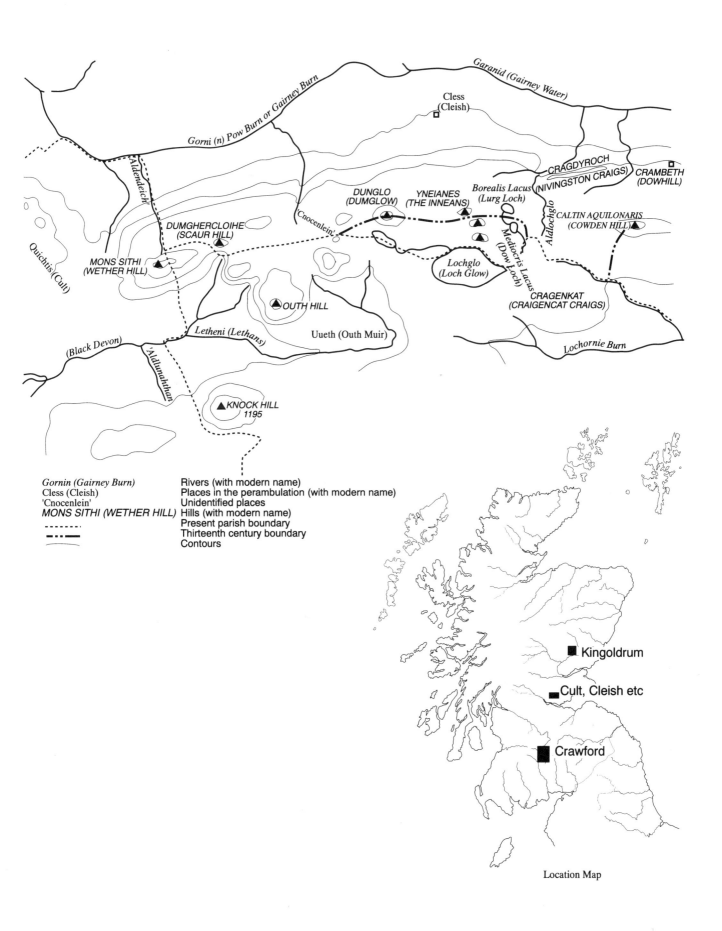

Perambulations: Cult, Cleish, Crambeth and the forest of Outh mid-thirteenth century

GWSB

Perambulations

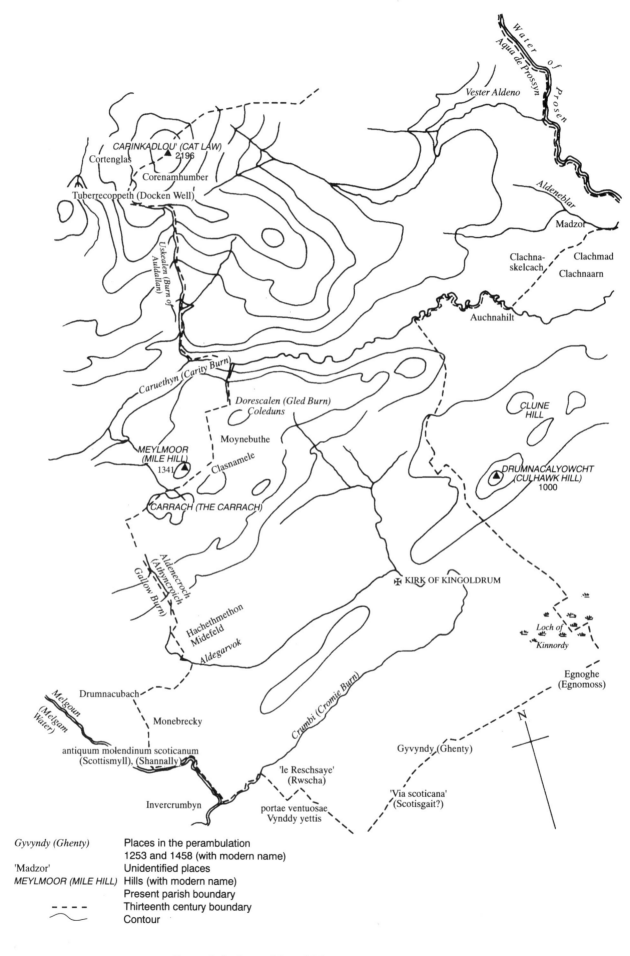

Perambulations: shire of Kingoldrum 1253 to 1458

GWSB

The Norman network

The most striking single fact about so-called 'Norman' families (often from Brittany, Ponthieu and Flanders rather than Normandy) taking part in the twelfth century feudal settlement of Scotland is that they were seldom in the first (or even second) rank among continental settlers in England, even where they can be shown to have held substantial English estates. Often the head of the Scottish branch of a family will be a younger son of the parent stem. A classic instance is the settlement north of the Channel of the Breton family descended from Flaald, seneschal of Dol. His son, Alan, got extensive lands in England, to which his second son succeeded, while his eldest son inherited the modest Breton estates. It was the third son, Walter, who received a vast estate in southern Scotland from David I, together with the royal stewardship, and became ancestors of the Stewarts whose chief of line in 1371 became king of Scots as Robert II.

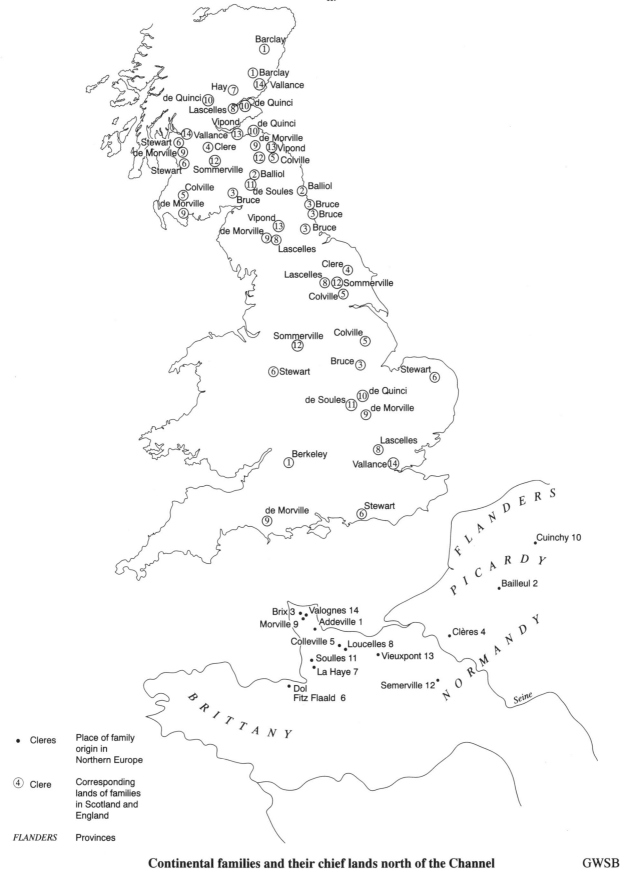

Continental families and their chief lands north of the Channel

GWSB

417

Anglo-Scottish landholding before the Wars of Independence

Anglo-Scottish landholding was important for almost 200 years before the Wars of Independence. The wider implications of this phenomenon cannot be pursued here. The most notable cross-Border landowners were the Scots kings and princes. But use of the first map depends on distinguishing between the war gains in England during Stephen's reign (1135-54) and their peaceful acquisitions, which were more characteristic of the relationship between the crowns. This distinction, however, cannot be drawn too sharply since the former included lands recognised by the Scots as being subject to English overlordship, at least for a while. The territories conceded in the north by the treaties of 1136 and 1139 were: Carlisle and its district, probably embracing Westmorland proper - i.e., Westmorland between Stainmore and the Eamont; Doncaster; the earldom of Northumberland except Bamburgh and Newcastle upon Tyne, and exclusive of any right over Hexhamshire and St Cuthbert's Land. All were probably to be held by King David I's son and heir Henry as a feudal vassal of the English crown. Then from 1141 David I and Earl Henry took over as King Stephen's enemies the whole of northern England to the Ribble and the Tees. Under them, William son of King Duncan II held three of the great north-western lordships: Allerdale, Copeland, and the honour of Skipton and Craven. The honour of Lancaster north of the Ribble, though granted to the earl of Chester in 1149, apparently remained subject to Scottish power. But by 1157 the English lands had been reduced to the honour of Huntingdon (acquired in marriage by David I in 1113, given to Earl Henry in 1136, and lost in 1141) and, in the north, to the 'liberty' of Tynedale. After Alexander II had renounced Scottish claims to the northern counties in 1237, he was granted Penrith with five other Cumberland manors. The superiority of Penrith, Tynedale, and the Huntingdon honour was held by the kings of Scots as tenants-in-chief owing homage to the English crown, although Huntingdon, with the title of earl, was treated as an appanage for Earl Henry's youngest son and his grandson, David (d. 1219) and John (d. 1237). On John's death it was partitioned among coheiresses. The earldom of Chester, John's private inheritance from 1232, remained undivided in possession of the English crown. (The external knights' fees held by John as part of the honour of Chester are not shown.) The last additions came shortly after 1286 for the brief period of John Balliol's effective reign (1292-6). The principal estates King John had previously inherited in England and Scotland are shown on the map which records the main outlines of the Anglo-Scottish estates held by magnates, or major nobles, on the eve of the Wars of Independence about 1290.

These men are defined here as earls and important lay barons, proprietors of course in England and Scotland but not necessarily enjoying the same dominant position in both countries. Most in fact held magnate rank only in Scotland where the magnates were generally lords of less substance than their counterparts in England. Any division between 'magnates' and lesser nobles must remain quite arbitrary, and some borderline cases have been included. In about 1290 Anglo-Scottish landowners nevertheless formed a very significant body among the higher nobility of Scotland, as is underlined by their prominence in the recognition of the Maid of Norway as heir to the throne (1284) and the Treaty of Birgham (1290). Almost all the Scottish estates represented are earldoms, 'provincial lordships', or baronies, though some had been partitioned. Again, some of the English baronies shown had been divided into fractions, but their lords remained entitled to baronial status. The other English estates are nearly all entire manors, a number being especially important. By varying the size of symbols a very rough guide is provided to the relative extent or significance of individual estates.

The map unavoidably underestimates the range and importance of cross-Border landholding. It obviously excludes lands held about 1290 in Ireland (Hastings, Vesci, Zouche), the Channel Islands (Wake), and France (Balliol of Bywell, Balliol of Urr). Otherwise, while the main features of estate complexes can be shown, the recording of actual estates is not exhaustive. Single symbols must also do duty for some large estates which in reality were widely dispersed. That applies particularly to England, with its highly complicated patchwork of landholding. Similarly, the map cannot even begin to tackle the complexities of the redistribution of the Huntingdon and de Quincy lands. In England alone they straggled across some 20 counties. The English lands of some magnates (e.g., Simon Fraser, William Melville) remain unidentified; likewise the Scottish lands of Ralph de Tosny. These men have all been excluded, as have those such as Andrew Murray of Petty who may never have realised their claims to English properties. Finally, the map is not designed to do justice to the many cross-Border estates held by the lesser nobility and the Church, though these were often founded through magnate patronage, or to fluctuations in the pattern of Anglo-Scottish landholding by the magnates themselves. In fact, there is some reason to believe that their influence had already begun to wane by c.1290.

Anglo-Scottish landholding before the Wars of Independence

Bamburgh

Northumberland

Newcastle upon Tyne

Tynedale

Carlisle

Penrith

Allerdale

Westmorland

Copeland

Kentdale

Burton in Lonsdale

Craven

Honour of Lancaster
(northern part)

Skipton

Doncaster

Chester

Nottingham

Leicester

Stamford

Huntingdon

Northampton

Bedford

St Cuthbert's Land

Hexhamshire

Limit of territorial control under King David, 1141 - 53

Approximate distribution of the lands of the honour of
Huntingdon (largely subinfeudated), about 1200

kms
0   25   50   75   100

0 10 20 30 40 50 60
miles

Lands of the Scottish kings and princes in England about 1100 to 1286

KJS

Anglo-Scottish landholding before the Wars of Independence

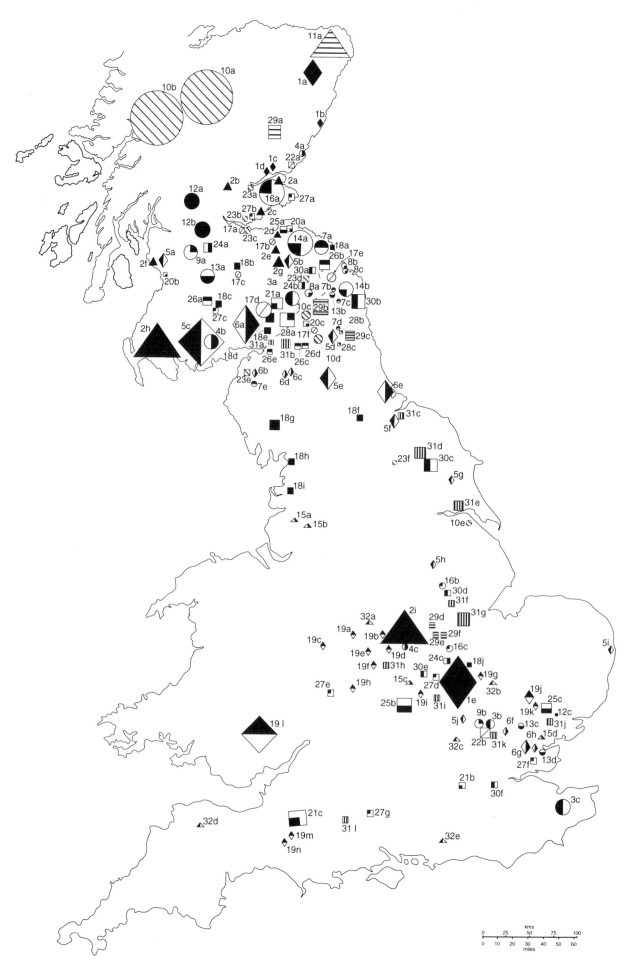

Anglo-Scottish landholding of the magnates about 1290

KJS

Anglo-Scottish landholding before the Wars of Independence

♦ 1. Coheirs of Earl John of Scotland, d. 1237 [Balliol of Bywell, Bruce, Hastings]

    a. Garioch, lordship
    b. Inverbervie (Bervie), barony
    c. Dundee, barony
    d. Longforgan, barony
    e. Huntingdon, honour
    (See also 5, 6, 19)

▲ 2. Coheirs of Earl Roger de Quincy, d. 1264 [Comyn of Buchan, Ferrers (of Groby), Zouche]

    a. Leuchars, barony
    b. Gask [also = Findo Gask], barony
    c. Dysart, barony
    d. Tranent, barony
    e. Heriot, barony
    f. Cunningham, lordship (part)
    g. Lauderdale, lordship (one half)
    h. Galloway, lordship (part)
    i. Leicester, honour (one half) [Ferrers of Groby held less than a full one sixth of the honour]
    (See also 11,15, 32)

◑ 3. Alexander de Balliol

    a. Cavers, barony
    b. Bennington, barony [also = honour of Valognes] (one third)
    c. Chilham, barony

◐ 4. Enguerrand de Balliol

    a. Redcastle (Inverkeilor), barony
    b. Urr, barony
    c. Foston

◆ 5. John de Balliol

    a. Cunningham, lordship (part)
    c. Galloway, lordship (main part + title 'lord of Galloway')
    d. Bywell, barony
    e. Barnard Castle, lordship
    f. Stokesley
    g. Driffield
    h. Torksey
    i. Lothingland
    j. Hitchin
    (See also 1)

◆ 6. Robert Bruce (d. 1295)

    a. Annandale, lordship
    b. Ireby
    c. Gamblesby
    d. Glassonby
    e. Hart and Hartness, lordship
    f. Hatfield Broad Oak [also = Hatfield Regis]
    g. Writtle, barony
    h. Great Baddow
    (See also 1)

◓ 7. Alexander of Bunkle

    a. Bunkle, barony
    b. Lilburn
    c. Shawdon
    d. Fenwick (Stamfordham)
    e. Uldale

◓ 8. Thomas Colville

    a. Oxnam, barony
    b. Budle
    c. Spindleston

◔ 9. Edmund Comyn

    a. Kilbride, barony
    b. Bennington, barony (one third)

◌ 10. John Comyn of Badenoch

    a. Badenoch, lordship
    b. Lochaber, lordship
    c. Tarset
    d. Thornton (Newbrough)
    e. Ulceby, Yarborough wapentake

△ 11. John Comyn, earl of Buchan

    a. Buchan, earldom
    (See also 2)

● 12. William Comyn

    a. Menteith, earldom lands (one half)
    b. Kirkintilloch, barony
    c. Groton

⊖ 13. William Douglas

    a. Douglas, barony
    b. Fawdon (Ingram)
    c. Stebbing
    d. Woodham Ferrers

◑ 14. Patrick, earl of Dunbar

    a. Dunbar, earldom
    b. Beanley, barony

▲ 15. William Ferrers (of Groby)

    a. Chorley
    b. Bolton-le-Moors
    c. Nobottle (Great Brington)
    d. Fairsted
    (See also 2)

◕ 16. Duncan, earl of Fife (d. 1288)

    a. Fife, earldom
    b. Carlton-le-Moorland
    c. Glapthorn

⊘ 17. Nicholas Graham

    a. Abercorn, barony
    b. Dalkeith, barony
    c. Kilbucho and Newlands, barony
    d. Eskdale, lordship
    e. Wooler, barony (one half)
    f. Simonburn

■ 18. Enguerrand de Guines

    a. Lamberton (Mordington)
    b. Skirling, barony
    c. Durisdeer, barony
    d. Westerkirk, barony
    e. Staplegordon (Westerkirk), barony
    f. Middleton Tyas
    g. Kendal, barony (one half)
    h. 'Moureholm' [= Warton]
    i. Garstang [also = Wyresdale]
    j. Molesworth

⬖ 19. John Hastings

    a. Wigginton
    b. Nailstone
    c. Worfield
    d. Burbage
    e. Fillongley
    f. Allesley
    g. Brampton
    h. Aston Cantlow
    i. Wootton
    j. Lidgate
    k. Badmondisfield (Wickhambrook)
    l. Abergavenny, lordship

Anglo-Scottish landholding: magnates and lands about 1290

m. Little Marston (West Camel)
n. Barwick
(See also 1)

20. Alexander Lindsay

    a. The Byres (Athelstaneford), barony
    b. Barnweill (Craigie)
    c. Chirdon

21. Hugh Lovel

    a. Hawick, barony
    b. Grove Barns (Staines)
    c. Castle Cary, barony

22. William Maule

    a. Panmure (Panbride), barony
    b. Bennington, barony (one third)

23. Geoffrey Mowbray

    a. Moncreiffe [also = Dunbarney]
    b. Inverkeithing, barony
    c. Dalmeny [also = Barnbougle], barony
    d. Eckford, barony
    e. Boltons
    f. Raskelf (Easingwold)

24. William Murray

    a. Bothwell, barony
    b. Crailing, barony
    c. Lilford

25. Robert Pinkney

    a. Ballencrieff + Luffness (Aberlady), baronies
    b. Weedon Pinkney [also = Weedon Lois], barony
    c. Cavendish, barony (one half)

26. Robert de Ros

    a. Sanquhar, barony
    b. Wark (Carham), barony
    c. Bellister
    d. Plenmeller
    e. Linstock (Stanwix)

27. Richard Siward

    a. Kellie (Carnbee), barony
    b. Aberdour, barony
    c. Tibbers (Durisdeer), barony
    d. Chelveston
    e. Crowle
    f. Burstead
    g. Clatford

28. William de Soules

    a. Liddesdale, lordship
    b. Stamfordham
    c. Stocksfield (Bywell St Andrew)

29. Gilbert de Umfraville, earl of Angus

    a. Angus, earldom
    b. Redesdale (+ Upper Coquetdale), 'liberty'
    c. Prudhoe, barony
    d. Market Overton
    e. Hambleton
    f. Normanton

30. William de Vesci

    a. Sprouston, barony
    b. Alnwick, barony
    c. Malton, 'honour'
    d. Caythorpe
    e. Faxton
    f. Eltham

31. John Wake

    a. Kirkandrews on Esk (now in England), barony
    b. Liddel Strength (Kirkandrews), barony
    c. Great Ayton
    d. Kirkby Moorside
    e. Cottingham, barony
    f. Kelby
    g. Bourne, barony
    h. Brinklow
    i. Stevington
    j. Wakes Colne
    k. Ware
    l. Winterbourne Stoke

32. Alan la Zouche

    a. Ashby-de-la-Zouch
    b. Swavesey
    c. Great Gaddesden
    d. North Molton
    e. 'Treve' [= River] (Tillington)
    (See also 2)

Anglo-Scottish landholding: magnates and lands about 1290

KJS

Landed influence in the late fifteenth century

The maps indicate the territorial power of several great families that played a leading part in Scottish politics between 1470 and 1513. The baronies held by the head of the family have been plotted and linked with the main family centre. No attempt has been made to show the baronies held by lesser members of the family. Even so, the complexity of the territorial basis of the power of these families is immediately apparent.

Although the power of a family was sometimes concentrated within a single region it was more often widely dispersed.

Thus the earl of Angus, in addition to his lands in Angus, held lands in the sheriffdoms of Ayr, Perth, Lanark, Dumfries, Roxburgh and Berwick. The earl of Bothwell held lands in the sheriffdoms of Lanark, Ayr, Dumfries, Roxburgh and Berwick and in the stewartry of Kirkcudbright. The earl of Huntly held lands in the sheriffdoms of Moray, Inverness, Banff, Aberdeen, Perth and Berwick. It was because these nobles drew their power from such a wide area that they and the families they headed could play a formidable part in politics and even try to impose their will upon the king.

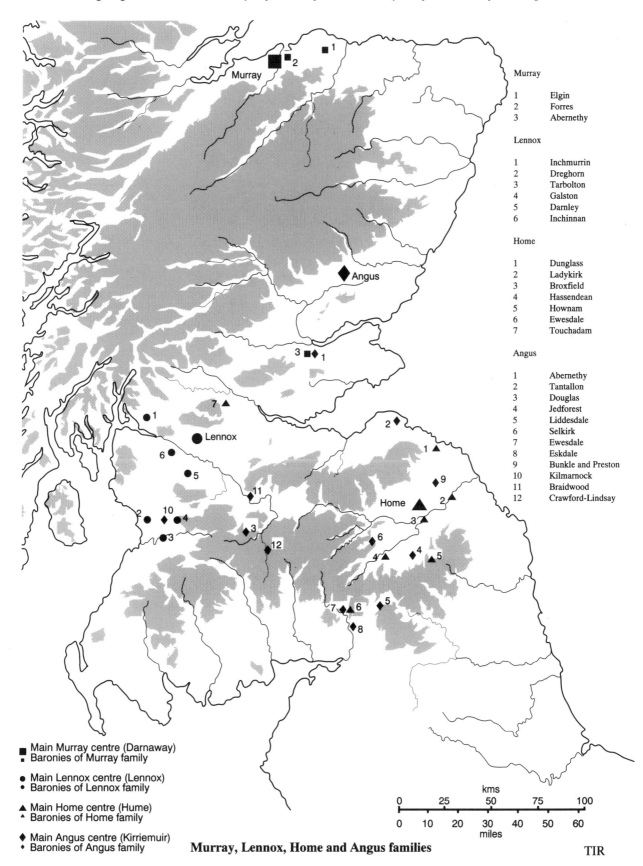

Murray

1 Elgin
2 Forres
3 Abernethy

Lennox

1 Inchmurrin
2 Dreghorn
3 Tarbolton
4 Galston
5 Darnley
6 Inchinnan

Home

1 Dunglass
2 Ladykirk
3 Broxfield
4 Hassendean
5 Hownam
6 Ewesdale
7 Touchadam

Angus

1 Abernethy
2 Tantallon
3 Douglas
4 Jedforest
5 Liddesdale
6 Selkirk
7 Ewesdale
8 Eskdale
9 Bunkle and Preston
10 Kilmarnock
11 Braidwood
12 Crawford-Lindsay

■ Main Murray centre (Darnaway)
▪ Baronies of Murray family

● Main Lennox centre (Lennox)
◆ Baronies of Lennox family

▲ Main Home centre (Hume)
▴ Baronies of Home family

◆ Main Angus centre (Kirriemuir)
◆ Baronies of Angus family

Murray, Lennox, Home and Angus families

TIR

423

Landed influence in the late fifteenth century

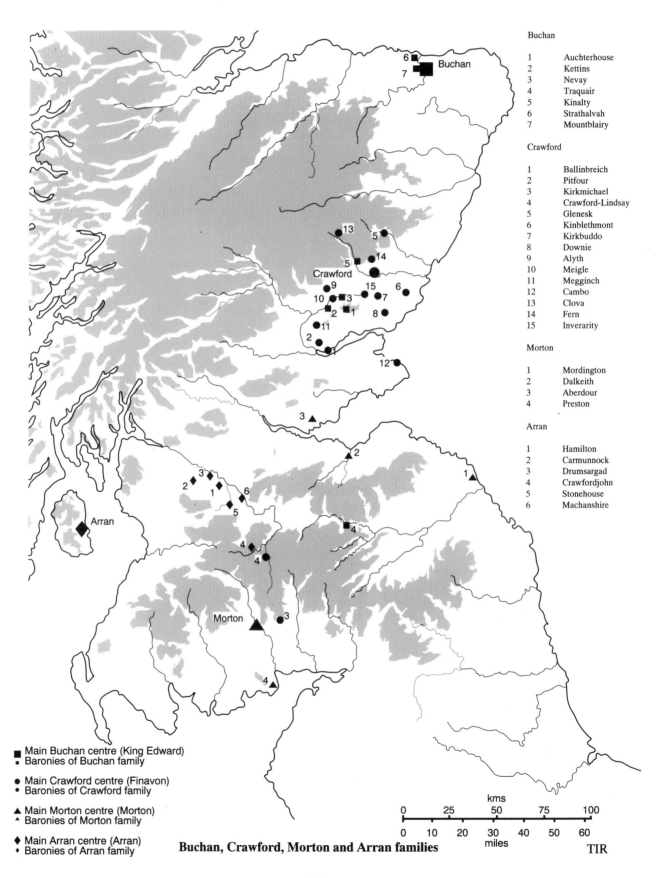

Buchan

1 Auchterhouse
2 Kettins
3 Nevay
4 Traquair
5 Kinalty
6 Strathalvah
7 Mountblairy

Crawford

1 Ballinbreich
2 Pitfour
3 Kirkmichael
4 Crawford-Lindsay
5 Glenesk
6 Kinblethmont
7 Kirkbuddo
8 Downie
9 Alyth
10 Meigle
11 Megginch
12 Cambo
13 Clova
14 Fern
15 Inverarity

Morton

1 Mordington
2 Dalkeith
3 Aberdour
4 Preston

Arran

1 Hamilton
2 Carmunnock
3 Drumsargad
4 Crawfordjohn
5 Stonehouse
6 Machanshire

■ Main Buchan centre (King Edward)
▪ Baronies of Buchan family

● Main Crawford centre (Finavon)
• Baronies of Crawford family

▲ Main Morton centre (Morton)
▴ Baronies of Morton family

◆ Main Arran centre (Arran)
♦ Baronies of Arran family

kms
0   25   50   75   100

0   10   20   30   40   50   60
miles

Buchan, Crawford, Morton and Arran families   TIR

Landed influence in the late fifteenth century

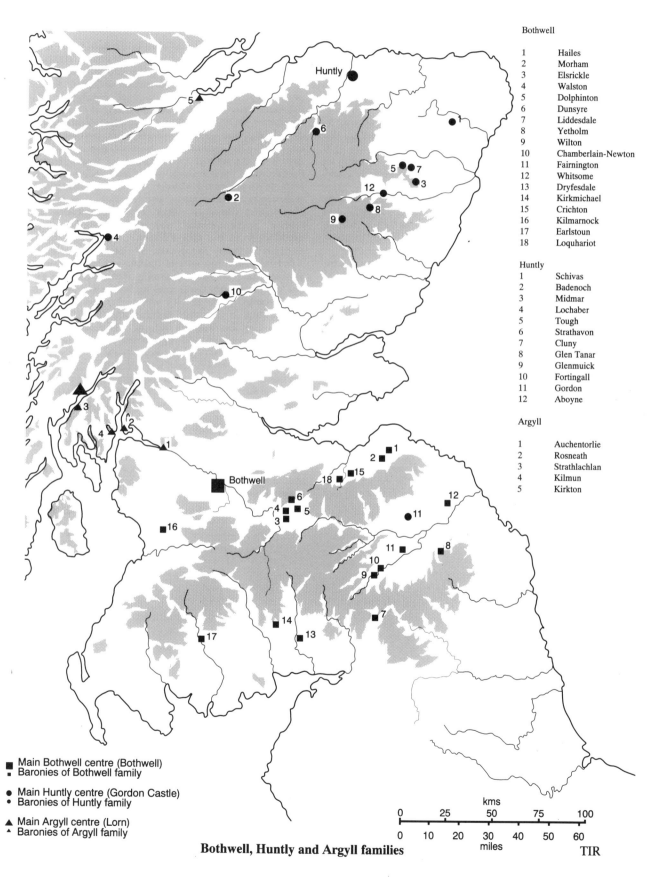

Bothwell

1 Hailes
2 Morham
3 Elsrickle
4 Walston
5 Dolphinton
6 Dunsyre
7 Liddesdale
8 Yetholm
9 Wilton
10 Chamberlain-Newton
11 Fairnington
12 Whitsome
13 Dryfesdale
14 Kirkmichael
15 Crichton
16 Kilmarnock
17 Earlstoun
18 Loquhariot

Huntly

1 Schivas
2 Badenoch
3 Midmar
4 Lochaber
5 Tough
6 Strathavon
7 Cluny
8 Glen Tanar
9 Glenmuick
10 Fortingall
11 Gordon
12 Aboyne

Argyll

1 Auchentorlie
2 Rosneath
3 Strathlachlan
4 Kilmun
5 Kirkton

Huntly

Bothwell

■ Main Bothwell centre (Bothwell)
▪ Baronies of Bothwell family

● Main Huntly centre (Gordon Castle)
• Baronies of Huntly family

▲ Main Argyll centre (Lorn)
▴ Baronies of Argyll family

Bothwell, Huntly and Argyll families

TIR

kms
0   25   50   75   100

0   10   20   30   40   50   60
miles

Linguistic changes

Gaelic is today widely spoken only in the north-west Highlands and islands. In the past, Gaelic was more widely spoken. Understanding the past extent of the *Gaidhealtachd* (Gaelic speaking region) before 1707 is hindered by the variable source material. Four principal categories of evidence may be distinguished: place names; medieval charters and documents which allow a conjectural positioning of the medieval Gaelic language border; localised sources on Gaelic in the seventeenth-century Highlands; and material of 1698 and 1705-1708 which allows the earliest picture of a nationwide *Gaidhealtachd*.

Gaelic was never everywhere spoken by all people in Scotland. Gaelic's decline begins from about A.D. 1100 as the result of several factors including the influence of the court; the authority of the Roman over the Celtic Church; the spread of·English-dominated trade; and the waning of Gaelic cultural prestige. By the later 1300s, these processes had led to the emergence of the Highlands as a distinct cultural and linguistic area.

South and east Scotland was particularly affected by these changes, the more isolated north and west less so. Yet the Gaelic notes in the Book of Deer, written between 1130 and 1150, suggest that Gaelic was still spoken quite widely in north-east Scotland at that period. Gaelic was probably extinct in Fife, Kinross, and Clackmannan by about 1350. Areas around Caputh and Abernyte in southern Perthshire were only partly Gaelic by the early sixteenth century. Gaelic was probably spoken in south-west Scotland until the late sixteenth century at least. But it should be emphasised that any definition of the medieval *Gaidhealtachd* must only be conjectural.

By the seventeenth century, the Gaelic language was the focus of direct legislative concern. One act spoke of 'English' schools 'rooting out the Irish language, [Gaelic], and other pious uses'. Several schools whose purpose was the teaching of English were in existence in the Highlands before 1696 and others are known in which Gaelic was used.

In the 1650s, Gaelic was the only language spoken by a large proportion of the population in the east central Highlands. In Watten in 1658-1659, there were over ninety Gaelic monoglots but no Gaelic-speaking minister. In some parishes along the upland margin, both Gaelic and English were spoken and used in religious administration. Southern Kintyre had a large English-speaking population. In Contin in 1651, Dores (1671), Kilmorack (1651), Kirkhill and Kiltearn (1680s), both Gaelic and English were preached. Gaelic and English services were held in Inverness burgh from 1639, from 1657 in Inveraray, and in Campbeltown from 1680. In several parishes which we must presume to have been largely Gaelic in the seventeenth century, ministers were settled who had little or no knowledge of the language.

In Perthshire in the 1660s, Gaelic was 'commonly in use' in the north-west upland parishes. Glenisla was Gaelic as was northern Alyth. In Glenshee and Strathardle, Gaelic was used in religious administration and was spoken in Lochlee and Lethnot and Navar parishes. It is likely other parishes in north-west Angus were at least partly Gaelic then. By piecing together this fragmentary evidence, we may suggest a conjectural boundary for the Gaidhealtachd in about 1660. It should be stressed that this boundary is not as clear cut on the ground as it is on a map. The first detailed extent of the Gaidhealtachd dates from 1698.

Evidence deriving from plans to distribute Gaelic scriptural texts throughout the late seventeenth-century Highlands provides the first detailed guide to parishes in which Gaelic was widely used in daily life and religious ordinance. Several parishes on the borders of, but not included in, the *Gaidhealtachd* of 1698 also contained numbers of Gaelic speakers. Sources of 1705-1708 allow a more exact identification of these parishes. The whole of Sutherland was reckoned Gaelic-speaking in 1706. Caithness was Gaelic-speaking in its western districts but we are told that 'the people of Week understand English also'. Inverness-shire was almost entirely Gaelic in 1706. In Nairn, Ardclach, Cawdor, and Edinkillie parishes, religious administration in Gaelic was 'absolutely necessary'. In Aberdeenshire, Glenmuick Tullich and Glengairn, Crathie and Braemar, Strathdon, Cabrach, and Mortlach were all strongly Gaelic in 1705 as was upland Perthshire. Several parishes in south-east Perthshire had pockets of Gaelic speakers in the period 1698-1708. The town of Dunkeld was 'divided equally' between Gaelic and English speakers in 1705. In Kirriemuir parish, Angus, over sixty Gaelic-speaking families were resident in the Glenprosen district in 1705 with smaller Gaelic communities elsewhere in the parish. Arrochar, Rhu [Row], Buchanan, Drymen, Luss and Rosneath were all 'Highland parishes' in 1708, but evidence of 1705 suggests that only one-quarter of the parish population actually spoke Gaelic in Drymen. In Rosneath, the figure was about one-half of the parish population Gaelic speaking. Gaelic and English were both commonly spoken on Bute and Arran, Gaelic prevailing on the west side of Arran, English on the east.

No definitive statements can be made on shifting social patterns of Gaelic before 1707, or on the numbers speaking Gaelic at this time since hearth and poll tax records give an incomplete coverage for the Highlands. The suggestion that about 30% of Scotland's population of about 900,000 persons in the late 1690s spoke Gaelic must be considered a rough approximation.

Linguistic changes

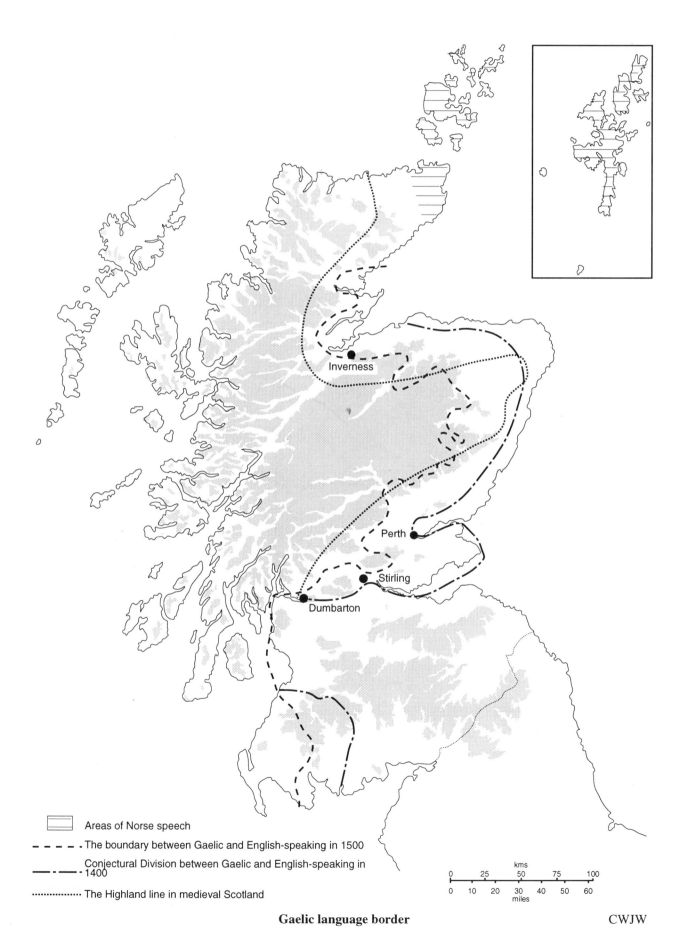

Areas of Norse speech

- - - - - The boundary between Gaelic and English-speaking in 1500

— · — · — Conjectural Division between Gaelic and English-speaking in 1400

················ The Highland line in medieval Scotland

Inverness

Perth

Stirling

Dumbarton

kms
0   25   50   75   100
0 10 20 30 40 50 60
miles

Gaelic language border

CWJW

427

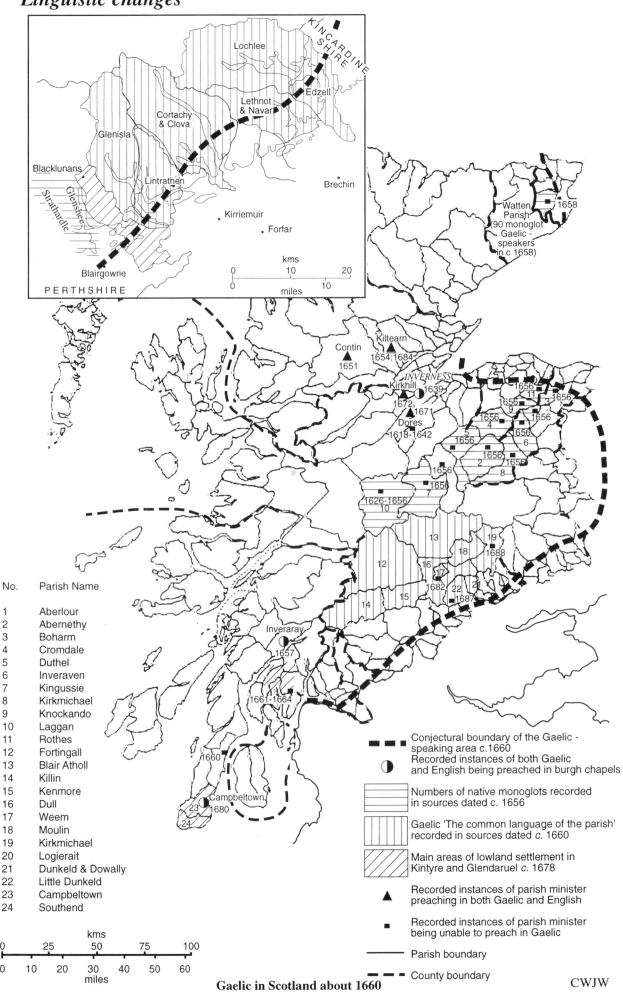

Linguistic changes

Linguistic changes

Lochlee

KINCARDINE SHIRE

Cortachy & Clova

Lethnot & Navar

Edzell

Glenisla

Blacklunans

Glenshee

Strathardle

Lintrathen

Brechin

Kirriemuir

Forfar

kms
0   10   20

miles
0   10

PERTHSHIRE

Blairgowrie

Watten Parish
(90 monoglot Gaelic-speakers in c 1658)
1658

Kiltearn
1654;1684

Contin
1651

INVERNESS
Kirkhill
1639
1672

Dores
1671
1618-1642

1656
11
1656
9
13   1656
1656
4
1656
5
1656
6
1656
2   1656
8
1656

1656

1626-1656
10

13
19
1688
18
12   16
1682   17   22   21
1687
14   15

Inveraray
1657

1661-1664

1660

Campbeltown
1680
23
24

No.	Parish Name
1	Aberlour
2	Abernethy
3	Boharm
4	Cromdale
5	Duthel
6	Inveraven
7	Kingussie
8	Kirkmichael
9	Knockando
10	Laggan
11	Rothes
12	Fortingall
13	Blair Atholl
14	Killin
15	Kenmore
16	Dull
17	Weem
18	Moulin
19	Kirkmichael
20	Logierait
21	Dunkeld & Dowally
22	Little Dunkeld
23	Campbeltown
24	Southend

– – – – Conjectural boundary of the Gaelic-speaking area c.1660

◑ Recorded instances of both Gaelic and English being preached in burgh chapels

Numbers of native monoglots recorded in sources dated c. 1656

Gaelic 'The common language of the parish' recorded in sources dated *c.* 1660

Main areas of lowland settlement in Kintyre and Glendaruel *c.* 1678

▲ Recorded instances of parish minister preaching in both Gaelic and English

■ Recorded instances of parish minister being unable to preach in Gaelic

——— Parish boundary

– – – – County boundary

kms
0   25   50   75   100

0   10   20   30   40   50   60
miles

Gaelic in Scotland about 1660

CWJW

428

Linguistic changes

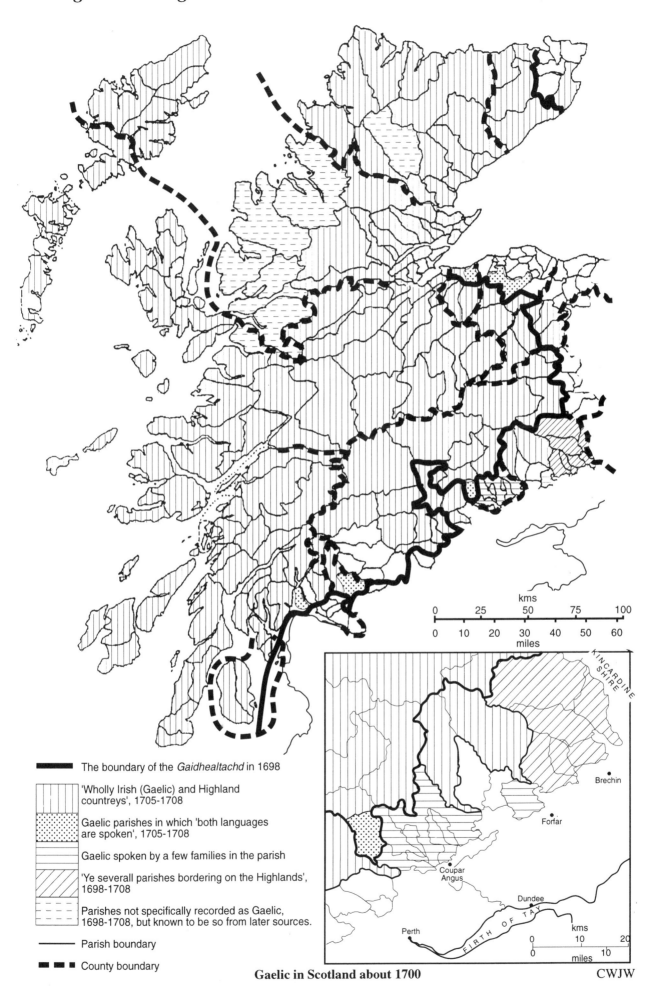

The boundary of the *Gaidhealtachd* in 1698

'Wholly Irish (Gaelic) and Highland countreys', 1705-1708

Gaelic parishes in which 'both languages are spoken', 1705-1708

Gaelic spoken by a few families in the parish

'Ye severall parishes bordering on the Highlands', 1698-1708

Parishes not specifically recorded as Gaelic, 1698-1708, but known to be so from later sources.

Parish boundary

County boundary

KINCARDINE SHIRE

Brechin

Forfar

Coupar Angus

Dundee

FIRTH OF TAY

Perth

kms
0   25   50   75   100
0 10 20 30 40 50 60
miles

kms
0   10   20
0   10
miles

Gaelic in Scotland about 1700   CWJW

Mottes

The motte or castle-mound is the best-known type of military fortification that is associated with the introduction into twelfth century Scotland of feudal land tenure and institutions. They survive most characteristically as scarped earthen mounds usually in the form of a truncated cone which often simply 'improves' a natural eminence or promontory. The summit area of the motte is usually circular on plan, but oval and rectilinear plan-types have been identified. The base of the mound is often defined by an encircling dry ditch, the upcast of which would probably be used in the construction of the motte itself. A number of mottes are set within, or lie adjacent to, enclosures or baileys, which are themselves often protected by independent systems of banks and ditches. Recent investigations have tended to suggest that in Scotland, as in other parts of the British Isles, there are roughly circular enclosures of a similar character known as ringworks. Archaeological excavations carried out at sites elsewhere in Britain have also demonstrated that a small ringwork or other structure or monument of earlier date may form the substructure of a motte, a building sequence which is now being taken into account in the study of early castles in Scotland.

Excavated sites represent only a very small proportion of the total number of mottes in Scotland, and the published archaeological evidence is still by no means sufficient to permit broad generalisations about their dating and character. The most recent national census produced a total of 318 known and possible motte-sites in Scotland, but this provisional list is being revised in the light of current fieldwork. The geographical distribution of these sites shows that by far the greatest concentration of mottes—more than half their total number-is

to be found in south-west Scotland between the Clyde and the Solway. There is a less dense but appreciable scatter of mottes in central Scotland and north from the River Forth to the coast of the Moray Firth. They are, however, more numerous in regions such as the semi-independent principality of Galloway where royal authority was less clearly acknowledged at this time.

In Galloway and in certain other areas the distribution of mottes extends beyond the detailed evidence of the feudal geography of the twelfth and thirteenth centuries that is provided by the written record. But in other regions for which there is rather more abundant documentary information, a greater proportion of surviving mottes can often be correlated with the centres of fiefs, and in these cases the motte-builders appear to have been private feudatories of varying ranks and social status. The relative profusion of mottes in Nithsdale and upper Clydesdale, for example, seems to reflect a tenurial structure of small fiefs, many of which are known to have been held directly of the Scottish crown. Mottes also occur in some numbers within some of the larger feudal estates such as the lordship of Annandale, where their distribution appears to coincide with both demesne lands and sub-infeudated tenancies. Conversely, however, surviving mottes and motte-sites, and possibly other comparable types of earthwork castle, are scarce in regions such as the Lothians and the Merse where fairly intensive feudal settlement is known to have taken place.

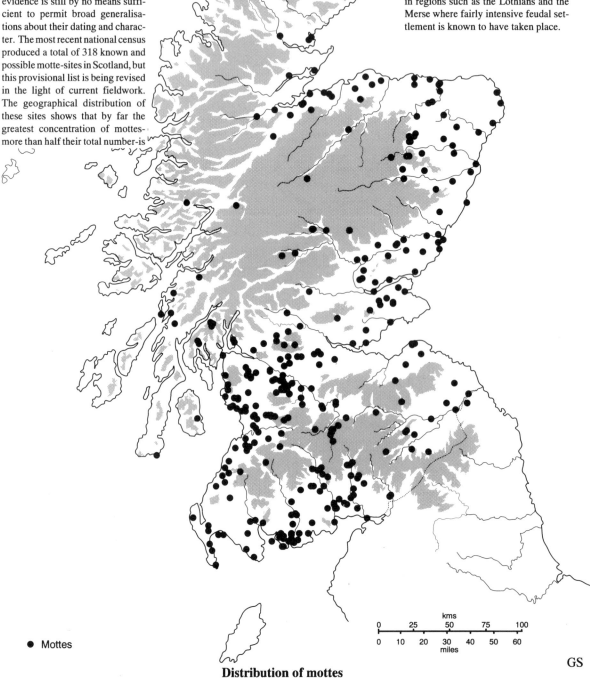

• Mottes

Distribution of mottes

GS

430

Moated sites

A moated site is defined here as an enclosure of medieval date, usually rectilinear on plan, surrounded by a broad ditch which may or may not have been water-filled. A number of problems attend their study in Scotland and only the most convincing sites have been included. For example, whilst moated sites possessed some defensive qualities they were not essentially military in character, and omitted from the map are those sites whose defences were developed to the point where they are better considered to be component parts of timber castles; there is inevitably a degree of subjectivity in deciding when that point has been reached. Omitted too are moats enclosing stone castles. To the south of the Forth identification is further complicated by the presence of large numbers of prehistoric rectilinear settlements which, on surface remains alone, may be indistinguishable from moated sites.

As yet not a great deal is known of the datespan within the medieval period of moated sites in Scotland, although they rarely occur outside the known areas of Anglo-Norman penetration. Those in England are thought to have their beginnings in the late twelfth century and their rate of construction to have reached its peak between about 1250 and 1350, declining thereafter. The scant evidence for Scotland is not inconsistent with these dates and also points to the seigneurial status, both secular and ecclesiastical, of the sites. The buildings which stood upon moated sites and the functions which were carried out from them, therefore, would have been primarily administrative, economic and domestic. In this regard they did not differ from estate centres which were enclosed, or enclosed only by a light stockade or wall, and which seem likely to have existed in far greater numbers, but to have left little or no discernible trace in the archaeological record.

- Moated sites

Distribution of moated sites

PC

431

Castles and strongpoints

This map shows castles, fortified towns and other strongpoints for which there is some evidence that they were in existence or played a part, however small, in the events of 1286 to 1315. In some cases (for example Kildrummy or Dunstaffnage) it is quite clear that the castle or strongpoint played a military part. In others there is no evidence other than, for example, that Edward I spent a night or two at a place where it is thought that there was a castle at that time. A broad definition of the word 'castle' is taken and range from the earthwork and drystone fortification of Dunaverty to sophisticated structures at Bothwell and Caerlaverock. Some 'strongpoints', such as Ancrum, Borders, Glenbervie, Grampian, Luffness and Livingston, Lothian may have been of less than castellar status but clear evidence is lacking. Castles such as Polmaise, Tullibody and Inverkeithing, planned but not known to have been built, are also mapped.

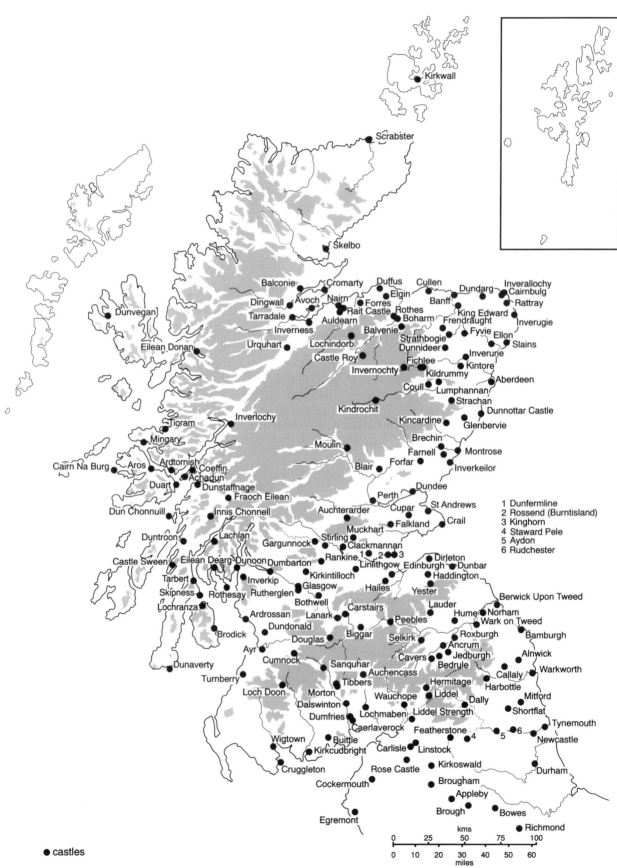

1 Dunfermline
2 Rossend (Burntisland)
3 Kinghorn
4 Staward Pele
5 Aydon
6 Rudchester

● castles

kms
0   25   50   75   100

0   10   20   30   40   50   60
miles

Castles and strongpoints in southern Scotland and northern England about 1286 to 1315   DJT

Defensible houses

In most areas the typical residence of the landed proprietor was the towerhouse, and buildings of this class were widely distributed throughout the lowlands, being particularly numerous in the rich agricultural lands of the Forth, Tay and Dee estuaries. Some of these towers had been erected during the fourteenth and fifteenth centuries but the majority were of sixteenth and seventeenth century date.

The survey of documentary and structural evidence for towerhouses in Scotland is incomplete and it is not yet practical to include a map of their distribution in the whole of Scotland. Work in the Borders and northern England, however, has shown that large towers were built only by men of the highest status. Smaller towers of sixteenth century date were numerous in the Scottish dales, and were occupied by the local lairds and their kindred.

English men of comparable local power were normally much poorer, the tenants of absentee lords, or of the crown, and built themselves small gabled defensible farmhouses, the pelehouses. These buildings are extremely rare in Scotland, and the rather larger and better-built bastle houses are also relatively uncommon. The latter were the homes of richer men who lived in towns or other places where defence could be subordinated to convenience of living, and the later bastle houses resemble the seventeenth century unfortified house of the southern lowlands.

In the north-west Highlands and the Western Isles, only the wealthiest lairds occupied even small tower-houses, and other types of stone castle, and lesser proprietors often made do with lake-dwellings. These structures, little different in essence from prehistoric crannogs, usually took the form of a small island, wholly or partly of artificial origin, situated close to the shore of an inland loch and sometimes joined to it by a causeway; typically they contained two or three single-storeyed buildings of dry-stone or timber construction, the perimeter of the island itself occasionally being enclosed by a defensive wall.

The sixteenth and seventeenth century defensible houses of Scotland, northern England and Ireland contrast with the contemporary buildings in Wales and southern England, where men of wealth did not expect to have to fortify their houses. In the former area, through lack of an effective central authority, self defence was necessary, and in the troubled Borders even relatively small landholders looked to their own protection.

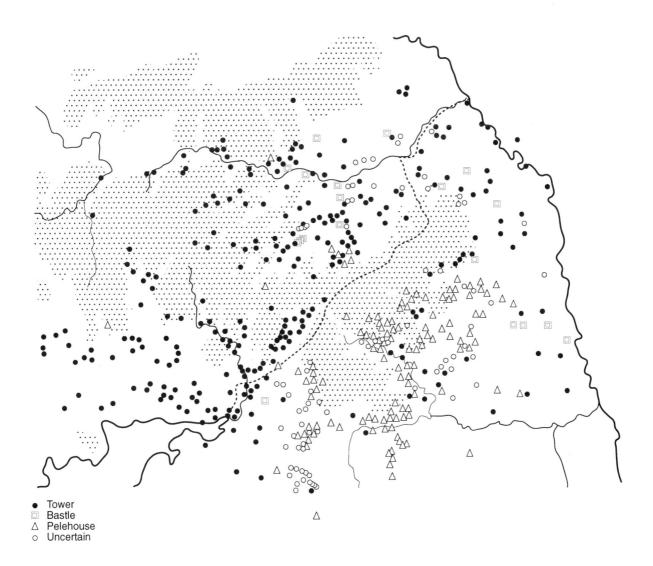

● Tower
▫ Bastle
△ Pelehouse
○ Uncertain

kms
0   25   50
0 10 20 30
miles

Defensible houses in southern Scotland and northern England about 1500 to 1625   PD, JGD

Defence with guns

The development of large artillery in the fifteenth century posed an enormous threat to traditional, high, stone-walled castles. It was also seen that guns had potential in defence. Several Scottish castles built from the late fifteenth century onwards show the influence of guns, typically the provision of embrasures for their use, but in a few cases like Dunbar blockhouse (about 1520) and the spurworks at Edinburgh and Stirling castles (1540s) a considerable departure from traditional castle design to withstand the impact of enemy artillery.

In the wars of the Rough Wooing (1547-50) a radically different type of fortification was introduced first by the English and then by the French forces in Scotland. *Trace italienne* fortifications with massive, low earthworks and large pointed bastions were a considerable improvement on traditional castles. They could mount large guns defensively and, most important, were so designed that all approaches could be raked with gunfire. These forts in Scotland performed well. The only one of strength overrun in a direct assault was the English fort at Balgillo outside Dundee, taken by a combined French and Scottish force in February 1550 after an artillery bombardment. On the other hand both the English in Haddington in 1548-9 and the French in Leith in 1559-60 withstood major assaults.

Trace italienne fortifications seem to have had practically no influence on Scottish fortifications in the sixteenth century. Of course, complicated earthworks may not have been deemed appropriate for many nobles' and lairds' houses but several did show a concern for defence which might have been better served by some such system. They could also have been applied to the major royal castles and some of the burghs. The 'French spur' at Stirling castle may be the responsibility of the French about 1559.

1	Noltland Castle
2	Earl's Palace, Birsay
3	Bishop's Palace, Kirkwall
4	Balvenie Castle
5	Tolquhon Castle
6	Aberdeen
7	Dunnottar Castle
8	Castle Menzies
9	Elcho Castle
10	Claypotts Castle
11	Balgillo Fort
12	St Andrews Castle
	St Andrews Cathedral
13	Burleigh Castle
14	Lochleven Castle
15	Macduff's Castle
16	Ravenscraig Castle
17	Burntisland Fort
18	Inchkeith Fort
19	Leith Fort
20	Edinburgh Castle
	Edinburgh Town Walls
21	Craigmillar Castle
22	Inchcolm Fort
23	Inchgarvie Castle
24	Blackness Castle
25	Linlithgow Palace
26	Kinneil House
27	Stirling Castle
	Stirling Town Walls
28	Inveresk Fort
29	Cadzow Castle
30	Craignethan Castle
31	Boghall Castle
32	Drochill Castle
33	Peebles Town Wall
34	Crichton Castle
35	Luffness Fort
36	Tantallon Castle
37	Haddington Fort
38	Barnes Castle
39	Dunbar Castle/Fort
40	Dunglass Fort
41	Eyemouth Fort
42	Lauder Fort
43	Newark Castle
44	Littledean Castle
45	Caelaverock Castle
46	Threave Castle
47	Castle Semple

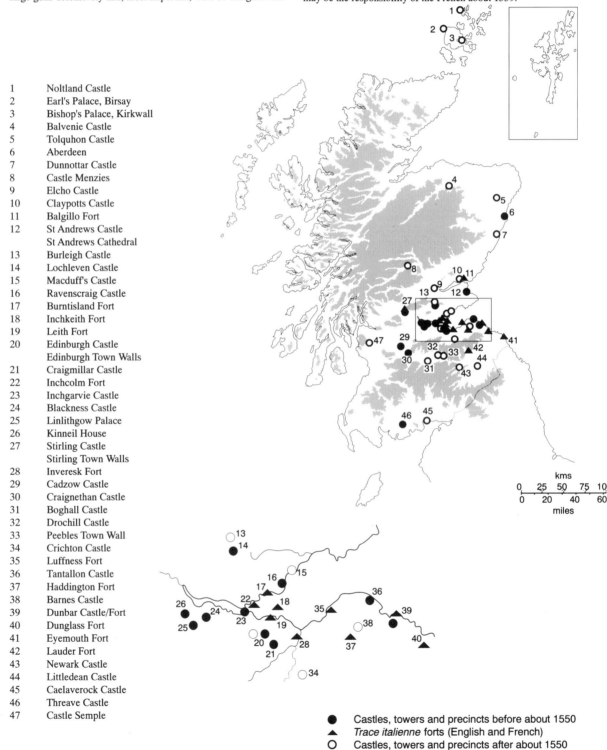

● Castles, towers and precincts before about 1550
▲ *Trace italienne* forts (English and French)
○ Castles, towers and precincts after about 1550

Defence with guns before about 1600

DHC

The Crusades

The Crusading movement had an impact which extended beyond the period of the Latin kingdom of Jerusalem (1099-1291) and which influenced many more people than the relatively small number of Scots who actually went on crusade. Its impact can be traced in oral tradition, propaganda, diplomacy, historiography in the endowment of religious institutions which had a crusading origin or raison d'etre, and in the survival and influence of these institution. The most notable of them were the Templars and Hospitallers but there also was a hospital of Bethlehemite canons at St Germains (East Lothian) a number of Trinitarian houses 'for the redemption of captives of the infidel' and endowments of the Lazarites and of the hospital of St Thomas of Acre. The crusading movement can be said to have had a significant art in bringing remote little Scotland into the fold of unified western Christendom in the twelfth and thirteenth centuries and thereafter the movement had a long history.

There are traces of a Scottish presence on the first Crusade (l095-99) and thereafter on all the major 'passages' to the Holy Land in the twelfth and thirteenth centuries. After the loss of Acre (1291), Scots are found fighting the heathen in Spain, Egypt and Turkey, and between mid-fourteenth century and the battle of Tannenberg (1410) a good number of Scottish aristocrats journeyed to Konigsberg to fight with the Teutonic Knights. There is a well-documented connection between Scotland and the Knights Hospitallers, first at Rhodes (1310-1522) and thereafter at Malta (from 1530); not only were there Scottish brother of the order serving at the convent and administering its Scottish properties, but also there are a number of examples of Scottish laymen engaged in military service with the Knights

The accompanying map shows some of the most important locations known to have been visited by Scots- engaged in crusading activities.

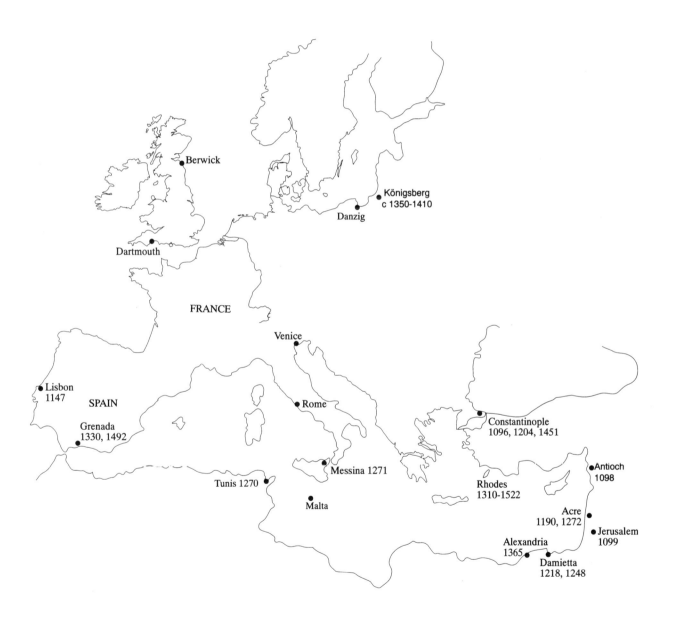

Places visited by Scots engaging in Crusading activities

AM

Military orders in Scotland

Writing about 1185, William of Tyre commented about the Knights Templars: 'There is not a province of the Christian world which has not granted a portion of its wealth to these brothers; and they may now be said to have wealth like the opulence of kings'. Together with their rivals the Knights Hospitallers they began to accumulate lands in Scotland from the first half of the twelfth century, which consisted of substantial baronies such as Temple and Torphichen, and also a large number of tiny tenements or 'templelands' scattered up and down the country. King Malcolm IV (1153-65) is said to have granted a toft in every royal burgh to the Hospitallers and another to the Templars, but the templelands are by no means restricted to the burghs. They are found in all parts of the country except in the Northern and Western Isles, Caithness and Sutherland, Wester Ross, western Inverness-shire, Argyll and Bute.

The Templars in Scotland had been suppressed in 1312 following the general suppression of the order throughout Europe, and their property passed to the Hospitallers between then and the end of Robert 1's reign (1306-29). It is not always easy to know what lands in Lindsay's rental had previously belonged to the Templars and what had belonged to the Hospitallers. In the sixteenth century the most dense concentrations of templelands are in Midlothian and West Lothian, Ayrshire, Fife and Angus, with areas of secondary density in Aberdeenshire, Perthshire, Dumbarton and Lennox, Lanarkshire and Galloway. More thinly spread are Dumfriesshire, Berwickshire, Mearns, the Border counties, and the coastal strip round the Moray Firth. In East Lothian, Peebles and probably also Renfrewshire the returns in the rental appear to be incomplete and the number of templelands cannot now be determined.

All in all, Lindsay's rental provides a fascinating picture of the estate management of a prosperous institution, partly religious but partly increasingly secularised, in the first half of the sixteenth century, at a time when religious and economic change was affecting the country. The distribution of the little templelands, taken together with that of the baronies, lands 'by thir baronys' and churches, shows the areas in which the work of the Military Orders during the Crusades had been most appreciated.

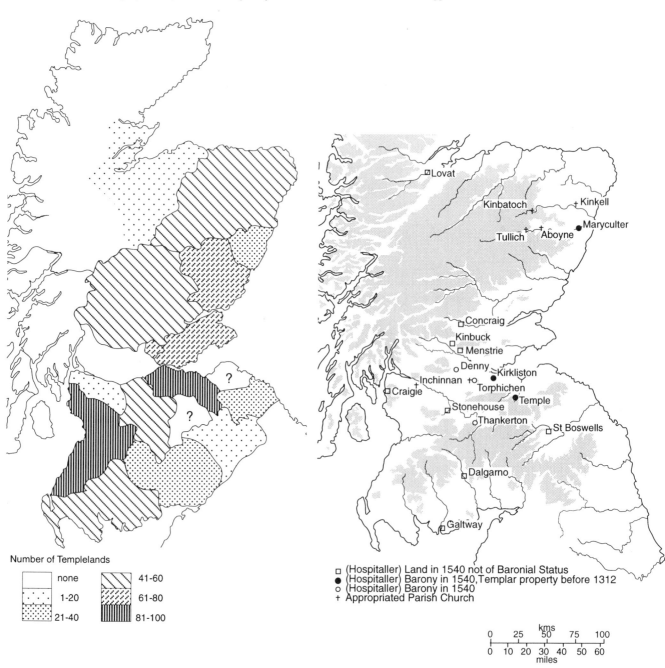

Number of Templelands

none	41-60
1-20	61-80
21-40	81-100

Temple lands, by county

□ (Hospitaller) Land in 1540 not of Baronial Status
● (Hospitaller) Barony in 1540, Templar property before 1312
○ (Hospitaller) Barony in 1540
+ Appropriated Parish Church

Temple properties

AM

Schools

This map records all documented schools before the first act of parliament (1633) which introduced an element of compulsion, omitting, however, highland schools as not acceptable of easy categorisation. It shows a much more nationwide spread than local historians of education are apt to reveal. The 1560 Book of Discipline planned a school in every parish, a prospect which the violence of Reformation conflict could only hinder. The first object was to restart medieval schools where extant, especially in towns, since there boarding facilities were more available. The post-Reformation reader replaced the chaplain as customary rural teacher, existing chaplains continuing sometimes as readers, though several parishes chose to have a separate schoolmaster. A full four-year grammar course was less usual than the more rudimentary Latin one of two years or so, yet Latin was a central Renaissance requirement, if not any longer for churchmen a vocational necessity. This vernacular education slowly took on greater prominence. Music teaching was revived with support for James VI and was more widely available as his reign proceeded: the figures for song schools hardly do justice to the basic musical education that seemingly went on. While most rural schools occupied a site in the parish kirk or a nearby chapel, a significant proportion of schools were 'adventure' schools sponsored to an extent at least by lay heritors. The unexpectedly large number of school sites must reflect population growth, though some may only have existed sporadically from lack of the sound maintenance called for in the submissions to the 1627 commissioners: though again these reports must be treated with caution. The relatively large number may also be related to the 1616 statute of privy council. Documentary dates assigned here however should not be relied upon as more than provisional indications, as our awareness of schools may be determined more by the increased documentation rather than by any other factor.

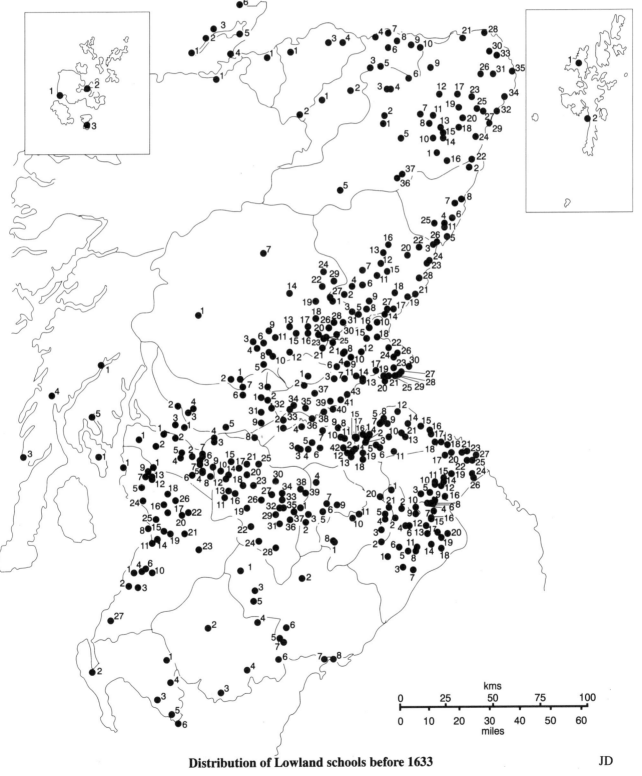

Distribution of Lowland schools before 1633

JD

437

Schools

•	School
1637	Date first recorded
C	Continued after the Reformation
nd	No date
P	Parish
RB	Royal burgh
G	Grammar school
V	Vernacular school
F	Fencing school
D	Dutch school
Fr	French school
SL	Song Latin school
H	Hospital school
W	Woman's school
Wr	Writing, school

Aberdeen

1. Auld Auchindoir 1633 P L
2. Rhynie 1626 P L
3. Dumbennan (Dunbennan) 1631 P
4. Huntly 1613 L
5. Alford 1618 P
6. Forgue 1628 P L
7. Rayne 1602 P L
8. Chapel of Garioch >1631 PL
9. Turriff 1586 P L
10. Kemnay 1628 P
11. Pittodrie 1633 L
12. Fyvie 1633 PL
13. Inverurie 1606 P(RB) G
14. Kintore 1619 P(RB)
15. Kinkell 1602 P
16. Carnie 1630 P
17. Methlick 1614 P
18. Straloch 1621
19. Tarves 1621 P
20. Udny 1614 P
21. Aberdour 1574, 1563 P
22. Aberdeen C P(RB) G(2) S(2)
23. Drumwhindle 1617
24. Belhelvie 1628 P L
25. Ellon 1602 P L S Wr
26. Deer nd P
27. Logie Buchan 1610 P
28. Fraserburgh 1601 P G
29. Newburgh 1605
30. Lonmay 1613 P
31. Longside 1626 P L S
32. Slains 1608 P
33. Crimond 1601 P
34. Cruden 1606 P
35. Peterhead 1597 P L
36. Birse 1629 P L
37. Kincardine O'Neil 1625 P L

Angus

1. Kettins > 1602 P L
2. Newtyle 1622 P L
3. Liff 1626 P
4. Nevay 1623 P
5. Dundee C P(RB) G S
6. Glamis >1610
7. Kirriemuir 1598 PL
8. Balmuir Mill 1619
9. Tealing 1609 P
10. Mains 1613 P
11. Forfar 1576 P(RB) L
12. Oathlaw 1628 PL
11. Fern 1619 P L
14. Monifeith 1599 P L
15. Rescobie 1610 P
16. Menmuir 1628 PM
17. Barry 1598 P L
18. Carmyllie 1574 L
19. Arbirlot 1602 P L
20. Brechin nd P(RB)
21. Arbroath 1620 P(RB) L
22. Logie Montrose (now Logie Pert) nd P Fr K
23. Craig 1632
24. Montrose 1566 P(RB) G S
25. Fordoun 1609 P
26. Lauriston 1630 L
27. Ardestie 1631

28. Inverkeilor 1611 P L

Argyll

1. Inveraray 1619 P(RB) G
2. Kilmeny 1622 P
3 . Kilberry 1617 P L
4 . Kilmichael Glassary 1629 P L
5. Lochhead 1622

Ayr

1. Largs 1595 P L
2. Blair (Castle) 1625
3. Dailly 1630 P
4. Maybole 1602 P L
5. Dalry 1625 P L
6. Drumellan 1631
7. Kilbirnie 1617 P
8. Irvine 1586 P(RB) G
9. Ladyland 1600
10. Kirkmichael 1630 P
11. Ayr C P(BR) G S Wr
12. Beith 1617 P
13. Hessilhead 1604
14. St Quivox 1621
15. West Killbride 1603 P L
16. Kilmaurs 1614 P
17. Kilmarnock I591 PG
18. Stewarton > 1620 P L
19. Tarbolton 1601 P L
20. Galston 1627 P
21. Mauchline 1622 P L
22. Newmilns 1601 P L P
23. Cumnock 1599 P L
24. Kilwinning 1605 P L
25. Dundonald 1606 P
26. Fenwick 1638
27. Colmonell 1630 P L

Banff

1. Inveravon 1633 P L
2. Mortlach 1228 P L
3. Keith 1620 P L
4. Rathven 1600 P
5. Grange 1631 PL
6. Ordens 1633
7. Cullen C P(RB) G
8. Fordyce 1624 P L
9. Baldavie 1629
10. Alvah 1626 P L
11. Banff C P(RB)

Berwick

1. Lauder >1621 P(RB) L
2. Earlston 1607
3. Rumbletonlaw 1622 L
4. Hume 1612 P
5. Greenlaw >1633 P
6. Kennetsidehead 1629
7. Ednam 1560? P L
8. Hassington 1622
9. Hardacres 1620
10. Polwarth 1586 PL
11. Choicelee 1609
12. Fogo 1632
13. Cockburnspath 1619 P L
14. Langton 1600 P L
15. Duns 1600 P
16. Bughtrig 1605
17. Butterdean 1592?
18. Old Cambus 1620
19. Edrom 1630 P
20. West Renton 1618 P
21. Chirnside > 1629
22. East Reston 1993
23. Coldingham 1587 P
24. Foulden 1619 P
25. Ayton 1583 P?
26. Paxton 1619
27. Eyemouth 1594 L

Bute

1. Rothesay 1619

Caithness

1. Thurso 1628 P L
2. Wick 1617 P
3. Dornoch 1588 P(RB) G

Clackmannan

1. Alloa P
2. Clackmannan 1590 P G
3. Tillicoultry 1627 P

Dunbarton

1. Dunbarton 1576 P(RB) G S
2. Kilpatrick 1622 P L
3. Lenzie 1625 P
4. Kirkintilloch nd P L

Dumfries

1. Sanquhar 1598 P(RB) L
2. Moffat 1612 P G
3. Drumlanrig 1619
4. Dunscore 1629 P L
5. Dumfries C P(RB) G
6. Tinwald 1627 P
7. Annan 1628 P(RB) L
8. Dornock 1633 P

East Lothian

1. Prestonpans 1591 PG (3 tongues)
2. Elphinstone 1624 L
3. Tranent 1594 P
4. Seton 1633 P
5. Pencaitland 1613 P
6. Saltoun 1589 P
7. Aberlady 1615 P
8. Gullane 1598 P
9. Drem 1629 P
10. Haddington C P(RB) G S V W
11. Bothans 1606 P
12. North Berwick 1581 P(RB)
13. Whittinghame 1620 P
14. Tyninghame 1600 P L
15. Dunbar 1564 PGV
16. East Barns 1612
17. Innerwick 1630 P
18. Oldhamstocks > 1577 P L

Fife

1. Abdie 1624 P L
2. Newburgh 1597 P(RB) G
3. Leslie 1623 P
4. Falkland 1589 P(RB) G
5. Largo 1623 P L
6. Collessie 1631 P
7. Markinch >1622 PL
8. Monimail 1632 P
9. Kingskettle 1571 P L
10. Auchtermuchty 1570 P(RB) L
11. Kennoway 1575 P L
12. Cupar 1564 P(RB) G
13. Leven >1633 L
14. Scoonie 1626 P
15. Logie 1630 PL
16. Forgan 1599 (RB) G
17. Newburn 1630P
18. Leuchars 1594 P L
19. Kilconquhar 1594 P
20. Elie 1600 P
21. Abercrombie 1617 P L
22. St Andrews C P(RB) G(4) H S(20)V
23. Carnbee 1613 PL
24. Dunino 1631 PL
25. Pittenweem 1592 P G
26. Kinglassie 1630 P
27. Anstruther Easter 1624 (RB) L
28. Anstruther Wester 1595 (RB) L
29. Kilrenny 1625 P(RB) L
30. Crail C P(RB) G
31. Culross 1585 P(RB) G
32. Kincardine >1618
33. Torryburn 1620 P

Lowland schools before 1633

Schools

34. Carnock 1628 P L
35. Dunfermline C P(RB) G S W Wr
36. Inverkeithing C P(RB) G
37. Keltiehaugh 1627 Mixed
38. Aberdour >1629 P L
39. Auchtertool 1631 PL
40. Burntisland 1587 P(RB) G
41. Kirkcaldy nd P(RB) G
42. Kinghorn 1575 P(RB) G
43. Dysart 1579 P(RB) G

Inverness

1. Inverness C P(RB) G

Kincardine

1. Bervie 1614 P(RB) L
2. Banchory Devenick 1621 P L
3. Ecclesgreig 1620 P L
4. Arbuthnott
5. Benholm >1619 P L
6. Chapel of Barras 1623
7. Fetteresso 1628 P L
8. Urie 1618

Kinross

1. Kinross 1615 P
2. Cleish 1633 P

Kirkcudbright

1. Minnigaff 1622 P
2. Dalry (St John's Clachan) > 1626 P(RB)
3. Kirkcudbright 1577 P(RB) G W
4. Buittle 1631 P
5. Grennan 1631
6. New Abbey 1628 P
7. Craigend 1630

Lanark

1. Bothwell 1612 P
2. Govan 1614 P
3. Rutherglen 1590 P(RB) G
4. Peel 1616 L
5. Carmunnock 21607 P
6. Gorbal 1633
7. Glasgow C P(RB) G S V (1+)
8. East Kilbride 1591 P L
9. Cambuslang 1598 P
10. Blantyrel611 P
11. Strathaven 1626 P L
12. Earnock 1619
13. Glassford 1620 P
14. Hamilton 1570 P(RB) G S
15. Shirrel 1624
16. Stonehouse 1630 P
17. Carfin 1627
18. Dalserf 1619 P
19. Lesmahagow 1623 PL
20. Cambusnethan 1627 P
21. Meikle Hareshaw 1605
22. Douglas >1633 P
23. Carluke 1620 P L
24. Crawfordjohn 1599 P L
25. Shotts 1629 P
26. Lanark nd P(RB) G S
27. Carstairs 1619 P
28. Crawfordjohn 1630 P
29. Wiston 1612
30. Stobwood 1620
31. Lamington > 1622 P L
32. Covington 1620 P
33. Libberton 1631 P
34. Carnwath 1617 P L
35. Quothquan 163
36. Coulter 1620 P
37. Biggar 1608 P
38. Dunsyre 1626 P
39. Dolphinton 1624 P L

Midlothian

1. Canongate C P G
2. Newbattle 1617 P L S
3. Midcalder >1611 P L
4. Kirknewton 1627 P
5. Ratho 1599 P
6. Liberton 1598 P
7. Cramond 1599 P L
8. Leith (South) 1598 P
9. Leith 1598 P G S
10. Edinburgh C P(RB) D Fe Fr G S V(3+) Wr
11. Duddingston 1630 P
12. Lasswade 1615 PL
13. Cockpen 1602 P
14. Dalkeith 1591 PG
15. Fisherrow >1615
16. Inveresk >1615 P
17. Musselburgh 1580 (part of Inveresk) G S
18. Crichton 1627 P
19. Cranston 1631 P
20. Stow 1628 P
21. Hailes 1599 P (RB) G S

Moray

1. Forres 1582 P(RB) G
2. Cromdale 1627 P L
3. Elgin CP (RB) G S
4. Urquhart > 1631 P

Nairn

1. Auldearn 1582 P(RB) G

Orkney

1. Stromness 1630 P
2. Kirkwall C P (RB) G S
3. South Ronaldsay 1627 P

Peebles

1. Skirling 1632 P
2. Glenholm 1625 P
3. Broughton 1630 P
4. West Linton 1602 P
5. Stobo 1604 P
6. Brig of Lyne 1614
7. Lyne 1600
8. Henderland 1633
9. Peebles C P (RB) GS
10. Traquhair 1617 PL
11. Bold (=West Bold?) 1621

Perth

1. Killin 1627 P
2. Doune 1632 P
3. Balloch 1618
4. Muthill 1583 P
5. Blackford 1613 P (see also Strageath)
6. Strageath 1583 P L
7. Bonskeid 1621
8. Tullibardine 1599 P
9. Fowlis Wester 1616 P L
10. Auchterarder 1610 P
11. Madderty 1632 P
12. Dunning 1610 P
13. Methven 1632 P L
14. Dunkeld C P (RB) G
15. Tibbermore 1611 P
16. Perth C P (RB) G S
17. Scone 1610 P L
18. St Martins > 1629 P L
19. Kinclaven 1609 P L
20. Kinfauns 1613 P
21. Abernethy 1632 P L
22. Rattray 1606 P L
23. St Madoes 1595 P
24. Tullymurdoch 1603 L
25. Chapelhill 1622
26. Kilspindie 1614 P
27. Coupar Angus (formerly in Angus) 1581 PG
28. Kinnaird 1613 P L

29. Alyth 1607 P
30. Erroll >1626 P L
31. Inchture 1613 P

Renfrew.

1. Lochwinnoch 1622 P
2. Kilmacolm 1623 P
3. Inchinnan 1623 P L
4. Paisley C P G S V W
5. Renfrew 1595 P(RB) L
6. Mearns (now Mearnskirk) 1605 P
7. Cathcart 1603 P

Ross and Cromarty

1. Dingwall 1569 P(RB)
2. Kiltearn 1631 P L S
3. Alness 1628 P L
4. Ross Chanonry nd P(RB) G
5. Cromarty 1580 P(RB) G
6. Tain 1630 P(RB) G S (1595)

Roxburgh

1. Hawick 1592 P G
2. Melrose 1608 P L
3. Hobkirk 1619 P
4. Lessudden 1631 P
5. Bedrule 1618
6. Maxton 1611 P
7. Southdean 1620 P
8. Hundalee 1608
9. Smailholm 1622 P
10. Mellerstain 1605
11. Jedburgh 1569 P(RB)
12. Roxburgh 1631 P(RB)
13. Eckford 1608 P
14. Samieston >1619
15. Maxwellheugh 1628
16. Kelso 1585 PL(G?)
17. Caverton 1617
18. Hownam 1609 P
19. Morebattle 1628 P L
20. Primside Mill 1617
21. Colmslie 1622

Selkirk

1. Littlehope 1619
2. Ashkirk 1618 P
3. Selkirk 1608 P(RB) G
4. Boleside 1617 P
5. Galashiels >1630 P
6. Minto 1616 P

Shetland

1. Scalloway 1612 P L
2. Dore 1582

Stirling

1. Dunblane C P(RB) G
2. Drymen 1624 P
3. Killearn 1630 P L
4. Branshogle 1620
5. Kilsyth 1590 P
6. Stirling C P(RB) G S V(1 +)
7. Logie 1627 P G late V
8. Slamannan 1632 P
9. Falkirk 1594 P

West Lothiam

1. Linlithgow 1575 P(RB)
2. Bo'ness 1630 L
3. Livingston 1633 P
4. Abercorn 1620 P
5. Luffness 1626 P

Wigtown

1. Glenluce 1632 P
2. Stranraer 1614 P(RB)
3. Longcastle 1581 P
4. Wigtown 1583 P(RB) G
5. Whithorn 1628 P(RB)
6. Bysbie 1631

Lowland schools before 1633

Regional and local

Innse Gall in the thirteenth century

The Kingdom of the Isles, extending from the Calf of Man to the Butt of Lewis, emerged as a political unit in the tenth and eleventh centuries. Contemporary nomenclature by both Norwegian (the Sudreys) and Gael (Innse Gall - the Foreigners Isles) reflected a strong Scandinavian presence. By the twelfth century at latest, Norwegian overlordship in matters both secular and religious had been established, and was to continue until the treaty of Perth in 1266. The dynasty of Godred (or Godfrey) Crovan (d. about 1095), based in Man, originally ruled all the isles, but lost control (about 1156) of the Islay and Mull groups of islands and probably of the Uists also, to Somerled of Argyll. Somerled had married Godred's granddaughter and is the ancestor of the MacDougalls, the MacRuaris and the later MacDonald Lords of the Isles. The map indicates the likely division of territory between the kings of Man and the house of Somerled. The areas of the mainland where Somerled's descendants are known or believed to have been major landowners, subject to the king of Scots, are also shown. The list of castles should be regarded as tentative. The dating and classification of Hebridean castles is notoriously fraught with problems. The intention is to include stone castles (or, in the case of Cairnburg, Iselburg and Dun Chonnel, strongly fortified sites) probably in existence by the end of the thirteenth century. Without doubt, many older brochs and duns were also in at least occasional occupation then and later.

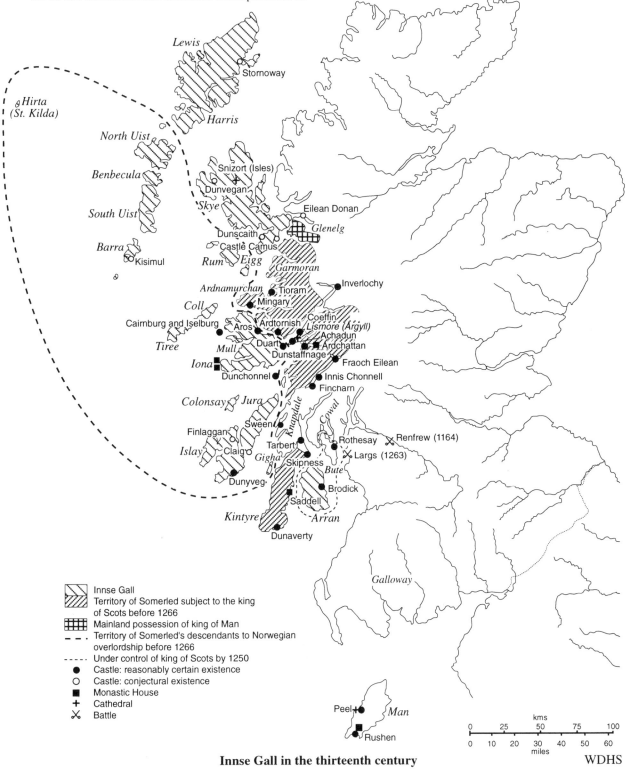

Innse Gall in the thirteenth century

WDHS

441

The Lordship of the Isles

The lands which belonged to the Lords of the Isles, descendants of Somerled of Argyll, in 1475 were acquired in a variety of ways and were all held from the king of Scots following the Treaty of Perth in 1266. Expanding from the family's base in Islay, some lands were granted or confirmed by Robert I and David II as reward for support in the wars of independence, partly at the expense of the MacDougalls. Others were acquired through the marriage of John, Lord of the Isles first with the heiress of the MacRuaris of Garmoran and later with a daughter of the Steward of Scotland (the future King Robert II), and of Donald, Lord of the Isles with the daughter of William, earl of Ross.

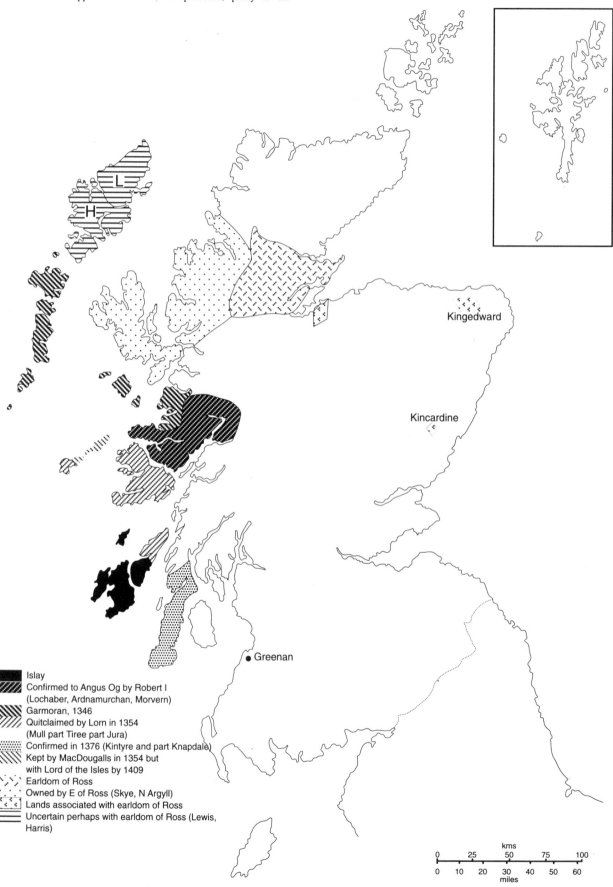

Islay

Confirmed to Angus Og by Robert I
(Lochaber, Ardnamurchan, Morvern)

Garmoran, 1346

Quitclaimed by Lorn in 1354
(Mull part Tiree part Jura)

Confirmed in 1376 (Kintyre and part Knapdale)

Kept by MacDougalls in 1354 but
with Lord of the Isles by 1409

Earldom of Ross

Owned by E of Ross (Skye, N Argyll)

Lands associated with earldom of Ross

Uncertain perhaps with earldom of Ross (Lewis, Harris)

kms
0   25   50   75   100
0   10   20   30   40   50   60
miles

The Lordship of the Isles: lands from 13th century to 1475   JM, RWM

442

The Lordship of the Isles

Most of the acts of the Lords of the Isles of which the texts survive record the place and date of issue. While the lordship was held along with the earldom of Ross - that is, from at least 1437 until 1475 - places within the mainland earldom predominate, even when the acts themselves relate to the Isles. Of the others, places of origin are scattered throughout the southern part of the lordship; if any were issued on the seaboard or islands north of Ardnamurchan, none is known to have survived.

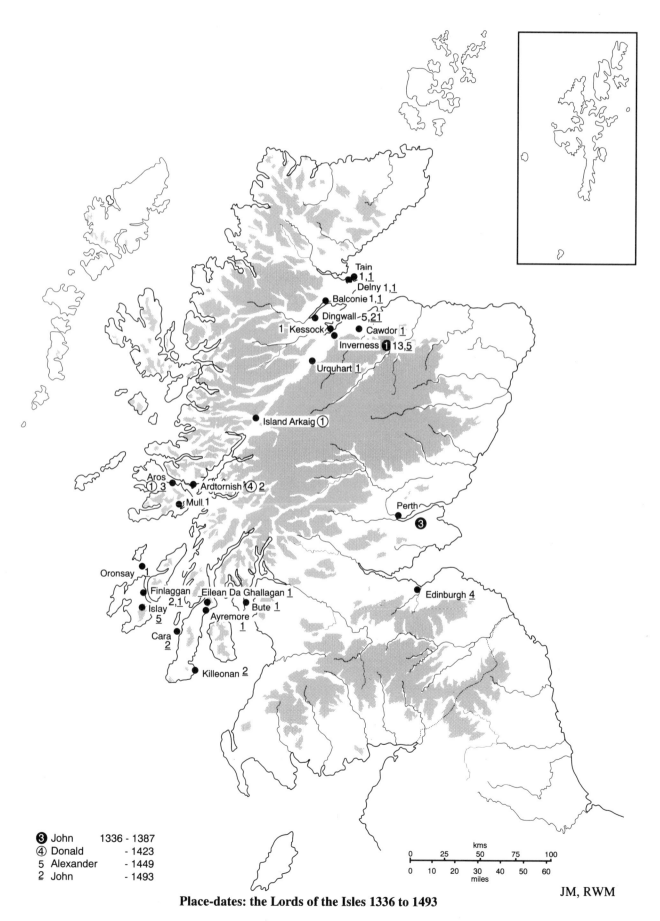

Tain 1,1
Delny 1,1
Balconie 1,1
Dingwall 5,21
Kessock 1
Cawdor 1
Inverness ❶ 13,5
Urquhart 1
Island Arkaig ①
Aros ① 3
Ardtornish ④ 2
Mull 1
Perth ❸
Oronsay 1
Finlaggan 2,1
Eilean Da Ghallagan 1
Islay 5
Bute 1
Ayremore 1
Cara 2
Killeonan 2
Edinburgh 4

❸ John   1336 - 1387
④ Donald   - 1423
5 Alexander   - 1449
2 John   - 1493

kms
0   25   50   75   100
0 10 20 30 40 50 60
miles

JM, RWM

Place-dates: the Lords of the Isles 1336 to 1493

The Lordship of the Isles

A remarkable series of stone castles built on the western seaboard and islands, where traffic in peace and war was essentially by sea, are evidence of the power and influence of the Lords of the Isles and their branch families and adherents. Many of the ruins are difficult to date, and some forts and duns of prehistoric origin show signs of later occupation and re-use. Those shown on the map are mentioned in documents, chronicles or topographical accounts written before 1550, when the last attempt to restore the Lordship of the Isles had ended.

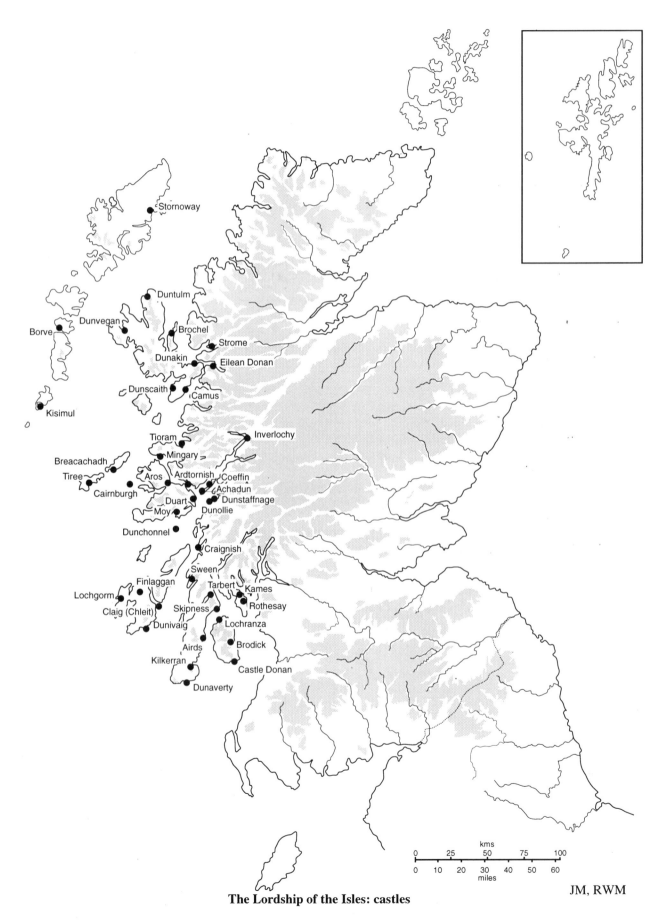

Stornoway

Duntulm

Dunvegan

Borve

Brochel

Strome

Dunakin

Eilean Donan

Dunscaith

Camus

Kisimul

Tioram

Inverlochy

Breacachadh

Mingary

Tiree

Aros

Ardtornish

Coeffin

Achadun

Cairnburgh

Duart

Dunstaffnage

Moy

Dunollie

Dunchonnel

Craignish

Sween

Finlaggan

Tarbert

Kames

Lochgorm

Rothesay

Claig (Chleit)

Skipness

Dunivaig

Lochranza

Airds

Brodick

Kilkerran

Castle Donan

Dunaverty

kms
0   25   50   75   100

0 10 20 30 40 50 60
miles

JM, RWM

The Lordship of the Isles: castles

The Lordship of the Isles

After the forfeiture of the earldom of Ross in 1475 and of the Lordship of the Isles in 1493, their territories were granted by the crown mainly to the heads of Clan Donald branches or other leading families who had held them from the forfeited superior. Charters in the Register of the Great Seal indicate those to whom the lands passed following the forfeitures.

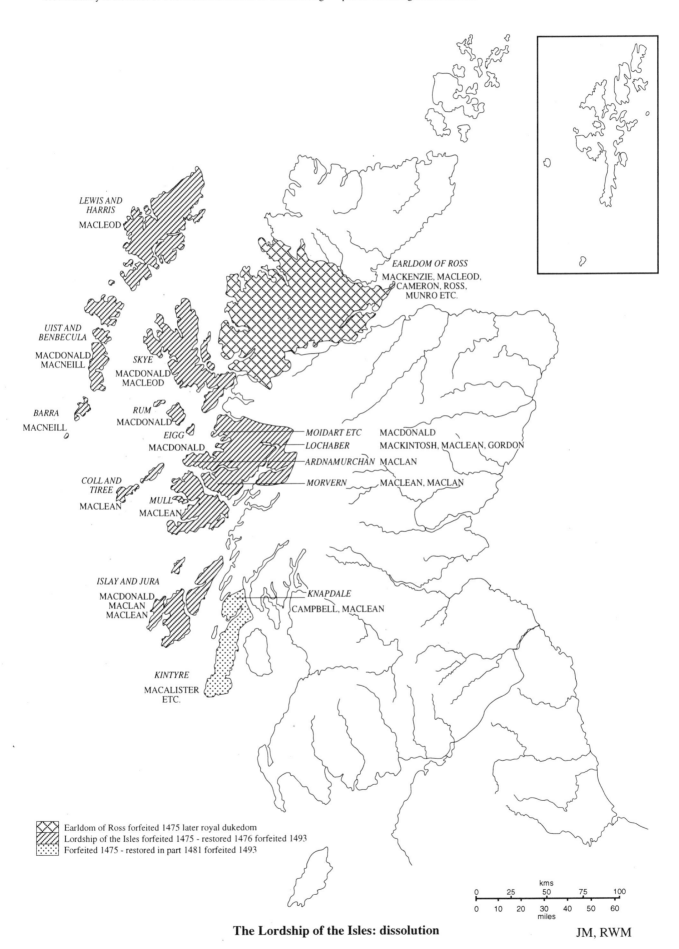

LEWIS AND
HARRIS
MACLEOD

EARLDOM OF ROSS
MACKENZIE, MACLEOD,
CAMERON, ROSS,
MUNRO ETC.

UIST AND
BENBECULA
MACDONALD
MACNEILL

SKYE
MACDONALD
MACLEOD

BARRA
MACNEILL

RUM
MACDONALD

EIGG
MACDONALD

MOIDART ETC   MACDONALD
LOCHABER   MACKINTOSH, MACLEAN, GORDON
ARDNAMURCHAN MACLAN
MORVERN   MACLEAN, MACLAN

COLL AND
TIREE
MACLEAN

MULL
MACLEAN

ISLAY AND JURA
MACDONALD
MACLAN
MACLEAN

KNAPDALE
CAMPBELL, MACLEAN

KINTYRE
MACALISTER
ETC.

Earldom of Ross forfeited 1475 later royal dukedom
Lordship of the Isles forfeited 1475 - restored 1476 forfeited 1493
Forfeited 1475 - restored in part 1481 forfeited 1493

kms
0   25   50   75   100
0   10 20 30 40 50 60
miles

The Lordship of the Isles: dissolution

JM, RWM

The Lords of Galloway

Following the death in 1234 of Alan, last of the male line of the Lords of Galloway, the demesne estates of the Lordship were partitioned between his three daughters and their husbands (see family tree). This arrangement lasted only until 1247, when the death without direct heirs of the second heiress, Christina, led to the redistribution of her estates between the surviving sisters. The nature of this original partition is unclear, but it would seem that the senior heiress, Helen, had gained most of the family estates around Kirkcudbright, the core of the early Lordship. Dervorguilla's principal interests were focused on eastern Galloway, with Buittle in the Urr Valley and a series of important estates lying in the Glenkens and Dee Valley areas falling to her lot. Outlying manors in western Galloway, remote from these main territorial blocks, may have pertained originally to Christina's portion, being redistributed to her surviving sisters after her death. The succession of heiresses to the de Quincy estates in 1264 saw a further subdivision of the Galloway demesne, with Helen's portion falling to the Comyn, earl of Buchan, husband of Helen's second daughter, succeeded in acquiring the largest share of the estates, including the key castle of Cruggleton. His dominant position in western Galloway was se-

cured by his acquisition of the office of sheriff of Wigtown, putting his family in general control of the country west of the Cree. The fragmentation of the de Quincy estates left the Balliols as the largest single landowning family in the Lordship, a position augmented by the exchange of land outwith Galloway for estates assigned originally to the other portioners.

The pattern of estates shown on the map below is drawn from a number of unrelated sources, there being no single survey of the Lordship demesne until the mid-15th century. The principal source for the Balliol lands is the series of documents in the Rotuli Scotiae relating to the ancestral lands of Edward Balliol, 'restored' to him by Edward III in 1334. For the de Quincy estates, the inquest into the lands of Helen de la Zouche, the youngest daughter of Helen de Quincy, held at Berwick in 1296, provided much information. The list, however, is incomplete due to the poverty of the sources. Certain estates, moreover, passed in and out of the lordly demesne, e.g. Lochkindeloch, which in 1273 became the principal endowment of Dervorguilla's abbey of Sweetheart, or Borgue (not shown on the map), which came into her possession in 1282 through the quit claim of the tenant.

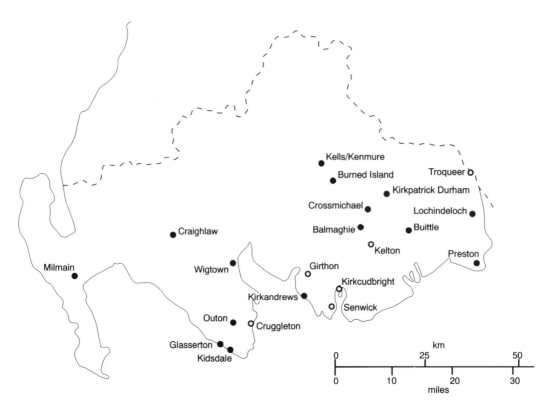

● Demesne estates of the lords of Galloway, Balliol lands
○ Demesne estates of the lords of Galloway, other than Balliol lands

The lords of Galloway : demesne lands of the later thirteenth century   RO

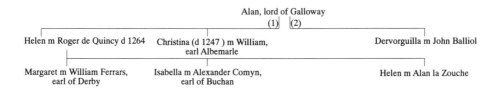

The lords of Galloway: genealogy   RO

Galloway: Douglas estates

The map below is based upon the list of forfeited Douglas estates in Galloway accounted for in September 1456 by Walter, Abbot of Dundrennan, royal chamberlain for Galloway. The map is incomplete, as certain of the land names in 1456 are no longer identifiable. In general, however, those places shown on the map correspond to modern farms or topographical features. The Douglas lands in the southwest developed out of the grant in 1325 of the former Balliol manor of Buittle to Sir James Douglas 'the Good', one of Robert I's principal adherents. This formed part of the entailed Douglas estates in 1342, but found its way into the possession of Sir William Douglas of Liddesdale. In 1367, on the death without heirs of his daughter, Mary Douglas, Buittle passed into the possession of her cousin, Sir James Douglas of Dalkeith. Rights to the estate were claimed by Archibald Douglas, illegitimate son of the 'Good Sir James', eventual head of the main line of the family, and the superiority was restored to him. This remained a major source of dispute with the Dalkeith line, but the right of superiority remained with the descendants of Archibald until their forfeiture in 1455. The component farms of the barony of Buittle formed one of the principal elements of the Douglas estate in Galloway, together with land in Balmaghie and Kelton forming the core of the demesne. The bulk

of the Douglas estates were acquired in 1369, when David II granted Archibald the Grim all royal lands between the Nith and Cree in free barony. These were composed principally of the former estates of the Balliols, focusing on Kells and Balmaclellan in the Glenkens and Balmaghie, lower down the Dee Valley, where Archibald built his fortress of Threave. At this time also, he may have secured possession of the Forest of Buchan, former Comyn territory which had been taken into the royal demesne by Robert I. Having achieved territorial dominance in eastern Galloway, Archibald turned to the lands of the Cree and in 1371 bought the earldom of Wigtown from Thomas Fleming. The latter had been unable to control the minor nobility of that region, but Archibald's firm administration of the law and superior landed base in eastern Galloway enabled him to assert his overlordship. His purchase of the earldom brought him a concentration of estates around Kirkinner, the main area of Fleming's interest, plus further portions of the former Balliol demesne in the southern Machars and Rhins, to a large extent reuniting the portions of the old Lordship of Galloway, divided since 1235. In 1388, Archibald succeeded to the earldom of Douglas and his lordship in Galloway was absorbed into the lands and titles of that dignity.

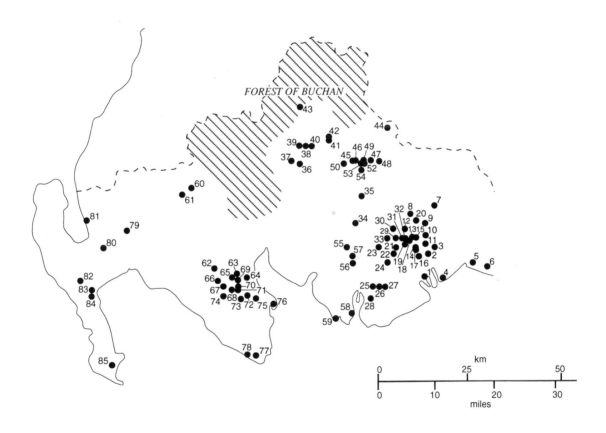

1	Almorness	18	Corra	35	Airds	52	Barlay	69	Barglass
2	Munches	19	Cuil	36	Craigenbay	53	Curse	70	Knockann
3	Little Richorn	20	Corbieton	37	Garrary	54	Craig	71	Blairmaken
4	Colvend	21	Kelton	38	Drumbuie	55	Miefield	72	Knockencur
5	Southwick	22	Slagnaw	39	Clenrie	56	Trostrie	73	Knockefferick
6	Preston	23	Dildawn	40	Largmore	57	Culcaigrie	74	Killdarroch
7	Culmain	24	Lochdougan	41	Barskeoch	58	Senwick	75	Corwar
8	Grange	25	Brockcleugh	42	Earlston	59	Dunrod Point	76	Eggerness
9	Mote of Urr	26	Balgreddan	43	Castlemaddy	60	Fintalloch	77	Arbrack
10	Firth Head	27	Marks	44	Craighuie	61	Tannilaggie	78	Kidsdale
11	Buittle	28	Galtway	45	Balmaclellan	62	Killadam	79	Larg
12	Halketleaths	29	Kelton Mains	46	Ironlosh	63	Kirwaugh	80	Cults
13	Meikle Knox	30	Threave	47	Lowes	64	Baldoon	81	Leffnoll
14	Little Knox	31	Carlingwark	48	Caldow	65	Clauchrie	82	Caldons
15	Guffog Land	32	Whitepark	49	Bartaggart	66	Kirbreen	83	Culgroat
16	Clone	33	Midpark	50	Cubbox	67	Clutag	84	Balgreggan
17	Cullinlaw	34	Cullenoch	51	Cassenvey	68	Barnbarroch	85	Alton
								86	Forest of Buchan

Douglas estates in Galloway 1456

RO

Orkney and Caithness

The earls of Orkney and Caithness strove to retain their traditional independence in an era of growing royal power, when the kings of Scotland were determined to extend their authority over the northernmost parts of the Scottish mainland. The earl who suffered particularly from this process was Harold Maddadson (1139-1206) who had to face two royal expeditions against his Scottish earldom; the first (1196/97) after he had led a raid into Moray and his son had fought a battle near Inverness against 'the King's vassals'; the second (1201/2) after he had led an attack on the Bishop of Caithness who was at his castle of Scrabster, near Thurso. Earl Harold survived by submitting to King William, although his successors were to lose much land to the foremost of the 'king's vassals' in the north, the de Moravia family. The earl's Norwegian overlords managed to maintain some authority in the Northern and Western Isles by periodic naval expeditions. The first historically authenticated was that of King Magnus in 1098 when he claimed all the islands off the Scottish coasts by sailing round them, even being dragged in a skiff across the neck of Kintyre. At the same time, he firmly subjected the earls of Orkney to his authority and even tried to establish some control in Ireland, where he was killed on a second expedition. Harold Maddadson also had to submit to his Norwegian overlords, being forced to pay tribute to King Eystein when taken by surprise in the harbour of Thurso in 1151, and after being involved in the unsuccessful Eyskeggjar rising against King Sverre in 1193. On the latter occasion he was allowed to keep his island earldom although losing control of judicial rights in Orkney and forfeiting Shetland. The final effort to retain authority by the King of Norway, in a changing world, ended with the skirmish at Largs in 1263 and the retreat of the Norwegian fleet to Orkney. Significantly, Earl Magnus of Orkney had disappeared during the king's progress south and was not even present in Orkney when King Hakon returned, to die, in December 1263.

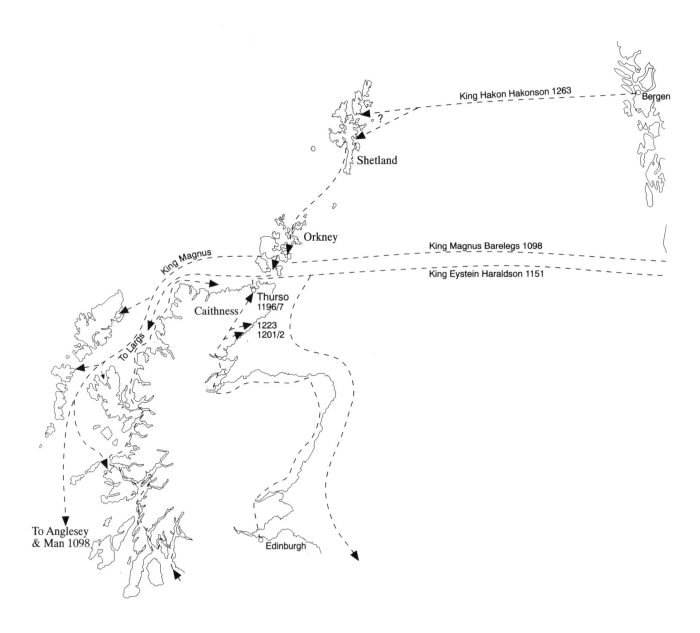

The expeditions to Orkney and Caithness by the kings of Norway and Scotland 1098 to 1263   BEC

Orkney and Caithness

The enormous loss of power and influence suffered by the Norse earls of Orkney and Caithness is illustrated in this map. The problems experienced by Harald Maddadson and the forfeiture of Shetland have been discussed in the commentary to the previous map. His son, Earl John, was antagonistic to the church's policy of tithe exaction and allowed himself to be associated with the attack on Bishop Adam which resulted in the bishop's death by burning in his own manor house at Halkirk in 1222, and the subsequent avenging expedition of King Alexander to the north. The immediate result was the imposition of a heavy fine and the loss of lands by both the earl and those men of Caithness convicted of responsibility for the crime. Another very significant result was the moving of the main diocesan church to a safer location in Sutherland, where a cathedral was built at Dornoch. This was done by Gilbert de Moravia, appointed Bishop Adam's successor, whose relatives were already in possession of lands and rights in Sutherland, which was detached from the earl of Caithness' sphere of influence and erected into a separate earldom about 1235. Finally, the Scottish king was able to benefit from a very confused period of inheritance of the Caithness and Orkney earldoms, when the direct line died out and heiresses from the Scottish house of Angus inherited, one of whom, *nobilis mulier domina Joanna*, was married to another member of the de Moravia family and given half of the earldom lands in Caithness, which can be traced in the hands of her descendants. The earls, left with a fraction of their former power and influence on the north Scottish mainland, were confined henceforth to the heartland of the former earls' dominion, the Orkney Islands.

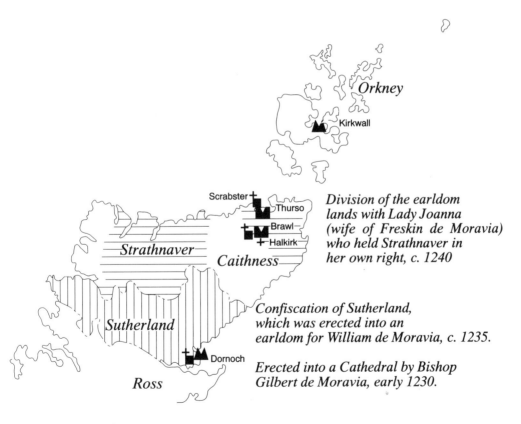

Shetland

Annexed by King Sverre of Norway 1195

Orkney

Kirkwall

Division of the earldom lands with Lady Joanna (wife of Freskin de Moravia) who held Strathnaver in her own right, c. 1240

Scrabster
Thurso
Brawl
Halkirk
Strathnaver
Caithness

Confiscation of Sutherland, which was erected into an earldom for William de Moravia, c. 1235.

Sutherland

Dornoch

Erected into a Cathedral by Bishop Gilbert de Moravia, early 1230.

Ross

▲▲ Cathedral
+ Church
⋈ Earldom castle
▟ Bishopric residence

kms
0   25   50   75   100
0 10 20 30 40 50 60
miles

Reduction of the earldoms of Orkney and Caithness   BEC

449

The Borders from the eleventh to the thirteenth centuries

The last independent King of Cumbria or Strathclyde, Owain (the Bald) son of Dyfnwal (Donald), died about 1018. His kingdom came under the control of Malcolm II, King of Scots, who set over it as ruler (probably not as king) his own son-in-law Duncan son of Crinan. Duncan succeeded as King of Scots in 1034 and even after his death six years later at the hands of Macbeth, Cumbria remained under Scottish rule, or at least within the Scottish sphere of influence. Its political history for the next two centuries was largely a matter of shifting boundaries and a tug-of-war between northern and southern influences. The northernmost portion, Lennox, strongly Gaelic when it emerges into record in the earlier 13th century, had almost certainly been absorbed within Scotia, i.e. Scotland north of Forth and Clyde, before 1000. In the south west, Galloway was effectively a distinct kingdom and culture. Only towards the east and south do the Cumbrians seem to have maintained their frontiers till the late eleventh century, although what emerges as Cumberland and Westmorland had received and been irreversibly affected by intensive Scandinavian settlement from the tenth century or earlier, while English-speaking settlers, pressing westward up Tweeddale and Teviotdale, had begun to spill over into the Annan and Clyde valleys by about 1100. William II Rufus, King of England, cut Cumbria in two in 1092, driving out the Scottish-backed lord, Dolfin, son of Cospatric and introducing southern English settlers to supply and support his new castle at Carlisle.

David I ruled Cumbria north of Solway in the reign of his brother Alexander I (1107-24), restoring the ancient see of Glasgow and bringing in feudatories of continental origin (Bruce, Morville, Stewart, Soules, etc.) who built the region's earliest castles. In 1136 David, now king of Scots, recovered 'English' Cumbria as far as Stainmore Common (the Rere or Rey Cross), and for a decade (1139-49) controlled the Honour of Lancaster as far south as the Ribble. In 1157, the situation reverted to what it had been from 1092 to 1136, for Henry II overawed the young King Malcolm IV and wrested control, permanently as it proved of Cumberland, Westmorland (and, for good measure, Northumberland) from the Scots, thus putting the Border back on the Solway-Tweed line. The twelfth century saw a thoroughgoing absorption of northern or 'Scottish' Cumbria into the kingdom of the Scots, while the northern English counties, despite William the Lion's strenuous attempt to recover them (1173-4), became steadily integrated within the shire-based English governmental system. The Treaty of York (1237) formally confirmed the Border essentially on the line which it was to keep until the present day, save that important adjustments were made between Esk and Sark on the west, while on the east, Scotland lost Berwick-upon-Tweed.

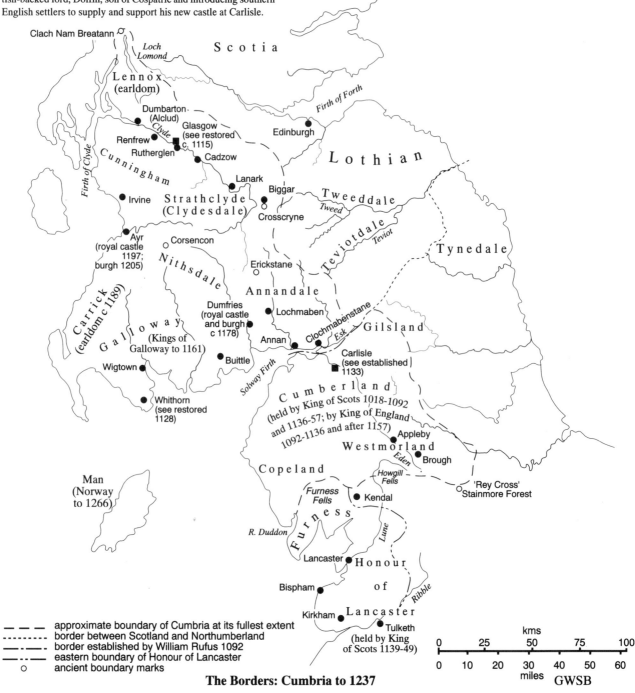

		approximate boundary of Cumbria at its fullest extent
		border between Scotland and Northumberland
		border established by William Rufus 1092
		eastern boundary of Honour of Lancaster
o		ancient boundary marks

The Borders: Cumbria to 1237

GWSB

The Borders from the thirteenth to the sixteenth centuries

By the mid-thirteenth century the Anglo-Scottish Border confirmed by the Treaty of York (1237), had settled down as a long-established feature of the political landscape, although its influence for social intercourse, landownership and settlement was relatively slight. Even politically, it must be noted that the treaty confirmed the Scottish king's lordship over the Liberty of Tynedale (i.e. the valleys of North and South Tyne), and added the Honour of Penrith, on either side of the River Eden. Yet, as the Laws of the Marches (revised and formally promulgated in 1249) make clear, the border was a true international frontier separating two distinct jurisdictions and administrative structures, punctuated by recognised crossing places - whether up-to-date like Berwick Bridge, or archaic like the Clochmabenstane, embodying the name of the Celtic pagan deity Maponus. Thus, in Penrith and Tynedale, the courts held by authority of the king of Scots followed English law and procedures and met with the same frequency as the

eyres of assizes for Cumberland and Northumberland. North of the Border the king's authority, when not exercised directly, was delegated to the justiciar of Lothian (sometimes reinforced by a justiciar of Galloway), below whom the key administrative officers were the sheriffs of Dumfries, Roxburgh and Berwick, normally appointed from powerful baronial families such as Lindsay, Maxwell or (rising fast in the thirteenth century) Randolph.

In keeping with the prevalence of peaceful relations between the death of King John of England (1216) and the reign of King John of Scotland (1292-6), the border was relatively unmilitarized and only thinly furnished with fortifications. On the Scottish side the king had important castles at Berwick-upon-Tweed, Roxburgh, Jedburgh and Dumfries. His backup defence consisted partly of a Tweed-Clyde line marked by castles, hardly first-rate, at Selkirk, Peebles, Lanark and Rutherglen, partly of the major castles at Ayr (New Castle-upon-Ayr founded 1197), Edinburgh and Stir-

Jedburgh ●   Royal centre
Glasgow ♰   Cathedral

⤨   The border
     with principal
     crossing places
BALLIOL   Some leading families
     and Lordships

The Borders about 1250: western side   GWSB

The Borders from the thirteenth to the sixteenth centuries

ling. Magnatial strongpoints included Dunbar (earl of Dunbar), Dirleton (Vaux of Scotland), Hermitage (Soules 1244?), Lochmaben (Bruce), Caerlaverock (Maxwell 1244?), Buittle (Balliol) and Crawford (Lindsay). On the English side, Newcastle and Carlisle were formidable strongholds, but represented a frontier withdrawn southward, especially in the east, to which the lesser castles of Warkworth and Bamburgh scarcely formed exceptions. The Bishop of Durham maintained a first-rate fortress at Norham, a bowshot from Scottish soil, but other magnatial castles, e.g. Wark on Tweed (Ros), Harbottle (Umfraville), Mitford (Bertram) Morpeth (Merlay then Greystoke), Brampton (Vaux of England) and Liddel Strength (Turgis of Brundis), were of less consequence and only the fine Umfraville castle at Prudhoe, south of Tyne, could compare with Norham or the royal strongholds. Wark on Tyne belonged to the king of Scots.

It is doubtful if what later became thought of as the Bor-

der region of southern Scotland was seen thus in the mid-thirteenth century. Scotland south of the Clyde-Forth line, save for Galloway, was by medieval standards populous and prosperous. The kings frequented the many royal castles, houses and hunting lodges in the area between the Forth and the Cheviot Hills, in Clydesdale, Tweeddale, Teviotdale and Lothian. This reflected a more fertile soil and favourable climate than characterized the northernmost counties of England, although the long Eden Valley and parts of the lower Tyne had much productive land. The biggest contrast between the Scottish and English border regions in the two or three generations before the first war of independence lay in the fact that the counties south of the frontier formed a remote and little-known part of the kingdom of England, whereas the sheriffdoms to the north constituted the Scottish realm's very heartland.

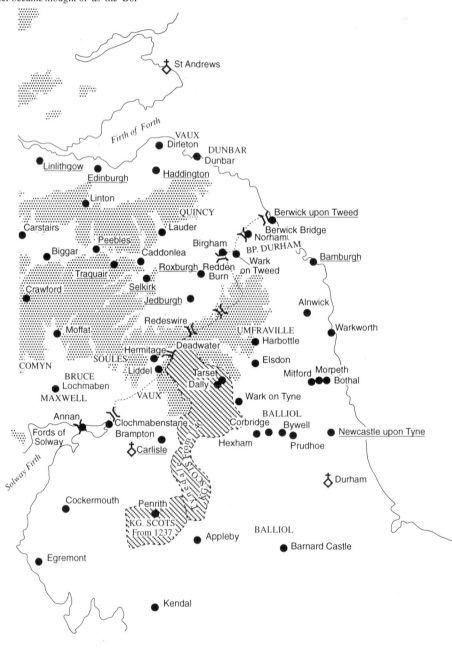

Jedburgh ● Royal centre
Glasgow ✠ Cathedral

⟩⟨ The border
with principal
crossing places
BALLIOL Some leading families
and Lordships
Penrith (hatched), King of Scots from 1237
Tynedale (hatched) King of Scots from about 1140

kms
0   25   50   75   100

0   10   20   30   40   50   60
miles

The Borders about 1250: eastern side   GWSB

The Borders from the thirteenth to the sixteenth centuries

The aims of Scottish frontier administration were adequate military defence and maintenance of law and order. The hilly terrain presented difficulties but warfare with England became less frequent in the sixteenth century. Peacetime administration was a matter for international control. All transgressions of the frontier, violent and non-violent, were expected to be submitted for settlement under the Laws of the Marches, which was administered by Scottish and English wardens of the Marches. There were three Marches on each side of the frontier - East, West and Middle - and each had its own warden, although at various times one warden might administer two marches. The Scottish middle March was divided during the sixteenth century and the Liddesdale area was separately administered by a keeper. Scottish and English wardens assembled at recognised meeting places to engage in diplomacy and dispense justice at 'days of truce', using procedures adapted so that the guilt or liability of defenders should be determined by their own countrymen.

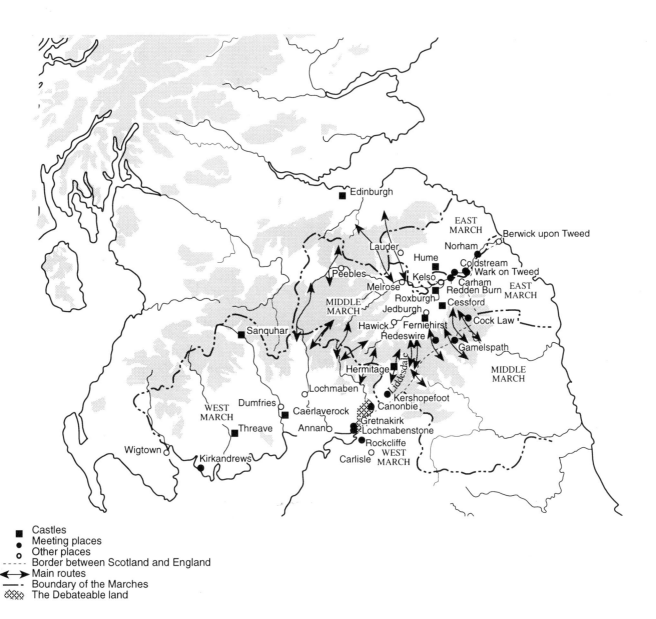

	Castles
	Meeting places
	Other places
-----	Border between Scotland and England
←→	Main routes
—·—	Boundary of the Marches
⬡⬡⬡	The Debateable land

The Borders in the sixteenth century

TIR(MM)

Forests

By 1214 Walter Steward held three reserves including Renfrew. In Renfrew the Stewards faced the same problem as the king faced in royal forests, namely, the difficulty of maintaining a forest as a hunting reserve while at the same time permitting economic activity, whether grazing, woodcutting or leasing within the forest. In the thirteenth century, pasture fines were carefully organised: the fine was heavier in the close season and a watch was set; but no distinction was made in the open season between tended and untended animals. In 1208 x 1214, Walter permitted Paisley to graze animals freely on their lands between the Old Patrick Water and the Espedair Burn; but these lands remained within his forest since he reserved the birds and beasts on them. James Steward, by 1294-5, has tackled this problem much in the same way as Robert I did after him. He created a *'foresta prohibita'* within his reserve where no economic activity was permitted, but liberated such exploitation in the rest of his reserve. The abbey had to pay the exactions - which had assumed the character of fines to a large extent - when their beasts were found on the unlet parts of the forest which presumably included the *foresta prohibita*. The map shows the Renfrew Forest and the other forests in the area with lands of the Stewards and Paisley Abbey.

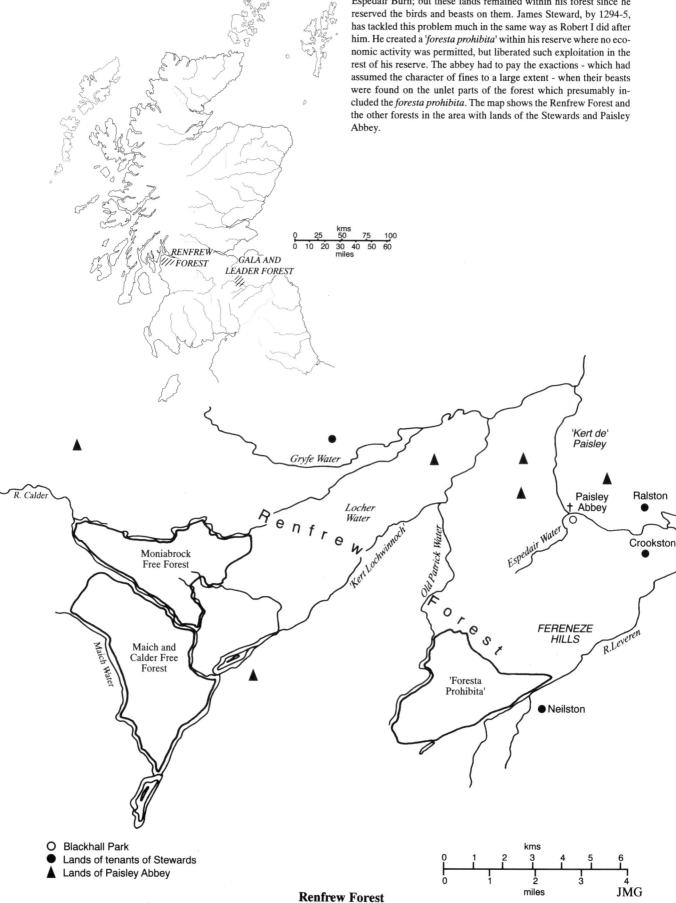

O Blackhall Park
● Lands of tenants of Stewards
▲ Lands of Paisley Abbey

Renfrew Forest

JMG

Forests

Hunting reserves were not only exploited by their owners. Some abbeys had exemptions from forest rights. The provision of fuel, the grazing of flocks, the construction of folds and shelters for the animals and of temporary shielings for the herdsmen must have made considerable inroads into a forest's vegetation and put pressure on the maintenance of a hunting reserve. Such pressure was exerted in several reserves including Gala and Leader.

The royal forest of Gala and Leader, first recorded in 1150 x 1152, must have been created shortly after 1136 when Melrose received pasture, pannage and the right to cut wood there. From its creation, this forest was subjected to the common activity of both laymen and ecclesiastics. Lands were held at Sorrowlessfield (by William Soroules), Kedslie (Alwin), Blainslie (William, son of Oein), lands near Kedslie (William de Lyndesay), lands near Blainslie (the Stewards) and Sorrowlessfield, Earlston and Lauder (earls of Dunbar). And the monks of Dryburgh held a grange at Kedslie with a right of pasture in the forest. It appears that there had been a dispute between the monks of Melrose and Richard de Moreville because he tried to share in Melrose's pasture rights in the royal forest and because the monks objected to Richard's

hunting throughout the forest (especially in Threepwood) and the monks tried to increase their buildings in the forest.

The first map gives an indication of the vegetation of the Gala and Leader Forest; and the second map shows the land use and routes in the forest.

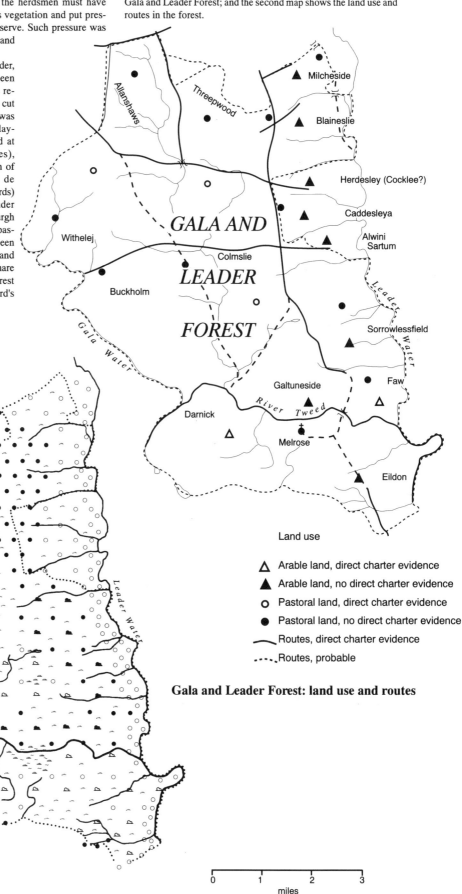

Gala and Leader Forest: land use and routes

Land use

△ Arable land, direct charter evidence

▲ Arable land, no direct charter evidence

○ Pastoral land, direct charter evidence

● Pastoral land, no direct charter evidence

—— Routes, direct charter evidence

······ Routes, probable

Woodland
Woodland scrub and grass
Moss-peat
Moor
Marsh
● ▲ Shaded symbols......Direct charter evidence

Gala and Leader Forest: vegetation

455

Burghs: development of Edinburgh 1550 to 1650

In 1400 Edinburgh had reportedly only 400 houses. Its population by 1558, when 736 merchants and 717 craftsmen (both with their apprentices and servants included) were recorded in a muster roll, was about 12,000. Although this was at least twice the size of any other Scottish town, it did not fully reflect either Edinburgh's position as an administrative capital or its growing stranglehold over Scotland's export trade.

Edinburgh was divided into four quarters and, also like other Scottish burghs, it was made up of only one parish - until 1592. In that year a census was conducted by the kirk session, which revealed 2,239 households and exactly 8,000 examinable persons (over 12 years of age) within the burgh walls. The kirk sought eight new model parishes, each with 1,000 communicants but had to settle, until the 1640s, for four, each based on one of the old quarters. By 1635, when a novel annuity tax, based on the valued rent of each household, was levied to pay for the burgh's ministers, the number of households had sharply increased, by 74 per cent, to 3,901; there were, in addition, a further 903 business premises. Its total population is likely to have been between 21,000 and 23, 500. And beyond its walls lay three other sizeable burghs - the Canongate and North and South Leith - making up 'greater Edinburgh'; its total population must have been in the region of 35,000.

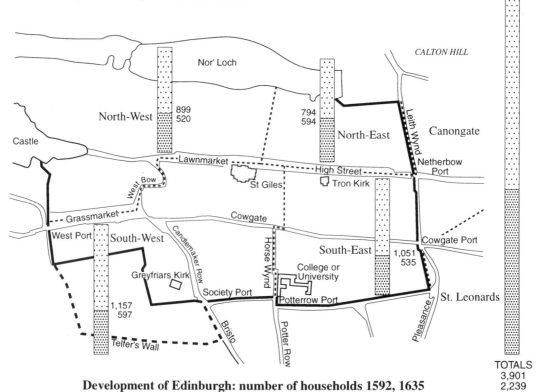

Development of Edinburgh: number of households 1592, 1635

ML

By 1635 each quarter had, for ease of administration, been divided into sub-thirds, which proceeded in a clockwise direction (North-west 1,2,3...) beginning and ending at the Grassmarket.

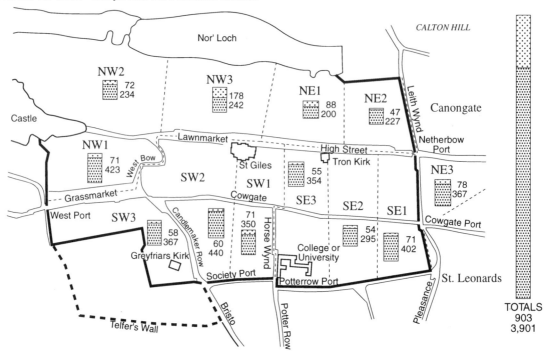

Development of Edinburgh: number of households and businesses 1635

ML

Burghs: development of Edinburgh 1550 to 1650

One reason for the markedly different rates of population increase between the southern and northern quarters of the town was terrain. On the steepest parts of the ridge, above St Giles' and to the north of the High Street, only well-built and expensive multi-storeyed tenements, such as Gladstone's Land which still stands, were likely to accommodate growing numbers. Further similar building, behind the market frontage of the Lawnmarket, had to wait until the 1670s. But two other patterns lay behind the population increase of 95% on the south side: cheaper building and the filling-in of backlands was more viable in the south-east quarter between the High Street and the Cowgate where the slope slackened; and growth made heavy demands on south-west 3 and north-west 1, where much of the town's stables and unpleasant industries had long been sited. The former was a novel pattern in burgh settlement, for rich and poor had until then mixed more closely together, often separated more by storeys of tenements (the poor at street level) rather than by richer and poorer geographic quarters.

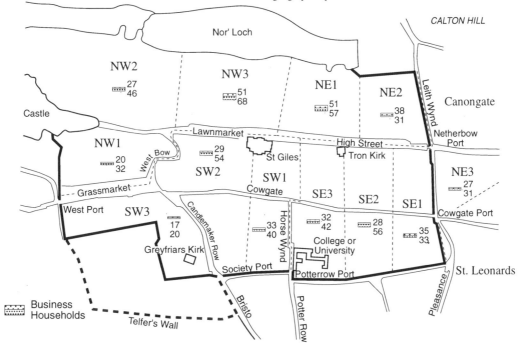

Development of Edinburgh: average rents of households 1635
ML

These more sharply defined divisions in settlement patterns are confirmed by different levels of household rent, which ranged from the £360 in the Lawnmarket to £4 barely 300 yards away, on the south side of Grassmarket. The varying levels of rent for business premises, too, reflect the gulf between the merchant's or moneylender's booth and the skinner's or candlemaker's workshop, typically pushed to the urban periphery.

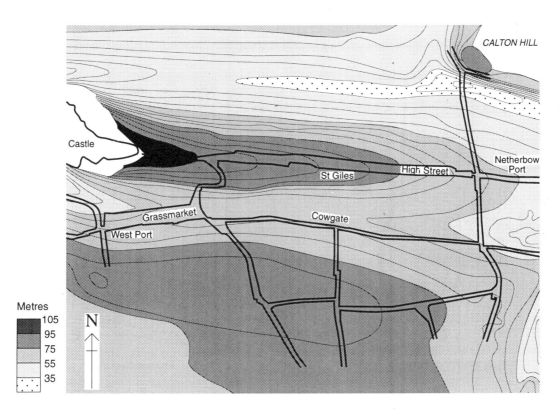

Development of Edinburgh: relief
ML

457

Settlement in burghs

Although the burgh as a formal institution was freshly imported into Scotland at the beginning of the twelfth century, it owed much, as a unit of human settlement, to the nucleated village familiar in Britain wherever Germanic settlers had established permanent agrarian communities; and it may have owed something, in purely physical terms, to at least the more simply planned among the trading towns ('Ports', 'boroughs') of England and Flanders. The plans given here are designed to show evolution of types of layout, from the pristine simplicity of Forres to the relative complexity of Glasgow or Berwick upon Tweed, and also the various ways in which burgh plans were adapted to physical problems of terrain or to changing historical circumstances. It will be noted that save at Perth (and to some extent at Berwick) Scots burghs were not enclosed by walls but relied on 'back dykes', often represented by modern roads and building plots, punctuated by gates ('ports') which marked the entry and exit points of principal highways. The peripheral yet associated placing of a castle, never itself a part of the burgh, is noteworthy, as is the siting- whether central as at Elgin, or peripheral as at Ayr - of the chief parish kirk.

These plans are derived from a detailed analysis of the property and street boundaries shown on eighteenth century plans of Perth. These early cartographic sources have then been compared in great detail with the first 1:500 Ordnance Survey plan of Perth in order to provide a standard accuracy of measurement. The careful identification of the largely man made boundaries within the town, has allowed the various phases in the towns growth to be identified.

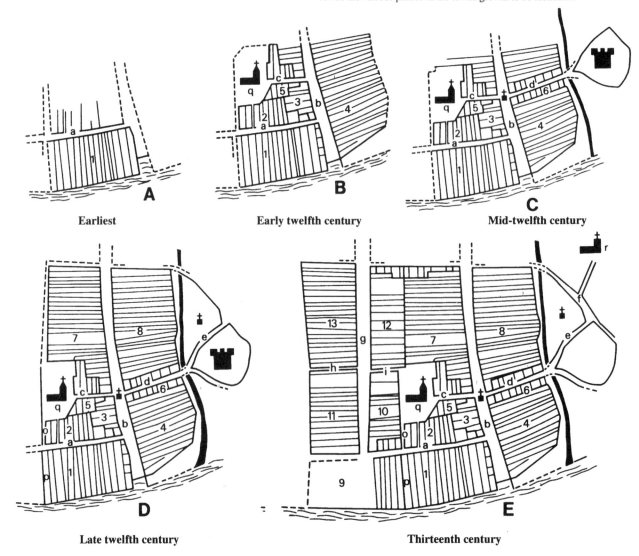

A Earliest

B Early twelfth century

C Mid-twelfth century

D Late twelfth century

E Thirteenth century

Settlement in Perth

RMS

458

Settlement in burghs

These plans are derived from a detailed analysis of the property and street boundaries shown on eighteenth century plans of Perth. These early cartographic sources have then been compared in great detail with the first 1:500 Ordnance Survey plan of Perth in order to provide a standard accuracy of measurement. The careful identification of the largely man made boundaries within the town, has allowed the various phases in the towns growth to be identified.

a	Watergate	k	Meal Vennel
b	High Street	l	Candlemakers Close
c	Kirkgate	m	New Row
d	Skinnergate	n	Mill Wynd
e	Castlegable	o	Baxter's Vennel
f	Curfew Row	p	Glen Close
g	South Street	q	St John's Church
h	Cow Vennel	r	Dominican Friary
i	Flesher's Close	s	Franciscan Friary
j	Roger's Close	t	Carthusian Monastery

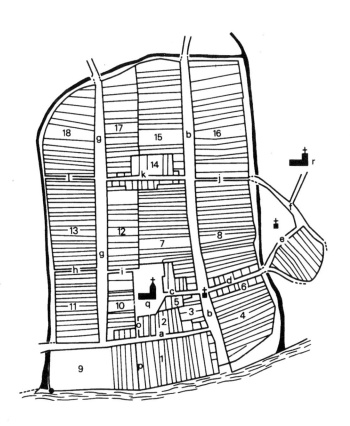

Early fourteenth century

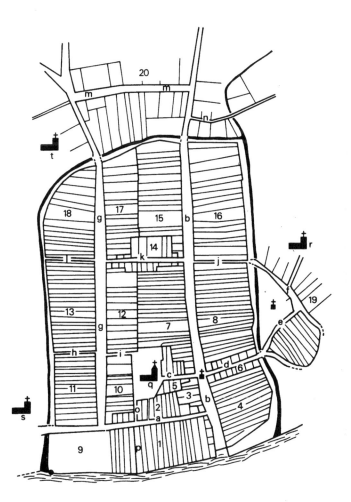

Fifteenth to sixteenth centuries

Settlement in Perth

RMS

Settlement in burghs

The development of settlement portrayed in this series above is largely based on documentary sources available for a study of the medieval burgh and on town plans produced between the seven- teenth and nineteenth centuries. Archaeological excavation, particularly the recent work of the Scottish Urban Archaeological Trust, has pro- vided supplementary evidence.

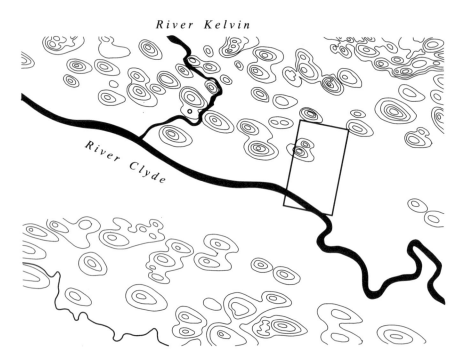

Location map, showing drumlins

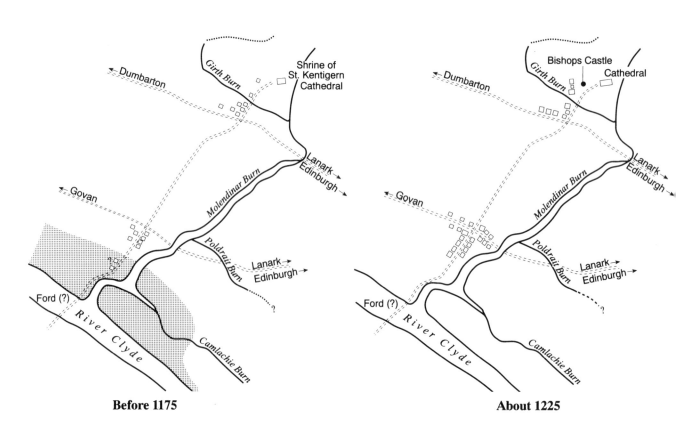

Before 1175

About 1225

Settlement in Glasgow

EPD

Settlement in burghs

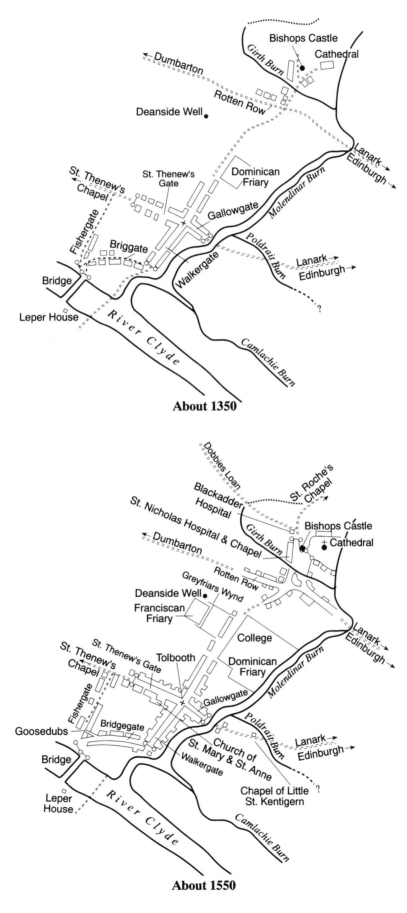

About 1350

About 1550

Settlement in Glasgow

EPD

Settlement in burghs

This series indicating the development of settlement is necessarily conjectural to some extent. Reliance has been placed on a relatively narrow range of source material since much of the documentation of early medieval Dundee has been lost. Archaeological evidence is minimal and likely to remain so. Town council minute books, burgh head court books, protocol books and records of the guild merchant, crafts, presbytery and kirk session have survived from the late sixteenth or early seventeenth centuries. These, together with maps dating from the seventeenth century to the nineteenth are the basic sources.

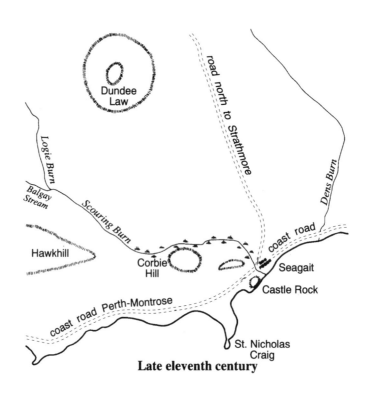

Late eleventh century

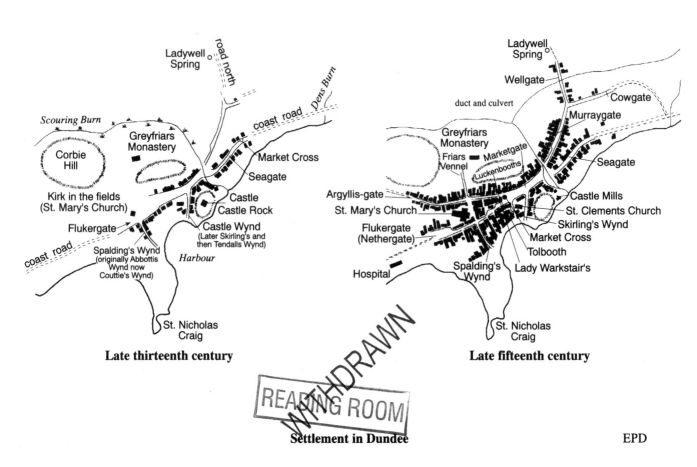

Late thirteenth century

Late fifteenth century

Settlement in Dundee

EPD